STRANGERS IN PARADISE

POCKET BOOK COLLECTION

art and story by

TERRY MOORE

1

publisher • Robyn Moore
colorist • Brian Miller

Published by
Abstract Studio, Inc.
P. O. Box 271487
Houston, TX 77277

ISBN: 1-892597-26-8

Printed in Canada

Visit the Strangers In Paradise website at
www.strangersinparadise.com

This book collects the complete works of Strangers in Paradise
Volume I (issues #1 – #3) and Volume II (issues #1 – #13).

STRANGERS IN PARADISE

POCKET BOOK COLLECTION

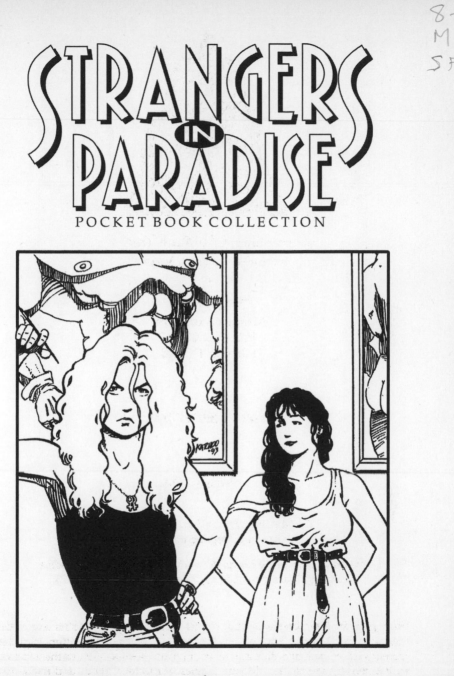

1

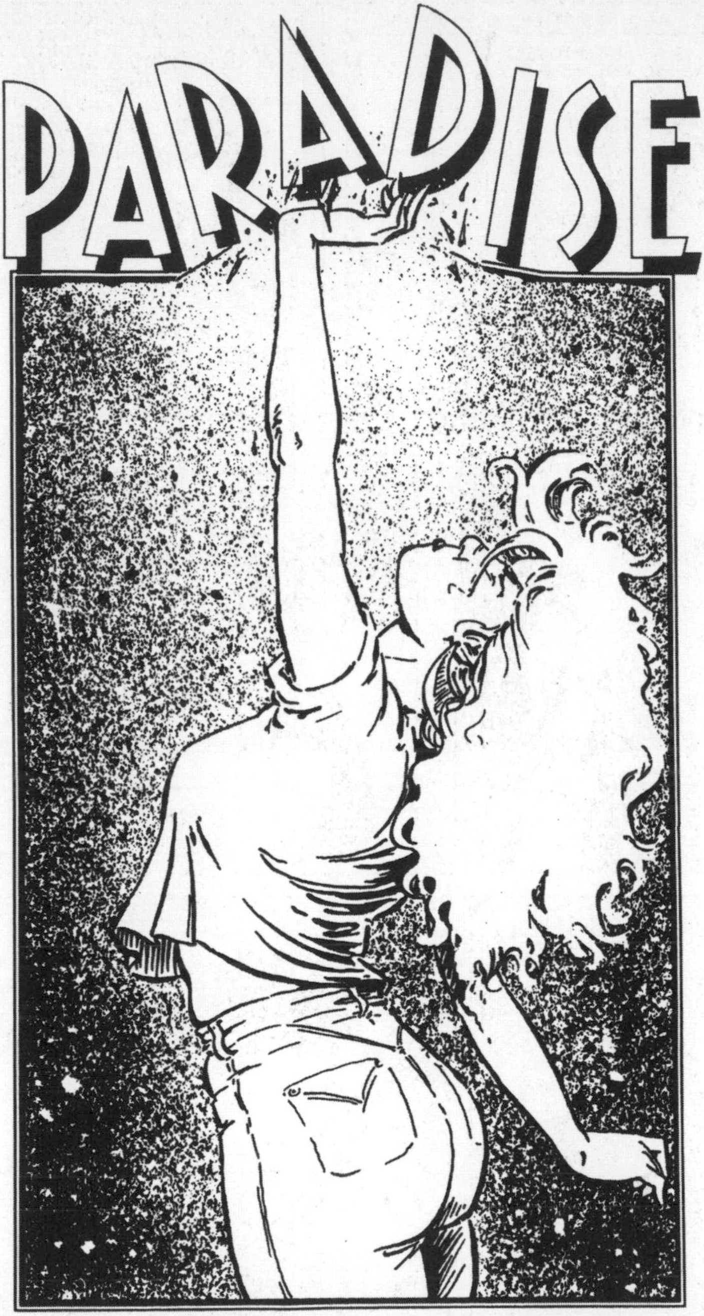
PARADISE

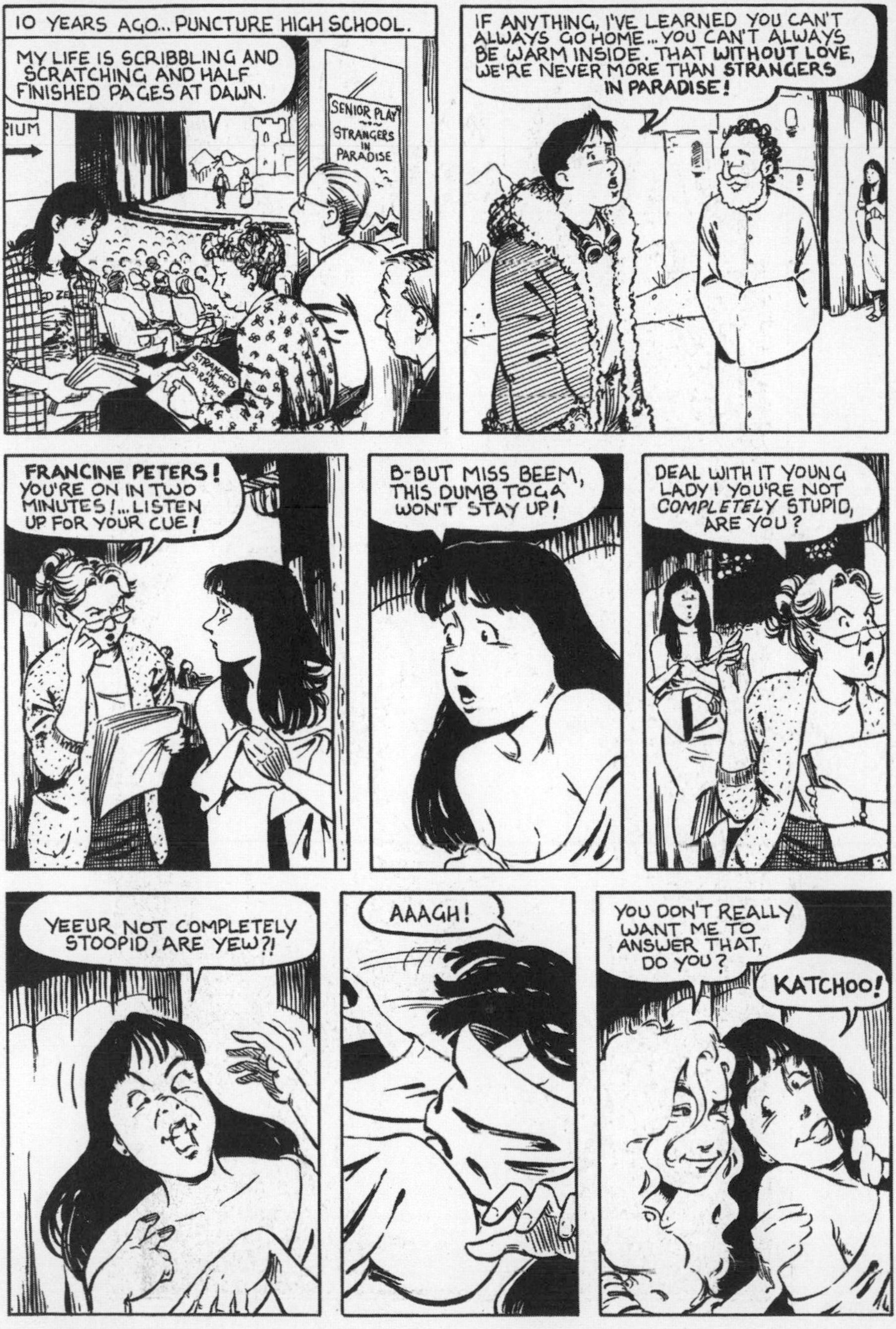
10 YEARS AGO... PUNCTURE HIGH SCHOOL.
MY LIFE IS SCRIBBLING AND SCRATCHING AND HALF FINISHED PAGES AT DAWN.
RIUM
SENIOR PLAY STRANGERS IN PARADISE
STRANGERS IN PARADISE
IF ANYTHING, I'VE LEARNED YOU CAN'T ALWAYS GO HOME... YOU CAN'T ALWAYS BE WARM INSIDE. THAT WITHOUT LOVE, WE'RE NEVER MORE THAN STRANGERS IN PARADISE!
FRANCINE PETERS! YOU'RE ON IN TWO MINUTES!... LISTEN UP FOR YOUR CUE!
B-BUT MISS BEEM, THIS DUMB TOGA WON'T STAY UP!
DEAL WITH IT YOUNG LADY! YOU'RE NOT COMPLETELY STUPID, ARE YOU?
YEEUR NOT COMPLETELY STOOPID, ARE YEW?!
AAAGH!
YOU DON'T REALLY WANT ME TO ANSWER THAT, DO YOU?
KATCHOO!

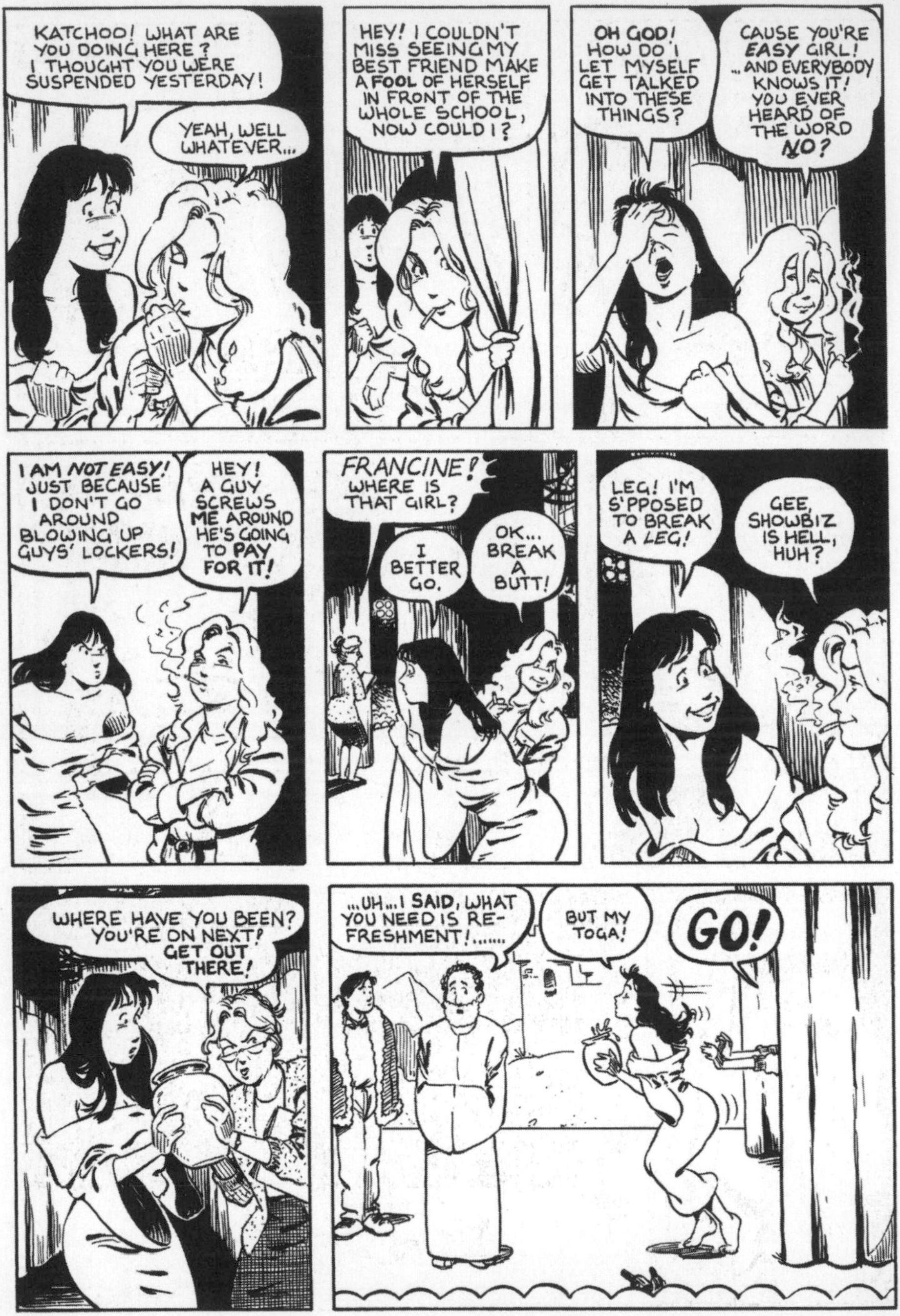
KATCHOO! WHAT ARE YOU DOING HERE? I THOUGHT YOU WERE SUSPENDED YESTERDAY!
YEAH, WELL WHATEVER...
HEY! I COULDN'T MISS SEEING MY BEST FRIEND MAKE A FOOL OF HERSELF IN FRONT OF THE WHOLE SCHOOL, NOW COULD I?
OH GOD! HOW DO I LET MYSELF GET TALKED INTO THESE THINGS?
CAUSE YOU'RE EASY GIRL! ...AND EVERYBODY KNOWS IT! YOU EVER HEARD OF THE WORD NO?
I AM NOT EASY! JUST BECAUSE I DON'T GO AROUND BLOWING UP GUYS' LOCKERS!
HEY! A GUY SCREWS ME AROUND HE'S GOING TO PAY FOR IT!
FRANCINE! WHERE IS THAT GIRL?
I BETTER GO.
OK... BREAK A BUTT!
LEG! I'M S'PPOSED TO BREAK A LEG!
GEE, SHOWBIZ IS HELL, HUH?
WHERE HAVE YOU BEEN? YOU'RE ON NEXT! GET OUT THERE!
...UH...I SAID, WHAT YOU NEED IS RE-FRESHMENT!......
BUT MY TOGA!
GO!

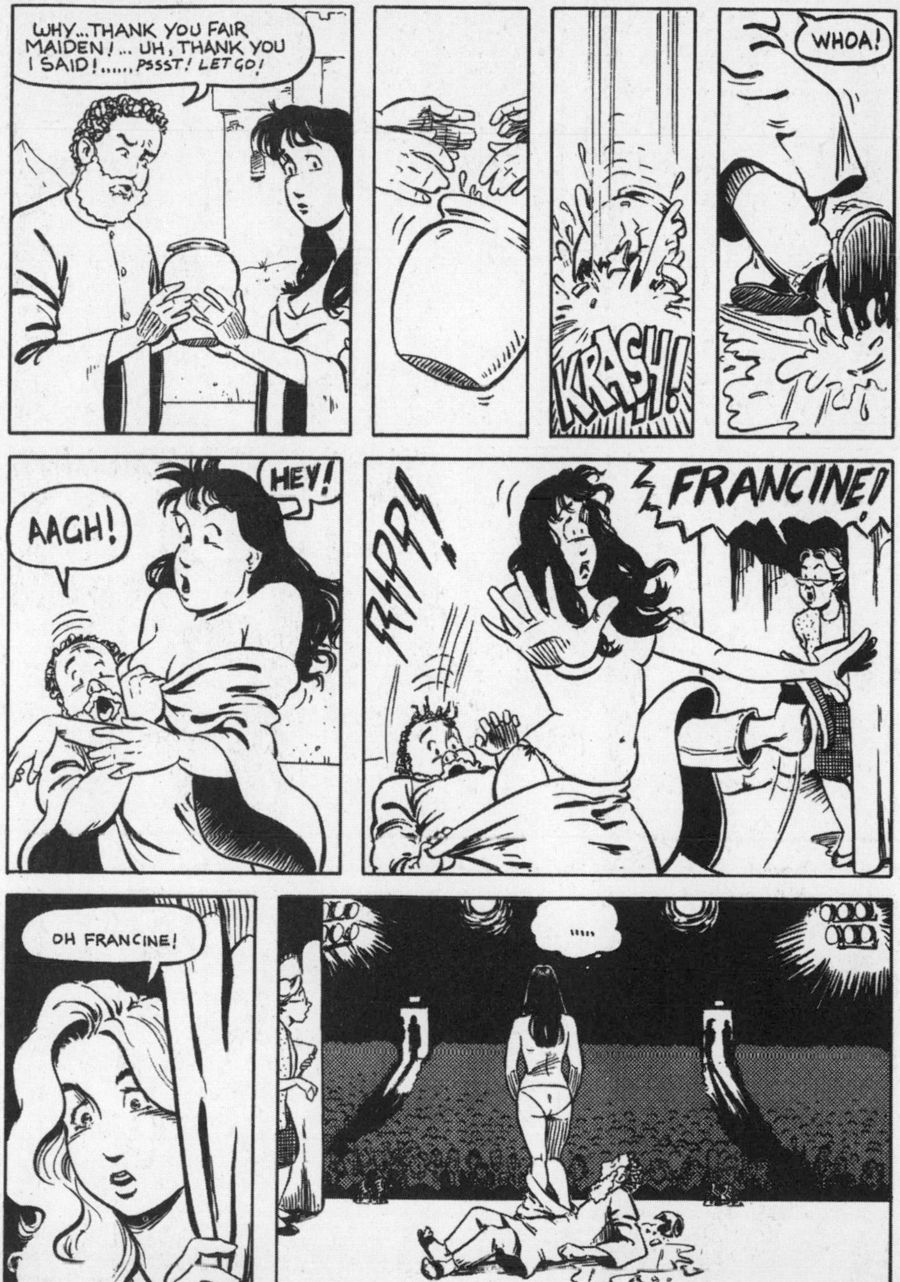
WHY...THANK YOU FAIR MAIDEN! ... UH, THANK YOU I SAID!...... PSSST! LET GO!
KRASH!
WHOA!
AAGH!
HEY!
RIPP!
FRANCINE!
OH FRANCINE!
.....
FADE TO BLACK...

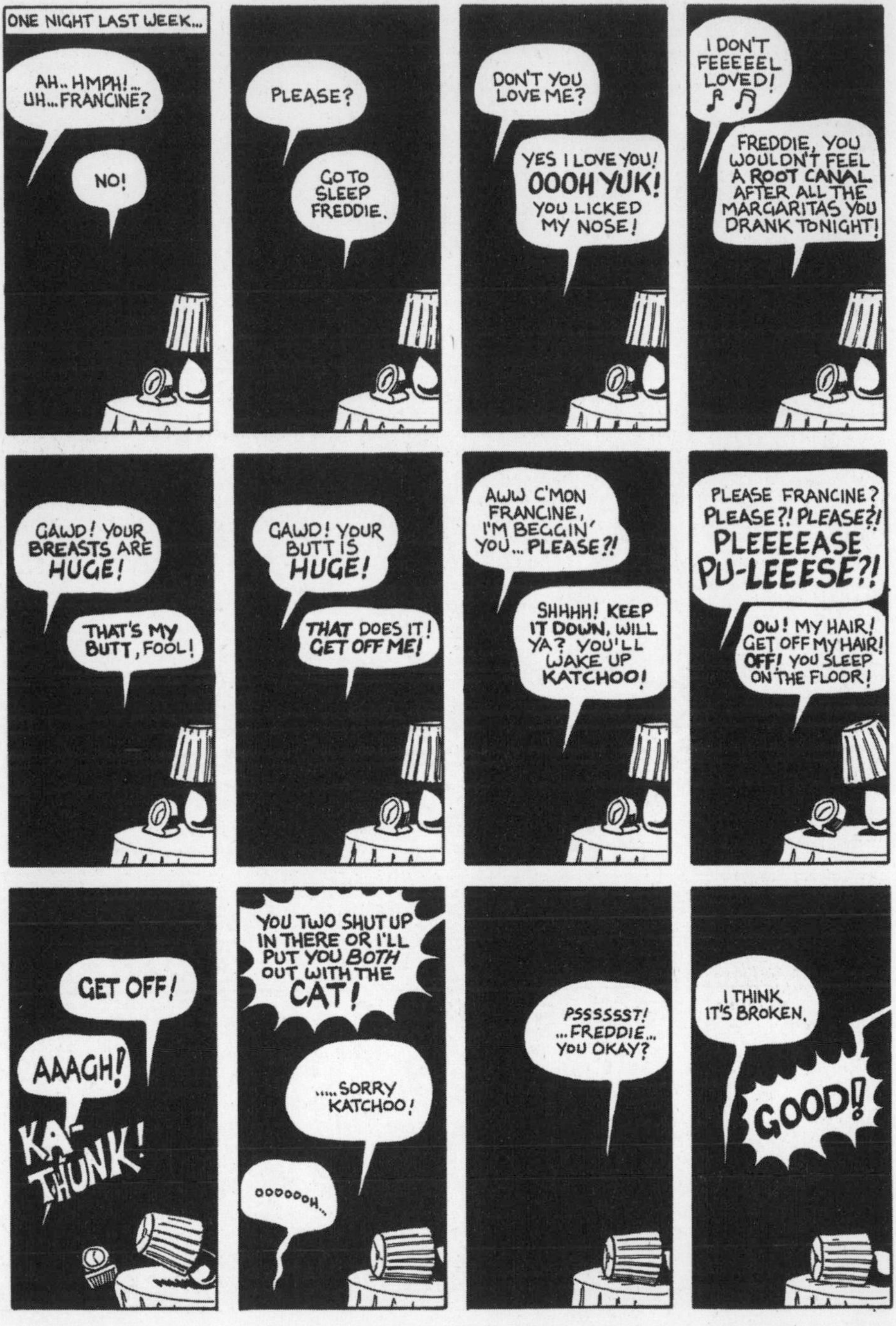
ONE NIGHT LAST WEEK...
AH.. HMPH!... UH... FRANCINE?
NO!
PLEASE?
GO TO SLEEP FREDDIE.
DON'T YOU LOVE ME?
YES I LOVE YOU! OOOH YUK! YOU LICKED MY NOSE!
I DON'T FEEEEEL LOVED!
FREDDIE, YOU WOULDN'T FEEL A ROOT CANAL AFTER ALL THE MARGARITAS YOU DRANK TONIGHT!
GAWD! YOUR BREASTS ARE HUGE!
THAT'S MY BUTT, FOOL!
GAWD! YOUR BUTT IS HUGE!
THAT DOES IT! GET OFF ME!
AWW C'MON FRANCINE, I'M BEGGIN' YOU... PLEASE?!
SHHHH! KEEP IT DOWN, WILL YA? YOU'LL WAKE UP KATCHOO!
PLEASE FRANCINE? PLEASE?! PLEASE?! PLEEEEASE PU-LEEESE?!
OW! MY HAIR! GET OFF MY HAIR! OFF! YOU SLEEP ON THE FLOOR!
GET OFF!
AAAGH!
KA-THUNK!
YOU TWO SHUT UP IN THERE OR I'LL PUT YOU BOTH OUT WITH THE CAT!
.....SORRY KATCHOO!
OOOOOOH...
PSSSSSST! ...FREDDIE... YOU OKAY?
I THINK IT'S BROKEN.
GOOD!

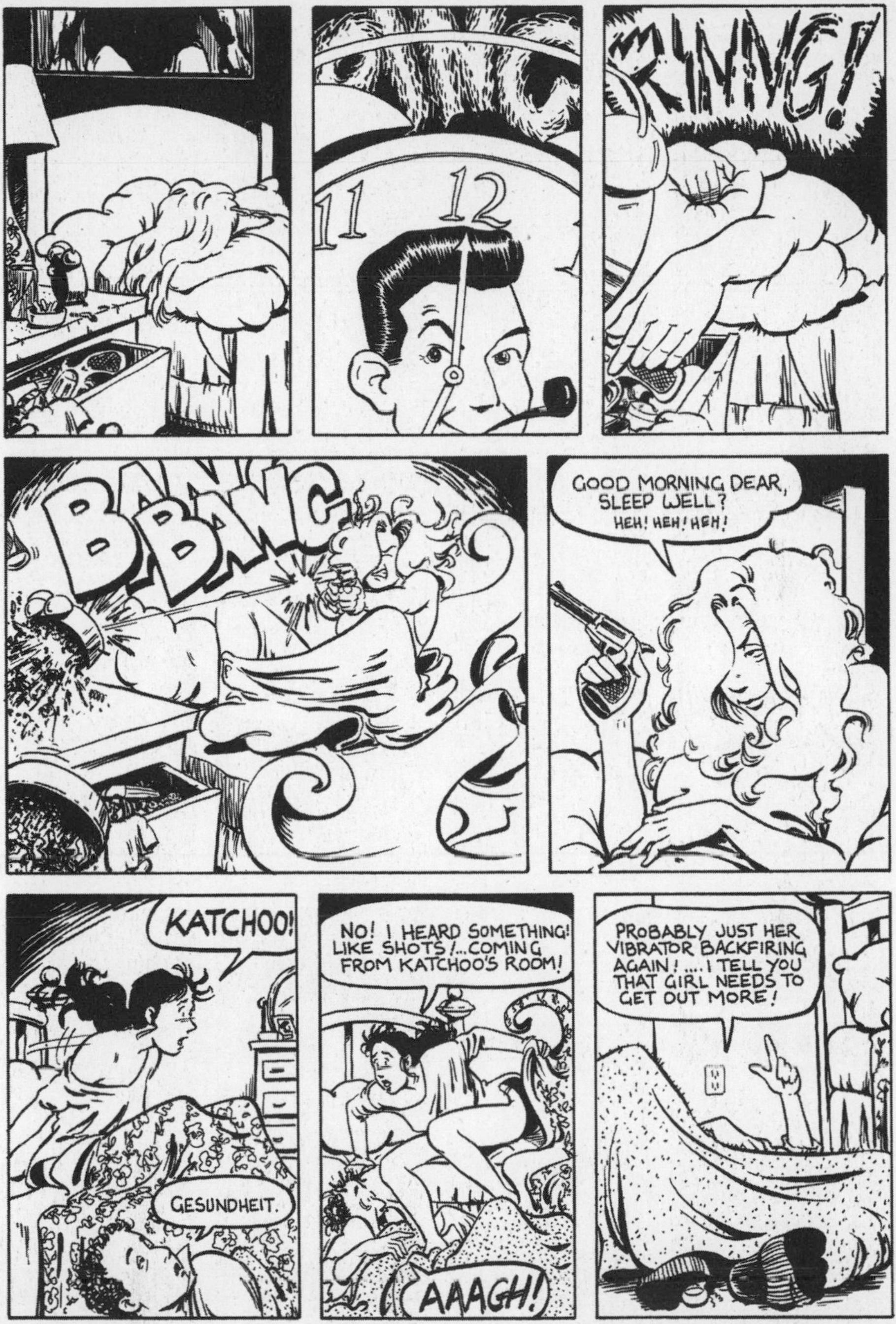
RINNG!
BANG
BANG
GOOD MORNING DEAR, SLEEP WELL? HEH! HEH! HEH!
KATCHOO!
GESUNDHEIT.
NO! I HEARD SOMETHING! LIKE SHOTS!...COMING FROM KATCHOO'S ROOM!
AAAGH!
PROBABLY JUST HER VIBRATOR BACKFIRING AGAIN! ....I TELL YOU THAT GIRL NEEDS TO GET OUT MORE!

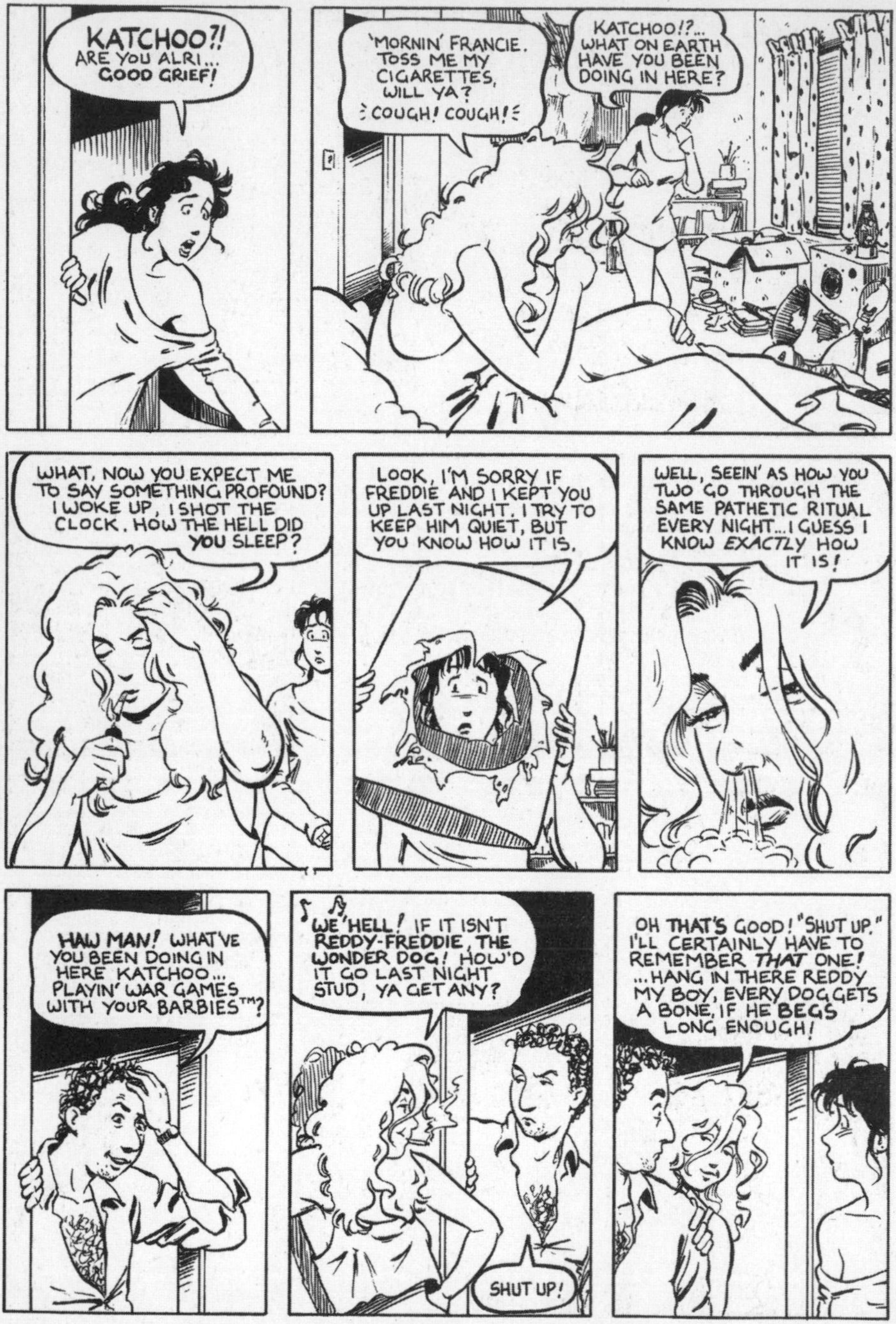
KATCHOO?! ARE YOU ALRI... GOOD GRIEF!
'MORNIN' FRANCIE. TOSS ME MY CIGARETTES, WILL YA?
COUGH! COUGH!
KATCHOO!?... WHAT ON EARTH HAVE YOU BEEN DOING IN HERE?
WHAT, NOW YOU EXPECT ME TO SAY SOMETHING PROFOUND? I WOKE UP, I SHOT THE CLOCK. HOW THE HELL DID YOU SLEEP?
LOOK, I'M SORRY IF FREDDIE AND I KEPT YOU UP LAST NIGHT. I TRY TO KEEP HIM QUIET, BUT YOU KNOW HOW IT IS.
WELL, SEEIN' AS HOW YOU TWO GO THROUGH THE SAME PATHETIC RITUAL EVERY NIGHT... I GUESS I KNOW EXACTLY HOW IT IS!
HAW MAN! WHAT'VE YOU BEEN DOING IN HERE KATCHOO... PLAYIN' WAR GAMES WITH YOUR BARBIES™?
WE'HELL! IF IT ISN'T REDDY-FREDDIE, THE WONDER DOG! HOW'D IT GO LAST NIGHT STUD, YA GET ANY?
SHUT UP!
OH THAT'S GOOD! "SHUT UP." I'LL CERTAINLY HAVE TO REMEMBER THAT ONE! ...HANG IN THERE REDDY MY BOY, EVERY DOG GETS A BONE, IF HE BEGS LONG ENOUGH!

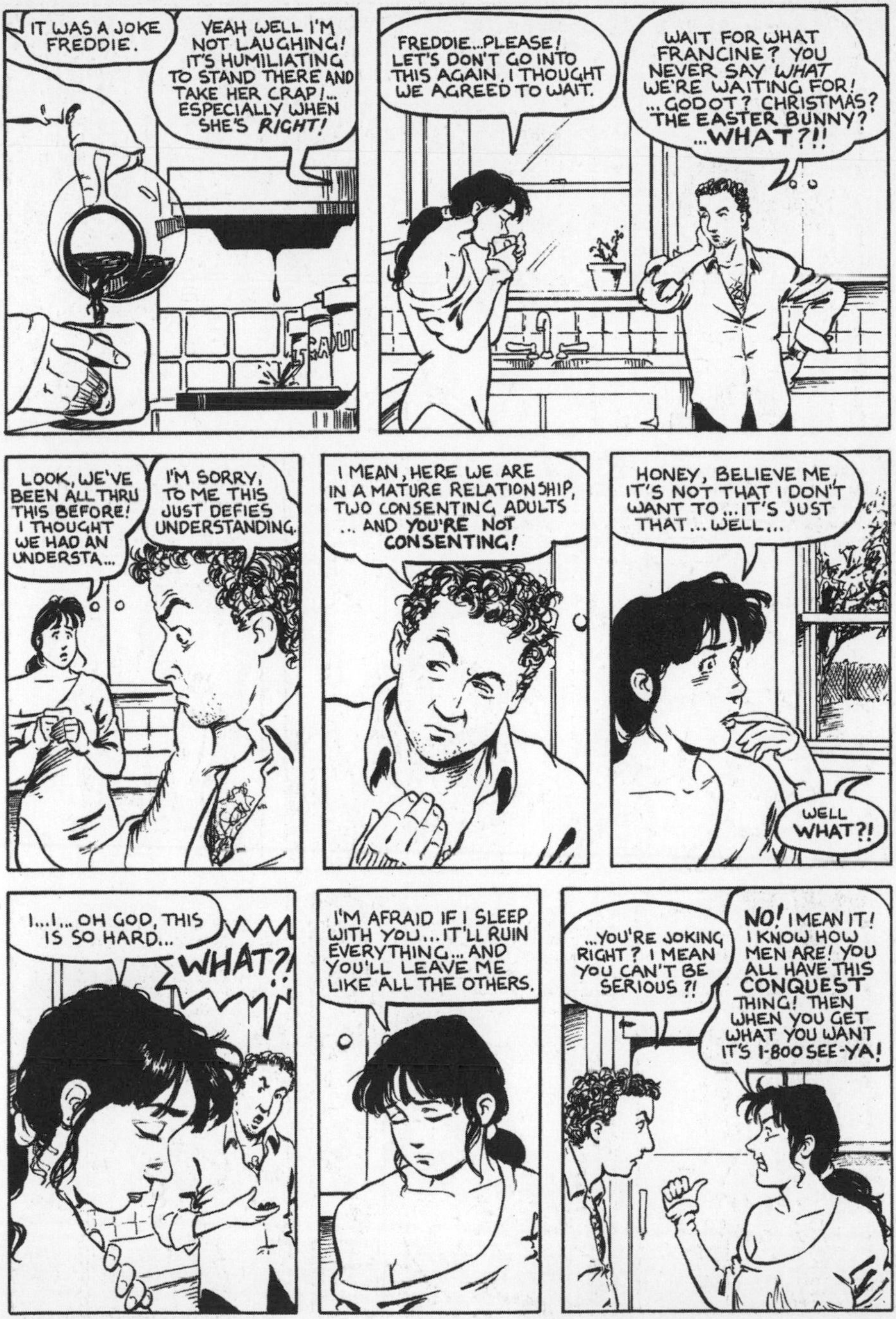
IT WAS A JOKE FREDDIE.
YEAH WELL I'M NOT LAUGHING! IT'S HUMILIATING TO STAND THERE AND TAKE HER CRAP!... ESPECIALLY WHEN SHE'S RIGHT!
FREDDIE...PLEASE! LET'S DON'T GO INTO THIS AGAIN. I THOUGHT WE AGREED TO WAIT.
WAIT FOR WHAT FRANCINE? YOU NEVER SAY WHAT WE'RE WAITING FOR! ...GODOT? CHRISTMAS? THE EASTER BUNNY? ...WHAT?!!
LOOK, WE'VE BEEN ALL THRU THIS BEFORE! I THOUGHT WE HAD AN UNDERSTA...
I'M SORRY, TO ME THIS JUST DEFIES UNDERSTANDING.
I MEAN, HERE WE ARE IN A MATURE RELATIONSHIP, TWO CONSENTING ADULTS ... AND YOU'RE NOT CONSENTING!
HONEY, BELIEVE ME IT'S NOT THAT I DON'T WANT TO...IT'S JUST THAT...WELL...
WELL WHAT?!
I...I... OH GOD, THIS IS SO HARD...
WHAT?!
I'M AFRAID IF I SLEEP WITH YOU...IT'LL RUIN EVERYTHING...AND YOU'LL LEAVE ME LIKE ALL THE OTHERS.
...YOU'RE JOKING RIGHT? I MEAN YOU CAN'T BE SERIOUS?!
NO! I MEAN IT! I KNOW HOW MEN ARE! YOU ALL HAVE THIS CONQUEST THING! THEN WHEN YOU GET WHAT YOU WANT IT'S 1-800 SEE-YA!

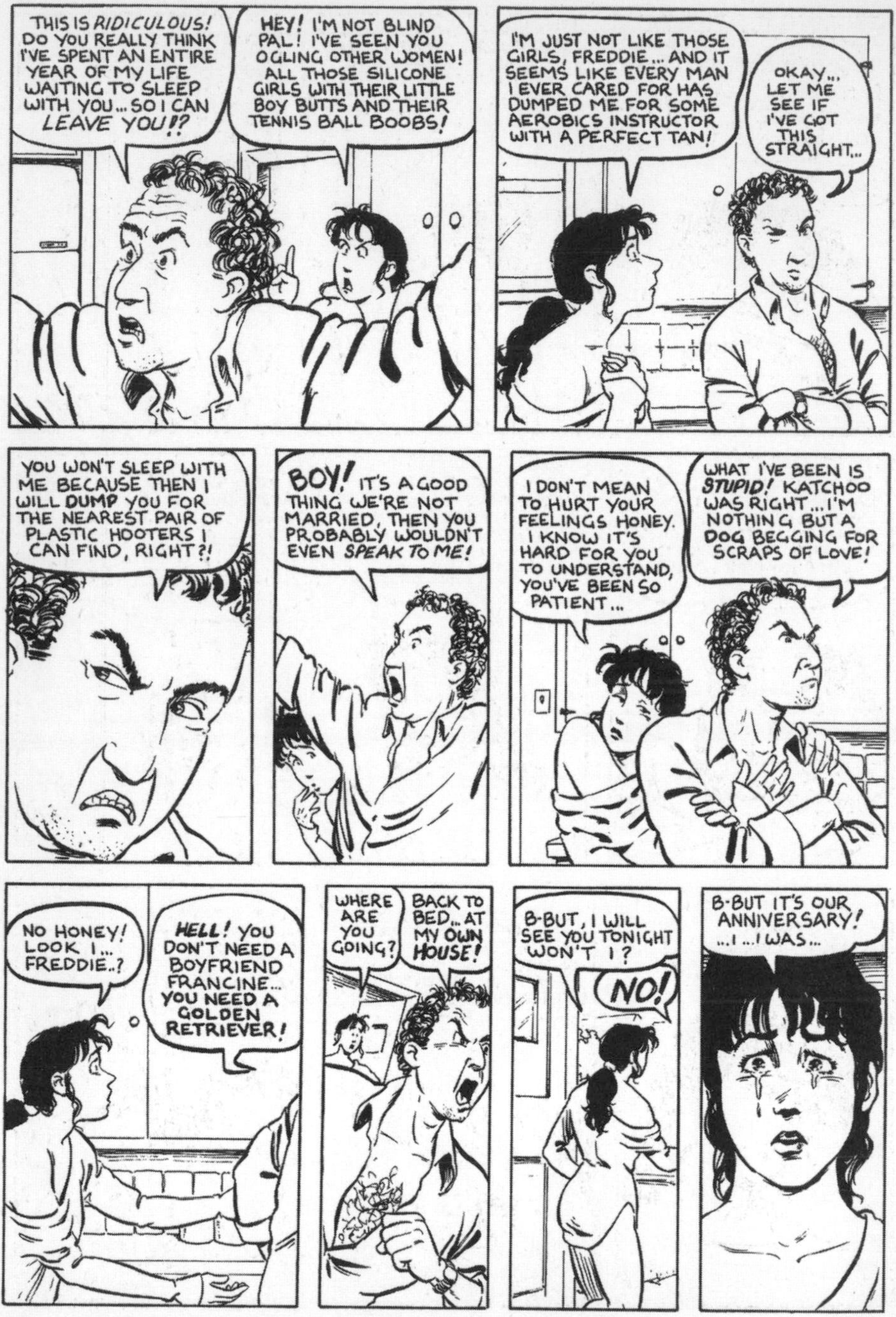
THIS IS RIDICULOUS! DO YOU REALLY THINK I'VE SPENT AN ENTIRE YEAR OF MY LIFE WAITING TO SLEEP WITH YOU... SO I CAN LEAVE YOU!?
HEY! I'M NOT BLIND PAL! I'VE SEEN YOU OGLING OTHER WOMEN! ALL THOSE SILICONE GIRLS WITH THEIR LITTLE BOY BUTTS AND THEIR TENNIS BALL BOOBS!
I'M JUST NOT LIKE THOSE GIRLS, FREDDIE... AND IT SEEMS LIKE EVERY MAN I EVER CARED FOR HAS DUMPED ME FOR SOME AEROBICS INSTRUCTOR WITH A PERFECT TAN!
OKAY... LET ME SEE IF I'VE GOT THIS STRAIGHT...
YOU WON'T SLEEP WITH ME BECAUSE THEN I WILL DUMP YOU FOR THE NEAREST PAIR OF PLASTIC HOOTERS I CAN FIND, RIGHT?!
BOY! IT'S A GOOD THING WE'RE NOT MARRIED, THEN YOU PROBABLY WOULDN'T EVEN SPEAK TO ME!
I DON'T MEAN TO HURT YOUR FEELINGS HONEY. I KNOW IT'S HARD FOR YOU TO UNDERSTAND, YOU'VE BEEN SO PATIENT...
WHAT I'VE BEEN IS STUPID! KATCHOO WAS RIGHT... I'M NOTHING BUT A DOG BEGGING FOR SCRAPS OF LOVE!
NO HONEY! LOOK I... FREDDIE..?
HELL! YOU DON'T NEED A BOYFRIEND FRANCINE... YOU NEED A GOLDEN RETRIEVER!
WHERE ARE YOU GOING?
BACK TO BED... AT MY OWN HOUSE!
B-BUT, I WILL SEE YOU TONIGHT WON'T I?
NO!
B-BUT IT'S OUR ANNIVERSARY! ...I ...I WAS...

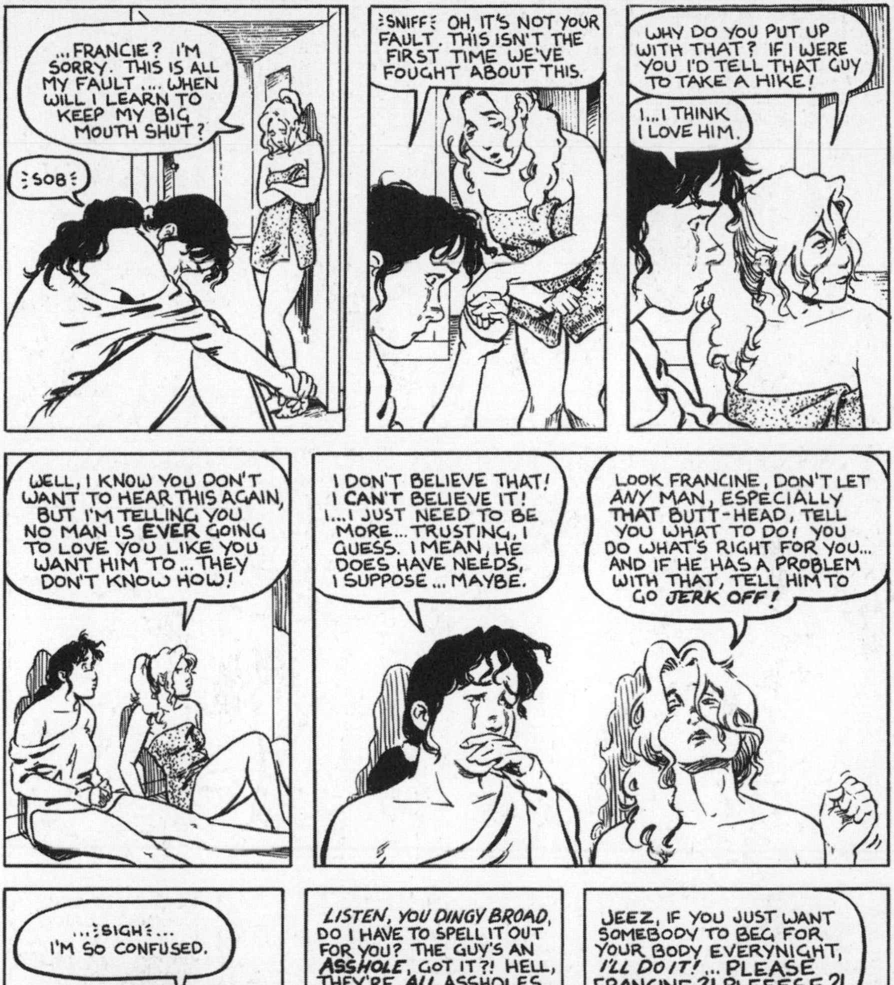
...FRANCIE? I'M SORRY. THIS IS ALL MY FAULT .... WHEN WILL I LEARN TO KEEP MY BIG MOUTH SHUT?
SOB
SNIFF OH, IT'S NOT YOUR FAULT. THIS ISN'T THE FIRST TIME WE'VE FOUGHT ABOUT THIS.
WHY DO YOU PUT UP WITH THAT? IF I WERE YOU I'D TELL THAT GUY TO TAKE A HIKE!
I...I THINK I LOVE HIM.
WELL, I KNOW YOU DON'T WANT TO HEAR THIS AGAIN, BUT I'M TELLING YOU NO MAN IS EVER GOING TO LOVE YOU LIKE YOU WANT HIM TO ... THEY DON'T KNOW HOW!
I DON'T BELIEVE THAT! I CAN'T BELIEVE IT! I...I JUST NEED TO BE MORE... TRUSTING, I GUESS. I MEAN, HE DOES HAVE NEEDS, I SUPPOSE ... MAYBE.
LOOK FRANCINE, DON'T LET ANY MAN, ESPECIALLY THAT BUTT-HEAD, TELL YOU WHAT TO DO! YOU DO WHAT'S RIGHT FOR YOU... AND IF HE HAS A PROBLEM WITH THAT, TELL HIM TO GO JERK OFF!
...SIGH... I'M SO CONFUSED.
LISTEN, YOU DINGY BROAD, DO I HAVE TO SPELL IT OUT FOR YOU? THE GUY'S AN ASSHOLE, GOT IT?! HELL, THEY'RE ALL ASSHOLES BUT THIS ONE'S CERTIFIED!!
JEEZ, IF YOU JUST WANT SOMEBODY TO BEG FOR YOUR BODY EVERYNIGHT, I'LL DO IT! ... PLEASE FRANCINE?! PLEEESE?! OH FRANCINE!
HAW!
HOOOOOWL!

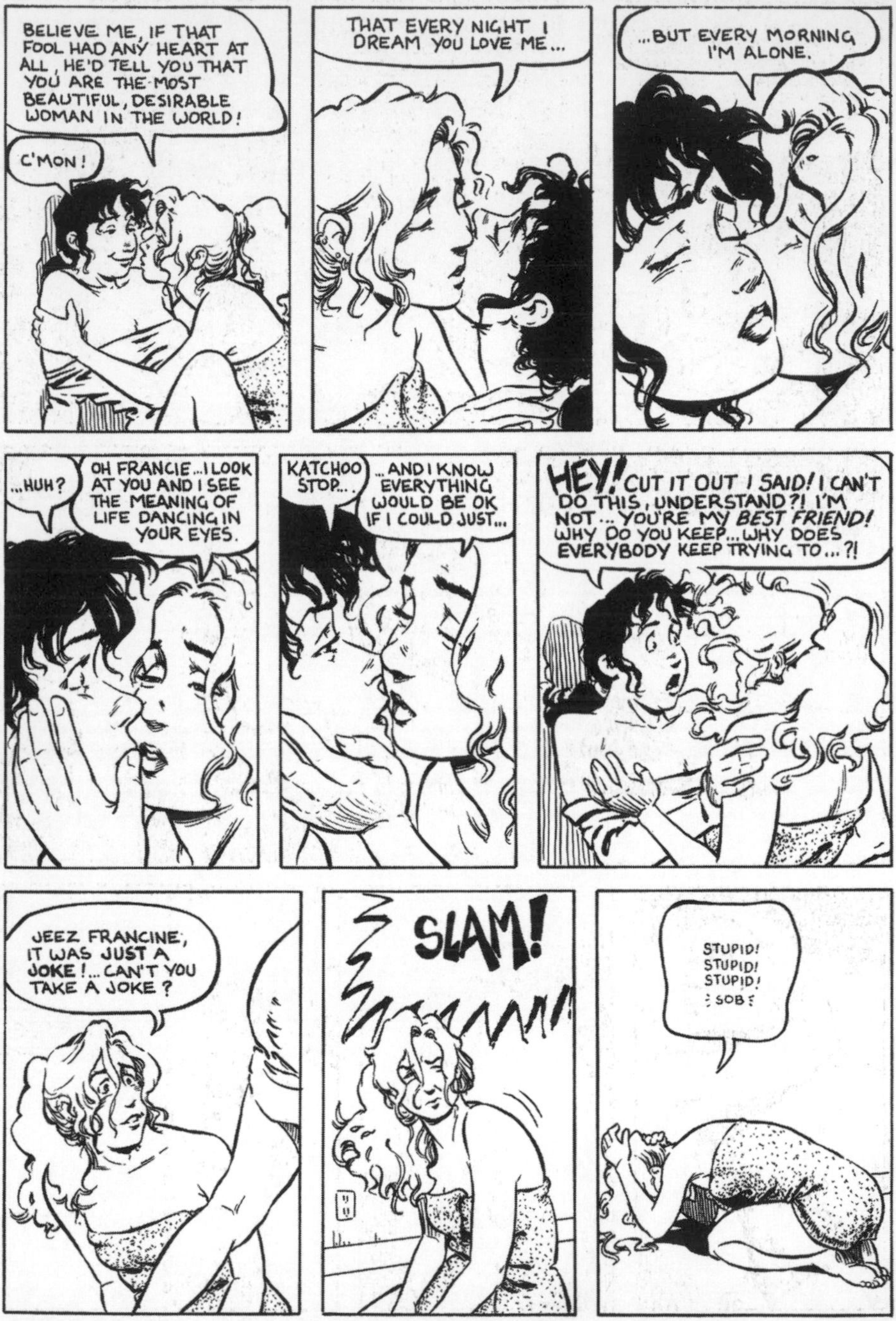
BELIEVE ME, IF THAT FOOL HAD ANY HEART AT ALL, HE'D TELL YOU THAT YOU ARE THE MOST BEAUTIFUL, DESIRABLE WOMAN IN THE WORLD!
C'MON!
THAT EVERY NIGHT I DREAM YOU LOVE ME...
...BUT EVERY MORNING I'M ALONE.
...HUH?
OH FRANCIE...I LOOK AT YOU AND I SEE THE MEANING OF LIFE DANCING IN YOUR EYES.
KATCHOO STOP...
...AND I KNOW EVERYTHING WOULD BE OK IF I COULD JUST...
HEY! CUT IT OUT I SAID! I CAN'T DO THIS, UNDERSTAND?! I'M NOT... YOU'RE MY BEST FRIEND! WHY DO YOU KEEP...WHY DOES EVERYBODY KEEP TRYING TO...?!
JEEZ FRANCINE, IT WAS JUST A JOKE!... CAN'T YOU TAKE A JOKE?
SLAM!
STUPID! STUPID! STUPID! SOB

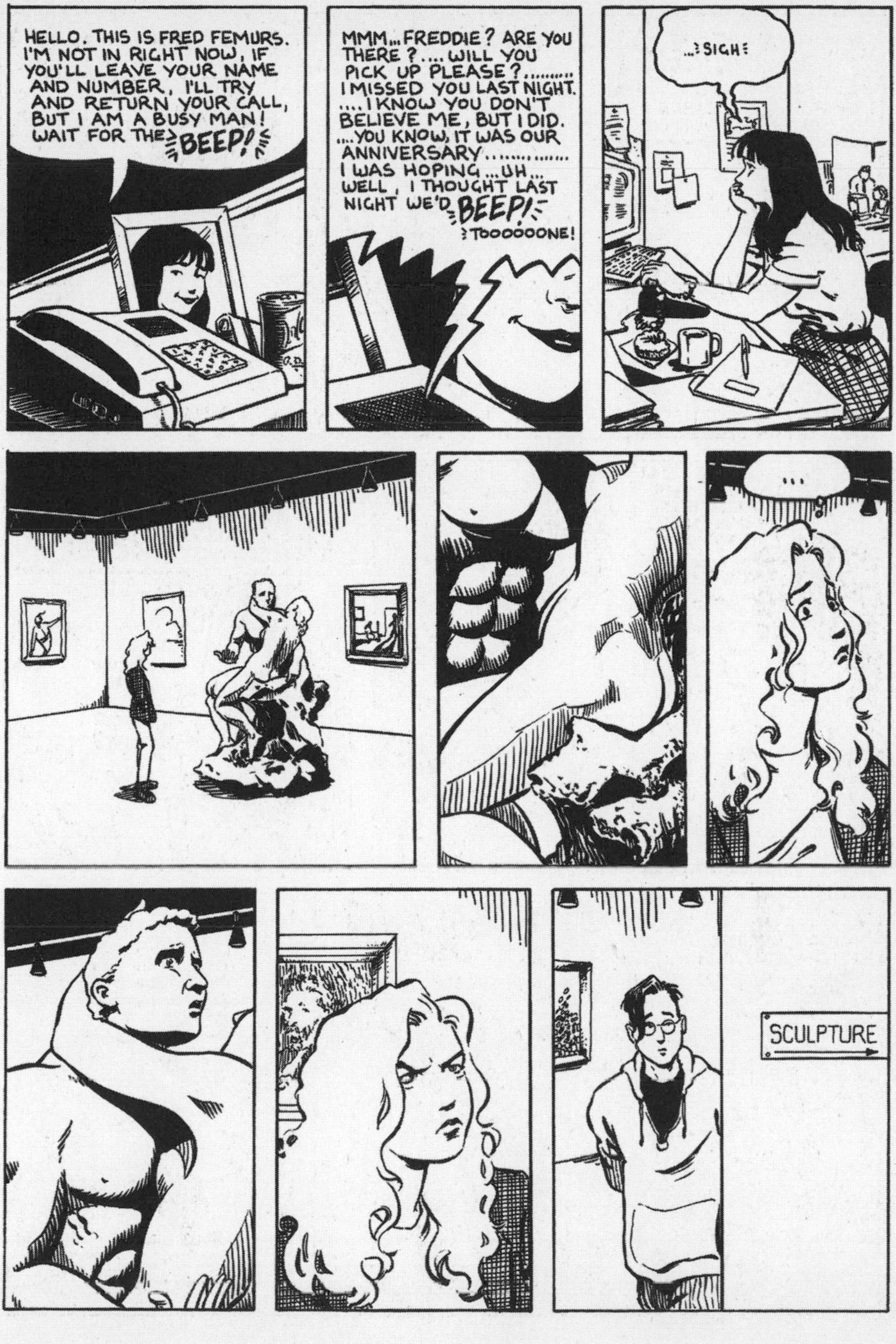
HELLO. THIS IS FRED FEMURS. I'M NOT IN RIGHT NOW, IF YOU'LL LEAVE YOUR NAME AND NUMBER, I'LL TRY AND RETURN YOUR CALL, BUT I AM A BUSY MAN! WAIT FOR THE BEEP!
MMM... FREDDIE? ARE YOU THERE?.... WILL YOU PICK UP PLEASE?......... I MISSED YOU LAST NIGHT. ....I KNOW YOU DON'T BELIEVE ME, BUT I DID. ...YOU KNOW, IT WAS OUR ANNIVERSARY.............. I WAS HOPING ...UH... WELL, I THOUGHT LAST NIGHT WE'D BEEP!
TOOOOOONE!
...SIGH
...
SCULPTURE

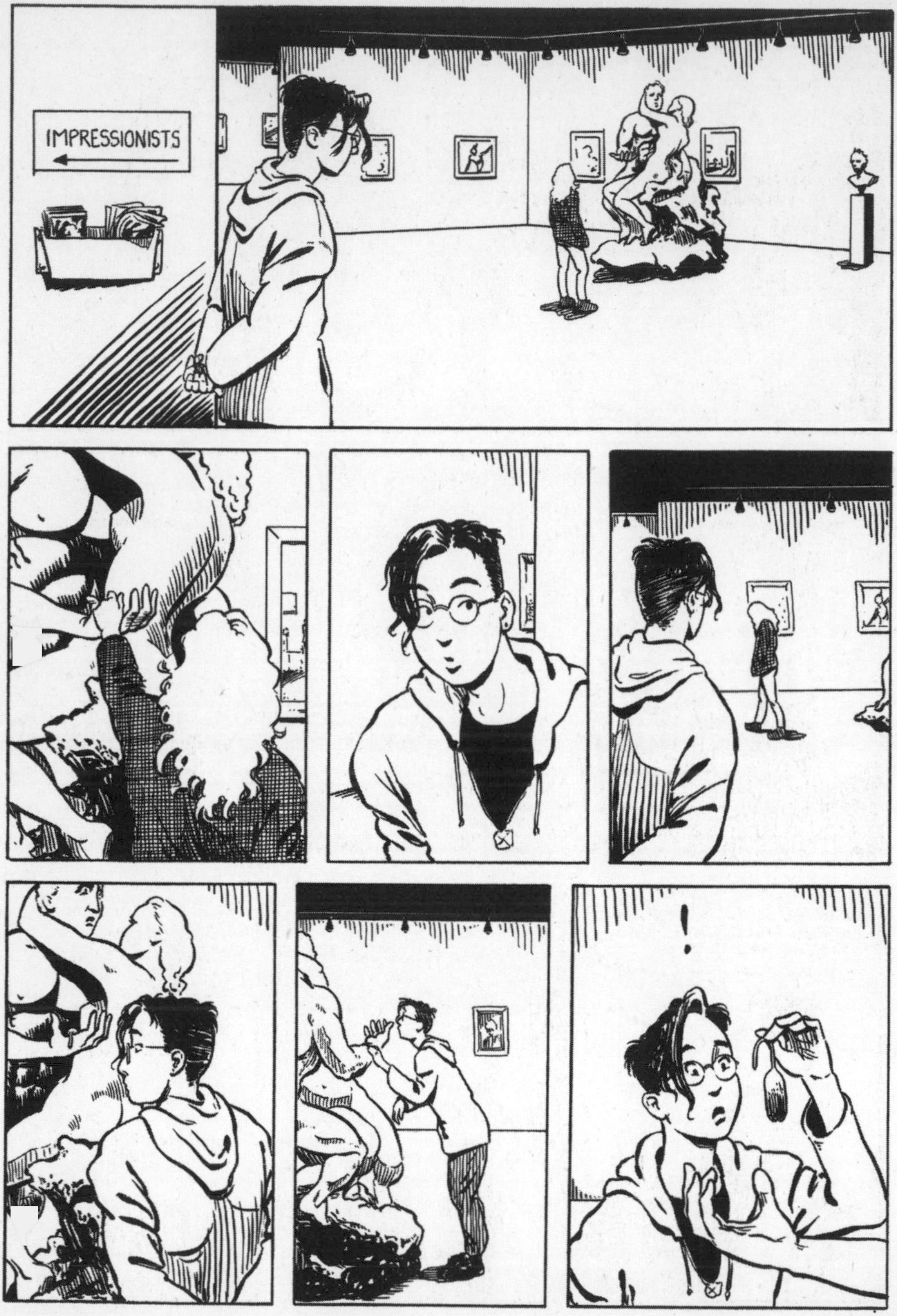
IMPRESSIONISTS
!

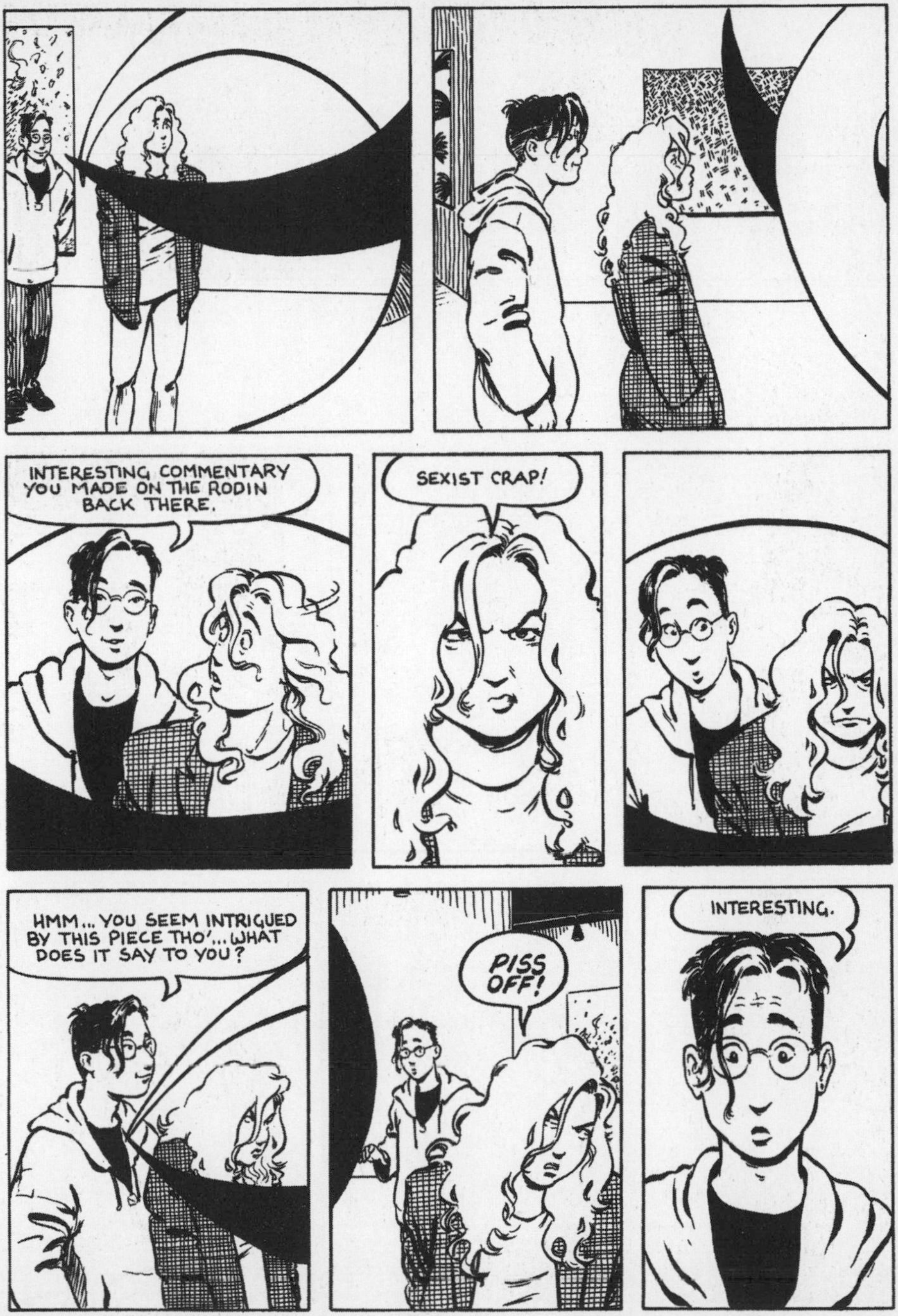
INTERESTING COMMENTARY YOU MADE ON THE RODIN BACK THERE.
SEXIST CRAP!
HMM... YOU SEEM INTRIGUED BY THIS PIECE THO'... WHAT DOES IT SAY TO YOU?
PISS OFF!
INTERESTING.

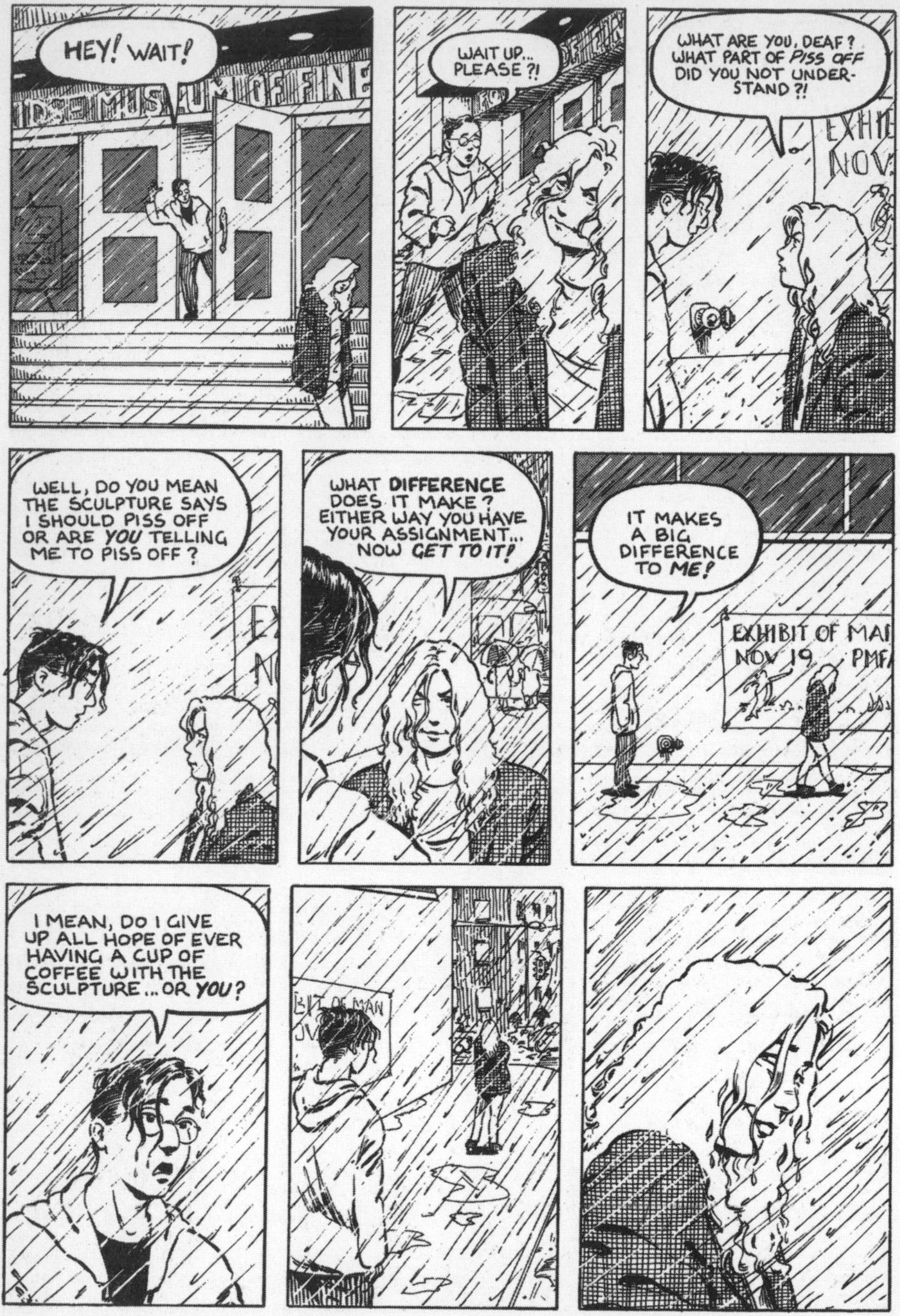
HEY! WAIT!
WAIT UP... PLEASE ?!
WHAT ARE YOU, DEAF ? WHAT PART OF *PISS OFF* DID YOU NOT UNDERSTAND ?!
WELL, DO YOU MEAN THE SCULPTURE SAYS I SHOULD PISS OFF OR ARE *YOU* TELLING ME TO PISS OFF ?
WHAT **DIFFERENCE** DOES IT MAKE ? EITHER WAY YOU HAVE YOUR ASSIGNMENT... NOW *GET TO IT!*
IT MAKES A BIG DIFFERENCE TO *ME!*
I MEAN, DO I GIVE UP ALL HOPE OF EVER HAVING A CUP OF COFFEE WITH THE SCULPTURE... OR *YOU*?

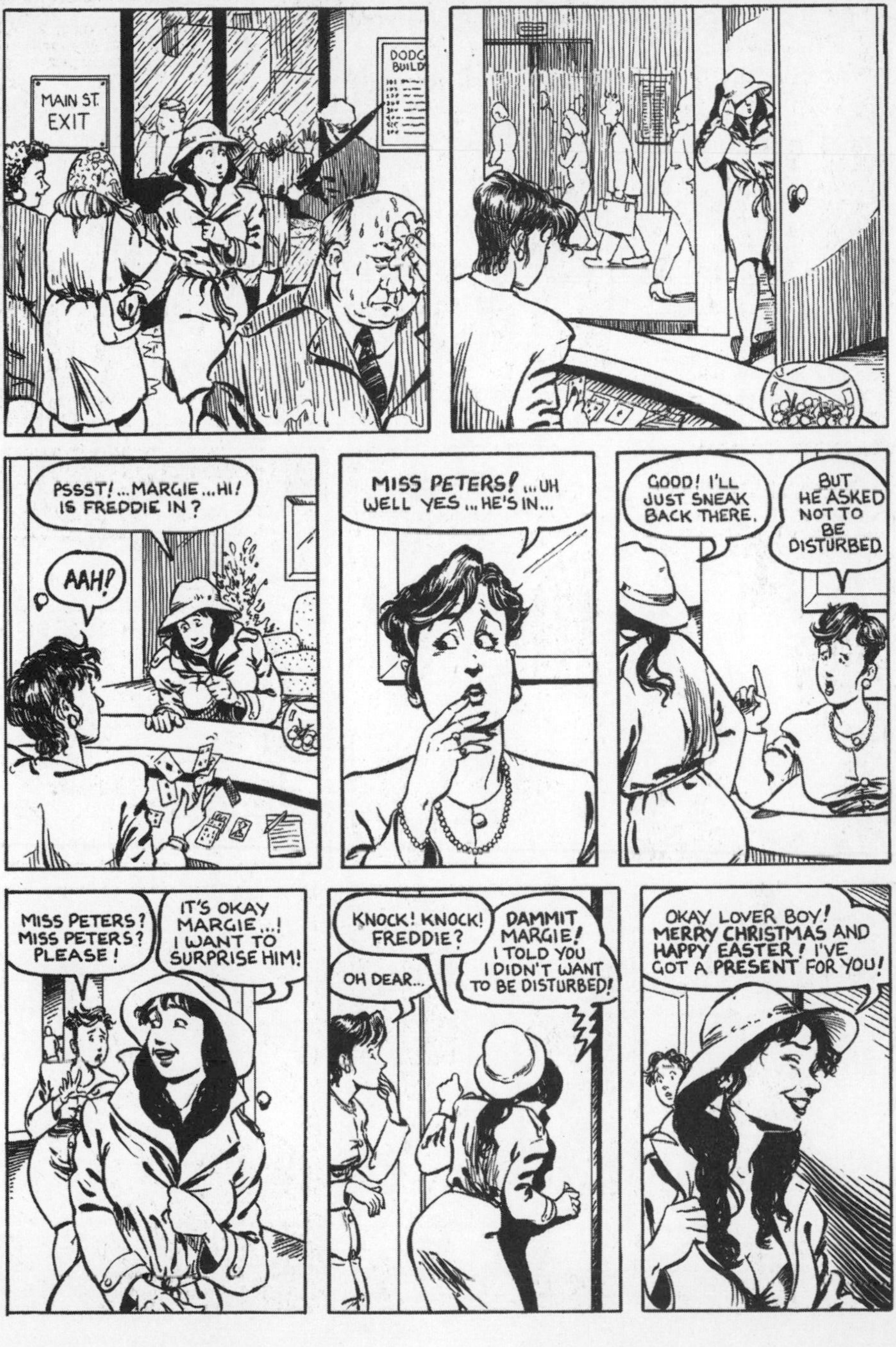
MAIN ST. EXIT
PSSST! ...MARGIE ...HI! IS FREDDIE IN ?
AAH!
MISS PETERS! ...UH WELL YES ... HE'S IN...
GOOD! I'LL JUST SNEAK BACK THERE.
BUT HE ASKED NOT TO BE DISTURBED.
MISS PETERS? MISS PETERS? PLEASE!
IT'S OKAY MARGIE...! I WANT TO SURPRISE HIM!
KNOCK! KNOCK! FREDDIE?
OH DEAR...
DAMMIT MARGIE! I TOLD YOU I DIDN'T WANT TO BE DISTURBED!
OKAY LOVER BOY! MERRY CHRISTMAS AND HAPPY EASTER! I'VE GOT A PRESENT FOR YOU!

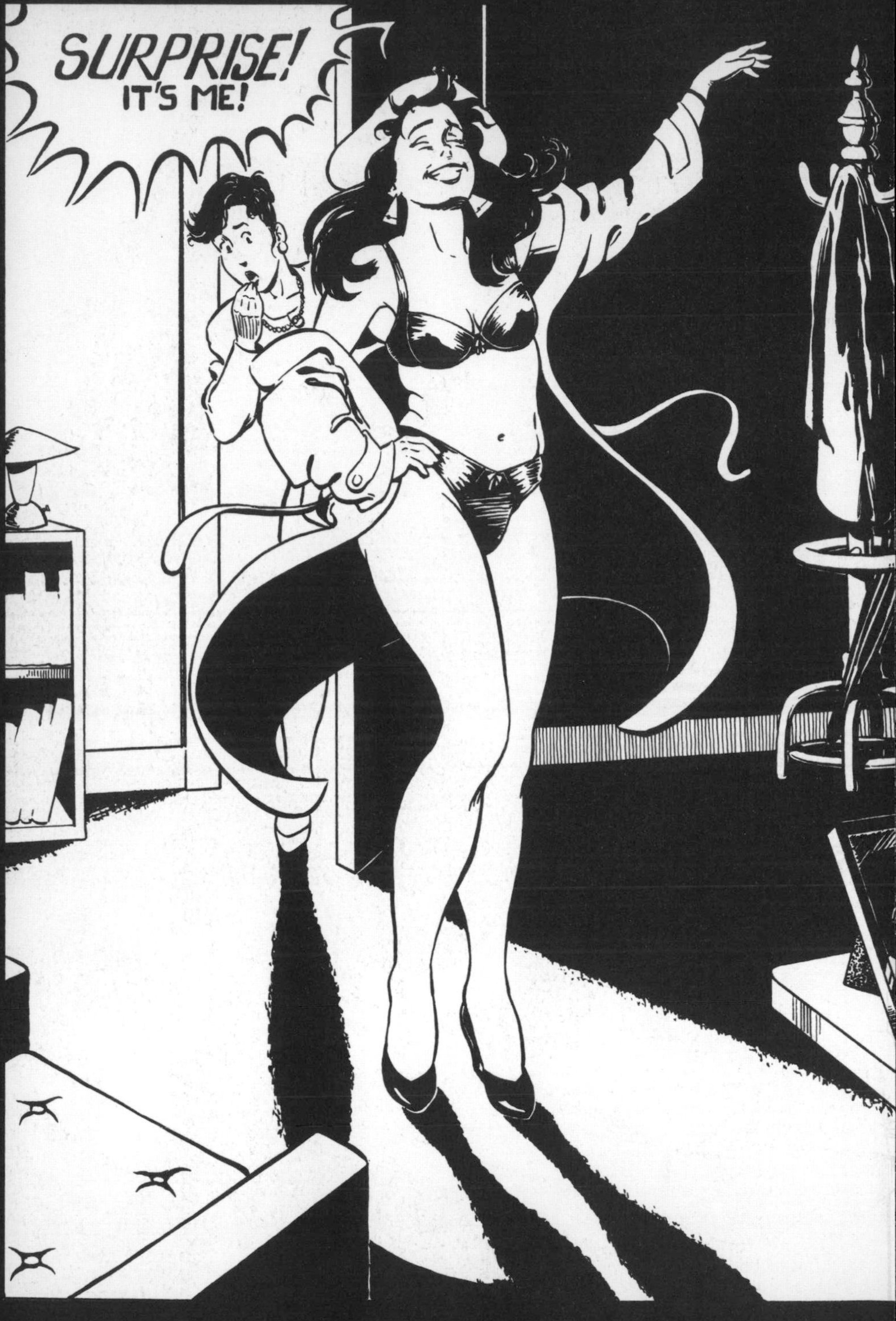
SURPRISE! IT'S ME!

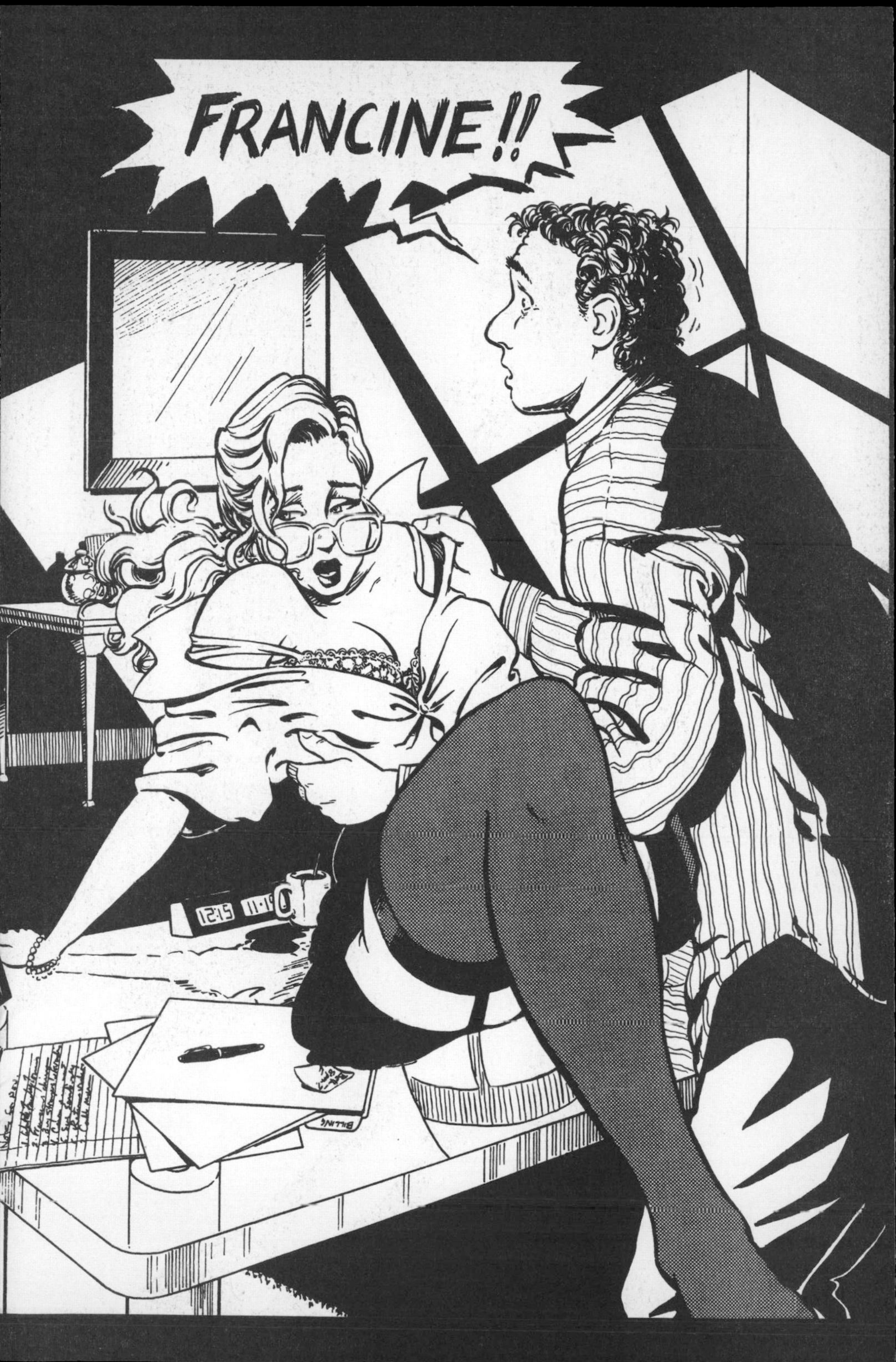
FRANCINE!!

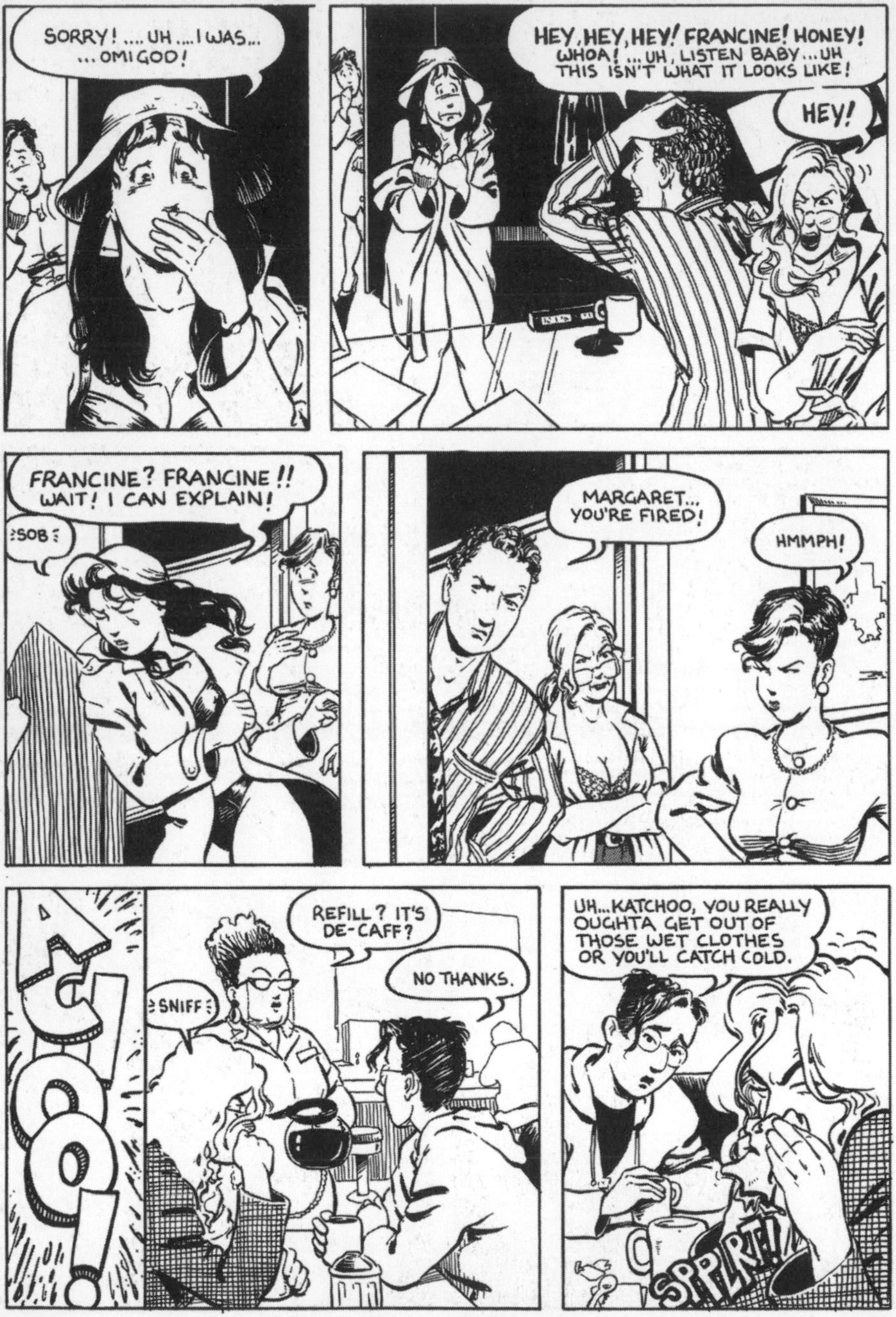
SORRY! ....UH ....I WAS... ...OMIGOD!
HEY, HEY, HEY! FRANCINE! HONEY! WHOA! ...UH, LISTEN BABY...UH THIS ISN'T WHAT IT LOOKS LIKE!
HEY!
FRANCINE? FRANCINE!! WAIT! I CAN EXPLAIN!
SOB
MARGARET... YOU'RE FIRED!
HMMPH!
ACHOO!
REFILL? IT'S DE-CAFF?
NO THANKS.
SNIFF
UH...KATCHOO, YOU REALLY OUGHTA GET OUT OF THOSE WET CLOTHES OR YOU'LL CATCH COLD.
SPPLRT!

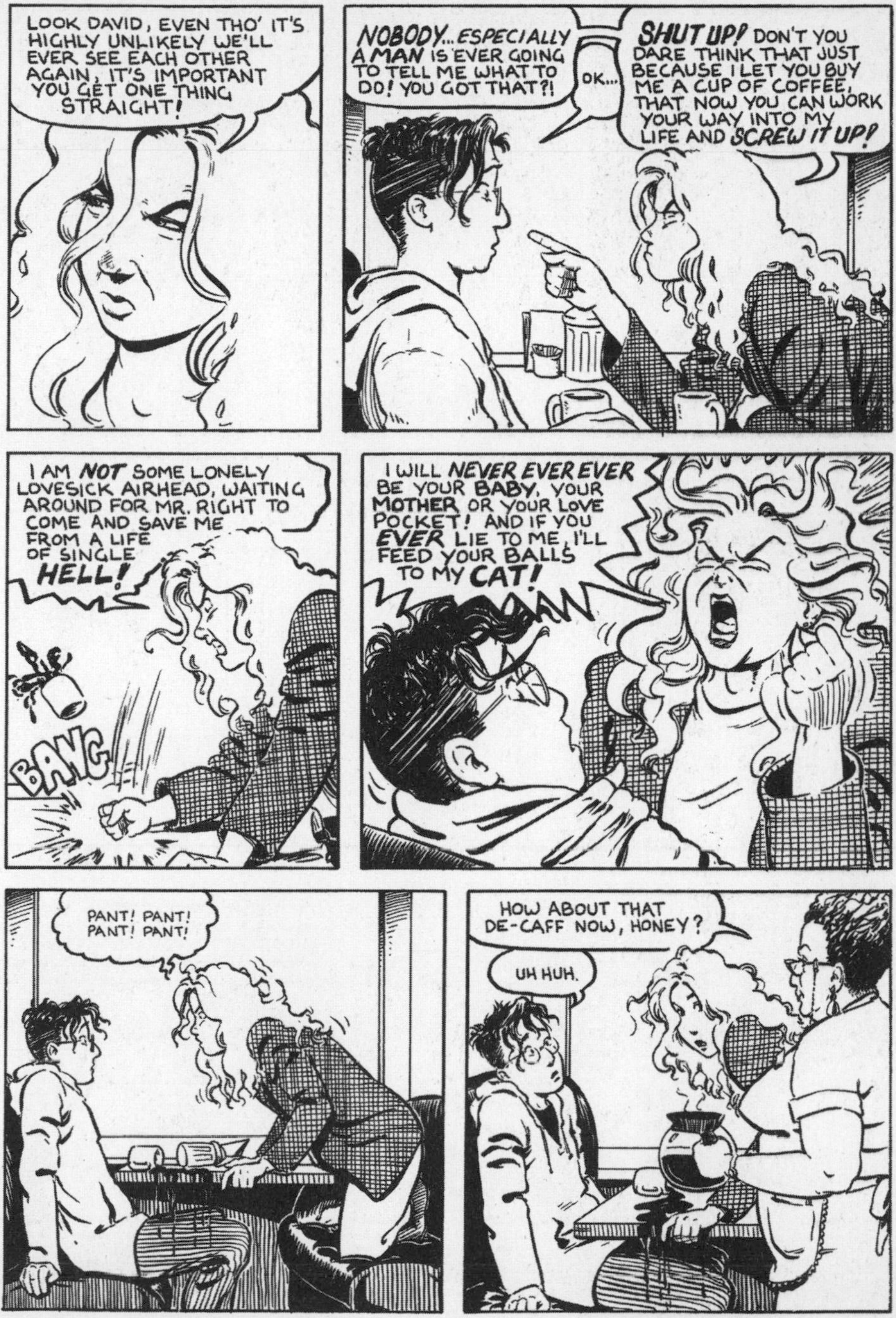
LOOK DAVID, EVEN THO' IT'S HIGHLY UNLIKELY WE'LL EVER SEE EACH OTHER AGAIN, IT'S IMPORTANT YOU GET ONE THING STRAIGHT!
NOBODY... ESPECIALLY A MAN IS EVER GOING TO TELL ME WHAT TO DO! YOU GOT THAT?!
OK...
SHUT UP! DON'T YOU DARE THINK THAT JUST BECAUSE I LET YOU BUY ME A CUP OF COFFEE, THAT NOW YOU CAN WORK YOUR WAY INTO MY LIFE AND SCREW IT UP!
I AM NOT SOME LONELY LOVESICK AIRHEAD, WAITING AROUND FOR MR. RIGHT TO COME AND SAVE ME FROM A LIFE OF SINGLE HELL!
BANG
I WILL NEVER EVER EVER BE YOUR BABY, YOUR MOTHER OR YOUR LOVE POCKET! AND IF YOU EVER LIE TO ME, I'LL FEED YOUR BALLS TO MY CAT!
PANT! PANT! PANT! PANT!
HOW ABOUT THAT DE-CAFF NOW, HONEY?
UH HUH.

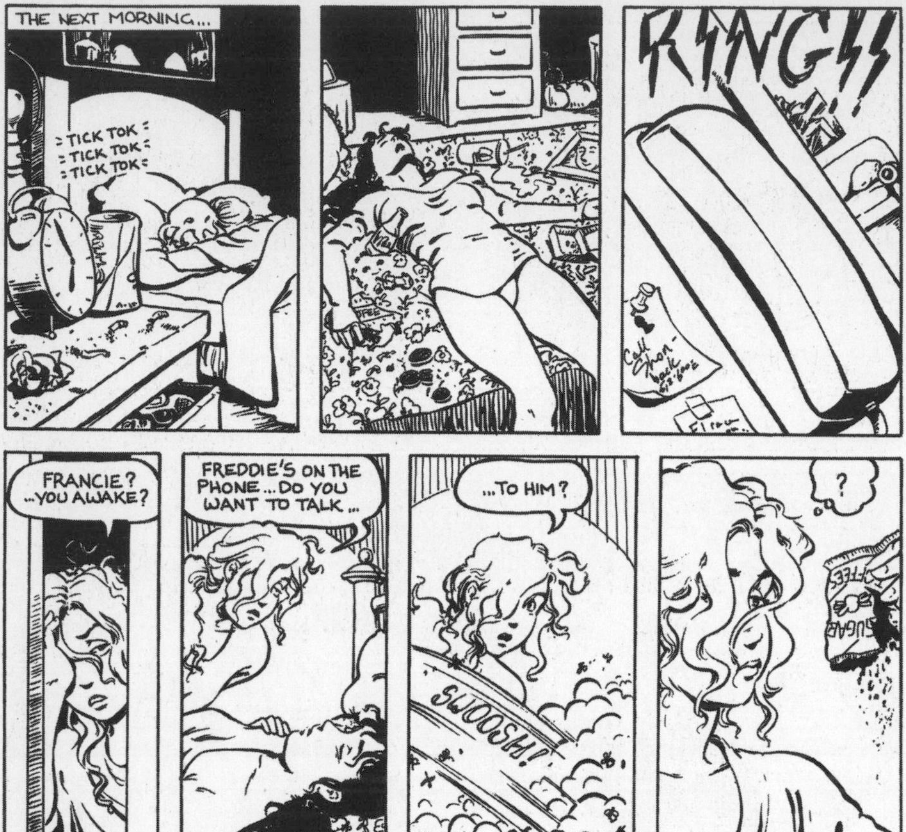

THE NEXT MORNING...
TICK TOK
TICK TOK
TICK TOK
RING!!
FRANCIE? ...YOU AWAKE?
FREDDIE'S ON THE PHONE... DO YOU WANT TO TALK...
...TO HIM?
SWOOSH!
?
HELLO? FREDDIE? ARE YOU THERE?!
FRANCINE, LISTEN, WE NEED TO TALK...
WHY DON'T YOU MEET ME FOR LUNCH... SAY AT THE PARK, OK? ....WELL, LOOK, LET'S WAIT AND TALK ABOUT IT THEN, OK? SEE YA.
DON'T WORRY BABS, THIS WON'T TAKE LONG, THEN WE'LL GO EAT.
GOOD, I'M FAMISHED!

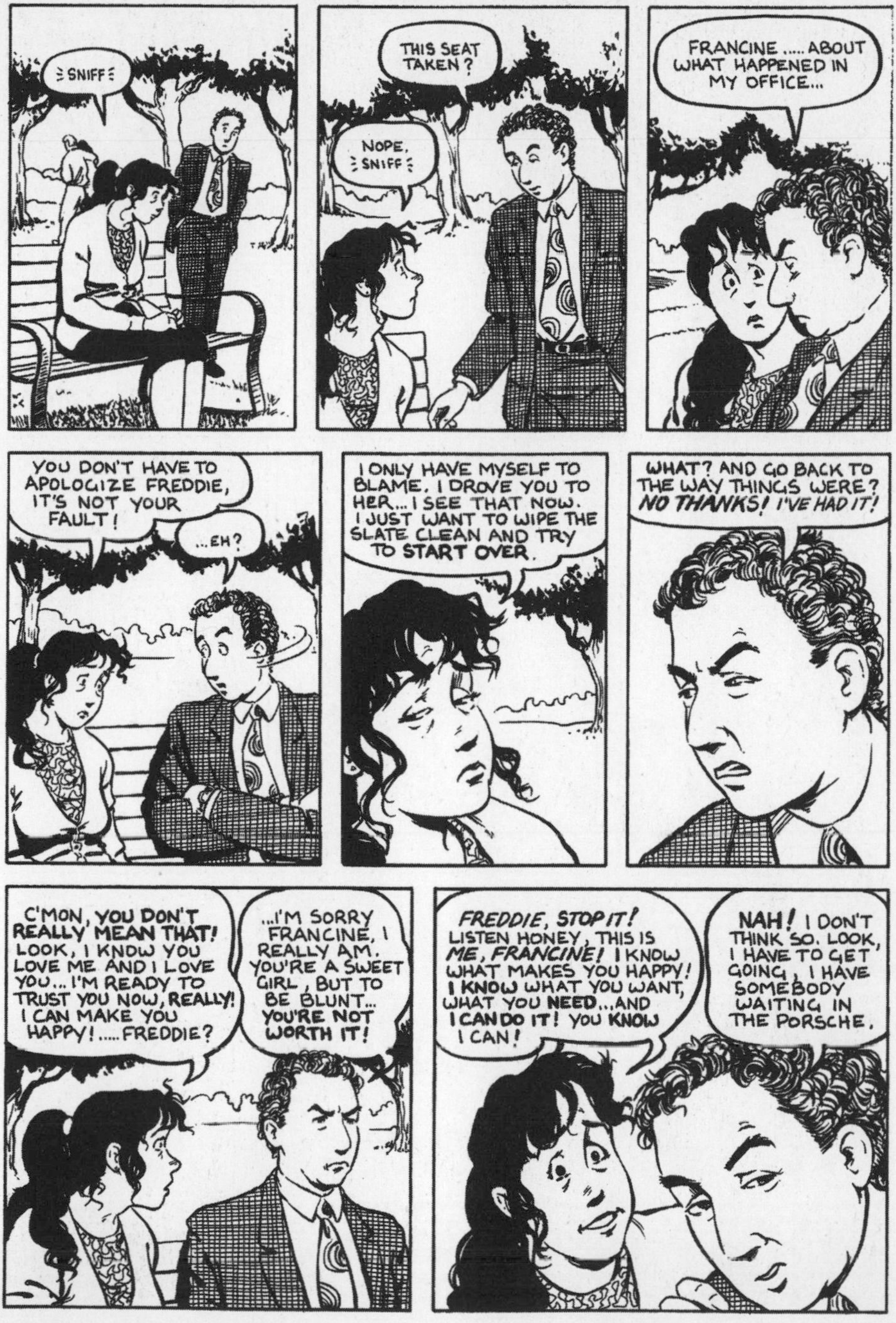
SNIFF
THIS SEAT TAKEN?
NOPE. SNIFF
FRANCINE ..... ABOUT WHAT HAPPENED IN MY OFFICE...
YOU DON'T HAVE TO APOLOGIZE FREDDIE, IT'S NOT YOUR FAULT!
...EH?
I ONLY HAVE MYSELF TO BLAME. I DROVE YOU TO HER... I SEE THAT NOW. I JUST WANT TO WIPE THE SLATE CLEAN AND TRY TO START OVER.
WHAT? AND GO BACK TO THE WAY THINGS WERE? NO THANKS! I'VE HAD IT!
C'MON, YOU DON'T REALLY MEAN THAT! LOOK, I KNOW YOU LOVE ME AND I LOVE YOU... I'M READY TO TRUST YOU NOW, REALLY! I CAN MAKE YOU HAPPY! ..... FREDDIE?
...I'M SORRY FRANCINE, I REALLY AM. YOU'RE A SWEET GIRL, BUT TO BE BLUNT... YOU'RE NOT WORTH IT!
FREDDIE, STOP IT! LISTEN HONEY, THIS IS ME, FRANCINE! I KNOW WHAT MAKES YOU HAPPY! I KNOW WHAT YOU WANT, WHAT YOU NEED... AND I CAN DO IT! YOU KNOW I CAN!
NAH! I DON'T THINK SO. LOOK, I HAVE TO GET GOING, I HAVE SOMEBODY WAITING IN THE PORSCHE.

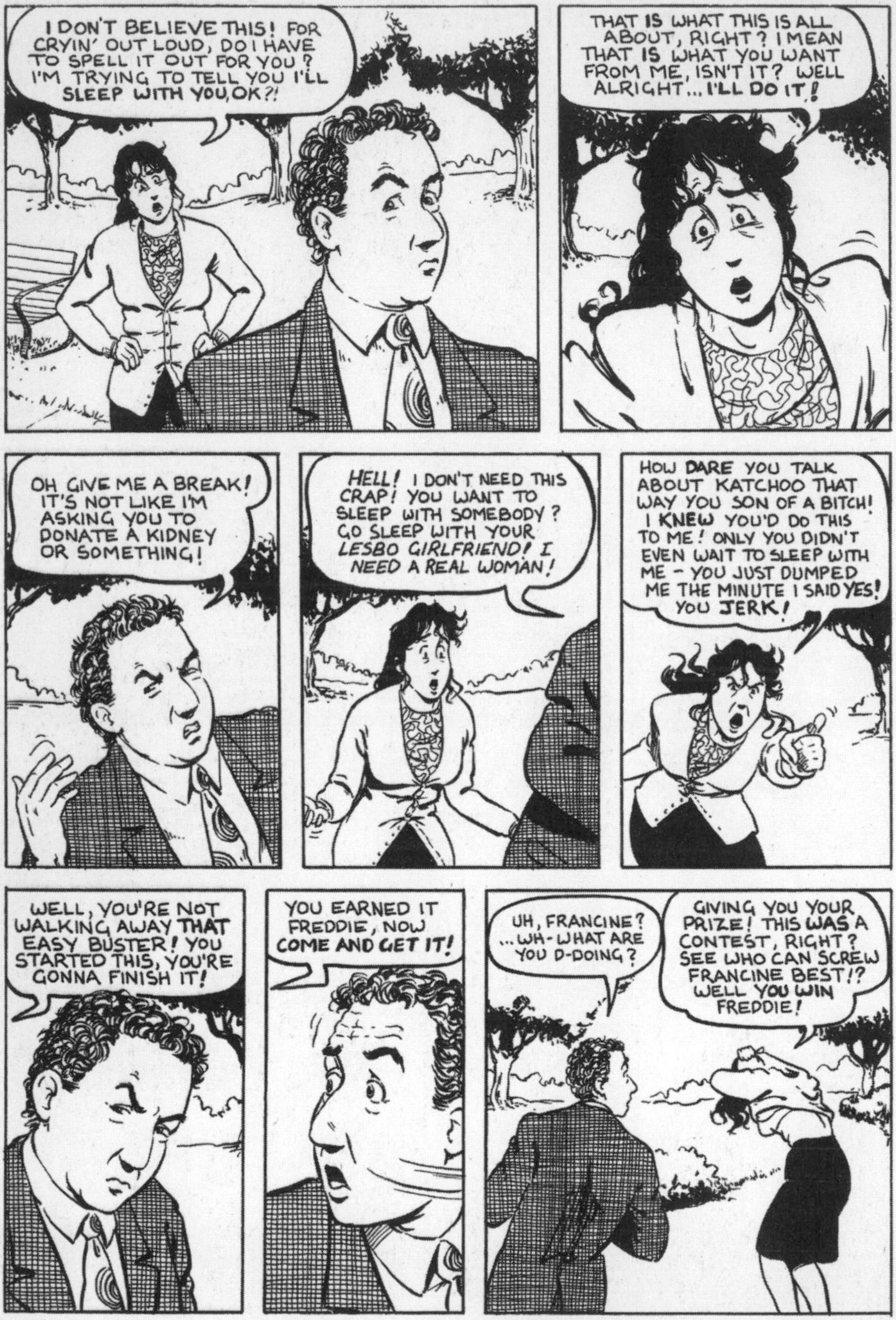
I DON'T BELIEVE THIS! FOR CRYIN' OUT LOUD, DO I HAVE TO SPELL IT OUT FOR YOU? I'M TRYING TO TELL YOU I'LL SLEEP WITH YOU, OK?!
THAT IS WHAT THIS IS ALL ABOUT, RIGHT? I MEAN THAT IS WHAT YOU WANT FROM ME, ISN'T IT? WELL ALRIGHT... I'LL DO IT!
OH GIVE ME A BREAK! IT'S NOT LIKE I'M ASKING YOU TO DONATE A KIDNEY OR SOMETHING!
HELL! I DON'T NEED THIS CRAP! YOU WANT TO SLEEP WITH SOMEBODY? GO SLEEP WITH YOUR LESBO GIRLFRIEND! I NEED A REAL WOMAN!
HOW DARE YOU TALK ABOUT KATCHOO THAT WAY YOU SON OF A BITCH! I KNEW YOU'D DO THIS TO ME! ONLY YOU DIDN'T EVEN WAIT TO SLEEP WITH ME - YOU JUST DUMPED ME THE MINUTE I SAID YES! YOU JERK!
WELL, YOU'RE NOT WALKING AWAY THAT EASY BUSTER! YOU STARTED THIS, YOU'RE GONNA FINISH IT!
YOU EARNED IT FREDDIE, NOW COME AND GET IT!
UH, FRANCINE? ...WH-WHAT ARE YOU D-DOING?
GIVING YOU YOUR PRIZE! THIS WAS A CONTEST, RIGHT? SEE WHO CAN SCREW FRANCINE BEST!? WELL YOU WIN FREDDIE!

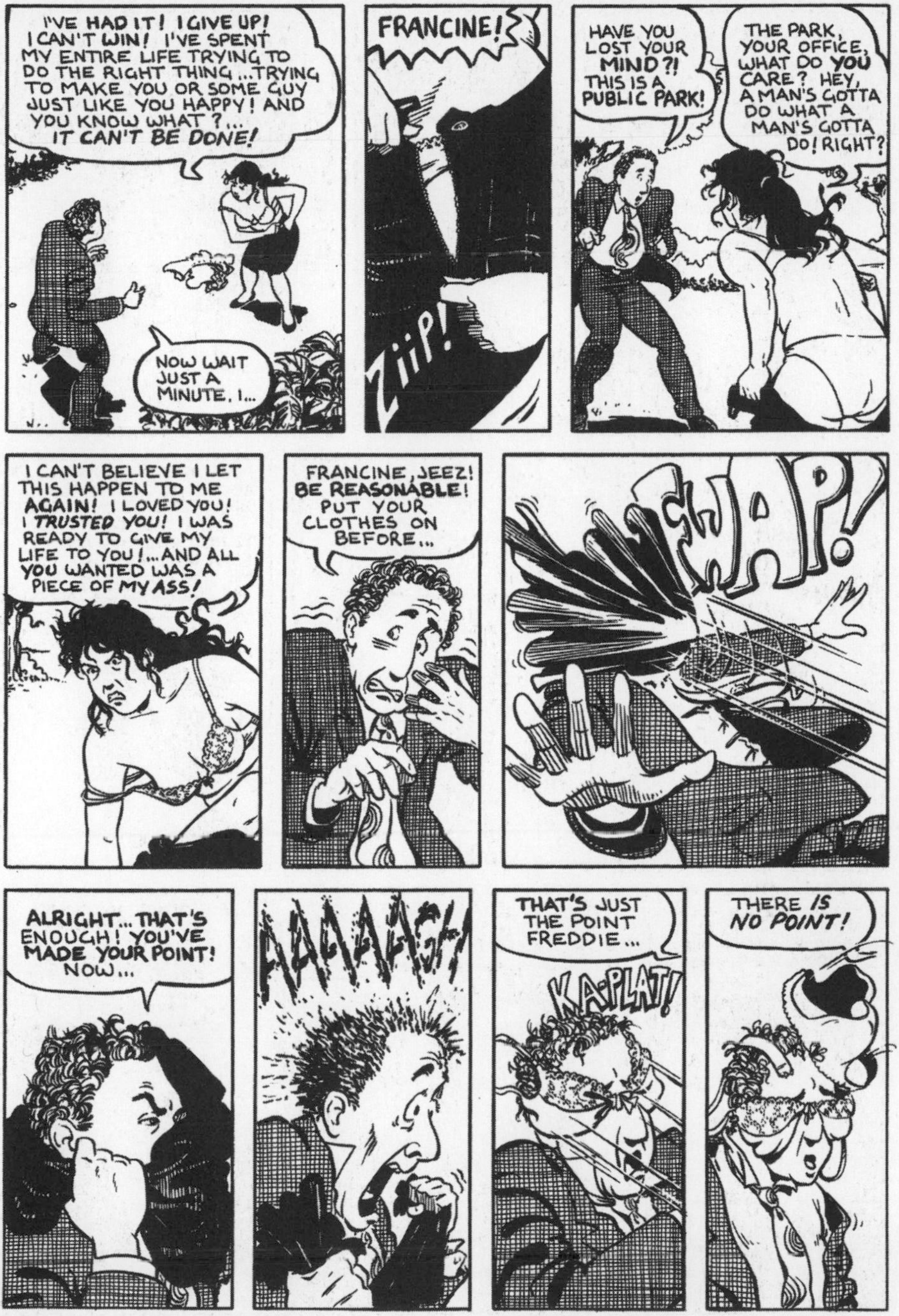
I'VE HAD IT! I GIVE UP! I CAN'T WIN! I'VE SPENT MY ENTIRE LIFE TRYING TO DO THE RIGHT THING ...TRYING TO MAKE YOU OR SOME GUY JUST LIKE YOU HAPPY! AND YOU KNOW WHAT?... IT CAN'T BE DONE!
NOW WAIT JUST A MINUTE. I...
FRANCINE!
ZiiP!
HAVE YOU LOST YOUR MIND?! THIS IS A PUBLIC PARK!
THE PARK, YOUR OFFICE, WHAT DO YOU CARE? HEY, A MAN'S GOTTA DO WHAT A MAN'S GOTTA DO! RIGHT?
I CAN'T BELIEVE I LET THIS HAPPEN TO ME AGAIN! I LOVED YOU! I TRUSTED YOU! I WAS READY TO GIVE MY LIFE TO YOU!...AND ALL YOU WANTED WAS A PIECE OF MY ASS!
FRANCINE, JEEZ! BE REASONABLE! PUT YOUR CLOTHES ON BEFORE...
SWAP!
ALRIGHT... THAT'S ENOUGH! YOU'VE MADE YOUR POINT! NOW...
AAGAAAGH
THAT'S JUST THE POINT FREDDIE...
KA-PLAT!
THERE IS NO POINT!

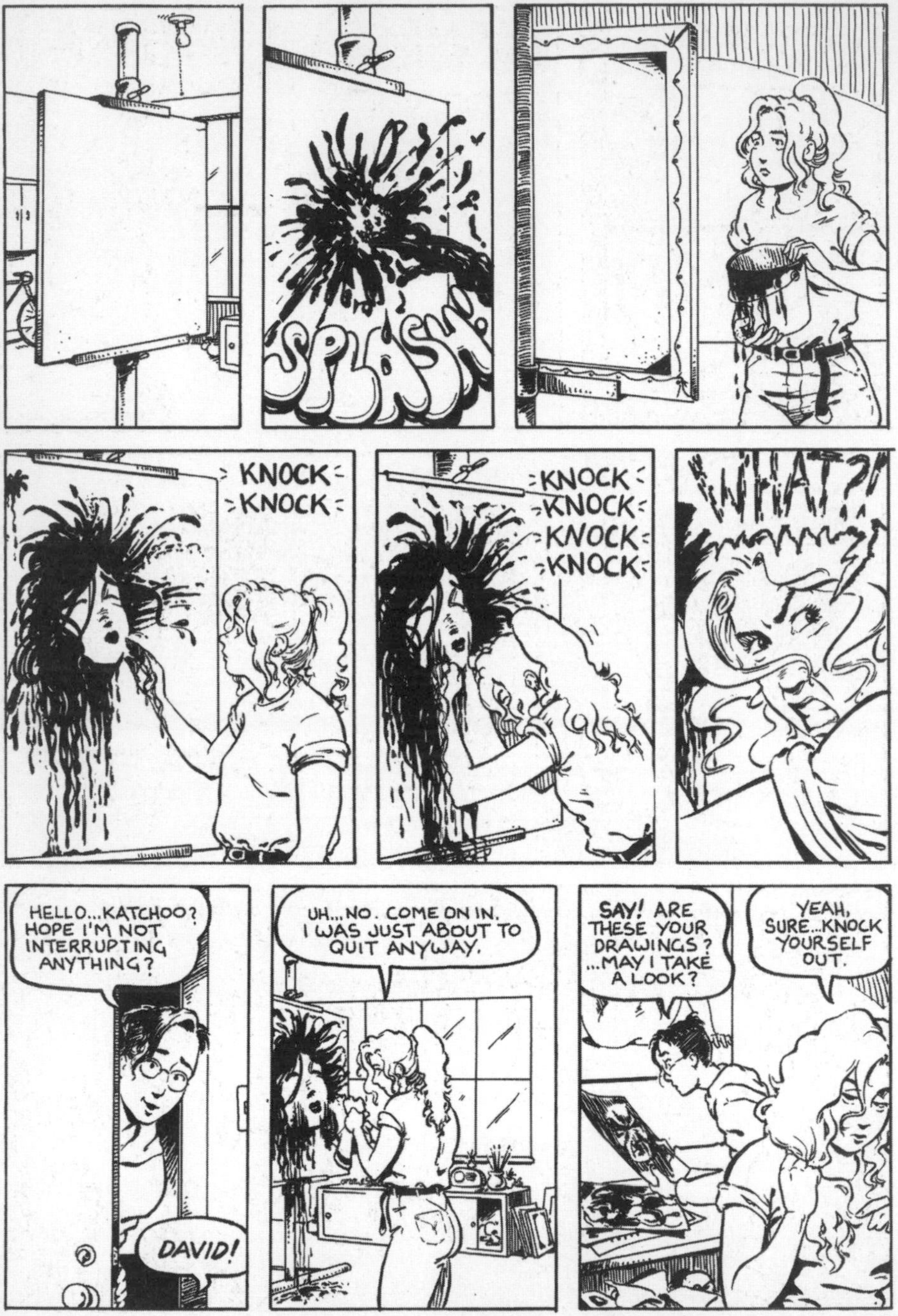
SPLASH
KNOCK KNOCK
KNOCK KNOCK KNOCK KNOCK
WHAT?!
HELLO...KATCHOO? HOPE I'M NOT INTERRUPTING ANYTHING?
DAVID!
UH...NO. COME ON IN. I WAS JUST ABOUT TO QUIT ANYWAY.
SAY! ARE THESE YOUR DRAWINGS? ...MAY I TAKE A LOOK?
YEAH, SURE...KNOCK YOURSELF OUT.

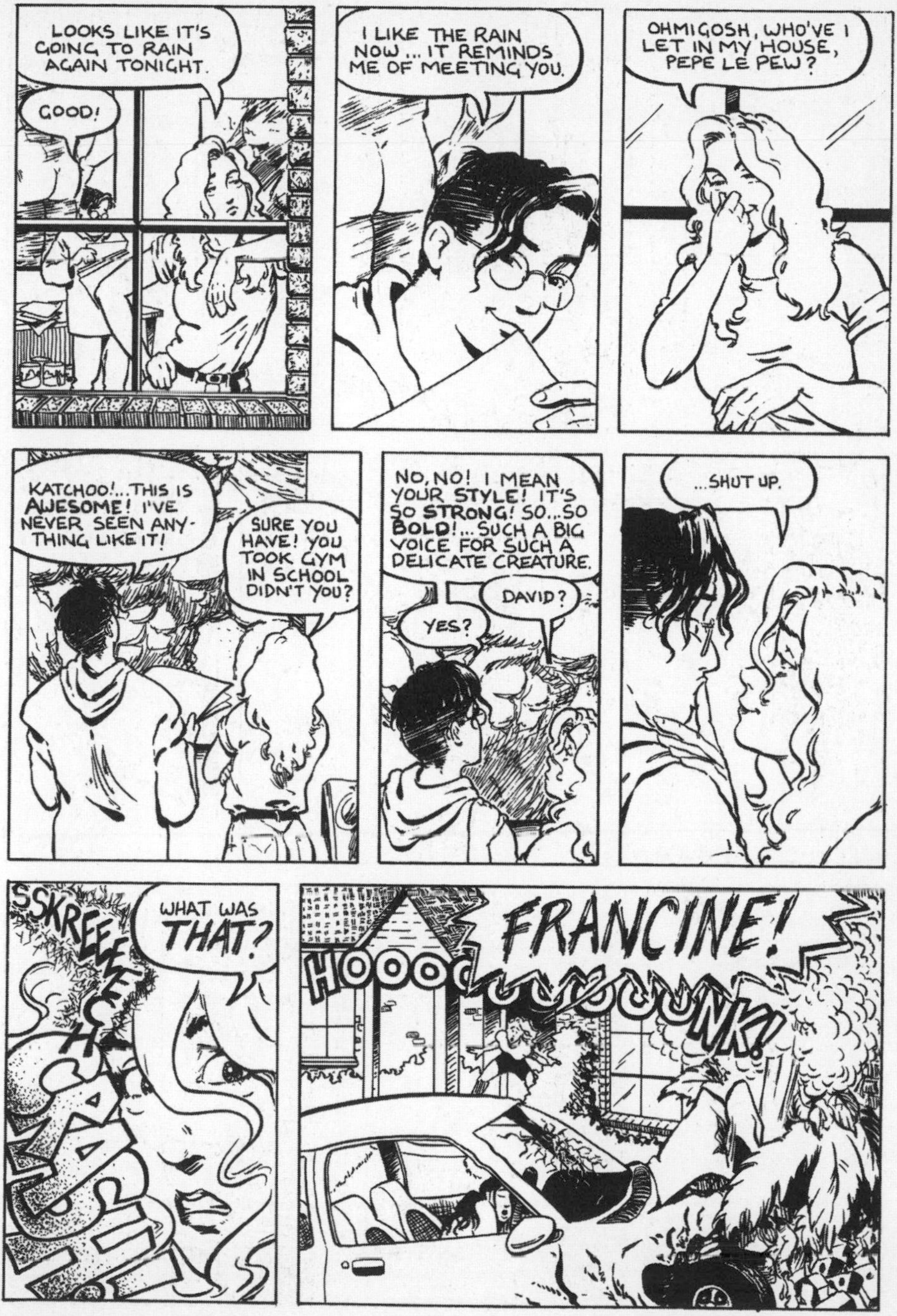
LOOKS LIKE IT'S GOING TO RAIN AGAIN TONIGHT.
GOOD!
I LIKE THE RAIN NOW... IT REMINDS ME OF MEETING YOU.
OHMIGOSH, WHO'VE I LET IN MY HOUSE, PEPE LE PEW?
KATCHOO!...THIS IS AWESOME! I'VE NEVER SEEN ANYTHING LIKE IT!
SURE YOU HAVE! YOU TOOK GYM IN SCHOOL DIDN'T YOU?
NO, NO! I MEAN YOUR STYLE! IT'S SO STRONG! SO...SO BOLD!...SUCH A BIG VOICE FOR SUCH A DELICATE CREATURE.
DAVID?
YES?
...SHUT UP.
SSKREEEEECH
WHAT WAS THAT?
FRANCINE!
HOOOOOOOOOONK!

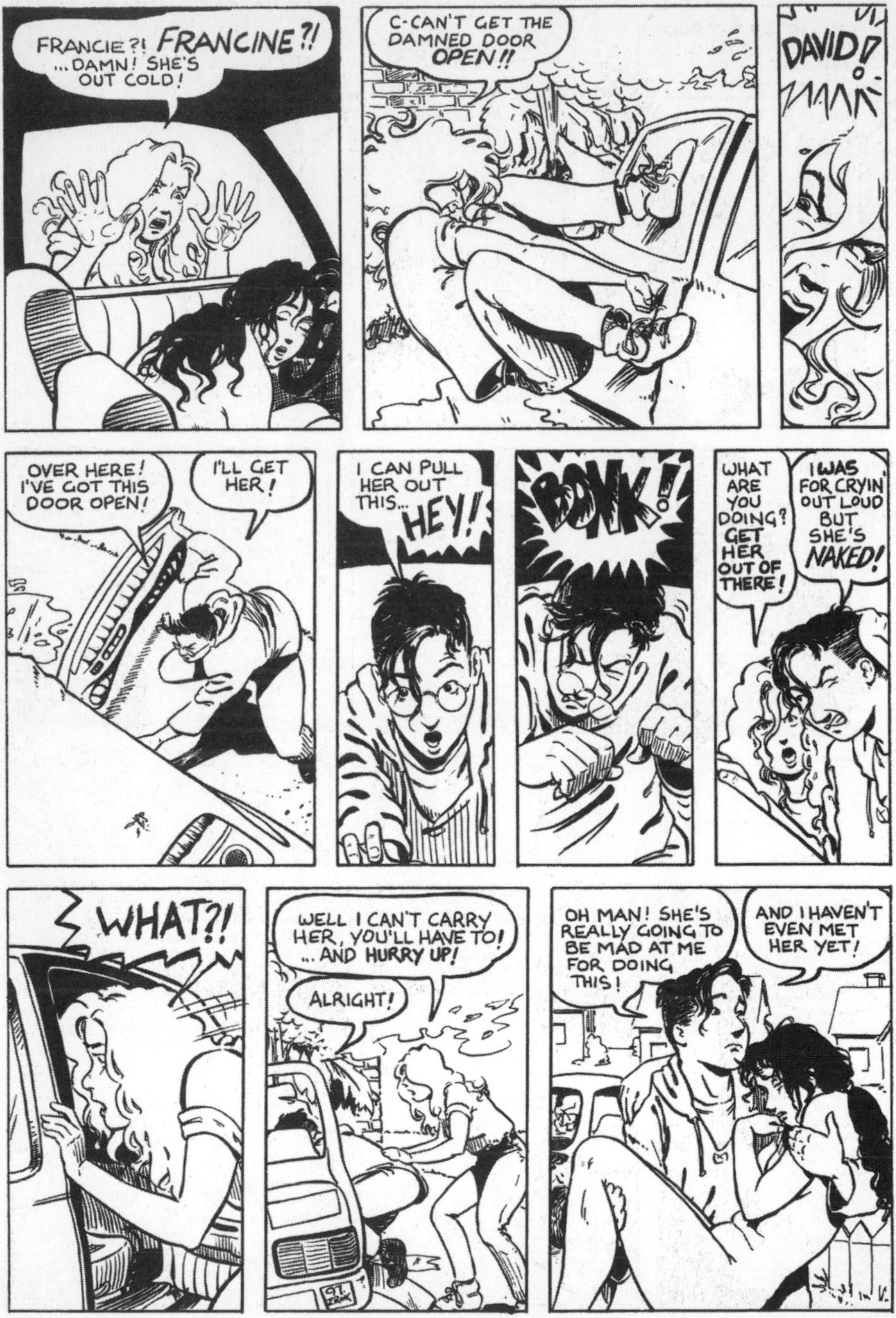
FRANCIE?! FRANCINE?! ...DAMN! SHE'S OUT COLD!
C-CAN'T GET THE DAMNED DOOR OPEN!!
DAVID!
OVER HERE! I'VE GOT THIS DOOR OPEN!
I'LL GET HER!
I CAN PULL HER OUT THIS... HEY!!
BONK!
WHAT ARE YOU DOING? GET HER OUT OF THERE!
I WAS FOR CRYIN' OUT LOUD BUT SHE'S NAKED!
WHAT?!
WELL I CAN'T CARRY HER, YOU'LL HAVE TO! ...AND HURRY UP!
ALRIGHT!
OH MAN! SHE'S REALLY GOING TO BE MAD AT ME FOR DOING THIS!
AND I HAVEN'T EVEN MET HER YET!

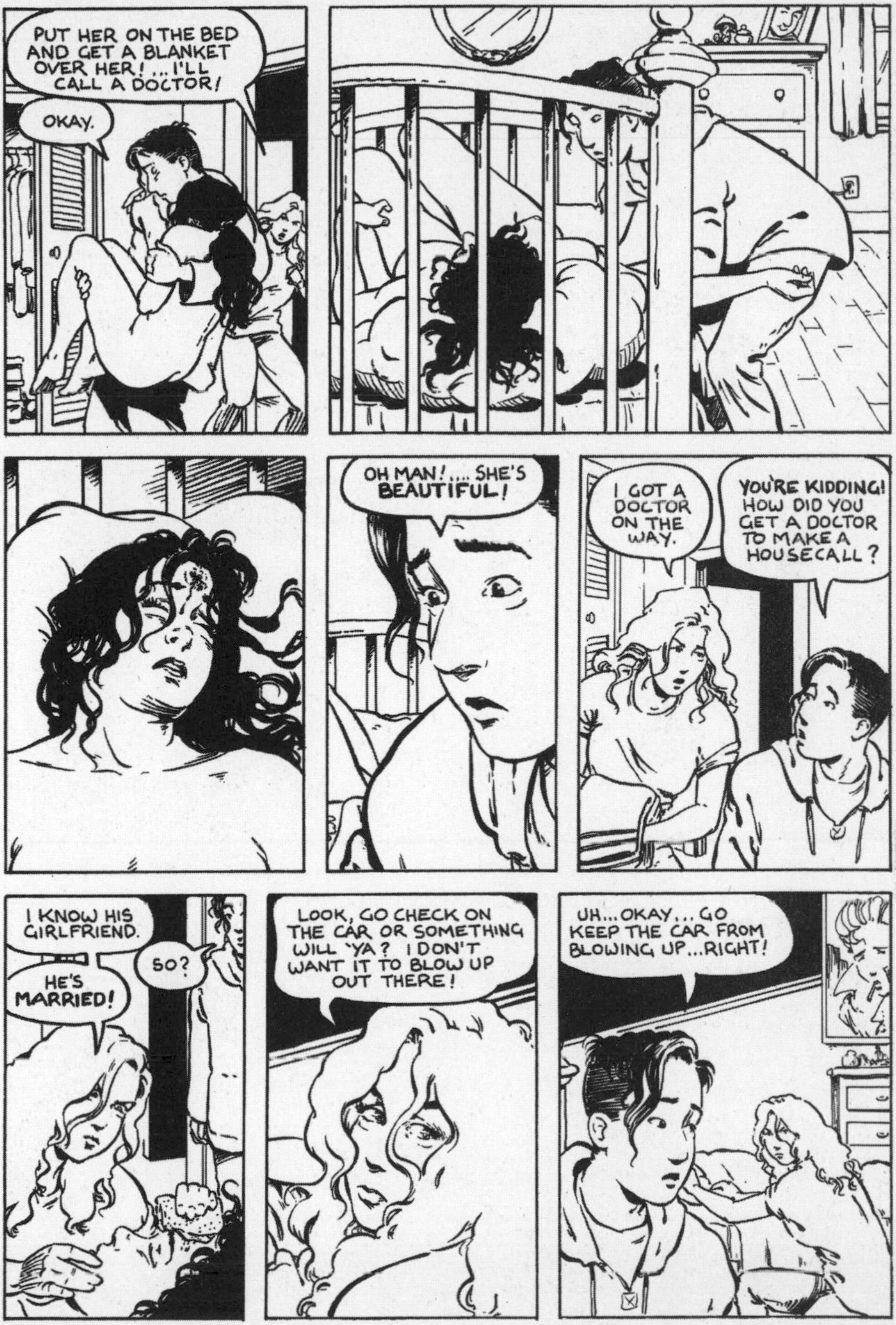
PUT HER ON THE BED AND GET A BLANKET OVER HER! ... I'LL CALL A DOCTOR!
OKAY.
OH MAN! .... SHE'S BEAUTIFUL!
I GOT A DOCTOR ON THE WAY.
YOU'RE KIDDING! HOW DID YOU GET A DOCTOR TO MAKE A HOUSECALL?
I KNOW HIS GIRLFRIEND.
SO?
HE'S MARRIED!
LOOK, GO CHECK ON THE CAR OR SOMETHING WILL 'YA? I DON'T WANT IT TO BLOW UP OUT THERE!
UH... OKAY,... GO KEEP THE CAR FROM BLOWING UP... RIGHT!

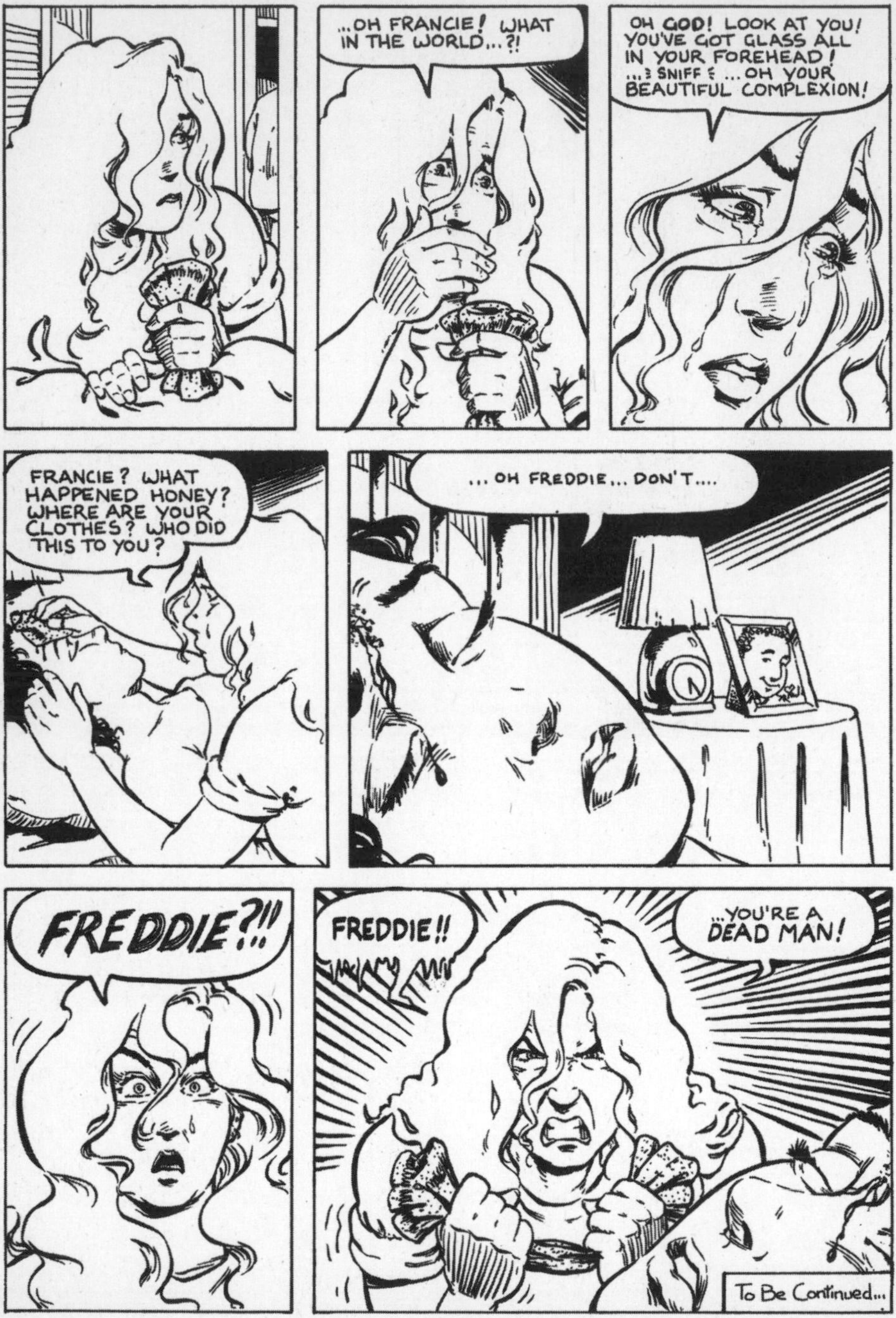
...OH FRANCIE! WHAT IN THE WORLD...?!
OH GOD! LOOK AT YOU! YOU'VE GOT GLASS ALL IN YOUR FOREHEAD! ...SNIFF ...OH YOUR BEAUTIFUL COMPLEXION!
FRANCIE? WHAT HAPPENED HONEY? WHERE ARE YOUR CLOTHES? WHO DID THIS TO YOU?
...OH FREDDIE... DON'T....
FREDDIE?!!
FREDDIE!!
...YOU'RE A DEAD MAN!
To Be Continued...

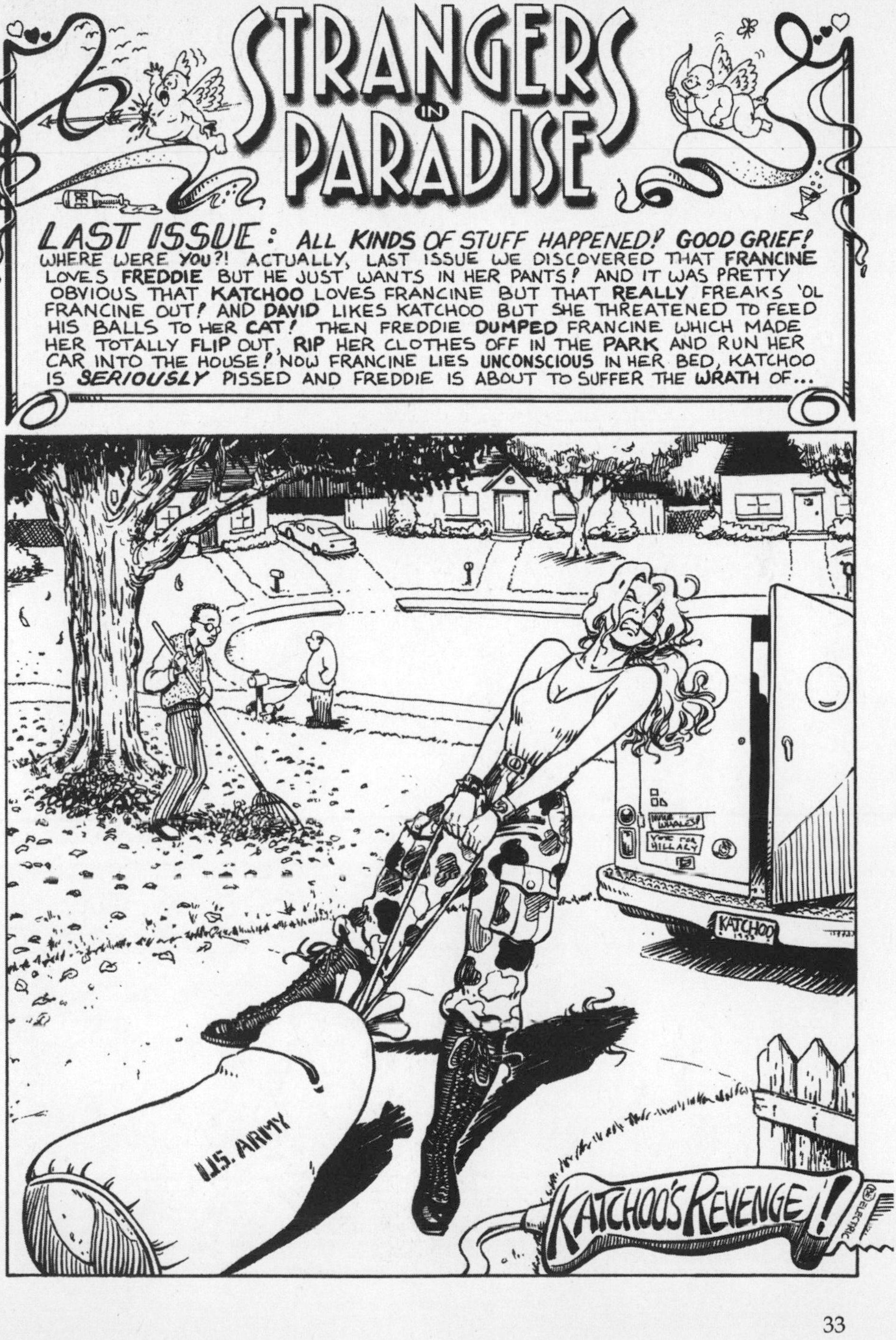
STRANGERS IN PARADISE
LAST ISSUE: ALL KINDS OF STUFF HAPPENED! GOOD GRIEF! WHERE WERE YOU?! ACTUALLY, LAST ISSUE WE DISCOVERED THAT FRANCINE LOVES FREDDIE BUT HE JUST WANTS IN HER PANTS! AND IT WAS PRETTY OBVIOUS THAT KATCHOO LOVES FRANCINE BUT THAT REALLY FREAKS 'OL FRANCINE OUT! AND DAVID LIKES KATCHOO BUT SHE THREATENED TO FEED HIS BALLS TO HER CAT! THEN FREDDIE DUMPED FRANCINE WHICH MADE HER TOTALLY FLIP OUT, RIP HER CLOTHES OFF IN THE PARK AND RUN HER CAR INTO THE HOUSE! NOW FRANCINE LIES UNCONSCIOUS IN HER BED, KATCHOO IS SERIOUSLY PISSED AND FREDDIE IS ABOUT TO SUFFER THE WRATH OF...
VOTE FOR HILLARY
KATCHOO
U.S. ARMY
KATCHOO'S REVENGE!

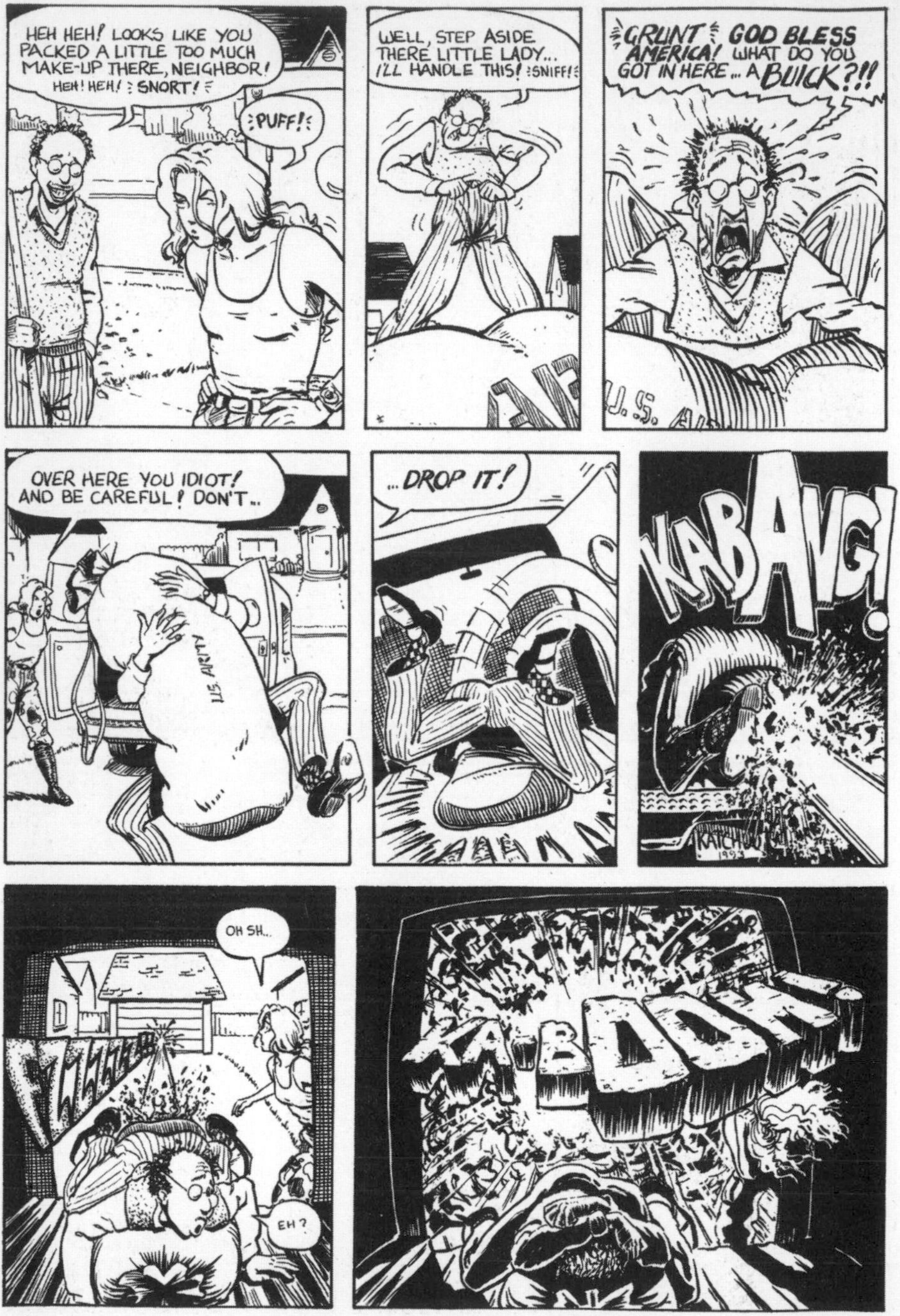
HEH HEH! LOOKS LIKE YOU PACKED A LITTLE TOO MUCH MAKE-UP THERE, NEIGHBOR! HEH! HEH! SNORT!
PUFF!
WELL, STEP ASIDE THERE LITTLE LADY... I'LL HANDLE THIS! SNIFF!
GRUNT GOD BLESS AMERICA! WHAT DO YOU GOT IN HERE... A BUICK?!!
U.S.
OVER HERE YOU IDIOT! AND BE CAREFUL! DON'T...
U.S. ARMY
...DROP IT!
KABANG!
KATCHOR 1993
OH SH..
EH?
KA-BOOM

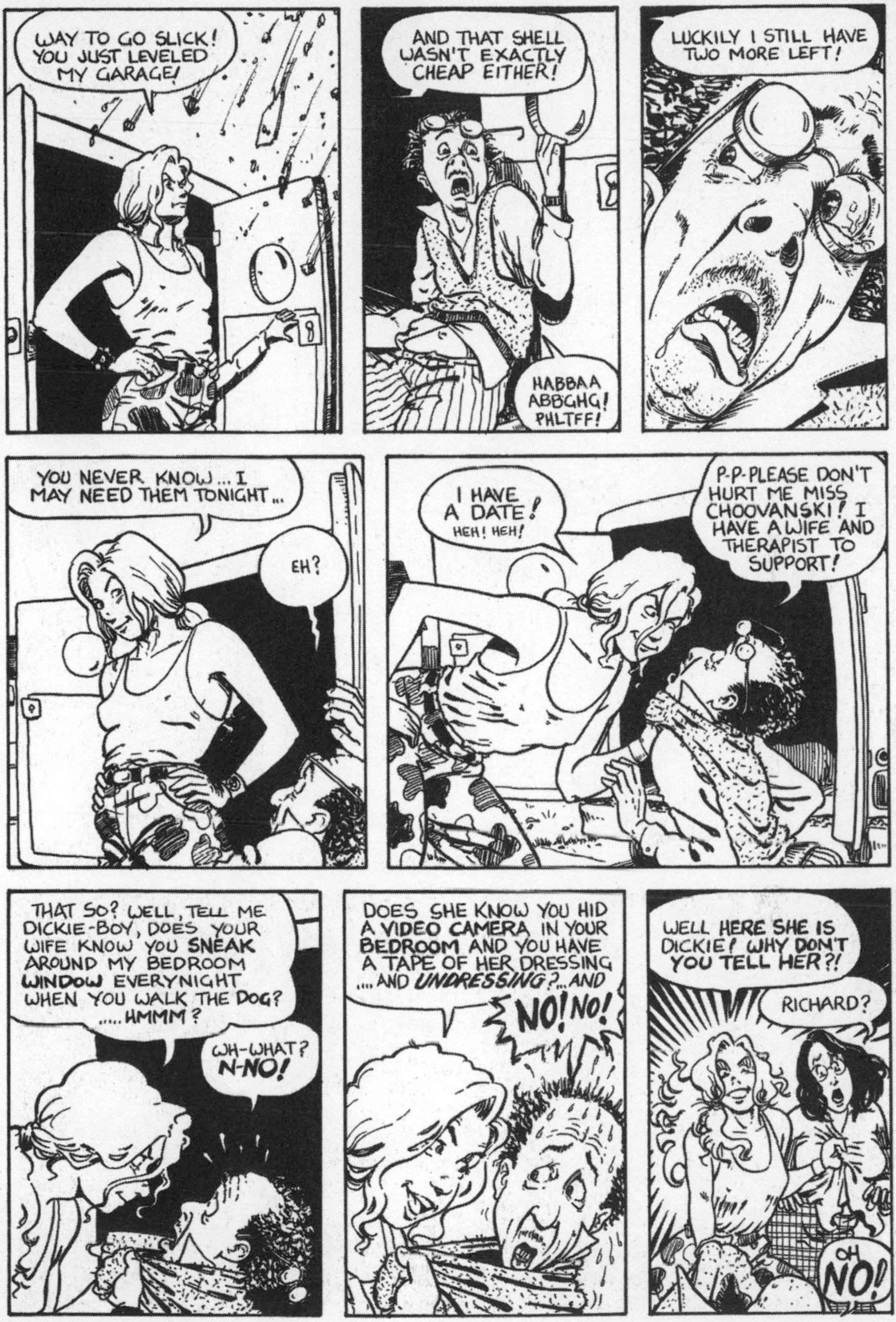
WAY TO GO SLICK! YOU JUST LEVELED MY GARAGE!
AND THAT SHELL WASN'T EXACTLY CHEAP EITHER!
HABBAA ABBGHG! PHLTFF!
LUCKILY I STILL HAVE TWO MORE LEFT!
YOU NEVER KNOW... I MAY NEED THEM TONIGHT...
EH?
I HAVE A DATE! HEH! HEH!
P-P-PLEASE DON'T HURT ME MISS CHOOVANSKI! I HAVE A WIFE AND THERAPIST TO SUPPORT!
THAT SO? WELL, TELL ME DICKIE-BOY, DOES YOUR WIFE KNOW YOU SNEAK AROUND MY BEDROOM WINDOW EVERYNIGHT WHEN YOU WALK THE DOG? .....HMMM?
WH-WHAT? N-NO!
DOES SHE KNOW YOU HID A VIDEO CAMERA IN YOUR BEDROOM AND YOU HAVE A TAPE OF HER DRESSING ....AND UNDRESSING?...AND
NO! NO!
WELL HERE SHE IS DICKIE! WHY DON'T YOU TELL HER?!
RICHARD?
OH NO!

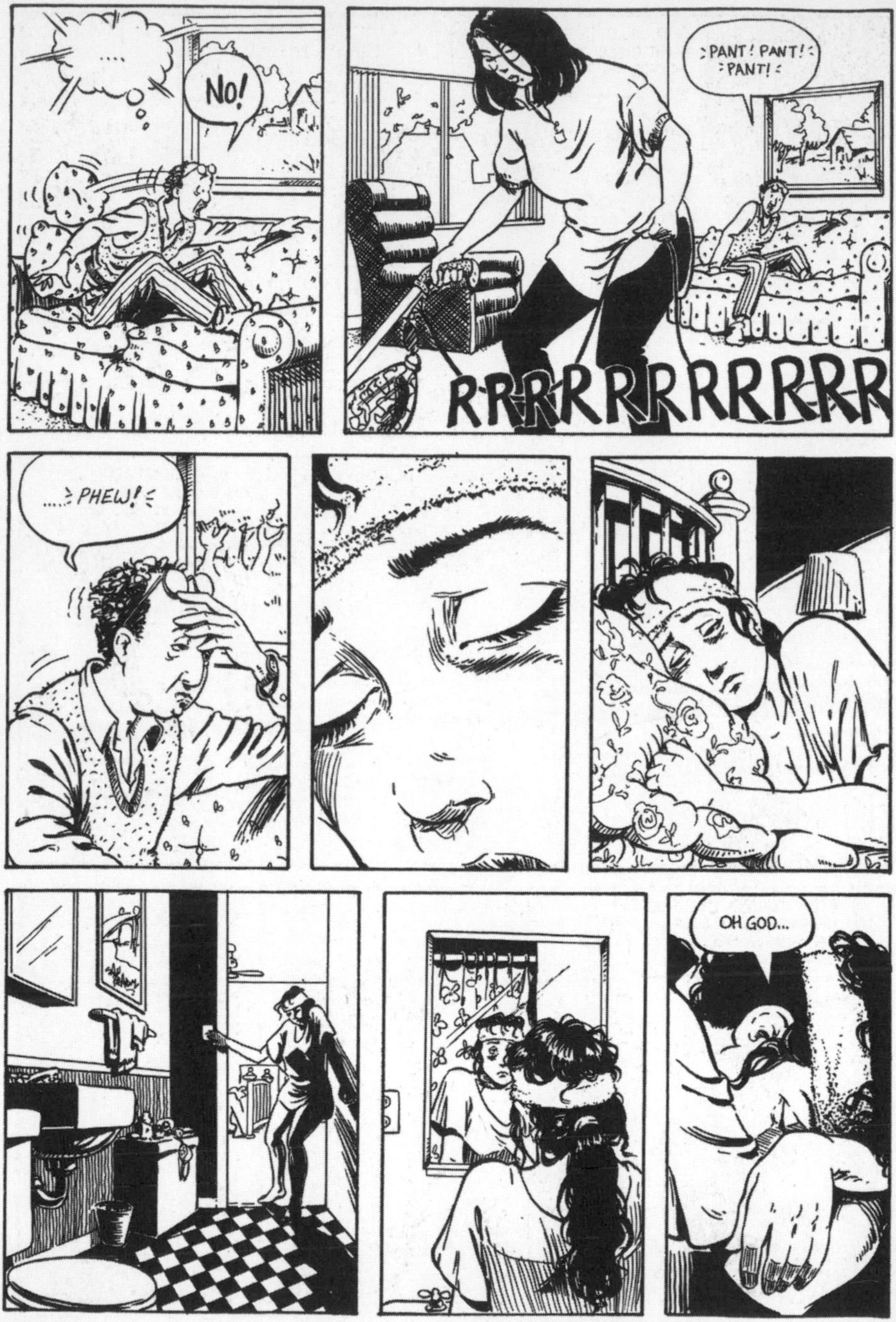
....
No!
PANT! PANT! PANT!
RRRRRRRRRRRR
.....PHEW!
OH GOD...

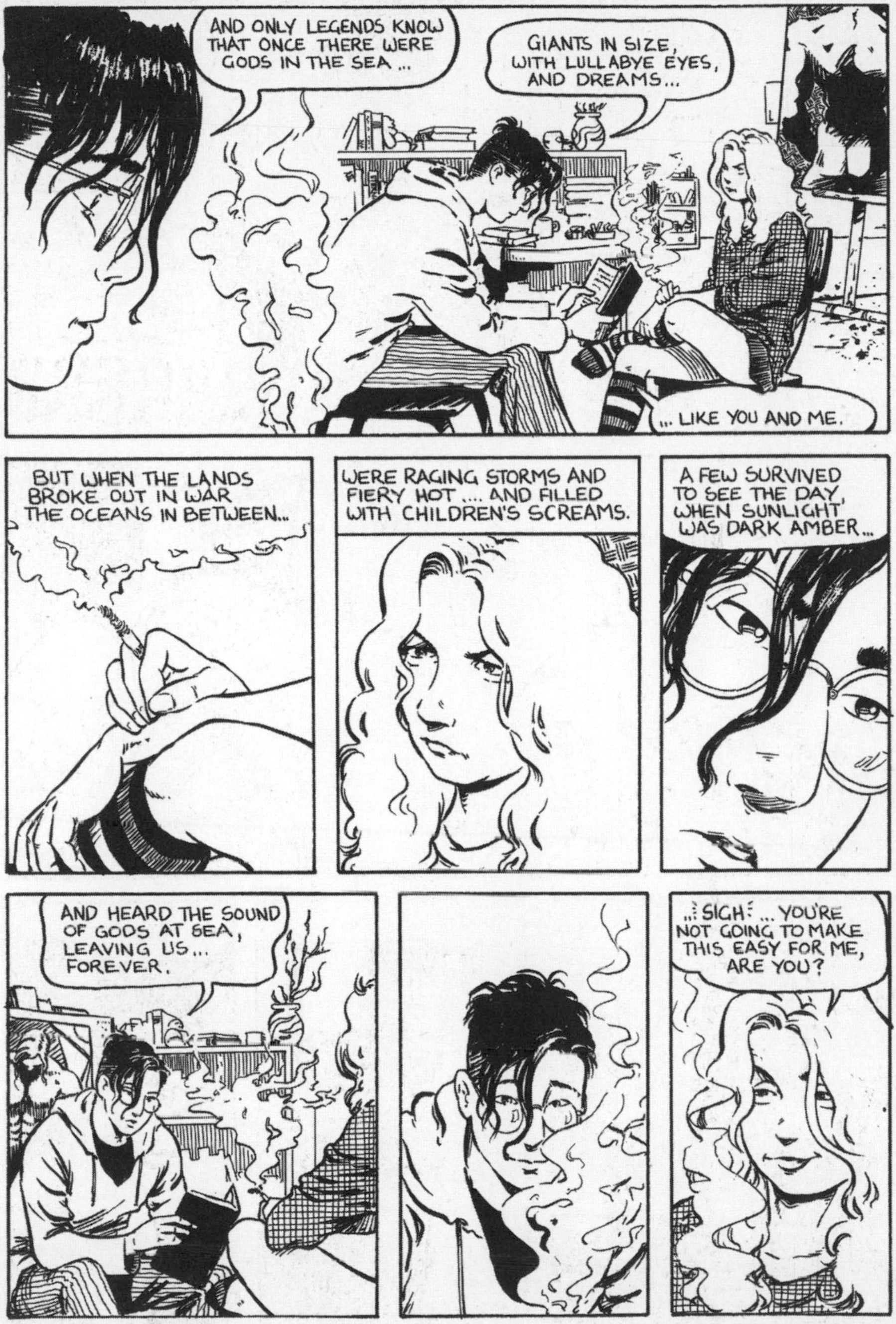

AND ONLY LEGENDS KNOW THAT ONCE THERE WERE GODS IN THE SEA ...
GIANTS IN SIZE, WITH LULLABYE EYES, AND DREAMS...
... LIKE YOU AND ME.
BUT WHEN THE LANDS BROKE OUT IN WAR THE OCEANS IN BETWEEN...
WERE RAGING STORMS AND FIERY HOT .... AND FILLED WITH CHILDREN'S SCREAMS.
A FEW SURVIVED TO SEE THE DAY, WHEN SUNLIGHT WAS DARK AMBER...
AND HEARD THE SOUND OF GODS AT SEA, LEAVING US... FOREVER.
...SIGH ... YOU'RE NOT GOING TO MAKE THIS EASY FOR ME, ARE YOU?

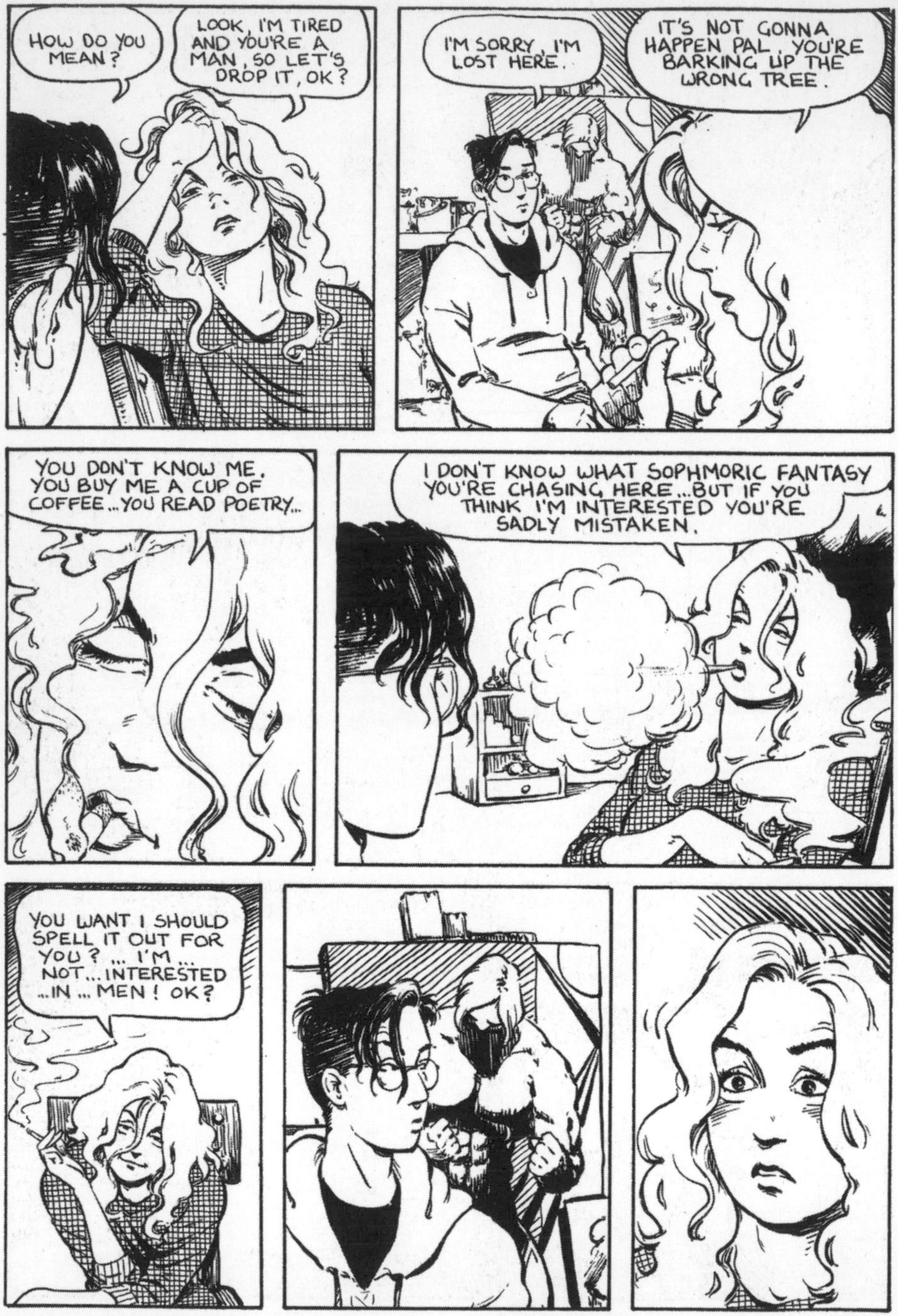
HOW DO YOU MEAN?
LOOK, I'M TIRED AND YOU'RE A MAN, SO LET'S DROP IT, OK?
I'M SORRY, I'M LOST HERE.
IT'S NOT GONNA HAPPEN PAL, YOU'RE BARKING UP THE WRONG TREE.
YOU DON'T KNOW ME. YOU BUY ME A CUP OF COFFEE... YOU READ POETRY...
I DON'T KNOW WHAT SOPHMORIC FANTASY YOU'RE CHASING HERE... BUT IF YOU THINK I'M INTERESTED YOU'RE SADLY MISTAKEN.
YOU WANT I SHOULD SPELL IT OUT FOR YOU? ... I'M ... NOT... INTERESTED ...IN ... MEN! OK?

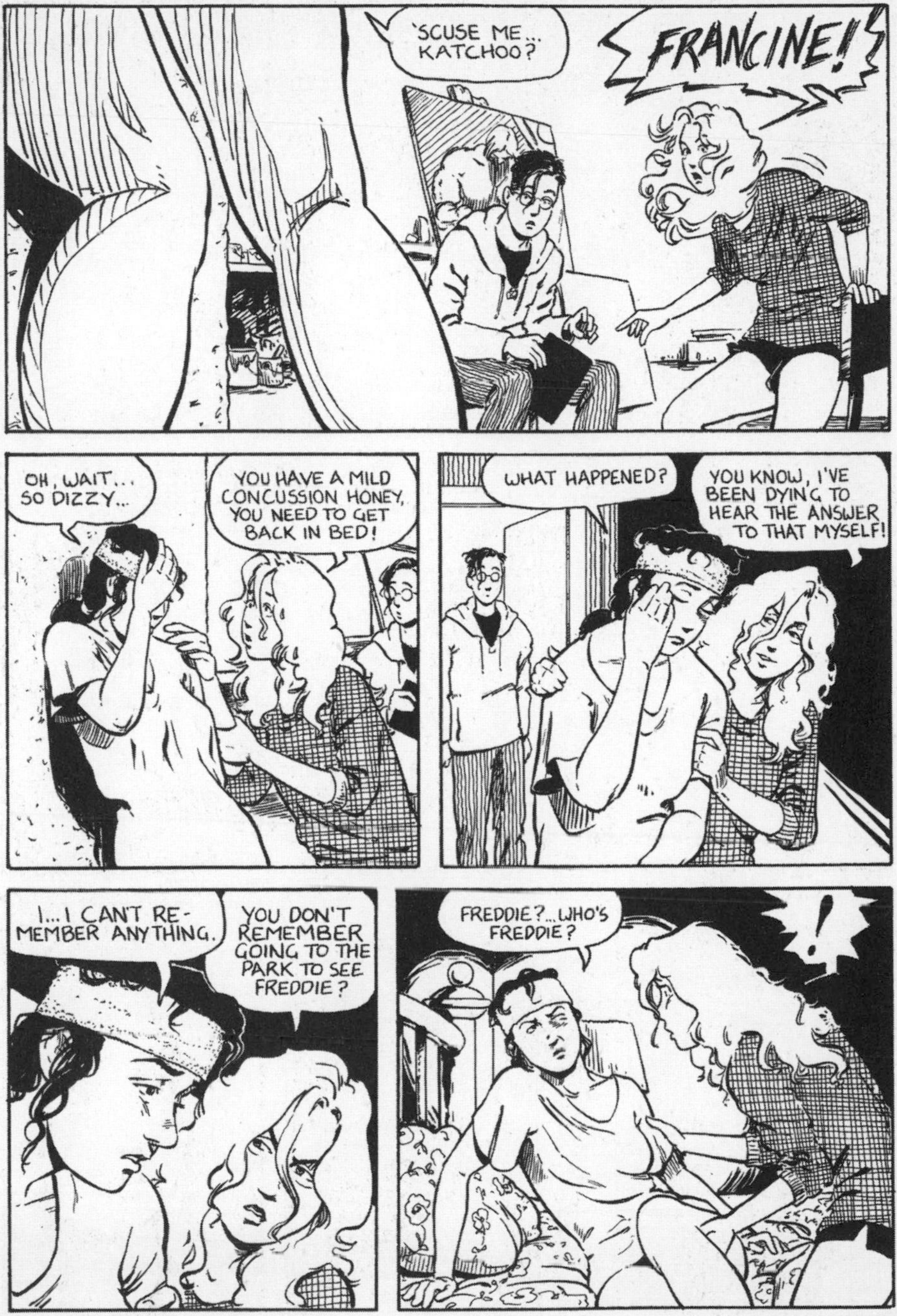
'SCUSE ME... KATCHOO?
FRANCINE!
OH, WAIT... SO DIZZY...
YOU HAVE A MILD CONCUSSION HONEY, YOU NEED TO GET BACK IN BED!
WHAT HAPPENED?
YOU KNOW, I'VE BEEN DYING TO HEAR THE ANSWER TO THAT MYSELF!
I... I CAN'T RE-MEMBER ANYTHING.
YOU DON'T REMEMBER GOING TO THE PARK TO SEE FREDDIE?
FREDDIE?... WHO'S FREDDIE?
!

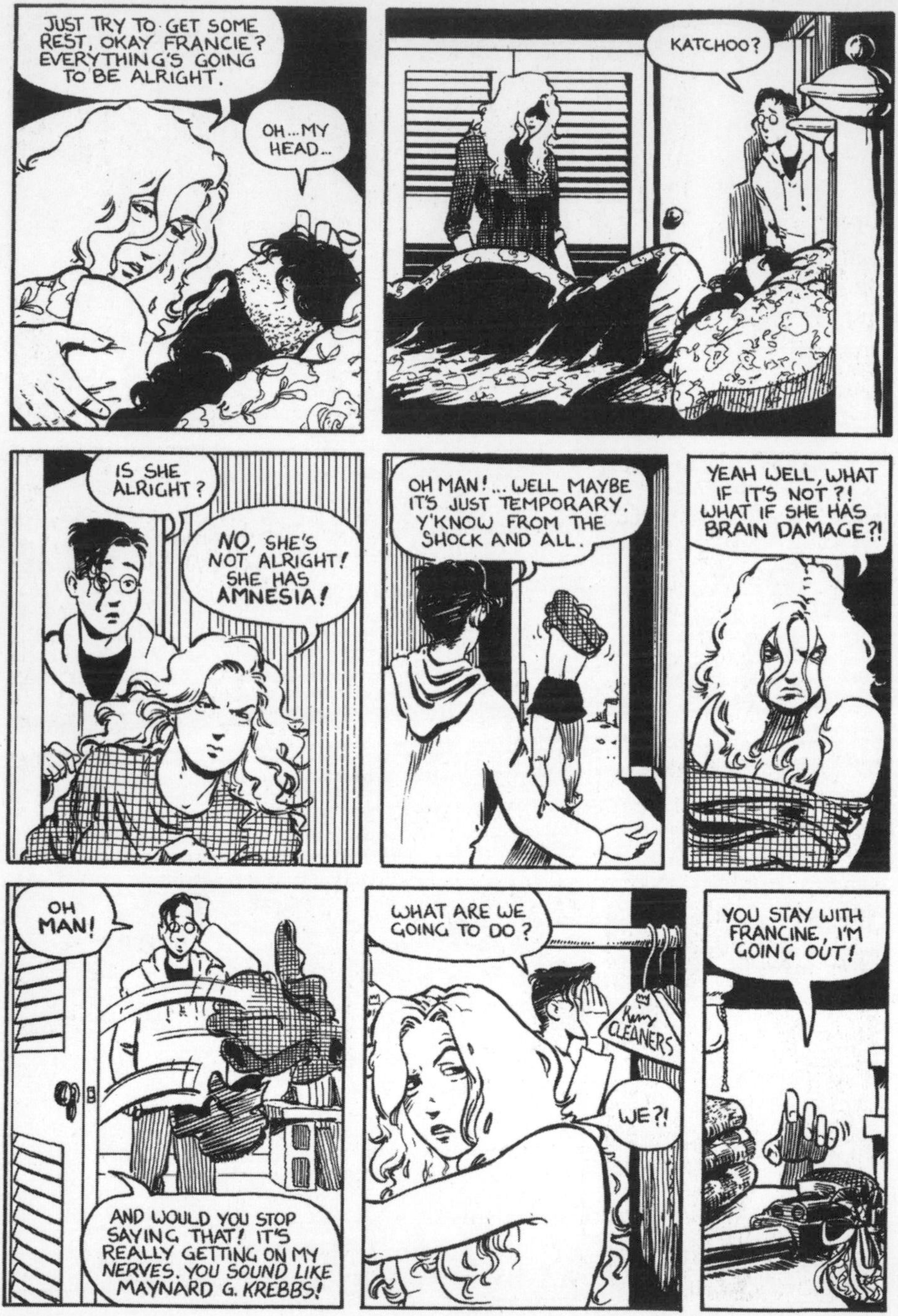
JUST TRY TO GET SOME REST, OKAY FRANCIE? EVERYTHING'S GOING TO BE ALRIGHT.
OH... MY HEAD...
KATCHOO?
IS SHE ALRIGHT?
NO, SHE'S NOT ALRIGHT! SHE HAS AMNESIA!
OH MAN!... WELL MAYBE IT'S JUST TEMPORARY. Y'KNOW FROM THE SHOCK AND ALL.
YEAH WELL, WHAT IF IT'S NOT?! WHAT IF SHE HAS BRAIN DAMAGE?!
OH MAN!
AND WOULD YOU STOP SAYING THAT! IT'S REALLY GETTING ON MY NERVES. YOU SOUND LIKE MAYNARD G. KREBBS!
WHAT ARE WE GOING TO DO?
CLEANERS
WE?!
YOU STAY WITH FRANCINE, I'M GOING OUT!

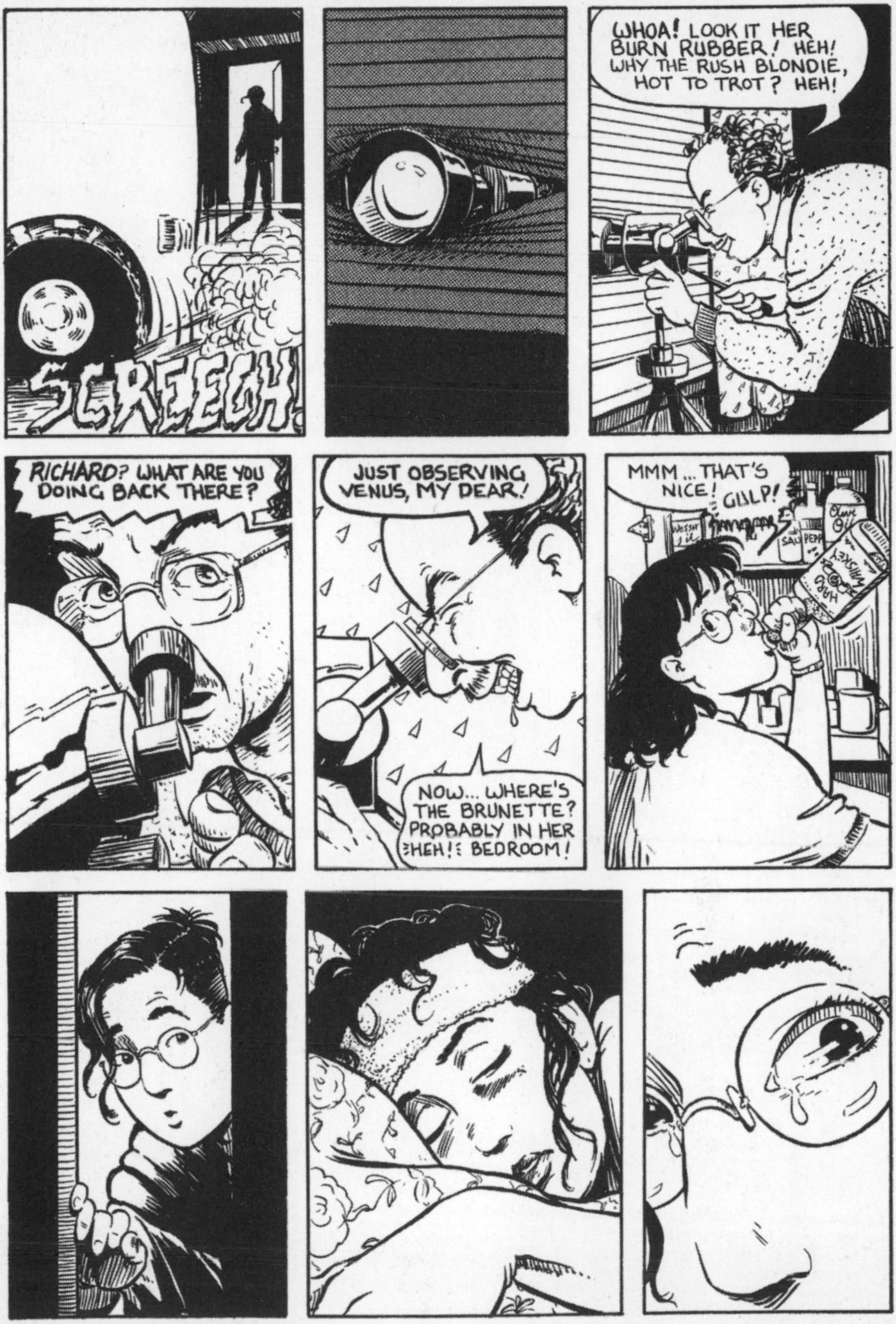
SCREECH!
WHOA! LOOK IT HER BURN RUBBER! HEH! WHY THE RUSH BLONDIE, HOT TO TROT? HEH!
RICHARD? WHAT ARE YOU DOING BACK THERE?
JUST OBSERVING VENUS, MY DEAR!
NOW... WHERE'S THE BRUNETTE? PROBABLY IN HER HEH! BEDROOM!
MMM... THAT'S NICE! GULP!
HARD WHISKEY

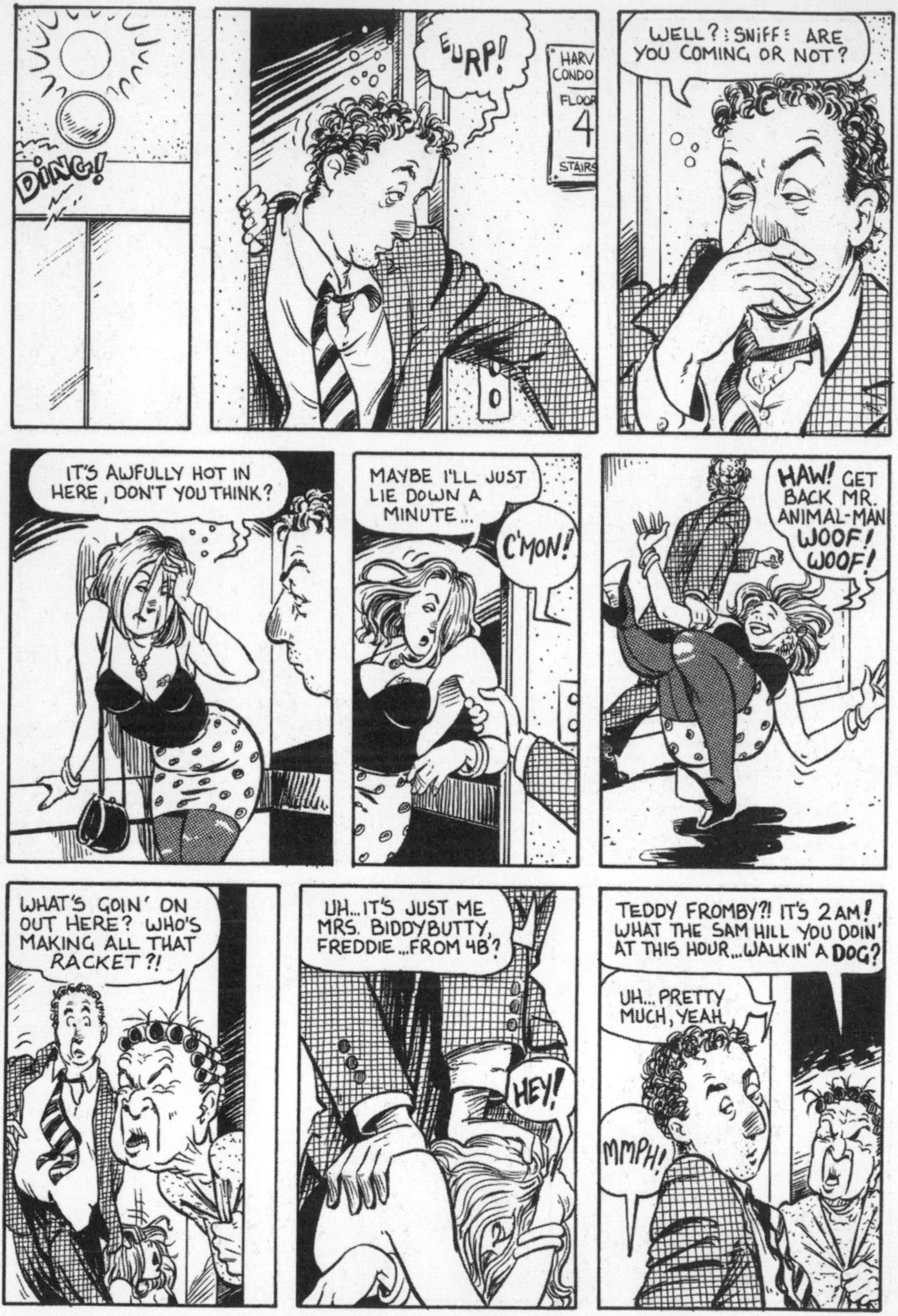
DING!
EURP!
HARV CONDO
FLOOR 4
STAIRS
WELL? :SNIFF: ARE YOU COMING OR NOT?
IT'S AWFULLY HOT IN HERE, DON'T YOU THINK?
MAYBE I'LL JUST LIE DOWN A MINUTE...
C'MON!
HAW! GET BACK MR. ANIMAL-MAN WOOF! WOOF!
WHAT'S GOIN' ON OUT HERE? WHO'S MAKING ALL THAT RACKET?!
UH...IT'S JUST ME MRS. BIDDYBUTTY, FREDDIE...FROM 4B?
HEY!
TEDDY FROMBY?! IT'S 2 AM! WHAT THE SAM HILL YOU DOIN' AT THIS HOUR...WALKIN' A DOG?
UH... PRETTY MUCH, YEAH.
MMPH!

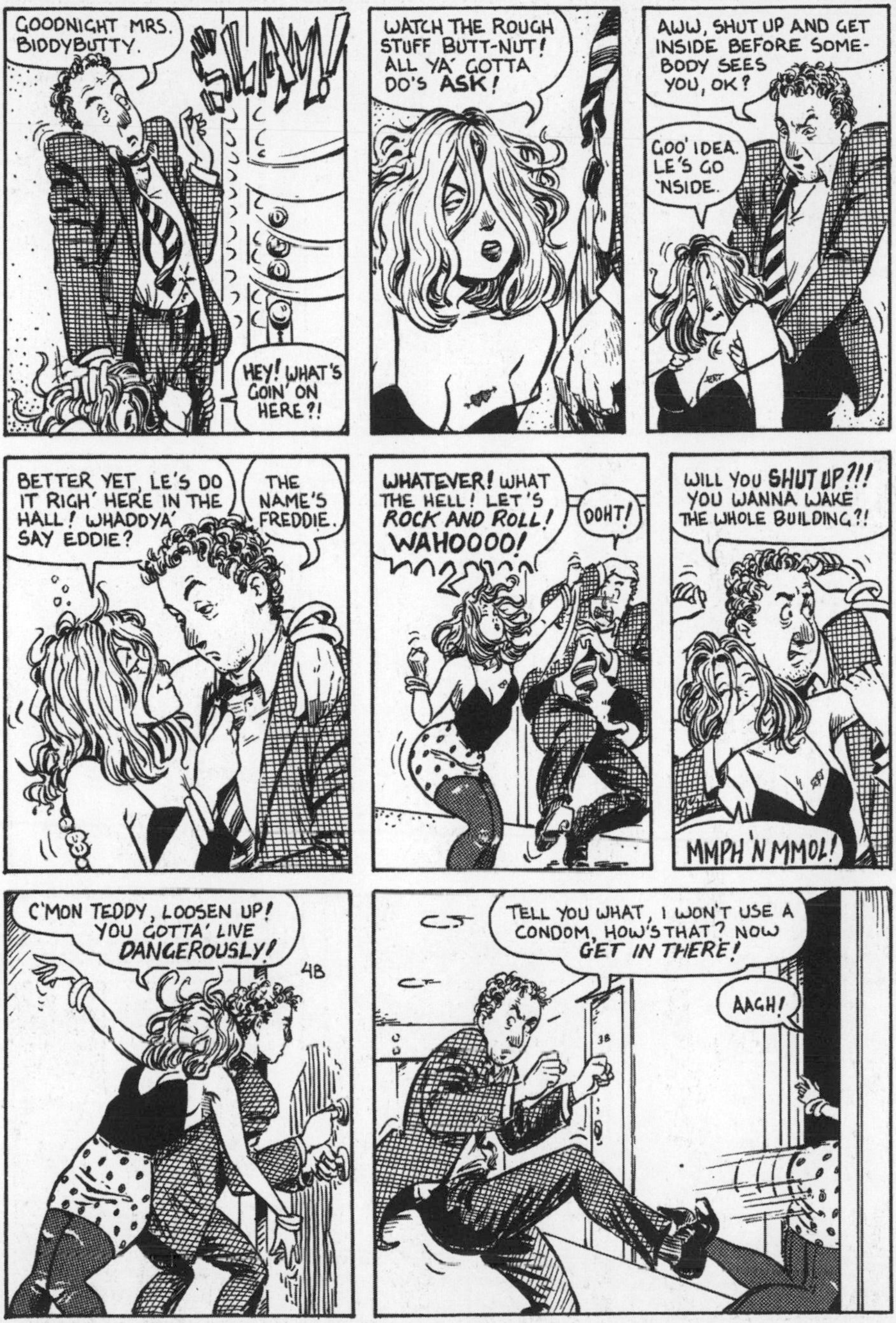
GOODNIGHT MRS. BIDDYBUTTY.
SLAM!
HEY! WHAT'S GOIN' ON HERE?!
WATCH THE ROUGH STUFF BUTT-NUT! ALL YA' GOTTA DO'S ASK!
AWW, SHUT UP AND GET INSIDE BEFORE SOME-BODY SEES YOU, OK?
GOO' IDEA. LE'S GO 'NSIDE.
BETTER YET, LE'S DO IT RIGH' HERE IN THE HALL! WHADDYA' SAY EDDIE?
THE NAME'S FREDDIE.
WHATEVER! WHAT THE HELL! LET'S ROCK AND ROLL! WAHOOOO!
DOHT!
WILL YOU SHUT UP?!! YOU WANNA WAKE THE WHOLE BUILDING?!
MMPH 'N MMOL!
C'MON TEDDY, LOOSEN UP! YOU GOTTA' LIVE DANGEROUSLY!
4B
TELL YOU WHAT, I WON'T USE A CONDOM, HOW'S THAT? NOW GET IN THERE!
AAGH!
3B

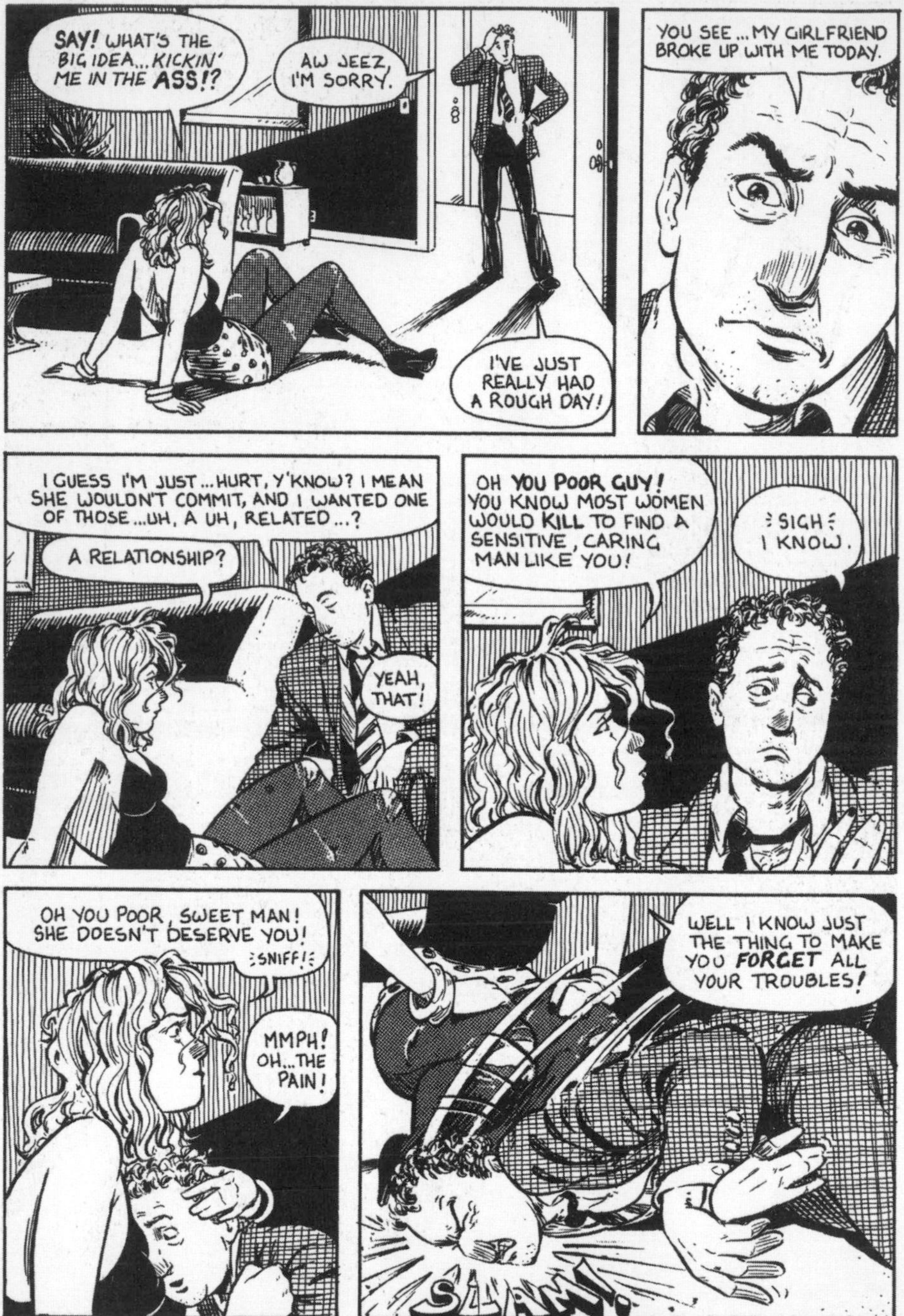
SAY! WHAT'S THE BIG IDEA...KICKIN' ME IN THE ASS!?
AW JEEZ, I'M SORRY.
I'VE JUST REALLY HAD A ROUGH DAY!
YOU SEE... MY GIRLFRIEND BROKE UP WITH ME TODAY.
I GUESS I'M JUST...HURT, Y'KNOW? I MEAN SHE WOULDN'T COMMIT, AND I WANTED ONE OF THOSE...UH, A UH, RELATED...?
A RELATIONSHIP?
YEAH, THAT!
OH YOU POOR GUY! YOU KNOW MOST WOMEN WOULD KILL TO FIND A SENSITIVE, CARING MAN LIKE YOU!
SIGH I KNOW.
OH YOU POOR, SWEET MAN! SHE DOESN'T DESERVE YOU!
SNIFF!
MMPH! OH...THE PAIN!
WELL I KNOW JUST THE THING TO MAKE YOU FORGET ALL YOUR TROUBLES!
SLAM!

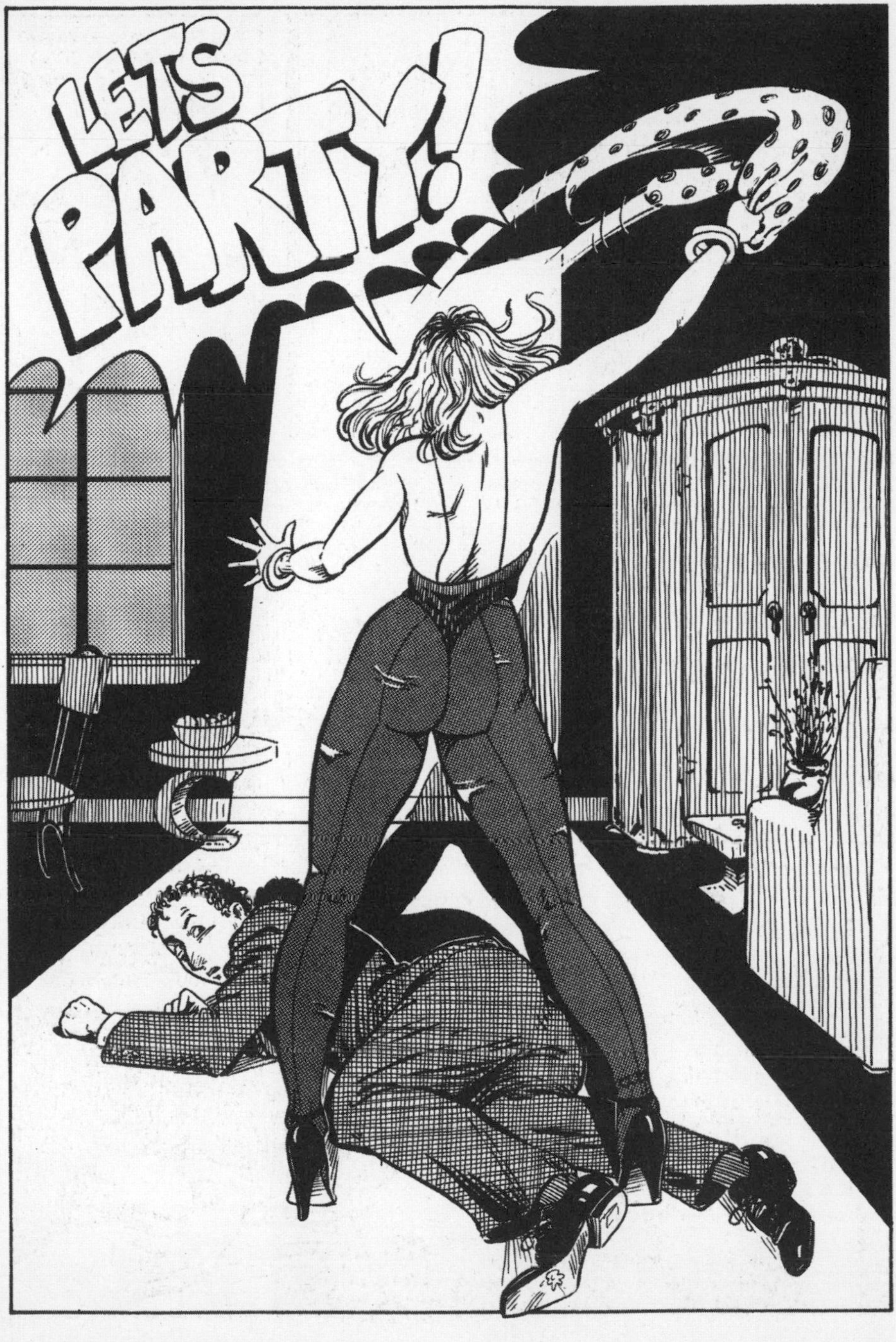
LETS PARTY!

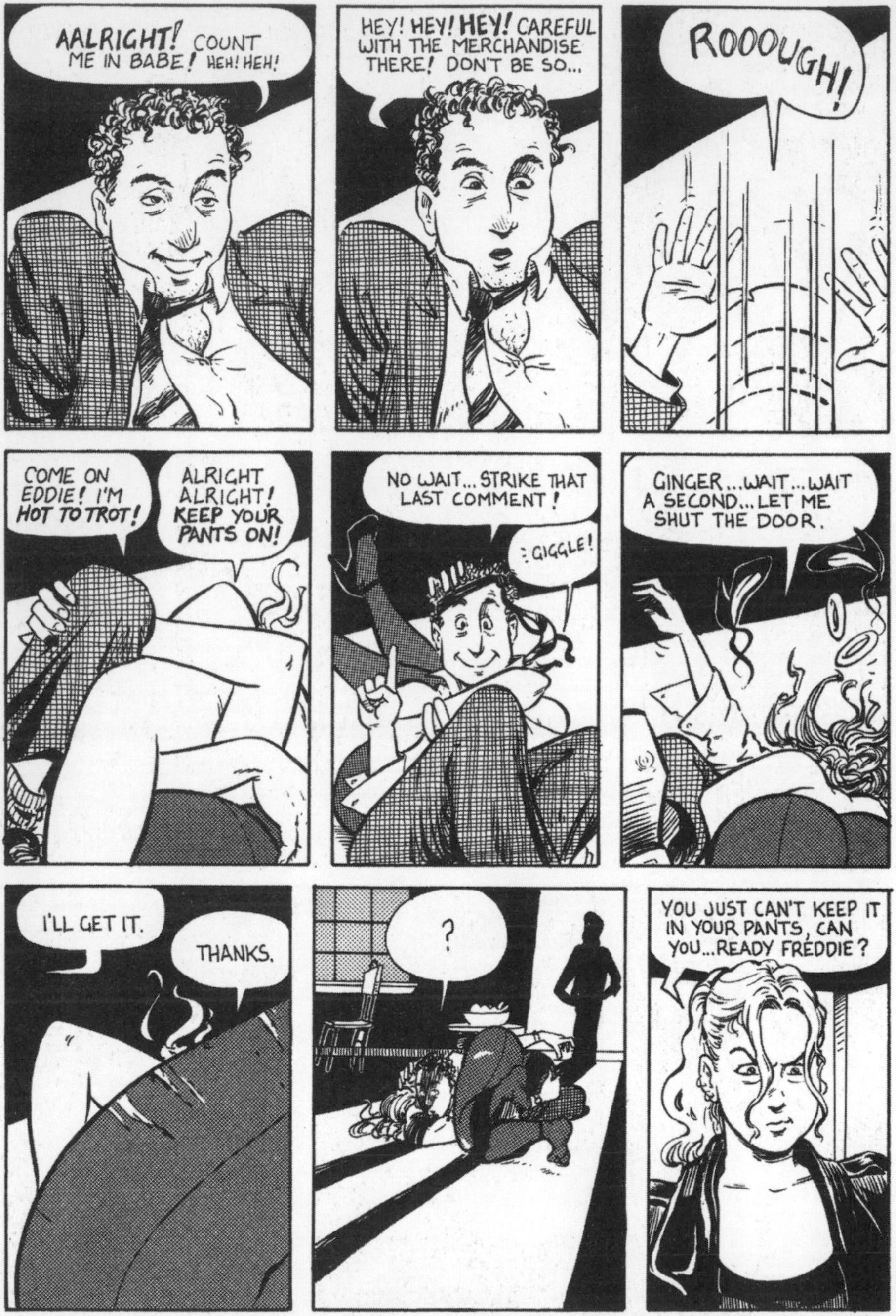
AALRIGHT! COUNT ME IN BABE! HEH! HEH!
HEY! HEY! HEY! CAREFUL WITH THE MERCHANDISE THERE! DON'T BE SO...
ROOOUGH!
COME ON EDDIE! I'M HOT TO TROT!
ALRIGHT ALRIGHT! KEEP YOUR PANTS ON!
NO WAIT... STRIKE THAT LAST COMMENT!
GIGGLE!
GINGER...WAIT...WAIT A SECOND...LET ME SHUT THE DOOR.
I'LL GET IT.
THANKS.
?
YOU JUST CAN'T KEEP IT IN YOUR PANTS, CAN YOU...READY FREDDIE?

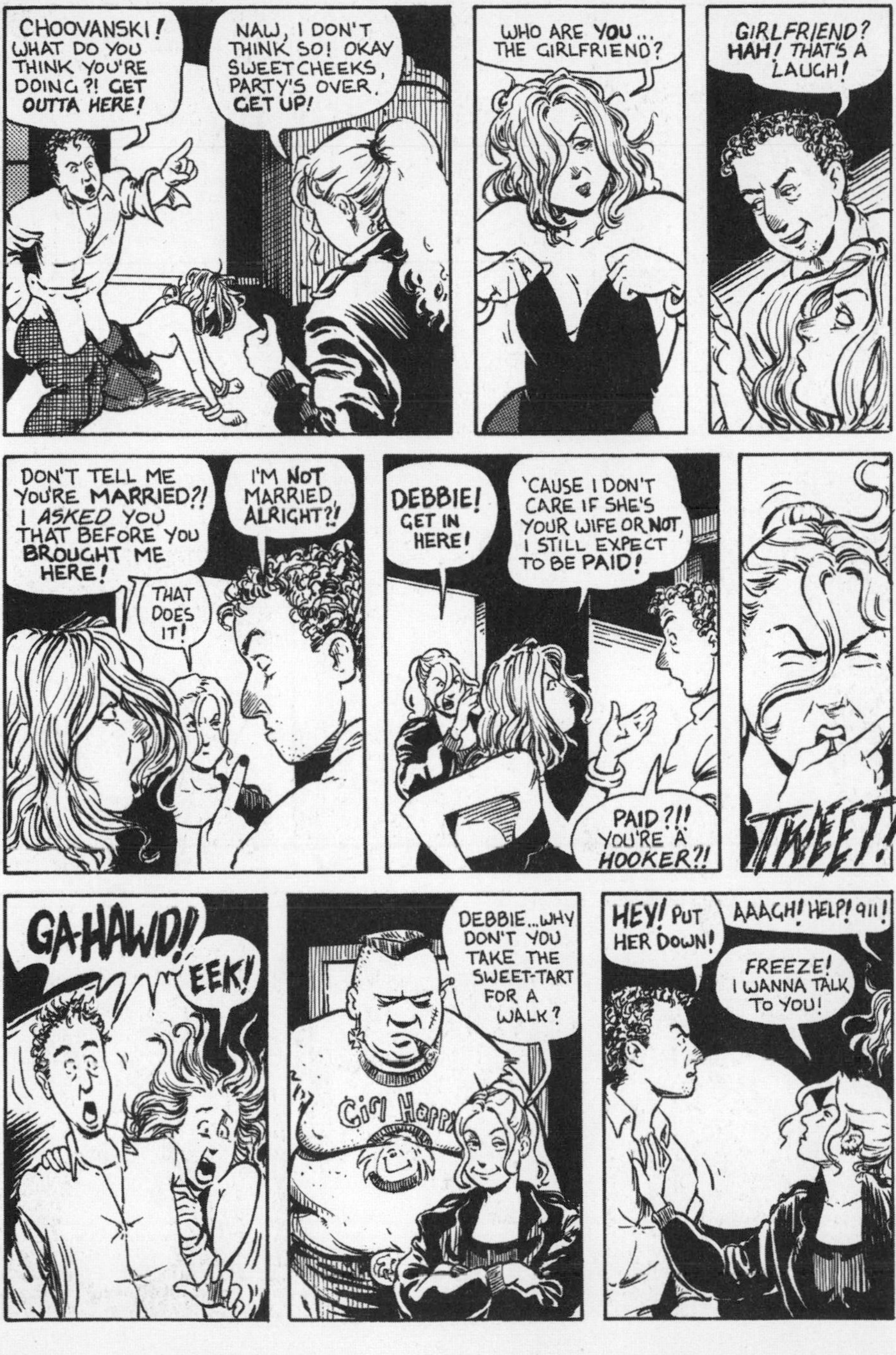

CHOOVANSKI! WHAT DO YOU THINK YOU'RE DOING?! GET OUTTA HERE!
NAW, I DON'T THINK SO! OKAY SWEETCHEEKS, PARTY'S OVER. GET UP!
WHO ARE YOU... THE GIRLFRIEND?
GIRLFRIEND? HAH! THAT'S A LAUGH!
DON'T TELL ME YOU'RE MARRIED?! I ASKED YOU THAT BEFORE YOU BROUGHT ME HERE!
I'M NOT MARRIED, ALRIGHT?!
THAT DOES IT!
DEBBIE! GET IN HERE!
'CAUSE I DON'T CARE IF SHE'S YOUR WIFE OR NOT, I STILL EXPECT TO BE PAID!
PAID?!! YOU'RE A HOOKER?!
TWEET!
GA-HAWD!
EEK!
DEBBIE...WHY DON'T YOU TAKE THE SWEET-TART FOR A WALK?
Girl Happy
HEY! PUT HER DOWN!
AAAGH! HELP! 911!
FREEZE! I WANNA TALK TO YOU!

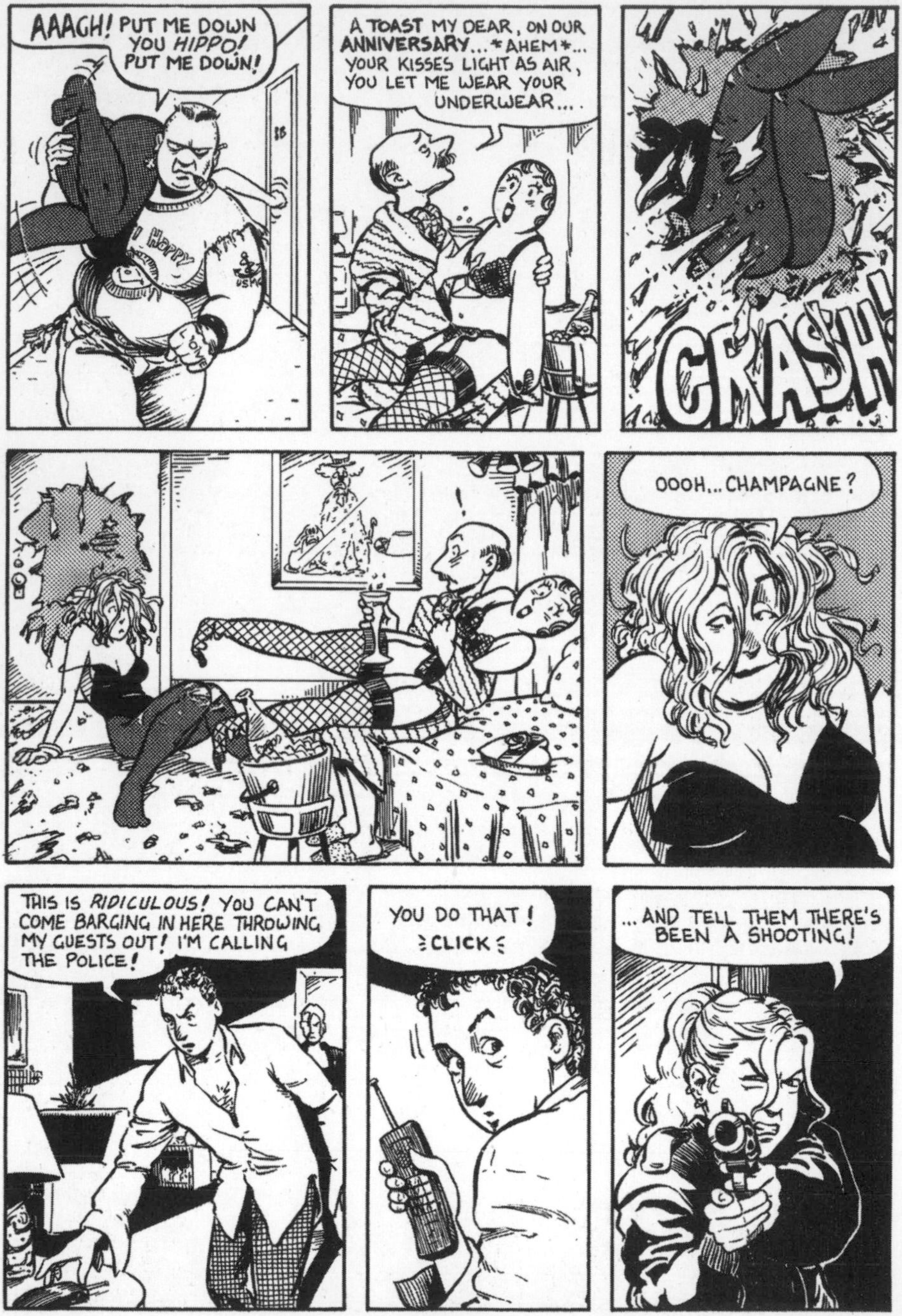
AAAGH! PUT ME DOWN YOU HIPPO! PUT ME DOWN!
A TOAST MY DEAR, ON OUR ANNIVERSARY... *AHEM*... YOUR KISSES LIGHT AS AIR, YOU LET ME WEAR YOUR UNDERWEAR....
CRASH!
OOOH... CHAMPAGNE?
THIS IS RIDICULOUS! YOU CAN'T COME BARGING IN HERE THROWING MY GUESTS OUT! I'M CALLING THE POLICE!
YOU DO THAT!
CLICK
... AND TELL THEM THERE'S BEEN A SHOOTING!

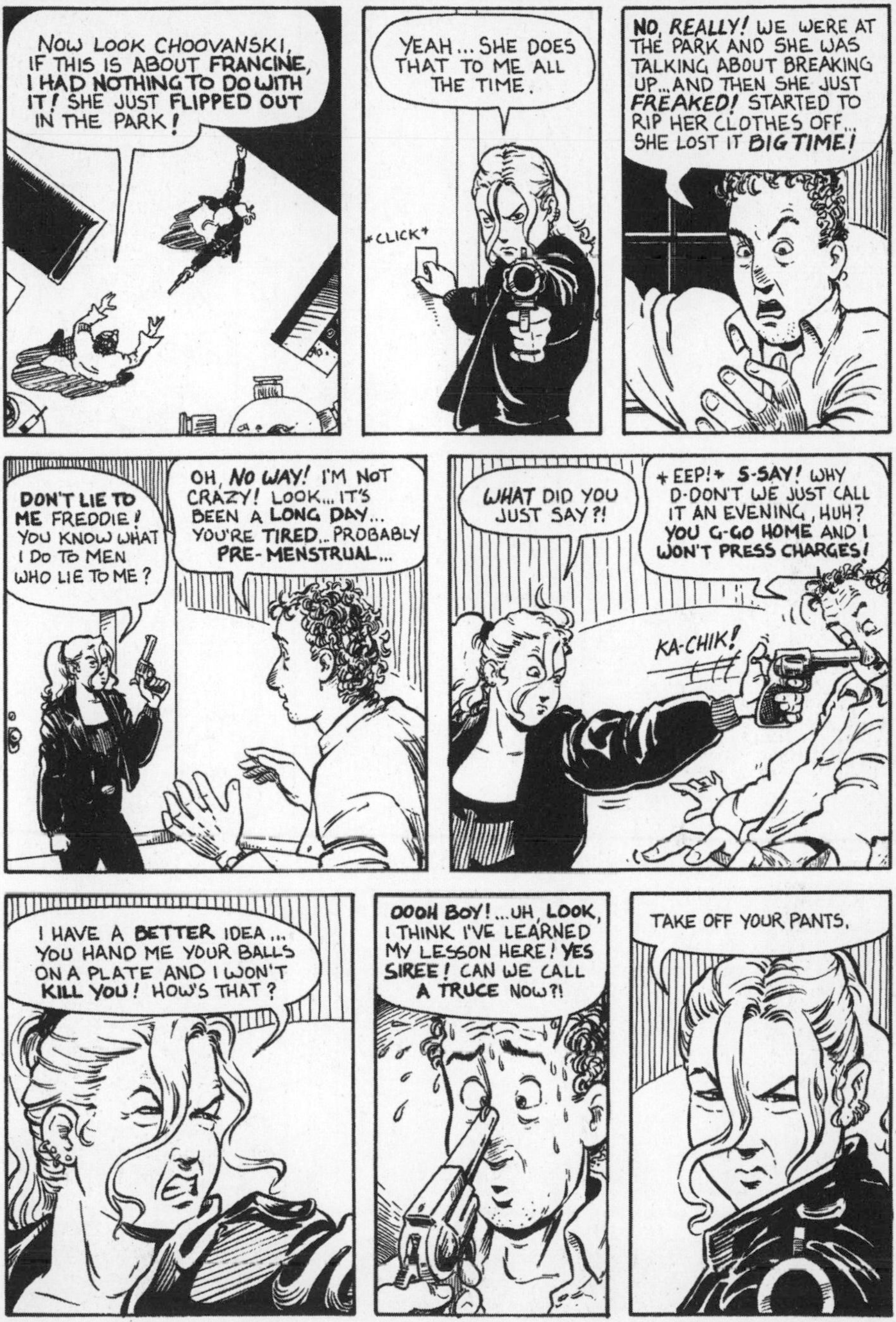
NOW LOOK CHOOVANSKI, IF THIS IS ABOUT FRANCINE, I HAD NOTHING TO DO WITH IT! SHE JUST FLIPPED OUT IN THE PARK!
YEAH... SHE DOES THAT TO ME ALL THE TIME.
CLICK
NO, REALLY! WE WERE AT THE PARK AND SHE WAS TALKING ABOUT BREAKING UP... AND THEN SHE JUST FREAKED! STARTED TO RIP HER CLOTHES OFF... SHE LOST IT BIG TIME!
DON'T LIE TO ME FREDDIE! YOU KNOW WHAT I DO TO MEN WHO LIE TO ME?
OH, NO WAY! I'M NOT CRAZY! LOOK... IT'S BEEN A LONG DAY... YOU'RE TIRED... PROBABLY PRE-MENSTRUAL...
WHAT DID YOU JUST SAY?!
EEP! S-SAY! WHY D-DON'T WE JUST CALL IT AN EVENING, HUH? YOU G-GO HOME AND I WON'T PRESS CHARGES!
KA-CHIK!
I HAVE A BETTER IDEA... YOU HAND ME YOUR BALLS ON A PLATE AND I WON'T KILL YOU! HOW'S THAT?
OOOH BOY! ...UH, LOOK, I THINK I'VE LEARNED MY LESSON HERE! YES SIREE! CAN WE CALL A TRUCE NOW?!
TAKE OFF YOUR PANTS.

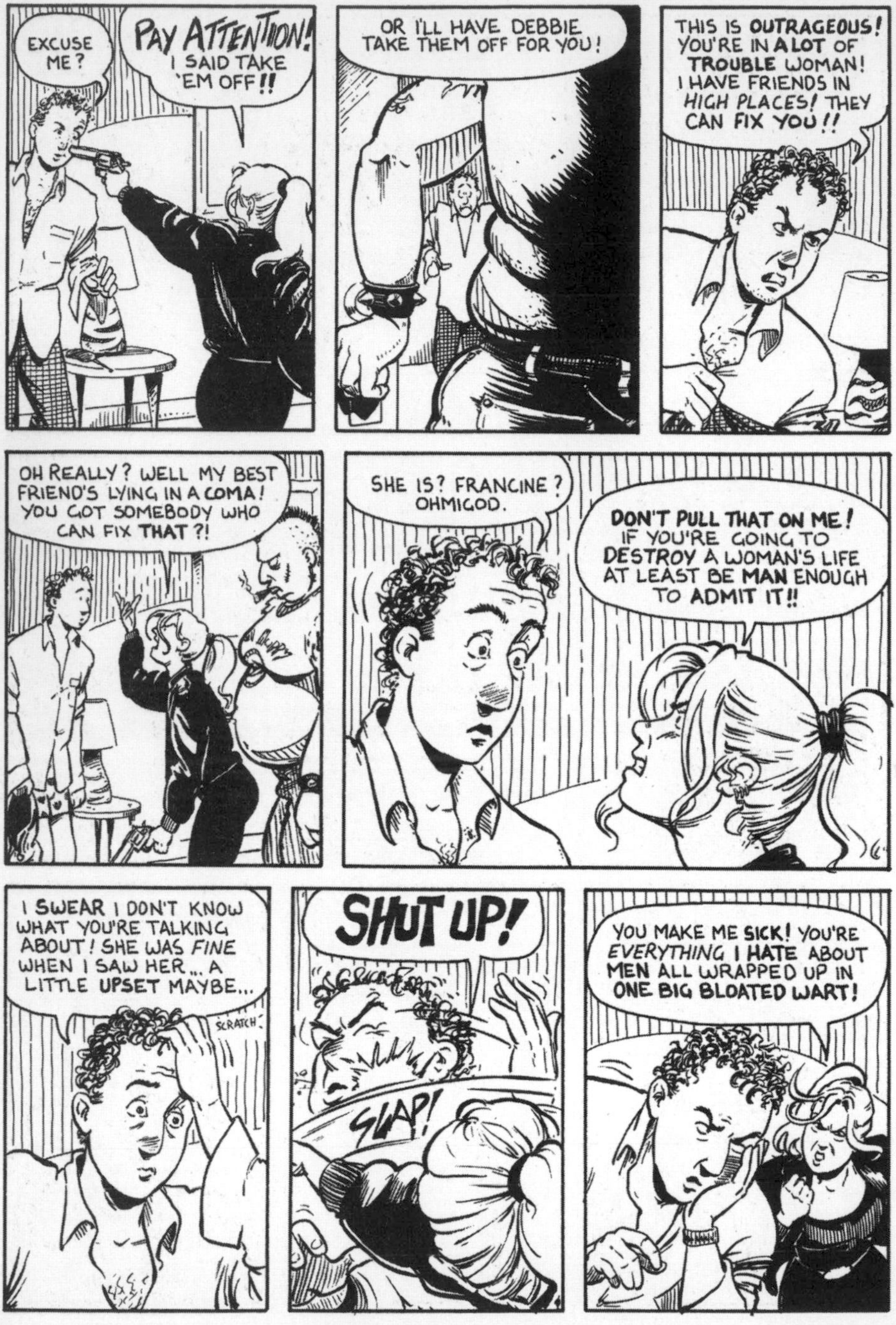
EXCUSE ME?
PAY ATTENTION! I SAID TAKE 'EM OFF!!
OR I'LL HAVE DEBBIE TAKE THEM OFF FOR YOU!
THIS IS OUTRAGEOUS! YOU'RE IN A LOT OF TROUBLE WOMAN! I HAVE FRIENDS IN HIGH PLACES! THEY CAN FIX YOU!!
OH REALLY? WELL MY BEST FRIEND'S LYING IN A COMA! YOU GOT SOMEBODY WHO CAN FIX THAT?!
SHE IS? FRANCINE? OHMIGOD.
DON'T PULL THAT ON ME! IF YOU'RE GOING TO DESTROY A WOMAN'S LIFE AT LEAST BE MAN ENOUGH TO ADMIT IT!!
I SWEAR I DON'T KNOW WHAT YOU'RE TALKING ABOUT! SHE WAS FINE WHEN I SAW HER... A LITTLE UPSET MAYBE...
SCRATCH
SHUT UP!
SLAP!
YOU MAKE ME SICK! YOU'RE EVERYTHING I HATE ABOUT MEN ALL WRAPPED UP IN ONE BIG BLOATED WART!

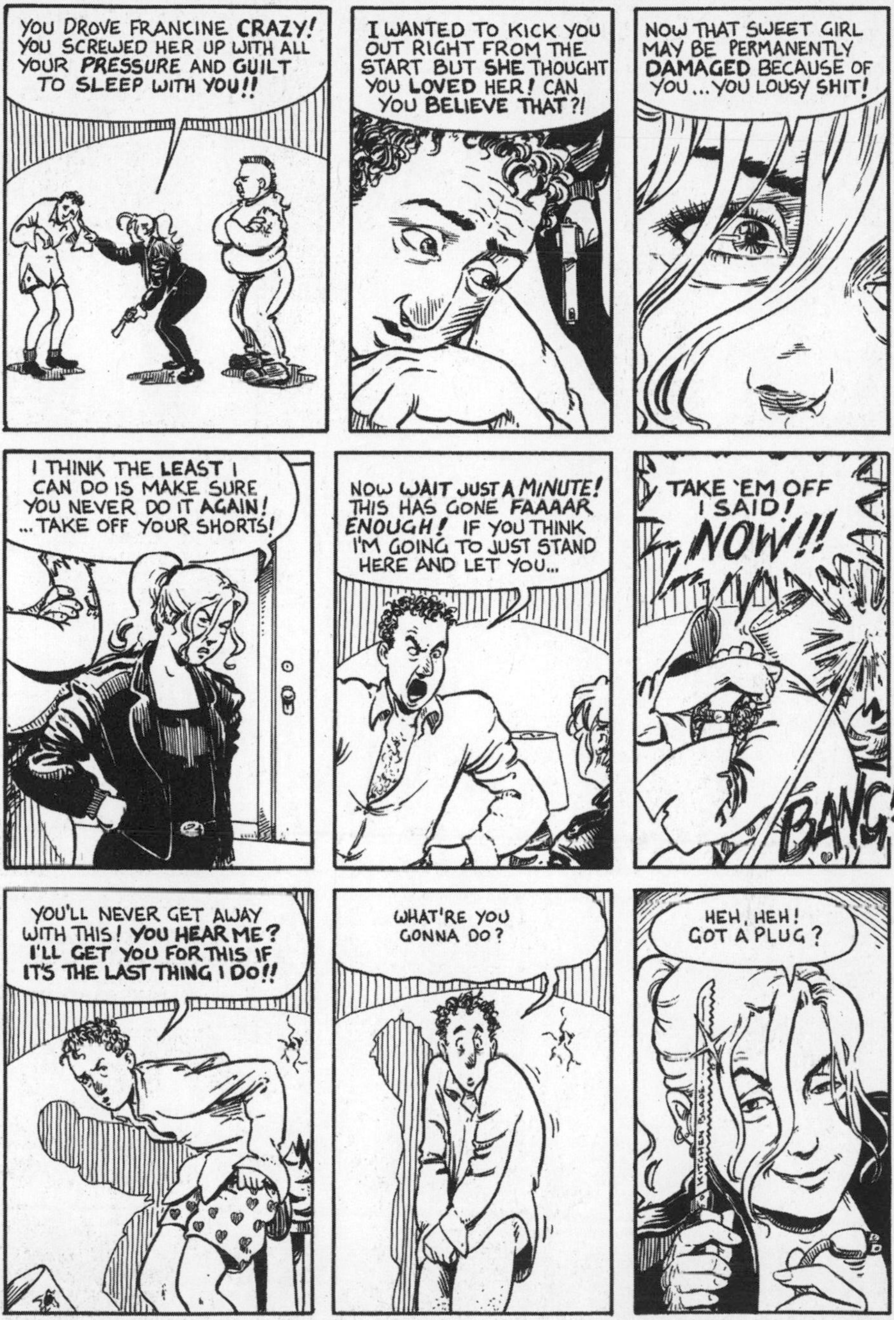
YOU DROVE FRANCINE CRAZY! YOU SCREWED HER UP WITH ALL YOUR PRESSURE AND GUILT TO SLEEP WITH YOU!!
I WANTED TO KICK YOU OUT RIGHT FROM THE START BUT SHE THOUGHT YOU LOVED HER! CAN YOU BELIEVE THAT?!
NOW THAT SWEET GIRL MAY BE PERMANENTLY DAMAGED BECAUSE OF YOU... YOU LOUSY SHIT!
I THINK THE LEAST I CAN DO IS MAKE SURE YOU NEVER DO IT AGAIN! ...TAKE OFF YOUR SHORTS!
NOW WAIT JUST A MINUTE! THIS HAS GONE FAAAAR ENOUGH! IF YOU THINK I'M GOING TO JUST STAND HERE AND LET YOU...
TAKE 'EM OFF I SAID! NOW!!
BANG!
YOU'LL NEVER GET AWAY WITH THIS! YOU HEAR ME? I'LL GET YOU FOR THIS IF IT'S THE LAST THING I DO!!
WHAT'RE YOU GONNA DO?
HEH, HEH! GOT A PLUG?
KITCHEN BLADE

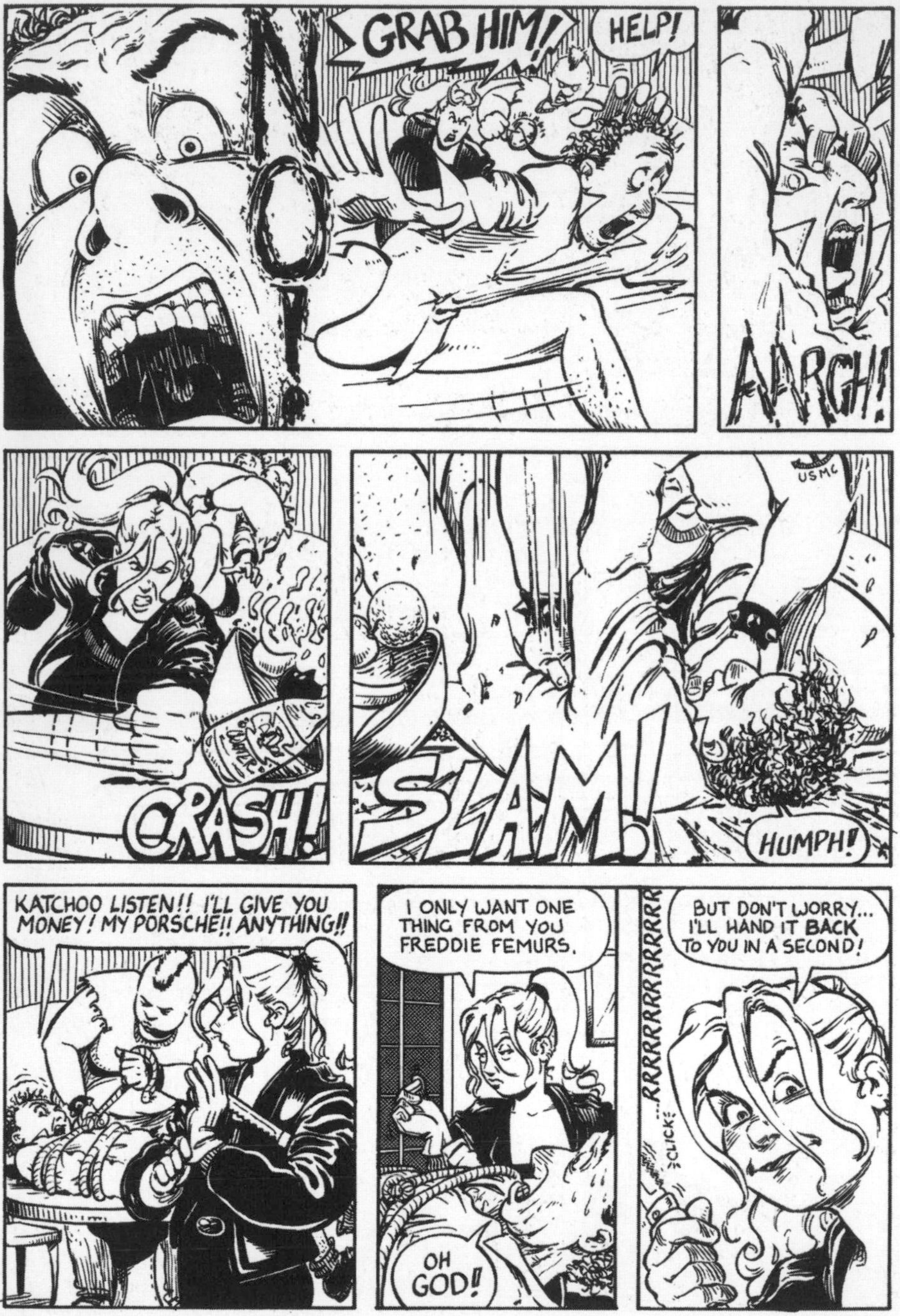
NO!
GRAB HIM!!
HELP!
AARGH!
CRASH!
USMC
SLAM!
HUMPH!
KATCHOO LISTEN!! I'LL GIVE YOU MONEY! MY PORSCHE!! ANYTHING!!
I ONLY WANT ONE THING FROM YOU FREDDIE FEMURS.
OH GOD!!
CLICK!
...RRRRRRRRRRRRRRR
BUT DON'T WORRY... I'LL HAND IT BACK TO YOU IN A SECOND!

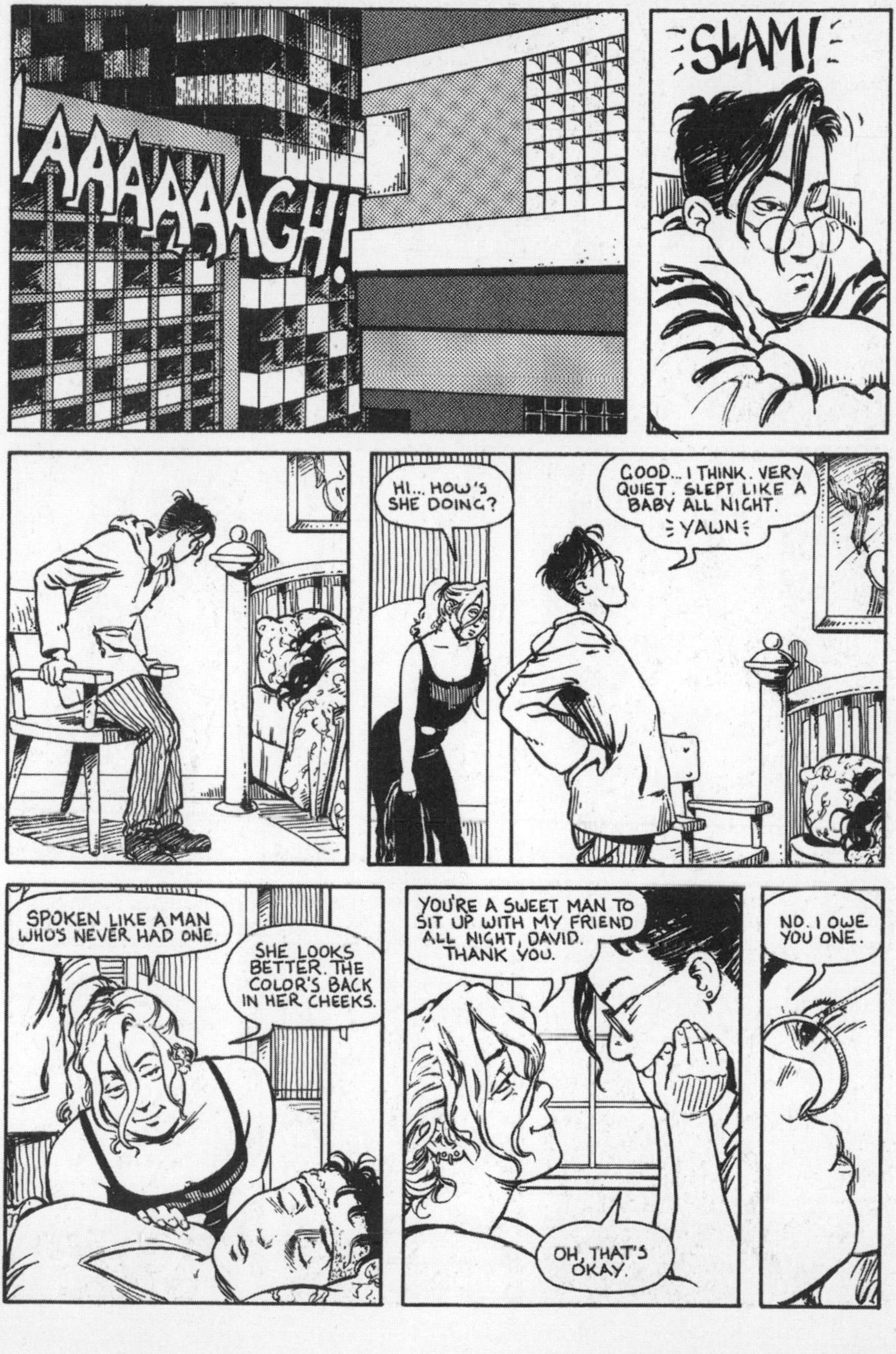
AAAAAAAGH!
SLAM!
HI... HOW'S SHE DOING?
GOOD... I THINK. VERY QUIET. SLEPT LIKE A BABY ALL NIGHT.
YAWN
SPOKEN LIKE A MAN WHO'S NEVER HAD ONE.
SHE LOOKS BETTER. THE COLOR'S BACK IN HER CHEEKS.
YOU'RE A SWEET MAN TO SIT UP WITH MY FRIEND ALL NIGHT, DAVID. THANK YOU.
OH, THAT'S OKAY.
NO. I OWE YOU ONE.

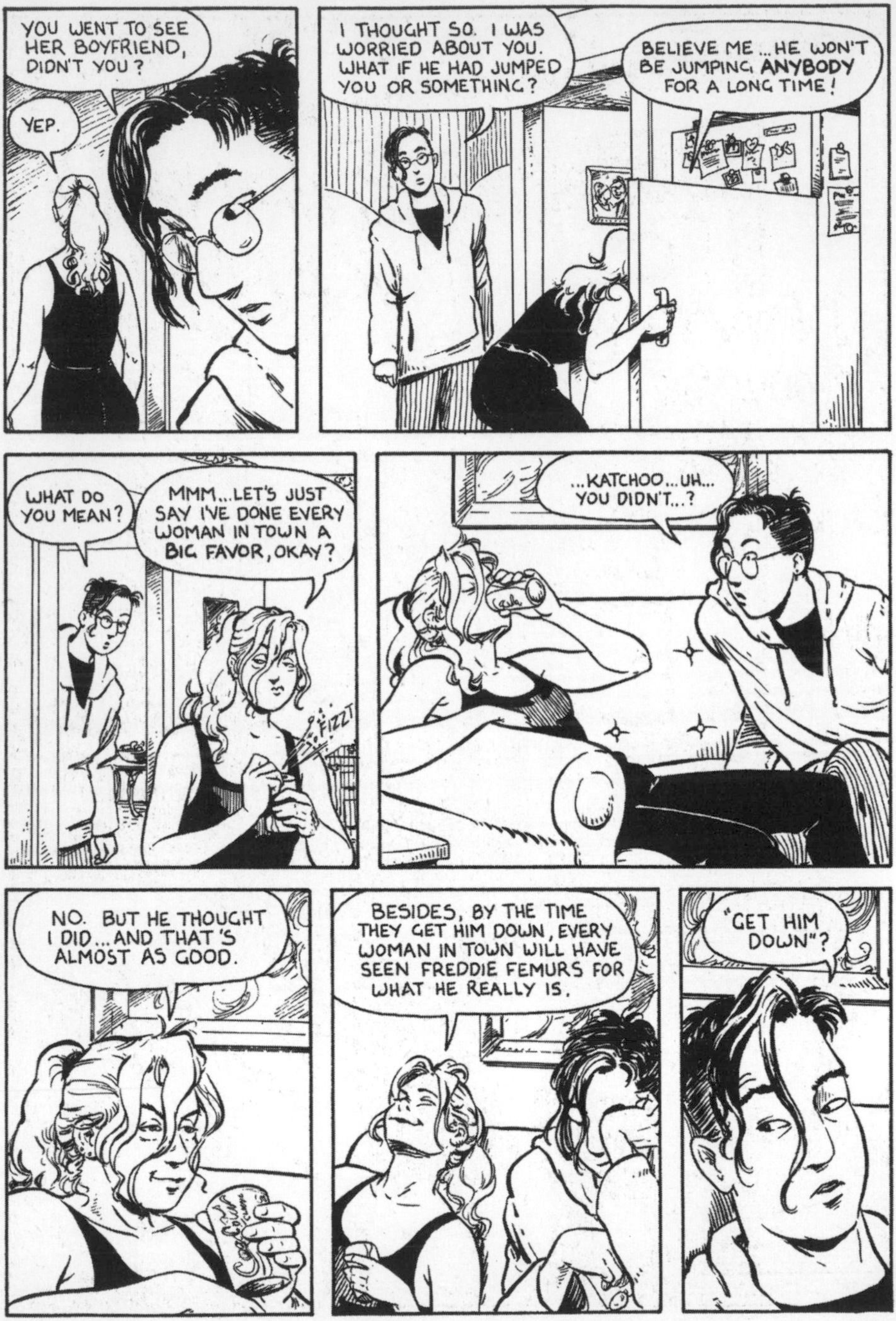
YOU WENT TO SEE HER BOYFRIEND, DIDN'T YOU?
YEP.
I THOUGHT SO. I WAS WORRIED ABOUT YOU. WHAT IF HE HAD JUMPED YOU OR SOMETHING?
BELIEVE ME ... HE WON'T BE JUMPING ANYBODY FOR A LONG TIME!
WHAT DO YOU MEAN?
MMM...LET'S JUST SAY I'VE DONE EVERY WOMAN IN TOWN A BIG FAVOR, OKAY?
FIZZT
...KATCHOO...UH... YOU DIDN'T...?
NO. BUT HE THOUGHT I DID...AND THAT'S ALMOST AS GOOD.
BESIDES, BY THE TIME THEY GET HIM DOWN, EVERY WOMAN IN TOWN WILL HAVE SEEN FREDDIE FEMURS FOR WHAT HE REALLY IS.
"GET HIM DOWN"?

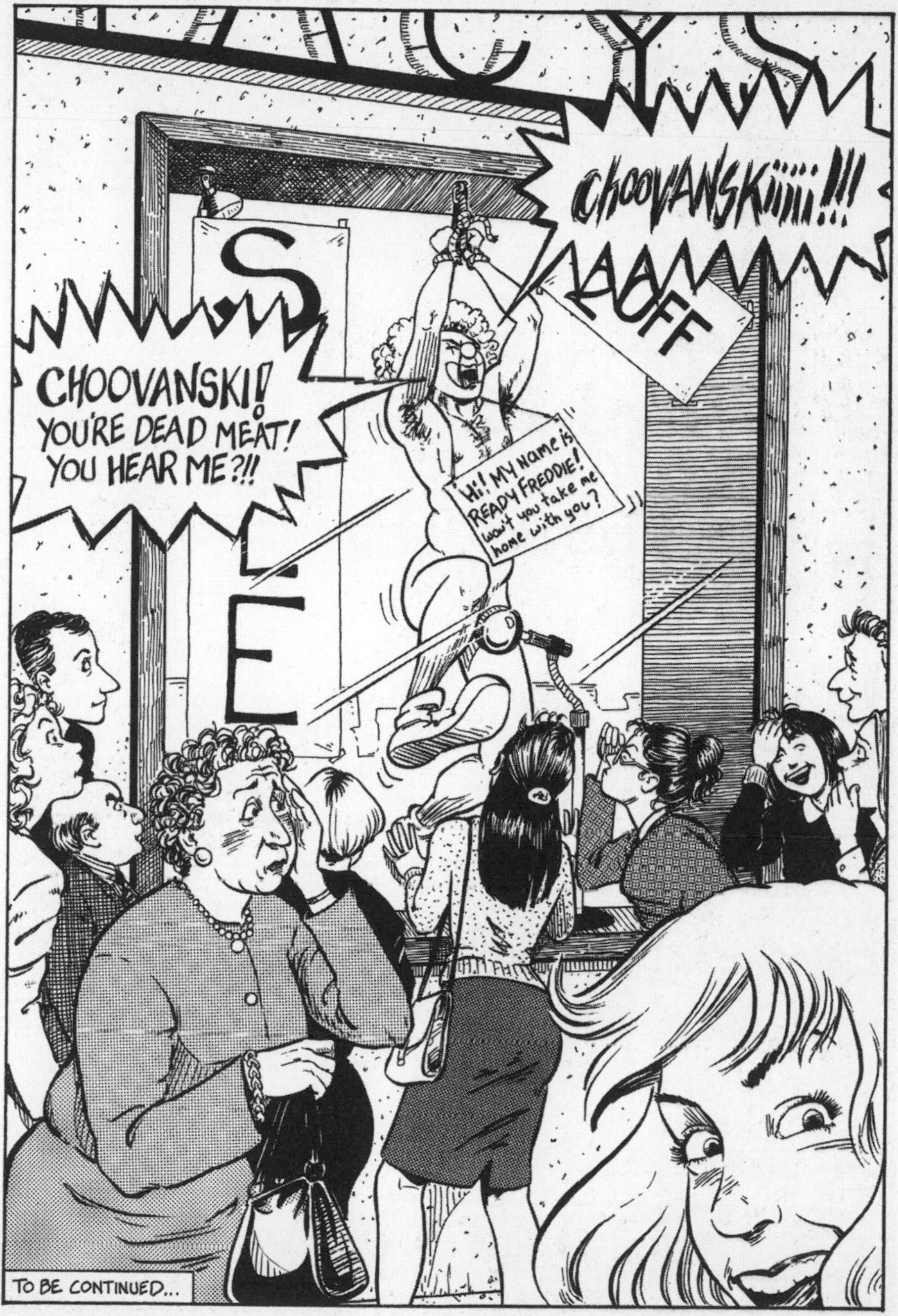
CHOOVANSKI! YOU'RE DEAD MEAT! YOU HEAR ME?!!
CHOOVANSKIiiii!!!
AAA
Hi! MY name is READY FREDDIE! won't you take me home with you?
TO BE CONTINUED...

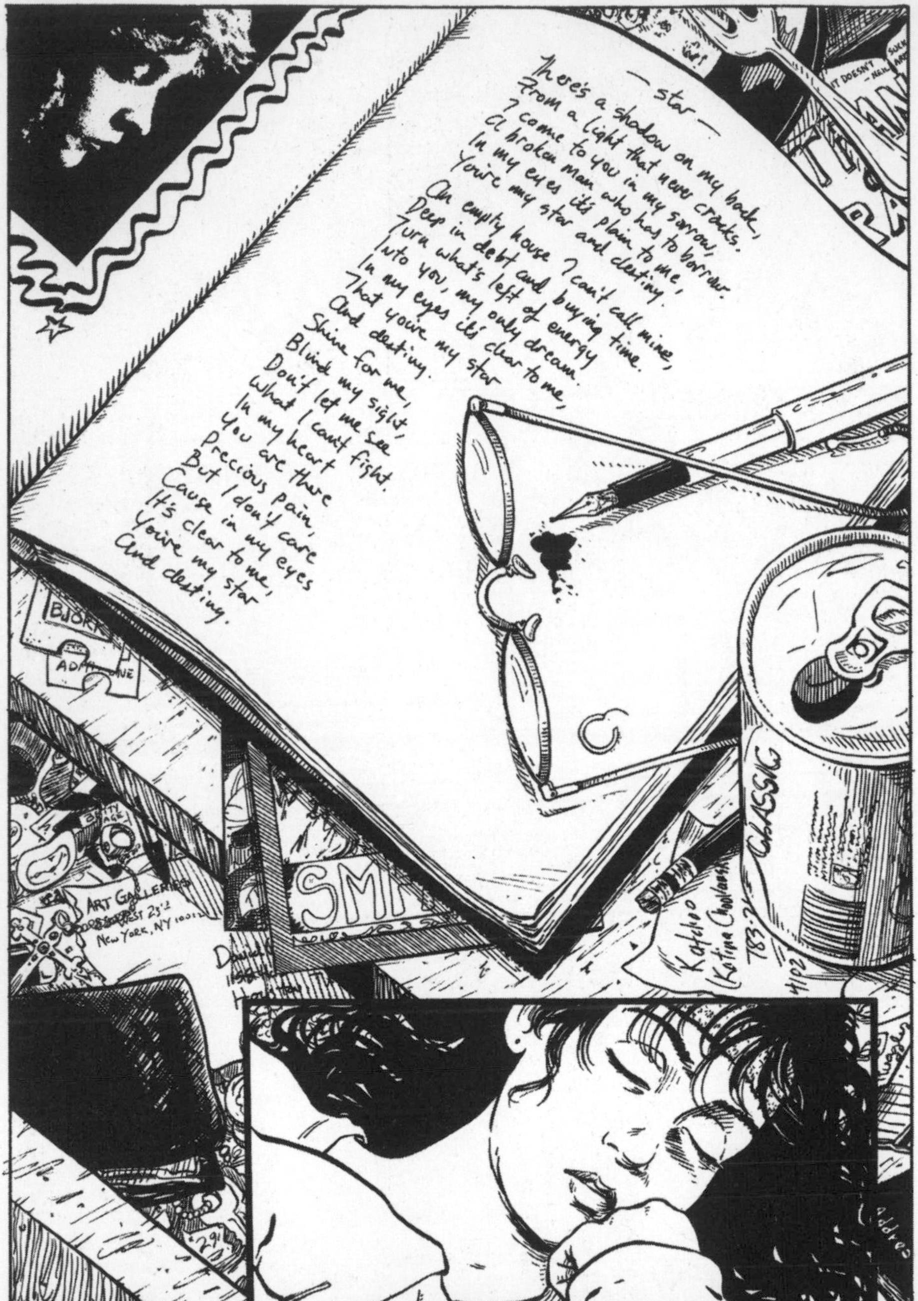
— star —
There's a shadow on my back,
From a light that never cracks.
I come to you in my sorrow,
A broken man who has to borrow.
In my eyes it's plain to me,
You're my star and destiny.
An empty house I can't call mine,
Deep in debt and buying time.
Turn what's left of energy
Into you, my only dream.
In my eyes it's clear to me,
That you're my star
And destiny.
Shine for me,
Blind my sight,
Don't let me see
What I can't fight.
In my heart
You are there
Precious pain,
But I don't care
Cause in my eyes
It's clear to me,
You're my star
And destiny.
BJÖRK
ART GALLERIES
NEW YORK, NY
CLASSIC

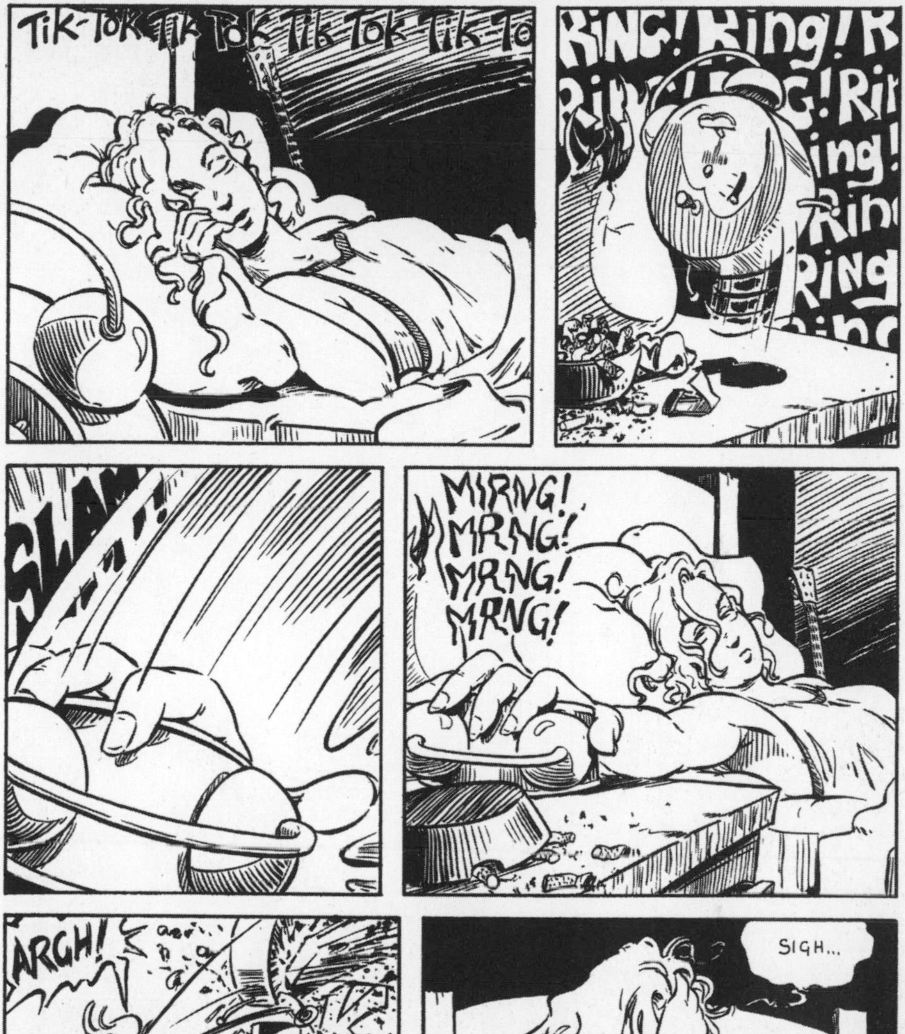
TIK-TOK TIK TOK TIK TOK TIK-TO
RING! RING! R
MRNG!
MRNG!
MRNG!
MRNG!
ARGH!
SIGH...

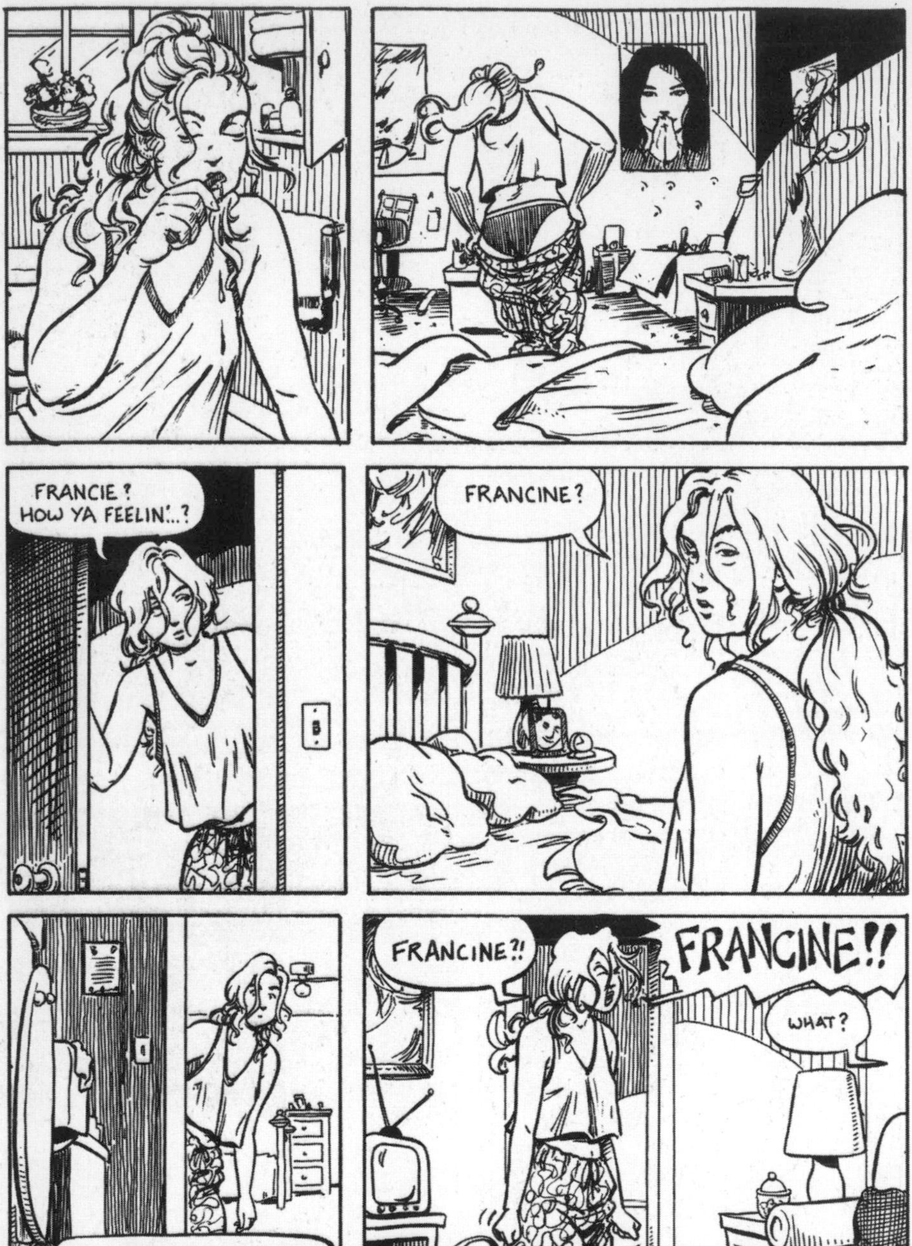
FRANCIE ? HOW YA FEELIN'...?
FRANCINE ?
FRANCINE?!
FRANCINE!!
WHAT ?

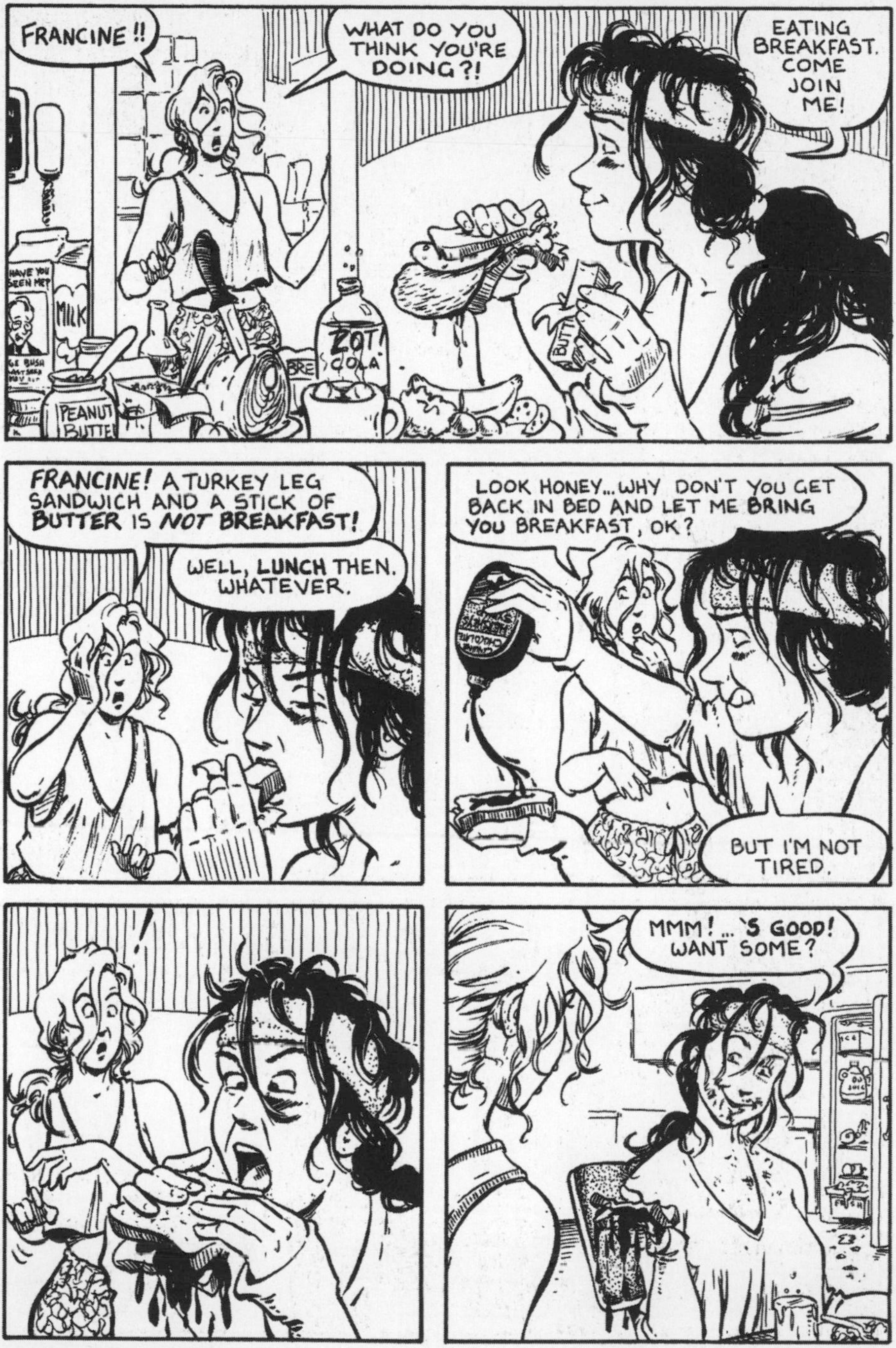

FRANCINE !!
WHAT DO YOU THINK YOU'RE DOING?!
EATING BREAKFAST. COME JOIN ME!
HAVE YOU SEEN ME?
MILK
PEANUT
ZOT! COLA
FRANCINE! A TURKEY LEG SANDWICH AND A STICK OF BUTTER IS NOT BREAKFAST!
WELL, LUNCH THEN. WHATEVER.
LOOK HONEY... WHY DON'T YOU GET BACK IN BED AND LET ME BRING YOU BREAKFAST, OK?
BUT I'M NOT TIRED.
!
MMM! ... 'S GOOD! WANT SOME?

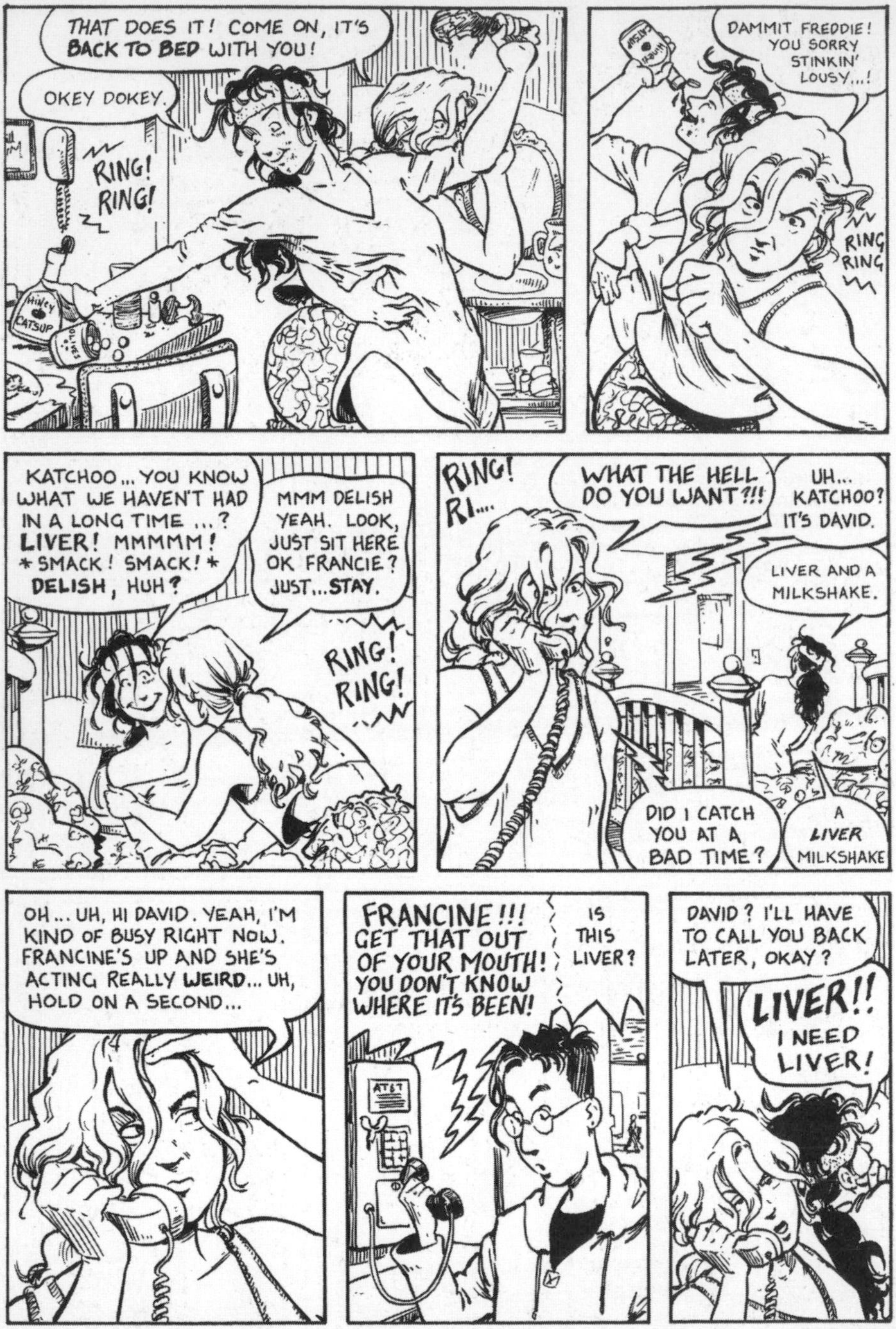
THAT DOES IT! COME ON, IT'S BACK TO BED WITH YOU!
OKEY DOKEY.
RING! RING!
DAMMIT FREDDIE! YOU SORRY STINKIN' LOUSY...!
RING RING
KATCHOO... YOU KNOW WHAT WE HAVEN'T HAD IN A LONG TIME ...? LIVER! MMMMM! *SMACK! SMACK!* DELISH, HUH?
MMM DELISH YEAH. LOOK, JUST SIT HERE OK FRANCIE? JUST... STAY.
RING! RING!
RING! RI....
WHAT THE HELL DO YOU WANT?!!
UH... KATCHOO? IT'S DAVID.
LIVER AND A MILKSHAKE.
DID I CATCH YOU AT A BAD TIME?
A LIVER MILKSHAKE
OH... UH, HI DAVID. YEAH, I'M KIND OF BUSY RIGHT NOW. FRANCINE'S UP AND SHE'S ACTING REALLY WEIRD... UH, HOLD ON A SECOND...
FRANCINE!!! GET THAT OUT OF YOUR MOUTH! YOU DON'T KNOW WHERE IT'S BEEN!
IS THIS LIVER?
DAVID? I'LL HAVE TO CALL YOU BACK LATER, OKAY?
LIVER!! I NEED LIVER!

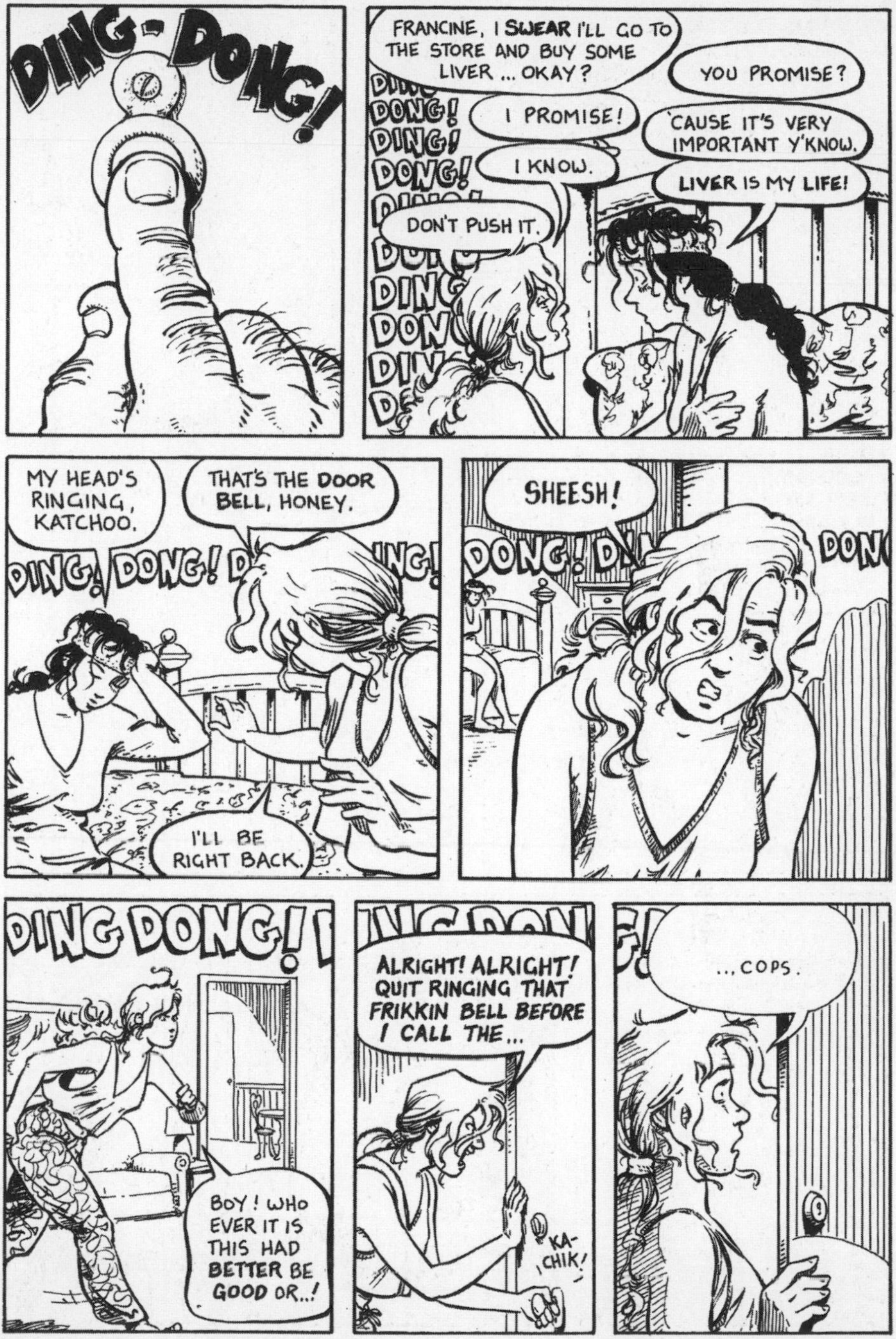
DING-DONG!
FRANCINE, I SWEAR I'LL GO TO THE STORE AND BUY SOME LIVER ... OKAY?
YOU PROMISE?
I PROMISE!
'CAUSE IT'S VERY IMPORTANT Y'KNOW.
I KNOW.
LIVER IS MY LIFE!
DON'T PUSH IT.
DONG! DING! DONG! DING DON
MY HEAD'S RINGING, KATCHOO.
THAT'S THE DOOR BELL, HONEY.
DING, DONG!
I'LL BE RIGHT BACK.
SHEESH!
DONG!
DING DONG!
ALRIGHT! ALRIGHT! QUIT RINGING THAT FRIKKIN BELL BEFORE I CALL THE...
KA-CHIK!
BOY! WHO EVER IT IS THIS HAD BETTER BE GOOD OR..!
...COPS.

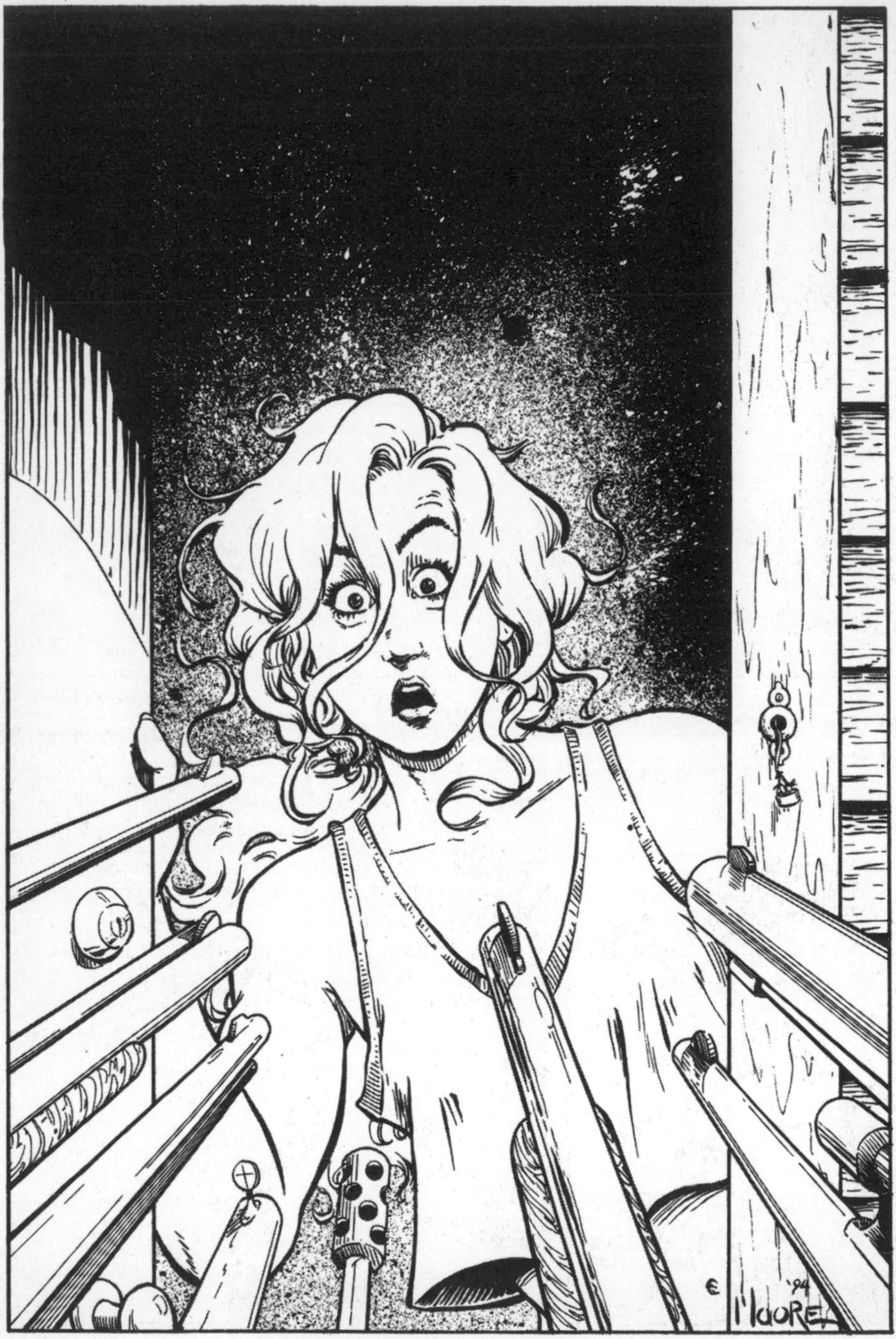
'94
MOORE

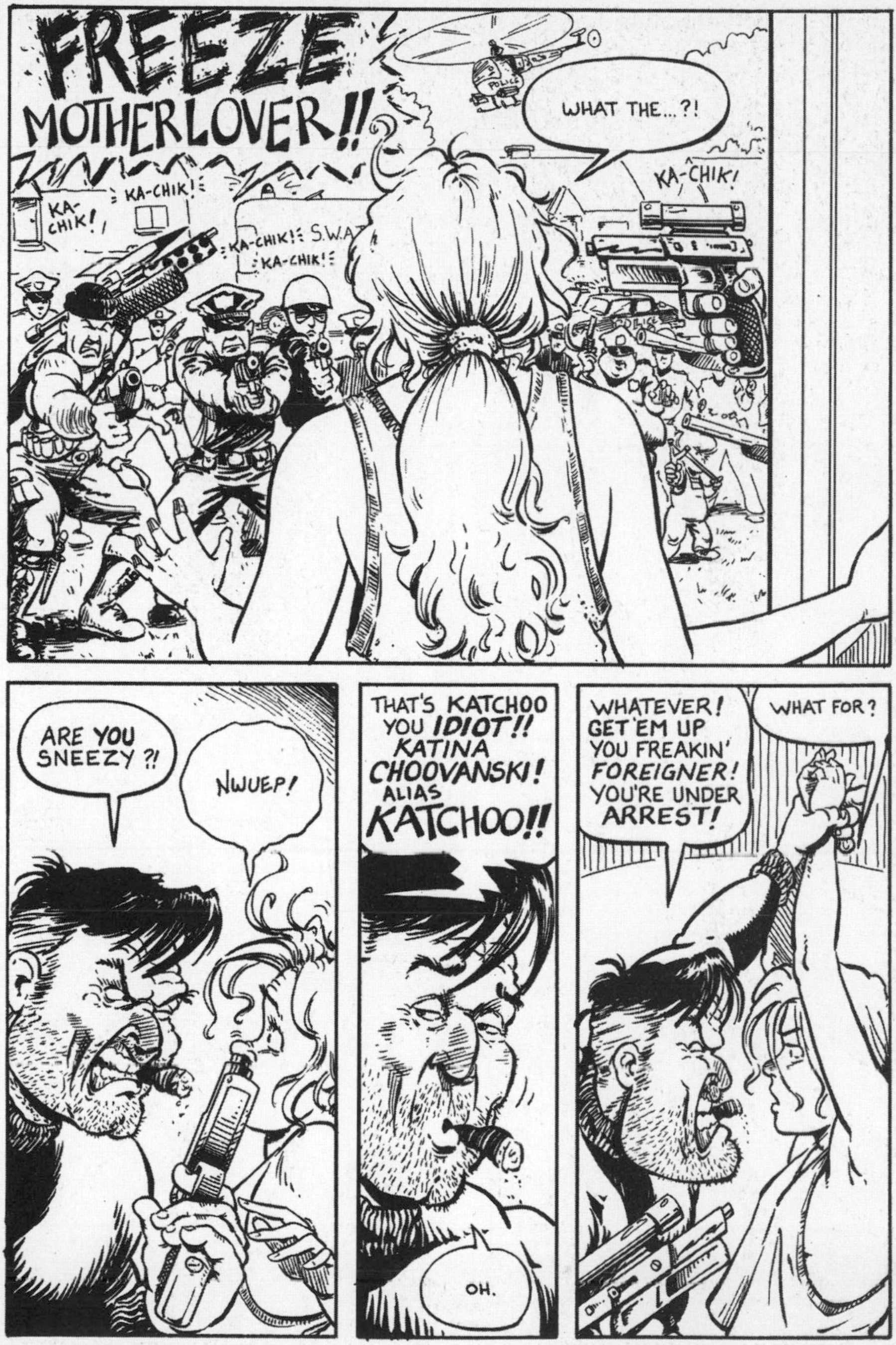
FREEZE MOTHERLOVER!!
WHAT THE...?!
KA-CHIK!
KA-CHIK!
KA-CHIK!
KA-CHIK!
S.W.A
KA-CHIK!
ARE YOU SNEEZY ?!
NWUEP!
THAT'S KATCHOO YOU IDIOT!! KATINA CHOOVANSKI! ALIAS KATCHOO!!
OH.
WHATEVER! GET 'EM UP YOU FREAKIN' FOREIGNER! YOU'RE UNDER ARREST!
WHAT FOR?

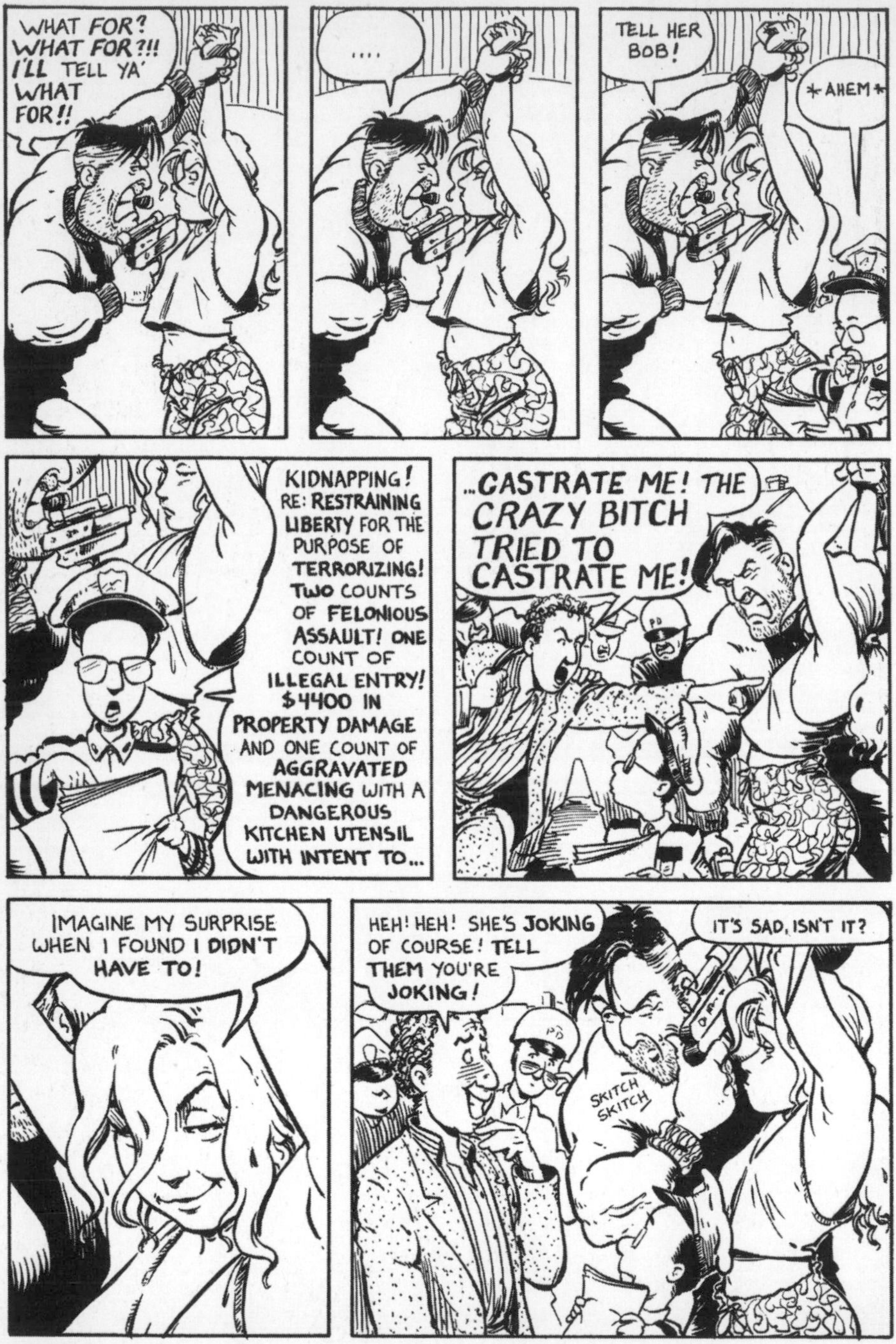
WHAT FOR? WHAT FOR?!! I'LL TELL YA' WHAT FOR!!
....
TELL HER BOB!
AHEM
KIDNAPPING! RE: RESTRAINING LIBERTY FOR THE PURPOSE OF TERRORIZING! TWO COUNTS OF FELONIOUS ASSAULT! ONE COUNT OF ILLEGAL ENTRY! $4400 IN PROPERTY DAMAGE AND ONE COUNT OF AGGRAVATED MENACING WITH A DANGEROUS KITCHEN UTENSIL WITH INTENT TO...
...CASTRATE ME! THE CRAZY BITCH TRIED TO CASTRATE ME!
PD
IMAGINE MY SURPRISE WHEN I FOUND I DIDN'T HAVE TO!
HEH! HEH! SHE'S JOKING OF COURSE! TELL THEM YOU'RE JOKING!
IT'S SAD, ISN'T IT?
PD
SKITCH SKITCH

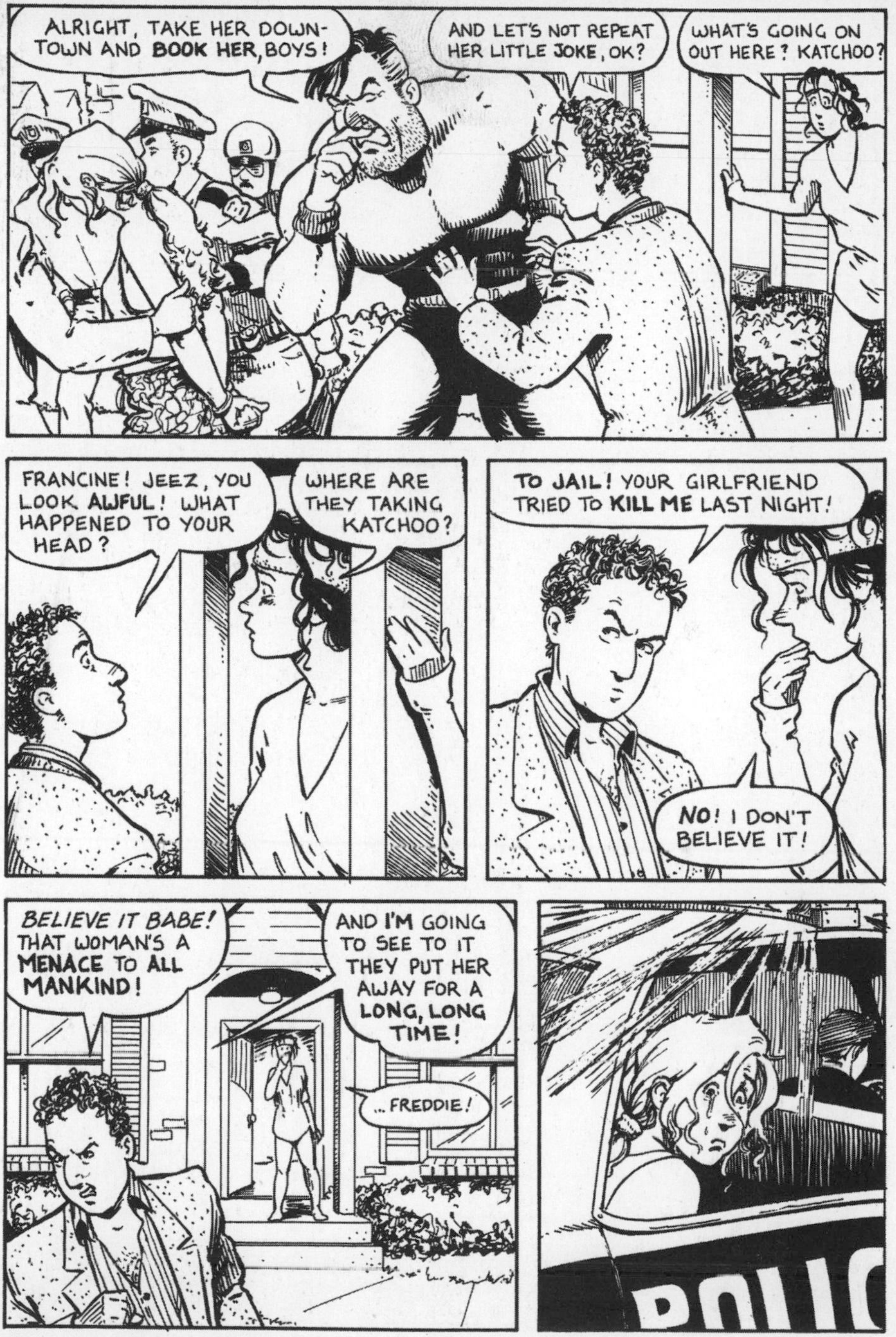
ALRIGHT, TAKE HER DOWNTOWN AND BOOK HER, BOYS!
AND LET'S NOT REPEAT HER LITTLE JOKE, OK?
WHAT'S GOING ON OUT HERE? KATCHOO?
FRANCINE! JEEZ, YOU LOOK AWFUL! WHAT HAPPENED TO YOUR HEAD?
WHERE ARE THEY TAKING KATCHOO?
TO JAIL! YOUR GIRLFRIEND TRIED TO KILL ME LAST NIGHT!
NO! I DON'T BELIEVE IT!
BELIEVE IT BABE! THAT WOMAN'S A MENACE TO ALL MANKIND!
AND I'M GOING TO SEE TO IT THEY PUT HER AWAY FOR A LONG, LONG TIME!
...FREDDIE!
POLIC

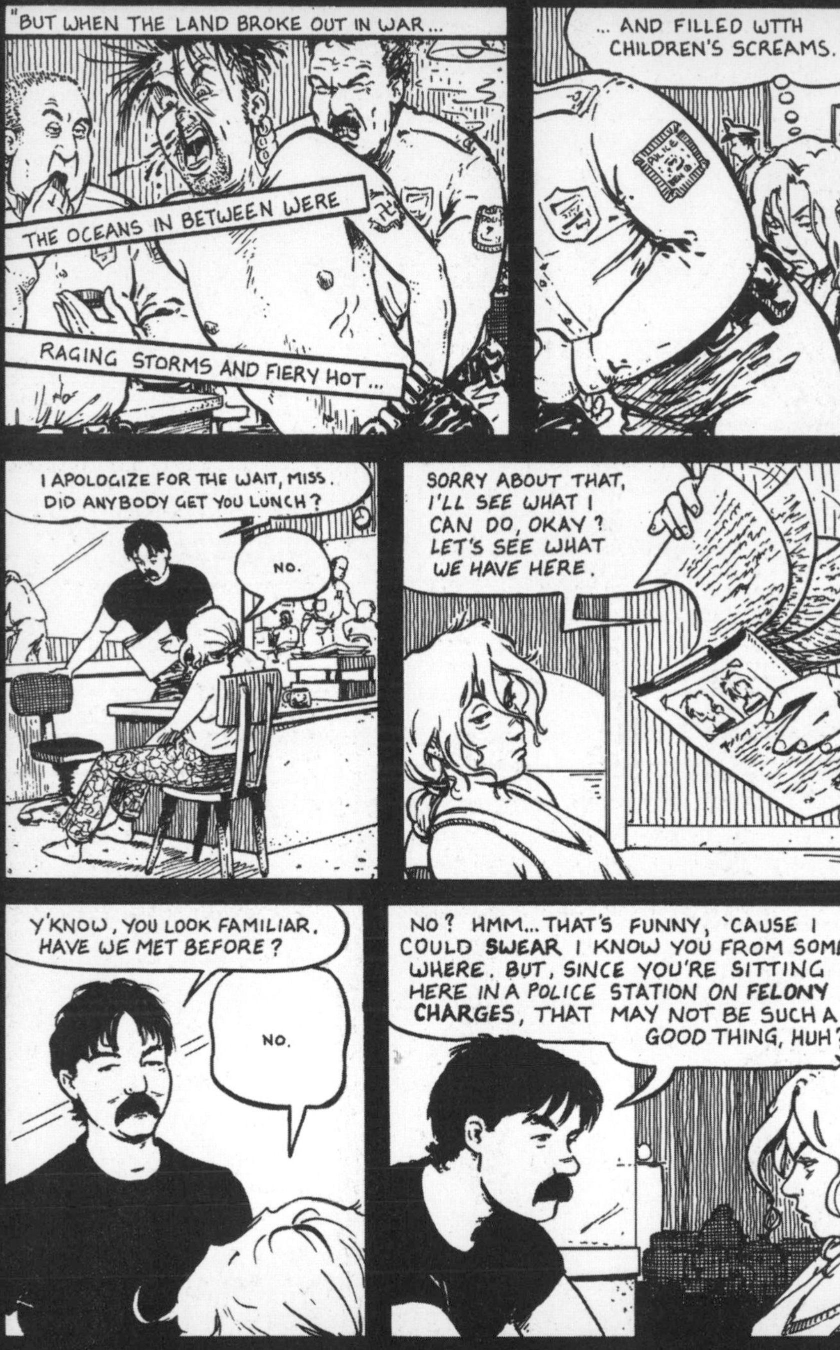
"BUT WHEN THE LAND BROKE OUT IN WAR...
THE OCEANS IN BETWEEN WERE
RAGING STORMS AND FIERY HOT...
... AND FILLED WITH CHILDREN'S SCREAMS."
I APOLOGIZE FOR THE WAIT, MISS. DID ANYBODY GET YOU LUNCH?
NO.
SORRY ABOUT THAT, I'LL SEE WHAT I CAN DO, OKAY? LET'S SEE WHAT WE HAVE HERE.
Y'KNOW, YOU LOOK FAMILIAR. HAVE WE MET BEFORE?
NO.
NO? HMM... THAT'S FUNNY, 'CAUSE I COULD SWEAR I KNOW YOU FROM SOMEWHERE. BUT, SINCE YOU'RE SITTING HERE IN A POLICE STATION ON FELONY CHARGES, THAT MAY NOT BE SUCH A GOOD THING, HUH?

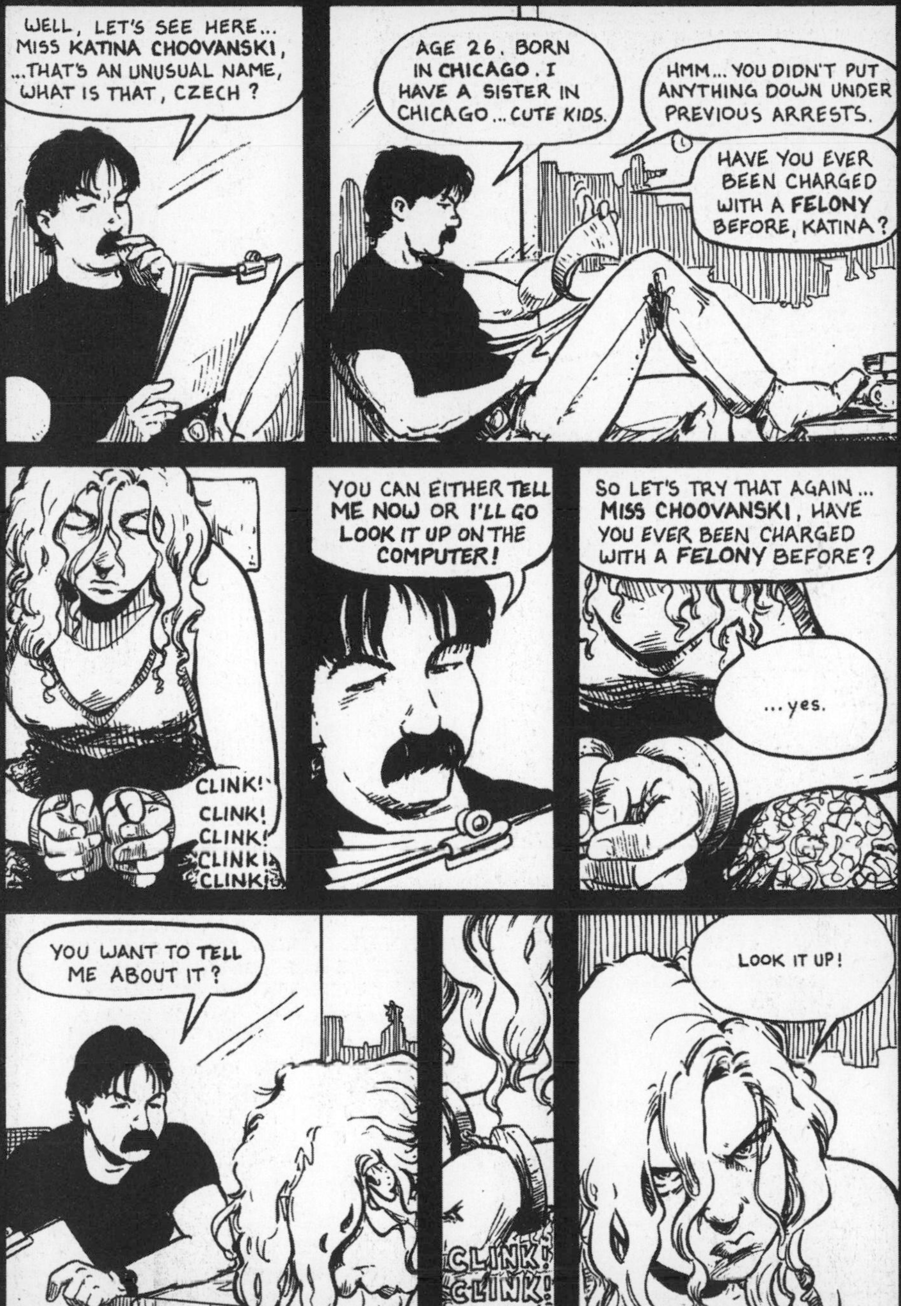
WELL, LET'S SEE HERE... MISS KATINA CHOOVANSKI, ...THAT'S AN UNUSUAL NAME, WHAT IS THAT, CZECH ?
AGE 26. BORN IN CHICAGO. I HAVE A SISTER IN CHICAGO... CUTE KIDS.
HMM... YOU DIDN'T PUT ANYTHING DOWN UNDER PREVIOUS ARRESTS.
HAVE YOU EVER BEEN CHARGED WITH A FELONY BEFORE, KATINA?
CLINK! CLINK! CLINK! CLINK! CLINK!
YOU CAN EITHER TELL ME NOW OR I'LL GO LOOK IT UP ON THE COMPUTER!
SO LET'S TRY THAT AGAIN... MISS CHOOVANSKI, HAVE YOU EVER BEEN CHARGED WITH A FELONY BEFORE?
...yes.
YOU WANT TO TELL ME ABOUT IT?
CLINK! CLINK! CLINK!
LOOK IT UP!

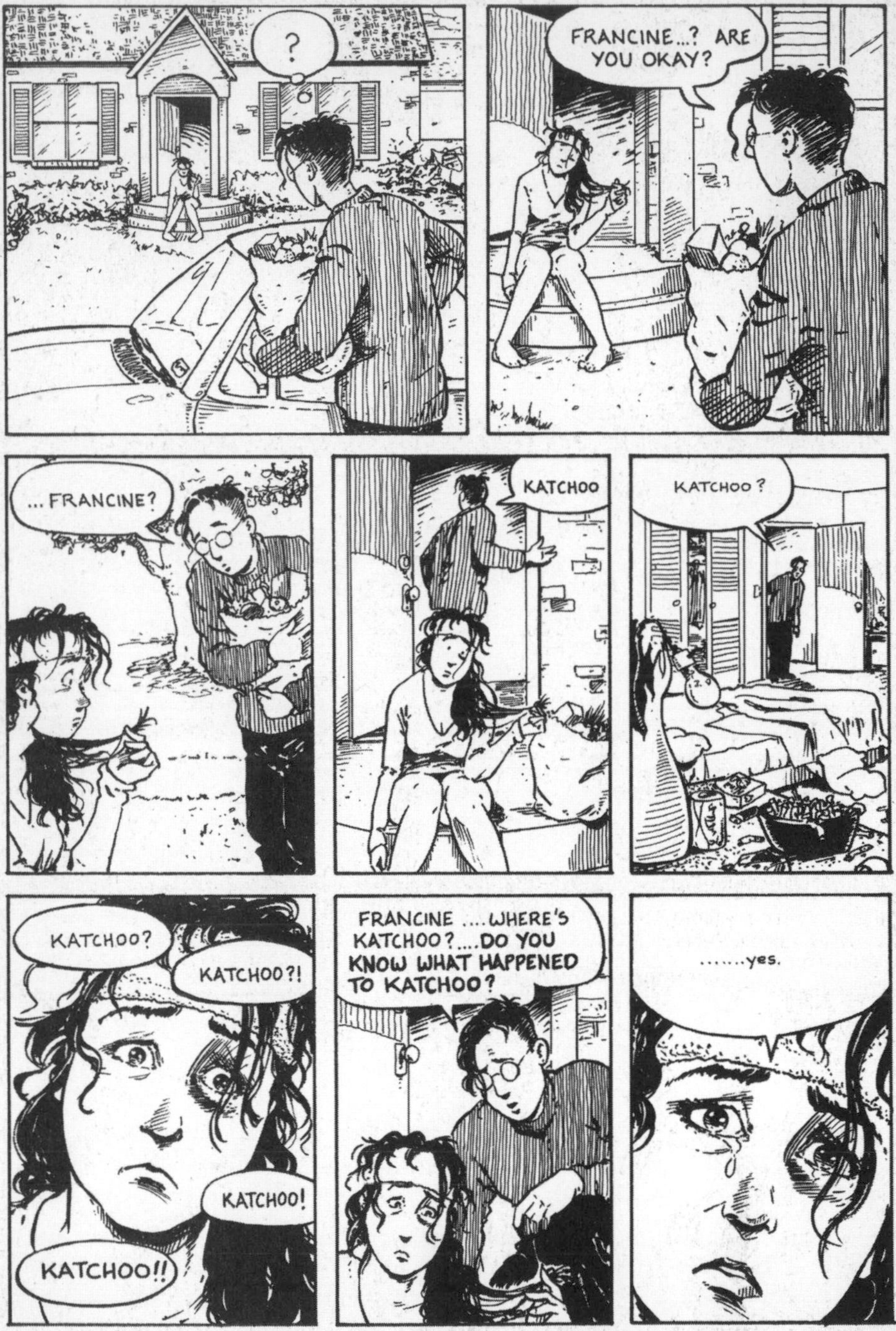
?
FRANCINE...? ARE YOU OKAY?
...FRANCINE?
KATCHOO
KATCHOO?
KATCHOO?
KATCHOO?!
KATCHOO!
KATCHOO!!
FRANCINE ....WHERE'S KATCHOO?....DO YOU KNOW WHAT HAPPENED TO KATCHOO?
.......yes.

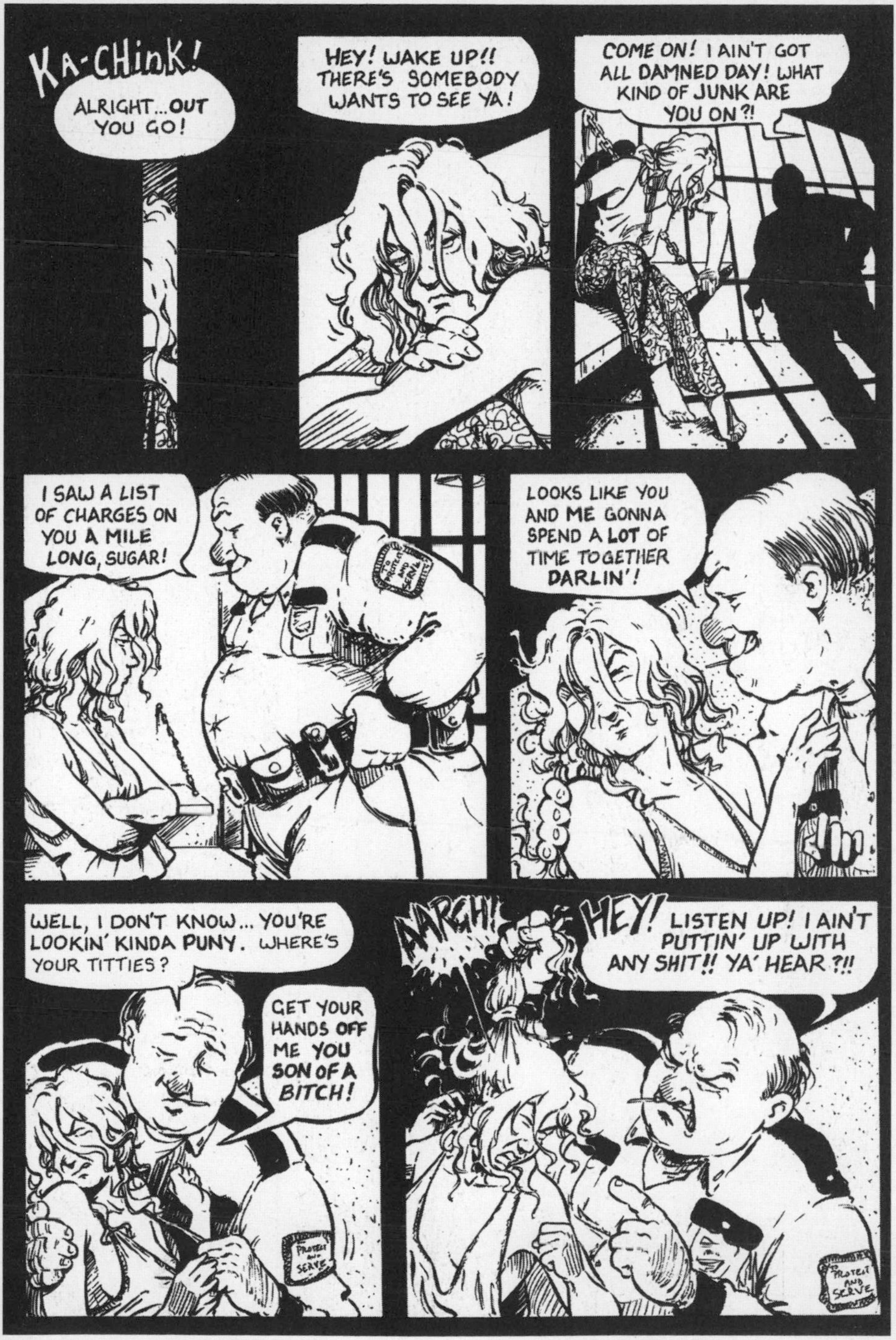
KA-CHINK!
ALRIGHT...OUT YOU GO!
HEY! WAKE UP!! THERE'S SOMEBODY WANTS TO SEE YA!
COME ON! I AIN'T GOT ALL DAMNED DAY! WHAT KIND OF JUNK ARE YOU ON?!
I SAW A LIST OF CHARGES ON YOU A MILE LONG, SUGAR!
TO PROTECT AND SERVE
LOOKS LIKE YOU AND ME GONNA SPEND A LOT OF TIME TOGETHER DARLIN'!
WELL, I DON'T KNOW... YOU'RE LOOKIN' KINDA PUNY. WHERE'S YOUR TITTIES?
GET YOUR HANDS OFF ME YOU SON OF A BITCH!
PROTECT AND SERVE
AARGH!
HEY! LISTEN UP! I AIN'T PUTTIN' UP WITH ANY SHIT!! YA' HEAR?!!
TO PROTECT AND SERVE

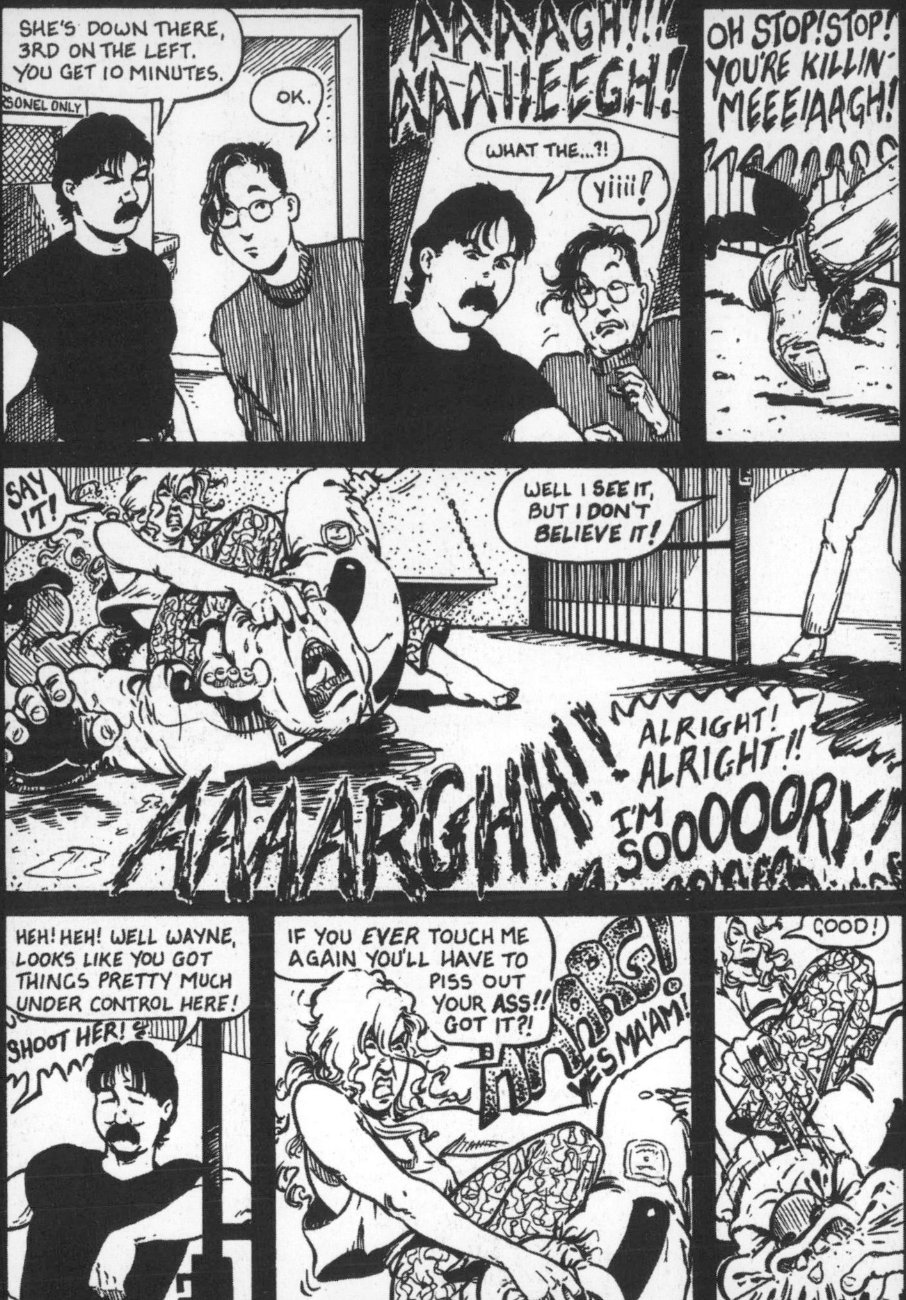
SHE'S DOWN THERE, 3RD ON THE LEFT. YOU GET 10 MINUTES.
SONEL ONLY
OK.
AAAAGH!!! AAAIIEEGH!
WHAT THE...?!
yiiii!
OH STOP! STOP! YOU'RE KILLIN' MEEE! AAGH!
SAY IT!
WELL I SEE IT, BUT I DON'T BELIEVE IT!
AAAARGHH!
ALRIGHT! ALRIGHT!!
I'M SOOOOORY!
HEH! HEH! WELL WAYNE, LOOKS LIKE YOU GOT THINGS PRETTY MUCH UNDER CONTROL HERE!
SHOOT HER!
IF YOU EVER TOUCH ME AGAIN YOU'LL HAVE TO PISS OUT YOUR ASS!! GOT IT?!
YES MA'AM!
GOOD!
KRUNCH!

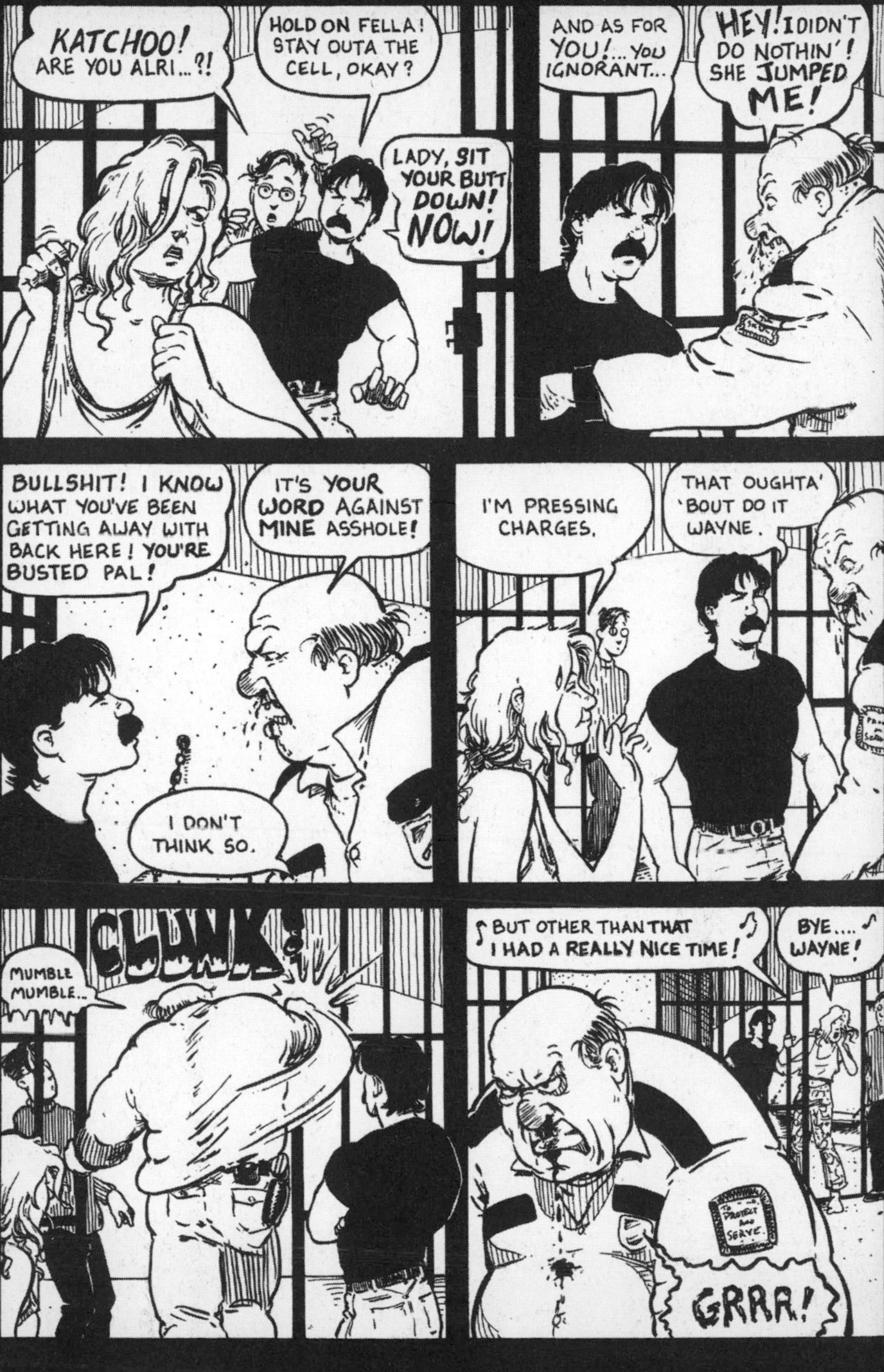
KATCHOO! ARE YOU ALRI...?!
HOLD ON FELLA! STAY OUTA THE CELL, OKAY?
LADY, SIT YOUR BUTT DOWN! NOW!
AND AS FOR YOU!... YOU IGNORANT...
HEY! I DIDN'T DO NOTHIN'! SHE JUMPED ME!
BULLSHIT! I KNOW WHAT YOU'VE BEEN GETTING AWAY WITH BACK HERE! YOU'RE BUSTED PAL!
IT'S YOUR WORD AGAINST MINE ASSHOLE!
I DON'T THINK SO.
I'M PRESSING CHARGES.
THAT OUGHTA' 'BOUT DO IT WAYNE.
CLUNK!
MUMBLE MUMBLE...
BUT OTHER THAN THAT I HAD A REALLY NICE TIME!
BYE.... WAYNE!
TO PROTECT AND SERVE
GRRR!

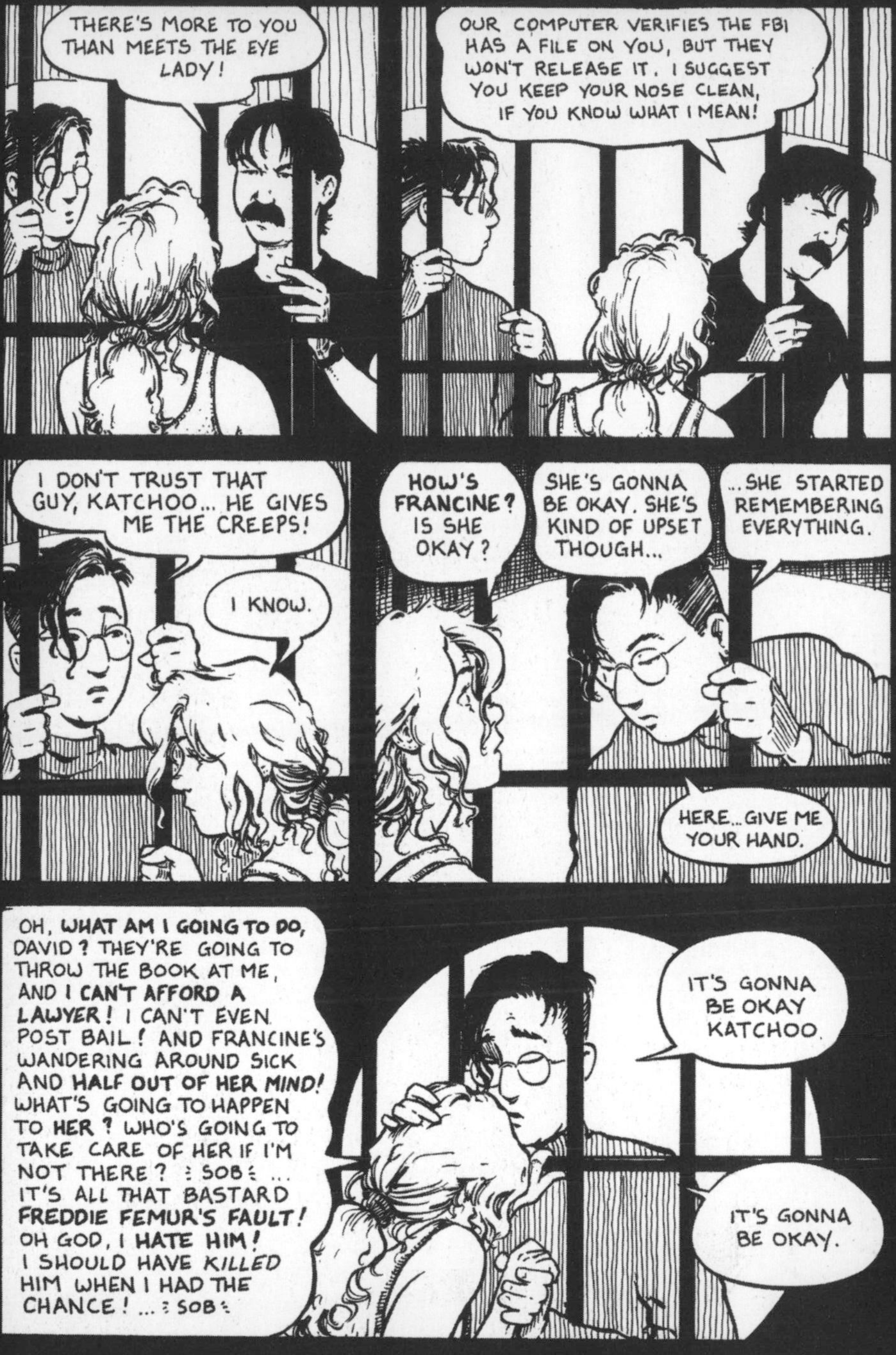
THERE'S MORE TO YOU THAN MEETS THE EYE LADY!
OUR COMPUTER VERIFIES THE FBI HAS A FILE ON YOU, BUT THEY WON'T RELEASE IT. I SUGGEST YOU KEEP YOUR NOSE CLEAN, IF YOU KNOW WHAT I MEAN!
I DON'T TRUST THAT GUY, KATCHOO... HE GIVES ME THE CREEPS!
I KNOW.
HOW'S FRANCINE? IS SHE OKAY?
SHE'S GONNA BE OKAY. SHE'S KIND OF UPSET THOUGH...
...SHE STARTED REMEMBERING EVERYTHING.
HERE... GIVE ME YOUR HAND.
OH, WHAT AM I GOING TO DO, DAVID? THEY'RE GOING TO THROW THE BOOK AT ME, AND I CAN'T AFFORD A LAWYER! I CAN'T EVEN POST BAIL! AND FRANCINE'S WANDERING AROUND SICK AND HALF OUT OF HER MIND! WHAT'S GOING TO HAPPEN TO HER? WHO'S GOING TO TAKE CARE OF HER IF I'M NOT THERE? :SOB: ... IT'S ALL THAT BASTARD FREDDIE FEMUR'S FAULT! OH GOD, I HATE HIM! I SHOULD HAVE KILLED HIM WHEN I HAD THE CHANCE! ... :SOB:
IT'S GONNA BE OKAY KATCHOO.
IT'S GONNA BE OKAY.

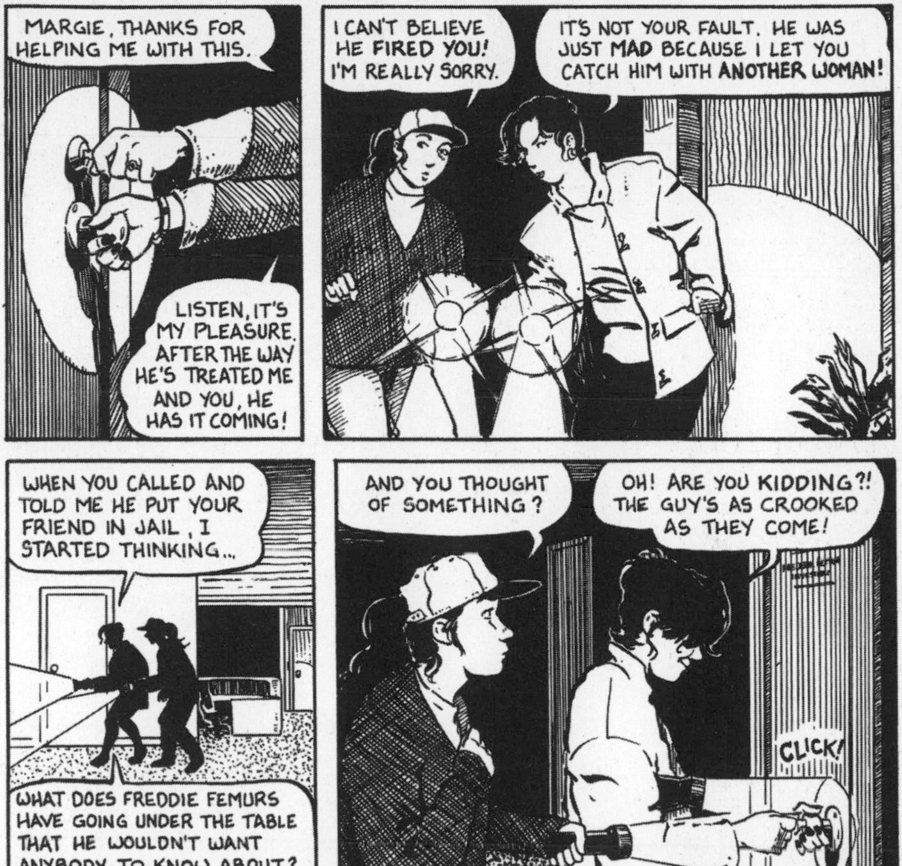
MARGIE, THANKS FOR HELPING ME WITH THIS.
LISTEN, IT'S MY PLEASURE. AFTER THE WAY HE'S TREATED ME AND YOU, HE HAS IT COMING!
I CAN'T BELIEVE HE FIRED YOU! I'M REALLY SORRY.
IT'S NOT YOUR FAULT. HE WAS JUST MAD BECAUSE I LET YOU CATCH HIM WITH ANOTHER WOMAN!
WHEN YOU CALLED AND TOLD ME HE PUT YOUR FRIEND IN JAIL, I STARTED THINKING...
WHAT DOES FREDDIE FEMURS HAVE GOING UNDER THE TABLE THAT HE WOULDN'T WANT ANYBODY TO KNOW ABOUT?
AND YOU THOUGHT OF SOMETHING?
OH! ARE YOU KIDDING?! THE GUY'S AS CROOKED AS THEY COME!
CLICK!
BUT THERE'S ONE ACCOUNT THAT REALLY TOPS THEM ALL... BERGER FOODS! HE'S BEEN OVERBIDDING THEIR JOBS AND POCKETING THE PROFITS FOR YEARS!
I KNOW HE KEEPS A SECRET RECORD OF HIS DEALINGS. IF I CAN JUST FIND...
...GOT IT!
SLAM!
SOMEBODY'S COMING!

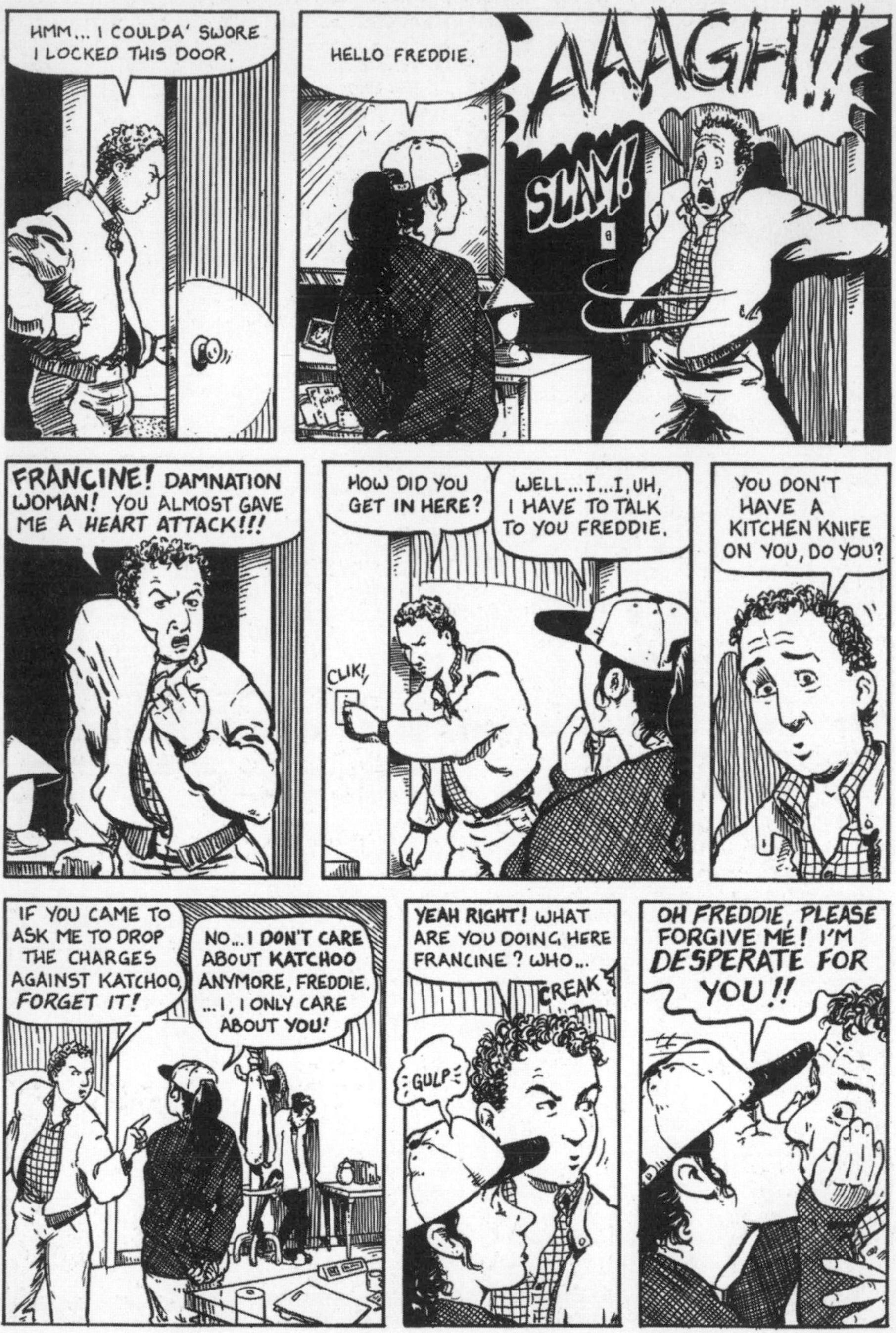
HMM... I COULDA' SWORE I LOCKED THIS DOOR.
HELLO FREDDIE.
AAAGH!!!
SLAM!
FRANCINE! DAMNATION WOMAN! YOU ALMOST GAVE ME A HEART ATTACK!!!
HOW DID YOU GET IN HERE?
CLIK!
WELL...I...I, UH, I HAVE TO TALK TO YOU FREDDIE.
YOU DON'T HAVE A KITCHEN KNIFE ON YOU, DO YOU?
IF YOU CAME TO ASK ME TO DROP THE CHARGES AGAINST KATCHOO, FORGET IT!
NO...I DON'T CARE ABOUT KATCHOO ANYMORE, FREDDIE. ...I, I ONLY CARE ABOUT YOU!
YEAH RIGHT! WHAT ARE YOU DOING HERE FRANCINE? WHO...
CREAK
GULP
OH FREDDIE, PLEASE FORGIVE ME! I'M DESPERATE FOR YOU!!

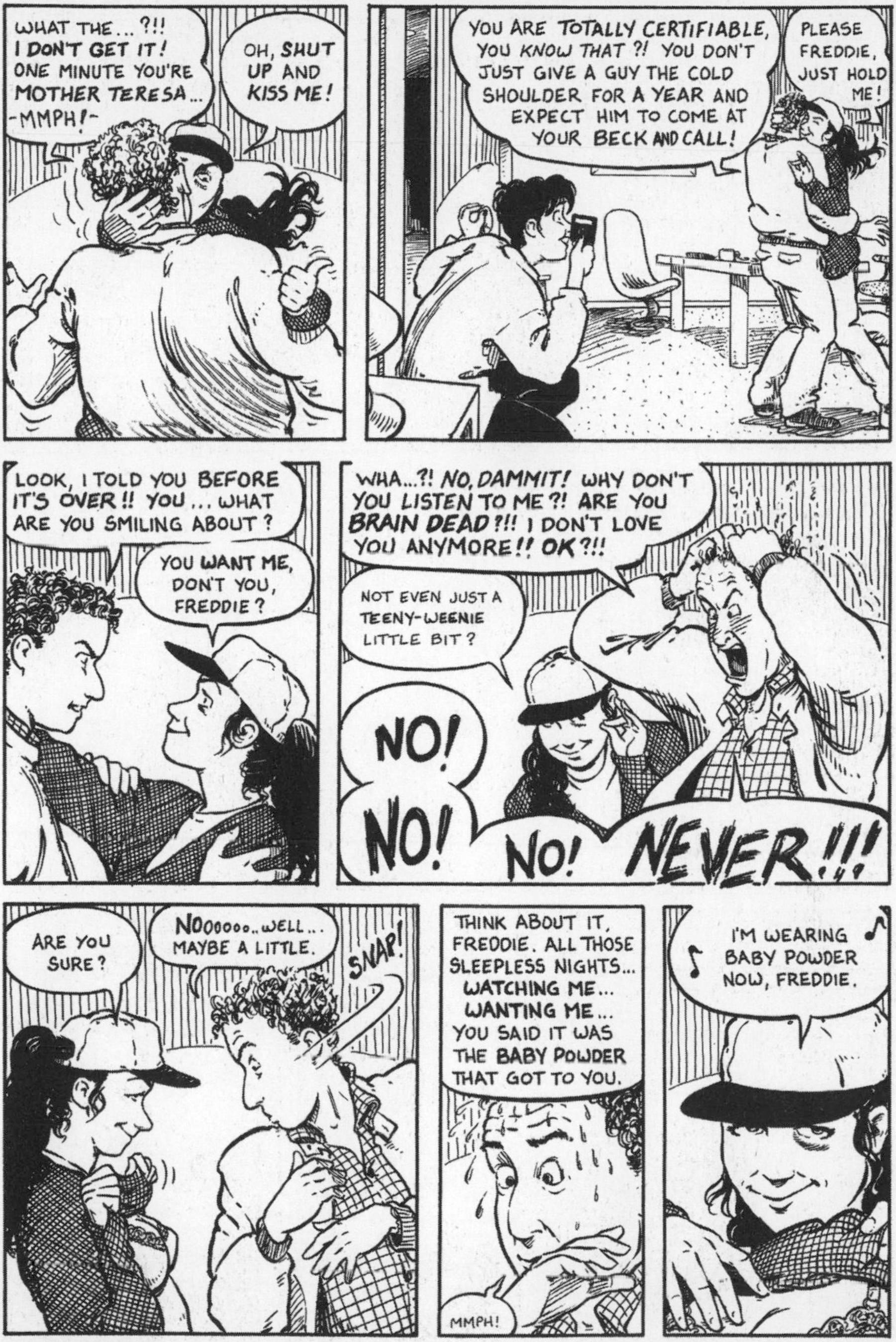
WHAT THE ... ?!! I DON'T GET IT! ONE MINUTE YOU'RE MOTHER TERESA ... -MMPH!-
OH, SHUT UP AND KISS ME!
YOU ARE TOTALLY CERTIFIABLE, YOU KNOW THAT ?! YOU DON'T JUST GIVE A GUY THE COLD SHOULDER FOR A YEAR AND EXPECT HIM TO COME AT YOUR BECK AND CALL!
PLEASE FREDDIE, JUST HOLD ME!
LOOK, I TOLD YOU BEFORE IT'S OVER!! YOU ... WHAT ARE YOU SMILING ABOUT?
YOU WANT ME, DON'T YOU, FREDDIE?
WHA...?! NO, DAMMIT! WHY DON'T YOU LISTEN TO ME?! ARE YOU BRAIN DEAD?!! I DON'T LOVE YOU ANYMORE!! OK?!!
NOT EVEN JUST A TEENY-WEENIE LITTLE BIT?
NO!
NO!
NO! NEVER!!!
ARE YOU SURE?
NOoooooo.. WELL... MAYBE A LITTLE.
SNAP!
THINK ABOUT IT, FREDDIE. ALL THOSE SLEEPLESS NIGHTS... WATCHING ME... WANTING ME... YOU SAID IT WAS THE BABY POWDER THAT GOT TO YOU.
MMPH!
I'M WEARING BABY POWDER NOW, FREDDIE.

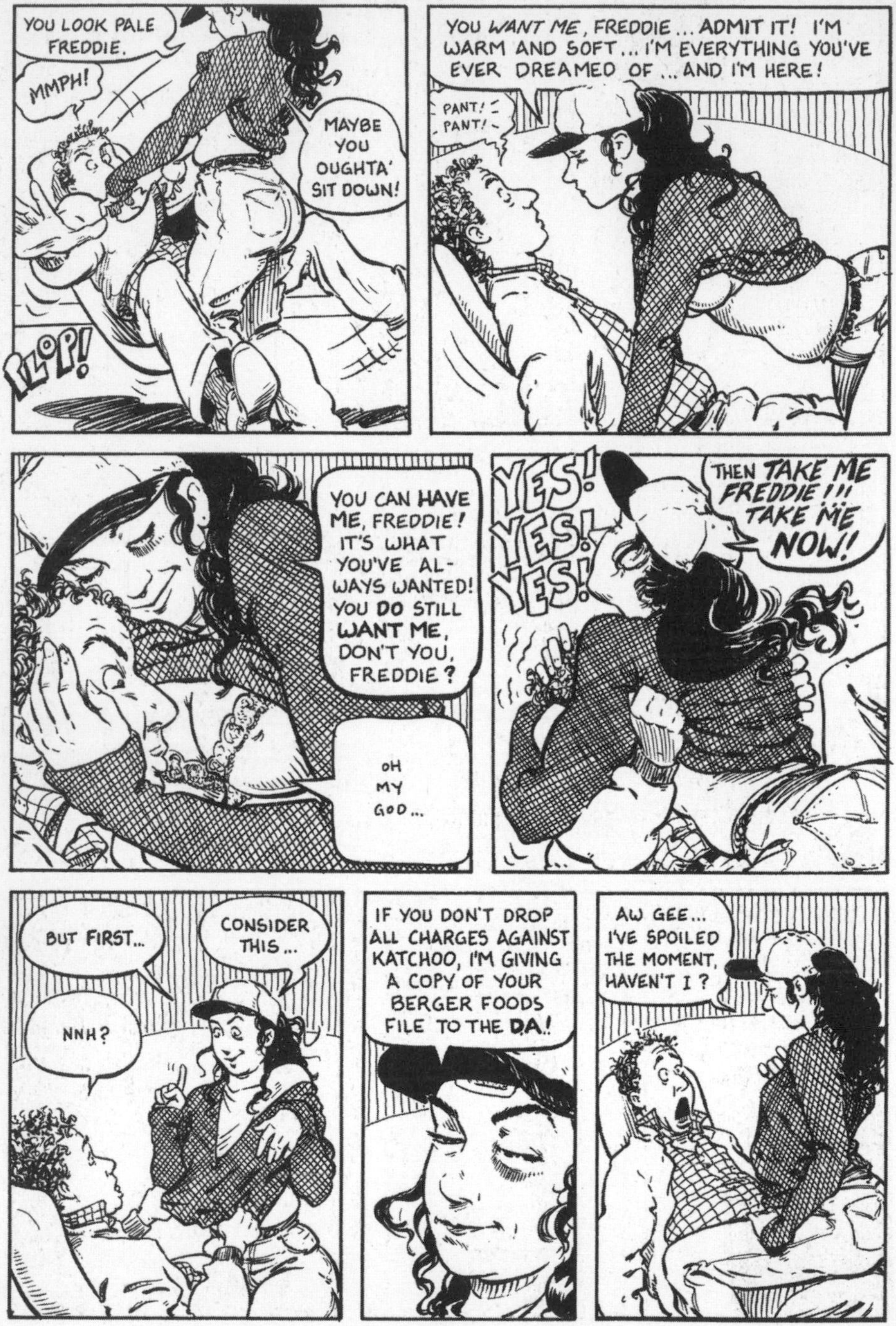
YOU LOOK PALE FREDDIE.
MMPH!
MAYBE YOU OUGHTA' SIT DOWN!
PLOP!
YOU WANT ME, FREDDIE... ADMIT IT! I'M WARM AND SOFT... I'M EVERYTHING YOU'VE EVER DREAMED OF... AND I'M HERE!
PANT! PANT!
YOU CAN HAVE ME, FREDDIE! IT'S WHAT YOU'VE ALWAYS WANTED! YOU DO STILL WANT ME, DON'T YOU, FREDDIE?
OH MY GOD...
YES! YES! YES!
THEN TAKE ME FREDDIE!!! TAKE ME NOW!
BUT FIRST...
CONSIDER THIS...
NNH?
IF YOU DON'T DROP ALL CHARGES AGAINST KATCHOO, I'M GIVING A COPY OF YOUR BERGER FOODS FILE TO THE DA!
AW GEE... I'VE SPOILED THE MOMENT, HAVEN'T I?

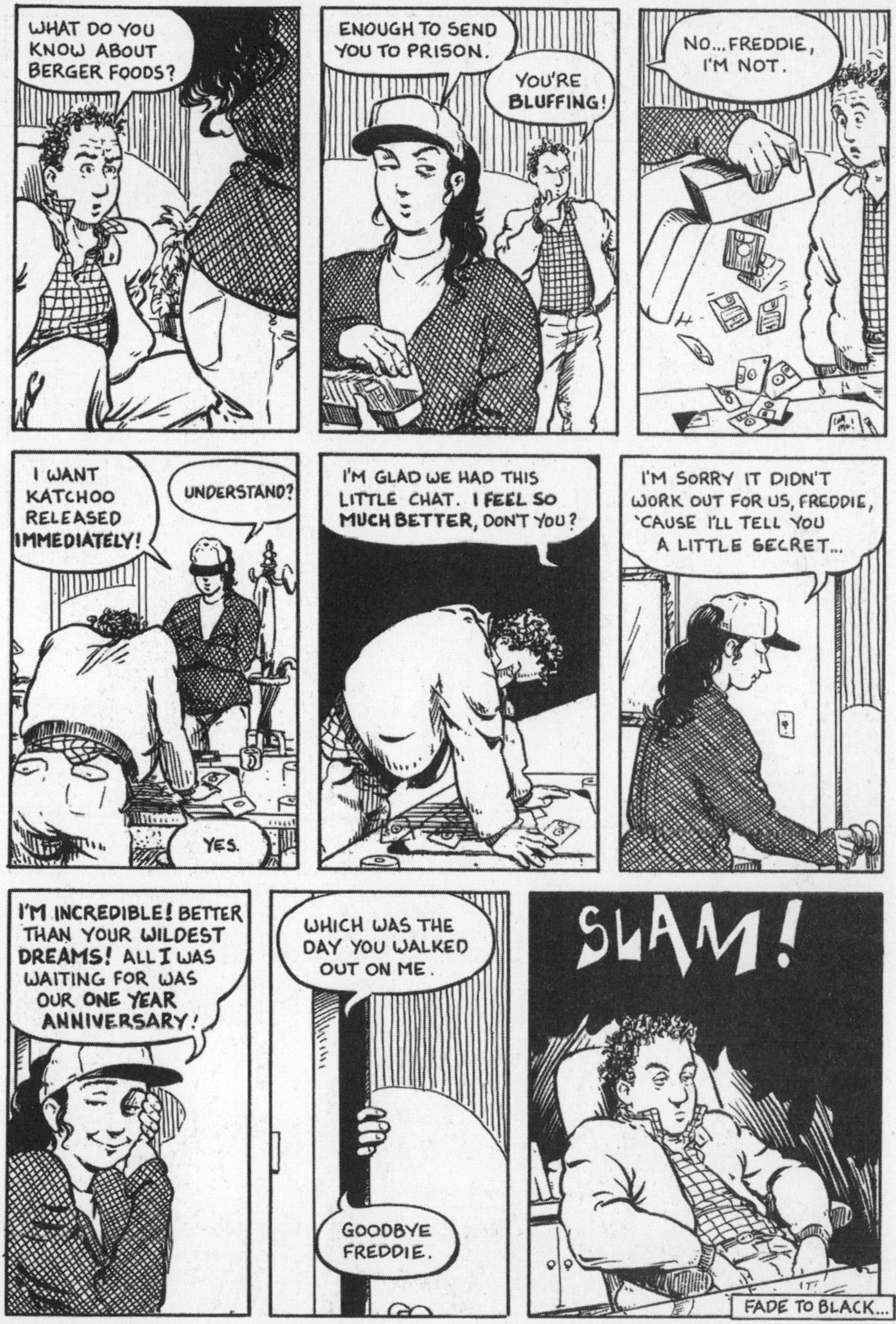
WHAT DO YOU KNOW ABOUT BERGER FOODS?
ENOUGH TO SEND YOU TO PRISON.
YOU'RE BLUFFING!
NO... FREDDIE, I'M NOT.
I WANT KATCHOO RELEASED IMMEDIATELY!
UNDERSTAND?
YES.
I'M GLAD WE HAD THIS LITTLE CHAT. I FEEL SO MUCH BETTER, DON'T YOU?
I'M SORRY IT DIDN'T WORK OUT FOR US, FREDDIE, 'CAUSE I'LL TELL YOU A LITTLE SECRET...
I'M INCREDIBLE! BETTER THAN YOUR WILDEST DREAMS! ALL I WAS WAITING FOR WAS OUR ONE YEAR ANNIVERSARY!
WHICH WAS THE DAY YOU WALKED OUT ON ME.
GOODBYE FREDDIE.
SLAM!
FADE TO BLACK...

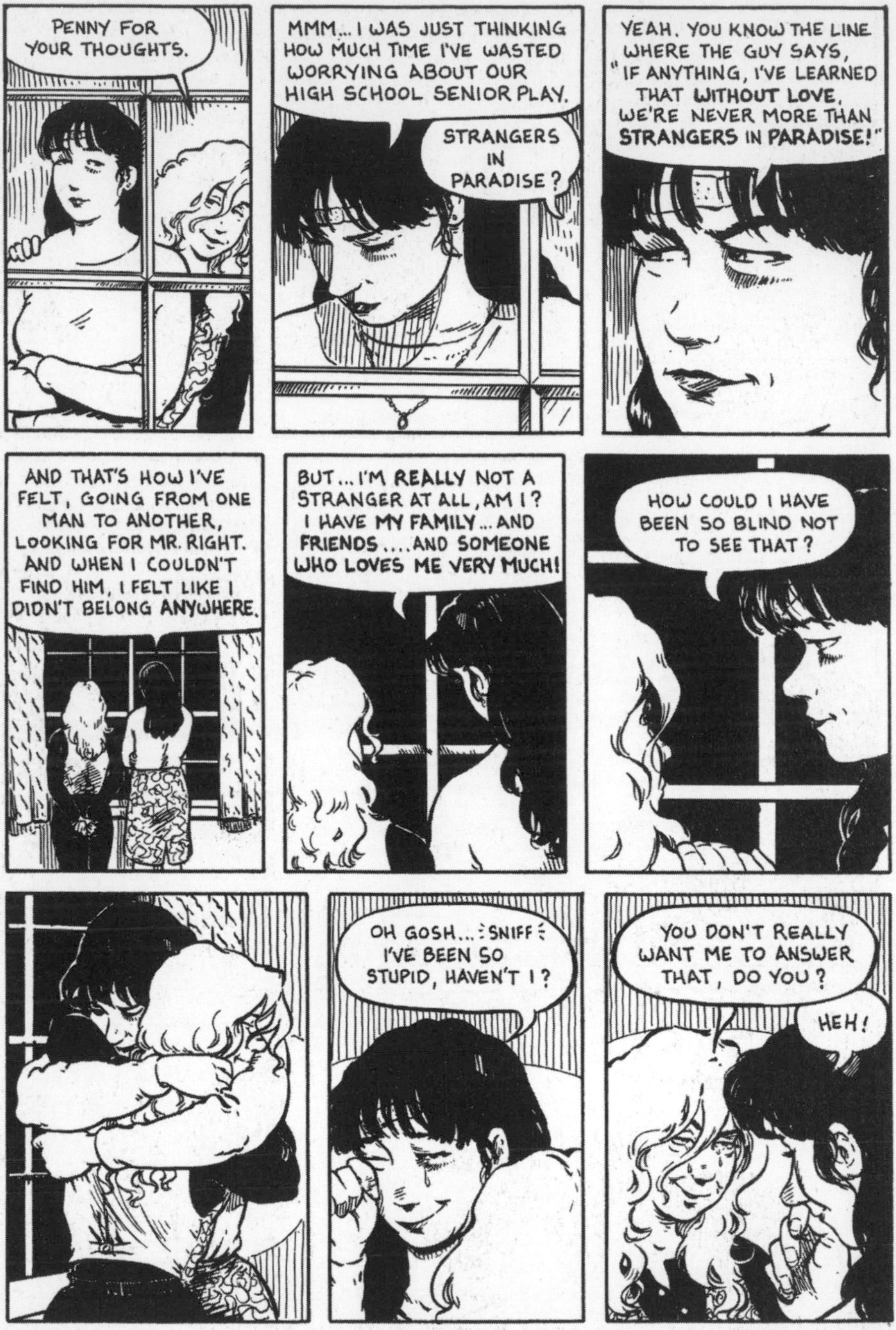
PENNY FOR YOUR THOUGHTS.
MMM... I WAS JUST THINKING HOW MUCH TIME I'VE WASTED WORRYING ABOUT OUR HIGH SCHOOL SENIOR PLAY.
STRANGERS IN PARADISE?
YEAH. YOU KNOW THE LINE WHERE THE GUY SAYS, "IF ANYTHING, I'VE LEARNED THAT WITHOUT LOVE, WE'RE NEVER MORE THAN STRANGERS IN PARADISE!"
AND THAT'S HOW I'VE FELT, GOING FROM ONE MAN TO ANOTHER, LOOKING FOR MR. RIGHT. AND WHEN I COULDN'T FIND HIM, I FELT LIKE I DIDN'T BELONG ANYWHERE.
BUT... I'M REALLY NOT A STRANGER AT ALL, AM I? I HAVE MY FAMILY... AND FRIENDS.... AND SOMEONE WHO LOVES ME VERY MUCH!
HOW COULD I HAVE BEEN SO BLIND NOT TO SEE THAT?
OH GOSH... SNIFF I'VE BEEN SO STUPID, HAVEN'T I?
YOU DON'T REALLY WANT ME TO ANSWER THAT, DO YOU?
HEH!

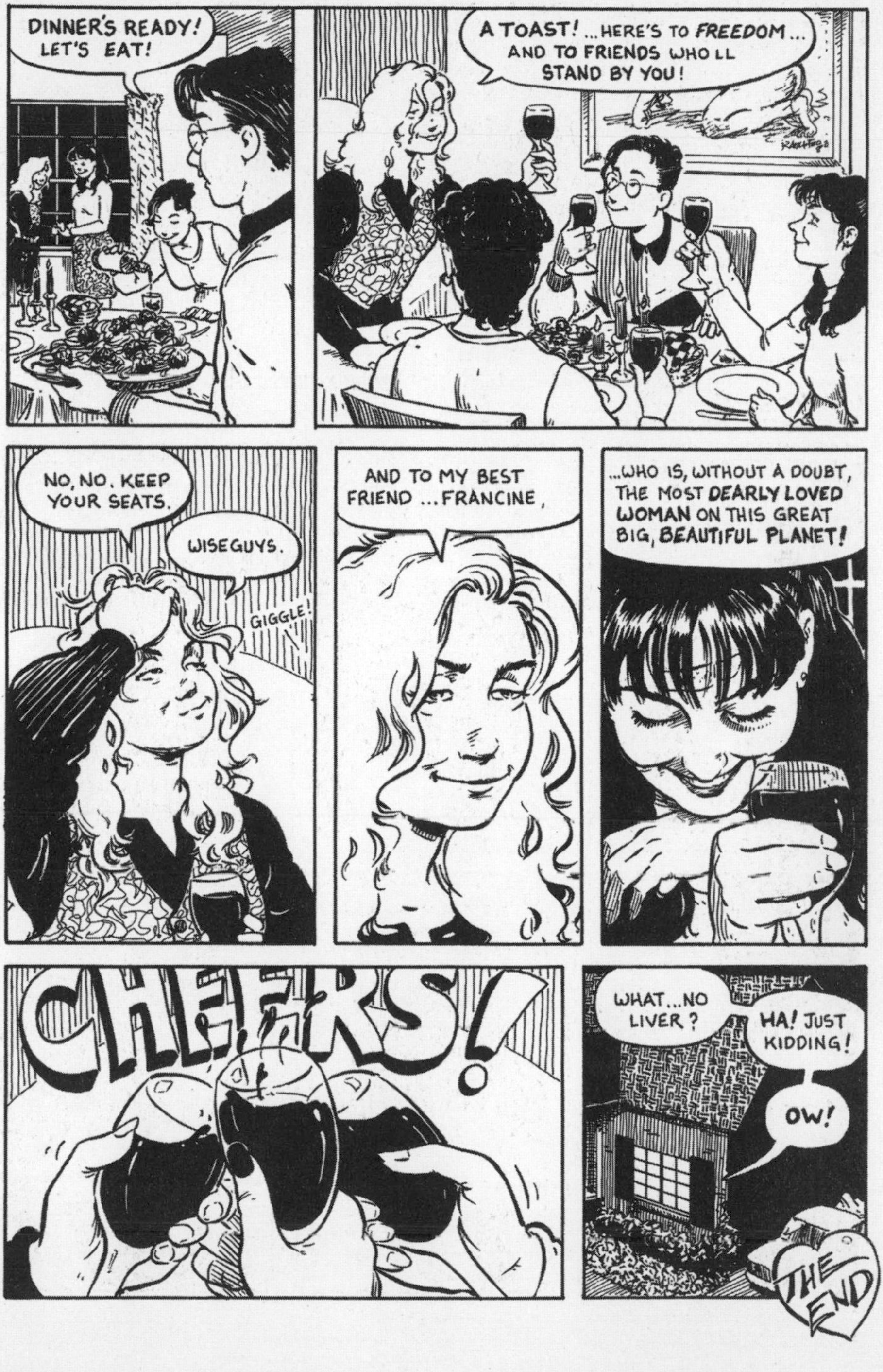
DINNER'S READY! LET'S EAT!
A TOAST! ...HERE'S TO FREEDOM... AND TO FRIENDS WHO'LL STAND BY YOU!
NO, NO. KEEP YOUR SEATS.
WISEGUYS.
GIGGLE!
AND TO MY BEST FRIEND ...FRANCINE,
...WHO IS, WITHOUT A DOUBT, THE MOST DEARLY LOVED WOMAN ON THIS GREAT BIG, BEAUTIFUL PLANET!
CHEERS!
WHAT...NO LIVER?
HA! JUST KIDDING!
OW!
THE END

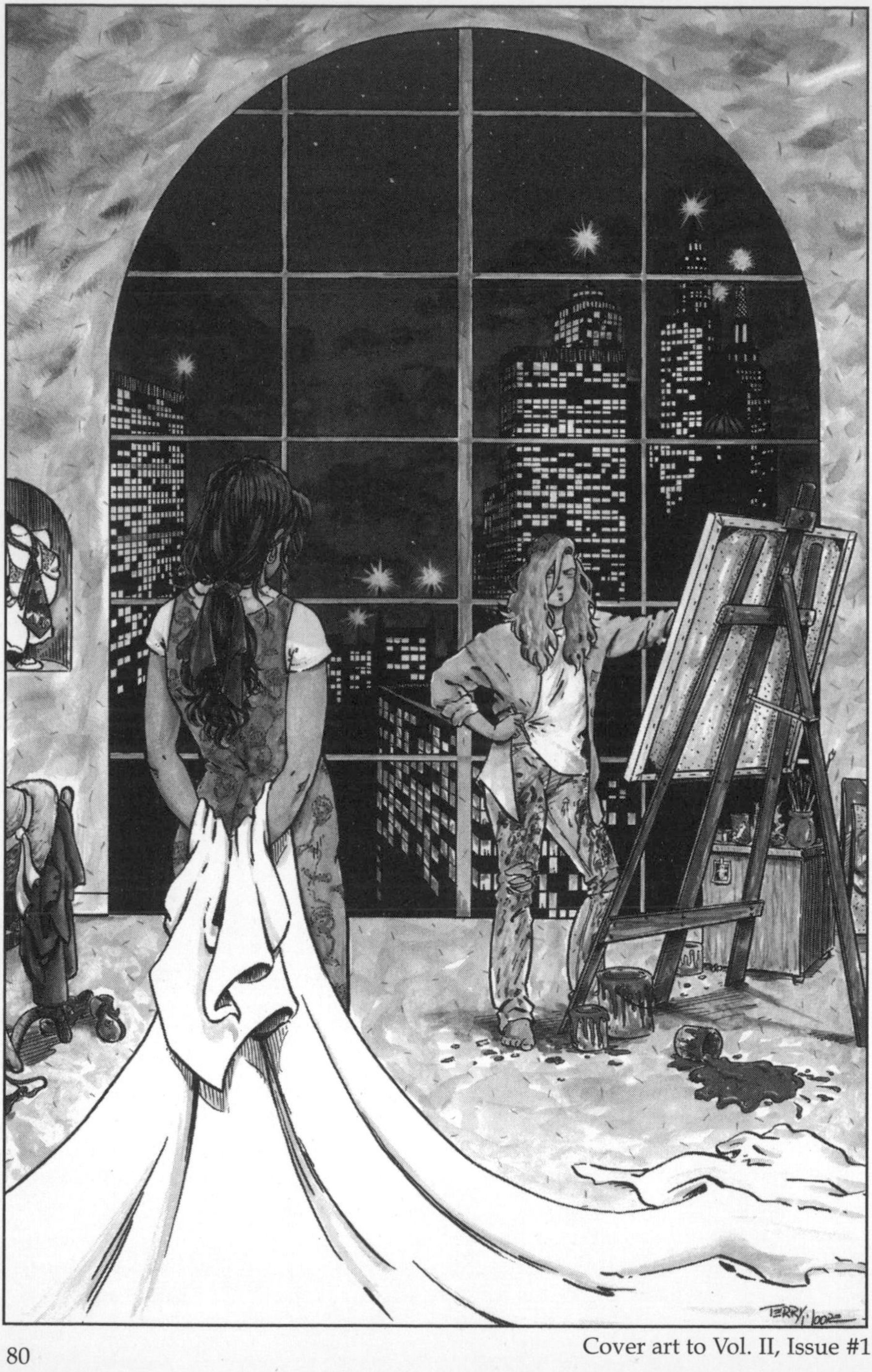

Cover art to Vol. II, Issue #1

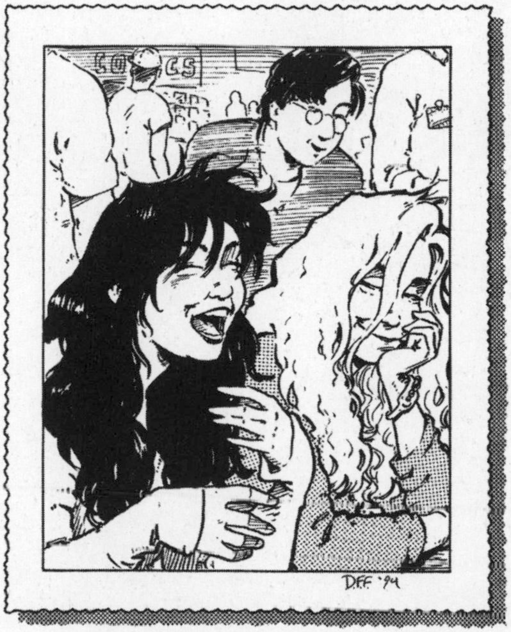
D.F.F. '94

The heart has its reasons, that reason cannot know.

—Pascal

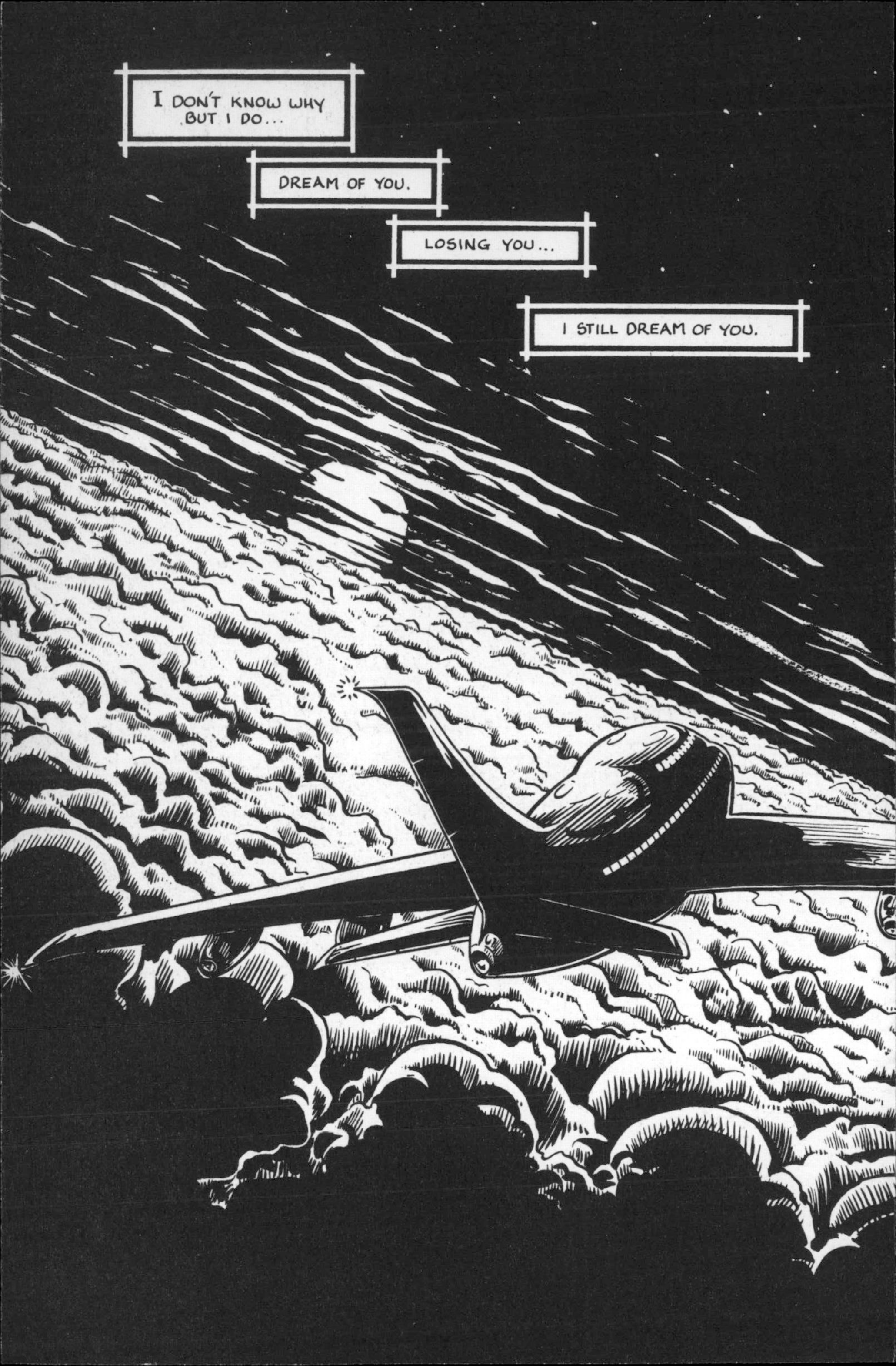
I DON'T KNOW WHY BUT I DO...
DREAM OF YOU.
LOSING YOU...
I STILL DREAM OF YOU.

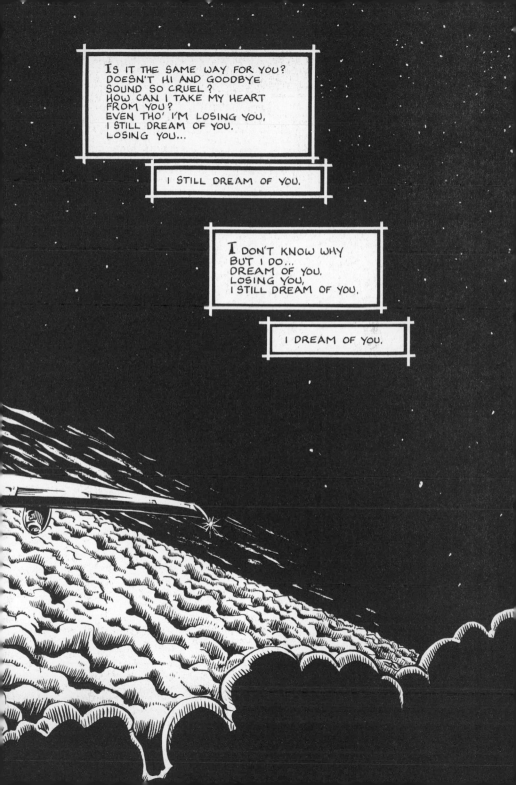

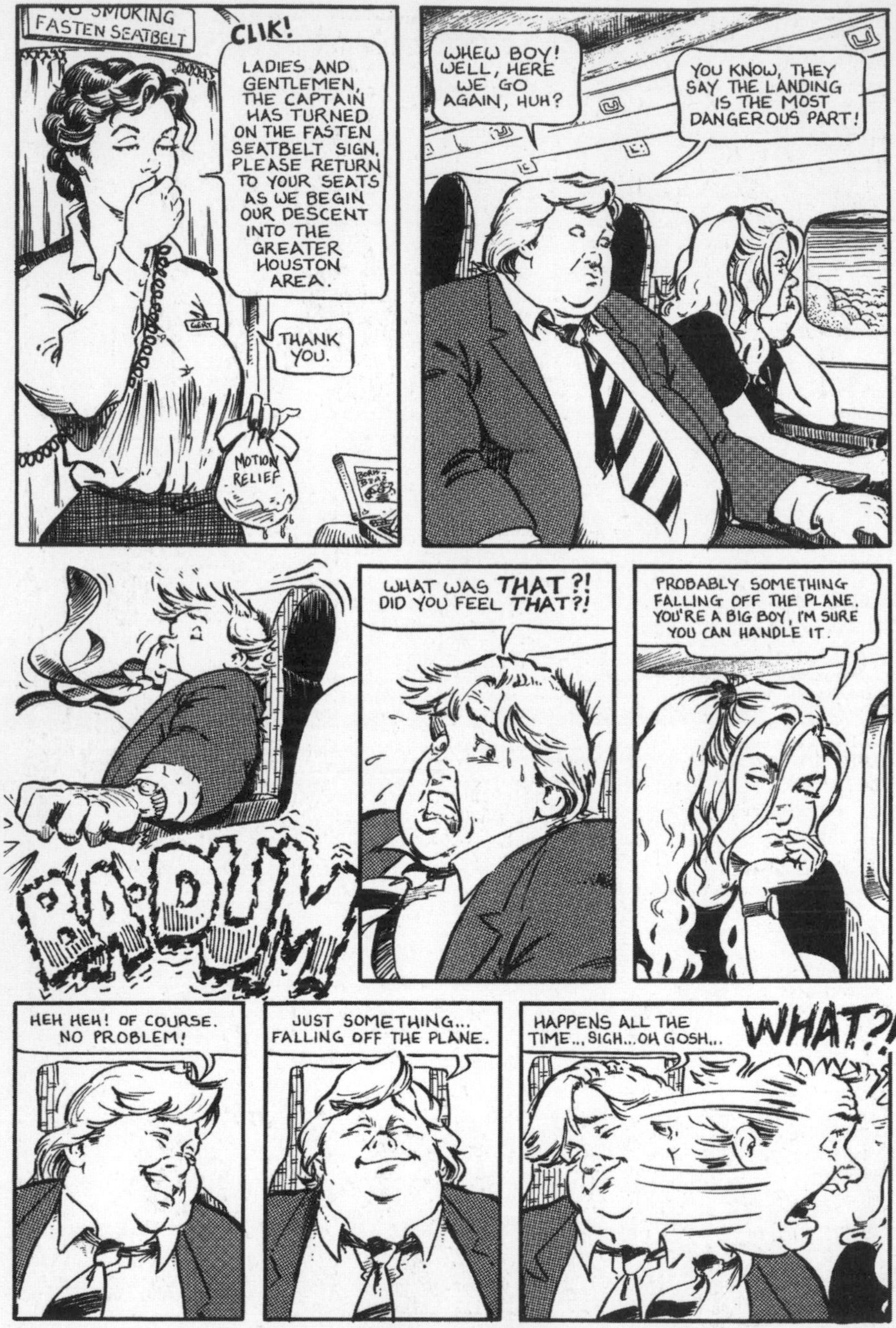
NO SMOKING
FASTEN SEATBELT
CLIK!
LADIES AND GENTLEMEN, THE CAPTAIN HAS TURNED ON THE FASTEN SEATBELT SIGN. PLEASE RETURN TO YOUR SEATS AS WE BEGIN OUR DESCENT INTO THE GREATER HOUSTON AREA.
THANK YOU.
MOTION RELIEF
WHEW BOY! WELL, HERE WE GO AGAIN, HUH?
YOU KNOW, THEY SAY THE LANDING IS THE MOST DANGEROUS PART!
BA-DUM
WHAT WAS THAT?! DID YOU FEEL THAT?!
PROBABLY SOMETHING FALLING OFF THE PLANE. YOU'RE A BIG BOY, I'M SURE YOU CAN HANDLE IT.
HEH HEH! OF COURSE. NO PROBLEM!
JUST SOMETHING... FALLING OFF THE PLANE.
HAPPENS ALL THE TIME... SIGH... OH GOSH...
WHAT?!

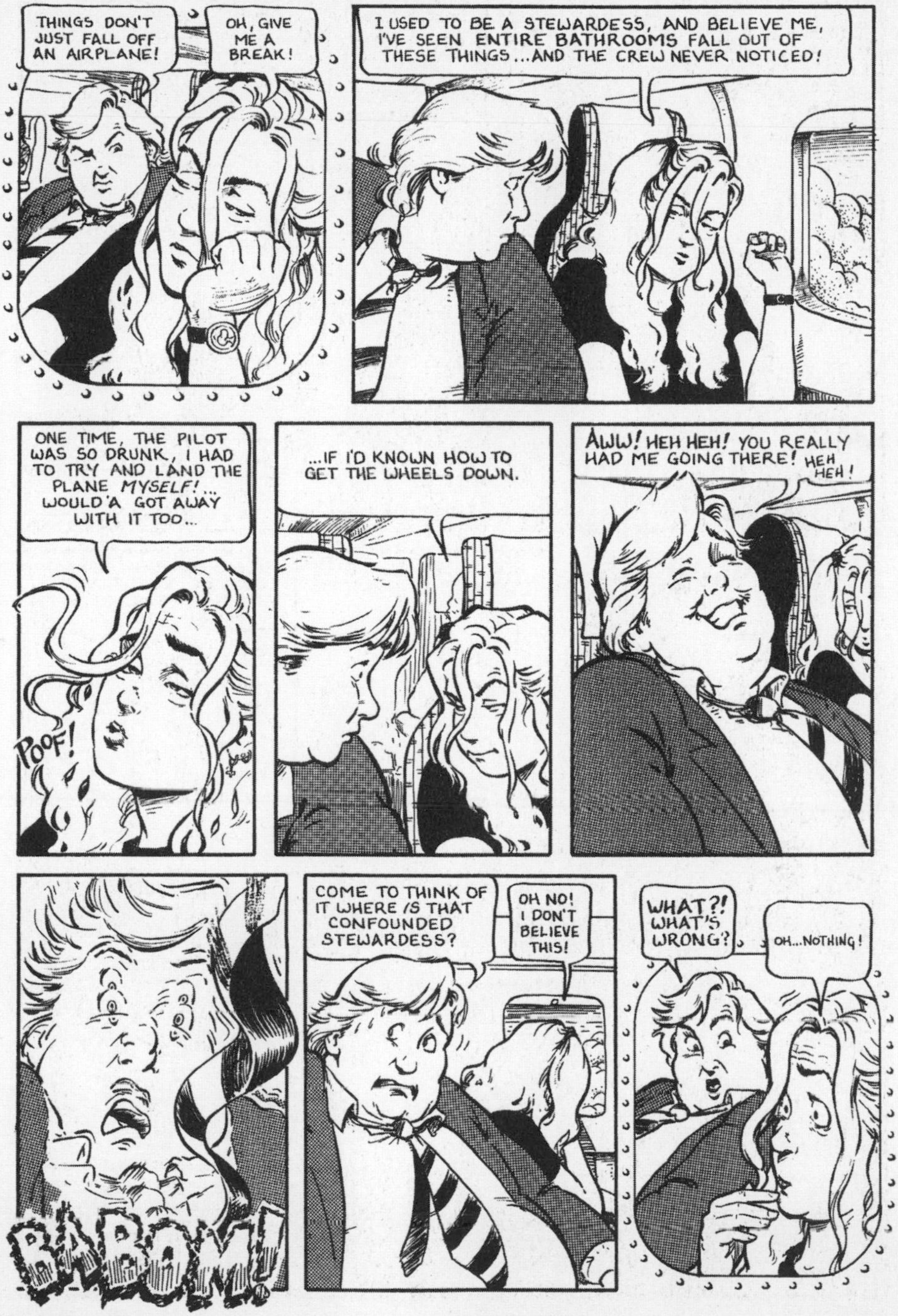
THINGS DON'T JUST FALL OFF AN AIRPLANE!
OH, GIVE ME A BREAK!
I USED TO BE A STEWARDESS, AND BELIEVE ME, I'VE SEEN ENTIRE BATHROOMS FALL OUT OF THESE THINGS...AND THE CREW NEVER NOTICED!
ONE TIME, THE PILOT WAS SO DRUNK, I HAD TO TRY AND LAND THE PLANE MYSELF!... WOULD'A GOT AWAY WITH IT TOO...
POOF!
...IF I'D KNOWN HOW TO GET THE WHEELS DOWN.
AWW! HEH HEH! YOU REALLY HAD ME GOING THERE! HEH HEH!
BABOM!
COME TO THINK OF IT WHERE IS THAT CONFOUNDED STEWARDESS?
OH NO! I DON'T BELIEVE THIS!
WHAT?! WHAT'S WRONG?
OH...NOTHING!

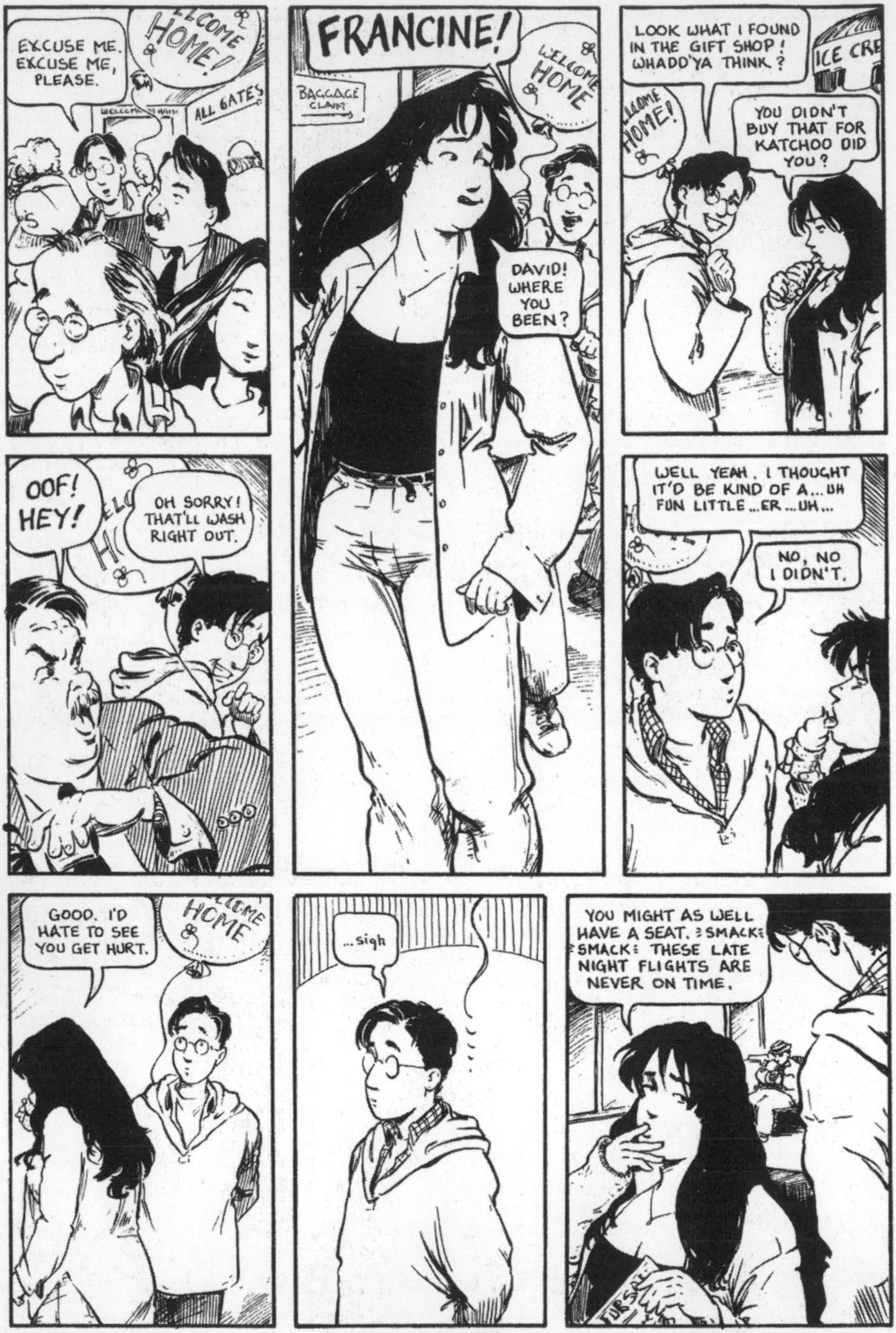
EXCUSE ME. EXCUSE ME, PLEASE.
WELCOME HOME!
ALL GATES
FRANCINE!
BAGGAGE CLAIM
WELCOME HOME
DAVID! WHERE YOU BEEN?
LOOK WHAT I FOUND IN THE GIFT SHOP! WHADD'YA THINK?
ICE CRE
WELCOME HOME!
YOU DIDN'T BUY THAT FOR KATCHOO DID YOU?
OOF! HEY!
OH SORRY! THAT'LL WASH RIGHT OUT.
WELL YEAH. I THOUGHT IT'D BE KIND OF A... UH FUN LITTLE... ER... UH...
NO, NO I DIDN'T.
GOOD. I'D HATE TO SEE YOU GET HURT.
WELCOME HOME
...sigh
YOU MIGHT AS WELL HAVE A SEAT. =SMACK= =SMACK= THESE LATE NIGHT FLIGHTS ARE NEVER ON TIME.

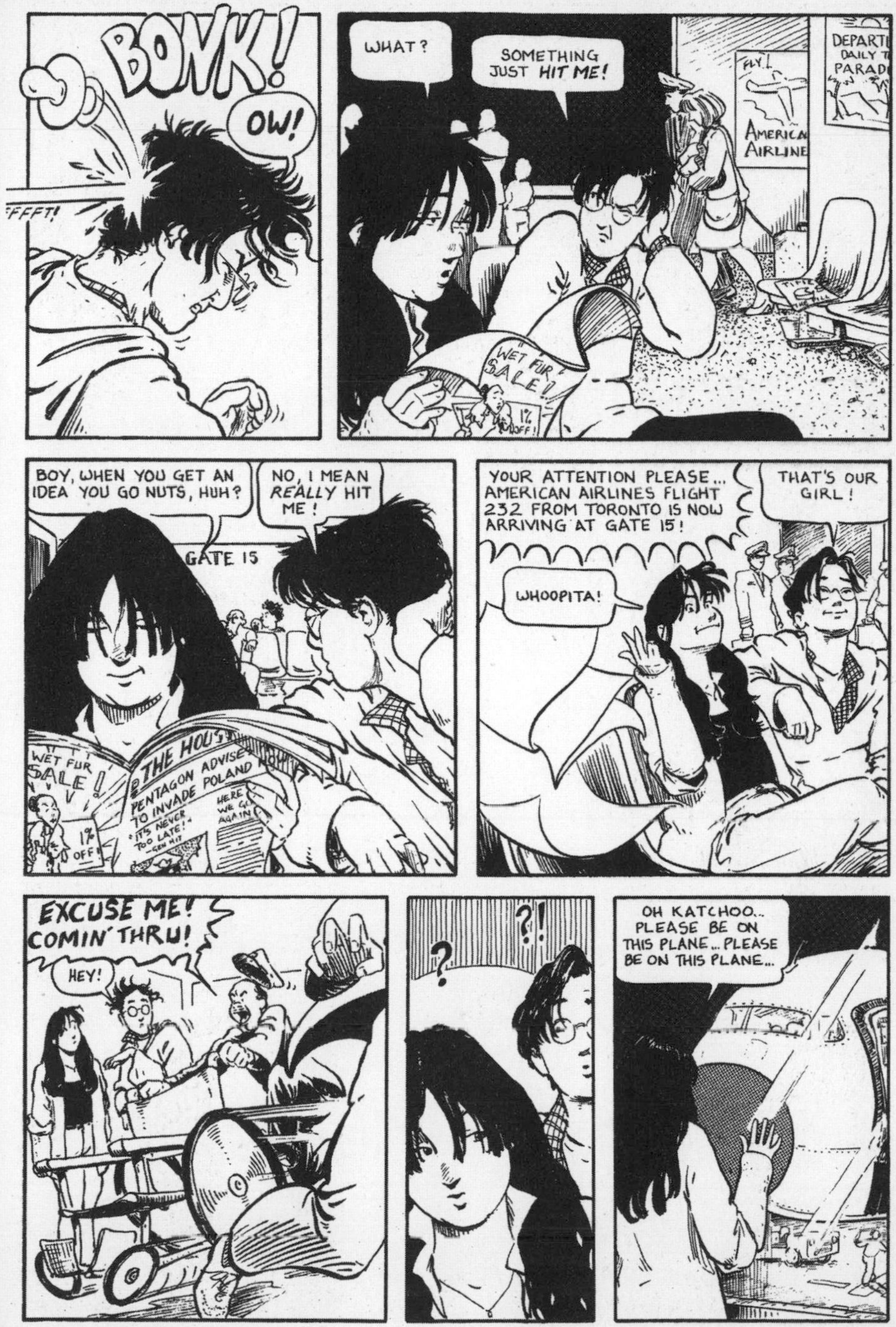
BONK!
OW!
FFFFT!
WHAT?
SOMETHING JUST HIT ME!
DEPARTS DAILY TO PARADI
FLY
AMERICAN AIRLINE
WET FUR SALE!
1% OFF!
BOY, WHEN YOU GET AN IDEA YOU GO NUTS, HUH?
NO, I MEAN REALLY HIT ME!
GATE 15
THE HOU
PENTAGON ADVISE TO INVADE POLAND
"IT'S NEVER TOO LATE!"
HERE WE GO AGAIN
WET FUR SALE!
1% OFF!
YOUR ATTENTION PLEASE... AMERICAN AIRLINES FLIGHT 232 FROM TORONTO IS NOW ARRIVING AT GATE 15!
THAT'S OUR GIRL!
WHOOPITA!
EXCUSE ME! COMIN' THRU!
HEY!
?!
?
OH KATCHOO... PLEASE BE ON THIS PLANE... PLEASE BE ON THIS PLANE...

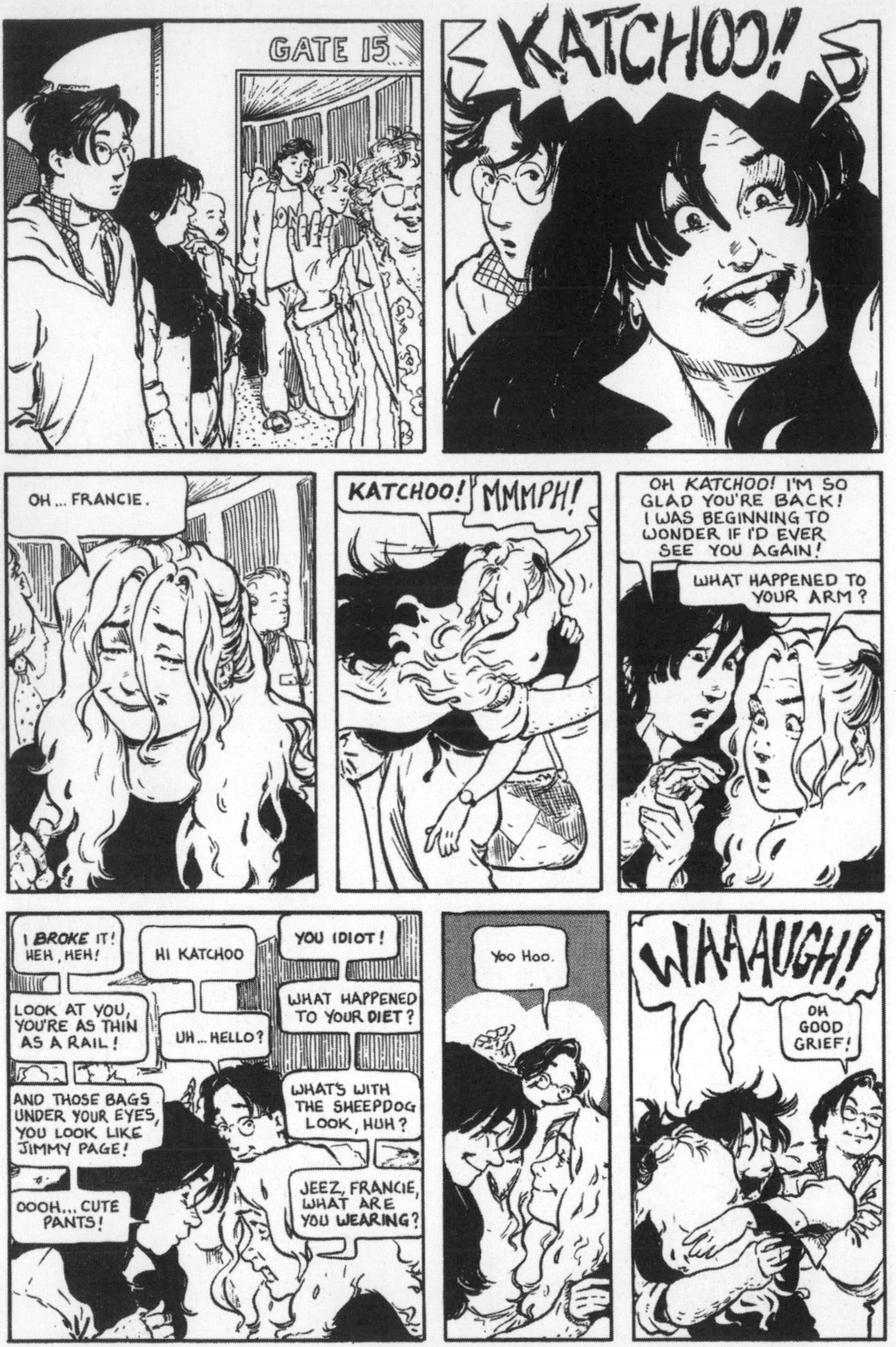

KATCHOO!
OH ... FRANCIE.
KATCHOO!
MMMPH!
OH KATCHOO! I'M SO GLAD YOU'RE BACK! I WAS BEGINNING TO WONDER IF I'D EVER SEE YOU AGAIN!
WHAT HAPPENED TO YOUR ARM?
I BROKE IT! HEH, HEH!
LOOK AT YOU, YOU'RE AS THIN AS A RAIL!
AND THOSE BAGS UNDER YOUR EYES, YOU LOOK LIKE JIMMY PAGE!
OOOH... CUTE PANTS!
HI KATCHOO
UH... HELLO?
YOU IDIOT!
WHAT HAPPENED TO YOUR DIET?
WHAT'S WITH THE SHEEPDOG LOOK, HUH?
JEEZ, FRANCIE, WHAT ARE YOU WEARING?
Yoo Hoo.
WAAAUGH!
OH GOOD GRIEF!

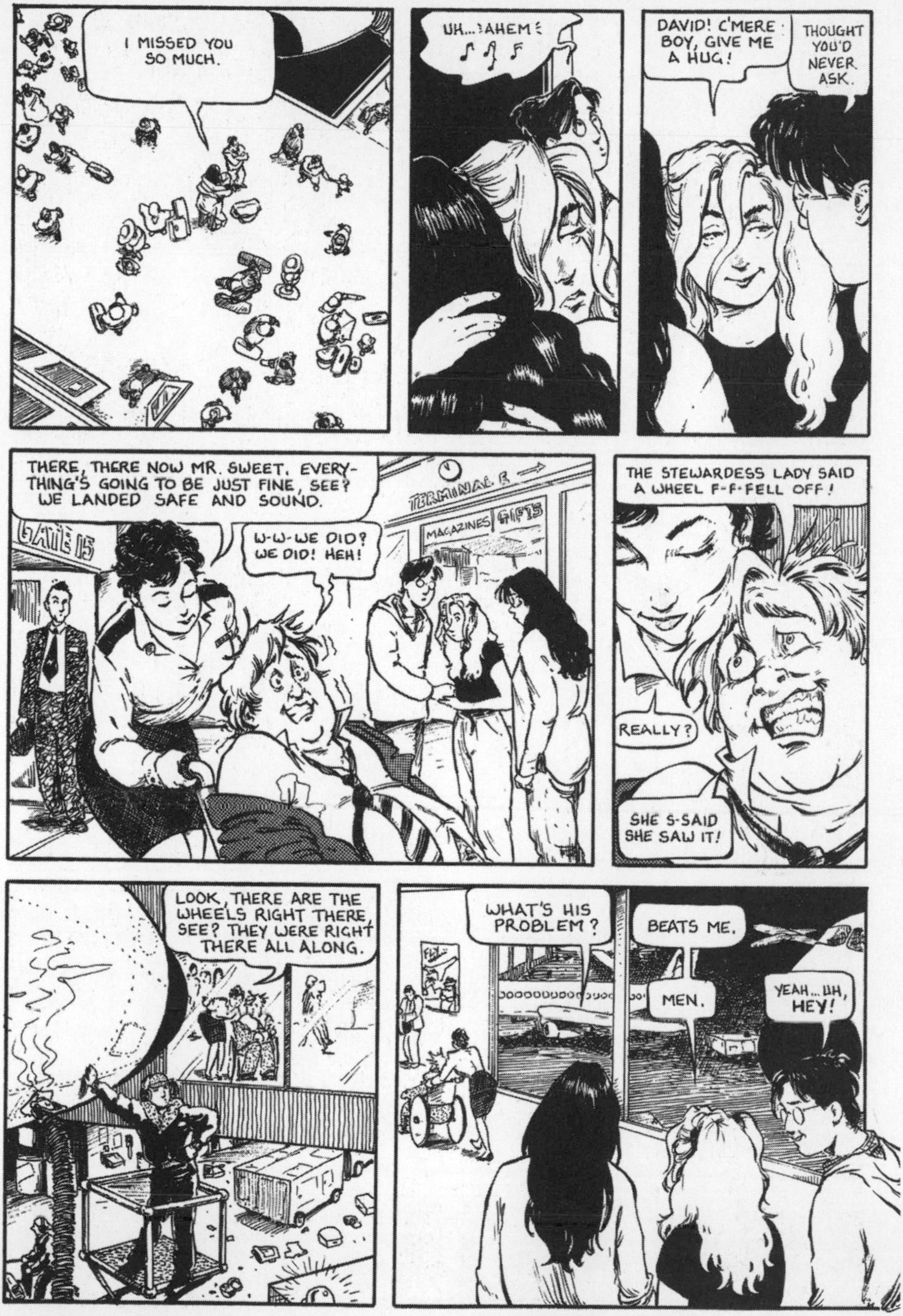
I MISSED YOU SO MUCH.
UH...AHEM
DAVID! C'MERE BOY, GIVE ME A HUG!
THOUGHT YOU'D NEVER ASK.
THERE, THERE NOW MR. SWEET. EVERYTHING'S GOING TO BE JUST FINE, SEE? WE LANDED SAFE AND SOUND.
TERMINAL B
GATE 15
MAGAZINES
GIFTS
W-W-WE DID? WE DID! HEH!
THE STEWARDESS LADY SAID A WHEEL F-F-FELL OFF!
REALLY?
SHE S-SAID SHE SAW IT!
LOOK, THERE ARE THE WHEELS RIGHT THERE, SEE? THEY WERE RIGHT THERE ALL ALONG.
WHAT'S HIS PROBLEM?
BEATS ME.
MEN.
YEAH... UH, HEY!

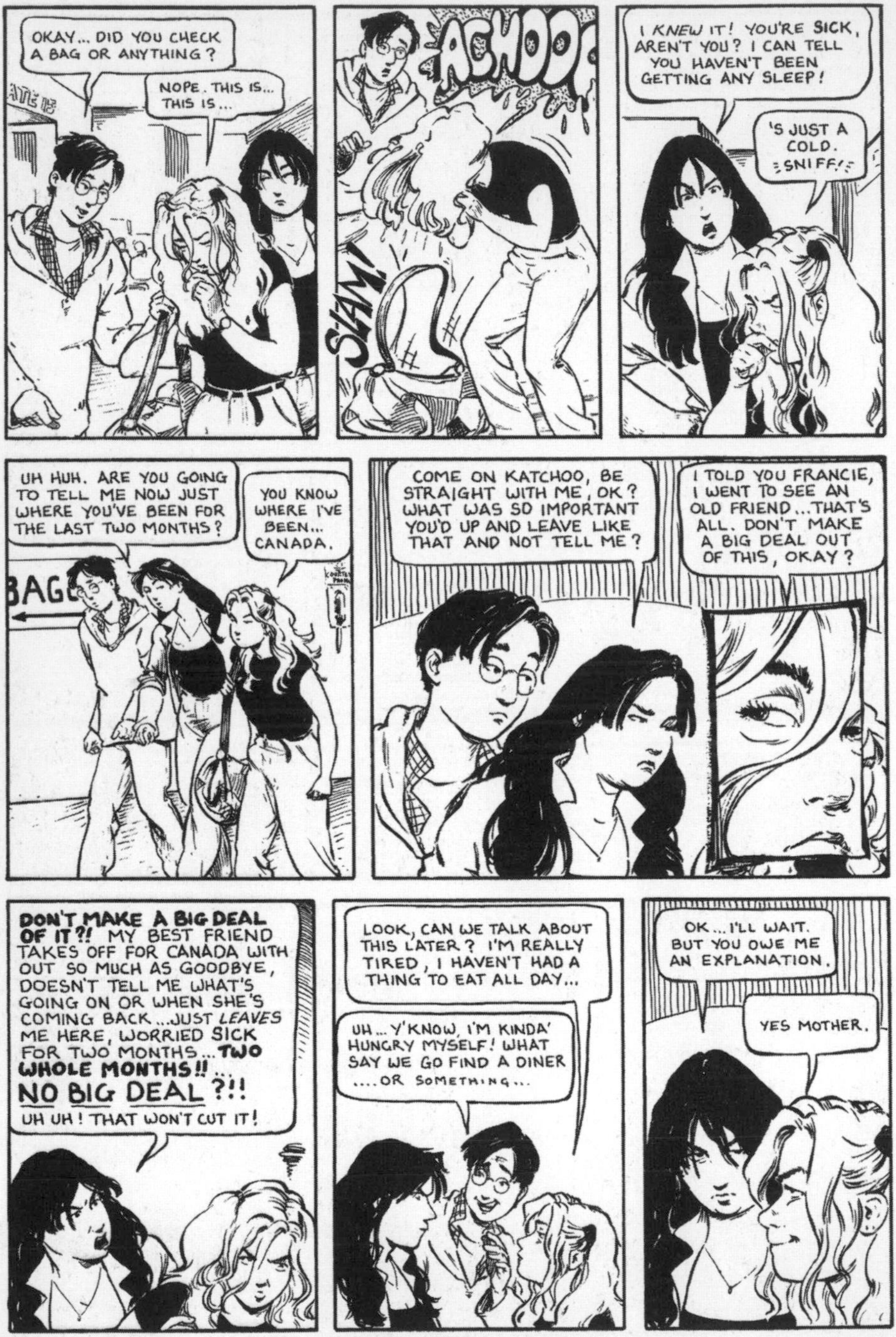
OKAY... DID YOU CHECK A BAG OR ANYTHING?
NOPE. THIS IS... THIS IS...
ACHOO!
SLAM!
I KNEW IT! YOU'RE SICK, AREN'T YOU? I CAN TELL YOU HAVEN'T BEEN GETTING ANY SLEEP!
'S JUST A COLD. SNIFF!
UH HUH. ARE YOU GOING TO TELL ME NOW JUST WHERE YOU'VE BEEN FOR THE LAST TWO MONTHS?
YOU KNOW WHERE I'VE BEEN... CANADA.
BAG
COME ON KATCHOO, BE STRAIGHT WITH ME, OK? WHAT WAS SO IMPORTANT YOU'D UP AND LEAVE LIKE THAT AND NOT TELL ME?
I TOLD YOU FRANCIE, I WENT TO SEE AN OLD FRIEND... THAT'S ALL. DON'T MAKE A BIG DEAL OUT OF THIS, OKAY?
DON'T MAKE A BIG DEAL OF IT?! MY BEST FRIEND TAKES OFF FOR CANADA WITH OUT SO MUCH AS GOODBYE, DOESN'T TELL ME WHAT'S GOING ON OR WHEN SHE'S COMING BACK... JUST LEAVES ME HERE, WORRIED SICK FOR TWO MONTHS... TWO WHOLE MONTHS!!... NO BIG DEAL?!! UH UH! THAT WON'T CUT IT!
LOOK, CAN WE TALK ABOUT THIS LATER? I'M REALLY TIRED, I HAVEN'T HAD A THING TO EAT ALL DAY...
UH... Y'KNOW, I'M KINDA' HUNGRY MYSELF! WHAT SAY WE GO FIND A DINER ....OR SOMETHING...
OK... I'LL WAIT. BUT YOU OWE ME AN EXPLANATION.
YES MOTHER.

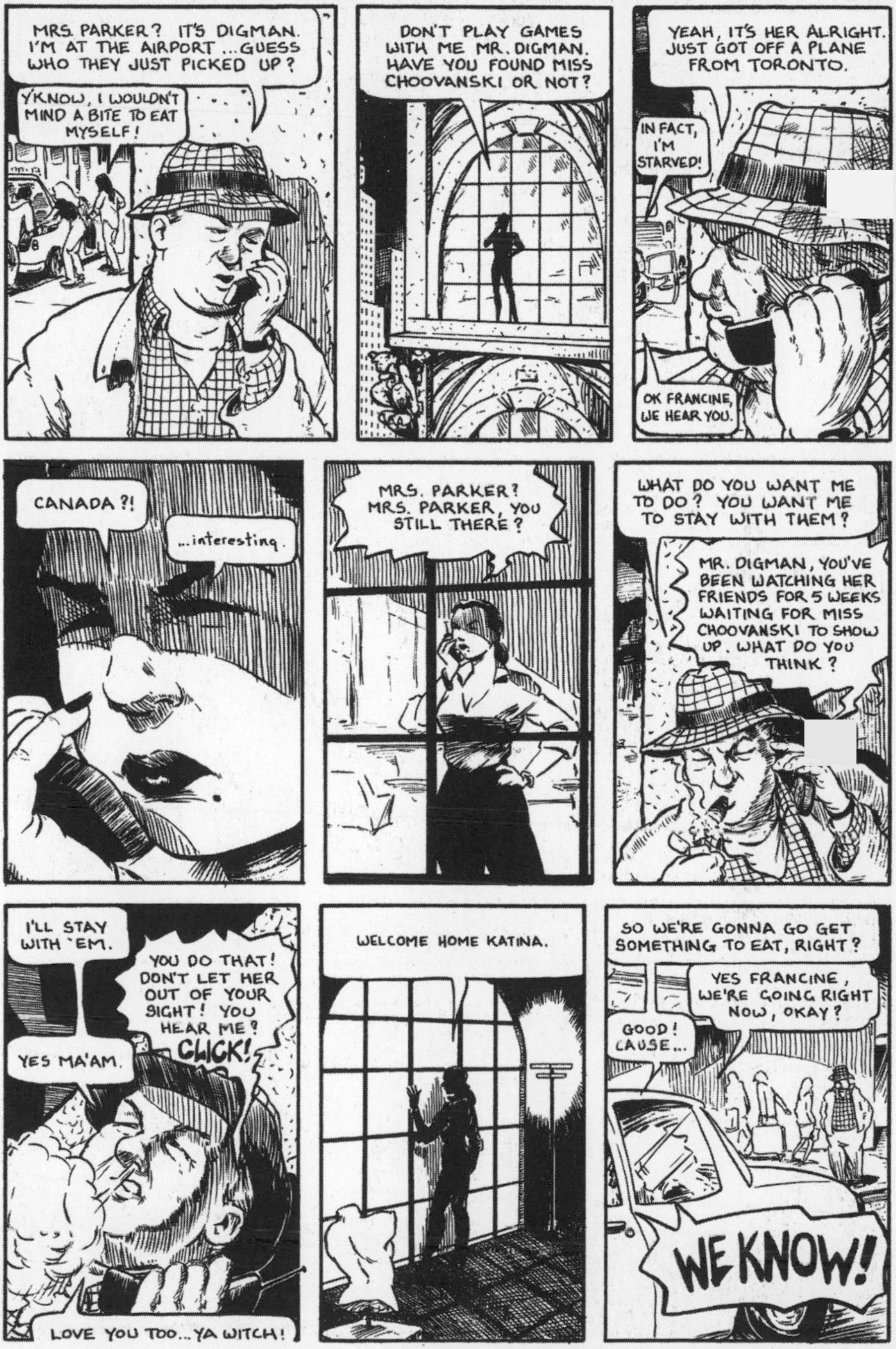
MRS. PARKER? IT'S DIGMAN. I'M AT THE AIRPORT ... GUESS WHO THEY JUST PICKED UP?
Y'KNOW, I WOULDN'T MIND A BITE TO EAT MYSELF!
DON'T PLAY GAMES WITH ME MR. DIGMAN. HAVE YOU FOUND MISS CHOOVANSKI OR NOT?
YEAH, IT'S HER ALRIGHT. JUST GOT OFF A PLANE FROM TORONTO.
IN FACT, I'M STARVED!
OK FRANCINE, WE HEAR YOU.
CANADA?!
...interesting.
MRS. PARKER? MRS. PARKER, YOU STILL THERE?
WHAT DO YOU WANT ME TO DO? YOU WANT ME TO STAY WITH THEM?
MR. DIGMAN, YOU'VE BEEN WATCHING HER FRIENDS FOR 5 WEEKS WAITING FOR MISS CHOOVANSKI TO SHOW UP. WHAT DO YOU THINK?
I'LL STAY WITH 'EM.
YOU DO THAT! DON'T LET HER OUT OF YOUR SIGHT! YOU HEAR ME?
CLICK!
YES MA'AM.
LOVE YOU TOO... YA WITCH!
WELCOME HOME KATINA.
SO WE'RE GONNA GO GET SOMETHING TO EAT, RIGHT?
YES FRANCINE, WE'RE GOING RIGHT NOW, OKAY?
GOOD! CAUSE...
WE KNOW!

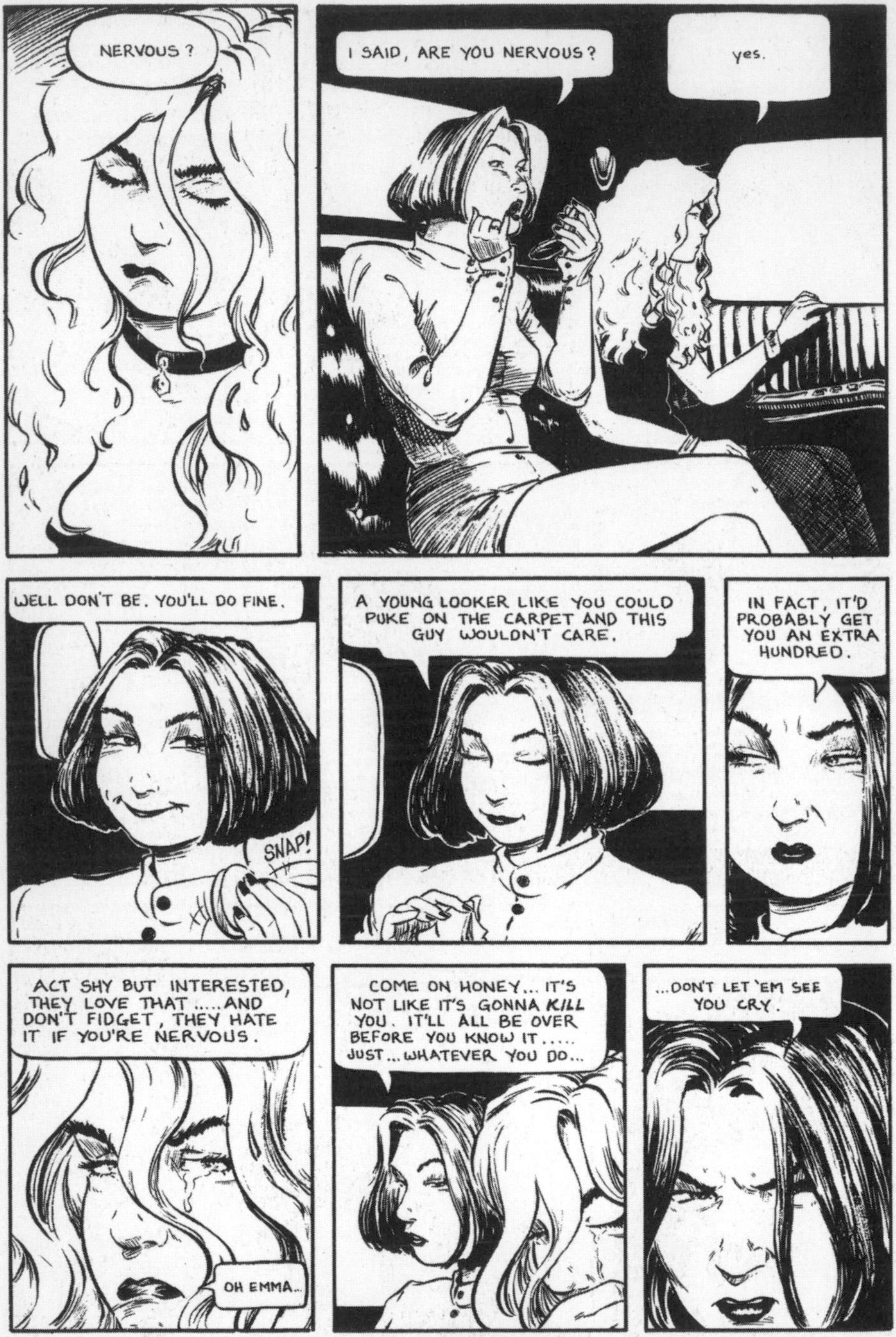
NERVOUS ?
I SAID, ARE YOU NERVOUS ?
yes.
WELL DON'T BE. YOU'LL DO FINE.
SNAP!
A YOUNG LOOKER LIKE YOU COULD PUKE ON THE CARPET AND THIS GUY WOULDN'T CARE.
IN FACT, IT'D PROBABLY GET YOU AN EXTRA HUNDRED.
ACT SHY BUT INTERESTED, THEY LOVE THAT .....AND DON'T FIDGET, THEY HATE IT IF YOU'RE NERVOUS.
OH EMMA..
COME ON HONEY... IT'S NOT LIKE IT'S GONNA *KILL* YOU. IT'LL ALL BE OVER BEFORE YOU KNOW IT..... JUST... WHATEVER YOU DO...
...DON'T LET 'EM SEE YOU CRY.

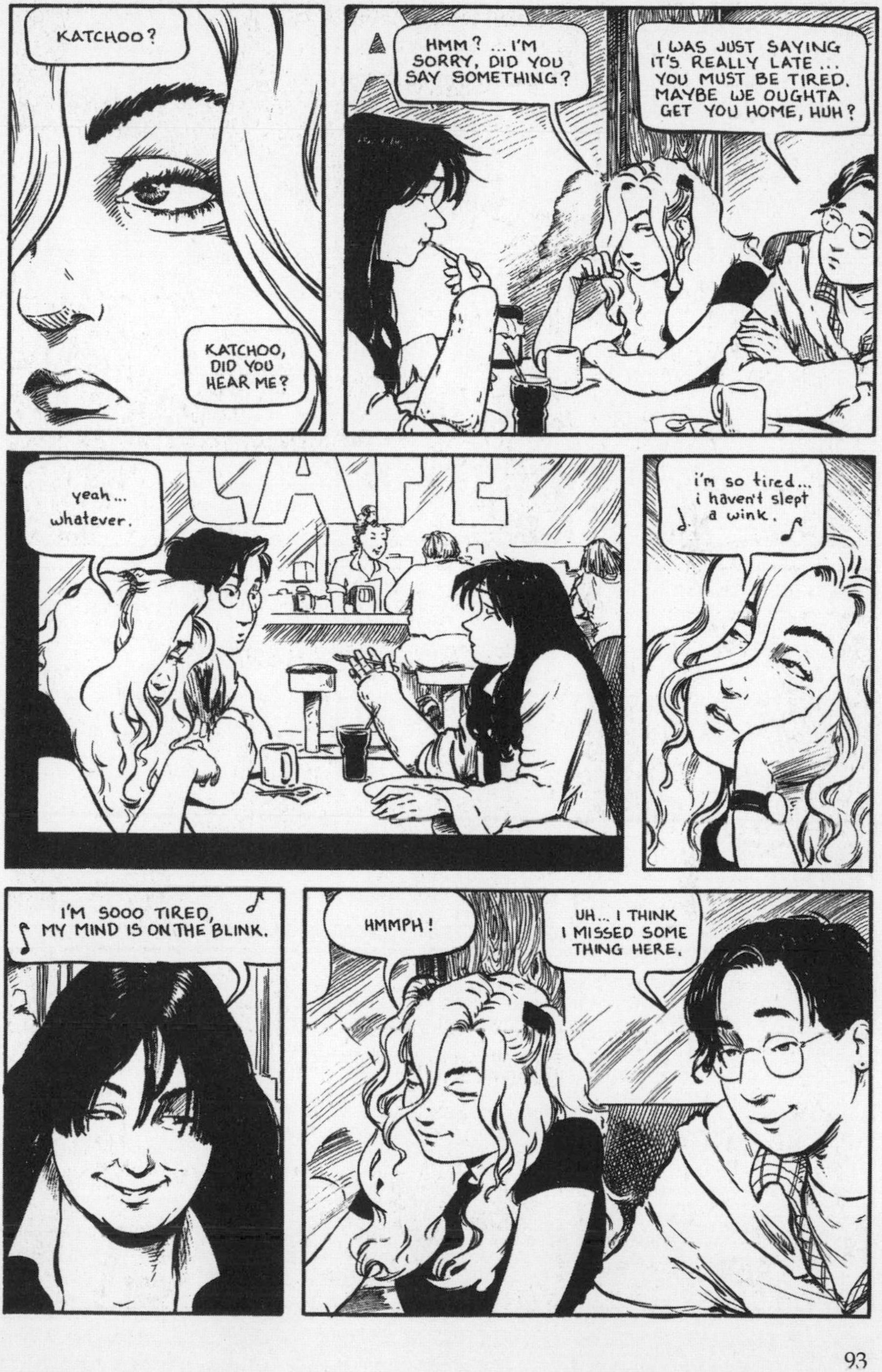
KATCHOO?
KATCHOO, DID YOU HEAR ME?
HMM? ... I'M SORRY, DID YOU SAY SOMETHING?
I WAS JUST SAYING IT'S REALLY LATE ... YOU MUST BE TIRED. MAYBE WE OUGHTA GET YOU HOME, HUH?
yeah... whatever.
CAFE
i'm so tired... i haven't slept a wink.
I'M SOOO TIRED, MY MIND IS ON THE BLINK.
HMMPH!
UH... I THINK I MISSED SOME THING HERE.

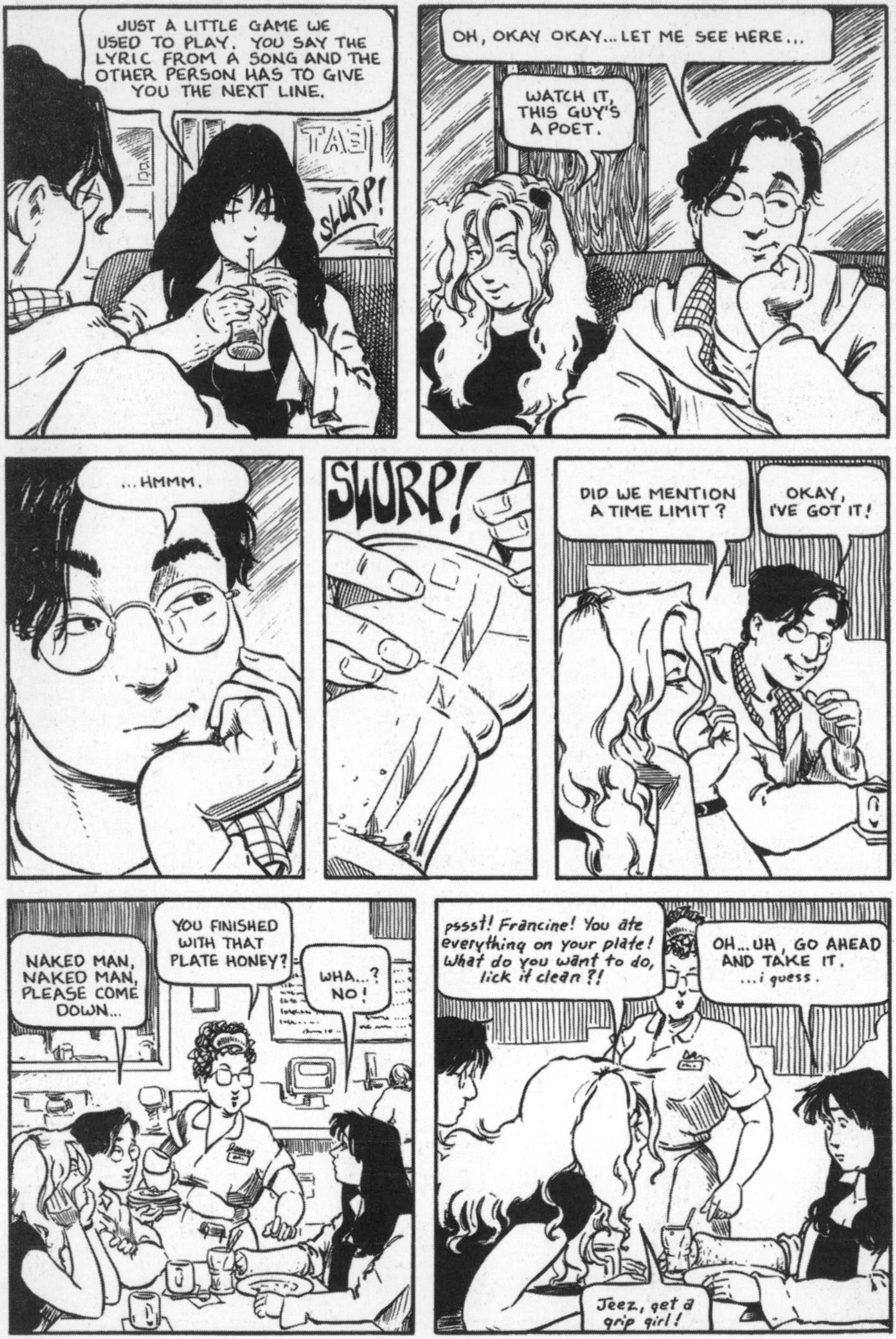

JUST A LITTLE GAME WE USED TO PLAY. YOU SAY THE LYRIC FROM A SONG AND THE OTHER PERSON HAS TO GIVE YOU THE NEXT LINE.
TAB
SLURP!
OH, OKAY OKAY... LET ME SEE HERE...
WATCH IT, THIS GUY'S A POET.
...HMMM.
SLURP!
DID WE MENTION A TIME LIMIT?
OKAY, I'VE GOT IT!
NAKED MAN, NAKED MAN, PLEASE COME DOWN...
YOU FINISHED WITH THAT PLATE HONEY?
WHA...? NO!
pssst! Francine! You ate everything on your plate! What do you want to do, lick it clean?!
OH...UH, GO AHEAD AND TAKE IT. ...i guess.
Jeez, get a grip girl!

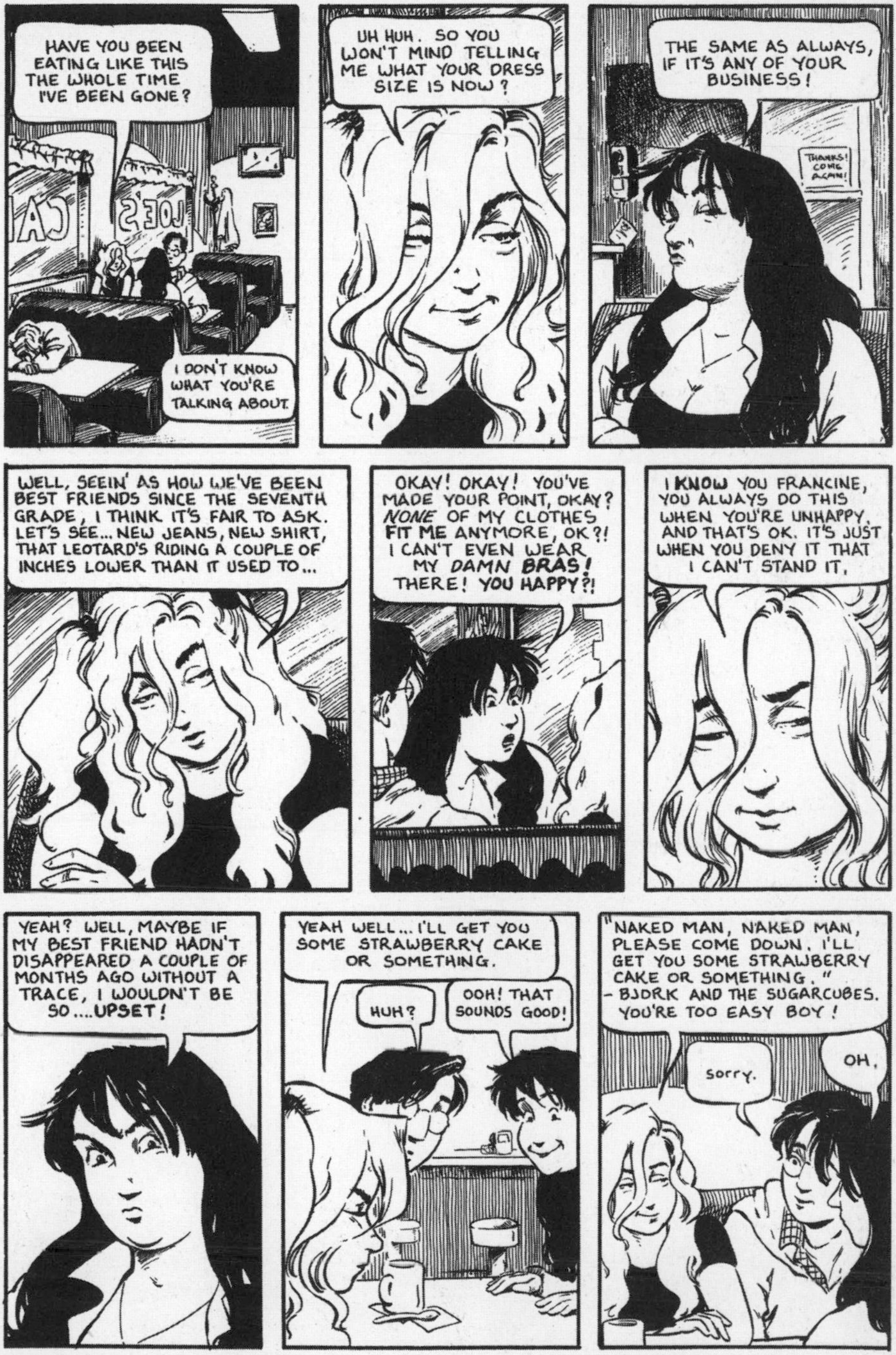
HAVE YOU BEEN EATING LIKE THIS THE WHOLE TIME I'VE BEEN GONE?
I DON'T KNOW WHAT YOU'RE TALKING ABOUT.
UH HUH. SO YOU WON'T MIND TELLING ME WHAT YOUR DRESS SIZE IS NOW?
THE SAME AS ALWAYS, IF IT'S ANY OF YOUR BUSINESS!
THANKS! COME AGAIN!
WELL, SEEIN' AS HOW WE'VE BEEN BEST FRIENDS SINCE THE SEVENTH GRADE, I THINK IT'S FAIR TO ASK. LET'S SEE... NEW JEANS, NEW SHIRT, THAT LEOTARD'S RIDING A COUPLE OF INCHES LOWER THAN IT USED TO...
OKAY! OKAY! YOU'VE MADE YOUR POINT, OKAY? *NONE* OF MY CLOTHES **FIT ME** ANYMORE, OK?! I CAN'T EVEN WEAR MY *DAMN* **BRAS**! THERE! **YOU HAPPY**?!
I **KNOW** YOU FRANCINE, YOU ALWAYS DO THIS WHEN YOU'RE UNHAPPY, AND THAT'S OK. IT'S JUST WHEN YOU DENY IT THAT I CAN'T STAND IT.
YEAH? WELL, MAYBE IF MY BEST FRIEND HADN'T DISAPPEARED A COUPLE OF MONTHS AGO WITHOUT A TRACE, I WOULDN'T BE SO.... **UPSET**!
YEAH WELL... I'LL GET YOU SOME STRAWBERRY CAKE OR SOMETHING.
HUH?
OOH! THAT SOUNDS GOOD!
"NAKED MAN, NAKED MAN, PLEASE COME DOWN. I'LL GET YOU SOME STRAWBERRY CAKE OR SOMETHING." - BJORK AND THE SUGARCUBES. YOU'RE TOO EASY BOY!
sorry.
OH.

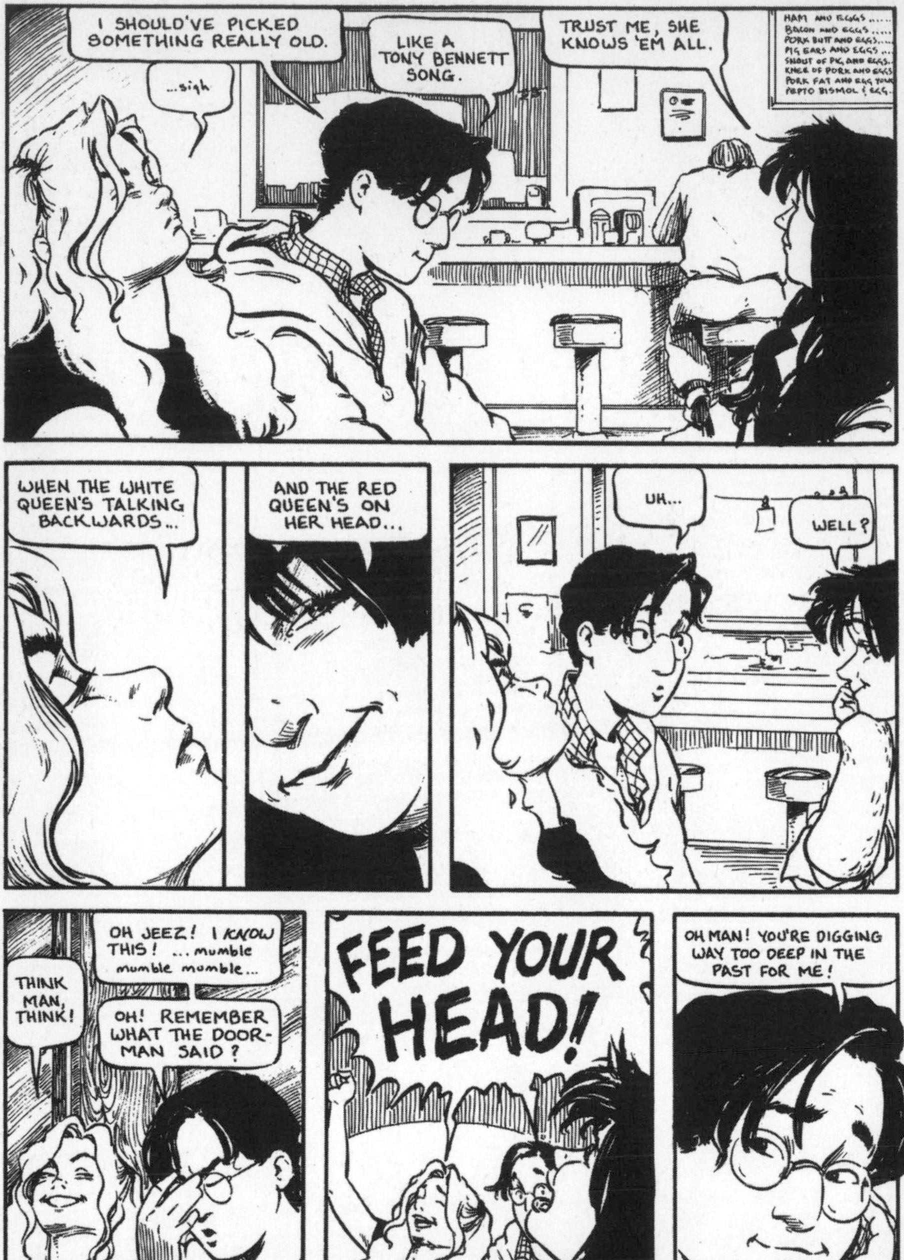

I SHOULD'VE PICKED SOMETHING REALLY OLD.
...sigh
LIKE A TONY BENNETT SONG.
TRUST ME, SHE KNOWS 'EM ALL.
HAM AND EGGS.....
BACON AND EGGS.....
PORK BUTT AND EGGS.....
PIG EARS AND EGGS...
SNOUT OF PIG AND EGGS..
KNEE OF PORK AND EGGS
PORK FAT AND EGG YOU
PEPTO BISMOL & EGG..
WHEN THE WHITE QUEEN'S TALKING BACKWARDS...
AND THE RED QUEEN'S ON HER HEAD...
UH...
WELL?
THINK MAN, THINK!
OH JEEZ! I KNOW THIS! ...mumble mumble mumble...
OH! REMEMBER WHAT THE DOOR-MAN SAID?
FEED YOUR HEAD!
OH MAN! YOU'RE DIGGING WAY TOO DEEP IN THE PAST FOR ME!

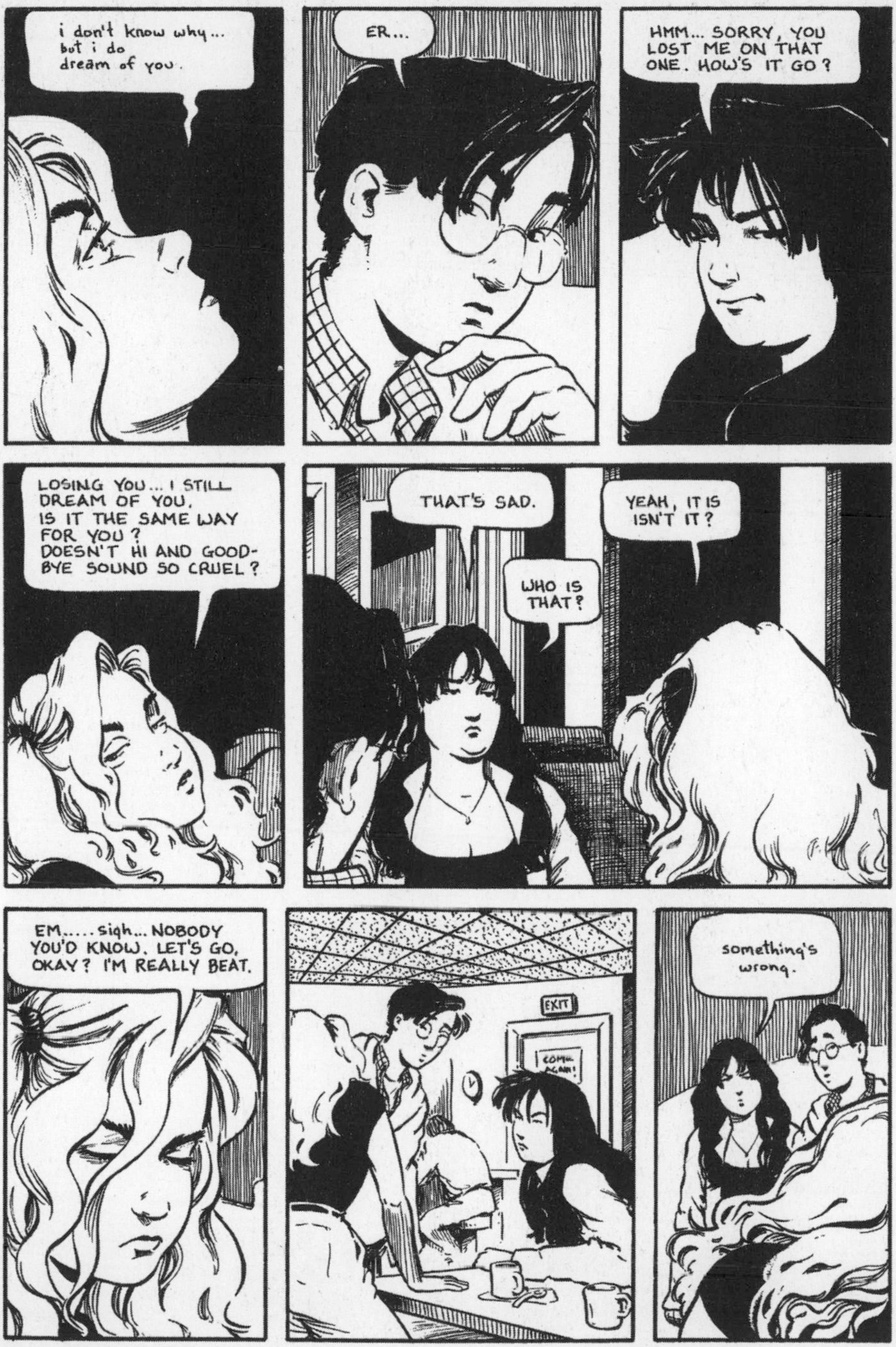
i don't know why... but i do dream of you.
ER...
HMM... SORRY, YOU LOST ME ON THAT ONE. HOW'S IT GO?
LOSING YOU... I STILL DREAM OF YOU. IS IT THE SAME WAY FOR YOU? DOESN'T HI AND GOOD-BYE SOUND SO CRUEL?
THAT'S SAD.
YEAH, IT IS ISN'T IT?
WHO IS THAT?
EM..... sigh... NOBODY YOU'D KNOW. LET'S GO, OKAY? I'M REALLY BEAT.
EXIT
something's wrong.

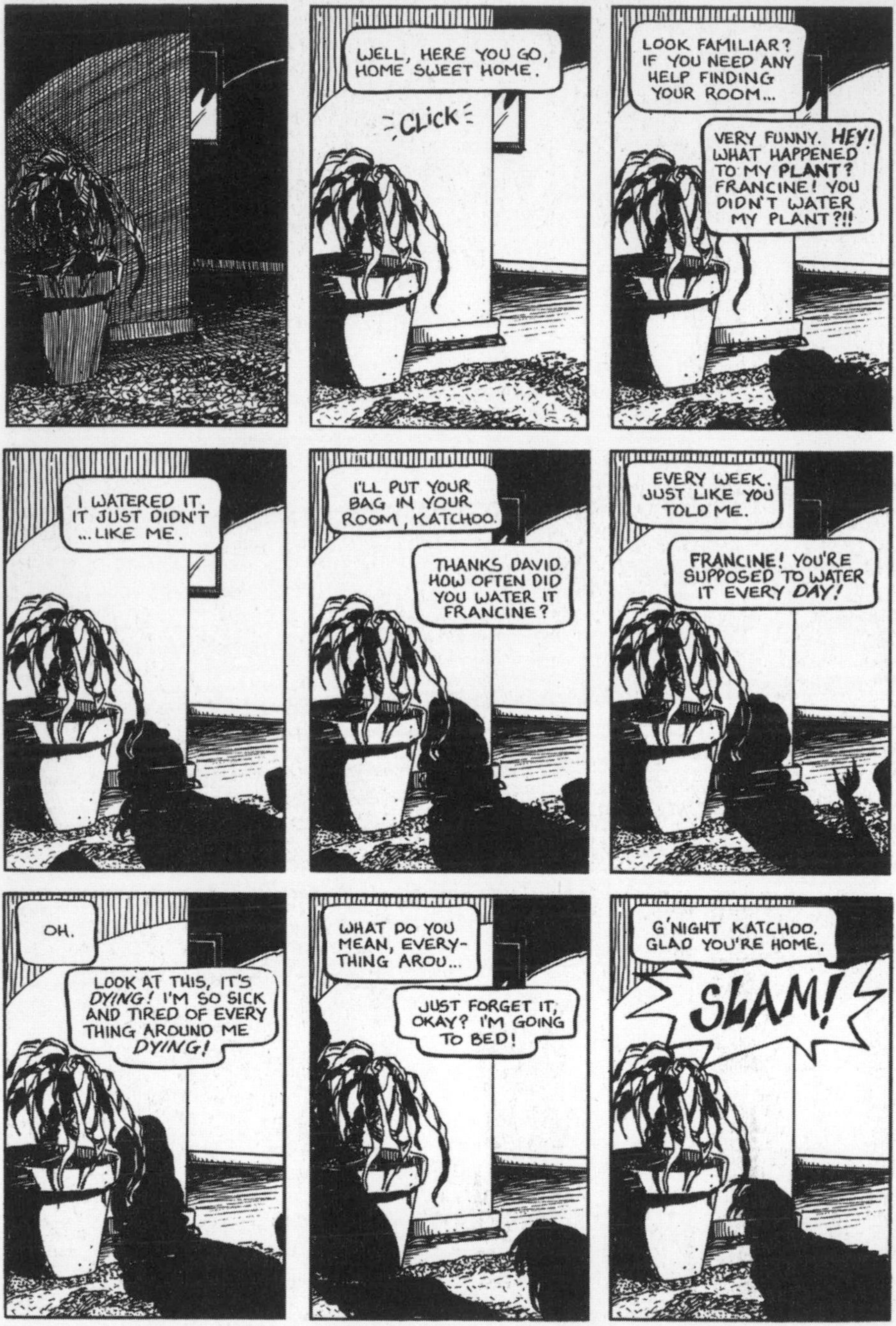
WELL, HERE YOU GO, HOME SWEET HOME.
CLICK
LOOK FAMILIAR? IF YOU NEED ANY HELP FINDING YOUR ROOM...
VERY FUNNY. HEY! WHAT HAPPENED TO MY PLANT? FRANCINE! YOU DIDN'T WATER MY PLANT?!!
I WATERED IT. IT JUST DIDN'T ...LIKE ME.
I'LL PUT YOUR BAG IN YOUR ROOM, KATCHOO.
THANKS DAVID. HOW OFTEN DID YOU WATER IT FRANCINE?
EVERY WEEK. JUST LIKE YOU TOLD ME.
FRANCINE! YOU'RE SUPPOSED TO WATER IT EVERY DAY!
OH.
LOOK AT THIS, IT'S DYING! I'M SO SICK AND TIRED OF EVERY THING AROUND ME DYING!
WHAT DO YOU MEAN, EVERY-THING AROU...
JUST FORGET IT, OKAY? I'M GOING TO BED!
G'NIGHT KATCHOO. GLAD YOU'RE HOME.
SLAM!

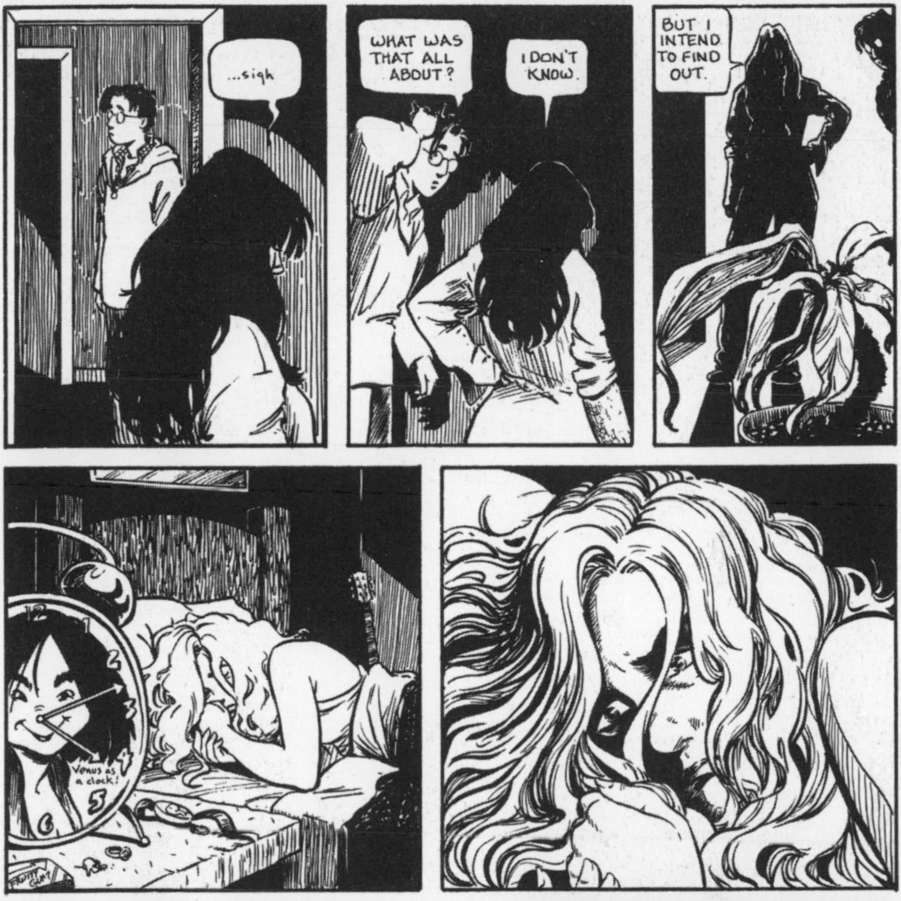
...sigh
WHAT WAS THAT ALL ABOUT?
I DON'T KNOW.
BUT I INTEND TO FIND OUT.
Venus as a clock!
...sigh

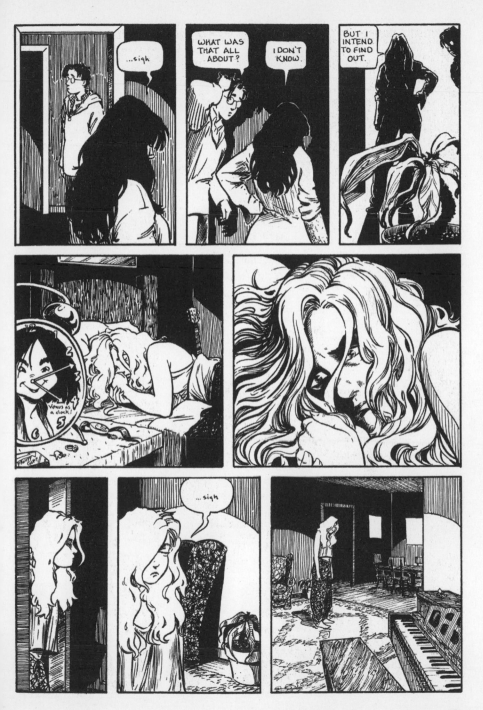

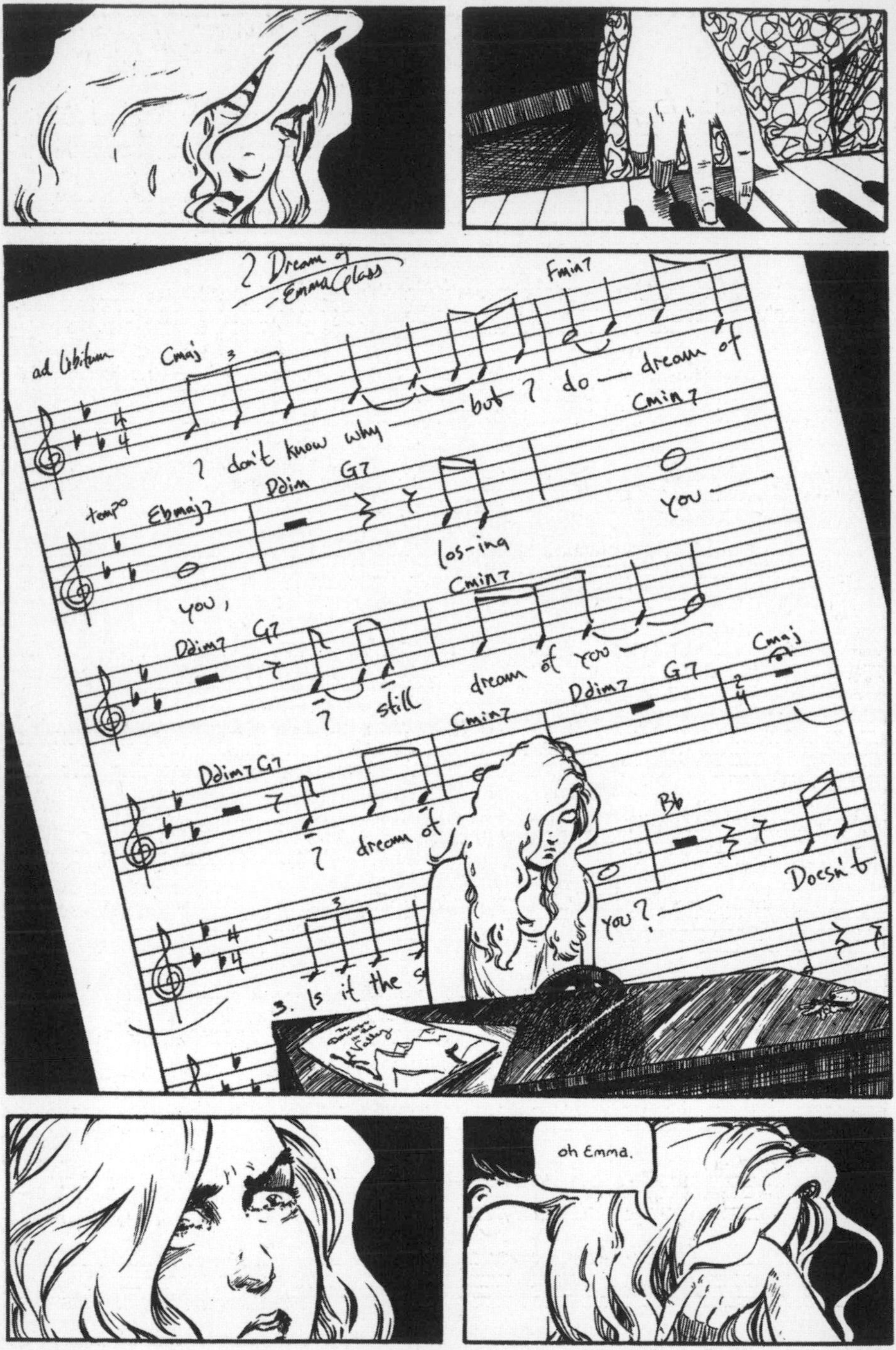
I Dream of
- Emma Glass
ad Libitum
Cmaj
Fmin7
I don't know why — but I do — dream of
Cmin7
tempo
Ebmaj7
Ddim
G7
you,
los-ing
you —
Ddim7
G7
Cmin7
I still dream of you —
Cmaj
Cmin7
Ddim7
G7
Ddim7 G7
I dream of
Bb
you? —
Doesn't
3. Is it the s
oh Emma.

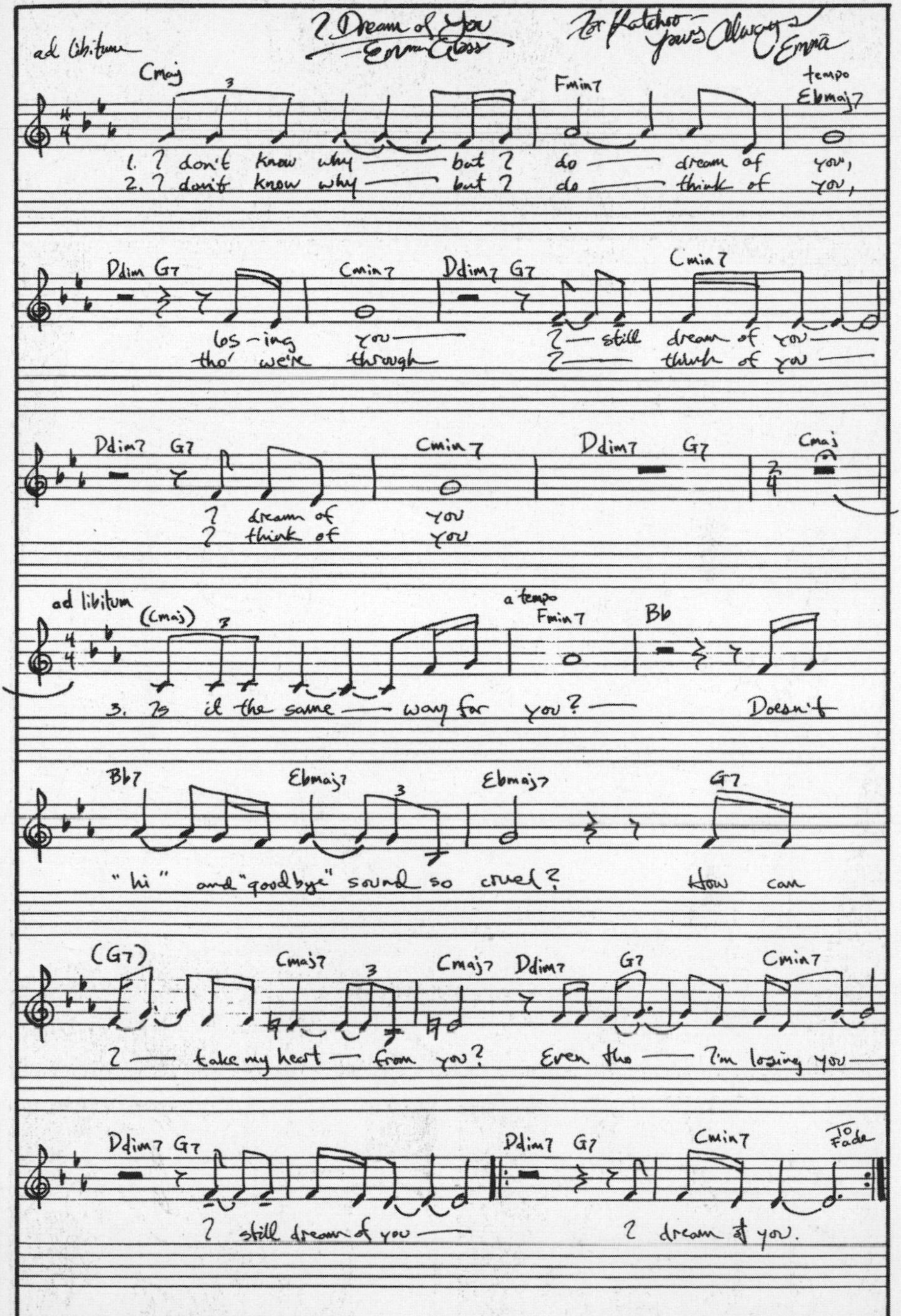
I Dream of You
Emma Glass
For Katchoo yours Always Emma
ad Libitum
Cmaj
Fmin7
tempo
Ebmaj7
1. I don't know why — but I do — dream of you,
2. I don't know why — but I do — think of you,
Ddim G7
Cmin7
Ddim7 G7
Cmin7
los-ing you —
tho' we're through —
I — still dream of you —
I — think of you —
Ddim7 G7
Cmin7
Ddim7 G7
Cmaj
I dream of you
I think of you
ad libitum
(Cmaj)
a tempo
Fmin7
Bb
3. Is it the same — way for you? — Doesn't
Bb7
Ebmaj7
Ebmaj7
G7
"hi" and "goodbye" sound so cruel? How can
(G7)
Cmaj7
Cmaj7 Ddim7
G7
Cmin7
I — take my heart — from you? Even tho — I'm losing you —
Ddim7 G7
Ddim7 G7
Cmin7
To Fade
I still dream of you —
I dream of you.

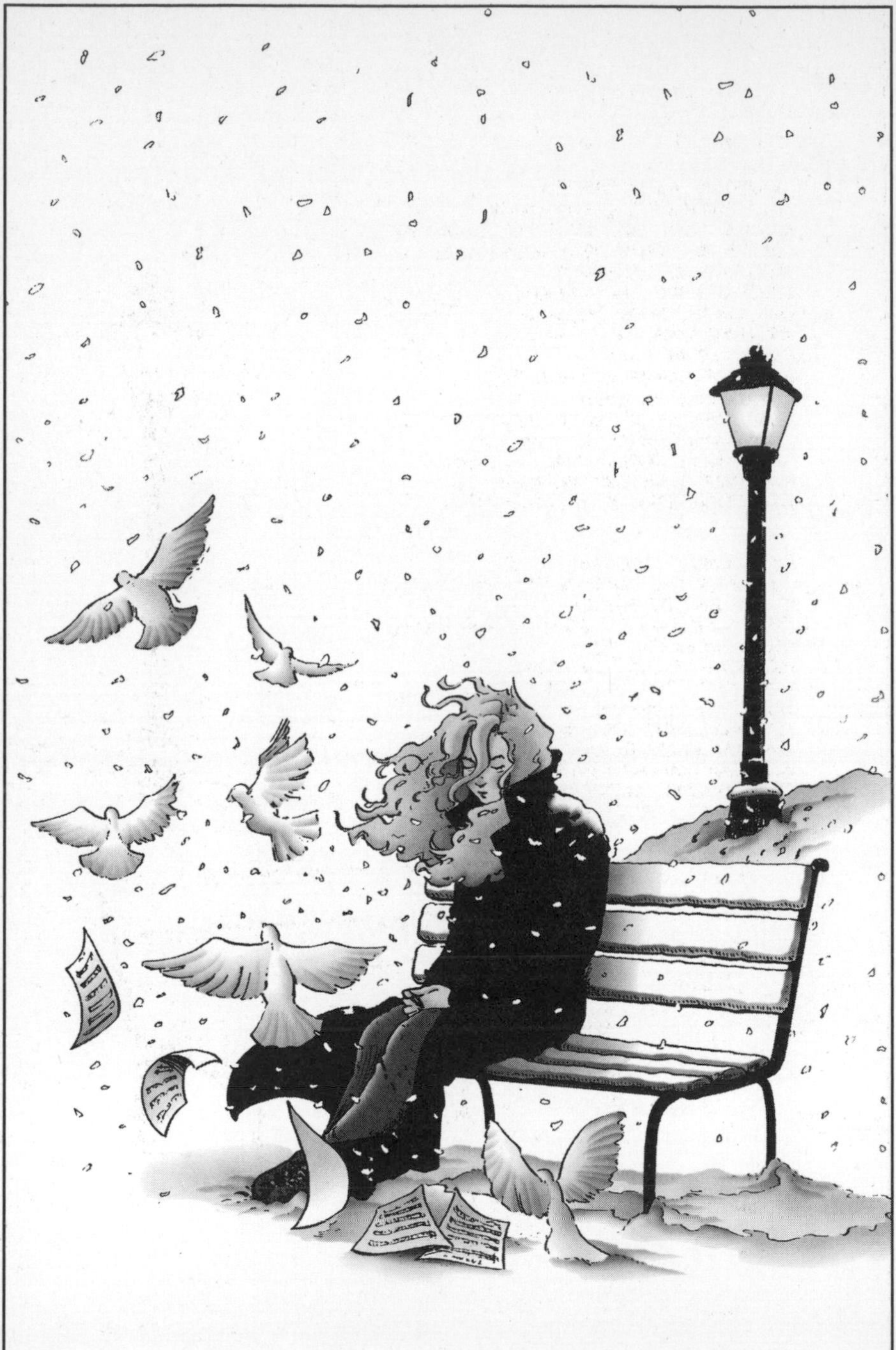

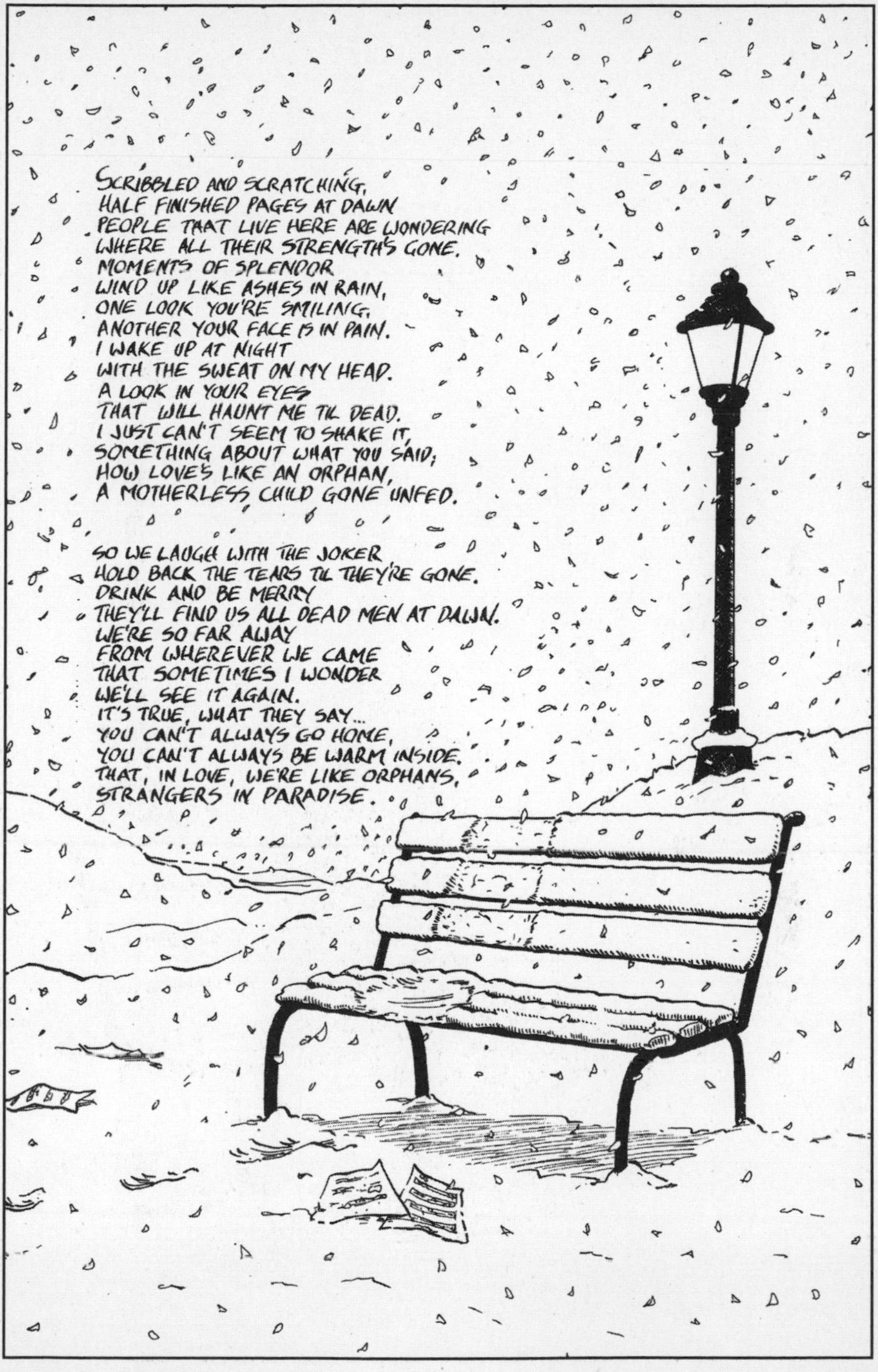
SCRIBBLED AND SCRATCHING,
HALF FINISHED PAGES AT DAWN
PEOPLE THAT LIVE HERE ARE WONDERING
WHERE ALL THEIR STRENGTH'S GONE.
MOMENTS OF SPLENDOR
WIND UP LIKE ASHES IN RAIN,
ONE LOOK YOU'RE SMILING,
ANOTHER YOUR FACE IS IN PAIN.
I WAKE UP AT NIGHT
WITH THE SWEAT ON MY HEAD.
A LOOK IN YOUR EYES
THAT WILL HAUNT ME TIL DEAD.
I JUST CAN'T SEEM TO SHAKE IT,
SOMETHING ABOUT WHAT YOU SAID;
HOW LOVE'S LIKE AN ORPHAN,
A MOTHERLESS CHILD GONE UNFED.

SO WE LAUGH WITH THE JOKER
HOLD BACK THE TEARS TIL THEY'RE GONE.
DRINK AND BE MERRY
THEY'LL FIND US ALL DEAD MEN AT DAWN.
WE'RE SO FAR AWAY
FROM WHEREVER WE CAME
THAT SOMETIMES I WONDER
WE'LL SEE IT AGAIN.
IT'S TRUE, WHAT THEY SAY...
YOU CAN'T ALWAYS GO HOME,
YOU CAN'T ALWAYS BE WARM INSIDE.
THAT, IN LOVE, WE'RE LIKE ORPHANS,
STRANGERS IN PARADISE.

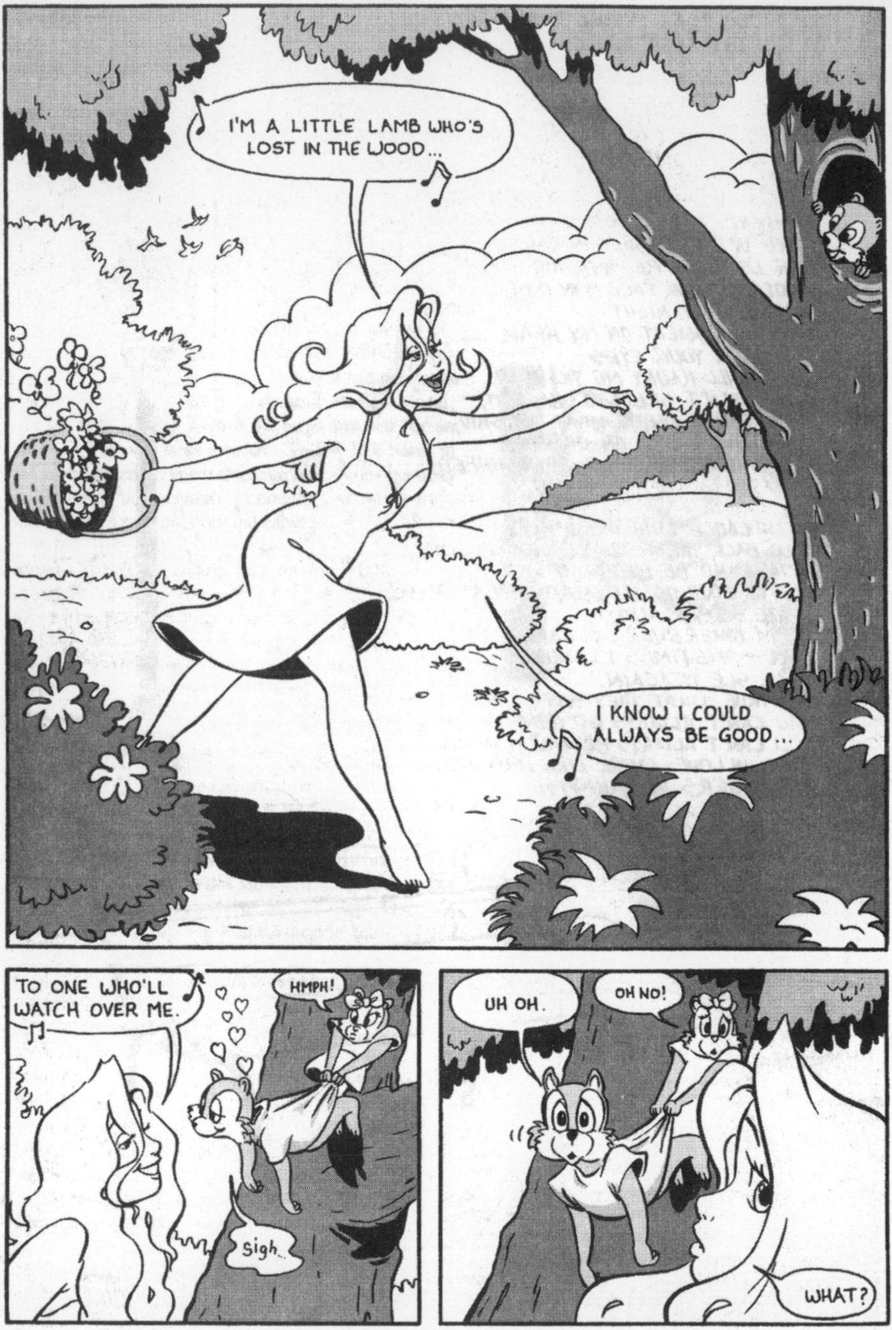
I'M A LITTLE LAMB WHO'S LOST IN THE WOOD...
I KNOW I COULD ALWAYS BE GOOD...
TO ONE WHO'LL WATCH OVER ME.
HMPH!
Sigh..
UH OH.
OH NO!
WHAT?

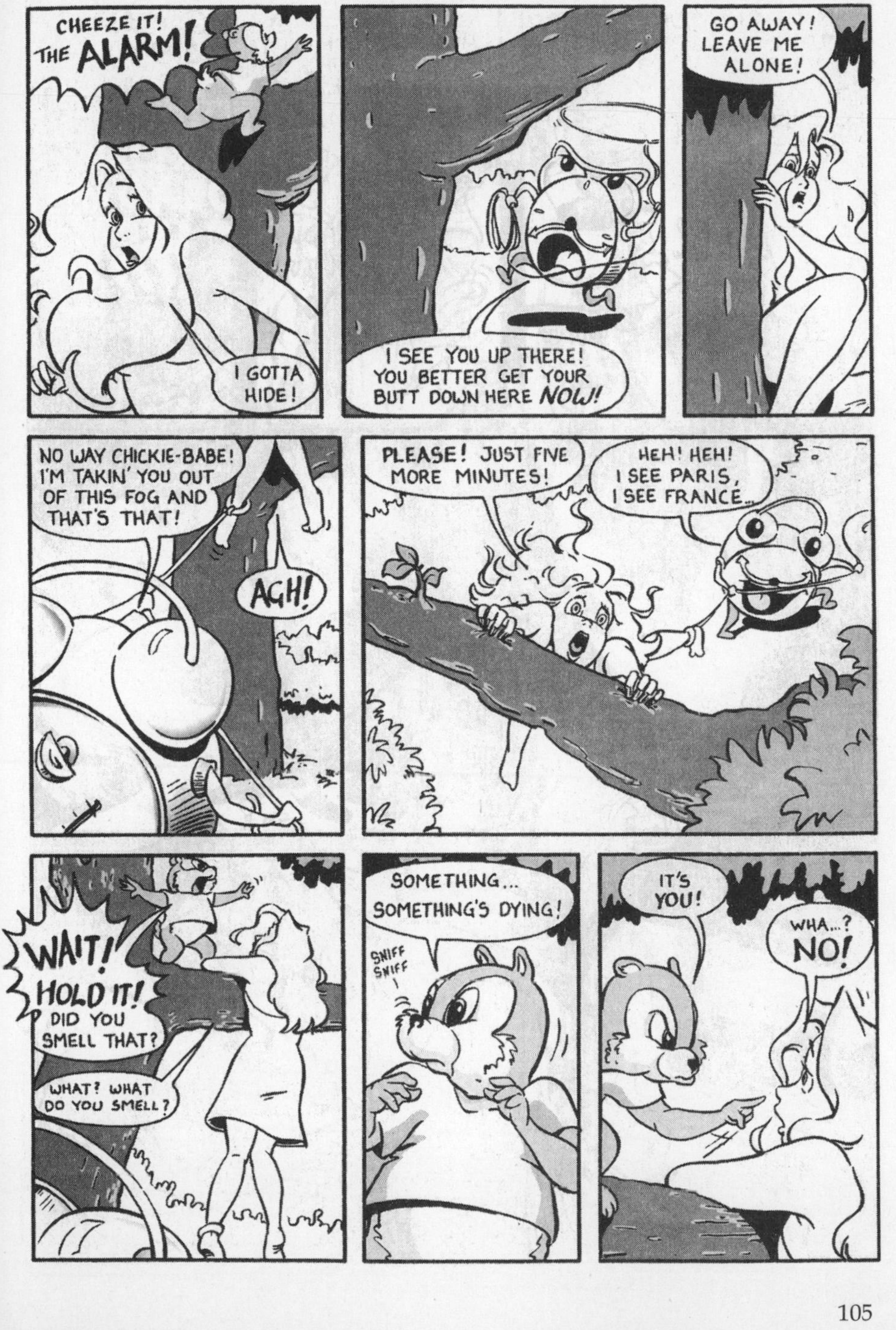
CHEEZE IT! THE ALARM!
I GOTTA HIDE!
I SEE YOU UP THERE! YOU BETTER GET YOUR BUTT DOWN HERE NOW!
GO AWAY! LEAVE ME ALONE!
NO WAY CHICKIE-BABE! I'M TAKIN' YOU OUT OF THIS FOG AND THAT'S THAT!
AGH!
PLEASE! JUST FIVE MORE MINUTES!
HEH! HEH! I SEE PARIS, I SEE FRANCE...
WAIT! HOLD IT! DID YOU SMELL THAT?
WHAT? WHAT DO YOU SMELL?
SOMETHING... SOMETHING'S DYING!
SNIFF SNIFF
IT'S YOU!
WHA...? NO!

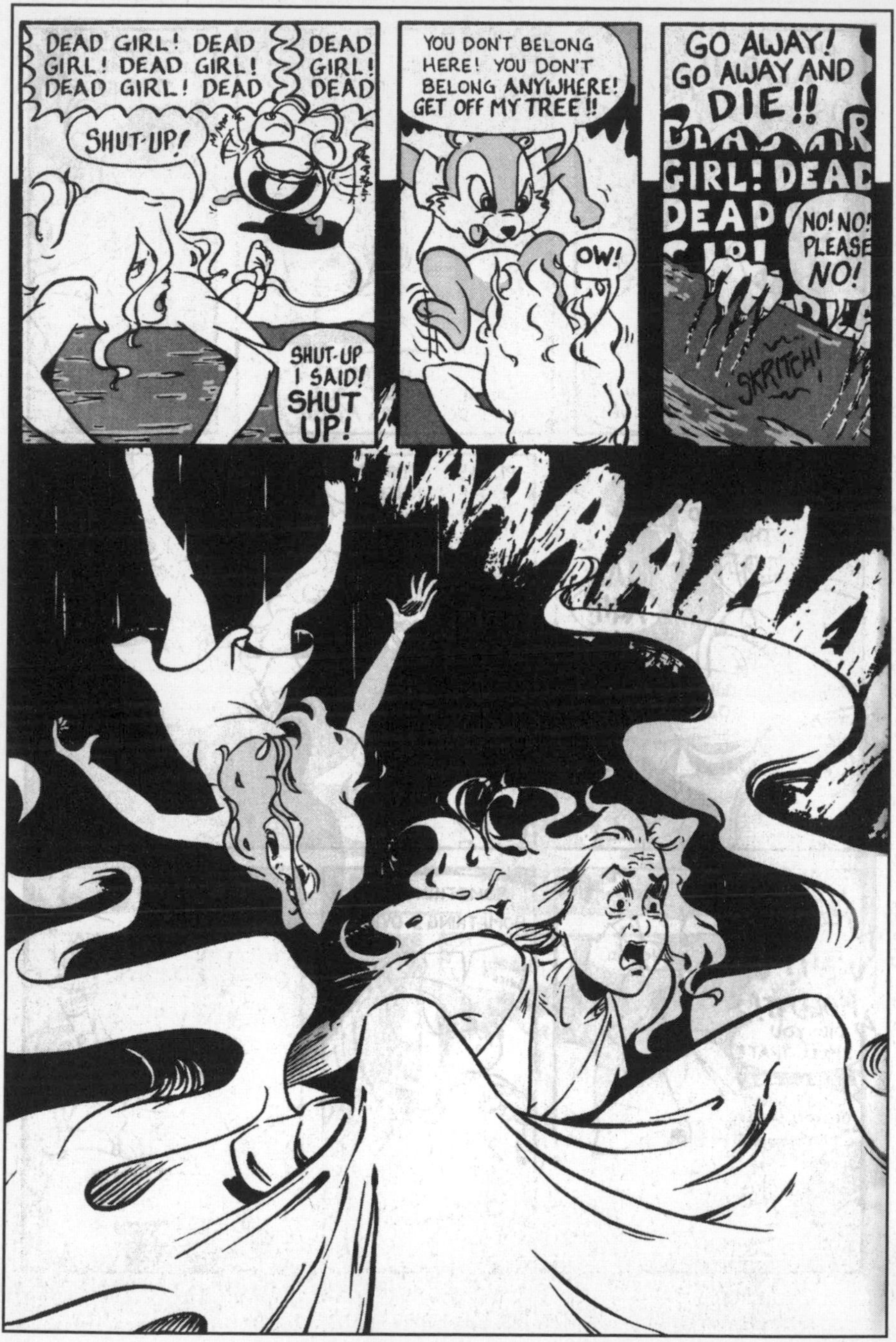
DEAD GIRL! DEAD GIRL! DEAD GIRL! DEAD GIRL! DEAD
DEAD GIRL! DEAD
SHUT-UP!
SHUT-UP I SAID! SHUT UP!
YOU DON'T BELONG HERE! YOU DON'T BELONG ANYWHERE! GET OFF MY TREE!!
OW!
GO AWAY! GO AWAY AND DIE!!
GIRL! DEAD
DEAD
NO! NO! PLEASE NO!
SKRITCH!
WAAAAA

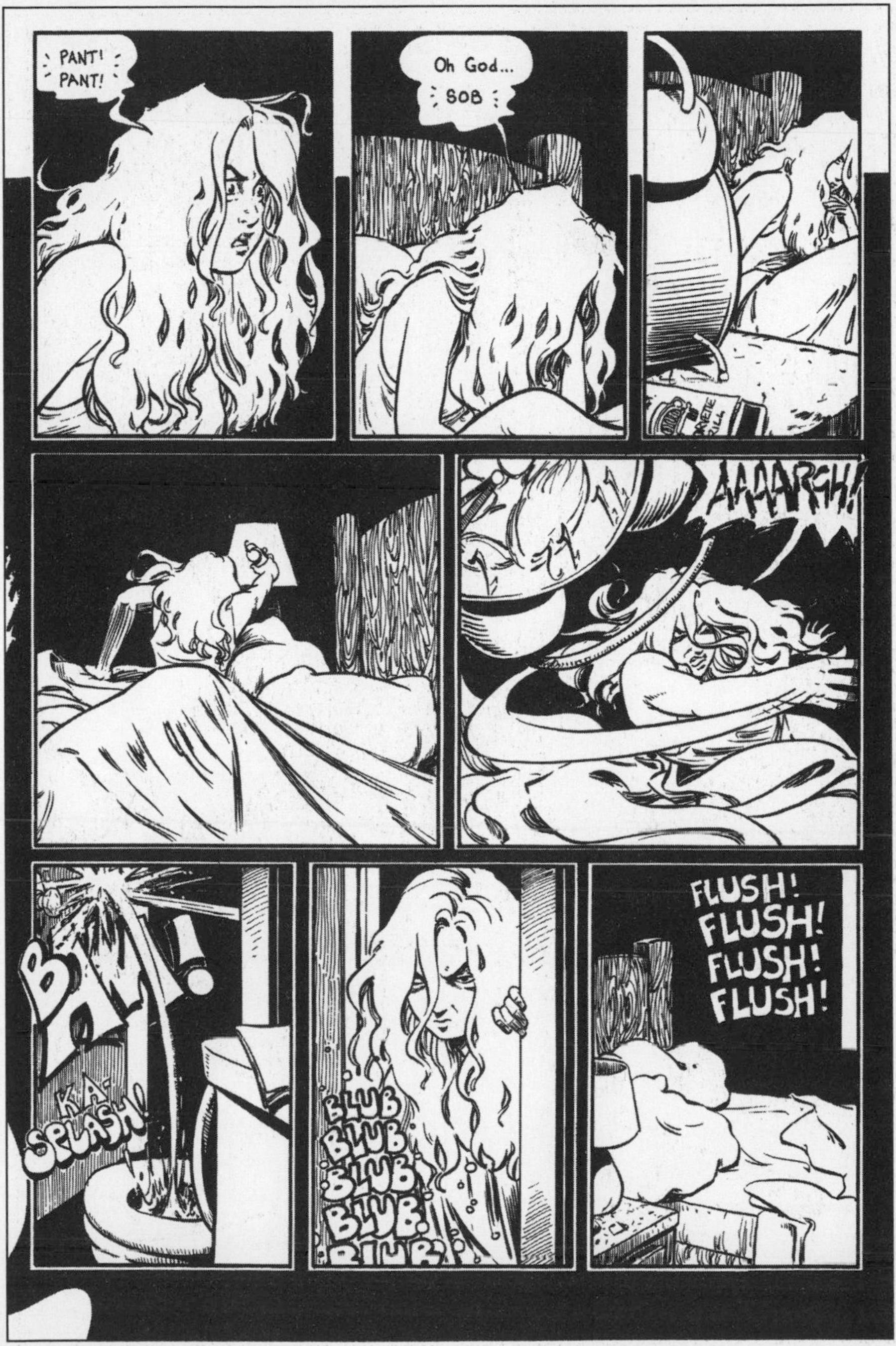
PANT! PANT!
Oh God... SOB
AAAARGH!
KA-SPLASH!
BLUB
BLUB
BLUB
BLUB
FLUSH!
FLUSH!
FLUSH!
FLUSH!

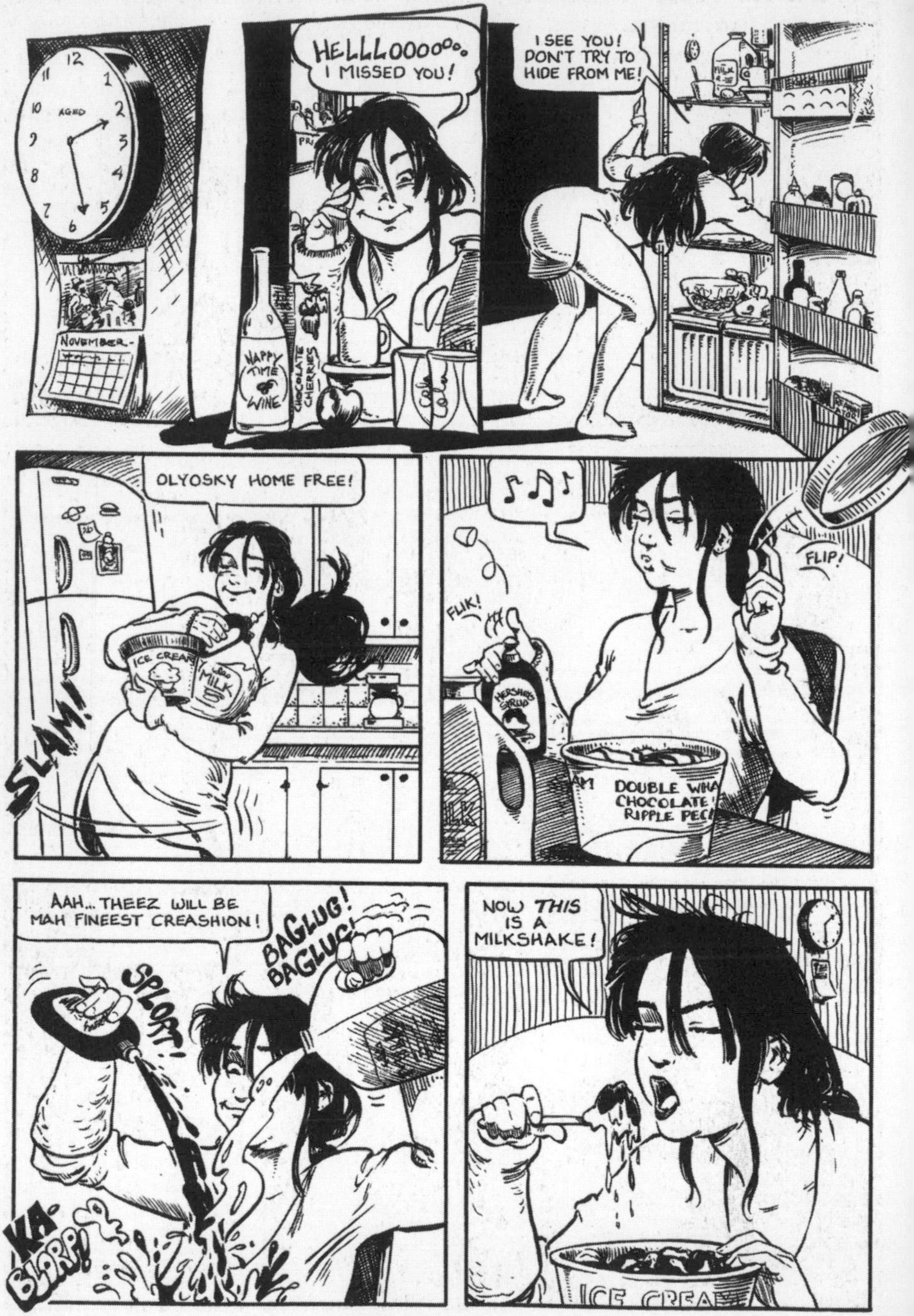
AGED
NOVEMBER
HELLLOOOOooo
I MISSED YOU!
NAPPY TIME WINE
CHOCOLATE CHERRIES
I SEE YOU! DON'T TRY TO HIDE FROM ME!
MILK
OLYOSKY HOME FREE!
ICE CREAM
MILK
SLAM!
♪♫♪
FLIP!
FLIK!
HERSHEY'S SYRUP
DOUBLE WHA
CHOCOLATE
RIPPLE PEC
AAH... THEEZ WILL BE MAH FINEEST CREASHION!
BAGLUG! BAGLUG!
SPLORT!
KA-BLORP!
NOW THIS IS A MILKSHAKE!
ICE CREA

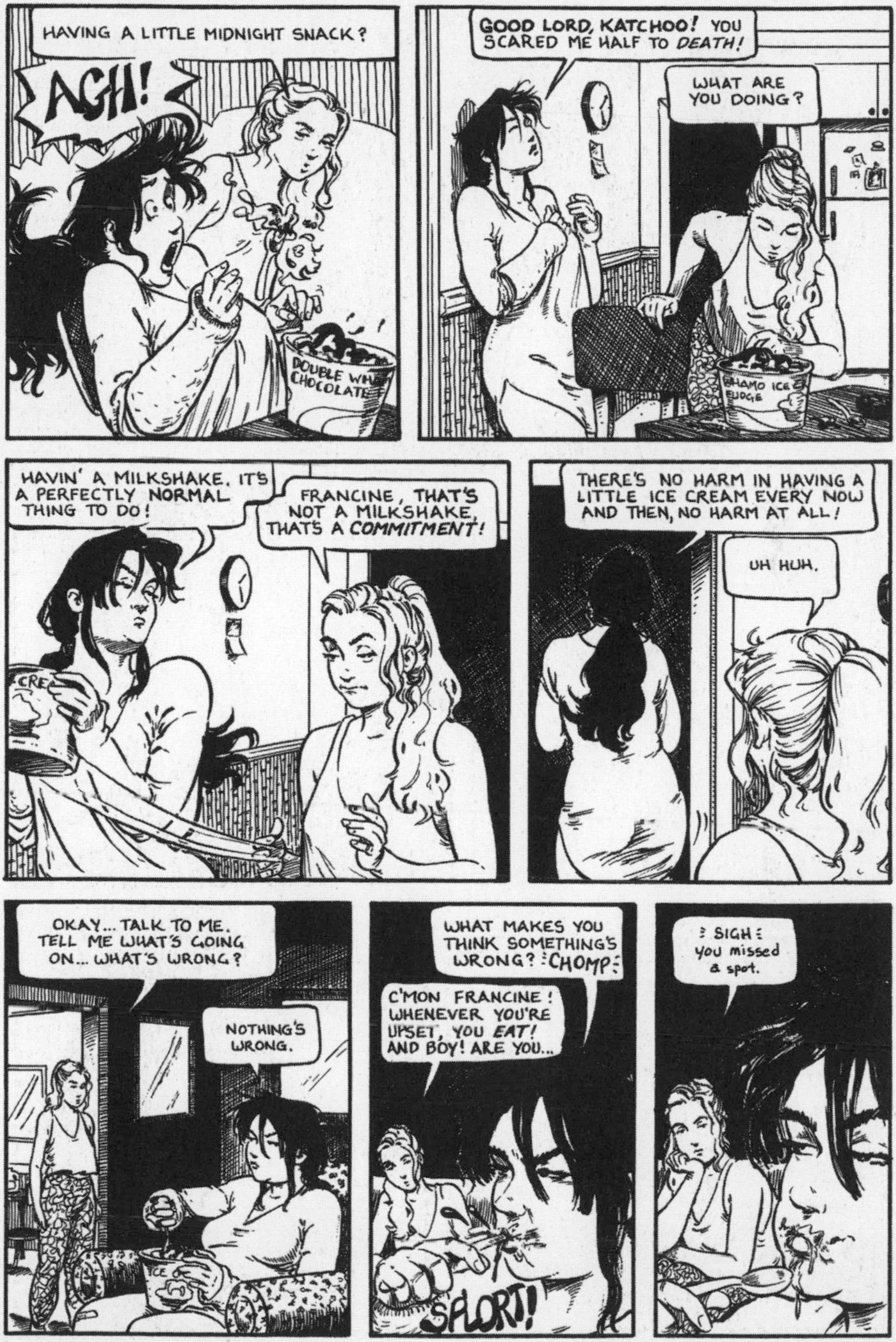
HAVING A LITTLE MIDNIGHT SNACK?
AGH!
DOUBLE WH CHOCOLATE
GOOD LORD, KATCHOO! YOU SCARED ME HALF TO *DEATH*!
WHAT ARE YOU DOING?
HAVIN' A MILKSHAKE. IT'S A PERFECTLY NORMAL THING TO DO!
FRANCINE, THAT'S NOT A MILKSHAKE, THAT'S A *COMMITMENT*!
THERE'S NO HARM IN HAVING A LITTLE ICE CREAM EVERY NOW AND THEN, NO HARM AT ALL!
UH HUH.
OKAY... TALK TO ME. TELL ME WHAT'S GOING ON... WHAT'S WRONG?
NOTHING'S WRONG.
WHAT MAKES YOU THINK SOMETHING'S WRONG? CHOMP
C'MON FRANCINE! WHENEVER YOU'RE UPSET, YOU *EAT*! AND BOY! ARE YOU...
SPLORT!
SIGH
you missed a spot.

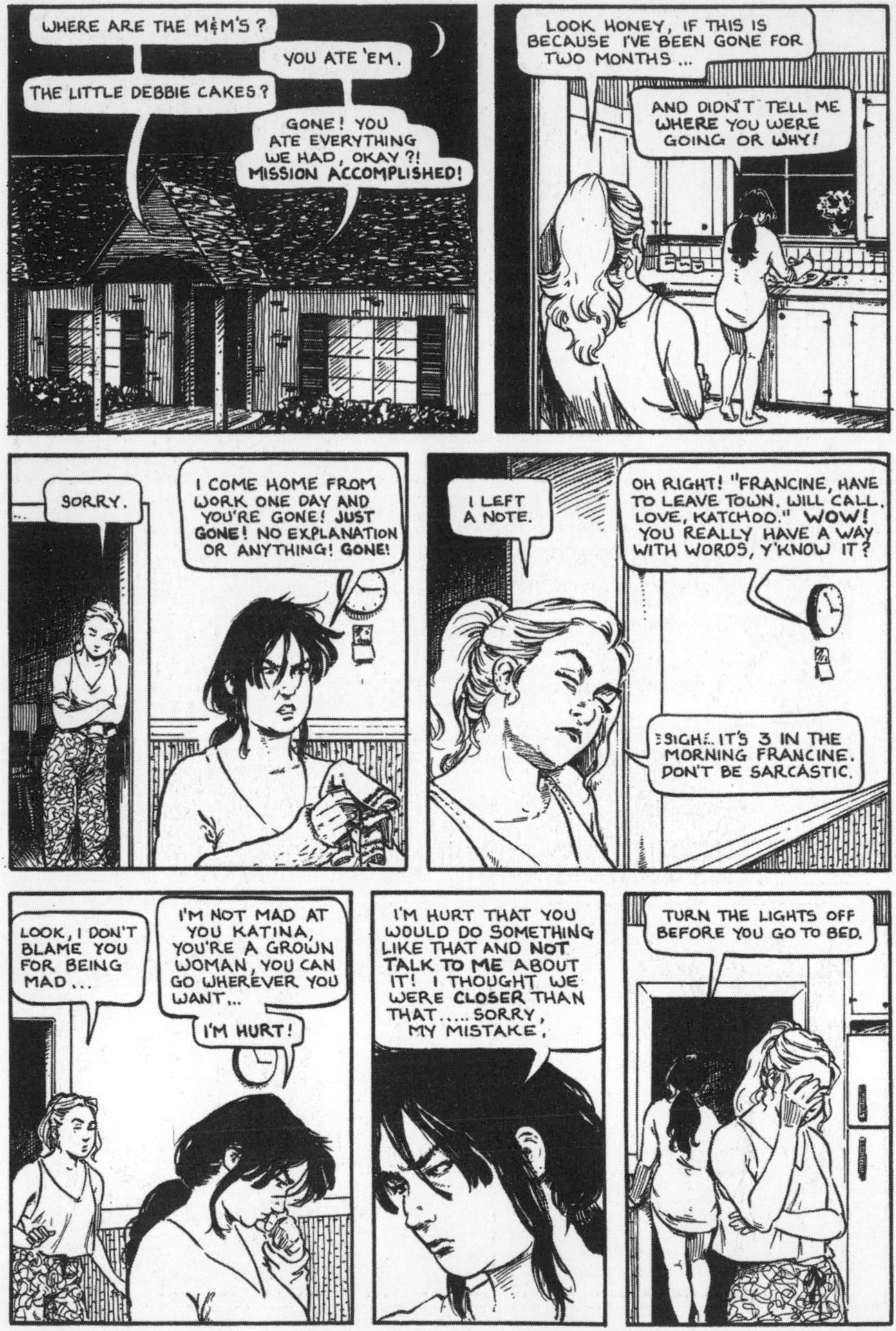
WHERE ARE THE M&M'S?
YOU ATE 'EM.
THE LITTLE DEBBIE CAKES?
GONE! YOU ATE EVERYTHING WE HAD, OKAY?! MISSION ACCOMPLISHED!
LOOK HONEY, IF THIS IS BECAUSE I'VE BEEN GONE FOR TWO MONTHS...
AND DIDN'T TELL ME WHERE YOU WERE GOING OR WHY!
SORRY.
I COME HOME FROM WORK ONE DAY AND YOU'RE GONE! JUST GONE! NO EXPLANATION OR ANYTHING! GONE!
I LEFT A NOTE.
OH RIGHT! "FRANCINE, HAVE TO LEAVE TOWN. WILL CALL. LOVE, KATCHOO." WOW! YOU REALLY HAVE A WAY WITH WORDS, Y'KNOW IT?
SIGH. IT'S 3 IN THE MORNING FRANCINE. DON'T BE SARCASTIC.
LOOK, I DON'T BLAME YOU FOR BEING MAD...
I'M NOT MAD AT YOU KATINA, YOU'RE A GROWN WOMAN, YOU CAN GO WHEREVER YOU WANT...
I'M HURT!
I'M HURT THAT YOU WOULD DO SOMETHING LIKE THAT AND NOT TALK TO ME ABOUT IT! I THOUGHT WE WERE CLOSER THAN THAT..... SORRY, MY MISTAKE.
TURN THE LIGHTS OFF BEFORE YOU GO TO BED.

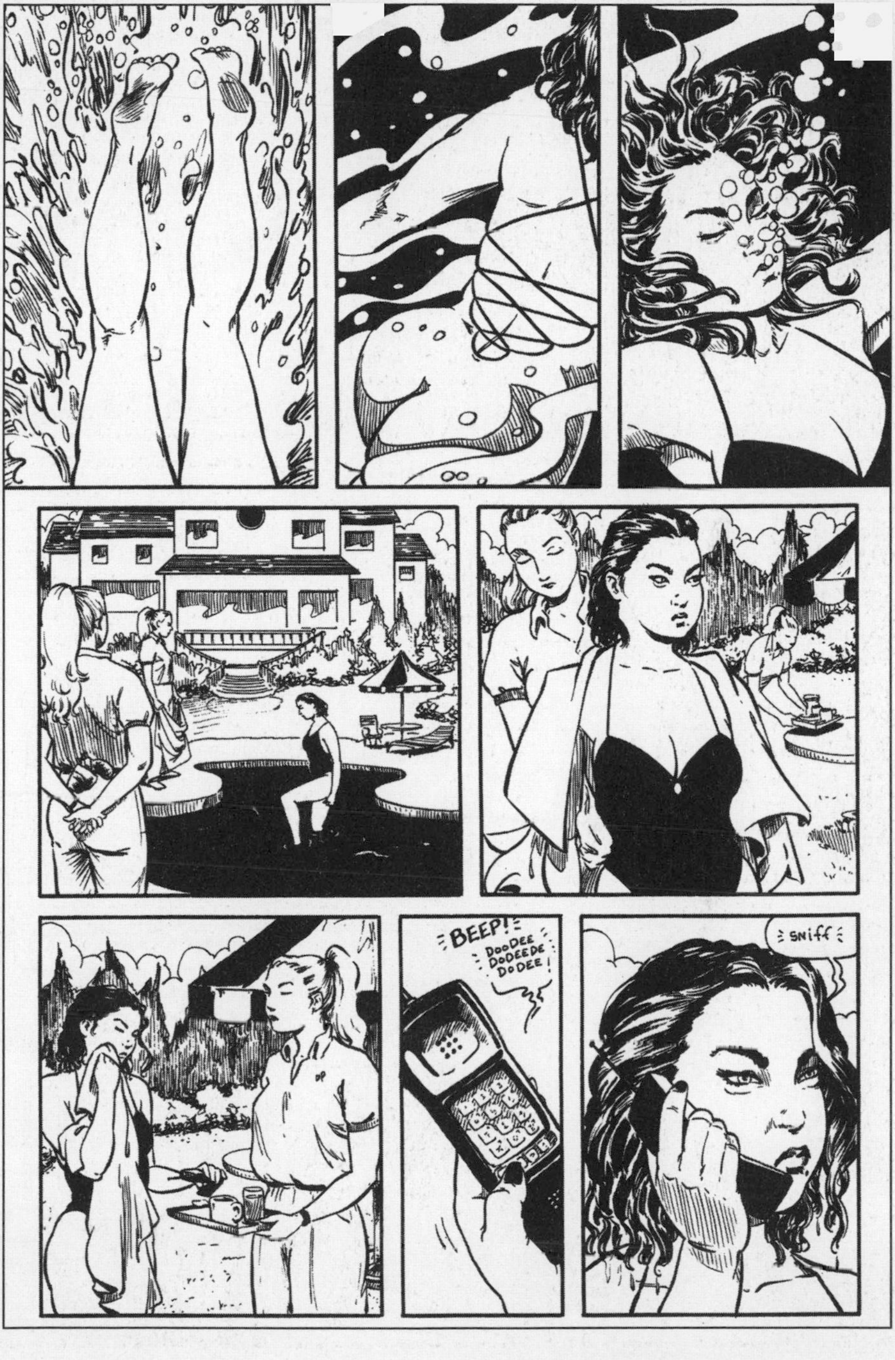
BEEP!
DOODEE DODEEDE DODEE!
SNIFF

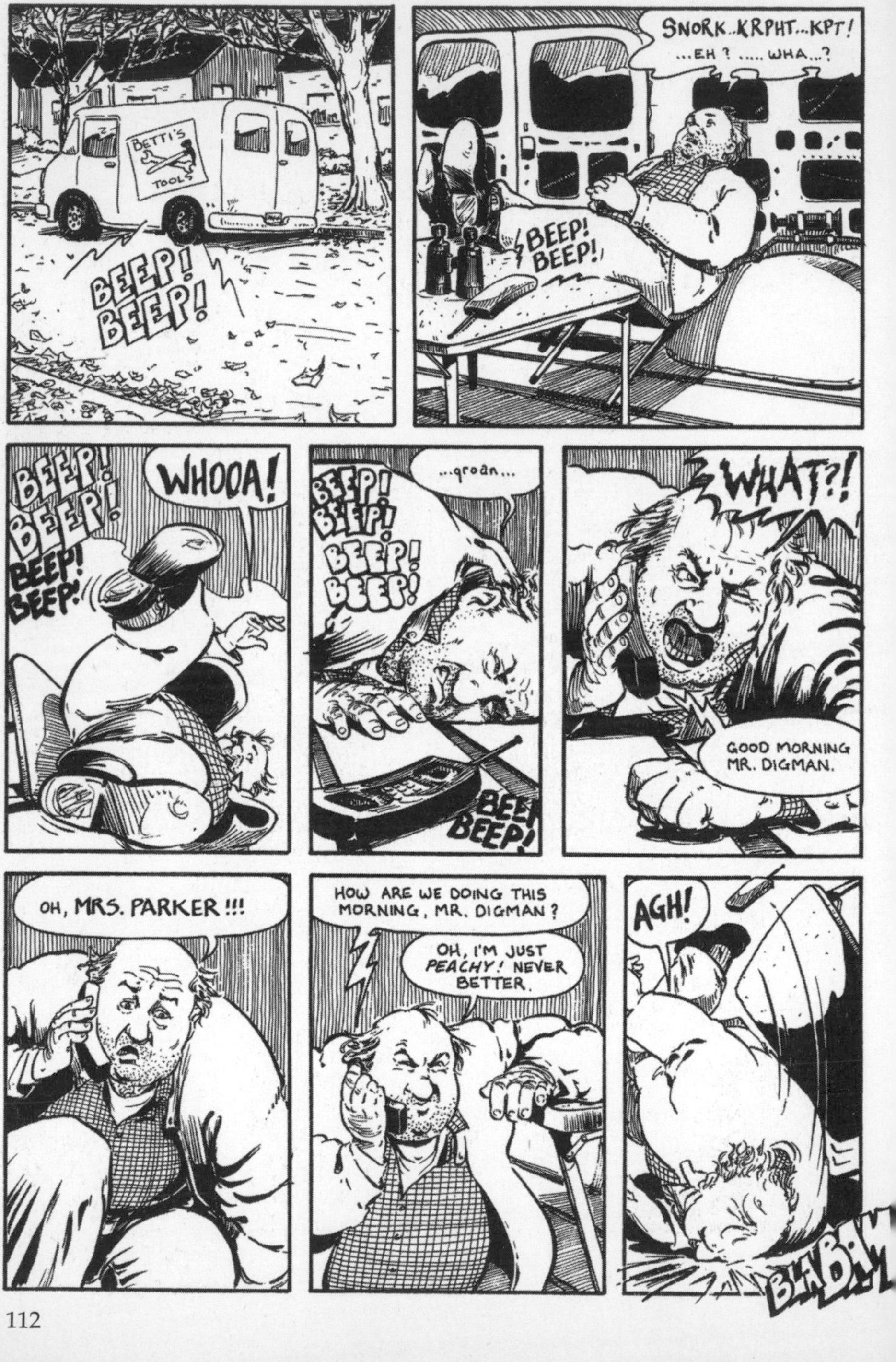
BETTI'S TOOLS
BEEP! BEEP!
SNORK..KRPHT...KPT! ...EH? ..... WHA...?
BEEP! BEEP!
BEEP! BEEP! BEEP! BEEP!
WHOOA!
BEEP! BEEP! BEEP! BEEP!
...groan...
BEEP!
WHAT?!
GOOD MORNING MR. DIGMAN.
OH, MRS. PARKER!!!
HOW ARE WE DOING THIS MORNING, MR. DIGMAN?
OH, I'M JUST *PEACHY!* NEVER BETTER.
AGH!
BLABAM

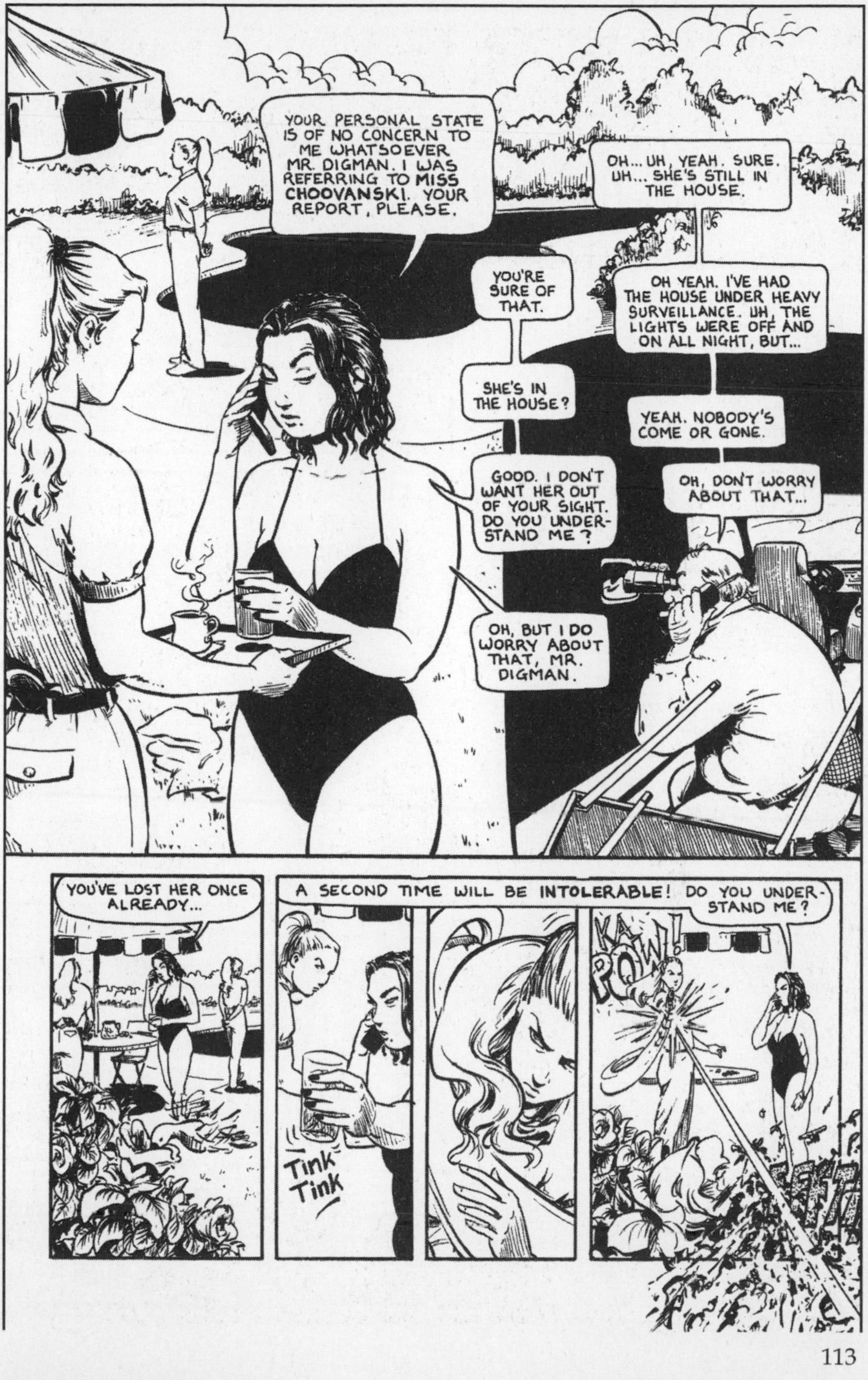
YOUR PERSONAL STATE IS OF NO CONCERN TO ME WHATSOEVER MR. DIGMAN. I WAS REFERRING TO MISS CHOOVANSKI. YOUR REPORT, PLEASE.
OH... UH, YEAH. SURE. UH... SHE'S STILL IN THE HOUSE.
YOU'RE SURE OF THAT.
OH YEAH. I'VE HAD THE HOUSE UNDER HEAVY SURVEILLANCE. UH, THE LIGHTS WERE OFF AND ON ALL NIGHT, BUT...
SHE'S IN THE HOUSE?
YEAH. NOBODY'S COME OR GONE.
GOOD. I DON'T WANT HER OUT OF YOUR SIGHT. DO YOU UNDERSTAND ME?
OH, DON'T WORRY ABOUT THAT...
OH, BUT I DO WORRY ABOUT THAT, MR. DIGMAN.
YOU'VE LOST HER ONCE ALREADY...
A SECOND TIME WILL BE INTOLERABLE! DO YOU UNDERSTAND ME?
Tink Tink
KA POW!

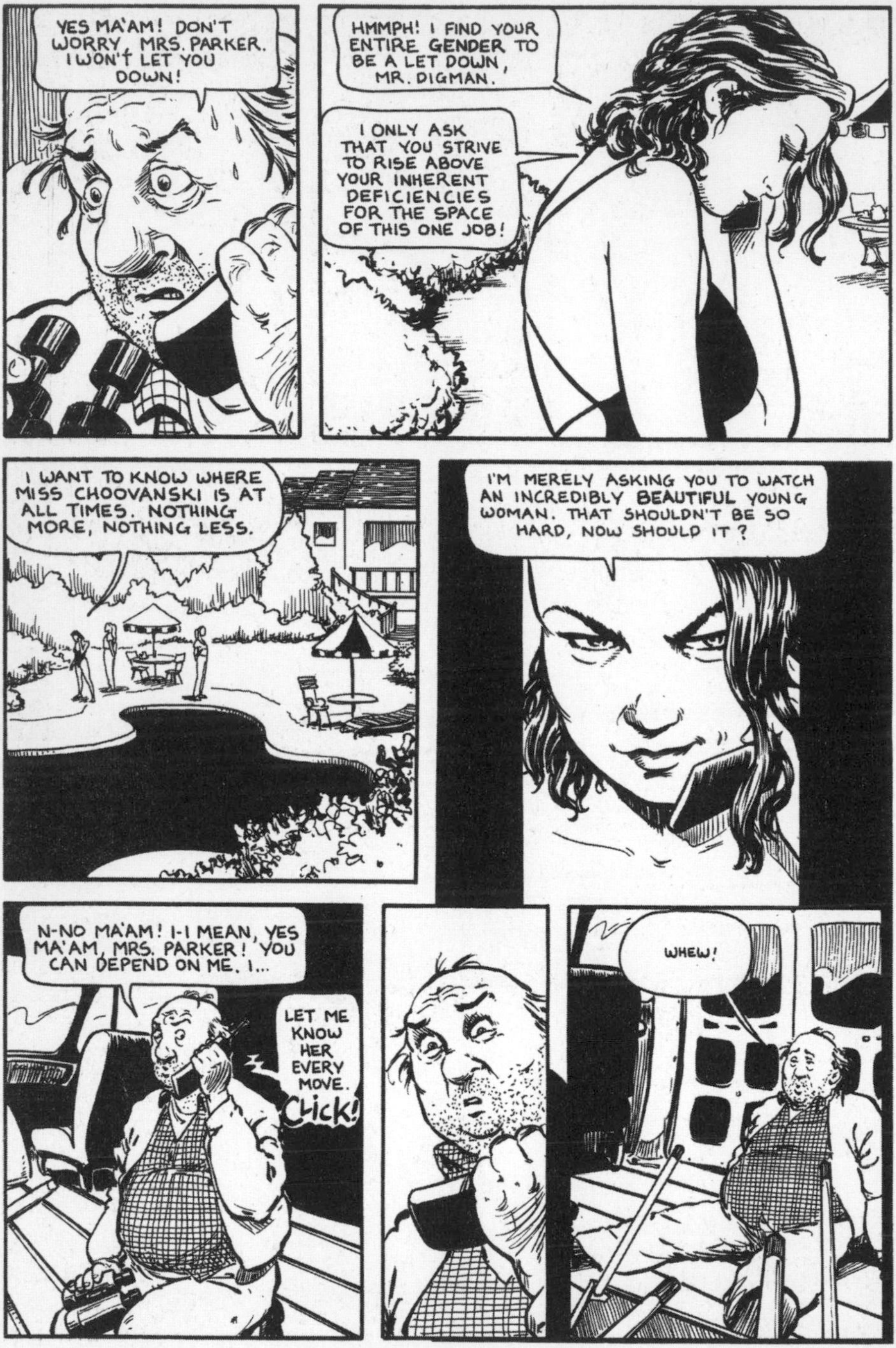
YES MA'AM! DON'T WORRY, MRS. PARKER. I WON'T LET YOU DOWN!
HMMPH! I FIND YOUR ENTIRE GENDER TO BE A LET DOWN, MR. DIGMAN.
I ONLY ASK THAT YOU STRIVE TO RISE ABOVE YOUR INHERENT DEFICIENCIES FOR THE SPACE OF THIS ONE JOB!
I WANT TO KNOW WHERE MISS CHOOVANSKI IS AT ALL TIMES. NOTHING MORE, NOTHING LESS.
I'M MERELY ASKING YOU TO WATCH AN INCREDIBLY BEAUTIFUL YOUNG WOMAN. THAT SHOULDN'T BE SO HARD, NOW SHOULD IT?
N-NO MA'AM! I-I MEAN, YES MA'AM, MRS. PARKER! YOU CAN DEPEND ON ME. I...
LET ME KNOW HER EVERY MOVE.
CLICK!
WHEW!

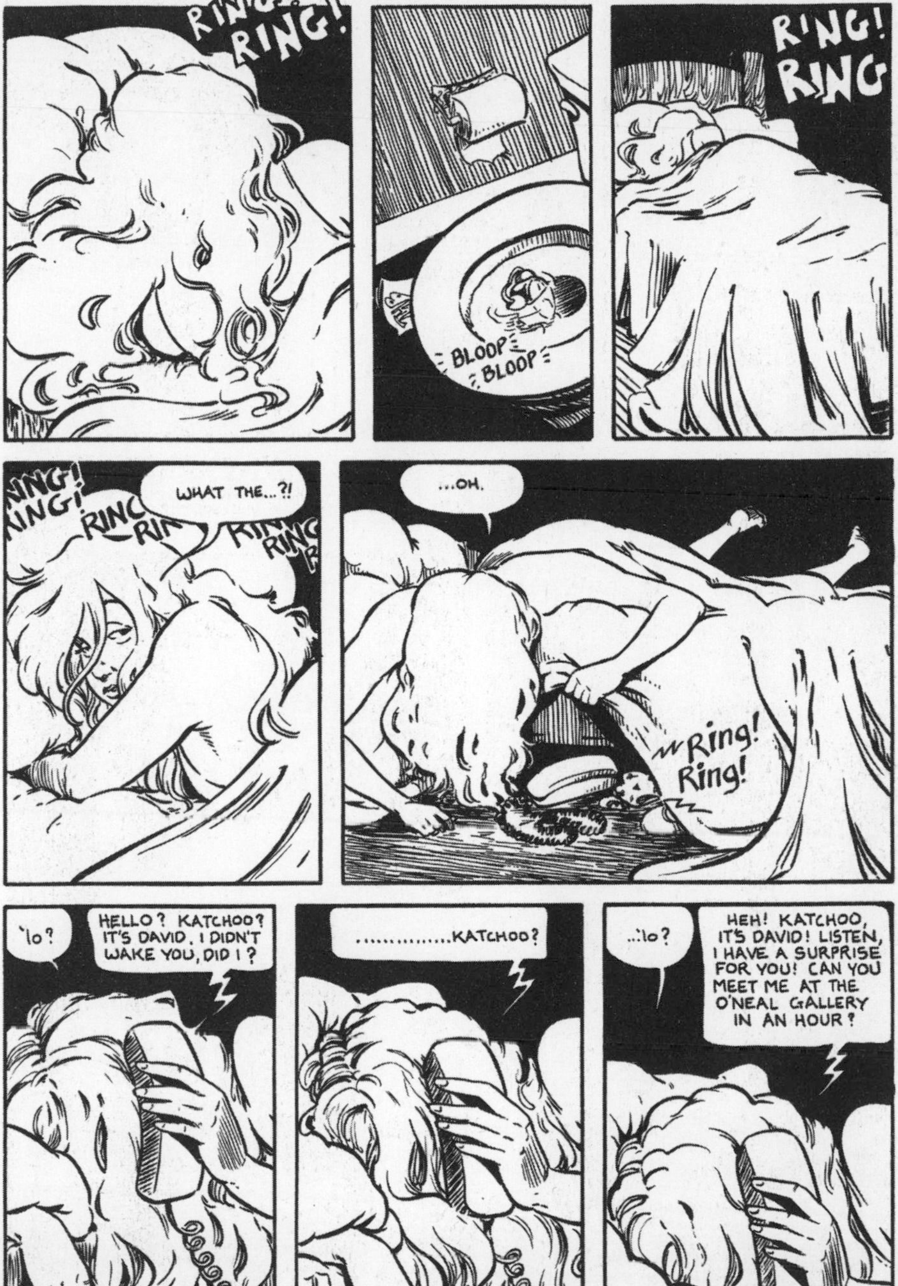
RING! RING!
BLOOP BLOOP
RING! RING
RING! RING! RING RI
WHAT THE...?!
...OH.
Ring! Ring!
'lo?
HELLO? KATCHOO? IT'S DAVID. I DIDN'T WAKE YOU, DID I?
...............KATCHOO?
..'lo?
HEH! KATCHOO, IT'S DAVID! LISTEN, I HAVE A SURPRISE FOR YOU! CAN YOU MEET ME AT THE O'NEAL GALLERY IN AN HOUR?

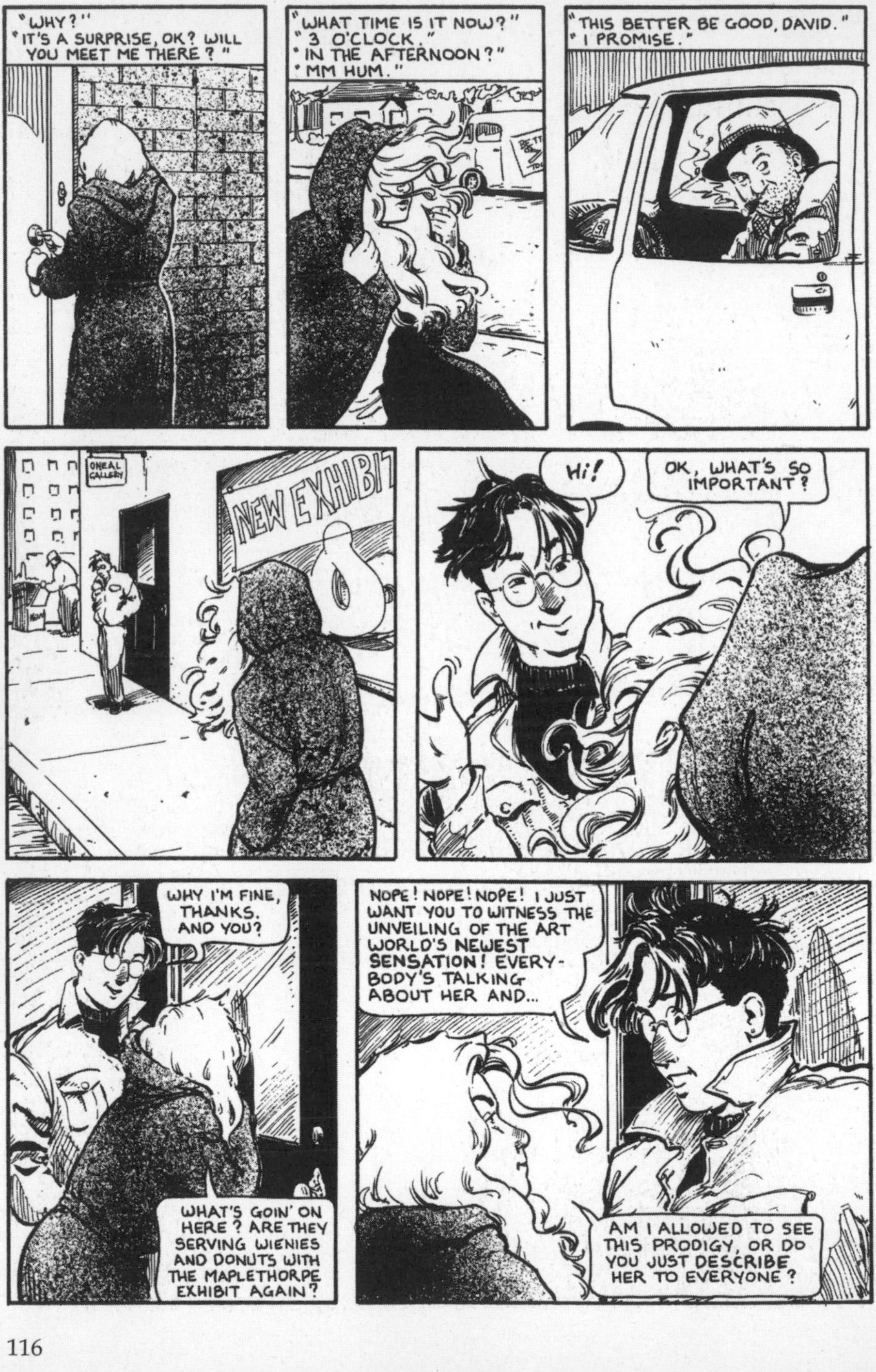
"WHY?"
"IT'S A SURPRISE, OK? WILL YOU MEET ME THERE?"
"WHAT TIME IS IT NOW?"
"3 O'CLOCK."
"IN THE AFTERNOON?"
"MM HUM."
"THIS BETTER BE GOOD, DAVID."
"I PROMISE."
ONEAL GALLERY
NEW EXHIBIT
HI!
OK, WHAT'S SO IMPORTANT?
WHY I'M FINE, THANKS. AND YOU?
WHAT'S GOIN' ON HERE? ARE THEY SERVING WIENIES AND DONUTS WITH THE MAPLETHORPE EXHIBIT AGAIN?
NOPE! NOPE! NOPE! I JUST WANT YOU TO WITNESS THE UNVEILING OF THE ART WORLD'S NEWEST SENSATION! EVERYBODY'S TALKING ABOUT HER AND...
AM I ALLOWED TO SEE THIS PRODIGY, OR DO YOU JUST DESCRIBE HER TO EVERYONE?

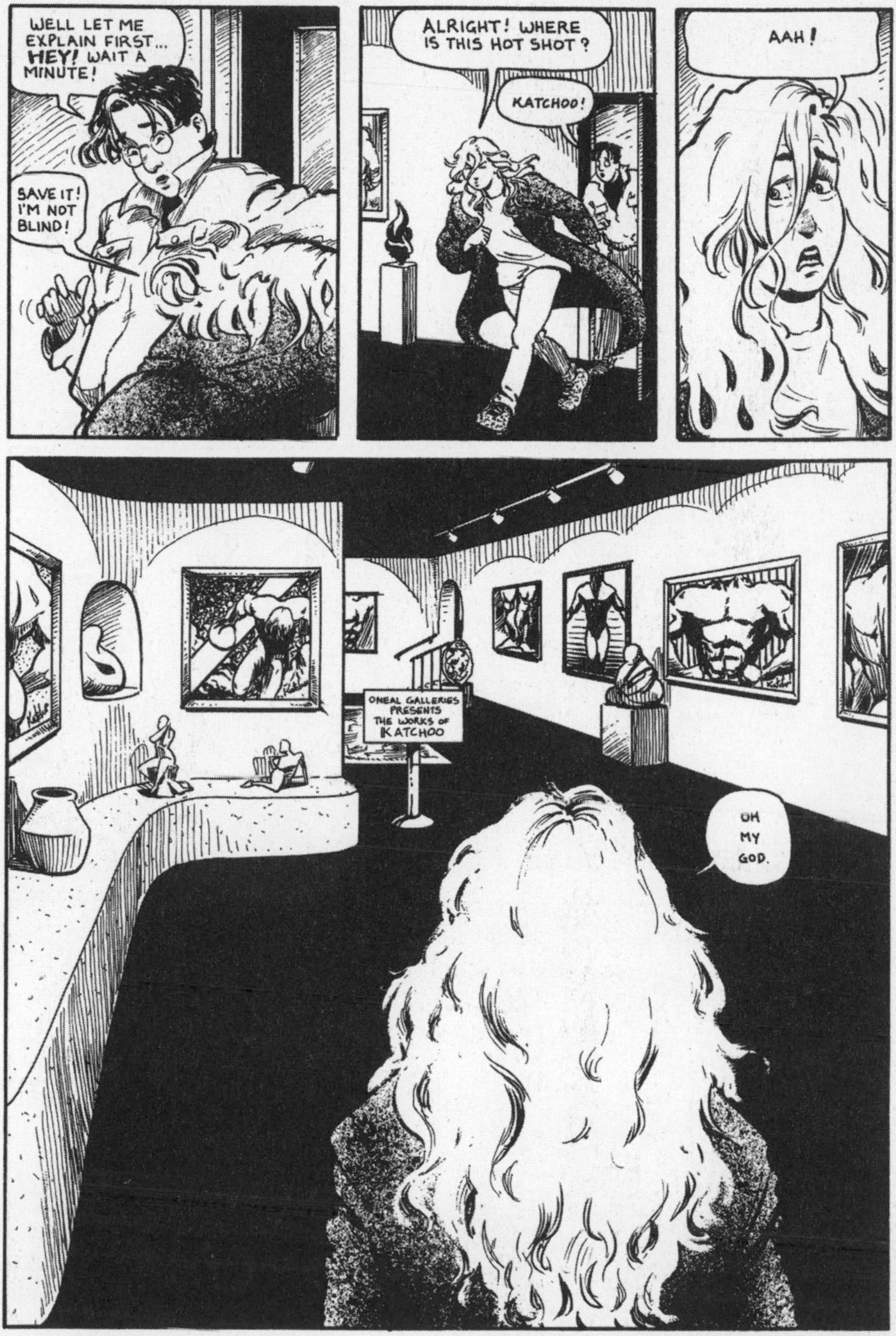
WELL LET ME EXPLAIN FIRST... HEY! WAIT A MINUTE!
SAVE IT! I'M NOT BLIND!
ALRIGHT! WHERE IS THIS HOT SHOT?
KATCHOO!
AAH!
ONEAL GALLERIES PRESENTS THE WORKS OF KATCHOO
OH MY GOD.

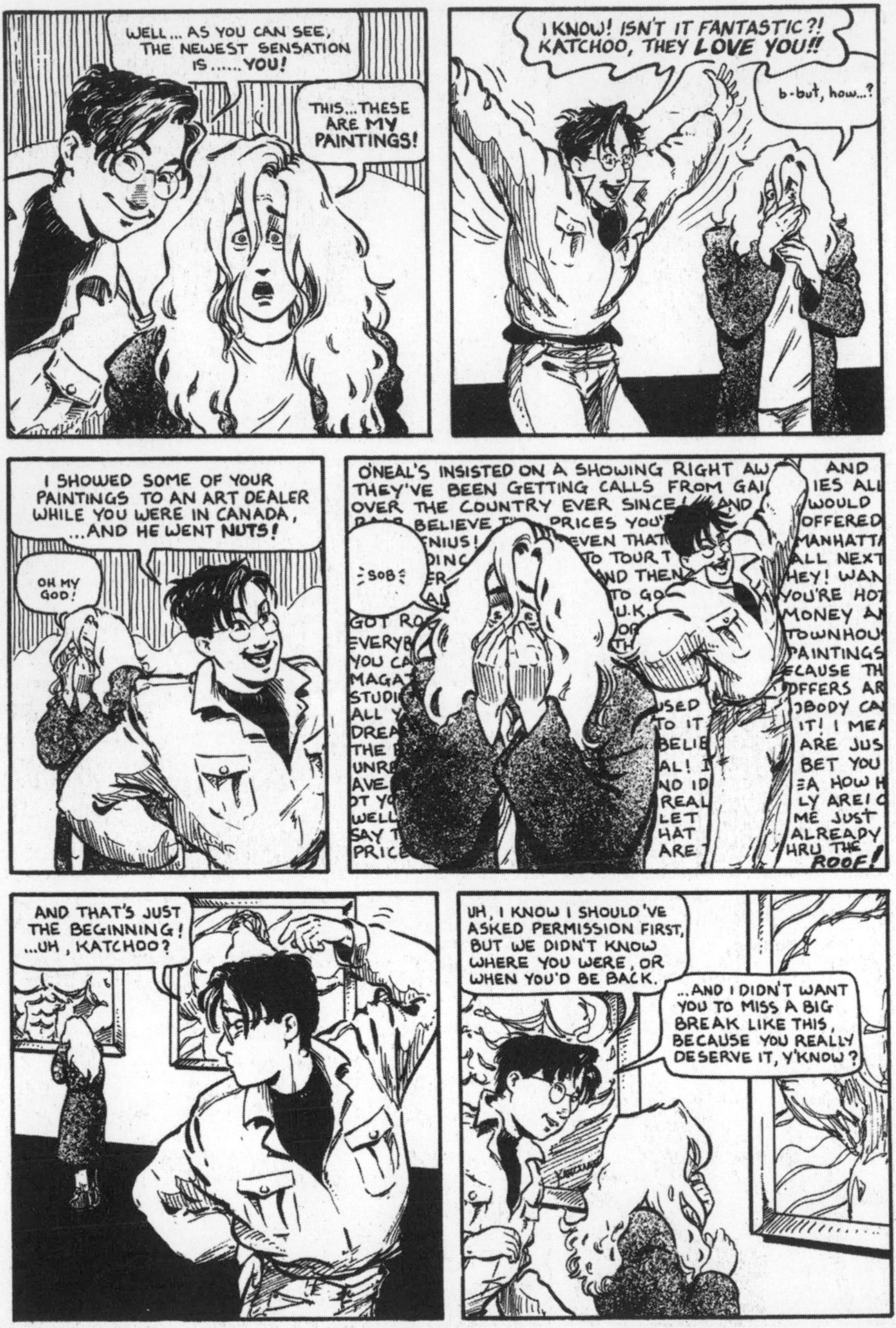
WELL... AS YOU CAN SEE, THE NEWEST SENSATION IS...... YOU!
THIS... THESE ARE MY PAINTINGS!
I KNOW! ISN'T IT FANTASTIC?! KATCHOO, THEY LOVE YOU!!
b-but, how...?
I SHOWED SOME OF YOUR PAINTINGS TO AN ART DEALER WHILE YOU WERE IN CANADA, ...AND HE WENT NUTS!
OH MY GOD!
O'NEAL'S INSISTED ON A SHOWING RIGHT AW
THEY'VE BEEN GETTING CALLS FROM GAL
OVER THE COUNTRY EVER SINCE!
SOB
ALREADY
THRU THE ROOF!
AND THAT'S JUST THE BEGINNING! ...UH, KATCHOO?
UH, I KNOW I SHOULD'VE ASKED PERMISSION FIRST, BUT WE DIDN'T KNOW WHERE YOU WERE, OR WHEN YOU'D BE BACK.
...AND I DIDN'T WANT YOU TO MISS A BIG BREAK LIKE THIS, BECAUSE YOU REALLY DESERVE IT, Y'KNOW?

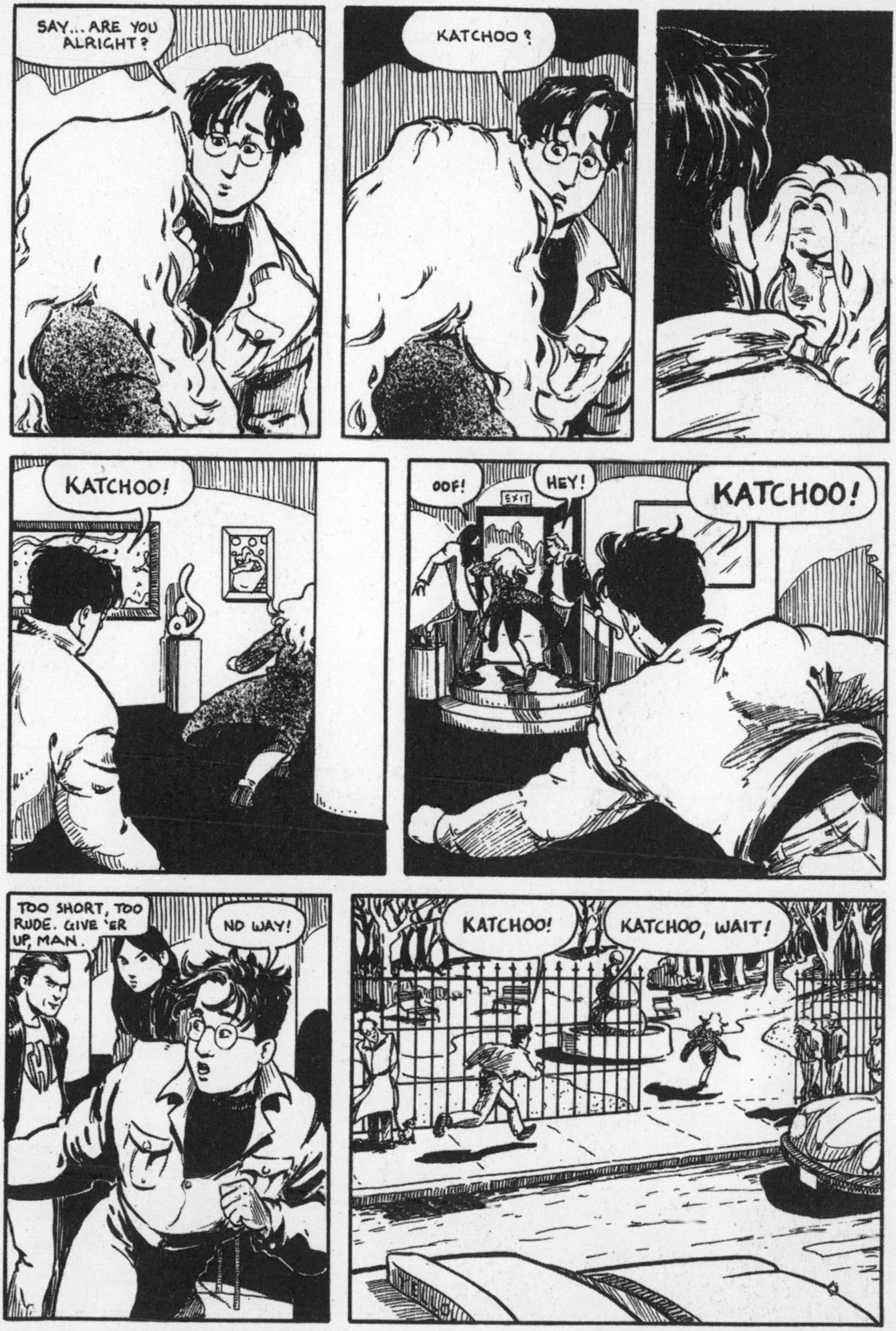
SAY... ARE YOU ALRIGHT?
KATCHOO?
KATCHOO!
OOF!
HEY!
EXIT
KATCHOO!
TOO SHORT, TOO RUDE. GIVE 'ER UP, MAN.
NO WAY!
KATCHOO!
KATCHOO, WAIT!

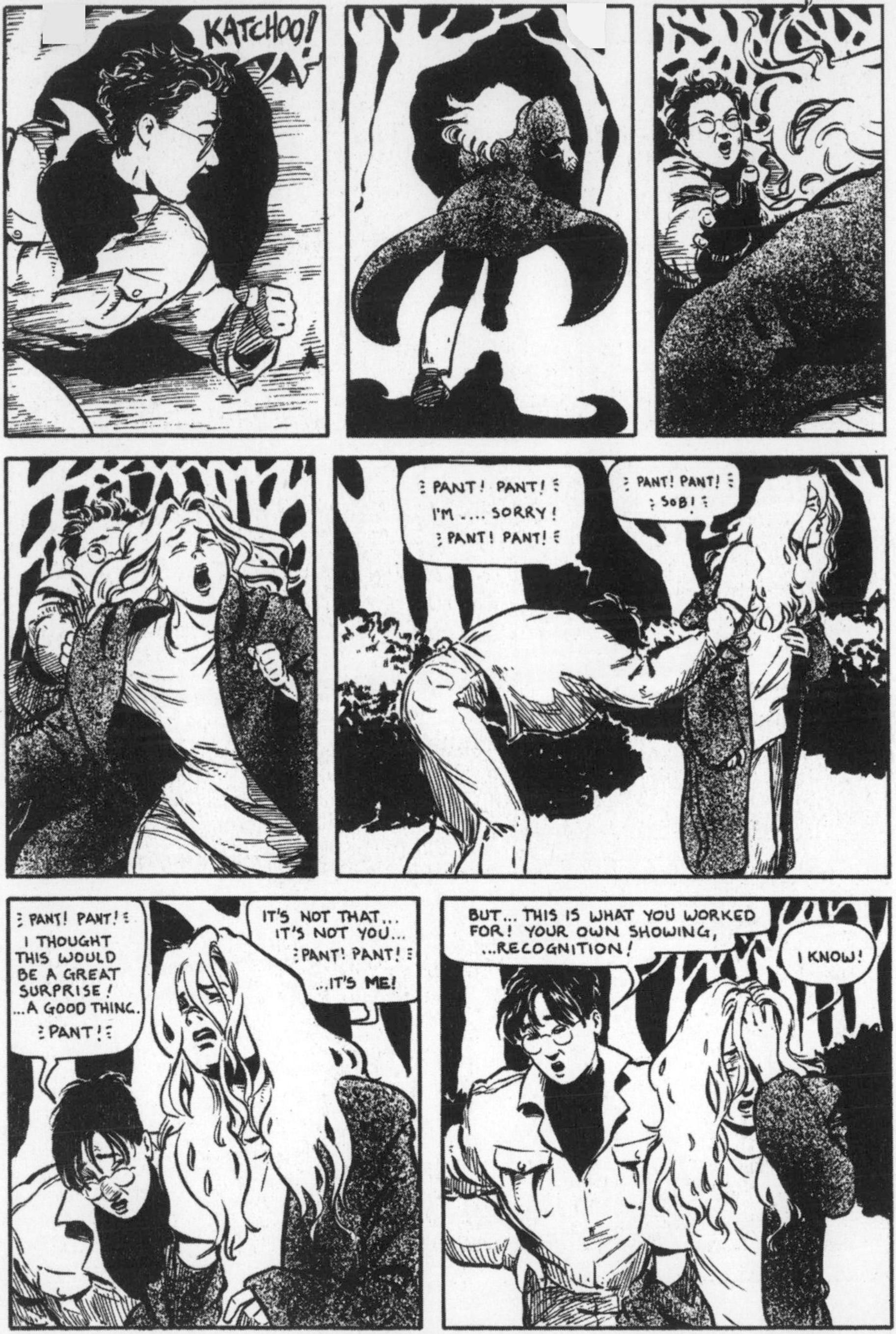
KATCHOO!
PANT! PANT!
I'M .... SORRY!
PANT! PANT!
PANT! PANT!
SOB!
PANT! PANT!
I THOUGHT THIS WOULD BE A GREAT SURPRISE! ...A GOOD THING.
PANT!
IT'S NOT THAT... IT'S NOT YOU...
PANT! PANT!
...IT'S ME!
BUT... THIS IS WHAT YOU WORKED FOR! YOUR OWN SHOWING, ...RECOGNITION!
I KNOW!

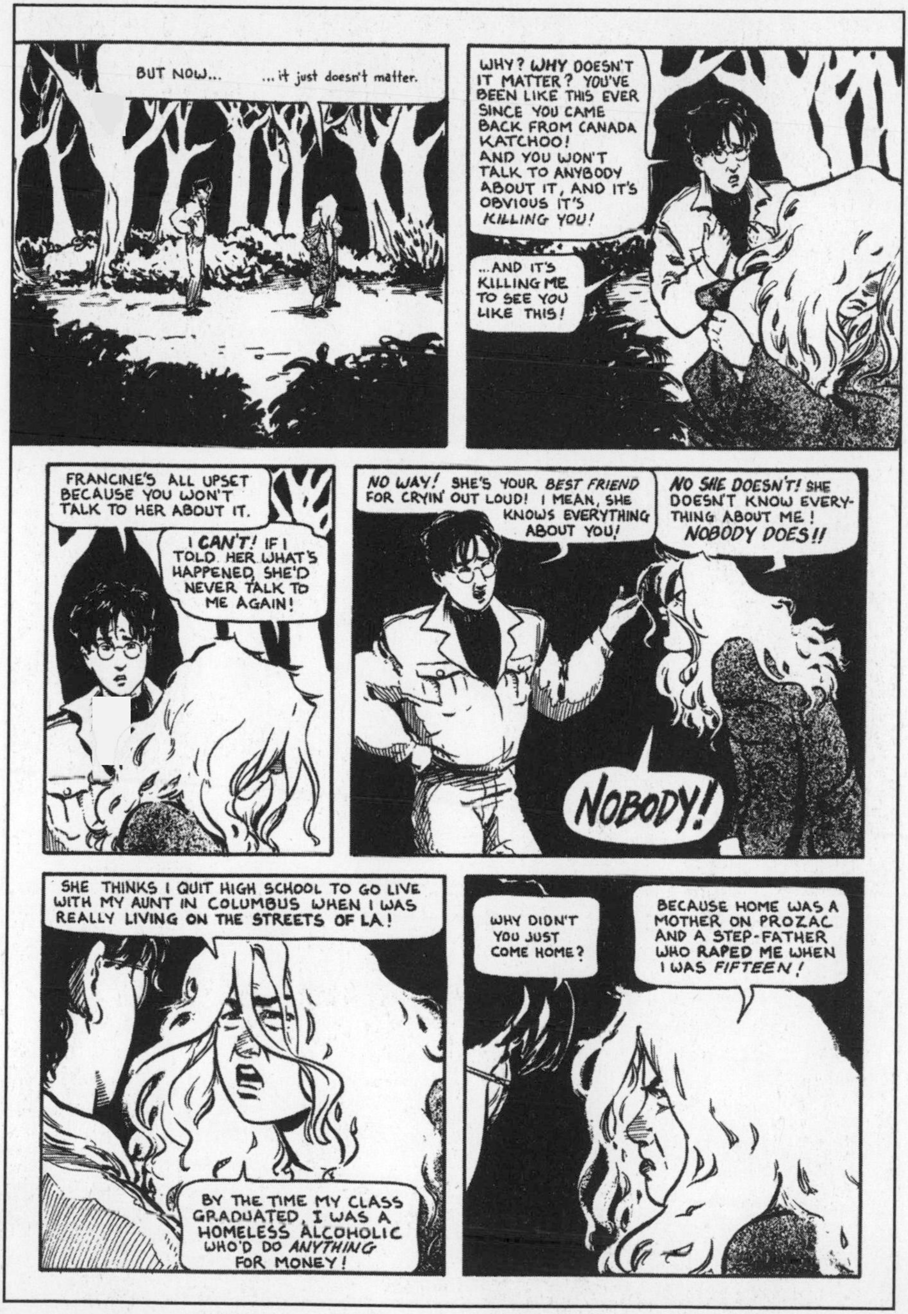
BUT NOW... ...it just doesn't matter.
WHY? WHY DOESN'T IT MATTER? YOU'VE BEEN LIKE THIS EVER SINCE YOU CAME BACK FROM CANADA KATCHOO! AND YOU WON'T TALK TO ANYBODY ABOUT IT, AND IT'S OBVIOUS IT'S KILLING YOU!
...AND IT'S KILLING ME TO SEE YOU LIKE THIS!
FRANCINE'S ALL UPSET BECAUSE YOU WON'T TALK TO HER ABOUT IT.
I CAN'T! IF I TOLD HER WHAT'S HAPPENED, SHE'D NEVER TALK TO ME AGAIN!
NO WAY! SHE'S YOUR BEST FRIEND FOR CRYIN' OUT LOUD! I MEAN, SHE KNOWS EVERYTHING ABOUT YOU!
NO SHE DOESN'T! SHE DOESN'T KNOW EVERYTHING ABOUT ME! NOBODY DOES!!
NOBODY!
SHE THINKS I QUIT HIGH SCHOOL TO GO LIVE WITH MY AUNT IN COLUMBUS WHEN I WAS REALLY LIVING ON THE STREETS OF LA!
BY THE TIME MY CLASS GRADUATED, I WAS A HOMELESS ALCOHOLIC WHO'D DO ANYTHING FOR MONEY!
WHY DIDN'T YOU JUST COME HOME?
BECAUSE HOME WAS A MOTHER ON PROZAC AND A STEP-FATHER WHO RAPED ME WHEN I WAS FIFTEEN!

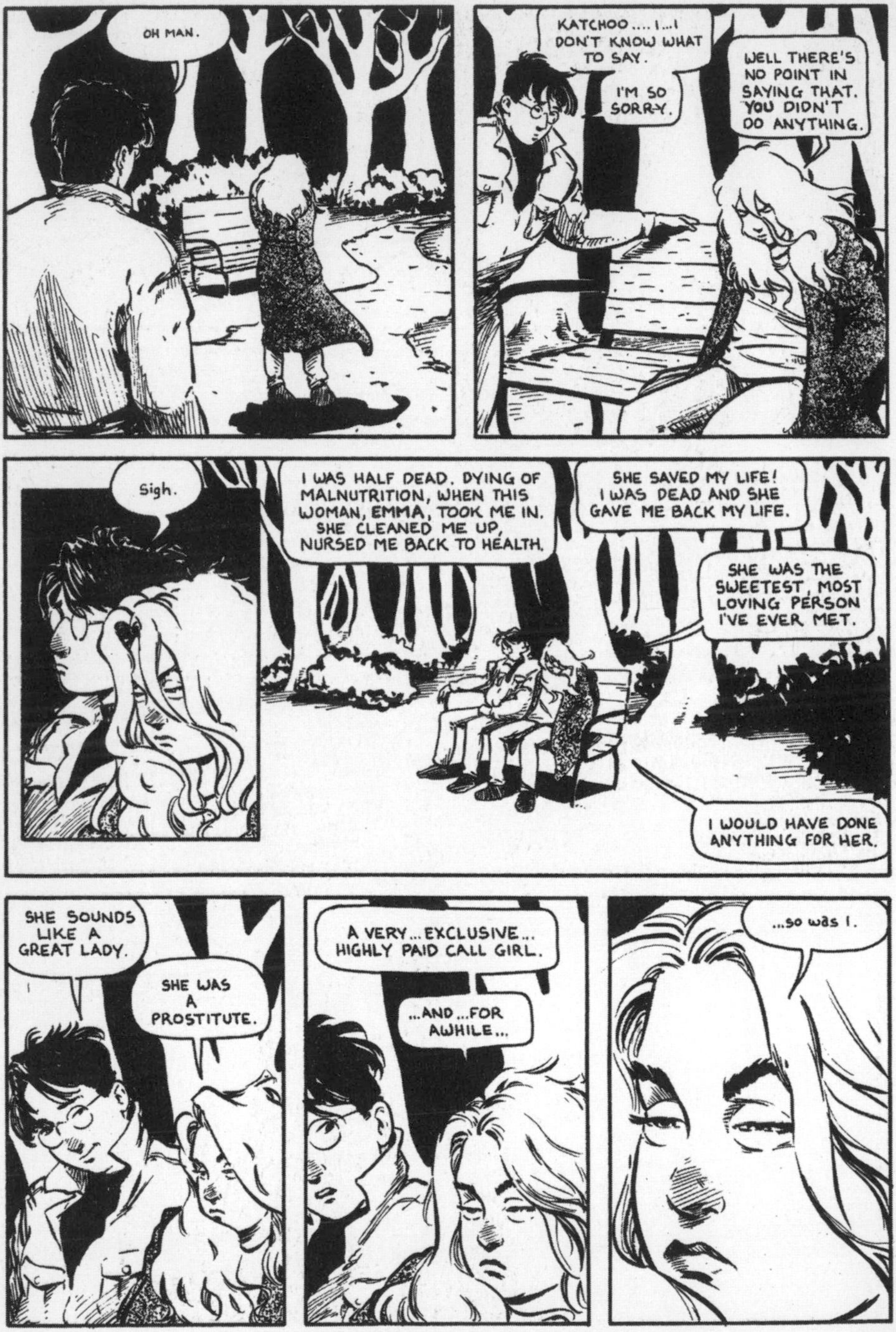

OH MAN.
KATCHOO.... I...I DON'T KNOW WHAT TO SAY.
I'M SO SORRY.
WELL THERE'S NO POINT IN SAYING THAT. YOU DIDN'T DO ANYTHING.
Sigh.
I WAS HALF DEAD, DYING OF MALNUTRITION, WHEN THIS WOMAN, EMMA, TOOK ME IN. SHE CLEANED ME UP, NURSED ME BACK TO HEALTH.
SHE SAVED MY LIFE! I WAS DEAD AND SHE GAVE ME BACK MY LIFE.
SHE WAS THE SWEETEST, MOST LOVING PERSON I'VE EVER MET.
I WOULD HAVE DONE ANYTHING FOR HER.
SHE SOUNDS LIKE A GREAT LADY.
SHE WAS A PROSTITUTE.
A VERY... EXCLUSIVE... HIGHLY PAID CALL GIRL.
...AND...FOR AWHILE...
...so was I.

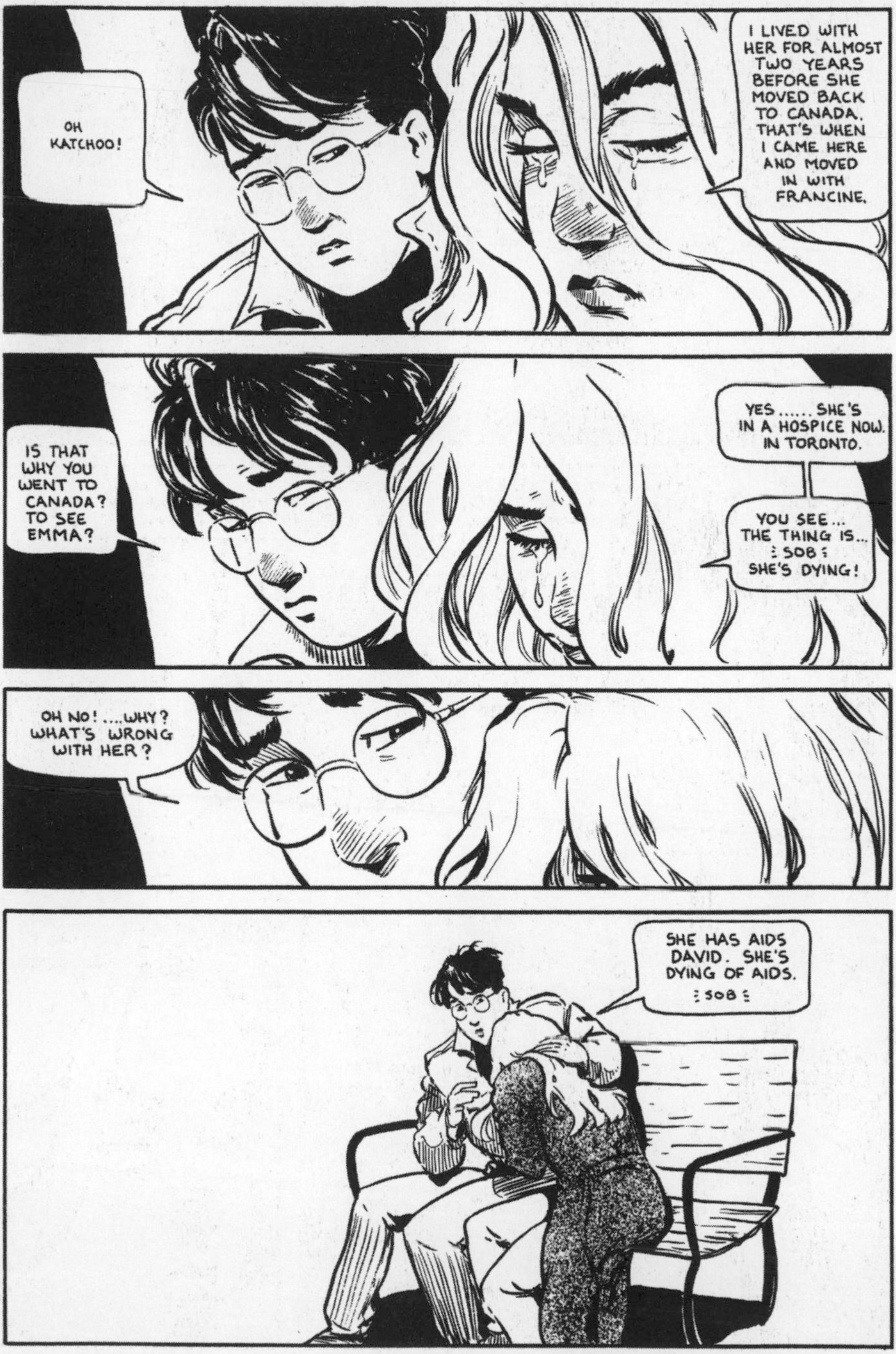
OH KATCHOO!
I LIVED WITH HER FOR ALMOST TWO YEARS BEFORE SHE MOVED BACK TO CANADA. THAT'S WHEN I CAME HERE AND MOVED IN WITH FRANCINE.
IS THAT WHY YOU WENT TO CANADA? TO SEE EMMA?
YES...... SHE'S IN A HOSPICE NOW. IN TORONTO.
YOU SEE... THE THING IS... SOB SHE'S DYING!
OH NO! ....WHY? WHAT'S WRONG WITH HER?
SHE HAS AIDS DAVID. SHE'S DYING OF AIDS.
SOB

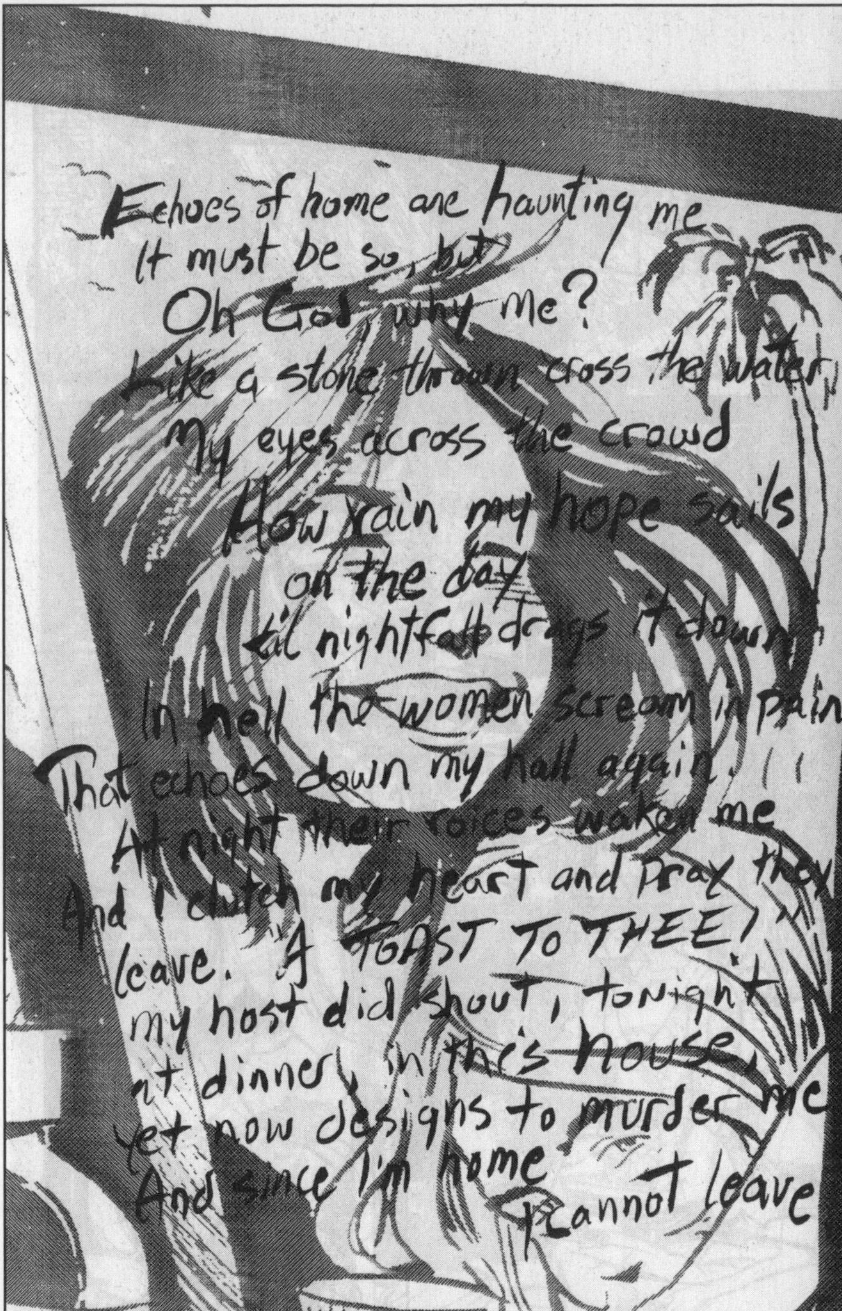
Echoes of home are haunting me
It must be so, but
Oh God, why me?
Like a stone thrown cross the water
My eyes across the crowd
How vain my hope sails
on the day
'til nightfall drags it down
In hell the women scream in pain
That echoes down my hall again
At night their voices waken me
And I clutch my heart and pray they
leave. "A TOAST TO THEE!"
my host did shout, tonight
at dinner, in this house,
yet now designs to murder me
And since I'm home
I cannot leave

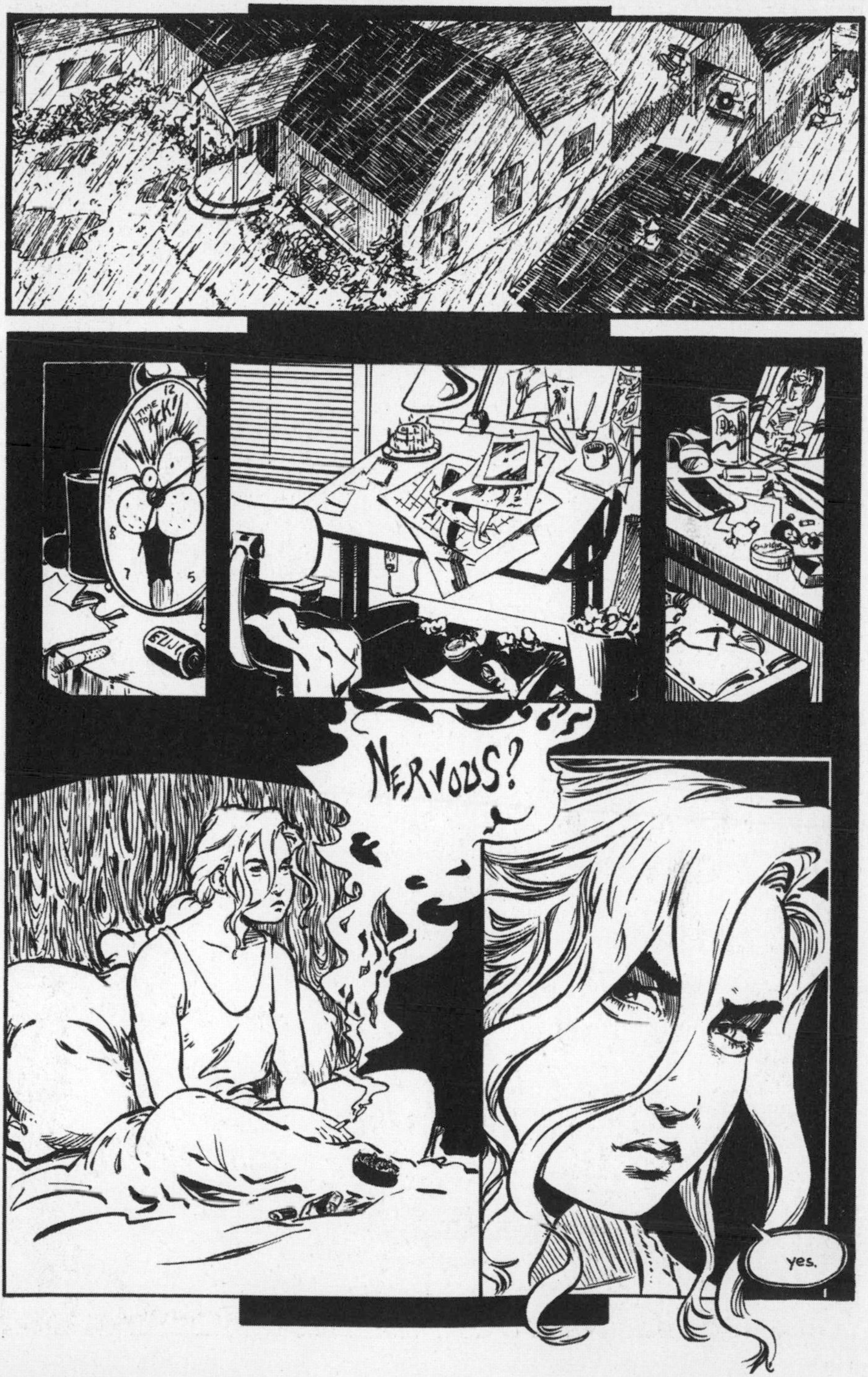
TIME TO ACK!
NERVOUS?
yes.

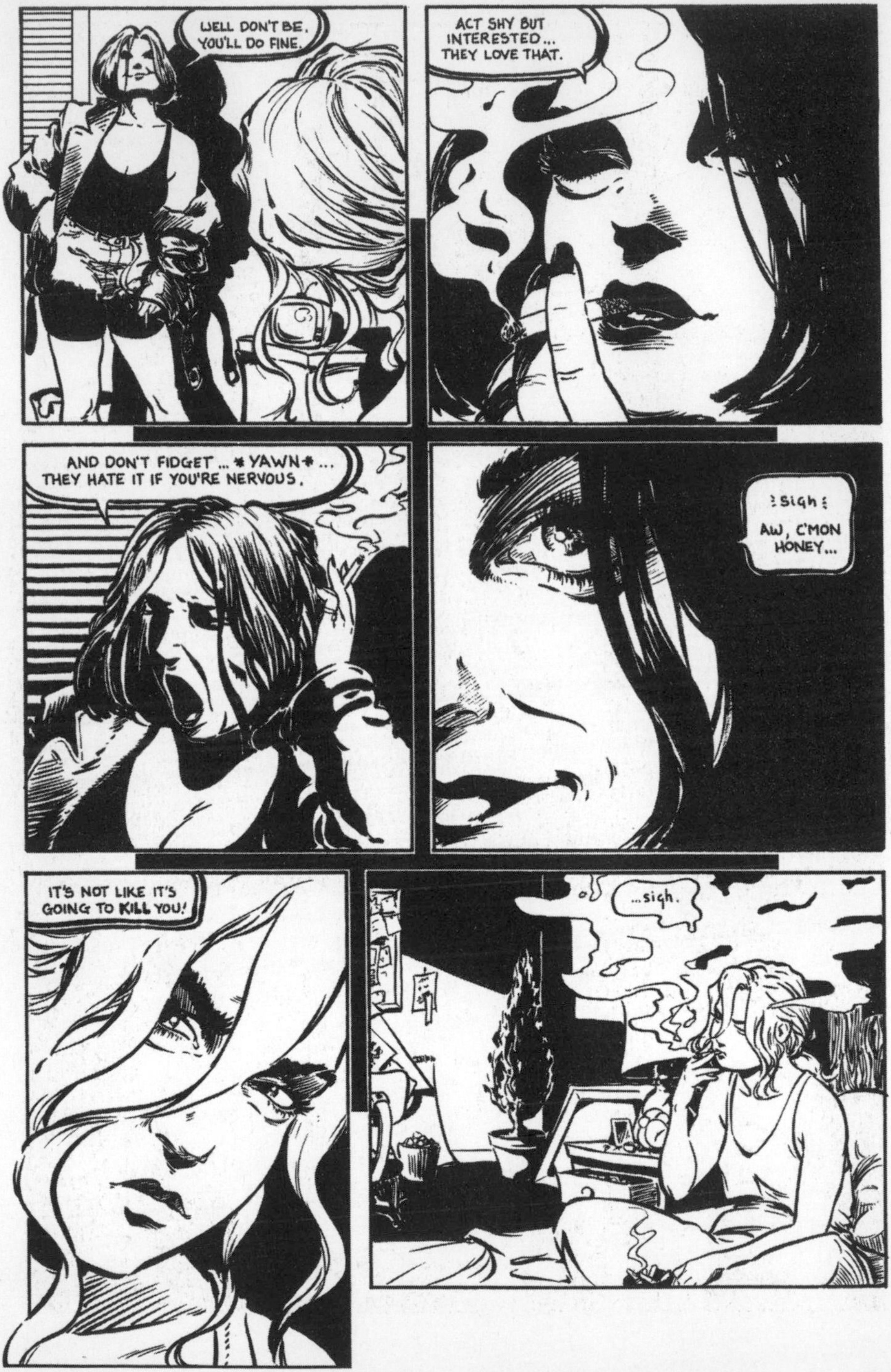
WELL DON'T BE. YOU'LL DO FINE.
ACT SHY BUT INTERESTED... THEY LOVE THAT.
AND DON'T FIDGET ... *YAWN* ... THEY HATE IT IF YOU'RE NERVOUS.
Sigh
AW, C'MON HONEY...
IT'S NOT LIKE IT'S GOING TO KILL YOU!
...sigh.

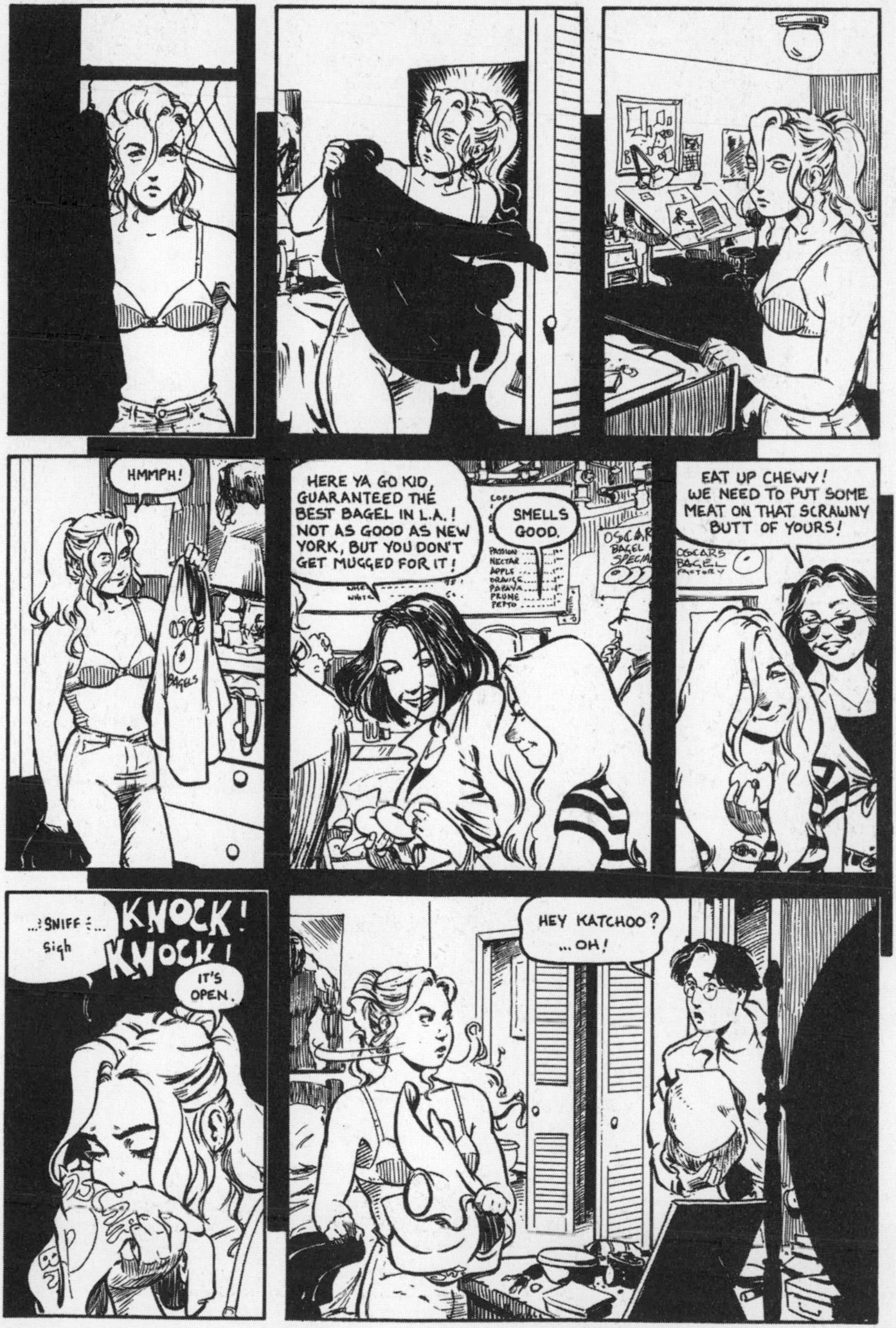
HMMPH!
HERE YA GO KID, GUARANTEED THE BEST BAGEL IN L.A.! NOT AS GOOD AS NEW YORK, BUT YOU DON'T GET MUGGED FOR IT!
SMELLS GOOD.
EAT UP CHEWY! WE NEED TO PUT SOME MEAT ON THAT SCRAWNY BUTT OF YOURS!
...SNIFF... Sigh
KNOCK! KNOCK!
IT'S OPEN.
HEY KATCHOO? ...OH!

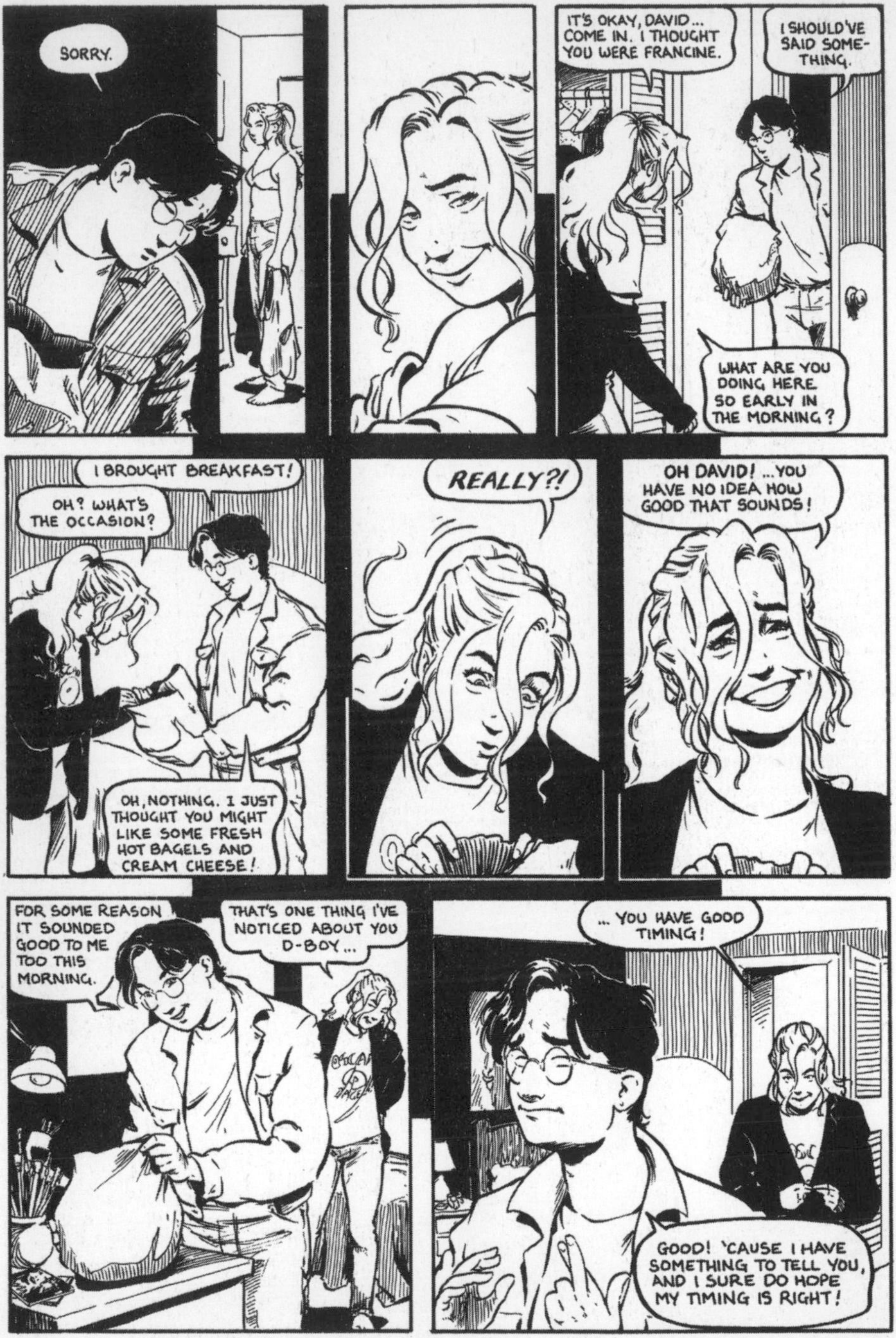
SORRY.
IT'S OKAY, DAVID... COME IN. I THOUGHT YOU WERE FRANCINE.
I SHOULD'VE SAID SOME-THING.
WHAT ARE YOU DOING HERE SO EARLY IN THE MORNING?
I BROUGHT BREAKFAST!
OH? WHAT'S THE OCCASION?
OH, NOTHING. I JUST THOUGHT YOU MIGHT LIKE SOME FRESH HOT BAGELS AND CREAM CHEESE!
REALLY?!
OH DAVID! ...YOU HAVE NO IDEA HOW GOOD THAT SOUNDS!
FOR SOME REASON IT SOUNDED GOOD TO ME TOO THIS MORNING.
THAT'S ONE THING I'VE NOTICED ABOUT YOU D-BOY...
... YOU HAVE GOOD TIMING!
GOOD! 'CAUSE I HAVE SOMETHING TO TELL YOU, AND I SURE DO HOPE MY TIMING IS RIGHT!

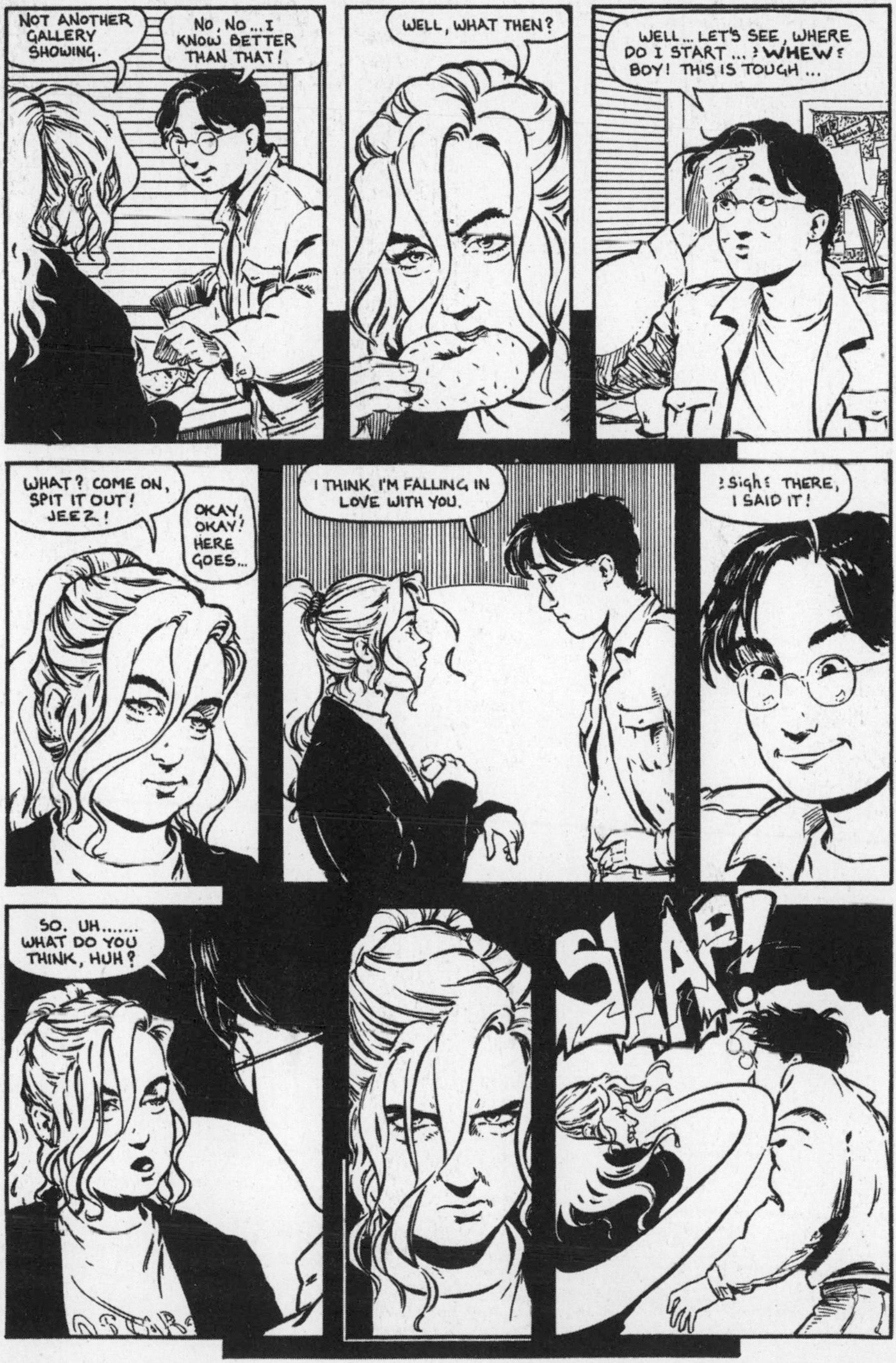
NOT ANOTHER GALLERY SHOWING.
NO, NO... I KNOW BETTER THAN THAT!
WELL, WHAT THEN?
WELL... LET'S SEE, WHERE DO I START... ⸮WHEW⸮ BOY! THIS IS TOUGH...
WHAT? COME ON, SPIT IT OUT! JEEZ!
OKAY, OKAY! HERE GOES...
I THINK I'M FALLING IN LOVE WITH YOU.
⸮Sigh⸮ THERE, I SAID IT!
SO. UH....... WHAT DO YOU THINK, HUH?
SLAP!

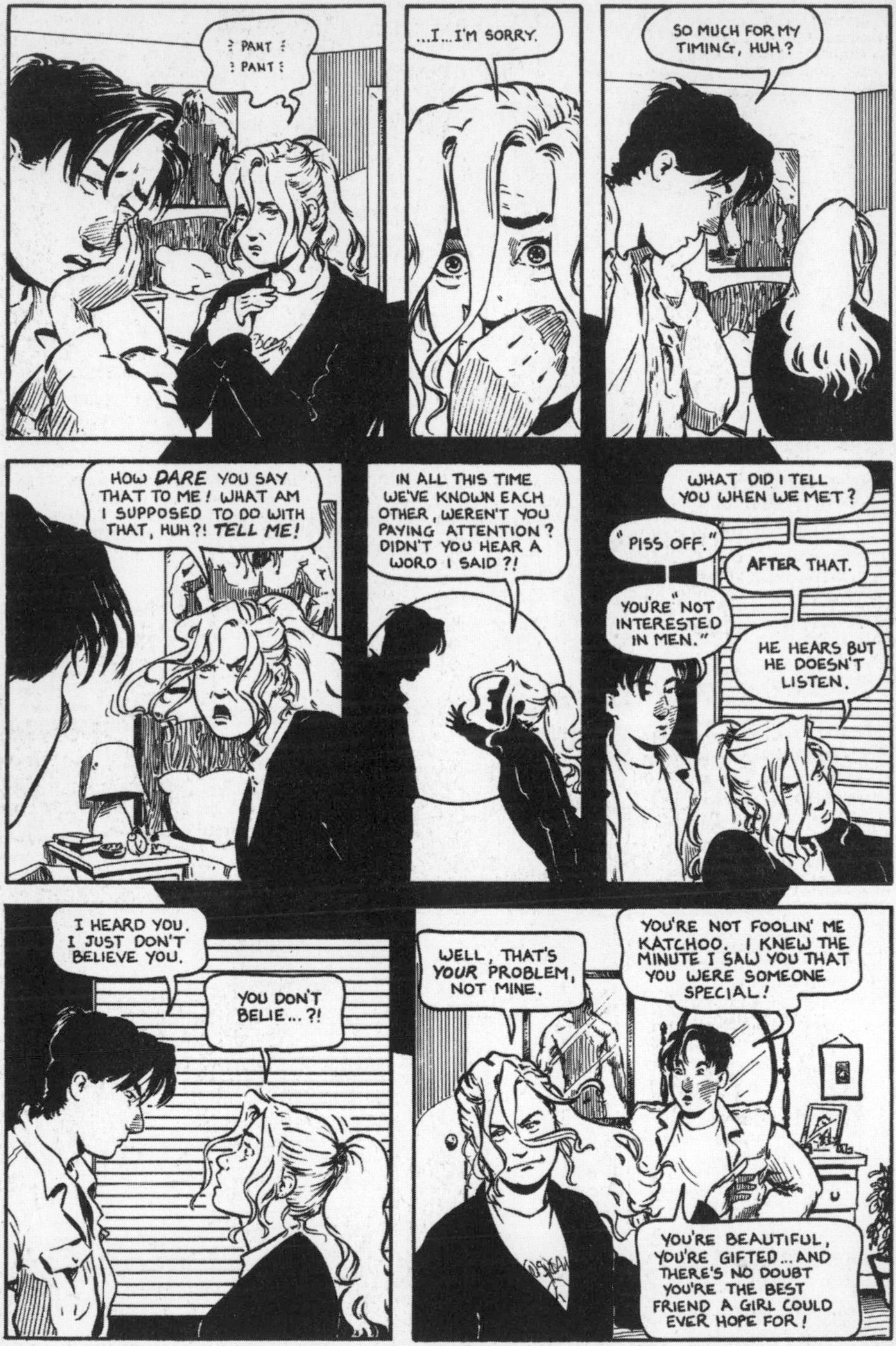

PANT
PANT
...I...I'M SORRY.
SO MUCH FOR MY TIMING, HUH?
HOW DARE YOU SAY THAT TO ME! WHAT AM I SUPPOSED TO DO WITH THAT, HUH?! TELL ME!
IN ALL THIS TIME WE'VE KNOWN EACH OTHER, WEREN'T YOU PAYING ATTENTION? DIDN'T YOU HEAR A WORD I SAID?!
WHAT DID I TELL YOU WHEN WE MET?
"PISS OFF."
AFTER THAT.
YOU'RE "NOT INTERESTED IN MEN."
HE HEARS BUT HE DOESN'T LISTEN.
I HEARD YOU. I JUST DON'T BELIEVE YOU.
YOU DON'T BELIE...?!
WELL, THAT'S YOUR PROBLEM, NOT MINE.
YOU'RE NOT FOOLIN' ME KATCHOO. I KNEW THE MINUTE I SAW YOU THAT YOU WERE SOMEONE SPECIAL!
YOU'RE BEAUTIFUL, YOU'RE GIFTED... AND THERE'S NO DOUBT YOU'RE THE BEST FRIEND A GIRL COULD EVER HOPE FOR!

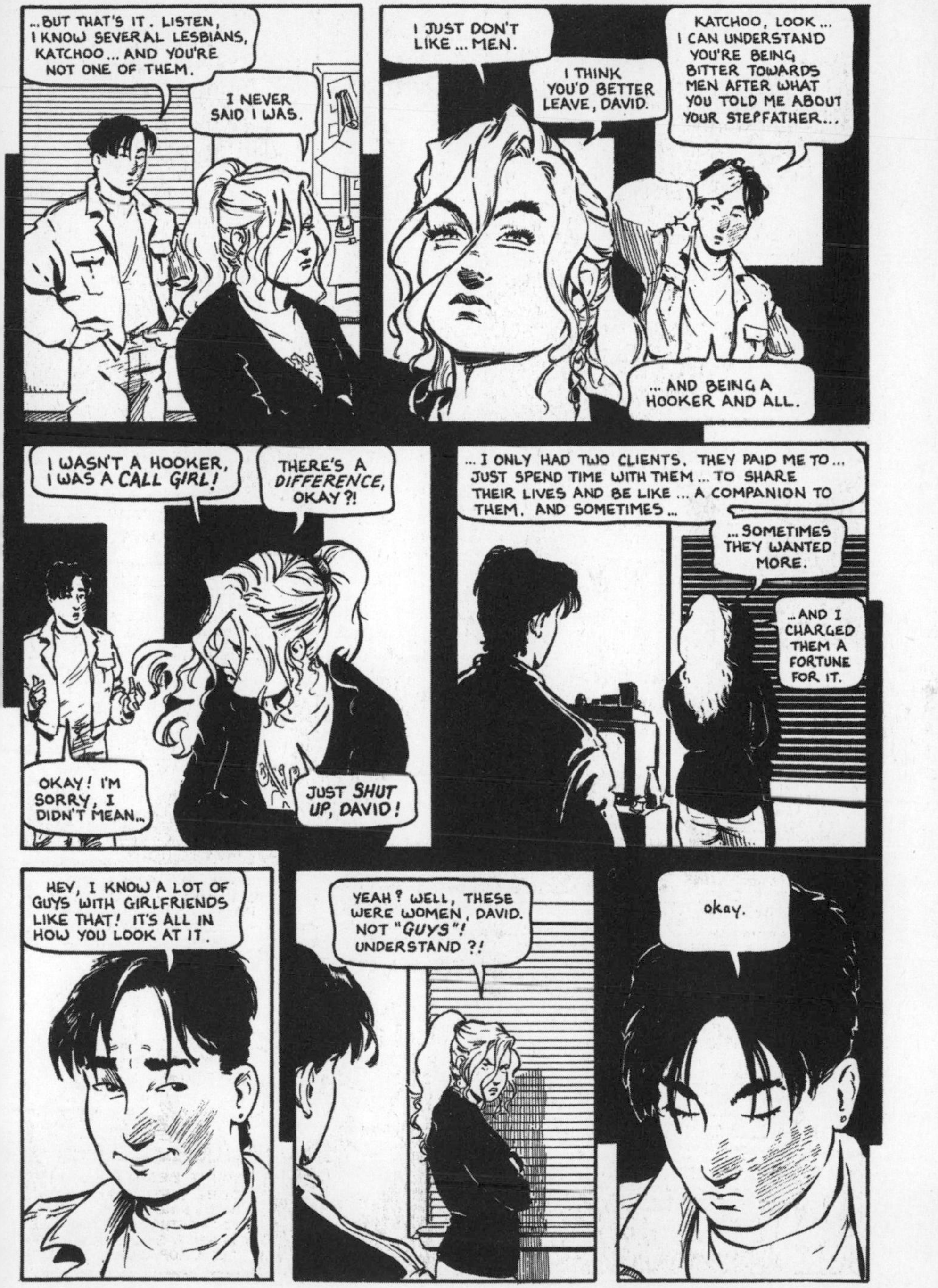
...BUT THAT'S IT. LISTEN, I KNOW SEVERAL LESBIANS, KATCHOO... AND YOU'RE NOT ONE OF THEM.
I NEVER SAID I WAS.
I JUST DON'T LIKE... MEN.
I THINK YOU'D BETTER LEAVE, DAVID.
KATCHOO, LOOK... I CAN UNDERSTAND YOU'RE BEING BITTER TOWARDS MEN AFTER WHAT YOU TOLD ME ABOUT YOUR STEPFATHER...
... AND BEING A HOOKER AND ALL.
I WASN'T A HOOKER, I WAS A *CALL GIRL!*
THERE'S A *DIFFERENCE*, OKAY?!
OKAY! I'M SORRY, I DIDN'T MEAN...
JUST *SHUT UP*, DAVID!
... I ONLY HAD TWO CLIENTS. THEY PAID ME TO... JUST SPEND TIME WITH THEM... TO SHARE THEIR LIVES AND BE LIKE... A COMPANION TO THEM. AND SOMETIMES...
... SOMETIMES THEY WANTED MORE.
... AND I CHARGED THEM A FORTUNE FOR IT.
HEY, I KNOW A LOT OF GUYS WITH GIRLFRIENDS LIKE THAT! IT'S ALL IN HOW YOU LOOK AT IT.
YEAH? WELL, THESE WERE WOMEN, DAVID. NOT "*GUYS*"! UNDERSTAND?!
okay.

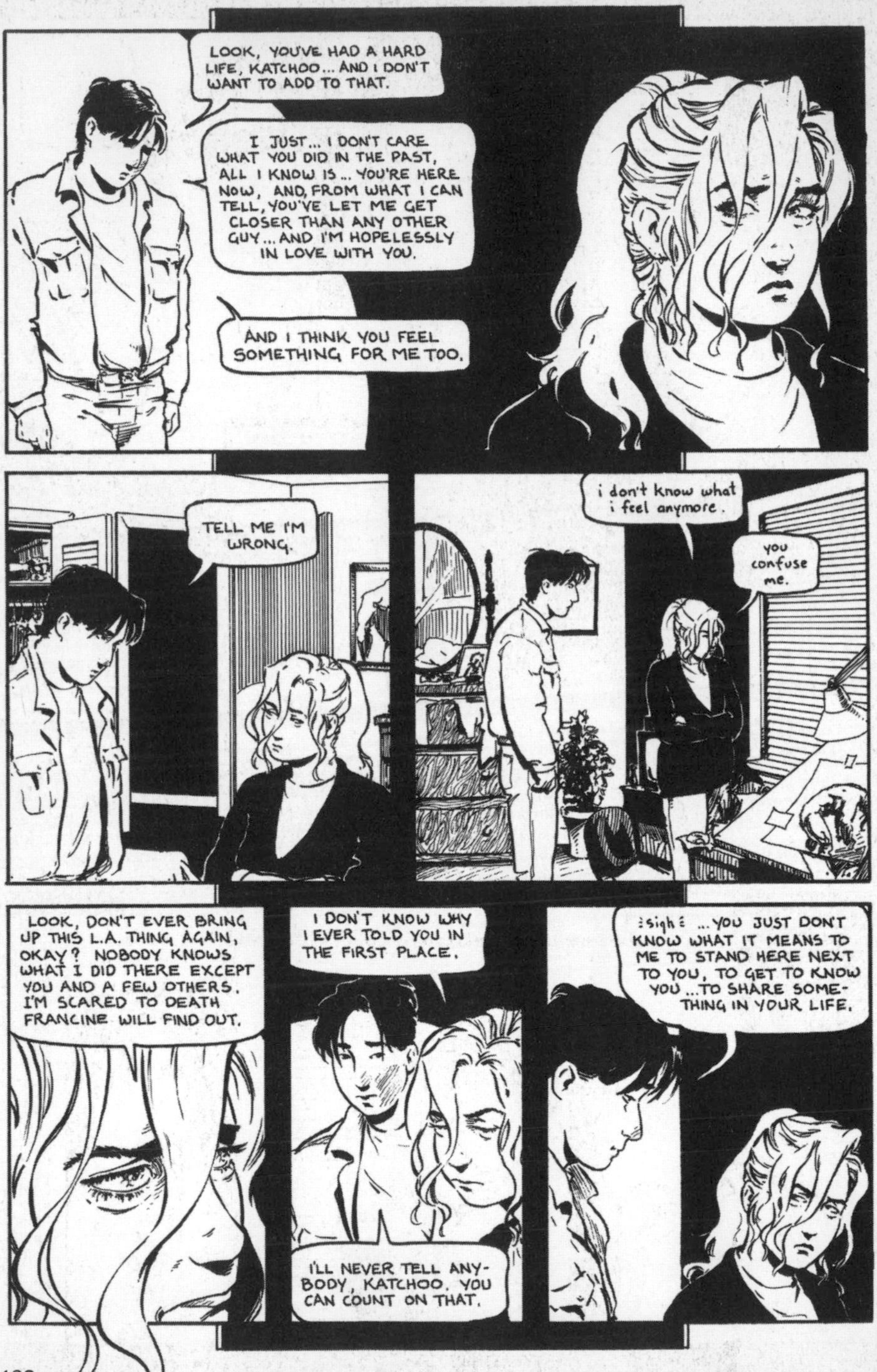
LOOK, YOU'VE HAD A HARD LIFE, KATCHOO... AND I DON'T WANT TO ADD TO THAT.
I JUST... I DON'T CARE WHAT YOU DID IN THE PAST, ALL I KNOW IS... YOU'RE HERE NOW, AND, FROM WHAT I CAN TELL, YOU'VE LET ME GET CLOSER THAN ANY OTHER GUY... AND I'M HOPELESSLY IN LOVE WITH YOU.
AND I THINK YOU FEEL SOMETHING FOR ME TOO.
TELL ME I'M WRONG.
i don't know what i feel anymore.
you confuse me.
LOOK, DON'T EVER BRING UP THIS L.A. THING AGAIN, OKAY? NOBODY KNOWS WHAT I DID THERE EXCEPT YOU AND A FEW OTHERS. I'M SCARED TO DEATH FRANCINE WILL FIND OUT.
I DON'T KNOW WHY I EVER TOLD YOU IN THE FIRST PLACE.
I'LL NEVER TELL ANYBODY, KATCHOO. YOU CAN COUNT ON THAT.
:sigh: ...YOU JUST DON'T KNOW WHAT IT MEANS TO ME TO STAND HERE NEXT TO YOU, TO GET TO KNOW YOU... TO SHARE SOMETHING IN YOUR LIFE.

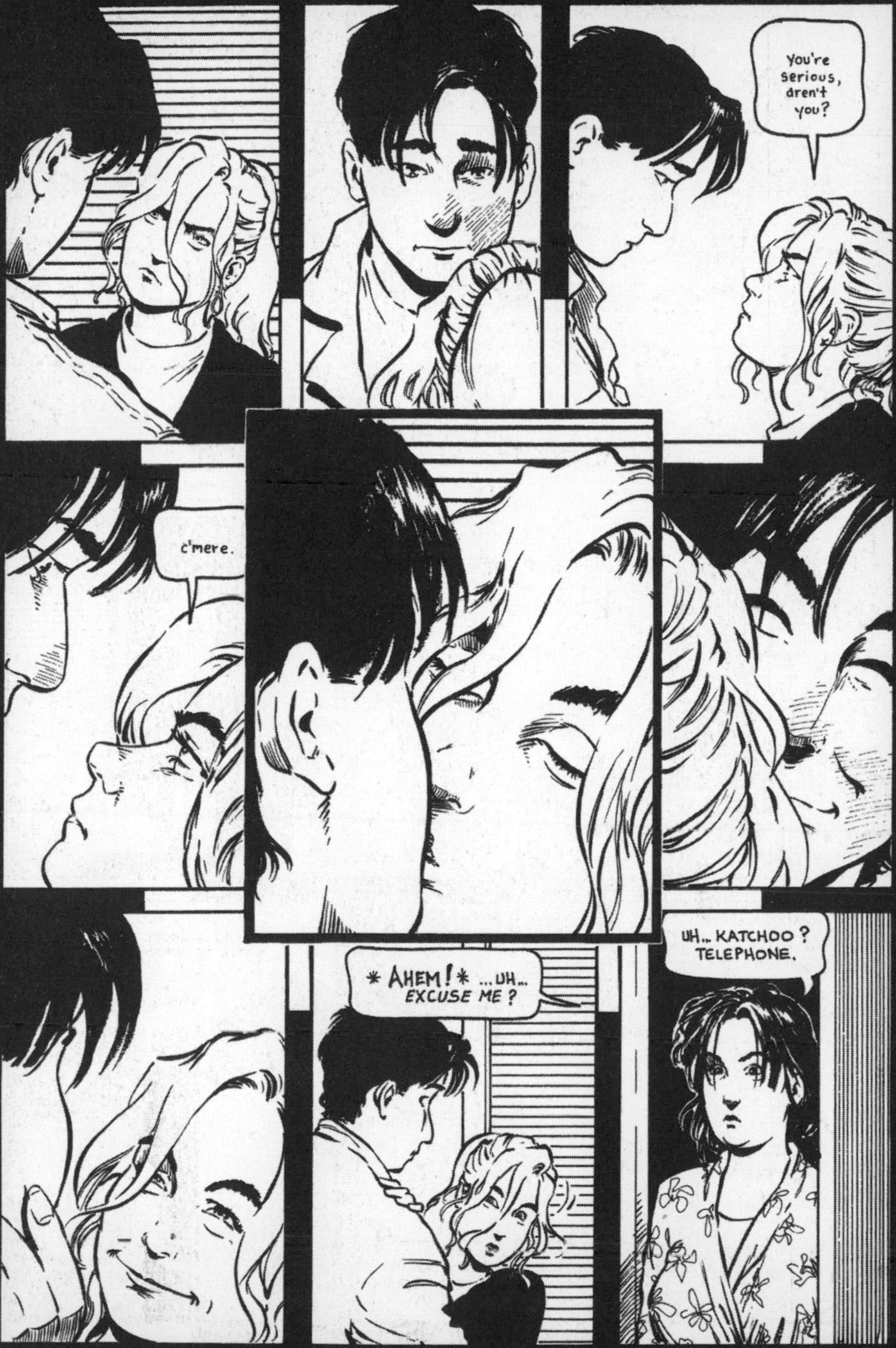
You're serious, aren't you?
c'mere.
AHEM! ...UH... EXCUSE ME?
UH... KATCHOO? TELEPHONE.

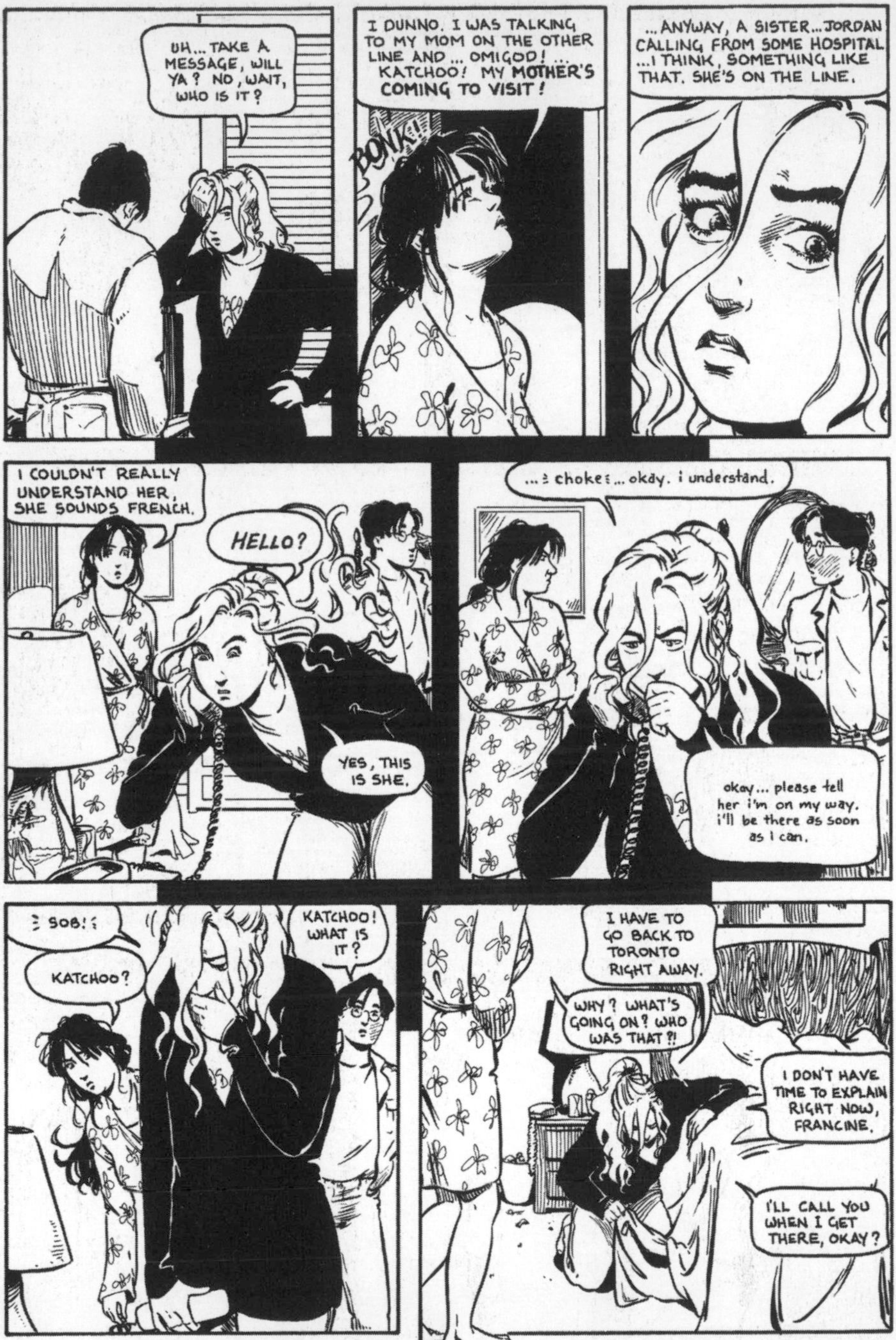

UH... TAKE A MESSAGE, WILL YA? NO, WAIT, WHO IS IT?
I DUNNO. I WAS TALKING TO MY MOM ON THE OTHER LINE AND ... OMIGOD! ... KATCHOO! MY MOTHER'S COMING TO VISIT!
BONK!!
...ANYWAY, A SISTER...JORDAN CALLING FROM SOME HOSPITAL ...I THINK, SOMETHING LIKE THAT. SHE'S ON THE LINE.
I COULDN'T REALLY UNDERSTAND HER, SHE SOUNDS FRENCH.
HELLO?
YES, THIS IS SHE.
...: choke:... okay. i understand.
okay... please tell her i'm on my way. i'll be there as soon as i can.
: SOB! :
KATCHOO?
KATCHOO! WHAT IS IT?
I HAVE TO GO BACK TO TORONTO RIGHT AWAY.
WHY? WHAT'S GOING ON? WHO WAS THAT?!
I DON'T HAVE TIME TO EXPLAIN RIGHT NOW, FRANCINE.
I'LL CALL YOU WHEN I GET THERE, OKAY?

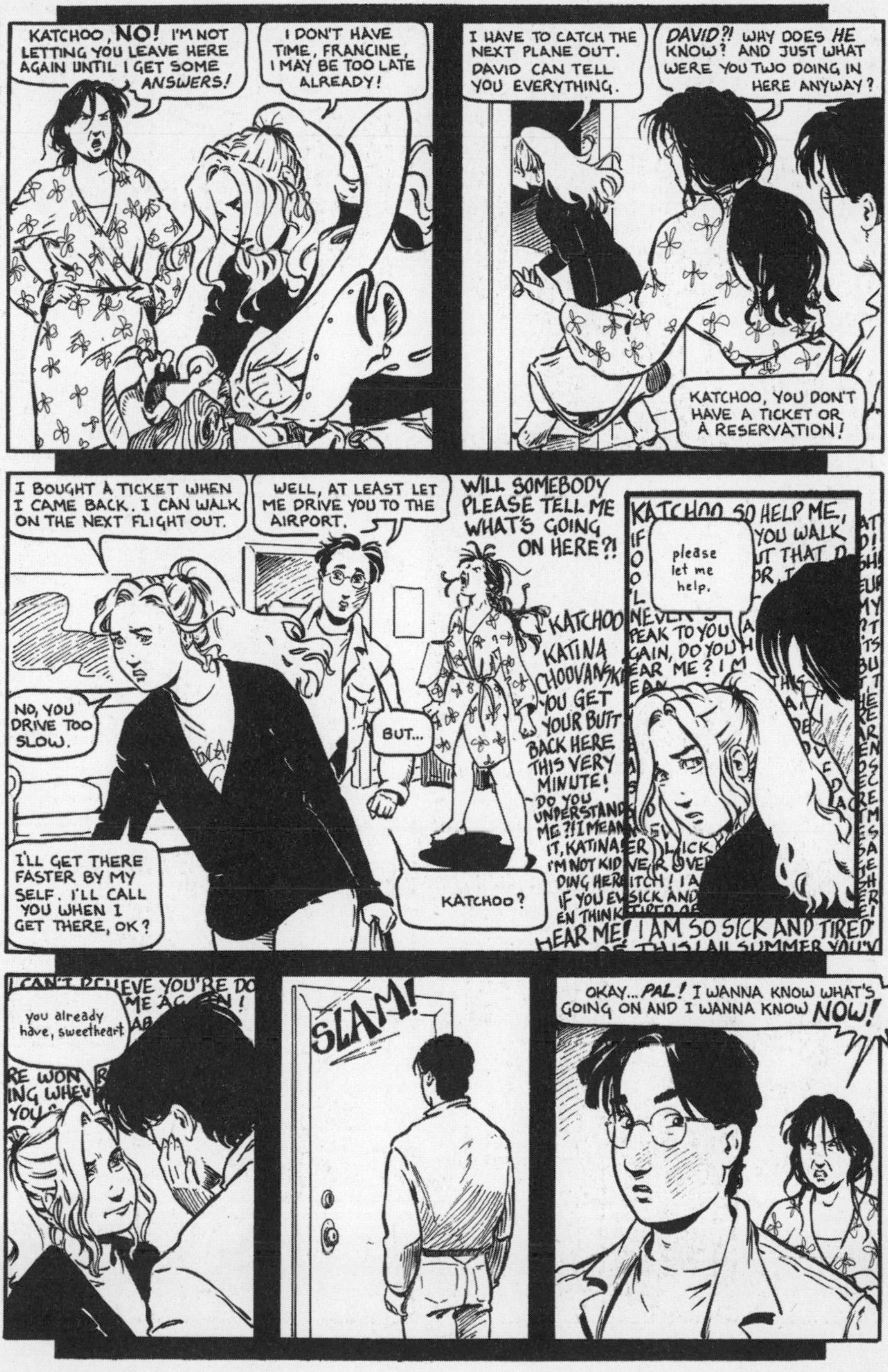

KATCHOO, NO! I'M NOT LETTING YOU LEAVE HERE AGAIN UNTIL I GET SOME ANSWERS!
I DON'T HAVE TIME, FRANCINE, I MAY BE TOO LATE ALREADY!
I HAVE TO CATCH THE NEXT PLANE OUT. DAVID CAN TELL YOU EVERYTHING.
DAVID?! WHY DOES HE KNOW? AND JUST WHAT WERE YOU TWO DOING IN HERE ANYWAY?
KATCHOO, YOU DON'T HAVE A TICKET OR A RESERVATION!
I BOUGHT A TICKET WHEN I CAME BACK. I CAN WALK ON THE NEXT FLIGHT OUT.
WELL, AT LEAST LET ME DRIVE YOU TO THE AIRPORT.
WILL SOMEBODY PLEASE TELL ME WHAT'S GOING ON HERE?!
NO, YOU DRIVE TOO SLOW.
BUT...
I'LL GET THERE FASTER BY MY SELF. I'LL CALL YOU WHEN I GET THERE, OK?
KATCHOO?
KATCHOO KATINA CHOOVANSKI YOU GET YOUR BUTT BACK HERE THIS VERY MINUTE!
please let me help.
I AM SO SICK AND TIRED
you already have, sweetheart
SLAM!
OKAY... PAL! I WANNA KNOW WHAT'S GOING ON AND I WANNA KNOW NOW!

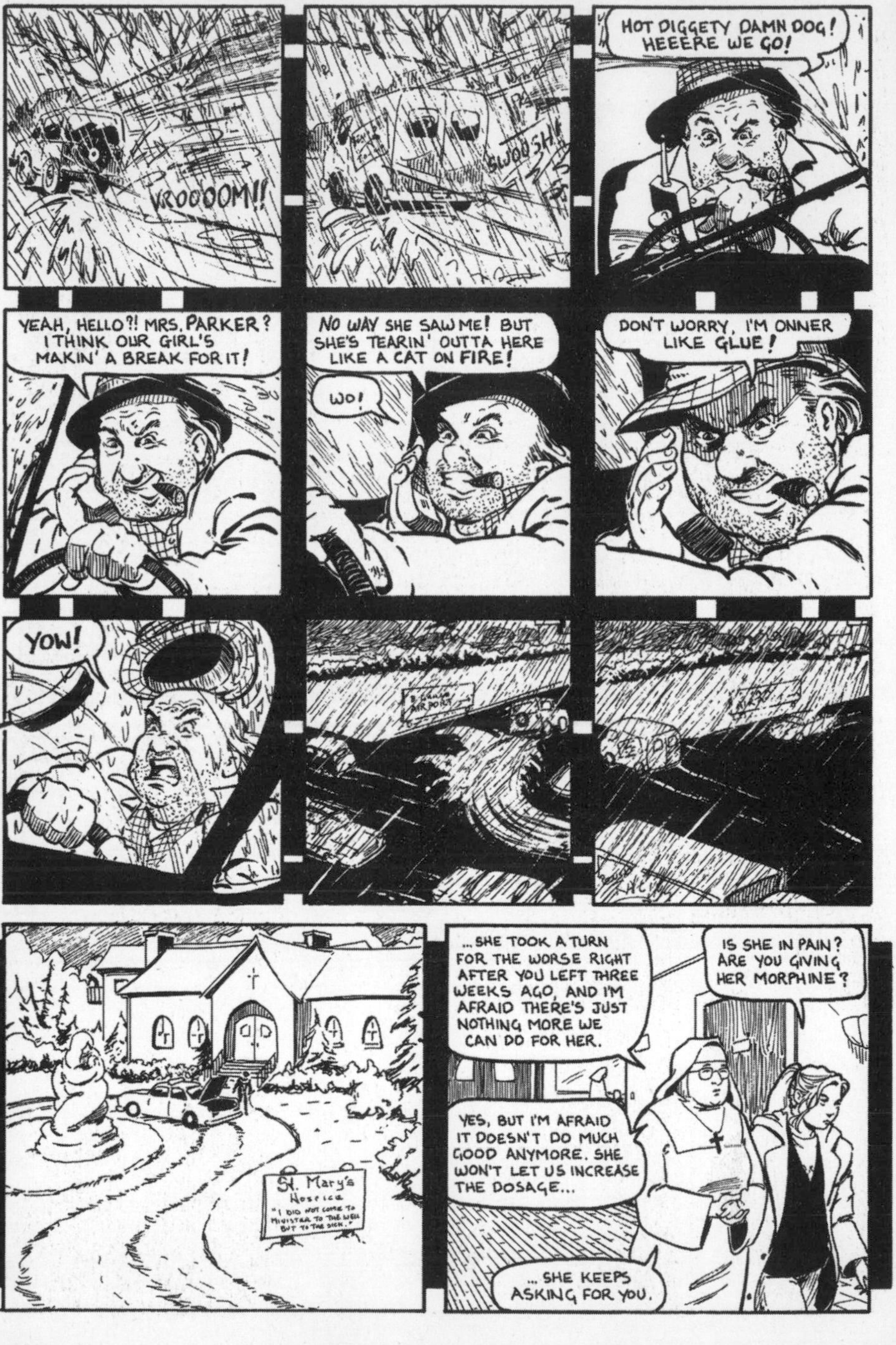
VROOOOM!!
SWOOSH!
HOT DIGGETY DAMN DOG! HEEERE WE GO!
YEAH, HELLO?! MRS. PARKER? I THINK OUR GIRL'S MAKIN' A BREAK FOR IT!
NO WAY SHE SAW ME! BUT SHE'S TEARIN' OUTTA HERE LIKE A CAT ON FIRE!
WO!
DON'T WORRY, I'M ONNER LIKE GLUE!
YOW!
St. Mary's
Hospice
"I DID NOT COME TO MINISTER TO THE WELL BUT TO THE SICK."
...SHE TOOK A TURN FOR THE WORSE RIGHT AFTER YOU LEFT THREE WEEKS AGO, AND I'M AFRAID THERE'S JUST NOTHING MORE WE CAN DO FOR HER.
IS SHE IN PAIN? ARE YOU GIVING HER MORPHINE?
YES, BUT I'M AFRAID IT DOESN'T DO MUCH GOOD ANYMORE. SHE WON'T LET US INCREASE THE DOSAGE...
...SHE KEEPS ASKING FOR YOU.

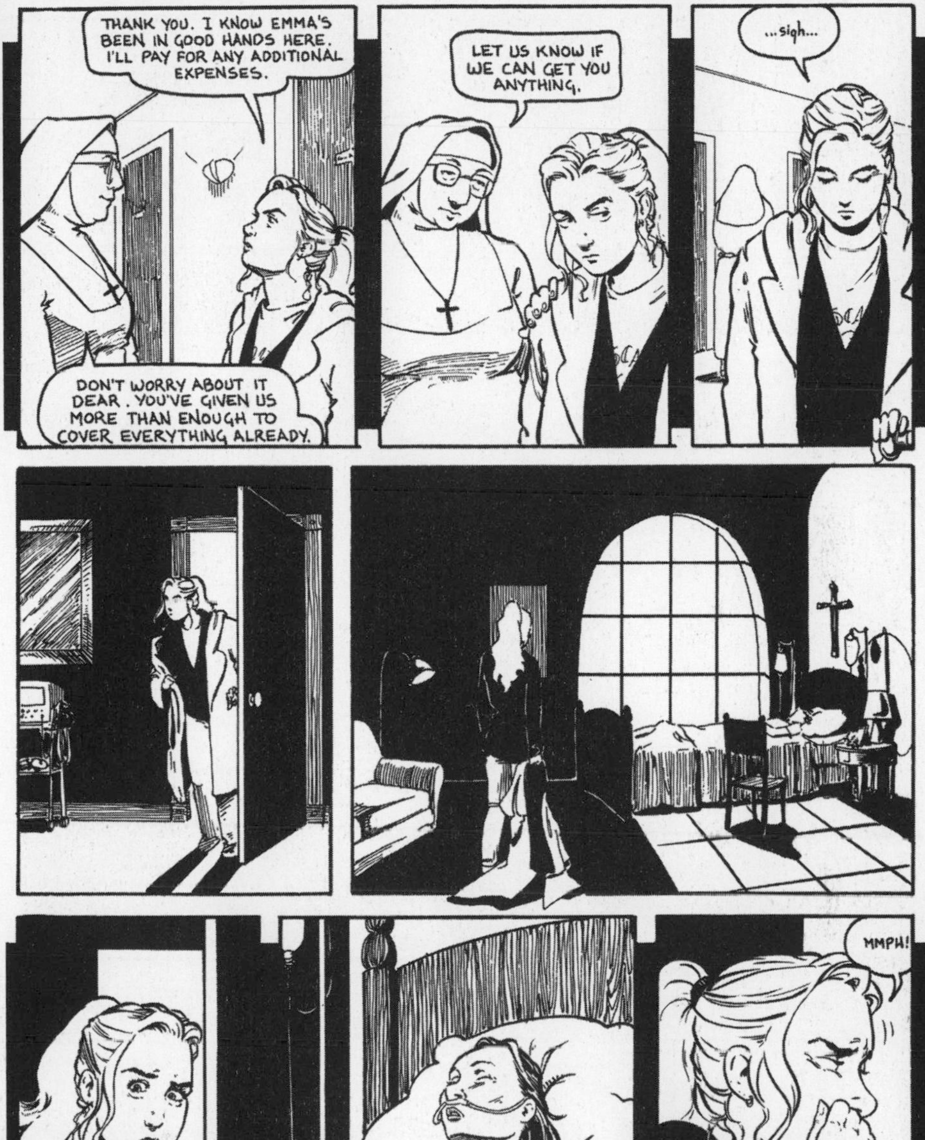
THANK YOU. I KNOW EMMA'S BEEN IN GOOD HANDS HERE. I'LL PAY FOR ANY ADDITIONAL EXPENSES.
DON'T WORRY ABOUT IT DEAR. YOU'VE GIVEN US MORE THAN ENOUGH TO COVER EVERYTHING ALREADY.
LET US KNOW IF WE CAN GET YOU ANYTHING.
...sigh...
MMPH!

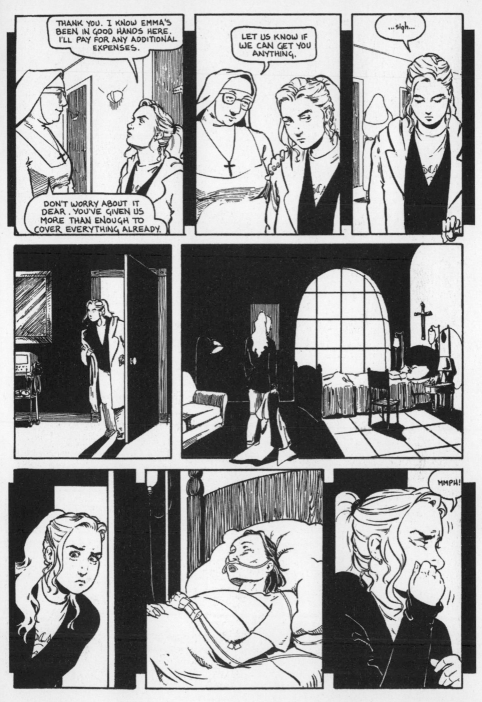

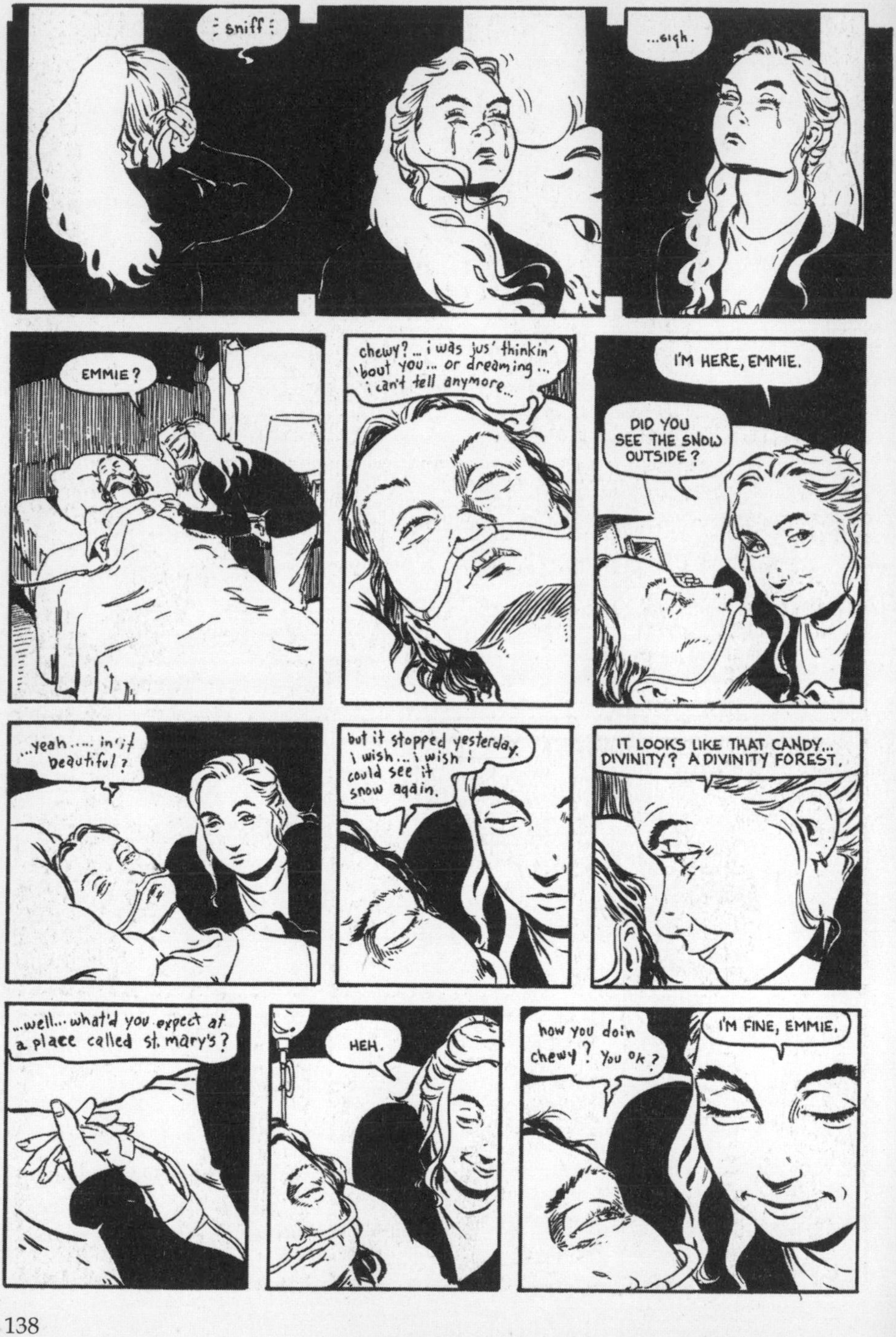
sniff
...sigh.
EMMIE?
chewy? ... i was jus' thinkin' 'bout you... or dreaming... i can't tell anymore...
I'M HERE, EMMIE.
DID YOU SEE THE SNOW OUTSIDE?
...yeah..... in'it beautiful?
but it stopped yesterday. i wish... i wish i could see it snow again.
IT LOOKS LIKE THAT CANDY... DIVINITY? A DIVINITY FOREST.
...well... what'd you expect at a place called st. mary's?
HEH.
how you doin chewy? You ok?
I'M FINE, EMMIE.

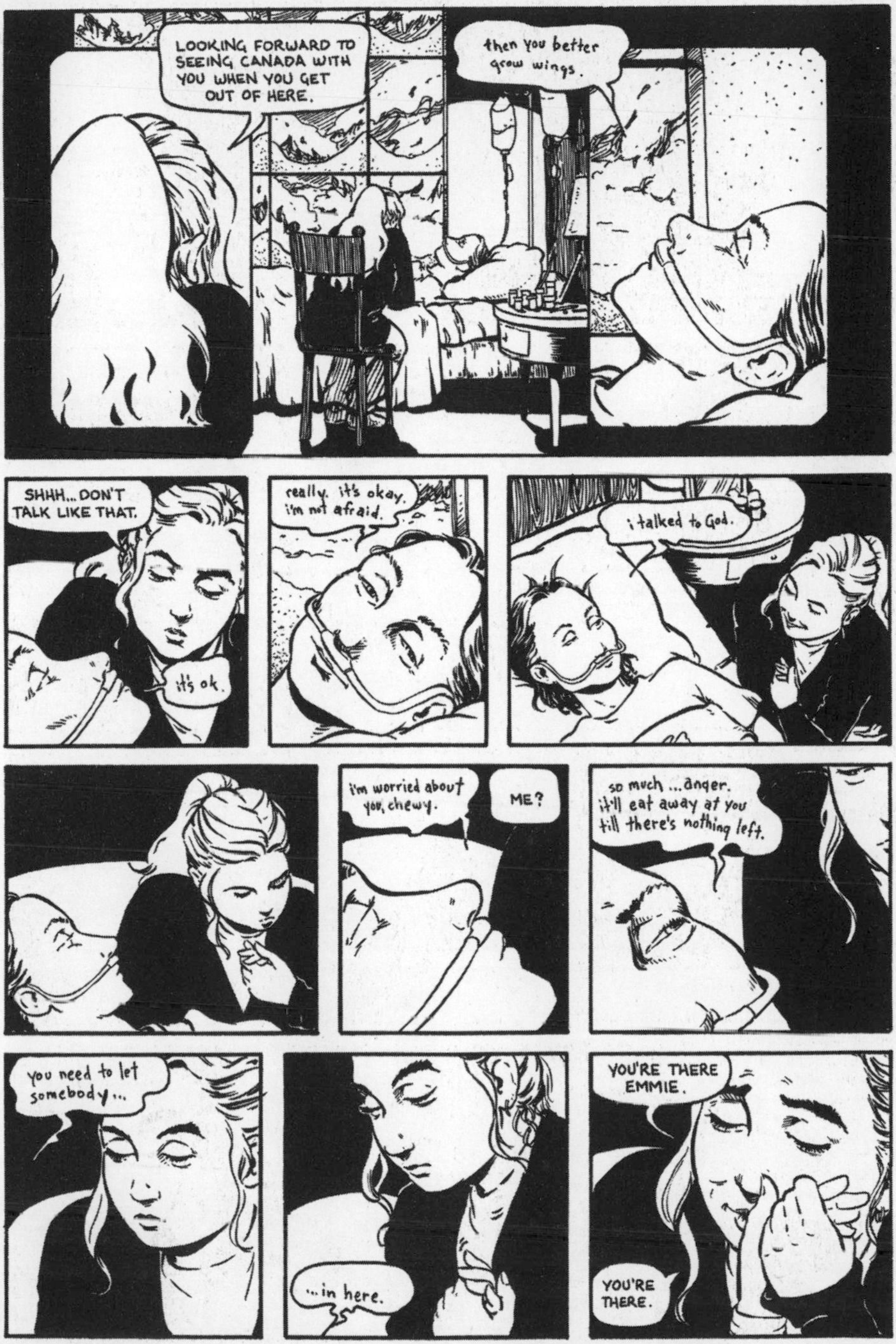

LOOKING FORWARD TO SEEING CANADA WITH YOU WHEN YOU GET OUT OF HERE.
then you better grow wings.
SHHH... DON'T TALK LIKE THAT.
it's ok.
really. it's okay. i'm not afraid.
i talked to God.
i'm worried about you, chewy.
ME?
so much ... anger. it'll eat away at you till there's nothing left.
you need to let somebody...
...in here.
YOU'RE THERE EMMIE.
YOU'RE THERE.

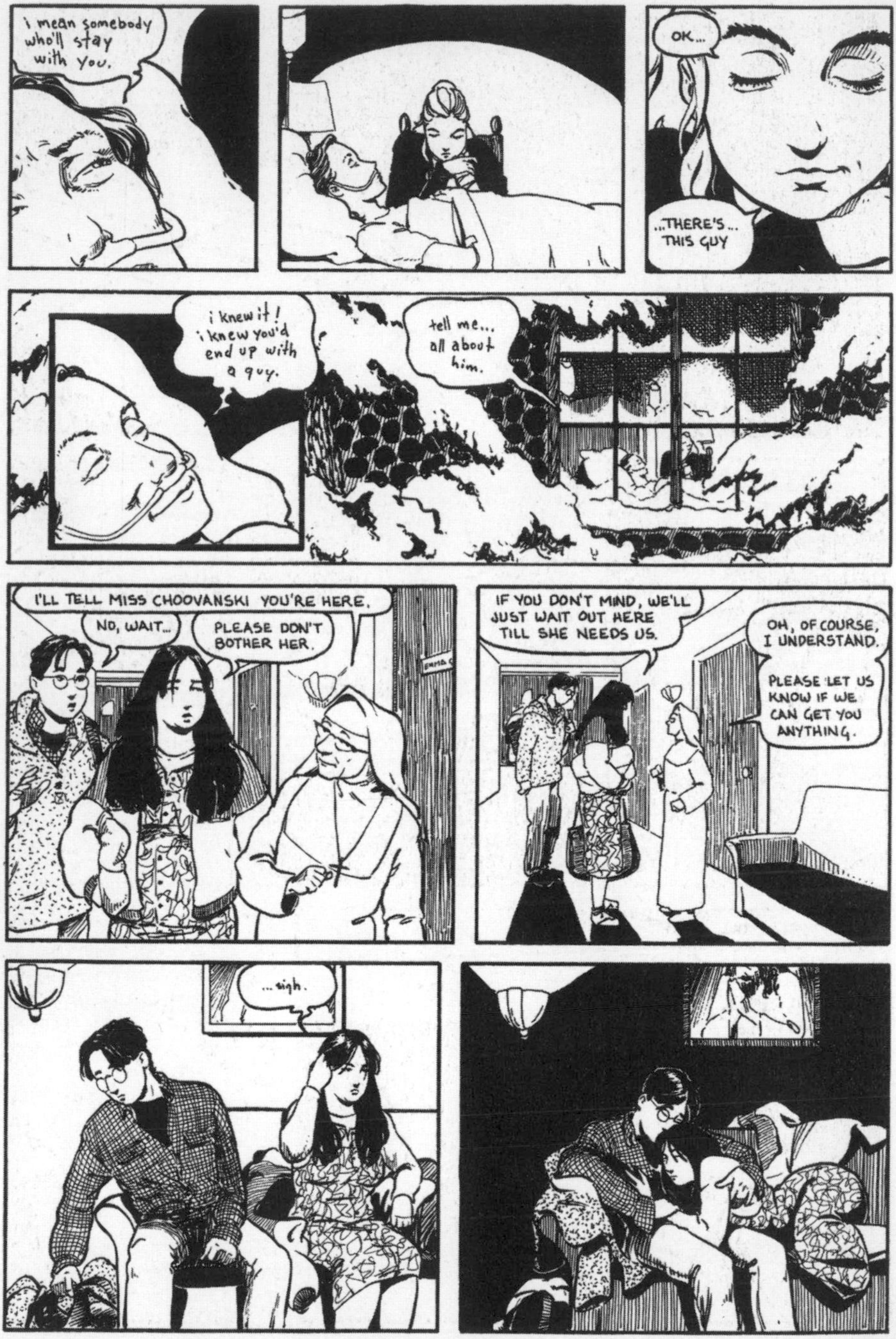
i mean somebody who'll stay with you.
OK...
...THERE'S... THIS GUY
i knew it! i knew you'd end up with a guy.
tell me... all about him.
I'LL TELL MISS CHOOVANSKI YOU'RE HERE.
NO, WAIT...
PLEASE DON'T BOTHER HER.
IF YOU DON'T MIND, WE'LL JUST WAIT OUT HERE TILL SHE NEEDS US.
OH, OF COURSE, I UNDERSTAND.
PLEASE LET US KNOW IF WE CAN GET YOU ANYTHING.
...sigh.

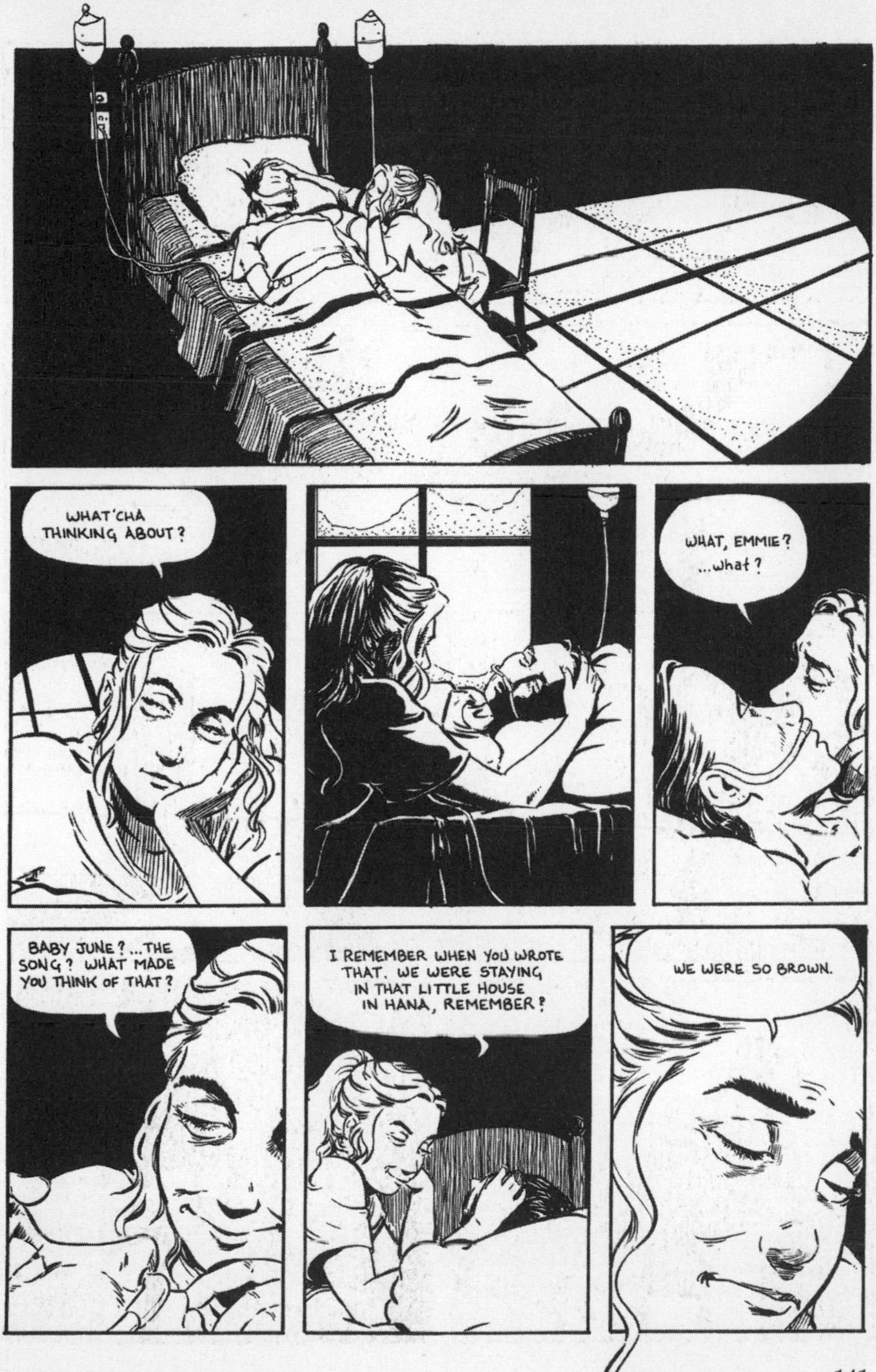
WHAT'CHA THINKING ABOUT?
WHAT, EMMIE? ...what?
BABY JUNE? ...THE SONG? WHAT MADE YOU THINK OF THAT?
I REMEMBER WHEN YOU WROTE THAT. WE WERE STAYING IN THAT LITTLE HOUSE IN HANA, REMEMBER?
WE WERE SO BROWN.

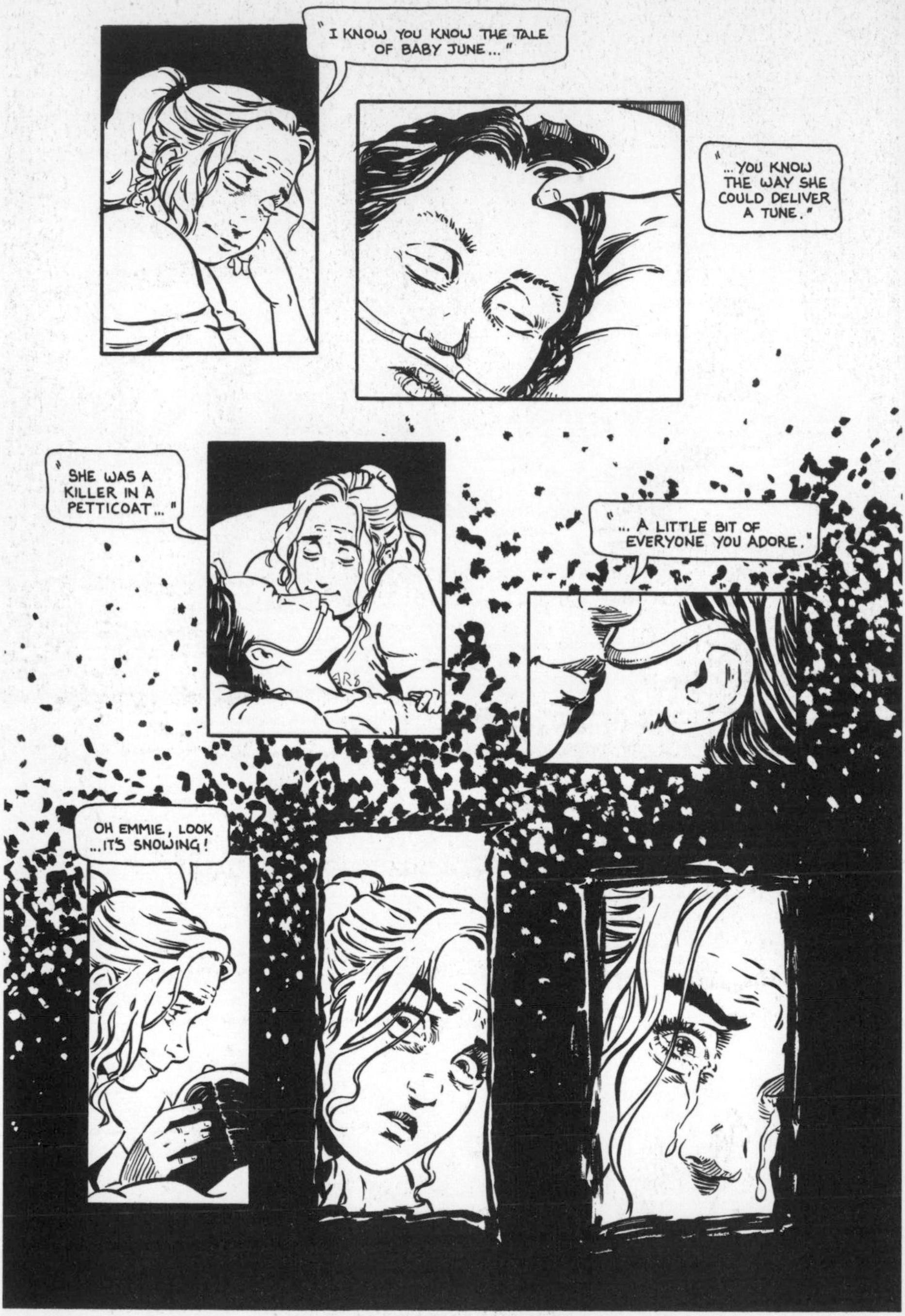
"I KNOW YOU KNOW THE TALE OF BABY JUNE..."
"...YOU KNOW THE WAY SHE COULD DELIVER A TUNE."
"SHE WAS A KILLER IN A PETTICOAT..."
"... A LITTLE BIT OF EVERYONE YOU ADORE."
OH EMMIE, LOOK ...IT'S SNOWING!

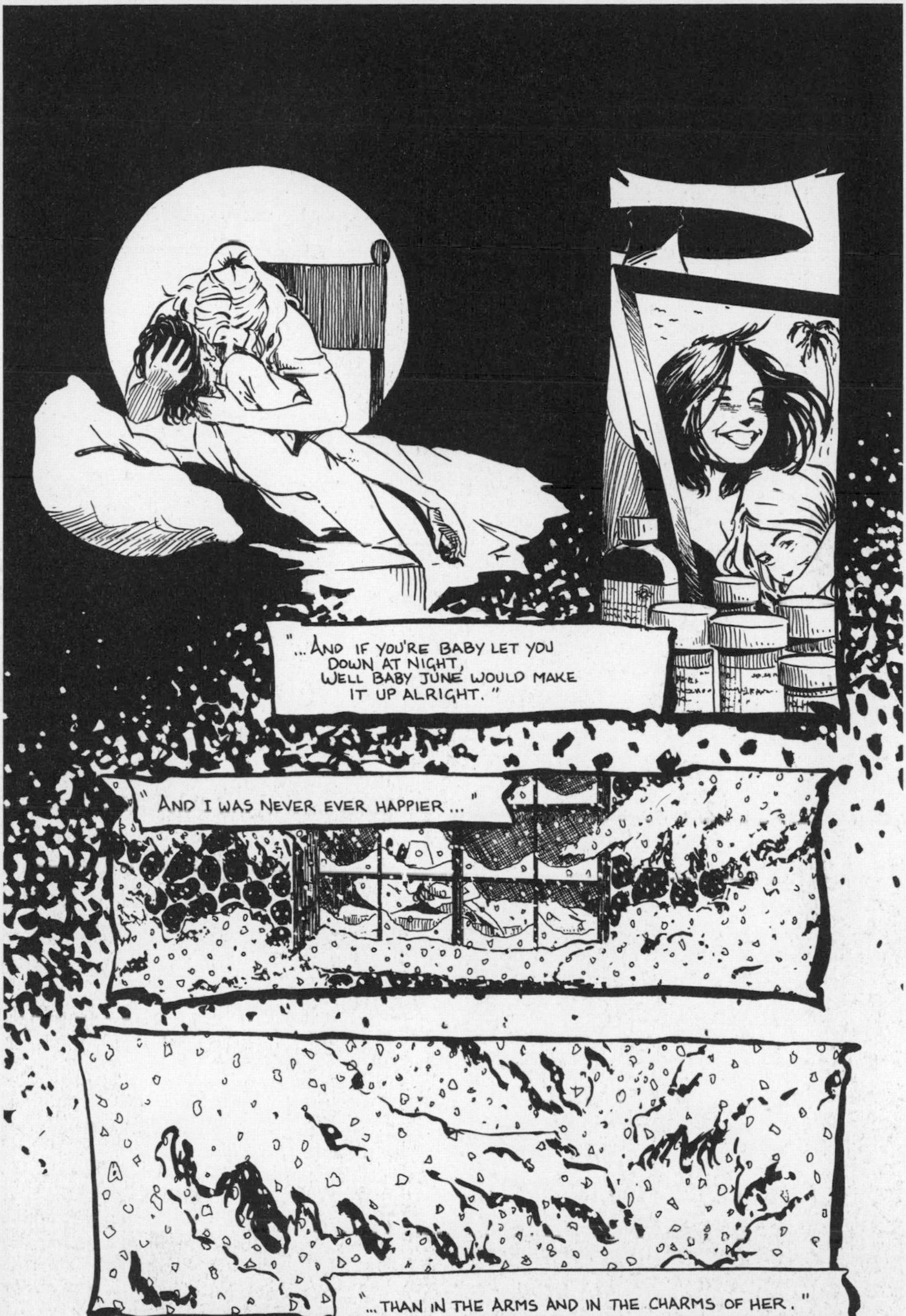
"... AND IF YOU'RE BABY LET YOU DOWN AT NIGHT, WELL BABY JUNE WOULD MAKE IT UP ALRIGHT."
"AND I WAS NEVER EVER HAPPIER ..."
"... THAN IN THE ARMS AND IN THE CHARMS OF HER."

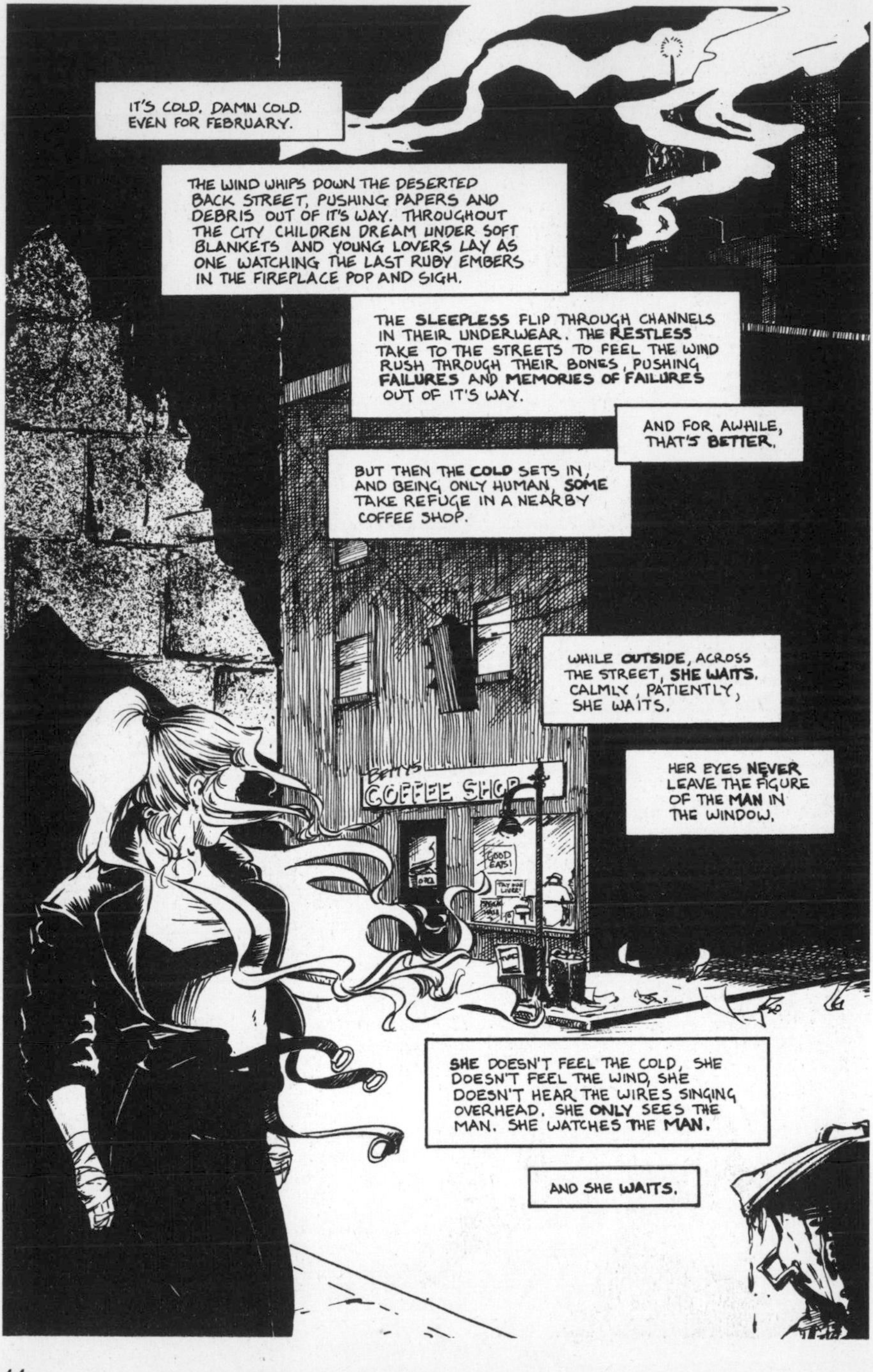
IT'S COLD. DAMN COLD. EVEN FOR FEBRUARY.
THE WIND WHIPS DOWN THE DESERTED BACK STREET, PUSHING PAPERS AND DEBRIS OUT OF IT'S WAY. THROUGHOUT THE CITY CHILDREN DREAM UNDER SOFT BLANKETS AND YOUNG LOVERS LAY AS ONE WATCHING THE LAST RUBY EMBERS IN THE FIREPLACE POP AND SIGH.
THE SLEEPLESS FLIP THROUGH CHANNELS IN THEIR UNDERWEAR. THE RESTLESS TAKE TO THE STREETS TO FEEL THE WIND RUSH THROUGH THEIR BONES, PUSHING FAILURES AND MEMORIES OF FAILURES OUT OF IT'S WAY.
AND FOR AWHILE, THAT'S BETTER.
BUT THEN THE COLD SETS IN, AND BEING ONLY HUMAN, SOME TAKE REFUGE IN A NEARBY COFFEE SHOP.
WHILE OUTSIDE, ACROSS THE STREET, SHE WAITS. CALMLY, PATIENTLY, SHE WAITS.
BETTY'S COFFEE SHOP
GOOD EATS!
HER EYES NEVER LEAVE THE FIGURE OF THE MAN IN THE WINDOW.
SHE DOESN'T FEEL THE COLD, SHE DOESN'T FEEL THE WIND, SHE DOESN'T HEAR THE WIRES SINGING OVERHEAD. SHE ONLY SEES THE MAN. SHE WATCHES THE MAN.
AND SHE WAITS.

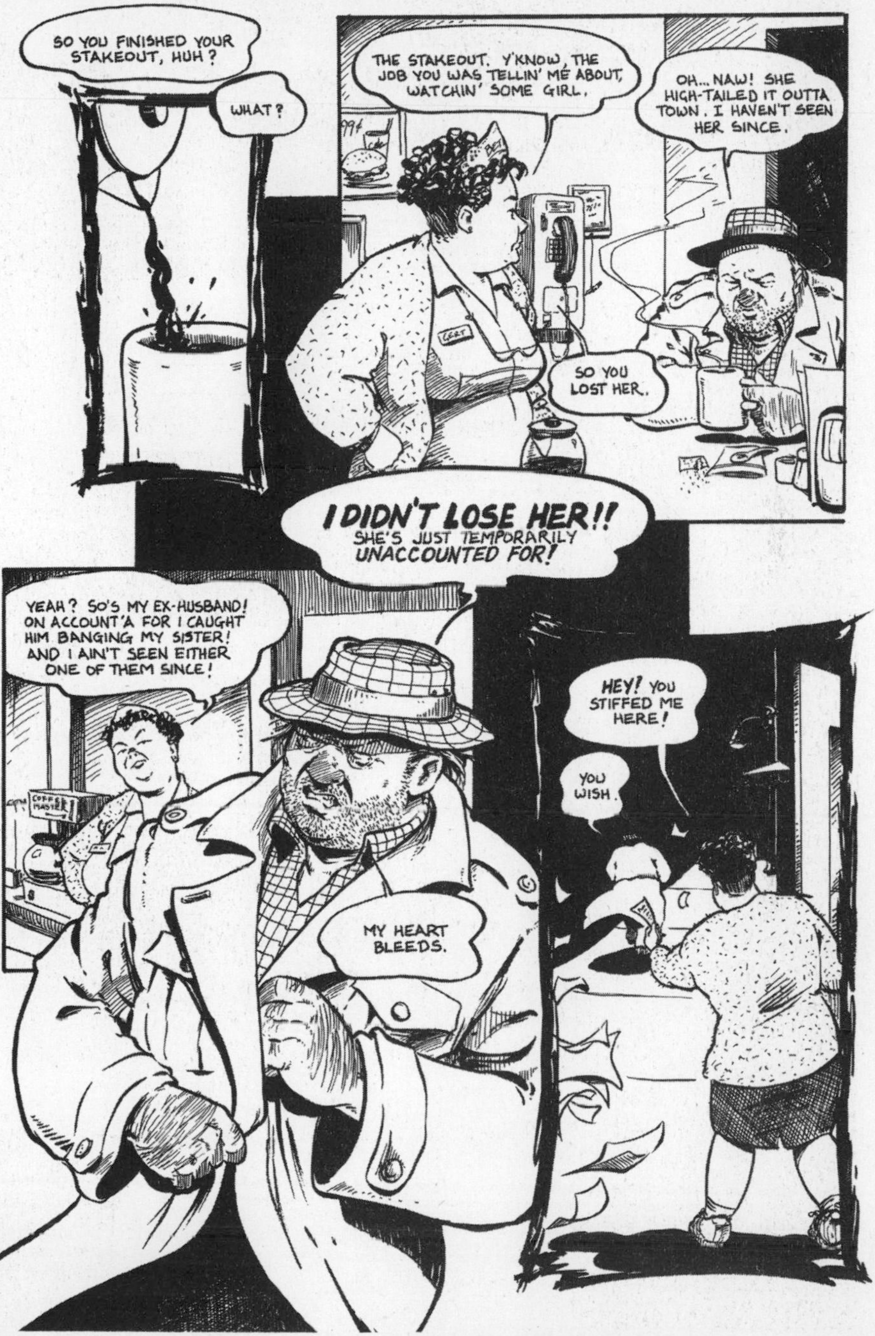
SO YOU FINISHED YOUR STAKEOUT, HUH?
WHAT?
THE STAKEOUT. Y'KNOW, THE JOB YOU WAS TELLIN' ME ABOUT, WATCHIN' SOME GIRL.
OH... NAW! SHE HIGH-TAILED IT OUTTA TOWN. I HAVEN'T SEEN HER SINCE.
GERT
SO YOU LOST HER.
I DIDN'T LOSE HER!! SHE'S JUST TEMPORARILY UNACCOUNTED FOR!
YEAH? SO'S MY EX-HUSBAND! ON ACCOUNT'A FOR I CAUGHT HIM BANGING MY SISTER! AND I AIN'T SEEN EITHER ONE OF THEM SINCE!
MY HEART BLEEDS.
HEY! YOU STIFFED ME HERE!
YOU WISH.

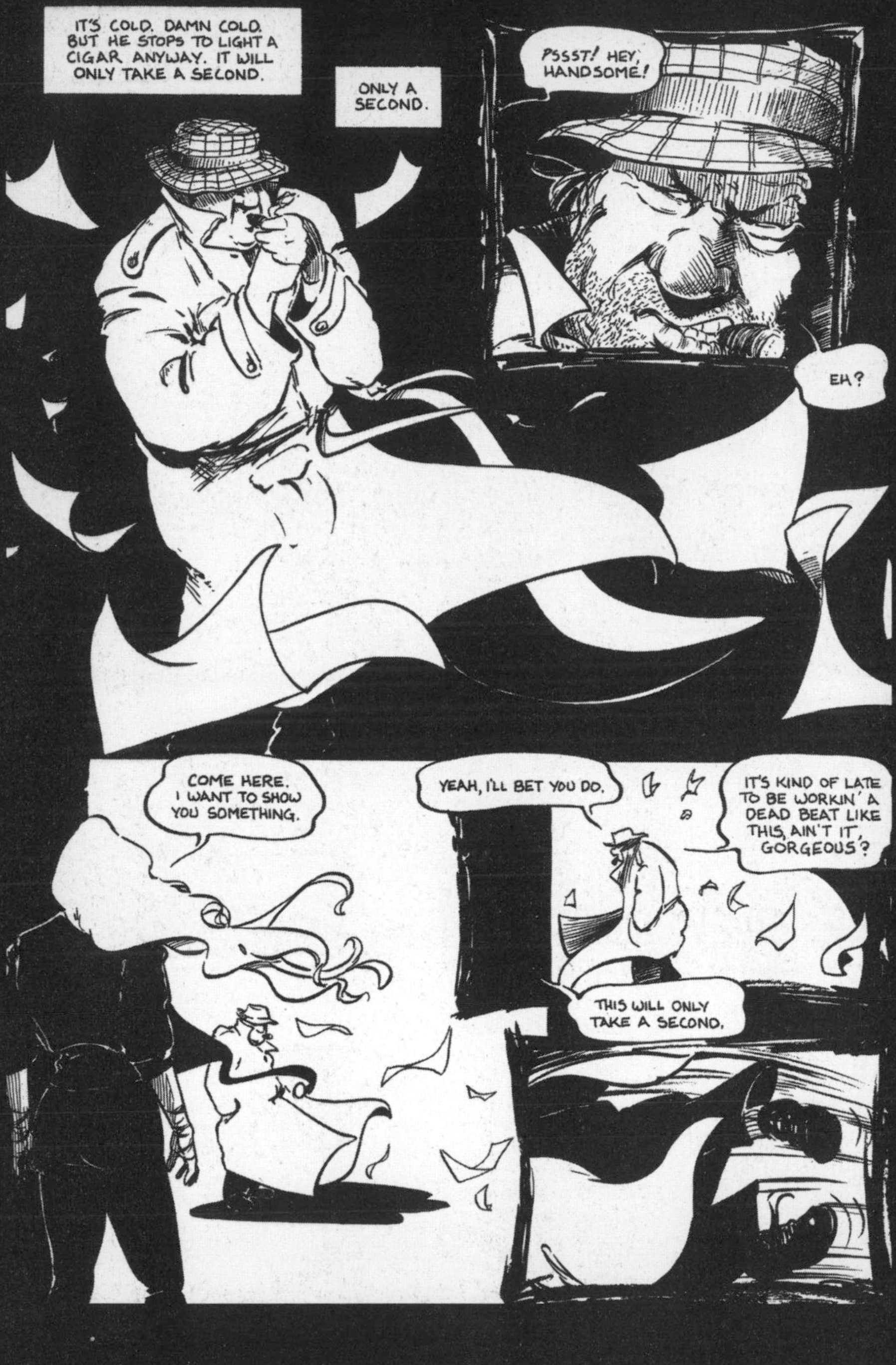
IT'S COLD. DAMN COLD. BUT HE STOPS TO LIGHT A CIGAR ANYWAY. IT WILL ONLY TAKE A SECOND.
ONLY A SECOND.
PSSST! HEY, HANDSOME!
EH?
COME HERE. I WANT TO SHOW YOU SOMETHING.
YEAH, I'LL BET YOU DO.
IT'S KIND OF LATE TO BE WORKIN' A DEAD BEAT LIKE THIS, AIN'T IT, GORGEOUS?
THIS WILL ONLY TAKE A SECOND.

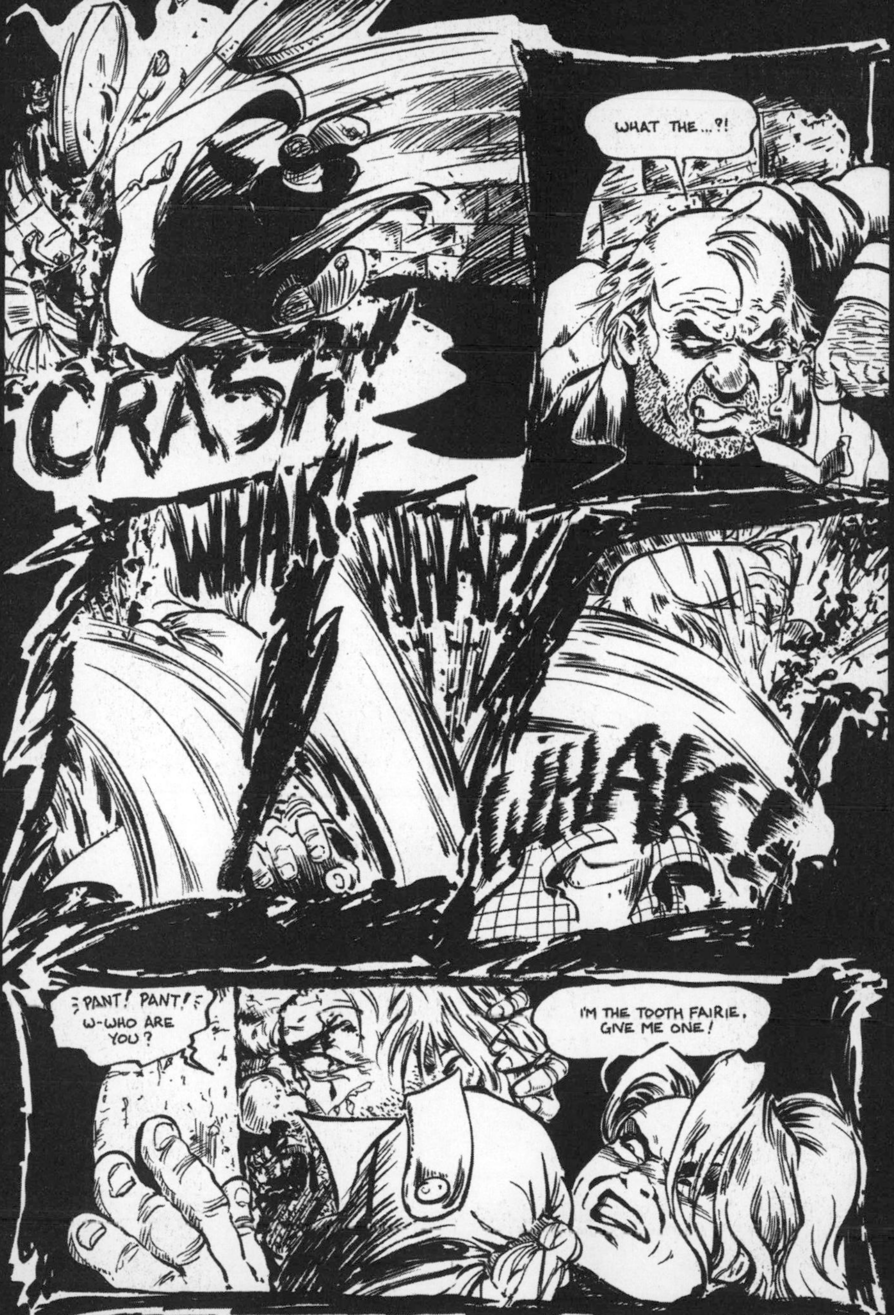
CRASH!
WHAT THE...?!
WHAK! WHAP!
WHAK!
PANT! PANT! W-WHO ARE YOU?
I'M THE TOOTH FAIRIE. GIVE ME ONE!

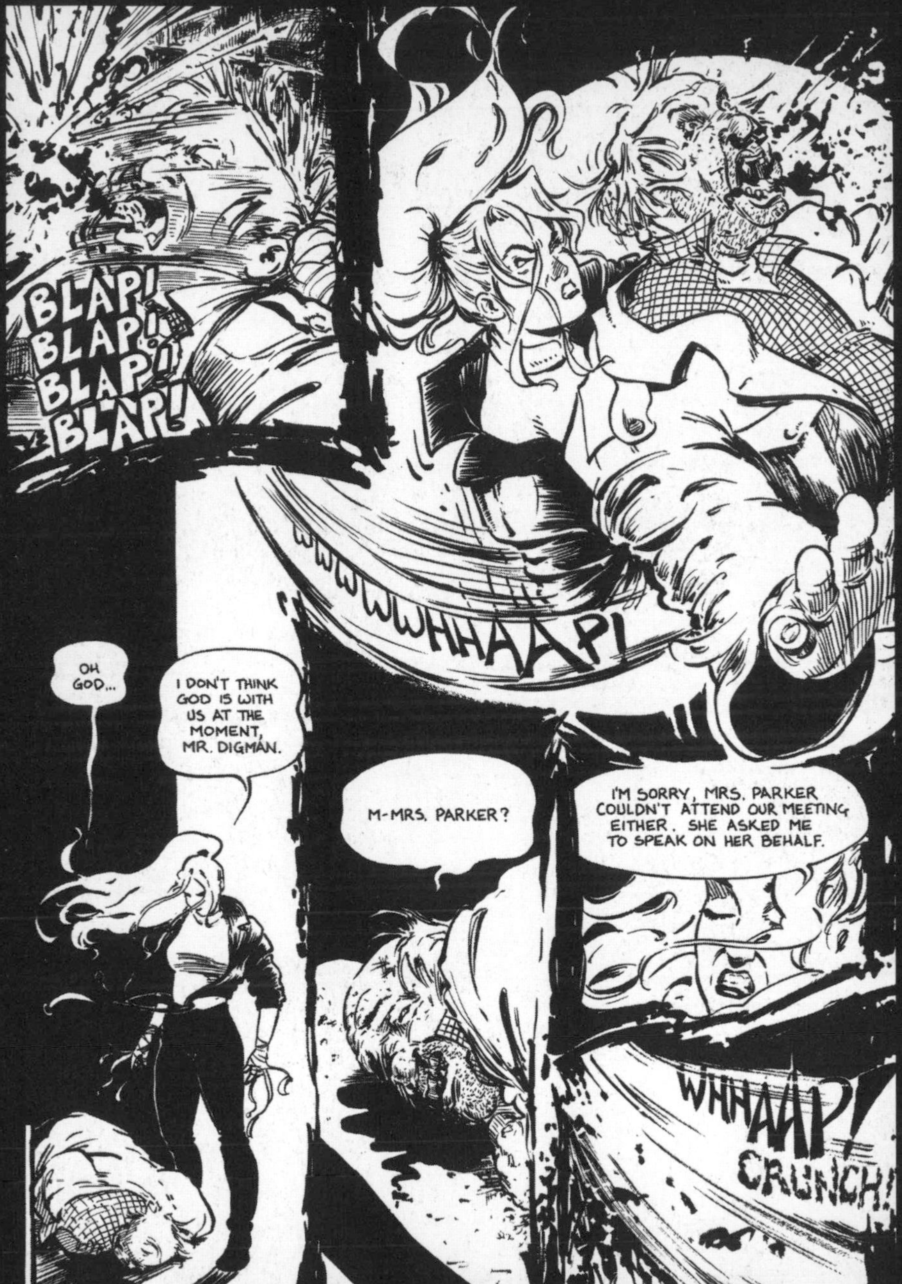
BLAP! BLAP! BLAP! BLAP!
WWWWWWHHAAP!
OH GOD...
I DON'T THINK GOD IS WITH US AT THE MOMENT, MR. DIGMAN.
M-MRS. PARKER?
I'M SORRY, MRS. PARKER COULDN'T ATTEND OUR MEETING EITHER. SHE ASKED ME TO SPEAK ON HER BEHALF.
WHHAAP!
CRUNCH!

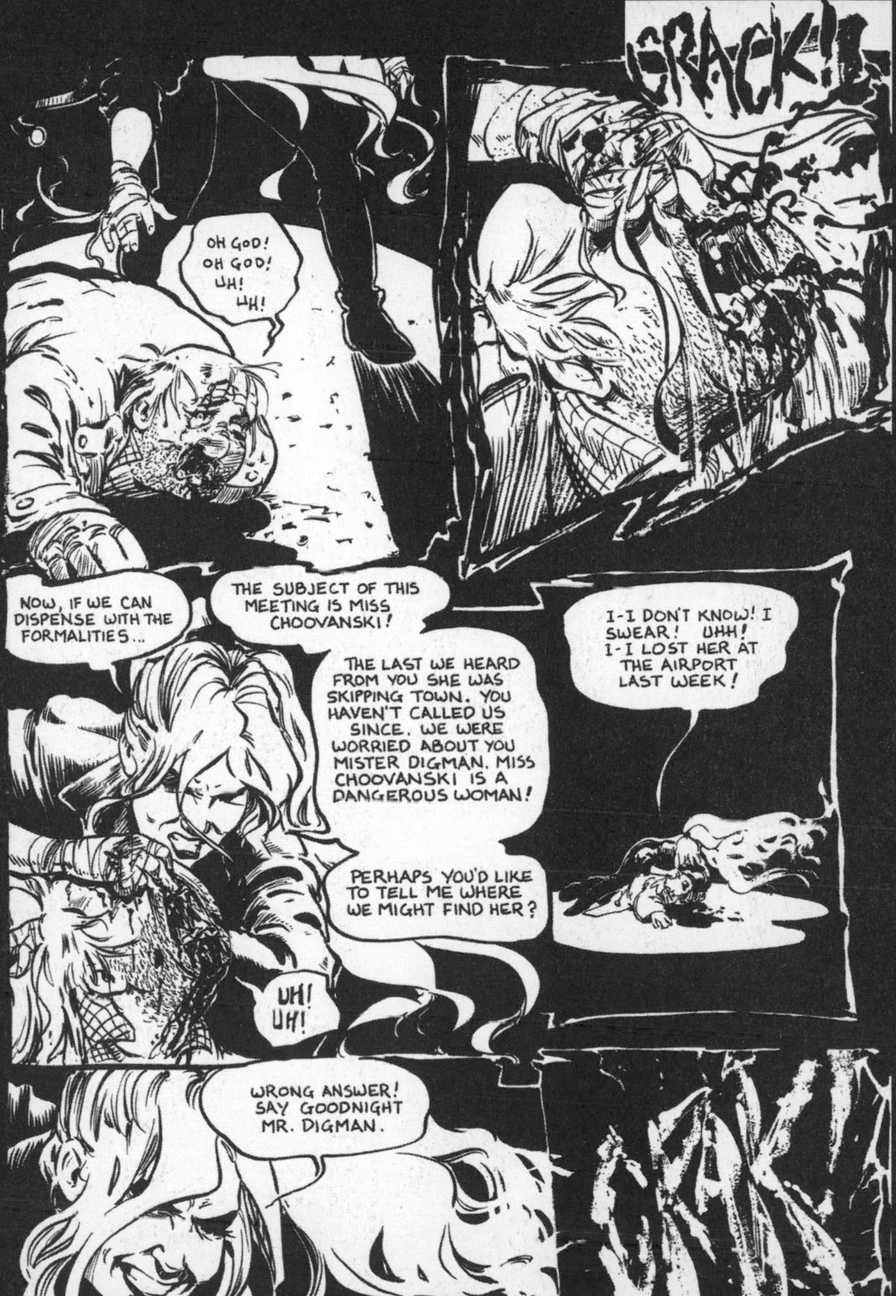
OH GOD! OH GOD! UH! UH!
CRACK!
NOW, IF WE CAN DISPENSE WITH THE FORMALITIES...
THE SUBJECT OF THIS MEETING IS MISS CHOOVANSKI!
THE LAST WE HEARD FROM YOU SHE WAS SKIPPING TOWN. YOU HAVEN'T CALLED US SINCE. WE WERE WORRIED ABOUT YOU MISTER DIGMAN. MISS CHOOVANSKI IS A DANGEROUS WOMAN!
PERHAPS YOU'D LIKE TO TELL ME WHERE WE MIGHT FIND HER?
UH! UH!
I-I DON'T KNOW! I SWEAR! UHH! I-I LOST HER AT THE AIRPORT LAST WEEK!
WRONG ANSWER! SAY GOODNIGHT MR. DIGMAN.
OH GOD...
CRACK!

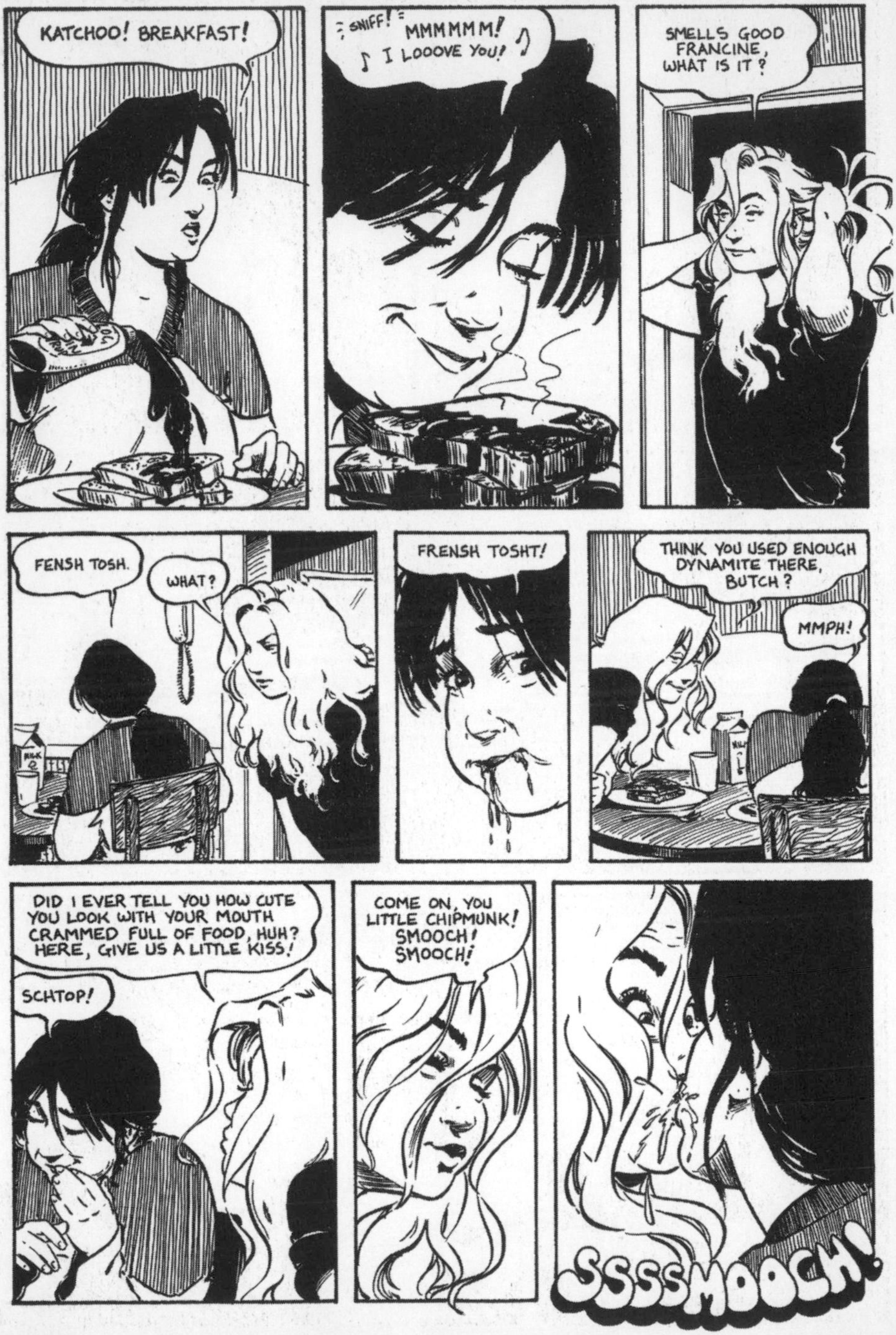
KATCHOO! BREAKFAST!
SNIFF!
MMMMMM! I LOOOVE YOU!
SMELLS GOOD FRANCINE, WHAT IS IT?
FENSH TOSH.
WHAT?
FRENSH TOSHT!
THINK YOU USED ENOUGH DYNAMITE THERE, BUTCH?
MMPH!
DID I EVER TELL YOU HOW CUTE YOU LOOK WITH YOUR MOUTH CRAMMED FULL OF FOOD, HUH? HERE, GIVE US A LITTLE KISS!
SCHTOP!
COME ON, YOU LITTLE CHIPMUNK! SMOOCH! SMOOCH!
SSSSMOOCH!

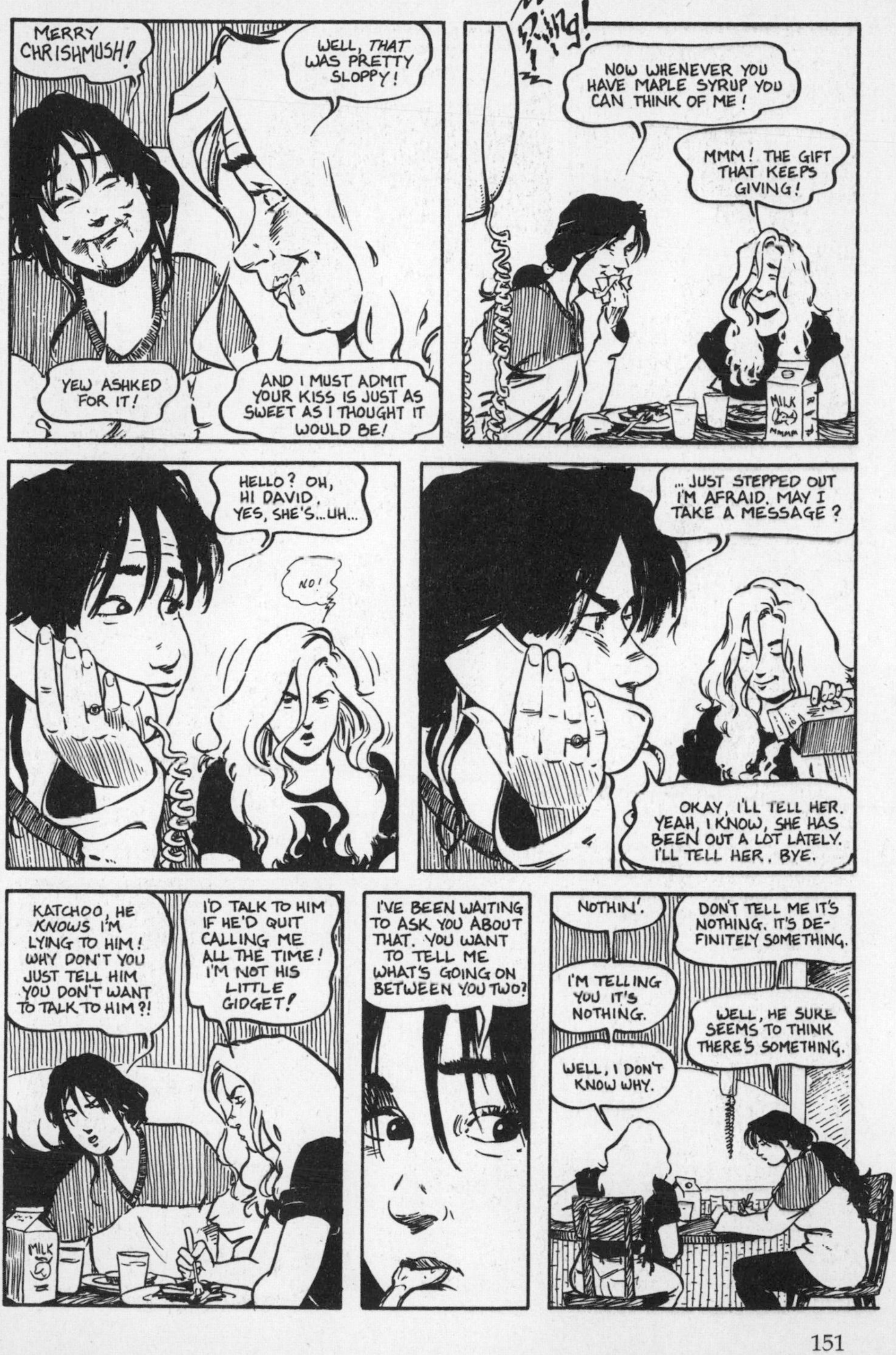
MERRY CHRISHMUSH!
WELL, THAT WAS PRETTY SLOPPY!
YEW ASHKED FOR IT!
AND I MUST ADMIT YOUR KISS IS JUST AS SWEET AS I THOUGHT IT WOULD BE!
Ring!
NOW WHENEVER YOU HAVE MAPLE SYRUP YOU CAN THINK OF ME!
MMM! THE GIFT THAT KEEPS GIVING!
MILK
HELLO? OH, HI DAVID. YES, SHE'S...UH...
NO!
...JUST STEPPED OUT I'M AFRAID. MAY I TAKE A MESSAGE?
OKAY, I'LL TELL HER. YEAH, I KNOW, SHE HAS BEEN OUT A LOT LATELY. I'LL TELL HER. BYE.
KATCHOO, HE KNOWS I'M LYING TO HIM! WHY DON'T YOU JUST TELL HIM YOU DON'T WANT TO TALK TO HIM?!
I'D TALK TO HIM IF HE'D QUIT CALLING ME ALL THE TIME! I'M NOT HIS LITTLE GIDGET!
MILK
I'VE BEEN WAITING TO ASK YOU ABOUT THAT. YOU WANT TO TELL ME WHAT'S GOING ON BETWEEN YOU TWO?
NOTHIN'.
DON'T TELL ME IT'S NOTHING. IT'S DEFINITELY SOMETHING.
I'M TELLING YOU IT'S NOTHING.
WELL, HE SURE SEEMS TO THINK THERE'S SOMETHING.
WELL, I DON'T KNOW WHY.

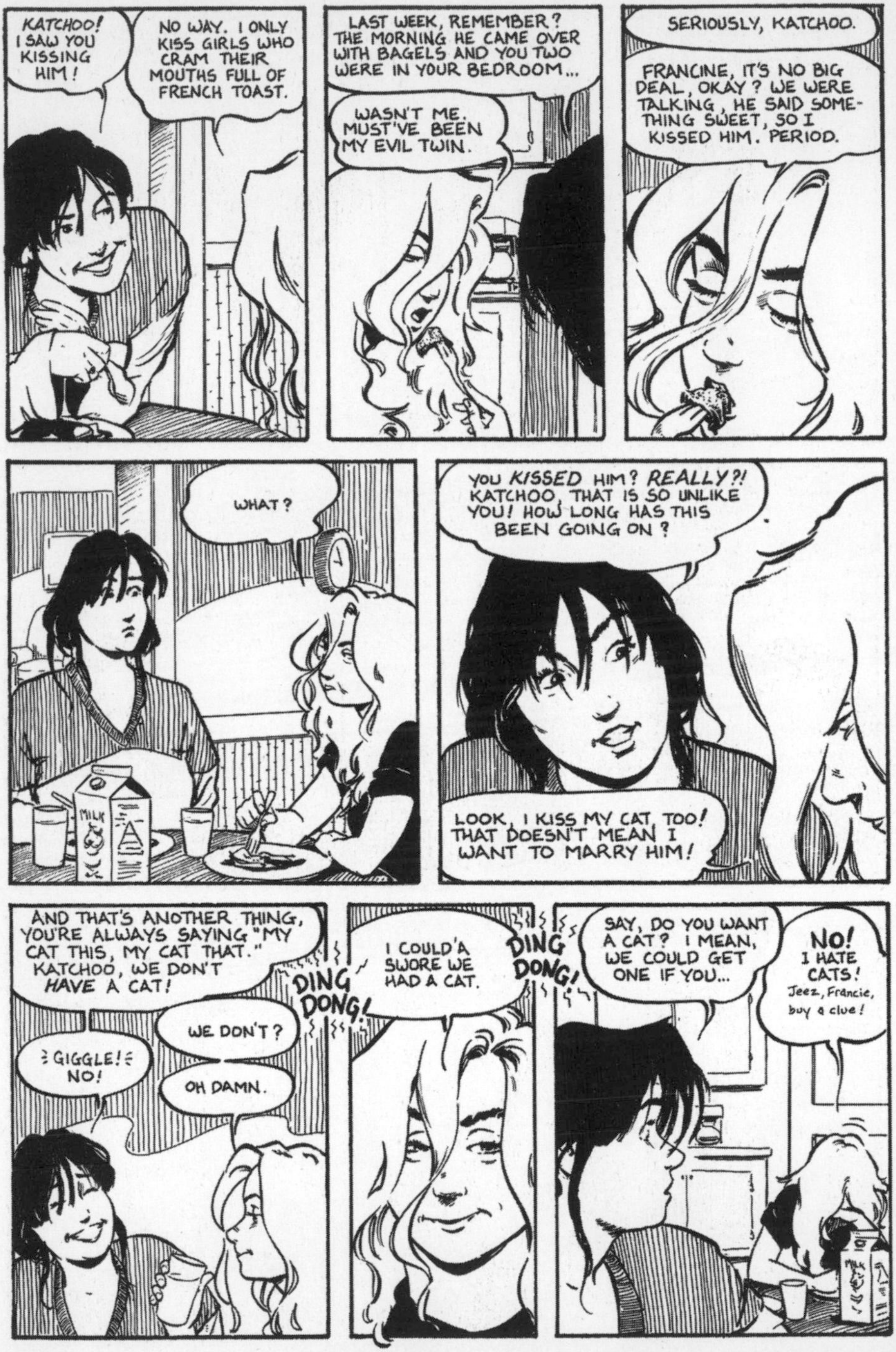
KATCHOO! I SAW YOU KISSING HIM!
NO WAY. I ONLY KISS GIRLS WHO CRAM THEIR MOUTHS FULL OF FRENCH TOAST.
LAST WEEK, REMEMBER? THE MORNING HE CAME OVER WITH BAGELS AND YOU TWO WERE IN YOUR BEDROOM...
WASN'T ME. MUST'VE BEEN MY EVIL TWIN.
SERIOUSLY, KATCHOO.
FRANCINE, IT'S NO BIG DEAL, OKAY? WE WERE TALKING, HE SAID SOMETHING SWEET, SO I KISSED HIM. PERIOD.
WHAT?
YOU KISSED HIM? REALLY?! KATCHOO, THAT IS SO UNLIKE YOU! HOW LONG HAS THIS BEEN GOING ON?
LOOK, I KISS MY CAT, TOO! THAT DOESN'T MEAN I WANT TO MARRY HIM!
AND THAT'S ANOTHER THING, YOU'RE ALWAYS SAYING "MY CAT THIS, MY CAT THAT." KATCHOO, WE DON'T HAVE A CAT!
WE DON'T?
GIGGLE! NO!
OH DAMN.
DING DONG!
I COULD'A SWORE WE HAD A CAT.
DING DONG!
SAY, DO YOU WANT A CAT? I MEAN, WE COULD GET ONE IF YOU...
NO! I HATE CATS! Jeez, Francie, buy a clue!

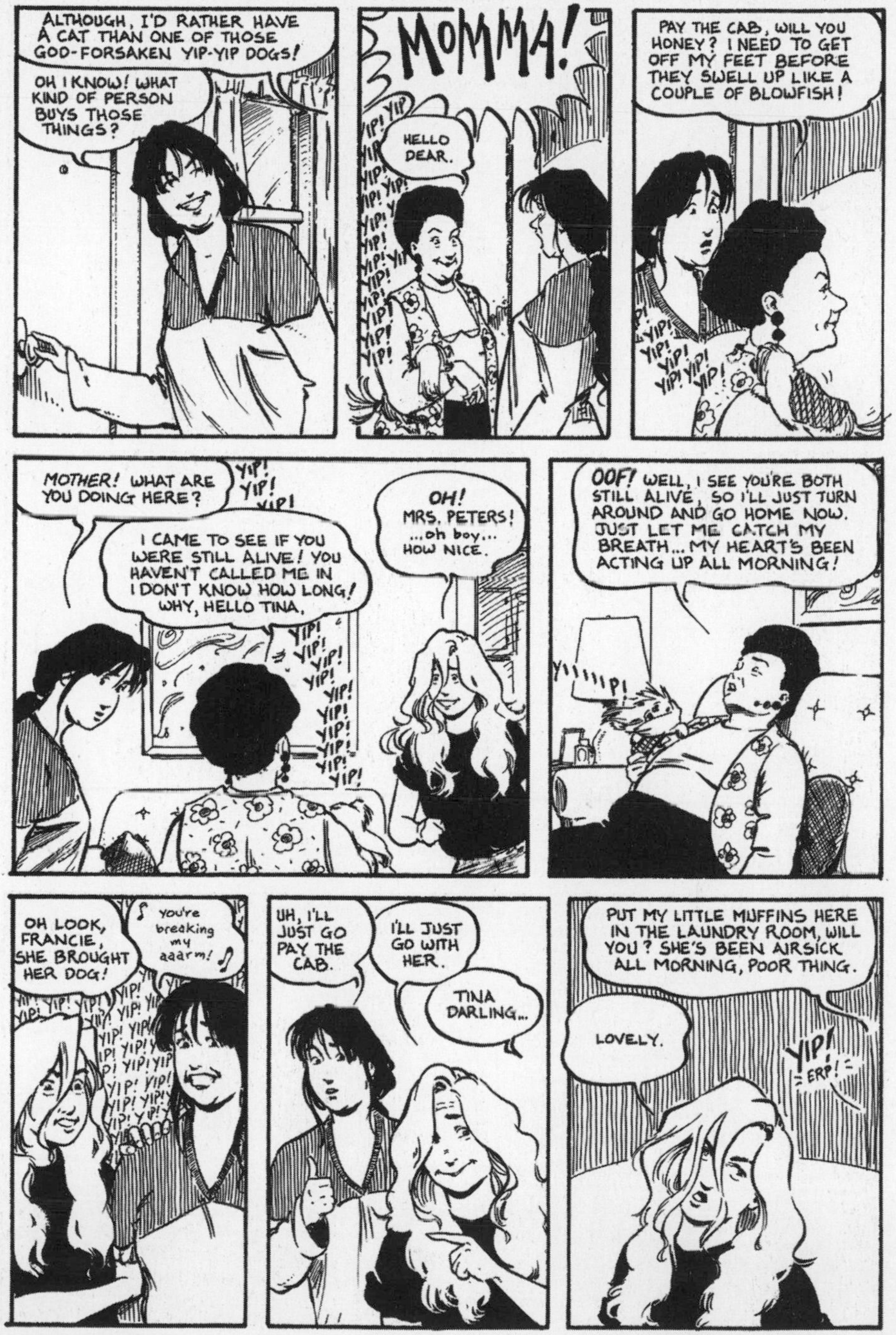
ALTHOUGH, I'D RATHER HAVE A CAT THAN ONE OF THOSE GOD-FORSAKEN YIP-YIP DOGS!
OH I KNOW! WHAT KIND OF PERSON BUYS THOSE THINGS?
MOMMA!
YIP! YIP!
HELLO DEAR.
YIP! YIP! YIP! YIP! YIP! YIP! YIP! YIP! YIP!
PAY THE CAB, WILL YOU HONEY? I NEED TO GET OFF MY FEET BEFORE THEY SWELL UP LIKE A COUPLE OF BLOWFISH!
YIP! YIP! YIP! YIP! YIP! YIP!
MOTHER! WHAT ARE YOU DOING HERE?
YIP! YIP! YIP!
I CAME TO SEE IF YOU WERE STILL ALIVE! YOU HAVEN'T CALLED ME IN I DON'T KNOW HOW LONG! WHY, HELLO TINA,
OH! MRS. PETERS! ...oh boy... HOW NICE.
YIP! YIP! YIP! YIP! YIP! YIP! YIP! YIP! YIP! YIP!
OOF! WELL, I SEE YOU'RE BOTH STILL ALIVE, SO I'LL JUST TURN AROUND AND GO HOME NOW. JUST LET ME CATCH MY BREATH... MY HEART'S BEEN ACTING UP ALL MORNING!
YIIIIIIP!
OH LOOK, FRANCIE, SHE BROUGHT HER DOG!
you're breaking my aaarm!
YIP! YIP! YIP! YIP! YIP! YIP! YIP!
UH, I'LL JUST GO PAY THE CAB.
I'LL JUST GO WITH HER.
TINA DARLING...
PUT MY LITTLE MUFFINS HERE IN THE LAUNDRY ROOM, WILL YOU? SHE'S BEEN AIRSICK ALL MORNING, POOR THING.
LOVELY.
YIP! ERP!

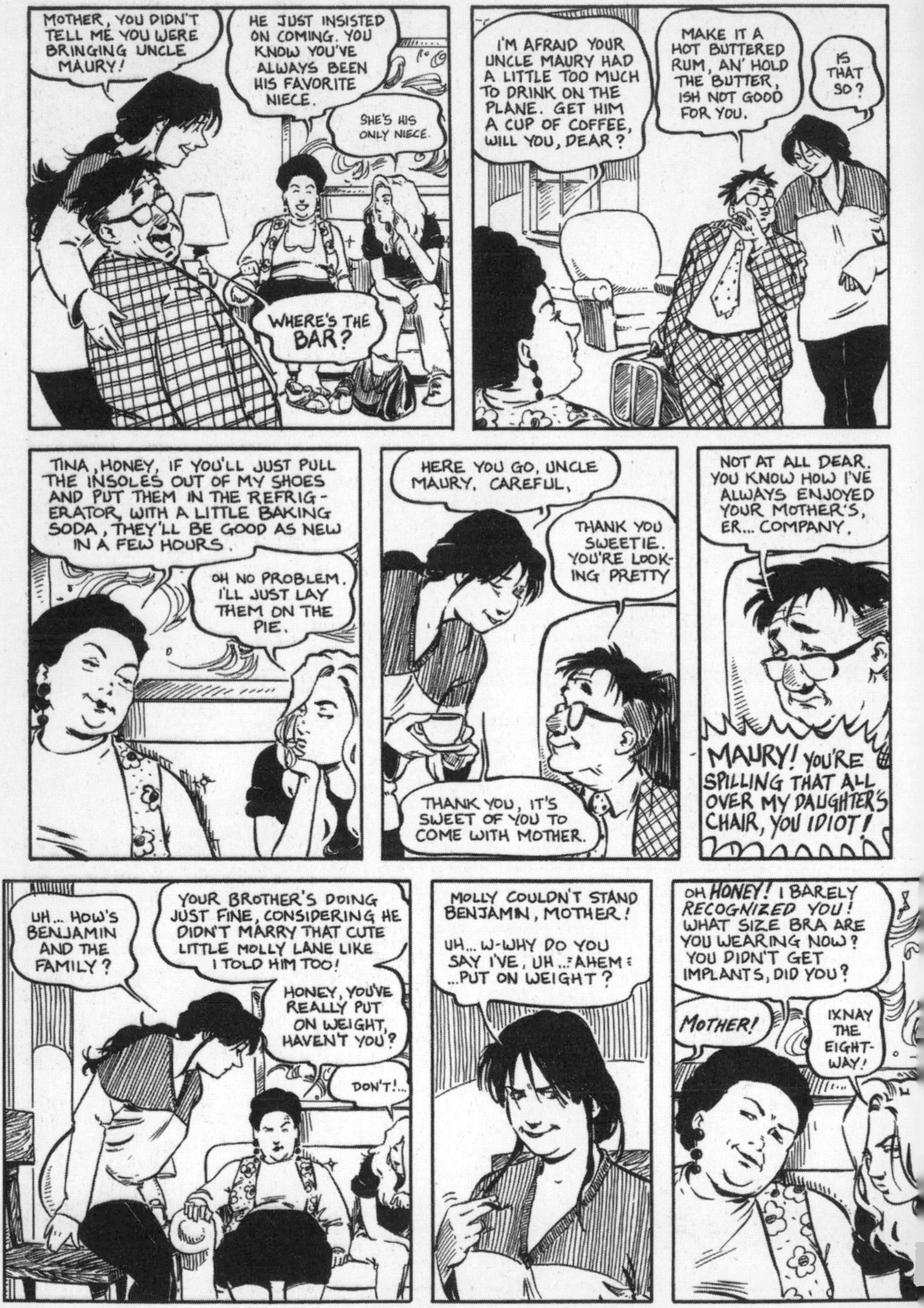
MOTHER, YOU DIDN'T TELL ME YOU WERE BRINGING UNCLE MAURY!
HE JUST INSISTED ON COMING. YOU KNOW YOU'VE ALWAYS BEEN HIS FAVORITE NIECE.
SHE'S HIS ONLY NIECE.
WHERE'S THE BAR?
I'M AFRAID YOUR UNCLE MAURY HAD A LITTLE TOO MUCH TO DRINK ON THE PLANE. GET HIM A CUP OF COFFEE, WILL YOU, DEAR?
MAKE IT A HOT BUTTERED RUM, AN' HOLD THE BUTTER, ISH NOT GOOD FOR YOU.
IS THAT SO?
TINA, HONEY, IF YOU'LL JUST PULL THE INSOLES OUT OF MY SHOES AND PUT THEM IN THE REFRIG-ERATOR, WITH A LITTLE BAKING SODA, THEY'LL BE GOOD AS NEW IN A FEW HOURS.
OH NO PROBLEM. I'LL JUST LAY THEM ON THE PIE.
HERE YOU GO, UNCLE MAURY, CAREFUL,
THANK YOU SWEETIE. YOU'RE LOOK-ING PRETTY
THANK YOU, IT'S SWEET OF YOU TO COME WITH MOTHER.
NOT AT ALL DEAR. YOU KNOW HOW I'VE ALWAYS ENJOYED YOUR MOTHER'S, ER... COMPANY.
MAURY! YOU'RE SPILLING THAT ALL OVER MY DAUGHTER'S CHAIR, YOU IDIOT!
UH... HOW'S BENJAMIN AND THE FAMILY?
YOUR BROTHER'S DOING JUST FINE, CONSIDERING HE DIDN'T MARRY THAT CUTE LITTLE MOLLY LANE LIKE I TOLD HIM TOO!
HONEY, YOU'VE REALLY PUT ON WEIGHT, HAVEN'T YOU?
DON'T!...
MOLLY COULDN'T STAND BENJAMIN, MOTHER!
UH... W-WHY DO YOU SAY I'VE, UH ... AHEM ...PUT ON WEIGHT?
OH HONEY! I BARELY RECOGNIZED YOU! WHAT SIZE BRA ARE YOU WEARING NOW? YOU DIDN'T GET IMPLANTS, DID YOU?
MOTHER!
IXNAY THE EIGHT-WAY!

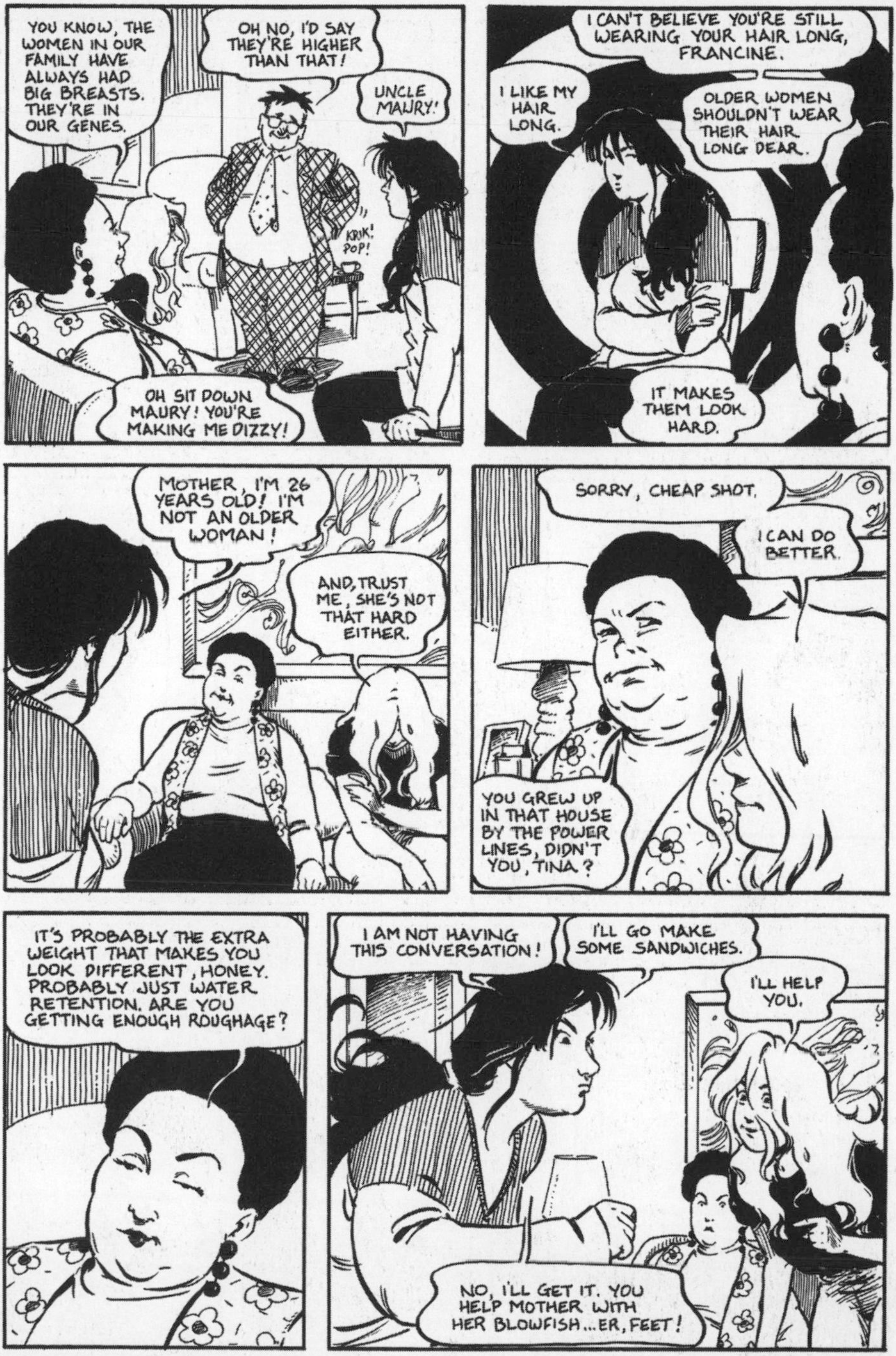
YOU KNOW, THE WOMEN IN OUR FAMILY HAVE ALWAYS HAD BIG BREASTS. THEY'RE IN OUR GENES.
OH NO, I'D SAY THEY'RE HIGHER THAN THAT!
UNCLE MAURY!
KRIK! POP!
OH SIT DOWN MAURY! YOU'RE MAKING ME DIZZY!
I CAN'T BELIEVE YOU'RE STILL WEARING YOUR HAIR LONG, FRANCINE.
I LIKE MY HAIR LONG.
OLDER WOMEN SHOULDN'T WEAR THEIR HAIR LONG DEAR.
IT MAKES THEM LOOK HARD.
MOTHER, I'M 26 YEARS OLD! I'M NOT AN OLDER WOMAN!
AND, TRUST ME, SHE'S NOT THAT HARD EITHER.
SORRY, CHEAP SHOT.
I CAN DO BETTER.
YOU GREW UP IN THAT HOUSE BY THE POWER LINES, DIDN'T YOU, TINA?
IT'S PROBABLY THE EXTRA WEIGHT THAT MAKES YOU LOOK DIFFERENT, HONEY. PROBABLY JUST WATER RETENTION. ARE YOU GETTING ENOUGH ROUGHAGE?
I AM NOT HAVING THIS CONVERSATION!
I'LL GO MAKE SOME SANDWICHES.
I'LL HELP YOU.
NO, I'LL GET IT. YOU HELP MOTHER WITH HER BLOWFISH...ER, FEET!

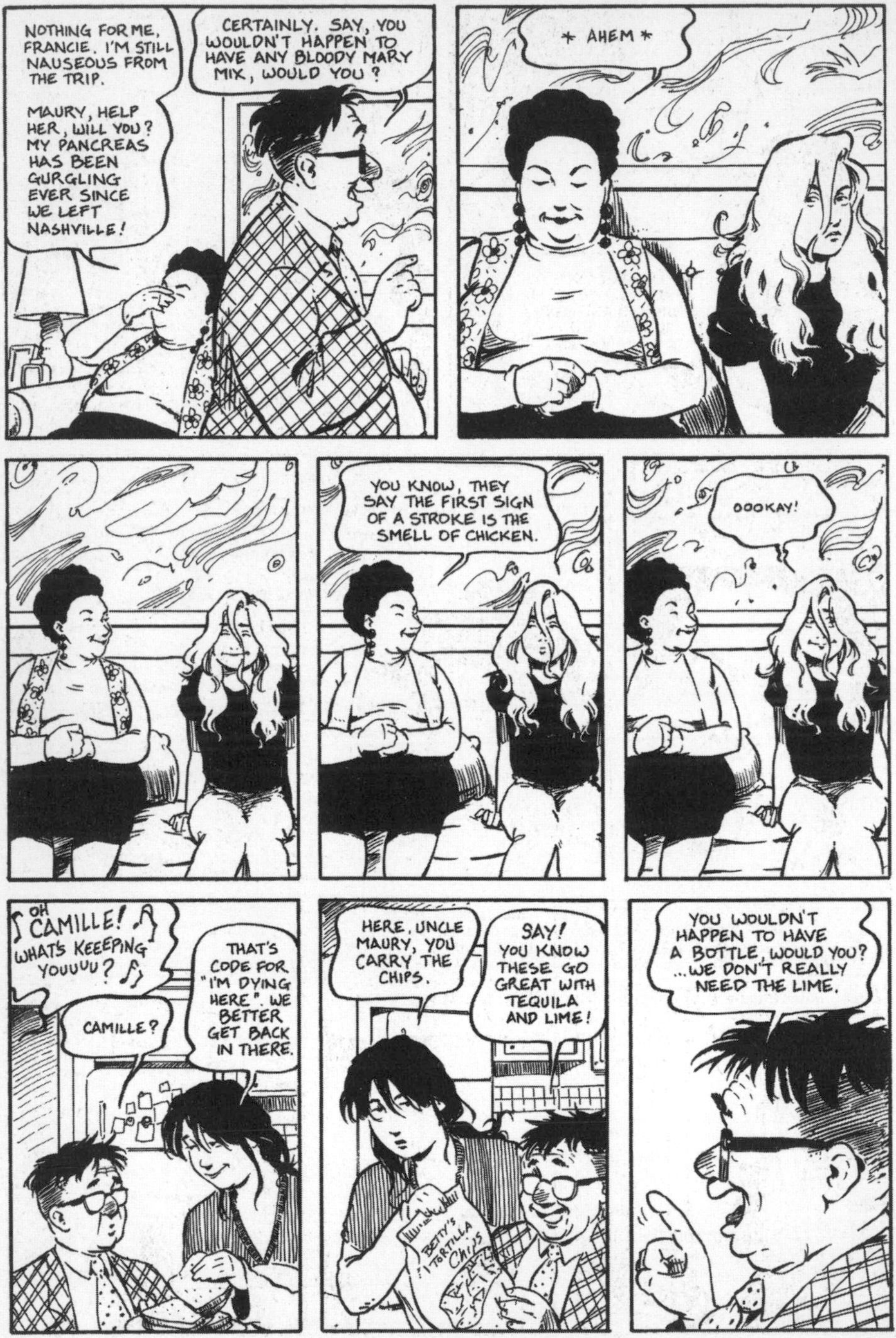
NOTHING FOR ME, FRANCIE. I'M STILL NAUSEOUS FROM THE TRIP.
MAURY, HELP HER, WILL YOU? MY PANCREAS HAS BEEN GURGLING EVER SINCE WE LEFT NASHVILLE!
CERTAINLY. SAY, YOU WOULDN'T HAPPEN TO HAVE ANY BLOODY MARY MIX, WOULD YOU?
* AHEM *
YOU KNOW, THEY SAY THE FIRST SIGN OF A STROKE IS THE SMELL OF CHICKEN.
OOOKAY!
OH CAMILLE! WHAT'S KEEEPING YOUUUU?
CAMILLE?
THAT'S CODE FOR "I'M DYING HERE". WE BETTER GET BACK IN THERE.
HERE, UNCLE MAURY, YOU CARRY THE CHIPS.
BETTY'S TORTILLA CHIPS
SAY! YOU KNOW THESE GO GREAT WITH TEQUILA AND LIME!
YOU WOULDN'T HAPPEN TO HAVE A BOTTLE, WOULD YOU? ...WE DON'T REALLY NEED THE LIME.

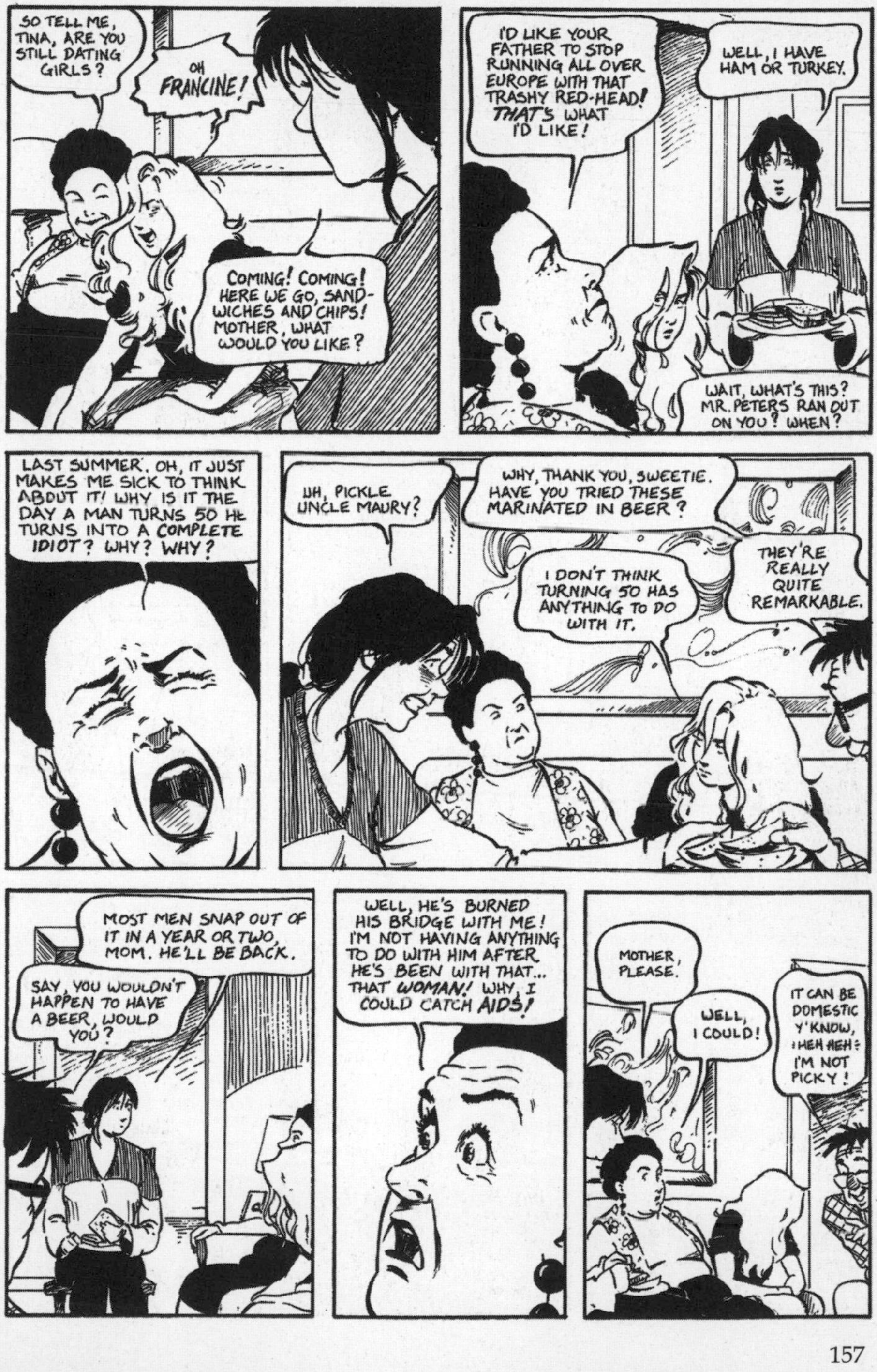
SO TELL ME, TINA, ARE YOU STILL DATING GIRLS?
OH FRANCINE!
COMING! COMING! HERE WE GO, SANDWICHES AND CHIPS! MOTHER, WHAT WOULD YOU LIKE?
I'D LIKE YOUR FATHER TO STOP RUNNING ALL OVER EUROPE WITH THAT TRASHY RED-HEAD! THAT'S WHAT I'D LIKE!
WELL, I HAVE HAM OR TURKEY.
WAIT, WHAT'S THIS? MR. PETERS RAN OUT ON YOU? WHEN?
LAST SUMMER. OH, IT JUST MAKES ME SICK TO THINK ABOUT IT! WHY IS IT THE DAY A MAN TURNS 50 HE TURNS INTO A COMPLETE IDIOT? WHY? WHY?
UH, PICKLE UNCLE MAURY?
WHY, THANK YOU, SWEETIE. HAVE YOU TRIED THESE MARINATED IN BEER?
I DON'T THINK TURNING 50 HAS ANYTHING TO DO WITH IT.
THEY'RE REALLY QUITE REMARKABLE.
MOST MEN SNAP OUT OF IT IN A YEAR OR TWO, MOM. HE'LL BE BACK.
SAY, YOU WOULDN'T HAPPEN TO HAVE A BEER, WOULD YOU?
WELL, HE'S BURNED HIS BRIDGE WITH ME! I'M NOT HAVING ANYTHING TO DO WITH HIM AFTER HE'S BEEN WITH THAT... THAT WOMAN! WHY, I COULD CATCH AIDS!
MOTHER, PLEASE.
WELL, I COULD!
IT CAN BE DOMESTIC Y'KNOW, HEH HEH I'M NOT PICKY!

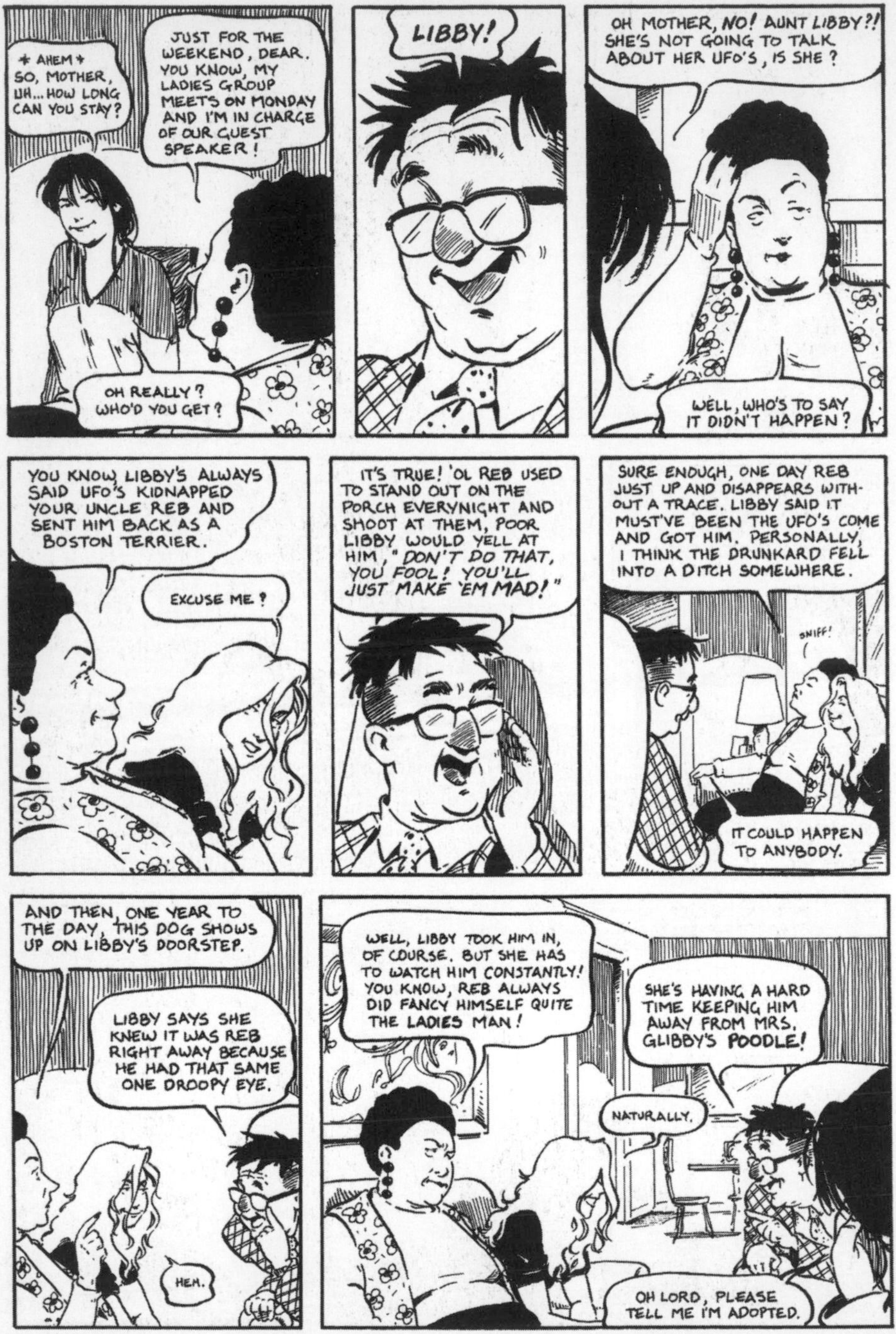
* AHEM * SO, MOTHER, UH... HOW LONG CAN YOU STAY?
JUST FOR THE WEEKEND, DEAR. YOU KNOW, MY LADIES GROUP MEETS ON MONDAY AND I'M IN CHARGE OF OUR GUEST SPEAKER!
OH REALLY? WHO'D YOU GET?
LIBBY!
OH MOTHER, NO! AUNT LIBBY?! SHE'S NOT GOING TO TALK ABOUT HER UFO'S, IS SHE?
WELL, WHO'S TO SAY IT DIDN'T HAPPEN?
YOU KNOW, LIBBY'S ALWAYS SAID UFO'S KIDNAPPED YOUR UNCLE REB AND SENT HIM BACK AS A BOSTON TERRIER.
EXCUSE ME?
IT'S TRUE! 'OL REB USED TO STAND OUT ON THE PORCH EVERYNIGHT AND SHOOT AT THEM, POOR LIBBY WOULD YELL AT HIM, "DON'T DO THAT, YOU FOOL! YOU'LL JUST MAKE 'EM MAD!"
SURE ENOUGH, ONE DAY REB JUST UP AND DISAPPEARS WITHOUT A TRACE. LIBBY SAID IT MUST'VE BEEN THE UFO'S COME AND GOT HIM. PERSONALLY, I THINK THE DRUNKARD FELL INTO A DITCH SOMEWHERE.
SNIFF!
IT COULD HAPPEN TO ANYBODY.
AND THEN, ONE YEAR TO THE DAY, THIS DOG SHOWS UP ON LIBBY'S DOORSTEP.
LIBBY SAYS SHE KNEW IT WAS REB RIGHT AWAY BECAUSE HE HAD THAT SAME ONE DROOPY EYE.
HEM.
WELL, LIBBY TOOK HIM IN, OF COURSE. BUT SHE HAS TO WATCH HIM CONSTANTLY! YOU KNOW, REB ALWAYS DID FANCY HIMSELF QUITE THE LADIES MAN!
SHE'S HAVING A HARD TIME KEEPING HIM AWAY FROM MRS. GLIBBY'S POODLE!
NATURALLY.
OH LORD, PLEASE TELL ME I'M ADOPTED.

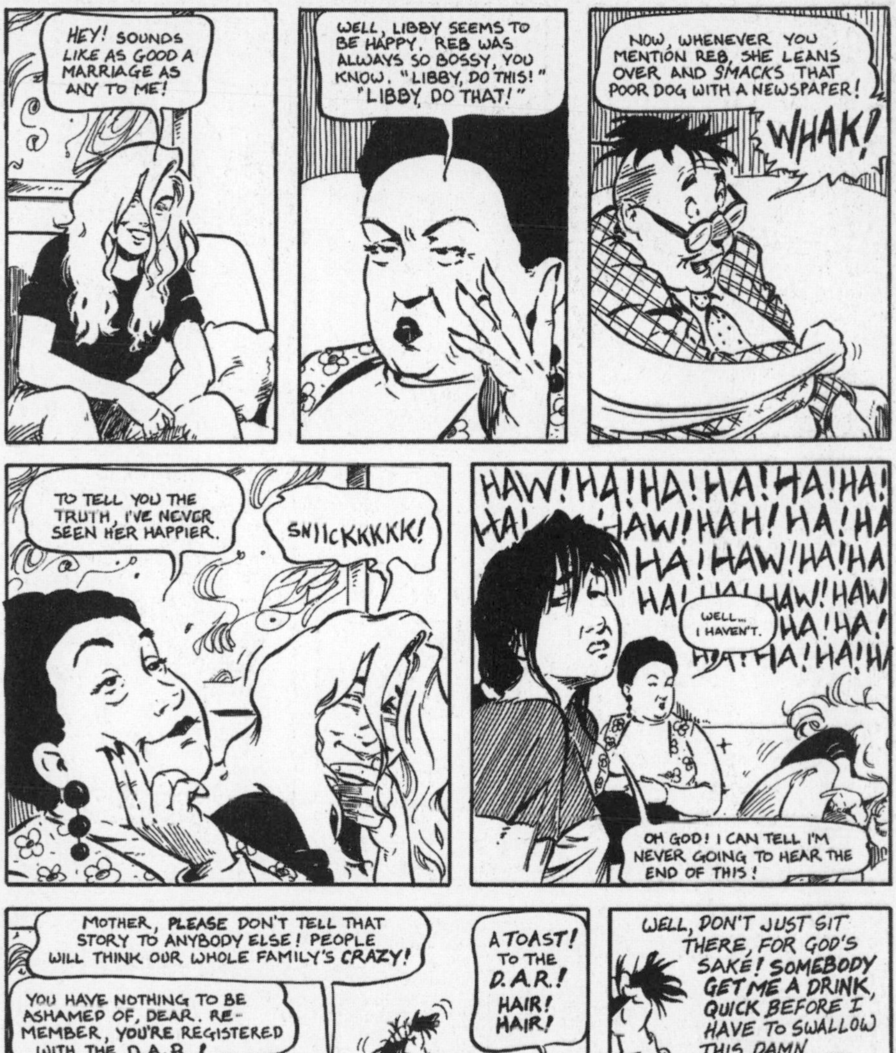
HEY! SOUNDS LIKE AS GOOD A MARRIAGE AS ANY TO ME!
WELL, LIBBY SEEMS TO BE HAPPY. REB WAS ALWAYS SO BOSSY, YOU KNOW. "LIBBY, DO THIS!" "LIBBY, DO THAT!"
NOW, WHENEVER YOU MENTION REB, SHE LEANS OVER AND SMACKS THAT POOR DOG WITH A NEWSPAPER!
WHAK!
TO TELL YOU THE TRUTH, I'VE NEVER SEEN HER HAPPIER.
SNIICKKKKK!
HAW! HA! HA! HA! HA! HA! HA! HAW! HAH! HA! HA HA! HAW! HA! HA HAW! HAW HA! HA! HA! HA! HA!
WELL... I HAVEN'T.
OH GOD! I CAN TELL I'M NEVER GOING TO HEAR THE END OF THIS!
MOTHER, PLEASE DON'T TELL THAT STORY TO ANYBODY ELSE! PEOPLE WILL THINK OUR WHOLE FAMILY'S CRAZY!
YOU HAVE NOTHING TO BE ASHAMED OF, DEAR. REMEMBER, YOU'RE REGISTERED WITH THE *D.A.R.!
HA! HA! HA! HA! HA! HA! HA! HA! HA! HA!
A TOAST! TO THE D.A.R.! HAIR! HAIR!
* DAUGHTERS OF THE AMERICAN REVOLUTION
WELL, DON'T JUST SIT THERE, FOR GOD'S SAKE! SOMEBODY GET ME A DRINK, QUICK BEFORE I HAVE TO SWALLOW THIS DAMN RUG!

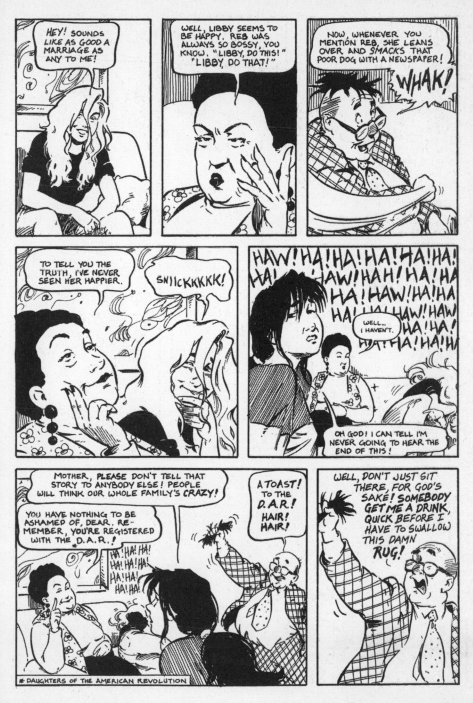

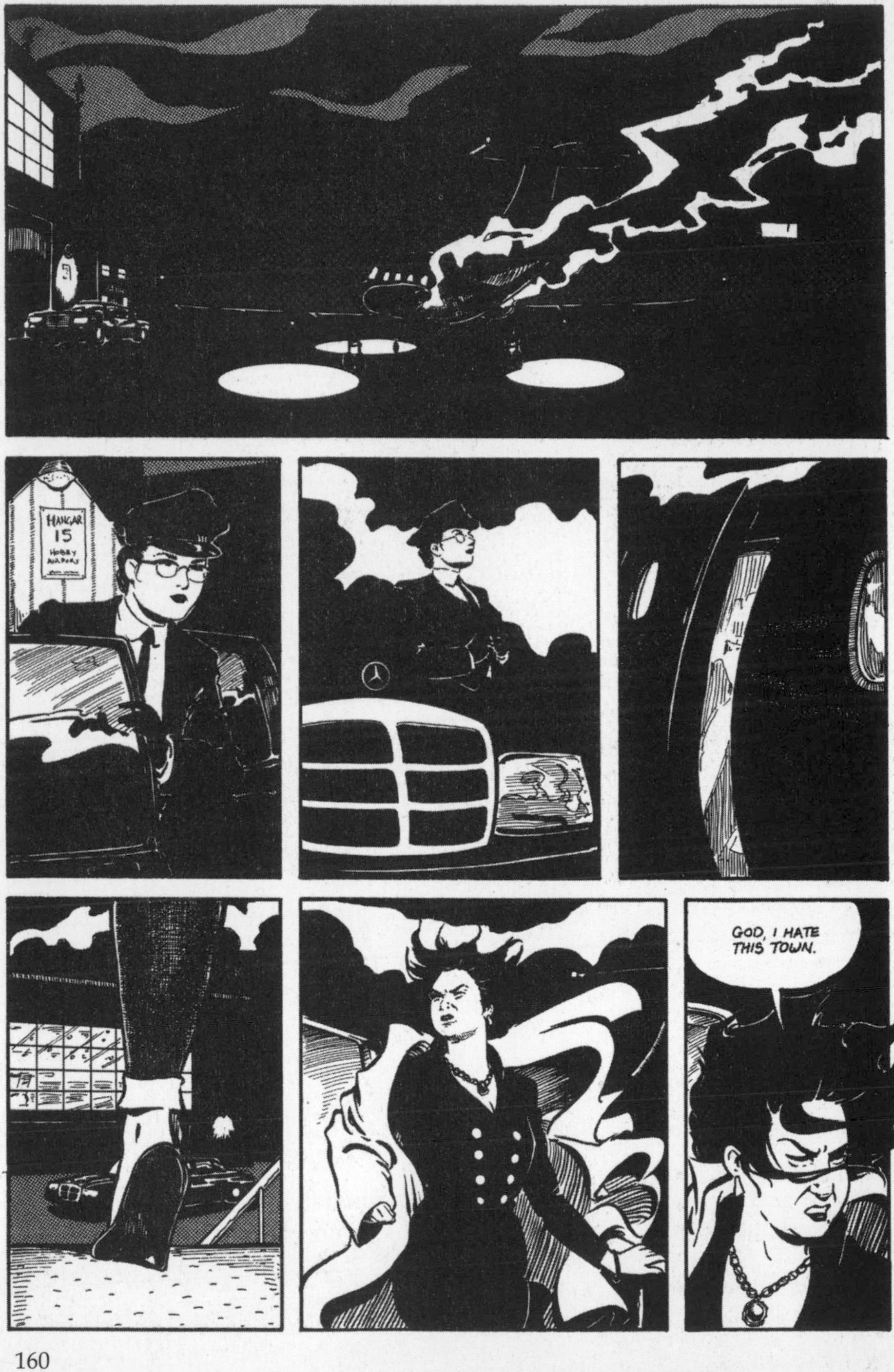
HANGAR
15
HOBBY
AIRPORT
GOD, I HATE
THIS TOWN.

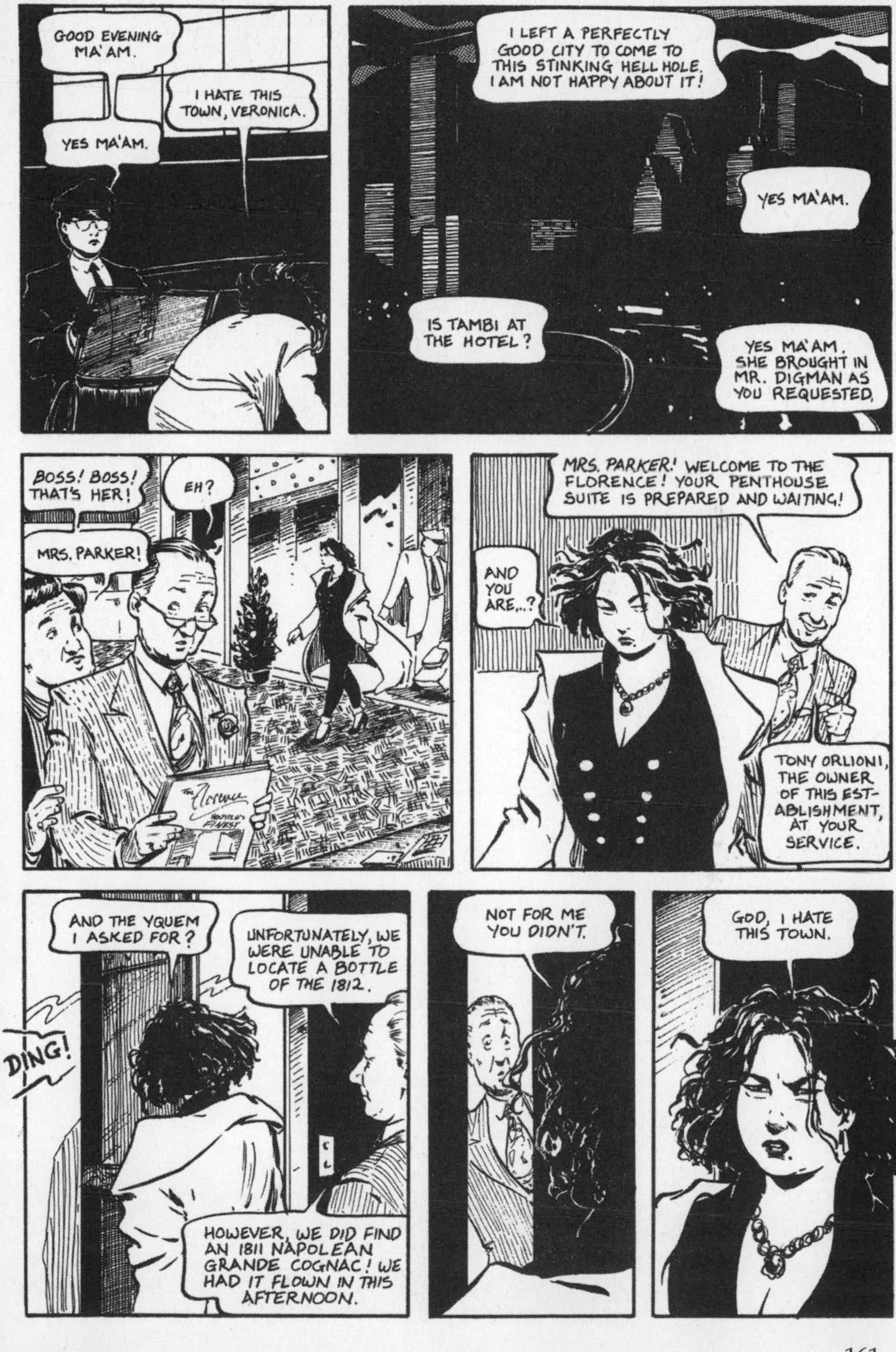
GOOD EVENING MA'AM.
I HATE THIS TOWN, VERONICA.
YES MA'AM.
I LEFT A PERFECTLY GOOD CITY TO COME TO THIS STINKING HELL HOLE. I AM NOT HAPPY ABOUT IT!
YES MA'AM.
IS TAMBI AT THE HOTEL?
YES MA'AM. SHE BROUGHT IN MR. DIGMAN AS YOU REQUESTED.
BOSS! BOSS! THAT'S HER!
EH?
MRS. PARKER!
MRS. PARKER! WELCOME TO THE FLORENCE! YOUR PENTHOUSE SUITE IS PREPARED AND WAITING!
AND YOU ARE...?
TONY ORLIONI, THE OWNER OF THIS ESTABLISHMENT, AT YOUR SERVICE.
AND THE YQUEM I ASKED FOR?
UNFORTUNATELY, WE WERE UNABLE TO LOCATE A BOTTLE OF THE 1812.
DING!
HOWEVER, WE DID FIND AN 1811 NAPOLEAN GRANDE COGNAC! WE HAD IT FLOWN IN THIS AFTERNOON.
NOT FOR ME YOU DIDN'T.
GOD, I HATE THIS TOWN.

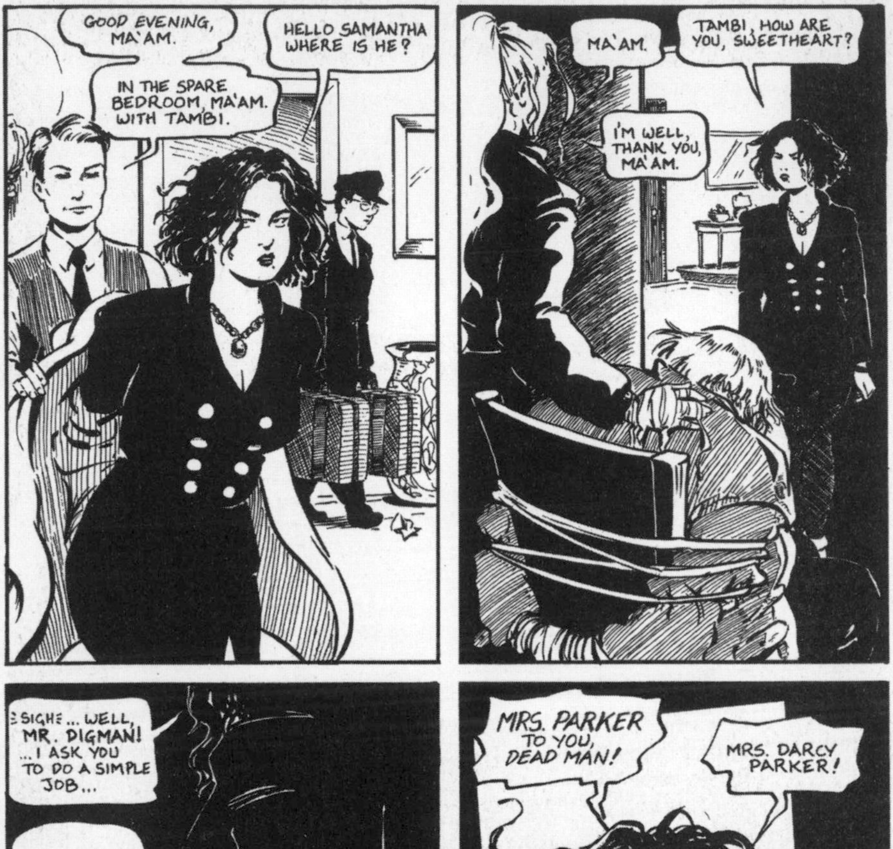
GOOD EVENING, MA'AM.
HELLO SAMANTHA WHERE IS HE?
IN THE SPARE BEDROOM, MA'AM. WITH TAMBI.
MA'AM.
TAMBI, HOW ARE YOU, SWEETHEART?
I'M WELL, THANK YOU, MA'AM.
≡SIGH≡ ... WELL, MR. DIGMAN! ...I ASK YOU TO DO A SIMPLE JOB...
...PARKER?
MRS. PARKER TO YOU, DEAD MAN!
MRS. DARCY PARKER!

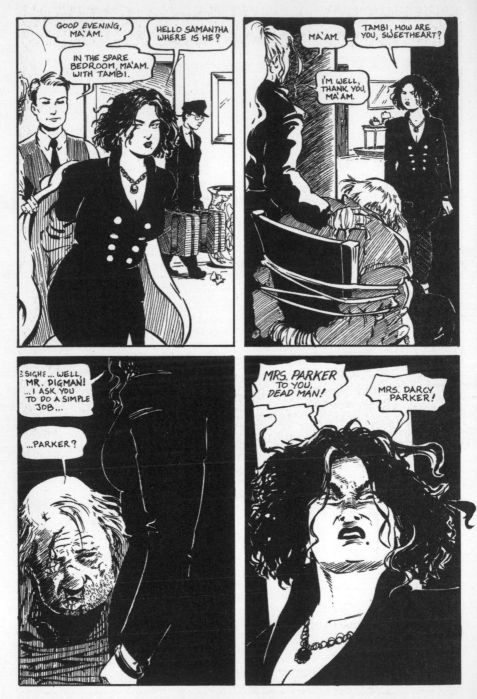

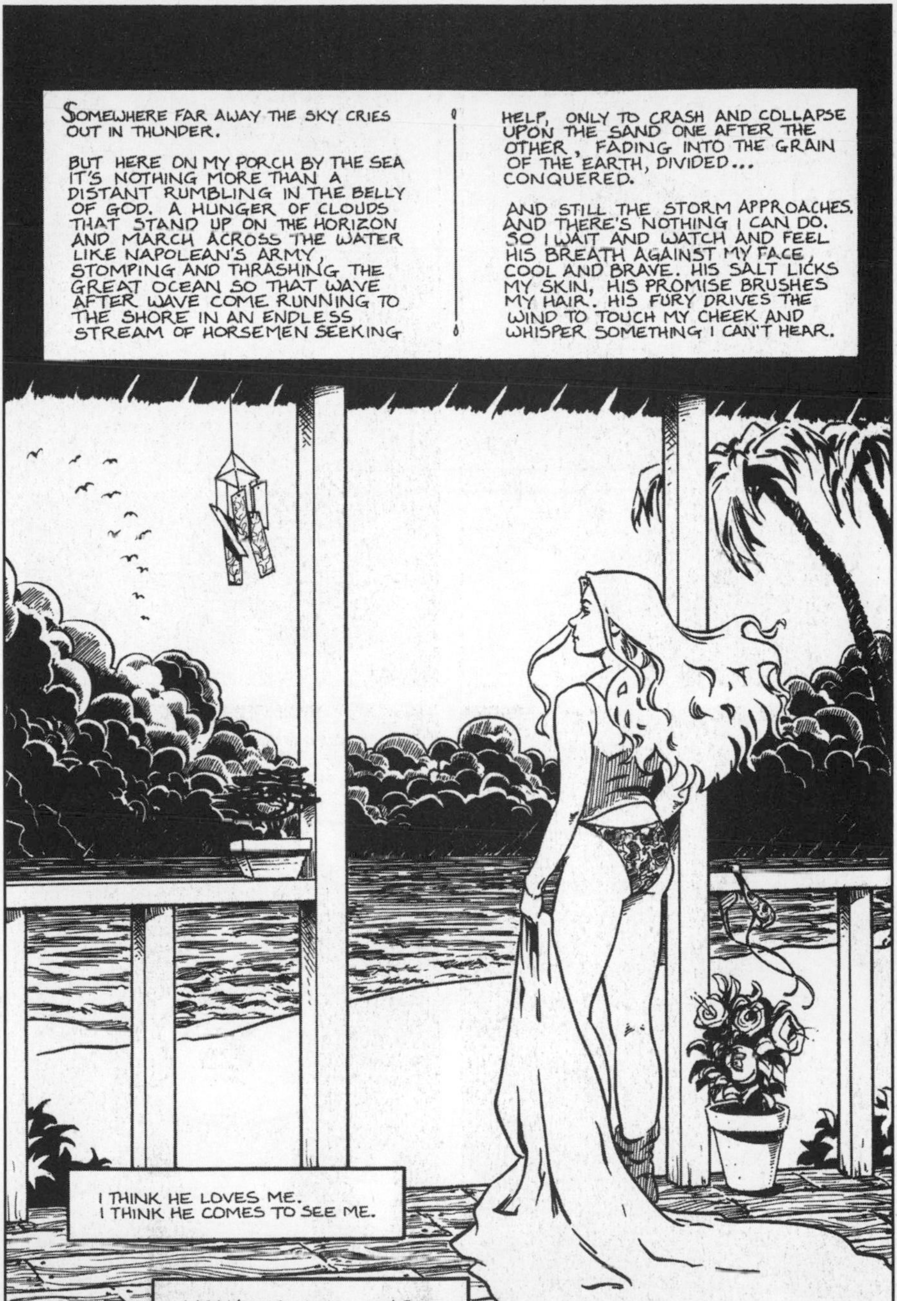
SOMEWHERE FAR AWAY THE SKY CRIES OUT IN THUNDER.
BUT HERE ON MY PORCH BY THE SEA IT'S NOTHING MORE THAN A DISTANT RUMBLING IN THE BELLY OF GOD. A HUNGER OF CLOUDS THAT STAND UP ON THE HORIZON AND MARCH ACROSS THE WATER LIKE NAPOLEAN'S ARMY, STOMPING AND THRASHING THE GREAT OCEAN SO THAT WAVE AFTER WAVE COME RUNNING TO THE SHORE IN AN ENDLESS STREAM OF HORSEMEN SEEKING HELP, ONLY TO CRASH AND COLLAPSE UPON THE SAND ONE AFTER THE OTHER, FADING INTO THE GRAIN OF THE EARTH, DIVIDED... CONQUERED.
AND STILL THE STORM APPROACHES. AND THERE'S NOTHING I CAN DO. SO I WAIT AND WATCH AND FEEL HIS BREATH AGAINST MY FACE, COOL AND BRAVE. HIS SALT LICKS MY SKIN, HIS PROMISE BRUSHES MY HAIR. HIS FURY DRIVES THE WIND TO TOUCH MY CHEEK AND WHISPER SOMETHING I CAN'T HEAR.
I THINK HE LOVES ME.
I THINK HE COMES TO SEE ME.
I AM YOUNG. I WILL LEARN.
2.

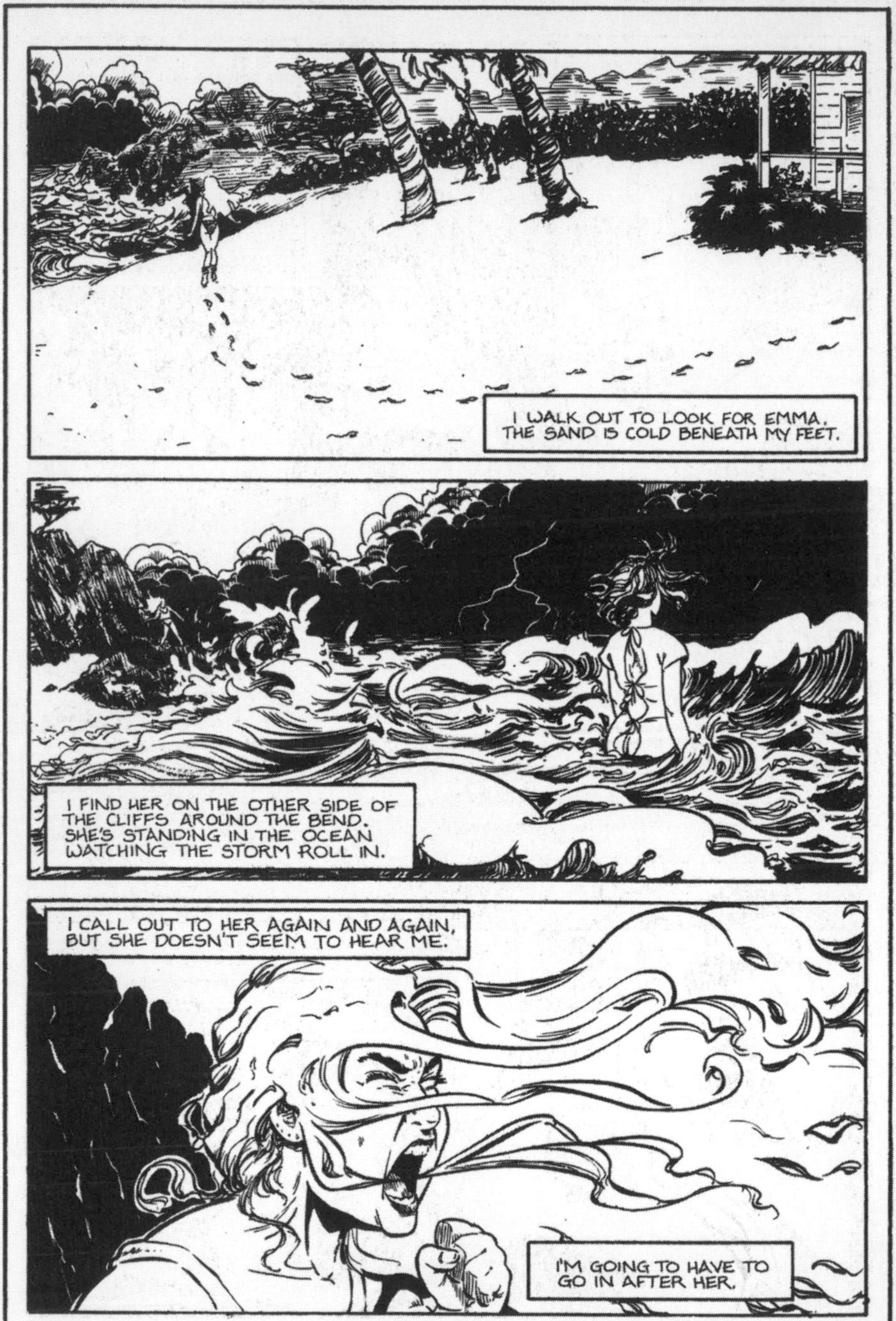
I WALK OUT TO LOOK FOR EMMA. THE SAND IS COLD BENEATH MY FEET.
I FIND HER ON THE OTHER SIDE OF THE CLIFFS AROUND THE BEND. SHE'S STANDING IN THE OCEAN WATCHING THE STORM ROLL IN.
I CALL OUT TO HER AGAIN AND AGAIN, BUT SHE DOESN'T SEEM TO HEAR ME.
I'M GOING TO HAVE TO GO IN AFTER HER.

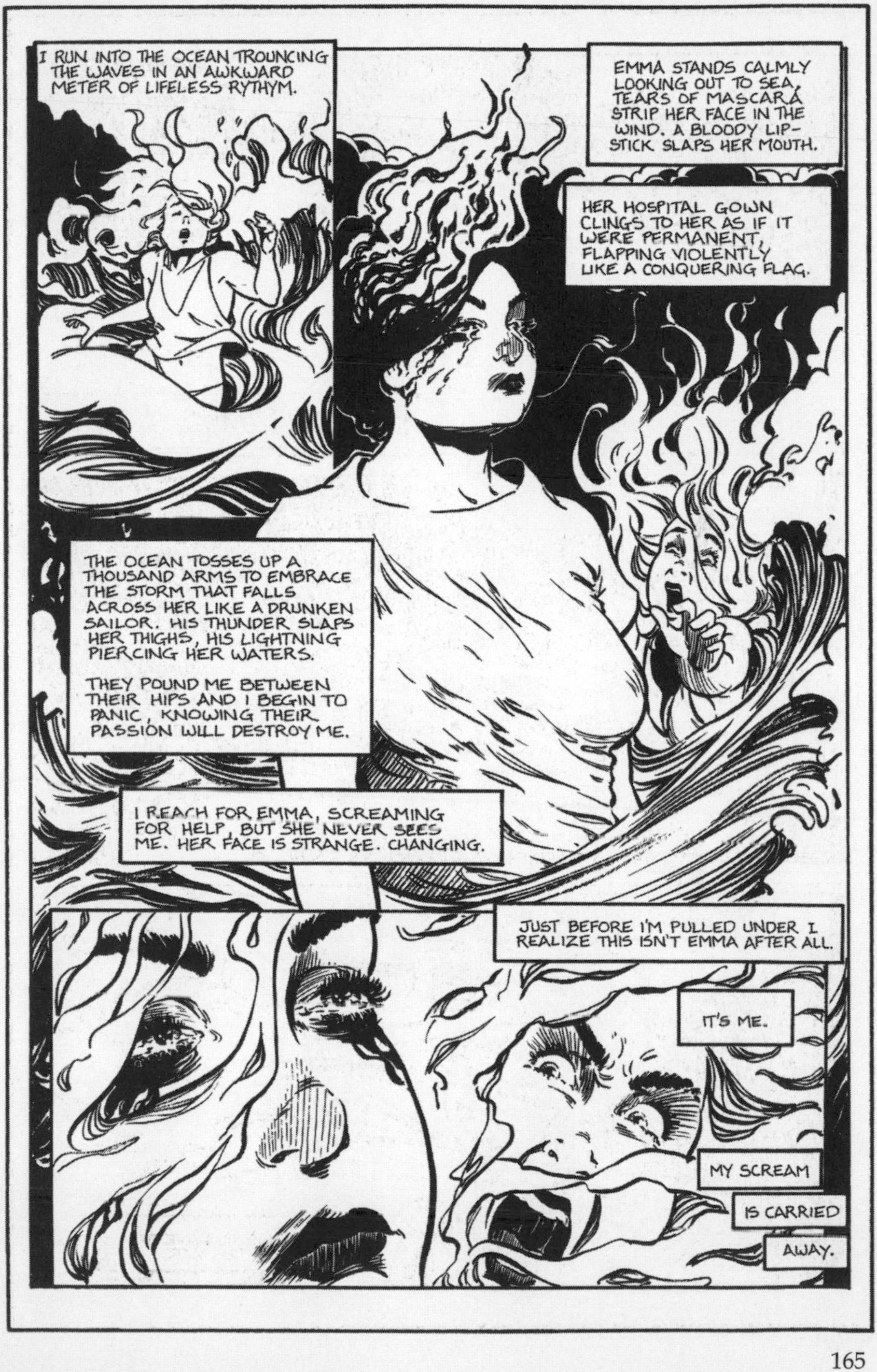
I RUN INTO THE OCEAN TROUNCING THE WAVES IN AN AWKWARD METER OF LIFELESS RYTHYM.
EMMA STANDS CALMLY LOOKING OUT TO SEA, TEARS OF MASCARA STRIP HER FACE IN THE WIND. A BLOODY LIP-STICK SLAPS HER MOUTH.
HER HOSPITAL GOWN CLINGS TO HER AS IF IT WERE PERMANENT, FLAPPING VIOLENTLY LIKE A CONQUERING FLAG.
THE OCEAN TOSSES UP A THOUSAND ARMS TO EMBRACE THE STORM THAT FALLS ACROSS HER LIKE A DRUNKEN SAILOR. HIS THUNDER SLAPS HER THIGHS, HIS LIGHTNING PIERCING HER WATERS.
THEY POUND ME BETWEEN THEIR HIPS AND I BEGIN TO PANIC, KNOWING THEIR PASSION WILL DESTROY ME.
I REACH FOR EMMA, SCREAMING FOR HELP, BUT SHE NEVER SEES ME. HER FACE IS STRANGE. CHANGING.
JUST BEFORE I'M PULLED UNDER I REALIZE THIS ISN'T EMMA AFTER ALL.
IT'S ME.
MY SCREAM
IS CARRIED
AWAY.

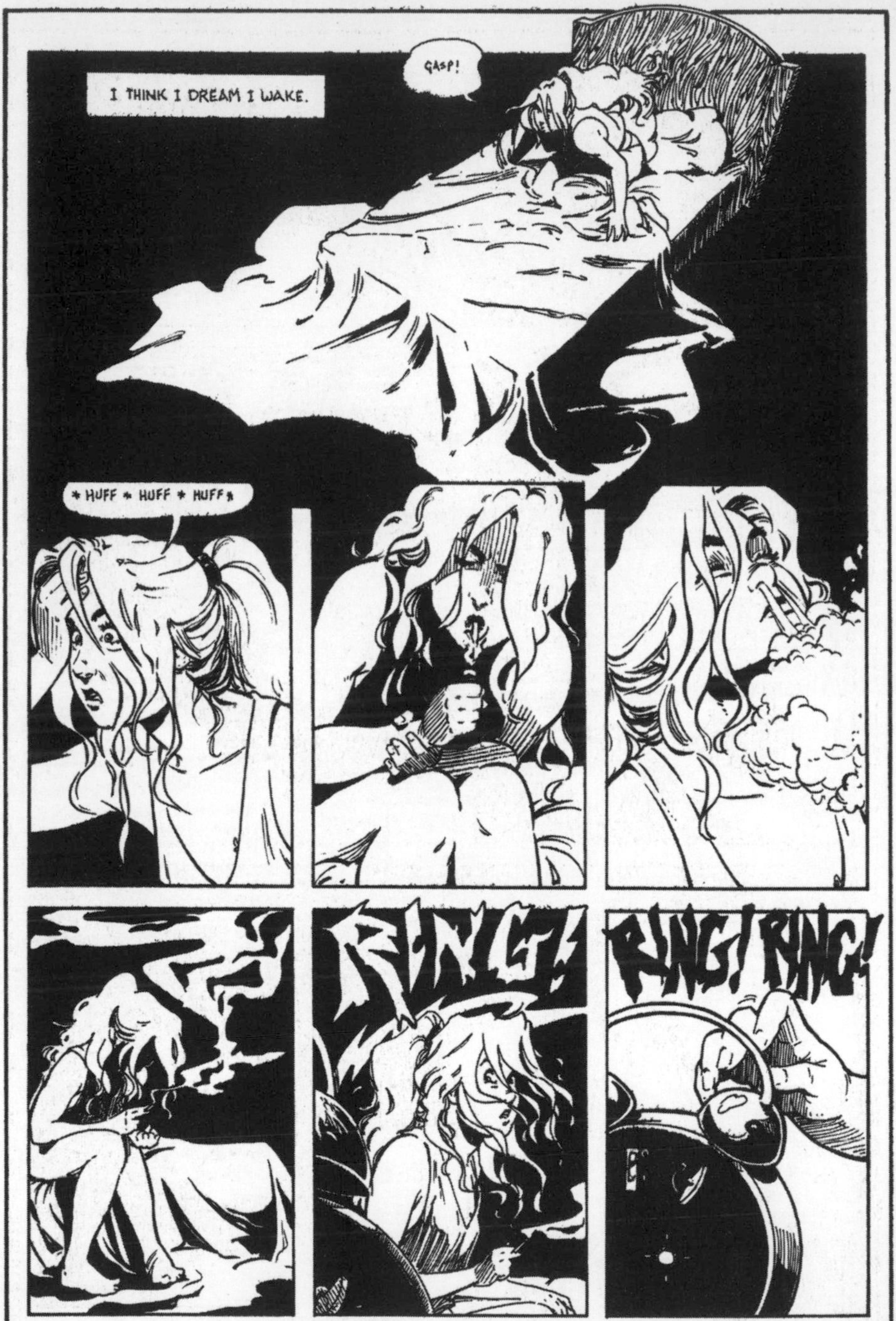
I THINK I DREAM I WAKE.
GASP!
* HUFF * HUFF * HUFF *
RING!
RING! RING!

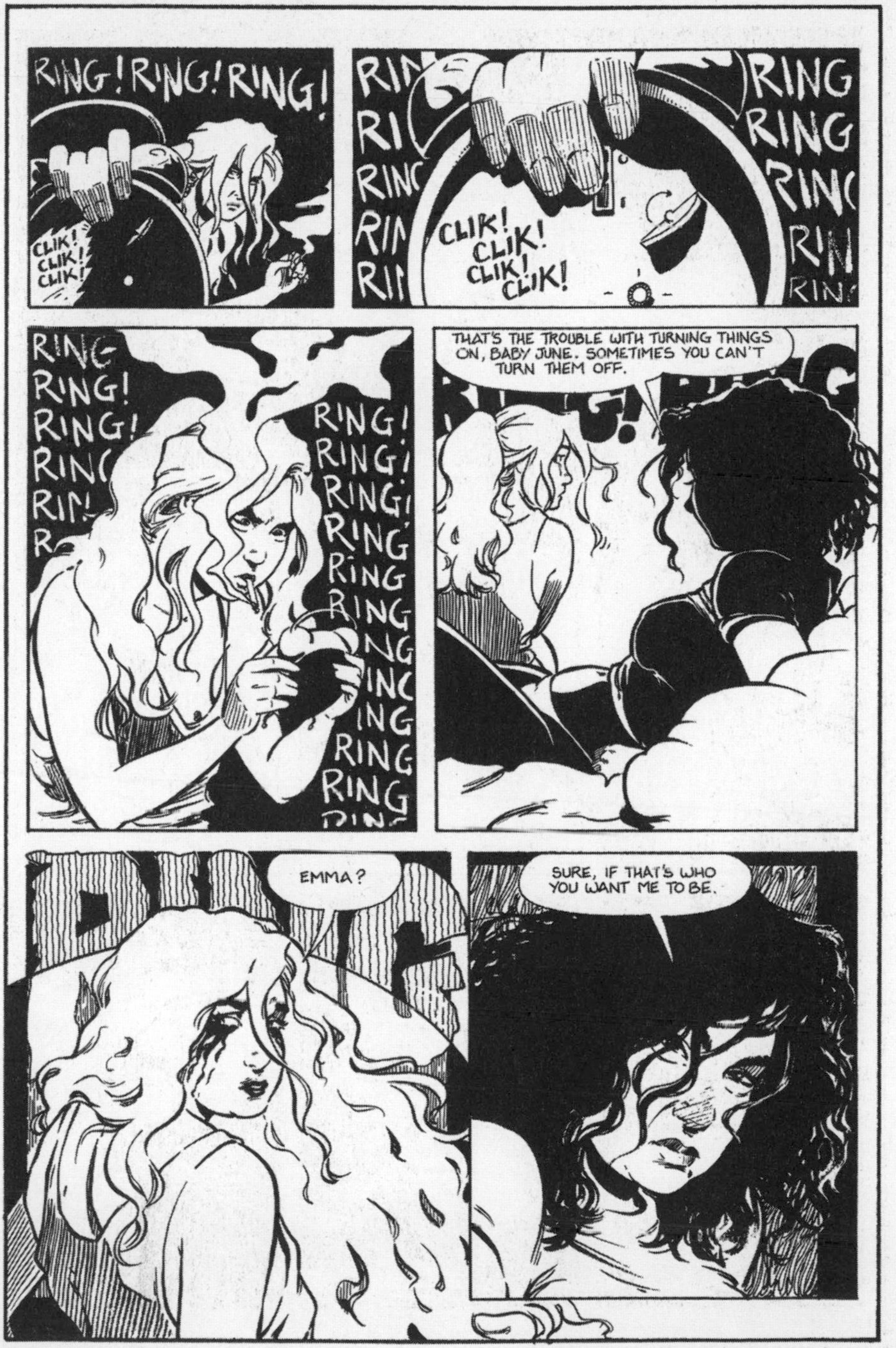

RING! RING! RING!
CLIK! CLIK! CLIK!
RING RING RING
CLIK! CLIK! CLIK! CLIK!
RING RING! RING! RING
RING! RING! RING! RING RING RING RING RING
THAT'S THE TROUBLE WITH TURNING THINGS ON, BABY JUNE. SOMETIMES YOU CAN'T TURN THEM OFF.
EMMA?
SURE, IF THAT'S WHO YOU WANT ME TO BE.

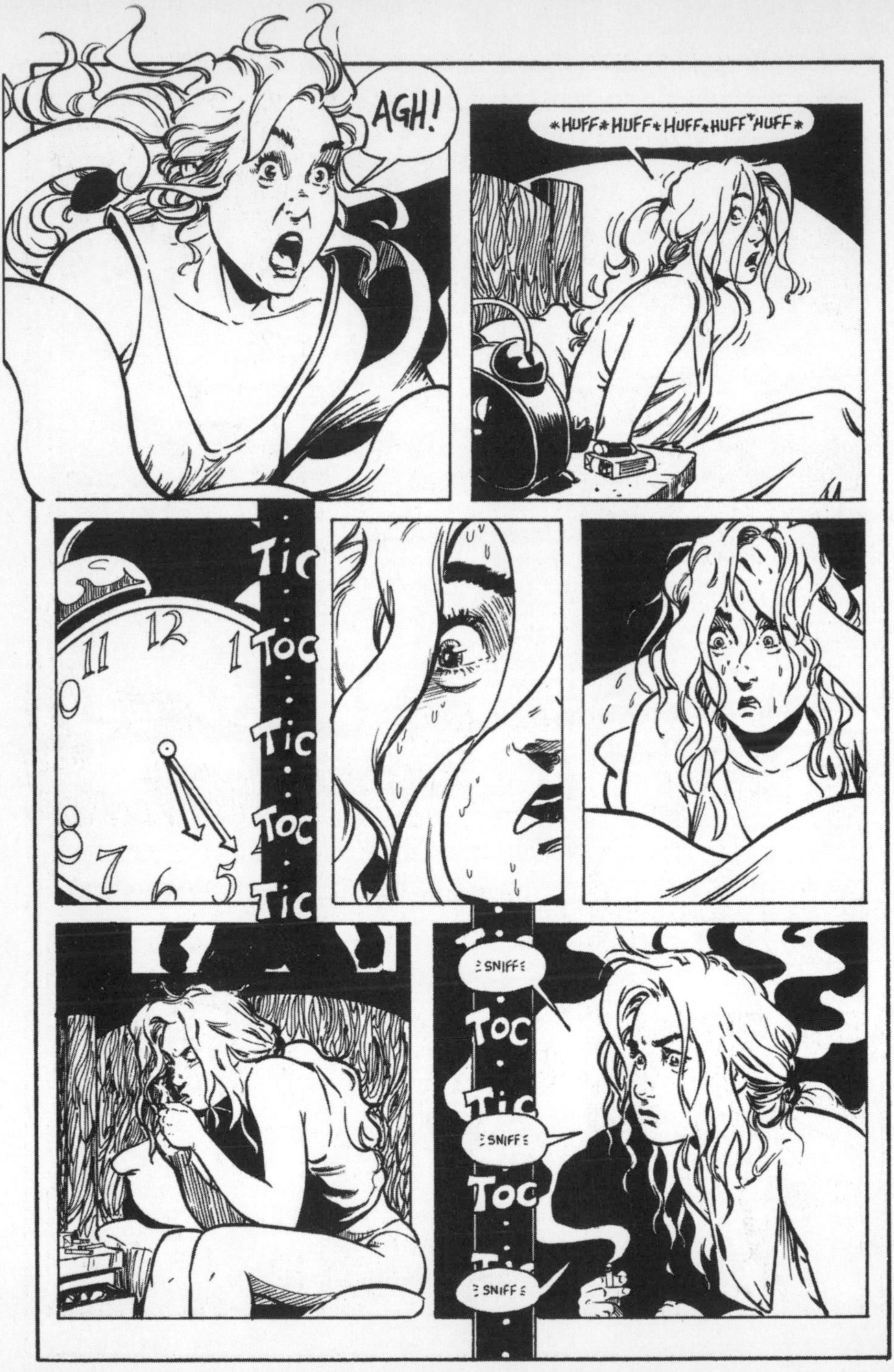
AGH!
*HUFF*HUFF*HUFF*HUFF*HUFF*
TIC
TOC
TIC
TOC
TIC
SNIFF
TOC
SNIFF
TOC
SNIFF

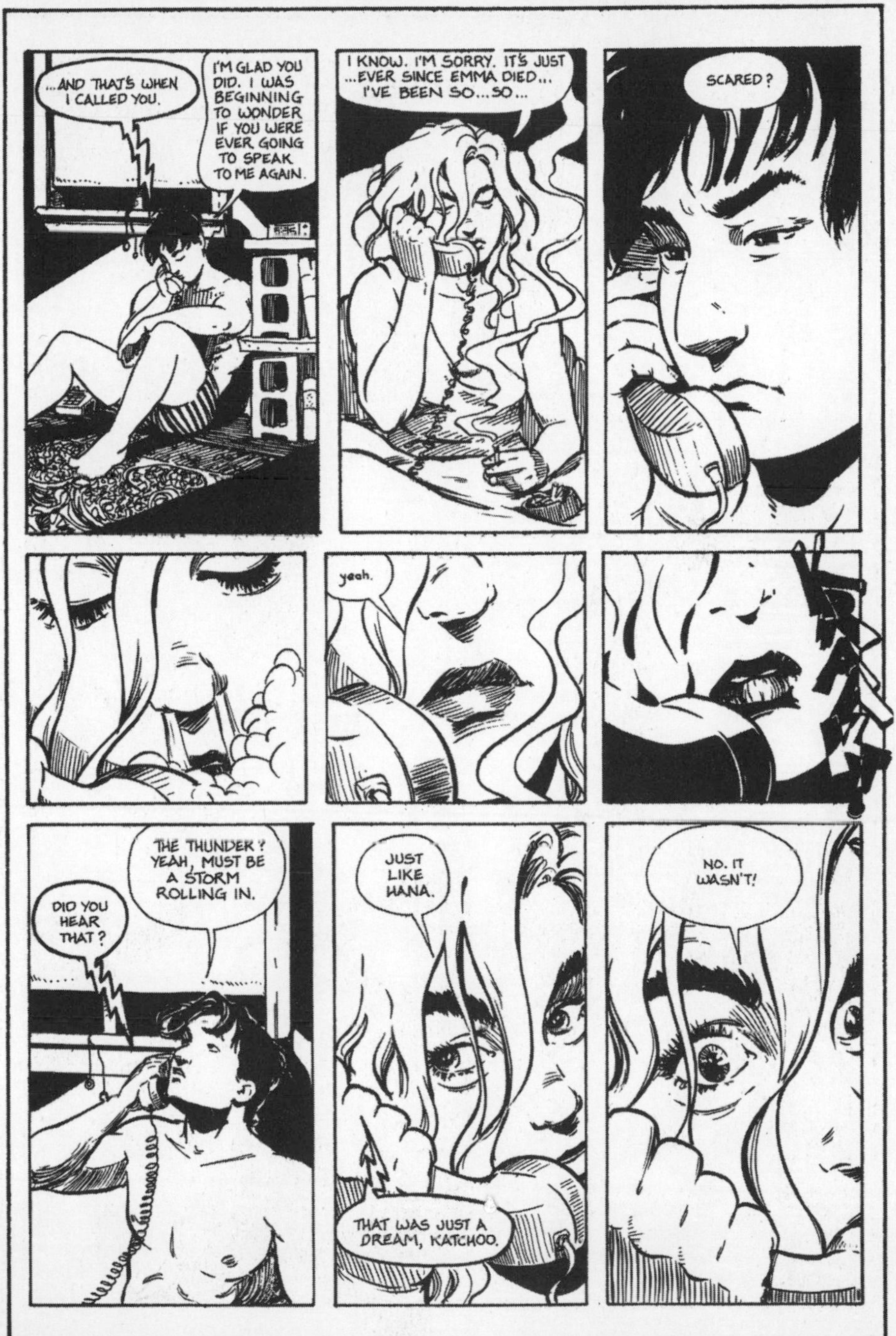
...AND THAT'S WHEN I CALLED YOU.
I'M GLAD YOU DID. I WAS BEGINNING TO WONDER IF YOU WERE EVER GOING TO SPEAK TO ME AGAIN.
I KNOW. I'M SORRY. IT'S JUST ...EVER SINCE EMMA DIED... I'VE BEEN SO...SO...
SCARED?
yeah.
DID YOU HEAR THAT?
THE THUNDER? YEAH, MUST BE A STORM ROLLING IN.
JUST LIKE HANA.
THAT WAS JUST A DREAM, KATCHOO.
NO. IT WASN'T!

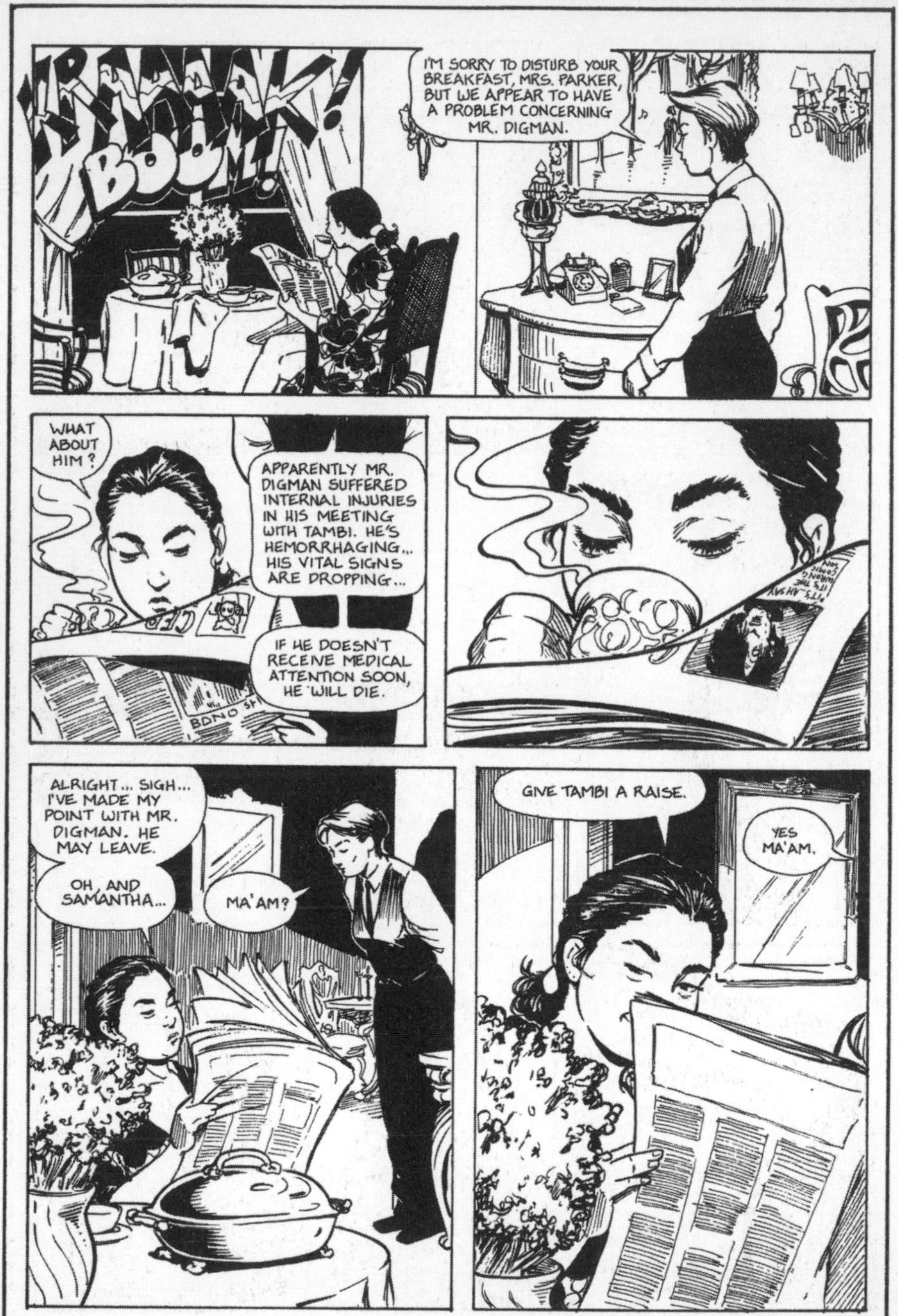
KRAAAAK!
BOOM!
I'M SORRY TO DISTURB YOUR BREAKFAST, MRS. PARKER, BUT WE APPEAR TO HAVE A PROBLEM CONCERNING MR. DIGMAN.
WHAT ABOUT HIM?
APPARENTLY MR. DIGMAN SUFFERED INTERNAL INJURIES IN HIS MEETING WITH TAMBI. HE'S HEMORRHAGING... HIS VITAL SIGNS ARE DROPPING...
IF HE DOESN'T RECEIVE MEDICAL ATTENTION SOON, HE WILL DIE.
ALRIGHT... SIGH... I'VE MADE MY POINT WITH MR. DIGMAN. HE MAY LEAVE.
OH, AND SAMANTHA...
MA'AM?
GIVE TAMBI A RAISE.
YES MA'AM.

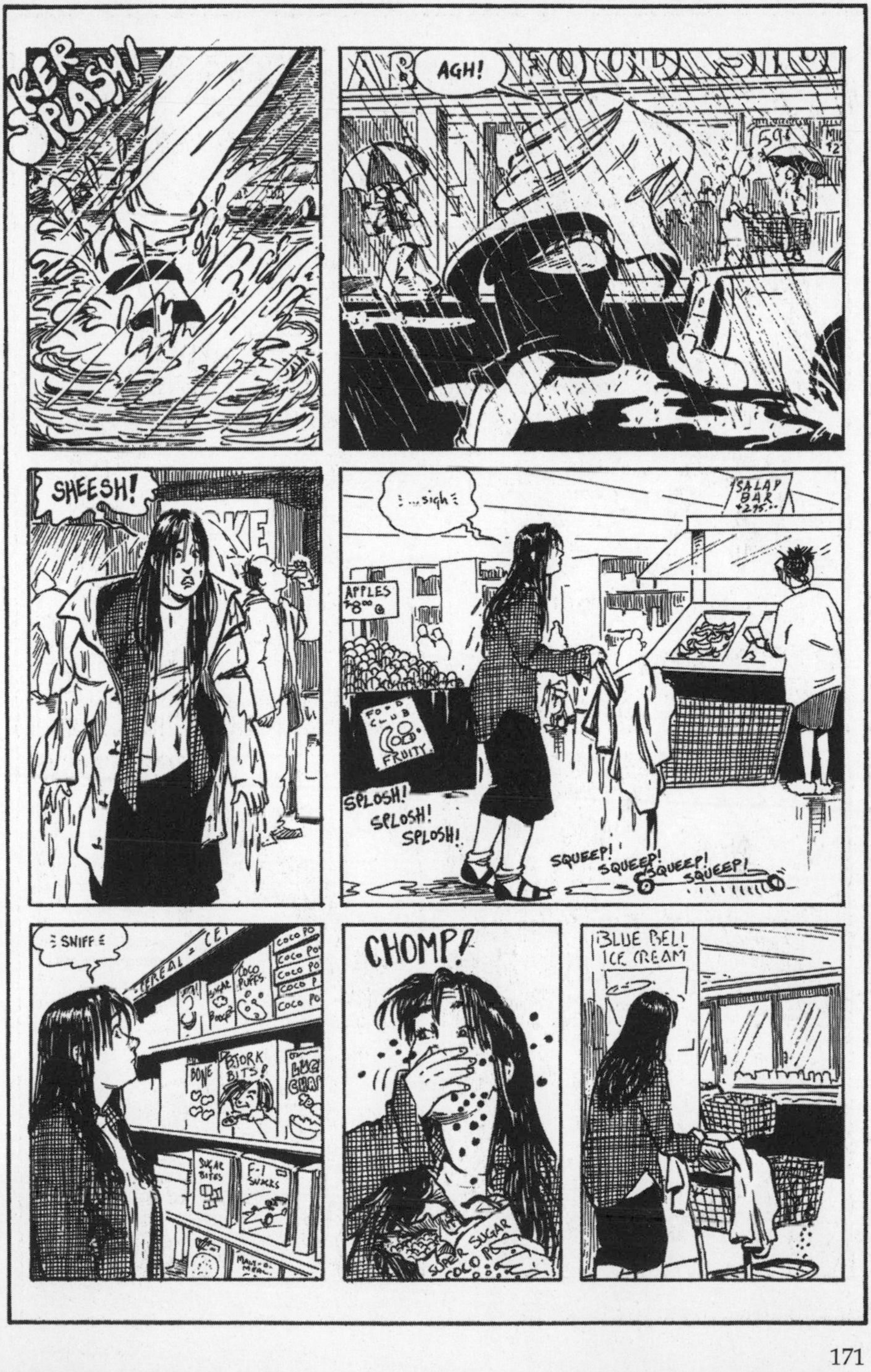
KER SPLASH!
AGH!
SHEESH!
...sigh
SALAD BAR
APPLES
FRUITY
SPLOSH!
SPLOSH!
SPLOSH!
SQUEEP!
SQUEEP!
SQUEEP!
SQUEEP!
SNIFF
COCO PUFFS
BJORK BITS!
BONE
SUGAR BITS
F-1 SNACKS
CHOMP!
SUPER SUGAR
BLUE BELL ICE CREAM

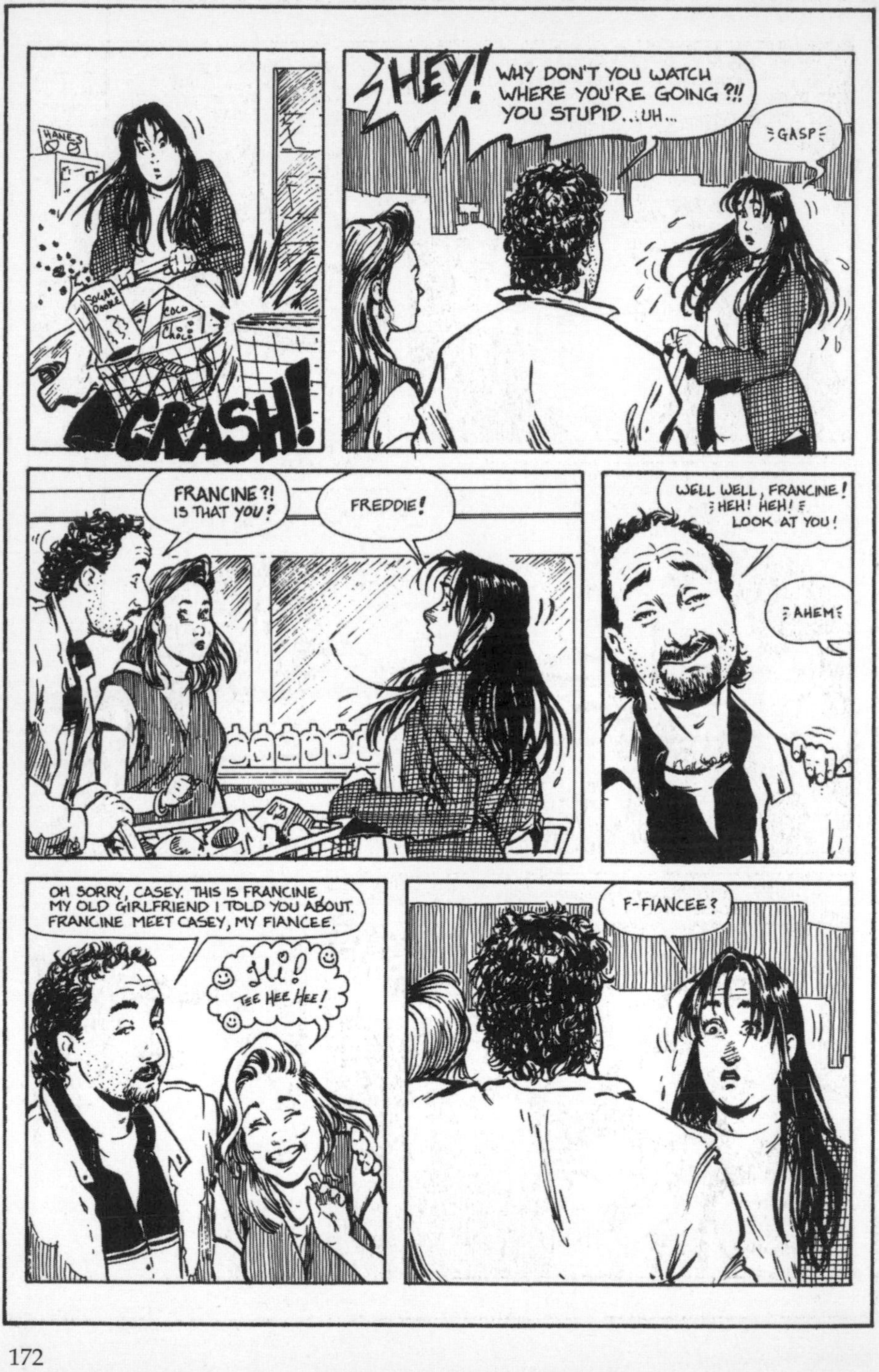
CRASH!
HEY!
WHY DON'T YOU WATCH WHERE YOU'RE GOING ?!! YOU STUPID...UH...
GASP
FRANCINE ?! IS THAT YOU ?
FREDDIE!
WELL WELL, FRANCINE! HEH! HEH! LOOK AT YOU!
AHEM
OH SORRY, CASEY. THIS IS FRANCINE MY OLD GIRLFRIEND I TOLD YOU ABOUT. FRANCINE MEET CASEY, MY FIANCEE.
Hi! TEE HEE HEE!
F-FIANCEE ?

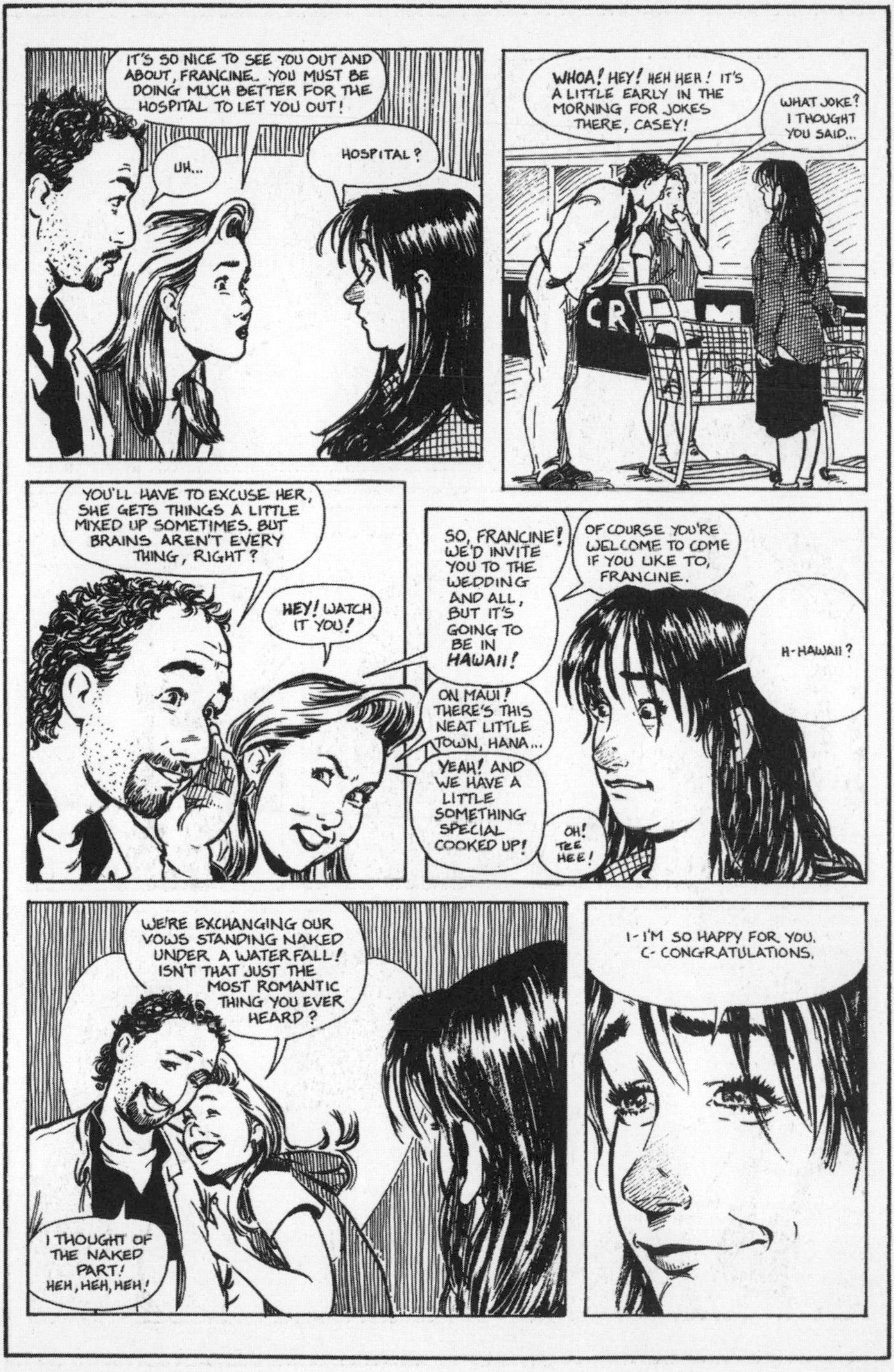
IT'S SO NICE TO SEE YOU OUT AND ABOUT, FRANCINE. YOU MUST BE DOING MUCH BETTER FOR THE HOSPITAL TO LET YOU OUT!
UH...
HOSPITAL?
WHOA! HEY! HEH HEH! IT'S A LITTLE EARLY IN THE MORNING FOR JOKES THERE, CASEY!
WHAT JOKE? I THOUGHT YOU SAID...
CR M
YOU'LL HAVE TO EXCUSE HER, SHE GETS THINGS A LITTLE MIXED UP SOMETIMES. BUT BRAINS AREN'T EVERY THING, RIGHT?
HEY! WATCH IT YOU!
SO, FRANCINE! WE'D INVITE YOU TO THE WEDDING AND ALL, BUT IT'S GOING TO BE IN HAWAII!
OF COURSE YOU'RE WELCOME TO COME IF YOU LIKE TO, FRANCINE.
H-HAWAII?
ON MAUI! THERE'S THIS NEAT LITTLE TOWN, HANA...
YEAH! AND WE HAVE A LITTLE SOMETHING SPECIAL COOKED UP!
OH! TEE HEE!
WE'RE EXCHANGING OUR VOWS STANDING NAKED UNDER A WATERFALL! ISN'T THAT JUST THE MOST ROMANTIC THING YOU EVER HEARD?
I THOUGHT OF THE NAKED PART! HEH, HEH, HEH!
I-I'M SO HAPPY FOR YOU. C-CONGRATULATIONS.

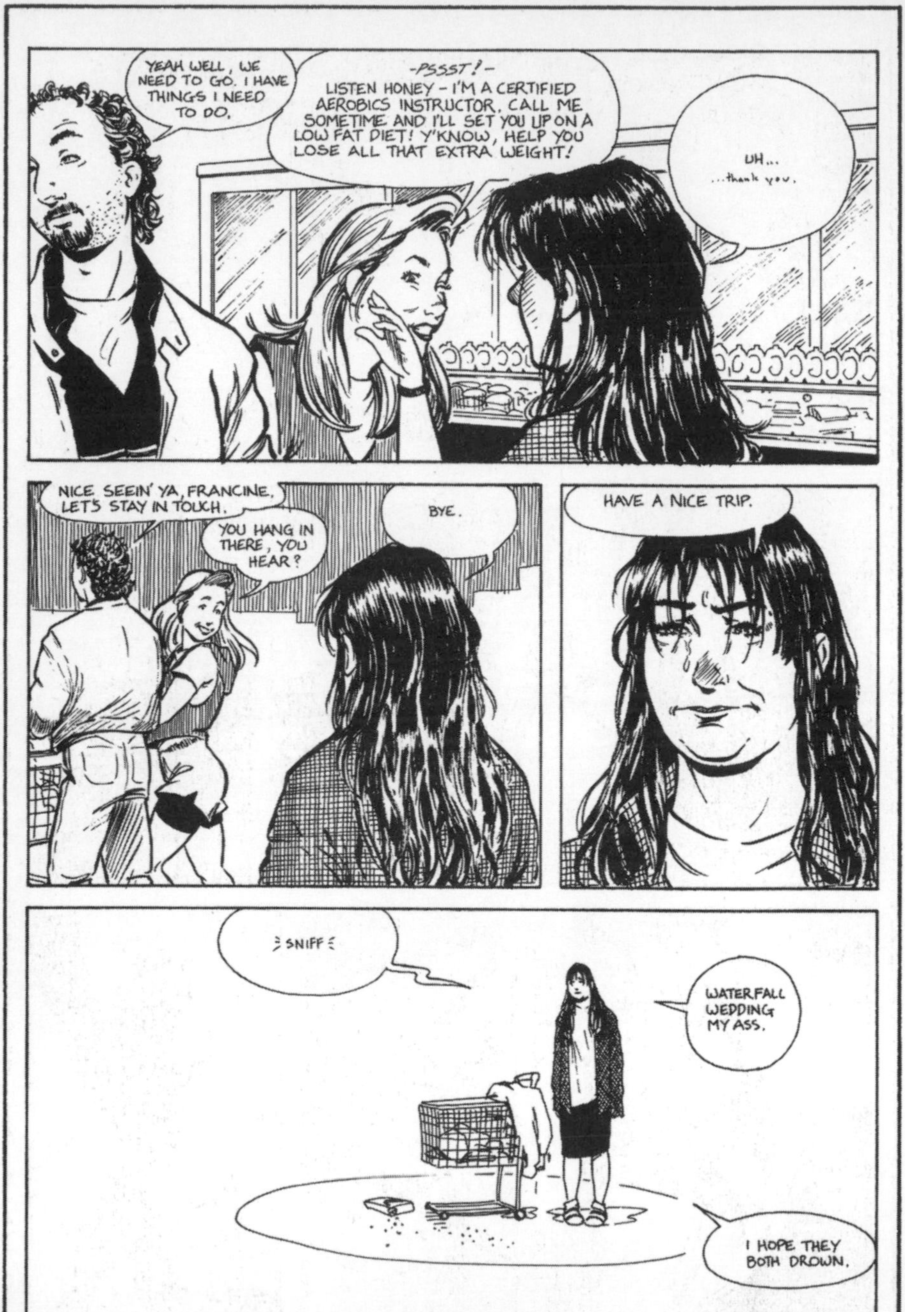
YEAH WELL, WE NEED TO GO. I HAVE THINGS I NEED TO DO.
-PSSST!-
LISTEN HONEY - I'M A CERTIFIED AEROBICS INSTRUCTOR. CALL ME SOMETIME AND I'LL SET YOU UP ON A LOW FAT DIET! Y'KNOW, HELP YOU LOSE ALL THAT EXTRA WEIGHT!
UH...
...thank you.
NICE SEEIN' YA, FRANCINE. LET'S STAY IN TOUCH.
YOU HANG IN THERE, YOU HEAR?
BYE.
HAVE A NICE TRIP.
SNIFF
WATERFALL WEDDING MY ASS.
I HOPE THEY BOTH DROWN.

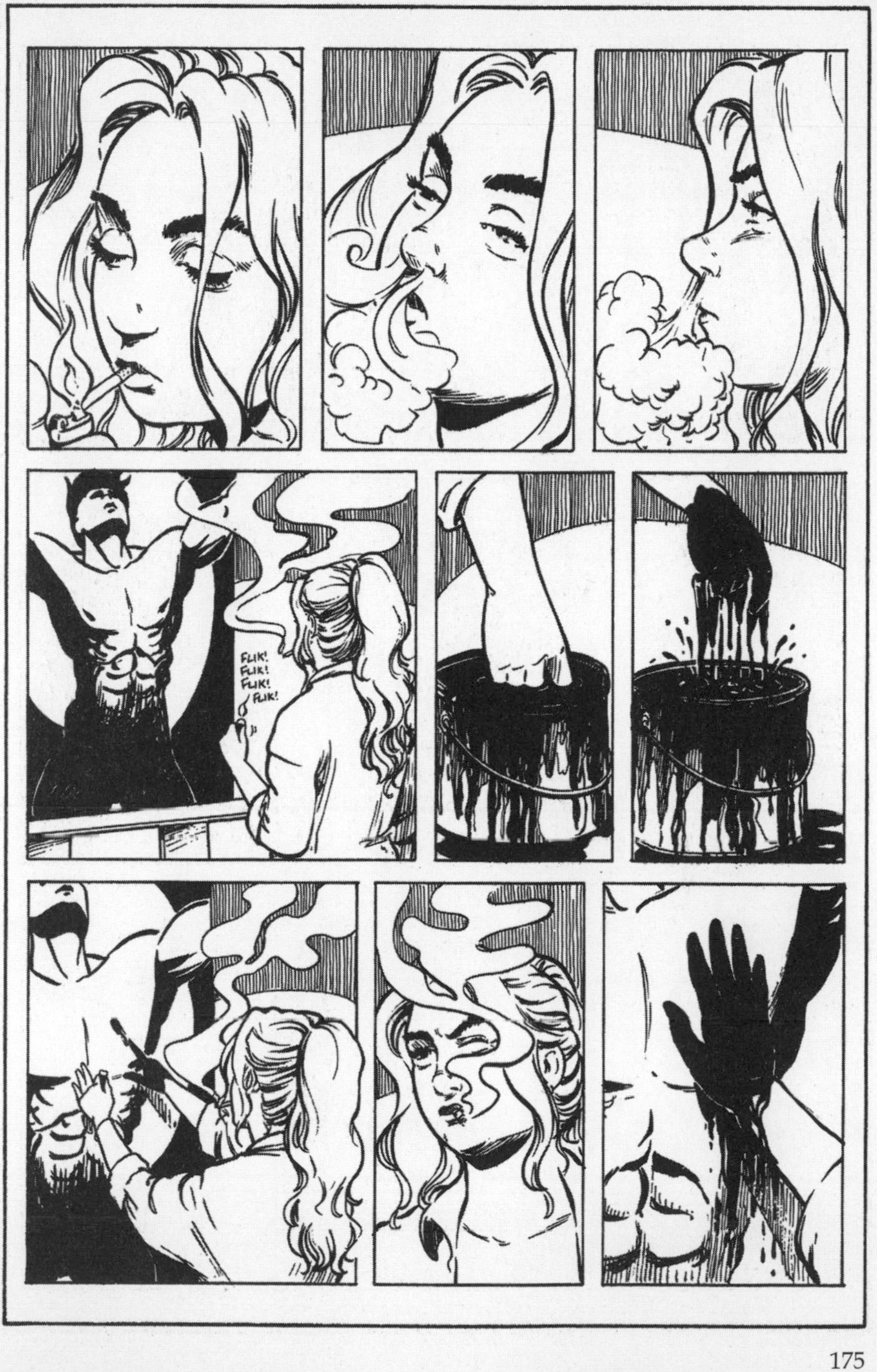

FLIK!
FLIK!
FLIK!
FLIK!

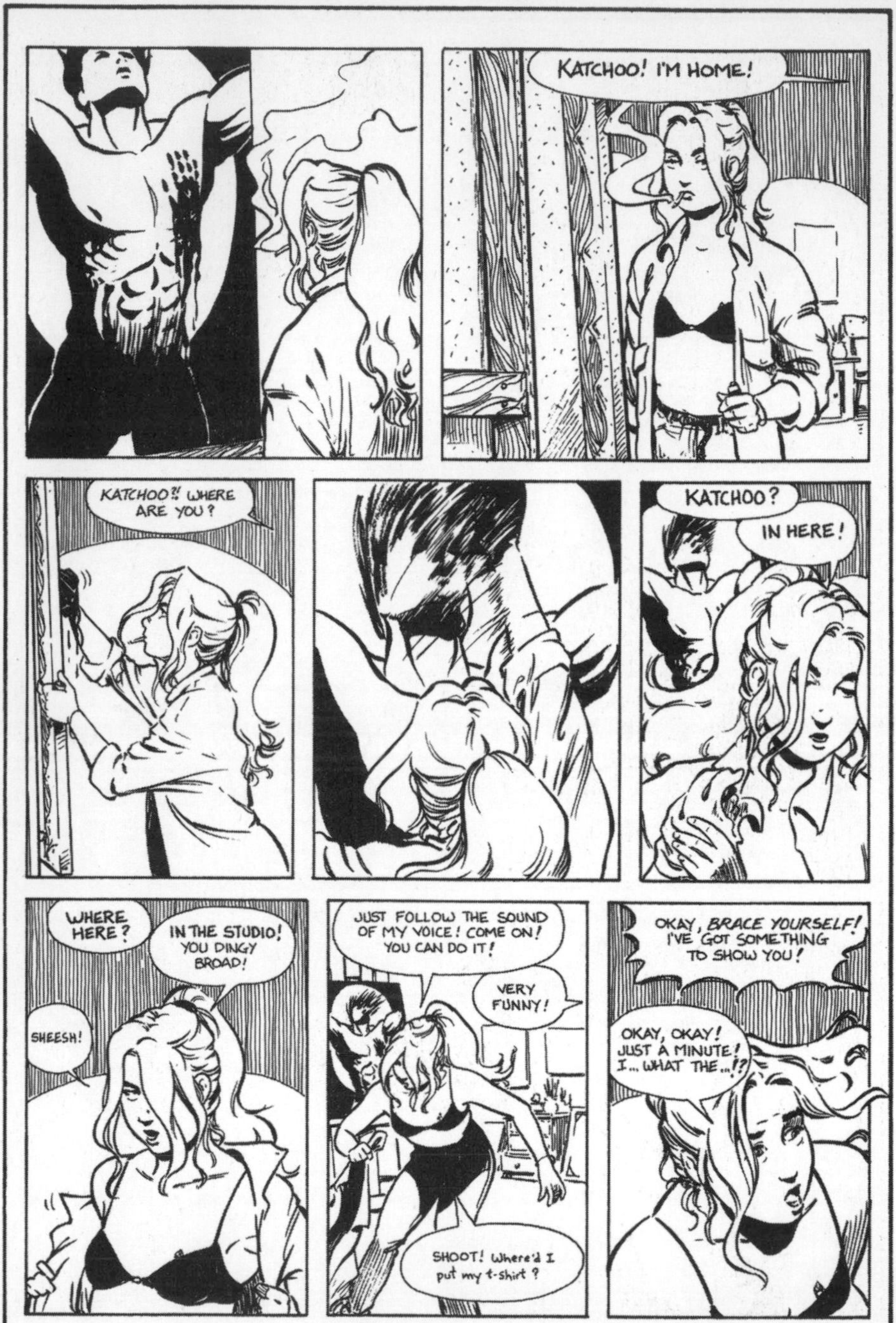
KATCHOO! I'M HOME!
KATCHOO?! WHERE ARE YOU?
KATCHOO?
IN HERE!
WHERE HERE?
IN THE STUDIO! YOU DINGY BROAD!
SHEESH!
JUST FOLLOW THE SOUND OF MY VOICE! COME ON! YOU CAN DO IT!
VERY FUNNY!
SHOOT! Where'd I put my t-shirt?
OKAY, BRACE YOURSELF! I'VE GOT SOMETHING TO SHOW YOU!
OKAY, OKAY! JUST A MINUTE! I... WHAT THE...!?

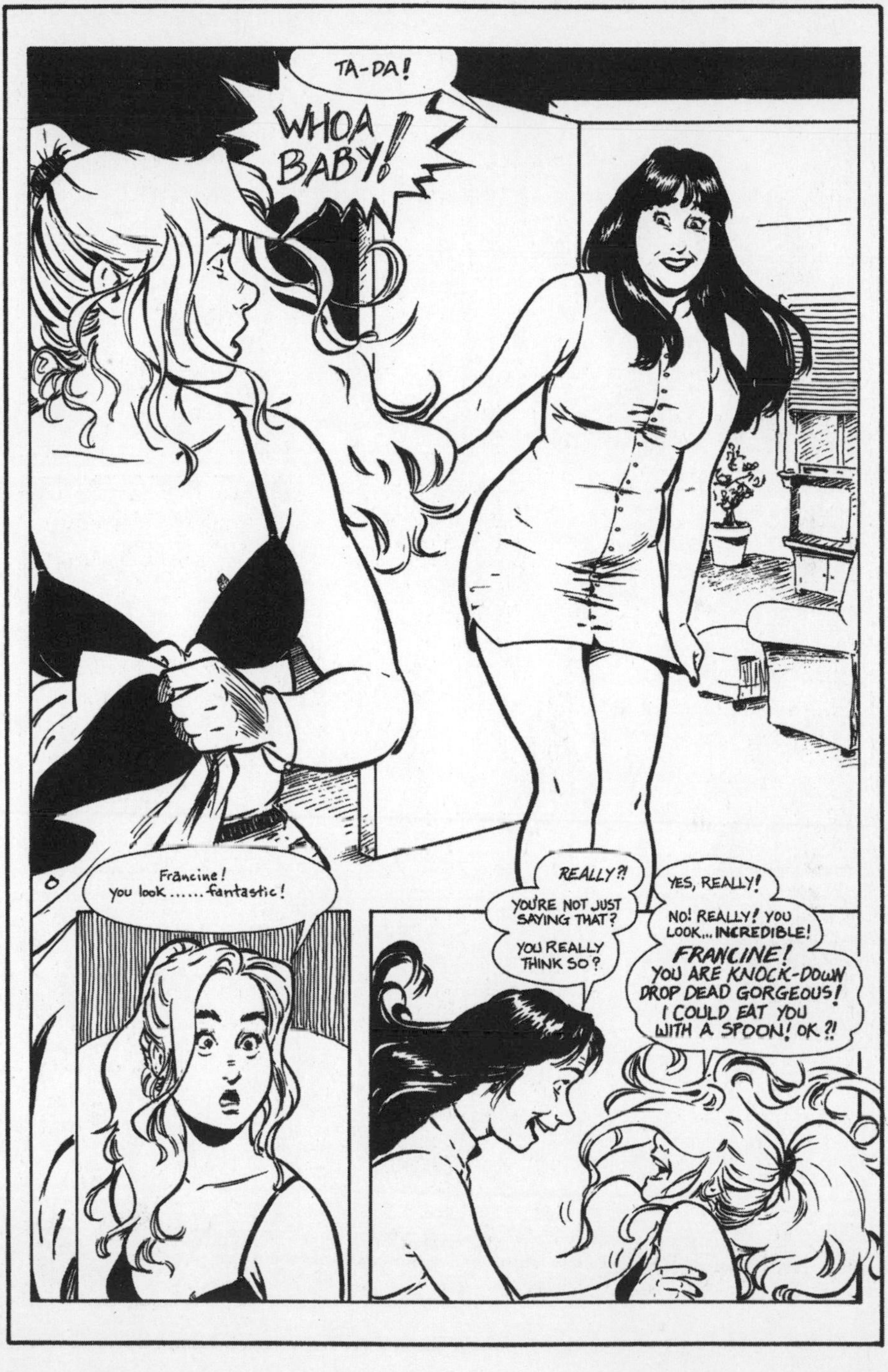
TA-DA!
WHOA BABY!
Francine! you look...... fantastic!
REALLY?!
YOU'RE NOT JUST SAYING THAT?
YOU REALLY THINK SO?
YES, REALLY!
NO! REALLY! YOU LOOK... INCREDIBLE!
FRANCINE! YOU ARE KNOCK-DOWN DROP DEAD GORGEOUS! I COULD EAT YOU WITH A SPOON! OK?!

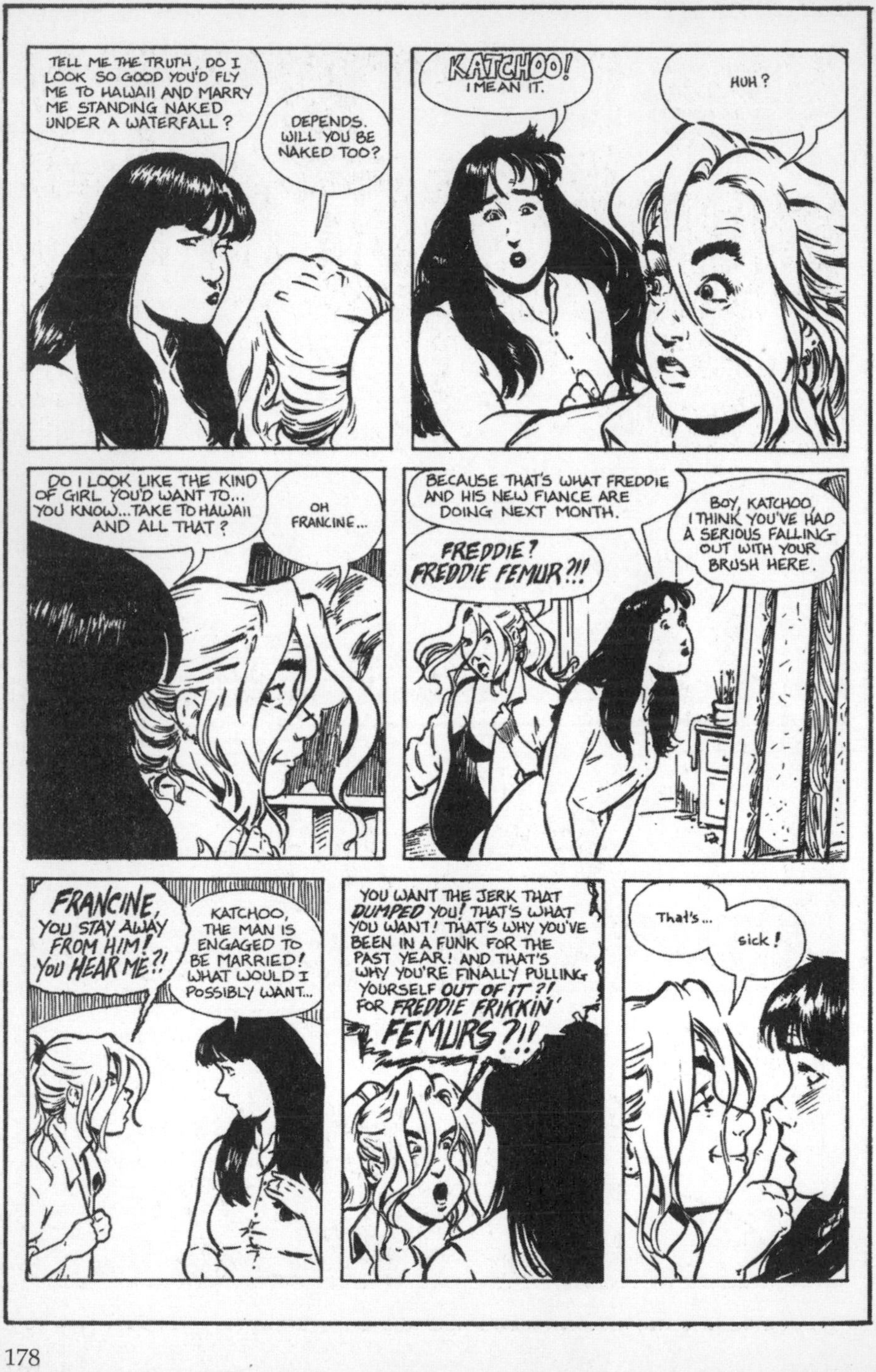
TELL ME THE TRUTH, DO I LOOK SO GOOD YOU'D FLY ME TO HAWAII AND MARRY ME STANDING NAKED UNDER A WATERFALL?
DEPENDS. WILL YOU BE NAKED TOO?
KATCHOO! I MEAN IT.
HUH?
DO I LOOK LIKE THE KIND OF GIRL YOU'D WANT TO... YOU KNOW...TAKE TO HAWAII AND ALL THAT?
OH FRANCINE...
BECAUSE THAT'S WHAT FREDDIE AND HIS NEW FIANCE ARE DOING NEXT MONTH.
FREDDIE? FREDDIE FEMUR?!!
BOY, KATCHOO, I THINK YOU'VE HAD A SERIOUS FALLING OUT WITH YOUR BRUSH HERE.
FRANCINE, YOU STAY AWAY FROM HIM! YOU HEAR ME?!
KATCHOO, THE MAN IS ENGAGED TO BE MARRIED! WHAT WOULD I POSSIBLY WANT...
YOU WANT THE JERK THAT DUMPED YOU! THAT'S WHAT YOU WANT! THAT'S WHY YOU'VE BEEN IN A FUNK FOR THE PAST YEAR! AND THAT'S WHY YOU'RE FINALLY PULLING YOURSELF OUT OF IT?! FOR FREDDIE FRIKKIN' FEMURS?!!
That's...
sick!

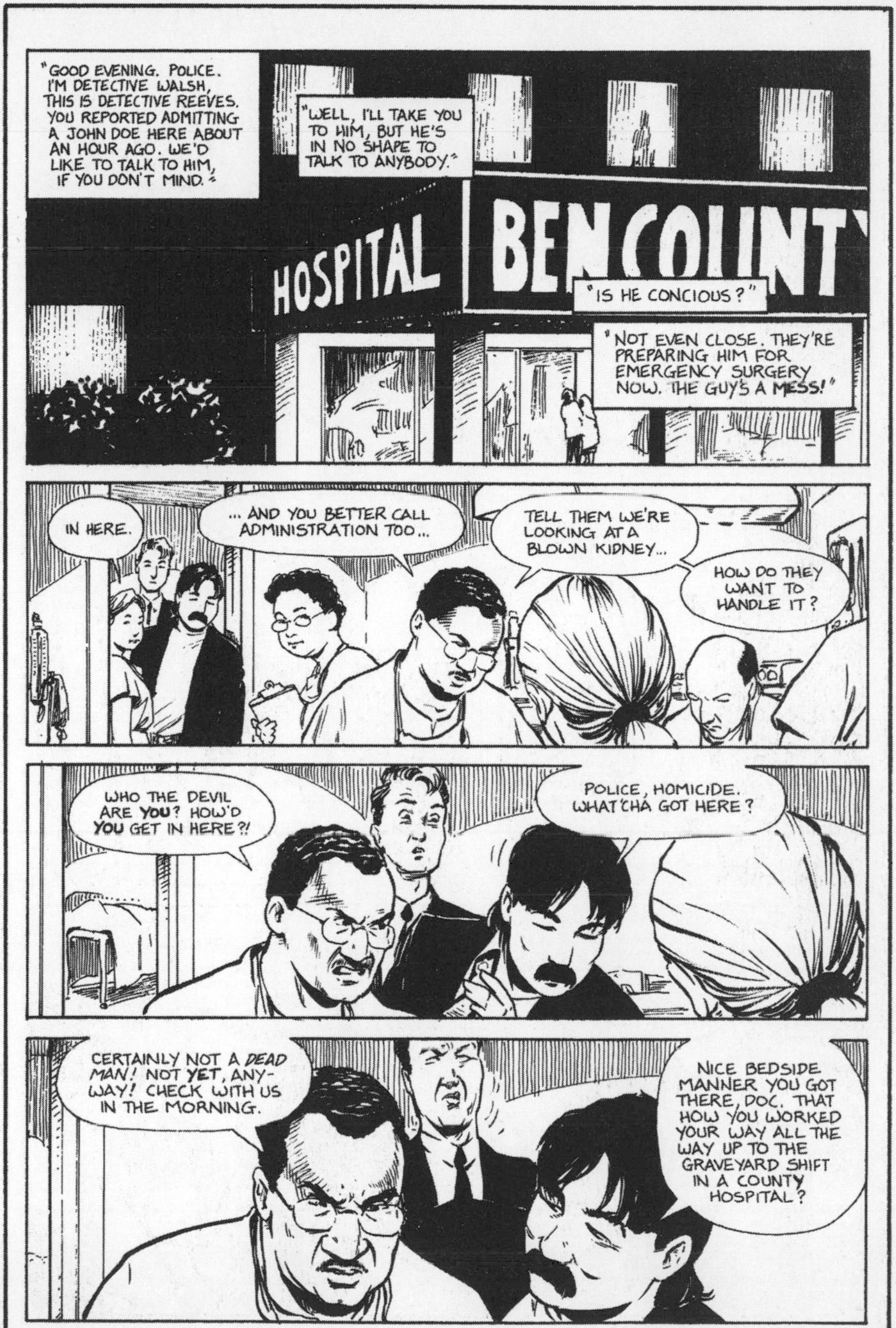
"GOOD EVENING. POLICE. I'M DETECTIVE WALSH, THIS IS DETECTIVE REEVES. YOU REPORTED ADMITTING A JOHN DOE HERE ABOUT AN HOUR AGO. WE'D LIKE TO TALK TO HIM, IF YOU DON'T MIND."
"WELL, I'LL TAKE YOU TO HIM, BUT HE'S IN NO SHAPE TO TALK TO ANYBODY."
HOSPITAL
BEN COUNTY
"IS HE CONCIOUS?"
"NOT EVEN CLOSE. THEY'RE PREPARING HIM FOR EMERGENCY SURGERY NOW. THE GUY'S A MESS!"
IN HERE.
... AND YOU BETTER CALL ADMINISTRATION TOO...
TELL THEM WE'RE LOOKING AT A BLOWN KIDNEY...
HOW DO THEY WANT TO HANDLE IT?
WHO THE DEVIL ARE YOU? HOW'D YOU GET IN HERE?!
POLICE, HOMICIDE. WHAT'CHA GOT HERE?
CERTAINLY NOT A DEAD MAN! NOT YET, ANYWAY! CHECK WITH US IN THE MORNING.
NICE BEDSIDE MANNER YOU GOT THERE, DOC. THAT HOW YOU WORKED YOUR WAY ALL THE WAY UP TO THE GRAVEYARD SHIFT IN A COUNTY HOSPITAL?

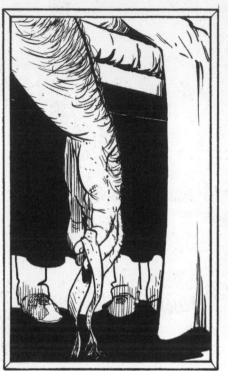

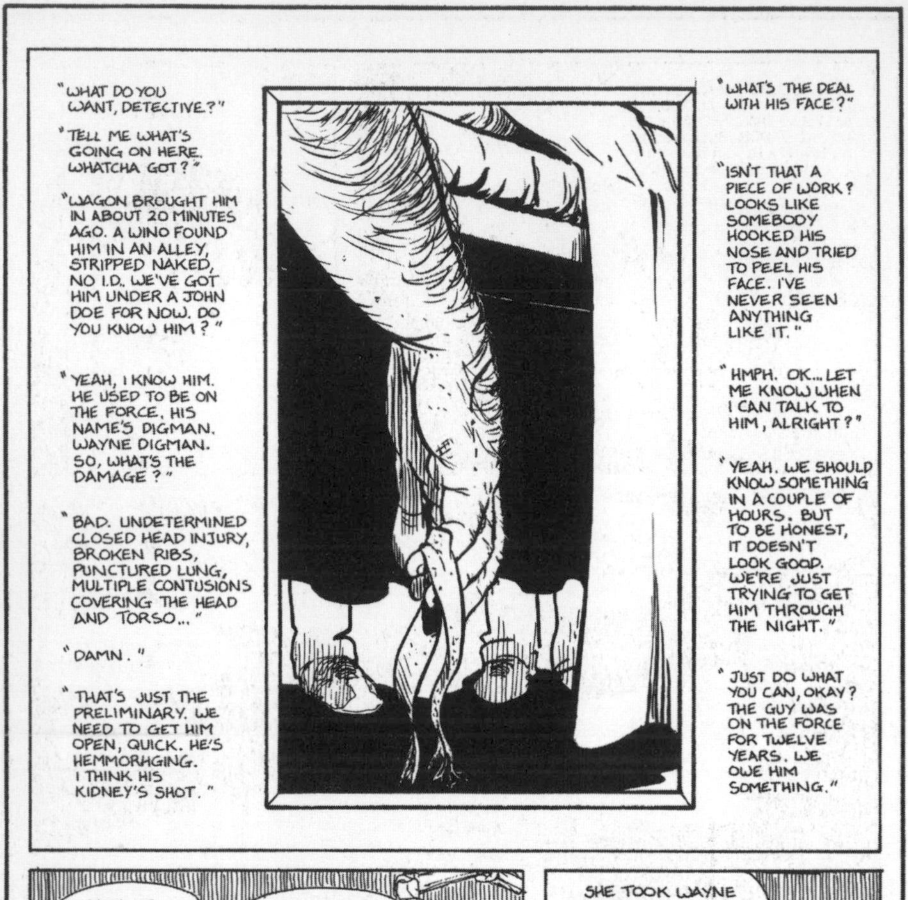

"WHAT DO YOU WANT, DETECTIVE?"

"TELL ME WHAT'S GOING ON HERE. WHATCHA GOT?"

"WAGON BROUGHT HIM IN ABOUT 20 MINUTES AGO. A WINO FOUND HIM IN AN ALLEY, STRIPPED NAKED, NO I.D. WE'VE GOT HIM UNDER A JOHN DOE FOR NOW. DO YOU KNOW HIM?"

"YEAH, I KNOW HIM. HE USED TO BE ON THE FORCE. HIS NAME'S DIGMAN. WAYNE DIGMAN. SO, WHAT'S THE DAMAGE?"

"BAD. UNDETERMINED CLOSED HEAD INJURY, BROKEN RIBS, PUNCTURED LUNG, MULTIPLE CONTUSIONS COVERING THE HEAD AND TORSO..."

"DAMN."

"THAT'S JUST THE PRELIMINARY. WE NEED TO GET HIM OPEN, QUICK. HE'S HEMMORHGING. I THINK HIS KIDNEY'S SHOT."

"WHAT'S THE DEAL WITH HIS FACE?"

"ISN'T THAT A PIECE OF WORK? LOOKS LIKE SOMEBODY HOOKED HIS NOSE AND TRIED TO PEEL HIS FACE. I'VE NEVER SEEN ANYTHING LIKE IT."

"HMPH. OK... LET ME KNOW WHEN I CAN TALK TO HIM, ALRIGHT?"

"YEAH. WE SHOULD KNOW SOMETHING IN A COUPLE OF HOURS. BUT TO BE HONEST, IT DOESN'T LOOK GOOD. WE'RE JUST TRYING TO GET HIM THROUGH THE NIGHT."

"JUST DO WHAT YOU CAN, OKAY? THE GUY WAS ON THE FORCE FOR TWELVE YEARS. WE OWE HIM SOMETHING."

MAN, HE LOOKS BAD.

YEAH. LISTEN, REMEMBER THE BLONDE WE HAD IN LAST SUMMER?

...TRIED TO CASTRATE HER ROOMMATE'S BOYFRIEND. HAD AN FBI FILE WE COULDN'T ACCESS?

YEAH?

SHE TOOK WAYNE DOWN IN A CELL ONE NIGHT WHEN HE TRIED TO GET CUTE WITH HER.

OH YEAH.

SHE HAD THIS BODACIOUS NOSE LOCK ON HIM.

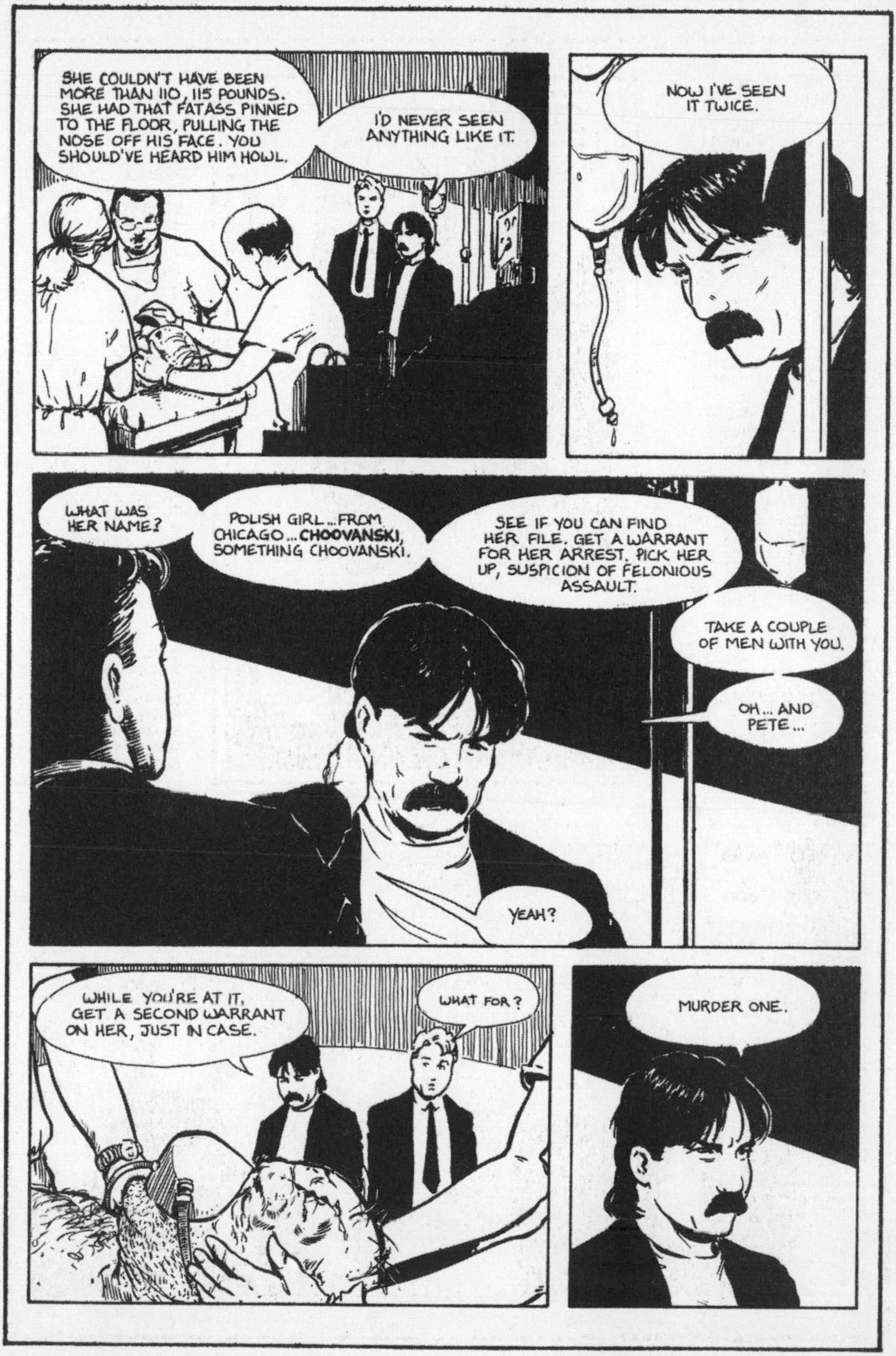
SHE COULDN'T HAVE BEEN MORE THAN 110, 115 POUNDS. SHE HAD THAT FATASS PINNED TO THE FLOOR, PULLING THE NOSE OFF HIS FACE. YOU SHOULD'VE HEARD HIM HOWL.
I'D NEVER SEEN ANYTHING LIKE IT.
NOW I'VE SEEN IT TWICE.
WHAT WAS HER NAME?
POLISH GIRL... FROM CHICAGO... CHOOVANSKI, SOMETHING CHOOVANSKI.
SEE IF YOU CAN FIND HER FILE. GET A WARRANT FOR HER ARREST. PICK HER UP, SUSPICION OF FELONIOUS ASSAULT.
TAKE A COUPLE OF MEN WITH YOU.
OH... AND PETE...
YEAH?
WHILE YOU'RE AT IT, GET A SECOND WARRANT ON HER, JUST IN CASE.
WHAT FOR?
MURDER ONE.

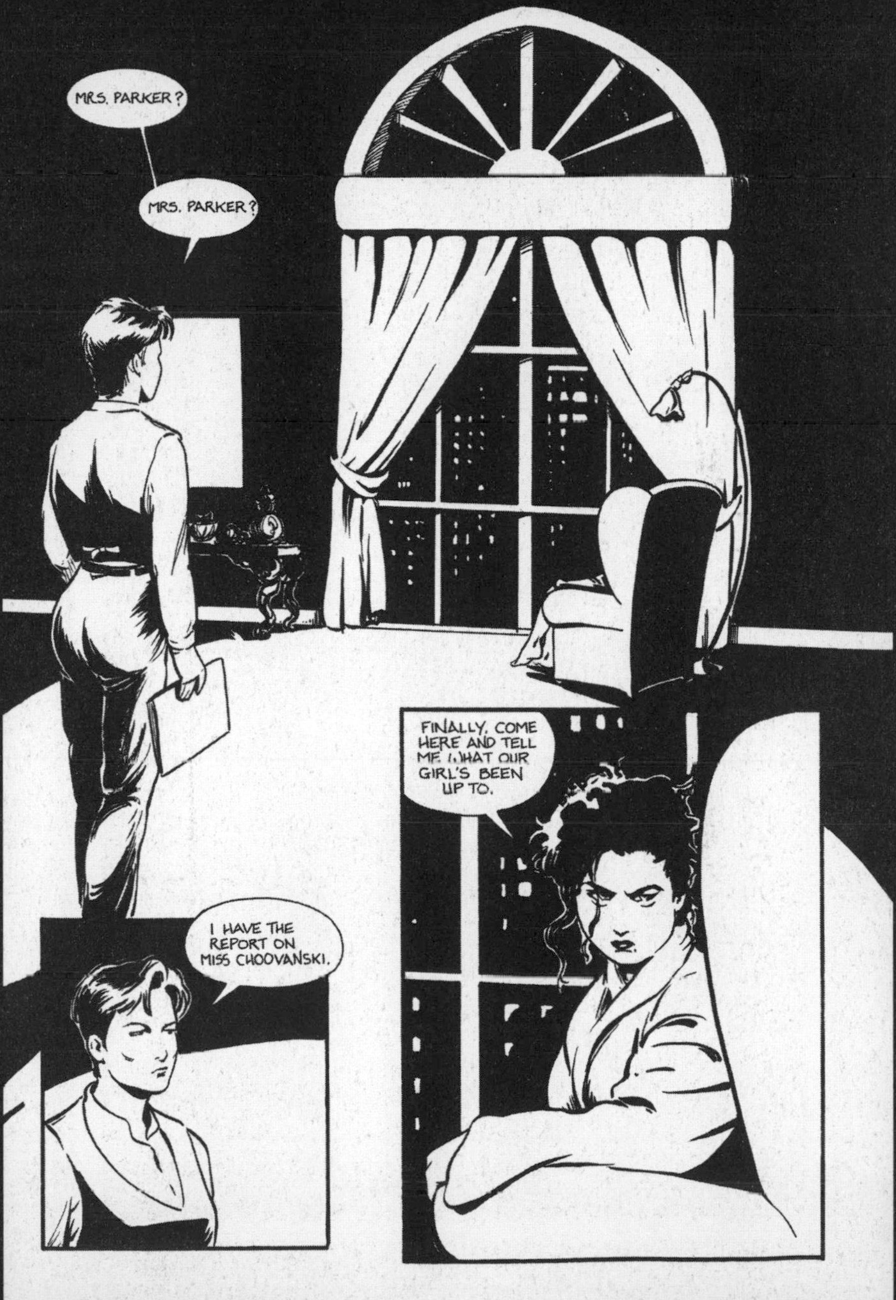
MRS. PARKER?
MRS. PARKER?
I HAVE THE REPORT ON MISS CHOOVANSKI.
FINALLY. COME HERE AND TELL ME WHAT OUR GIRL'S BEEN UP TO.

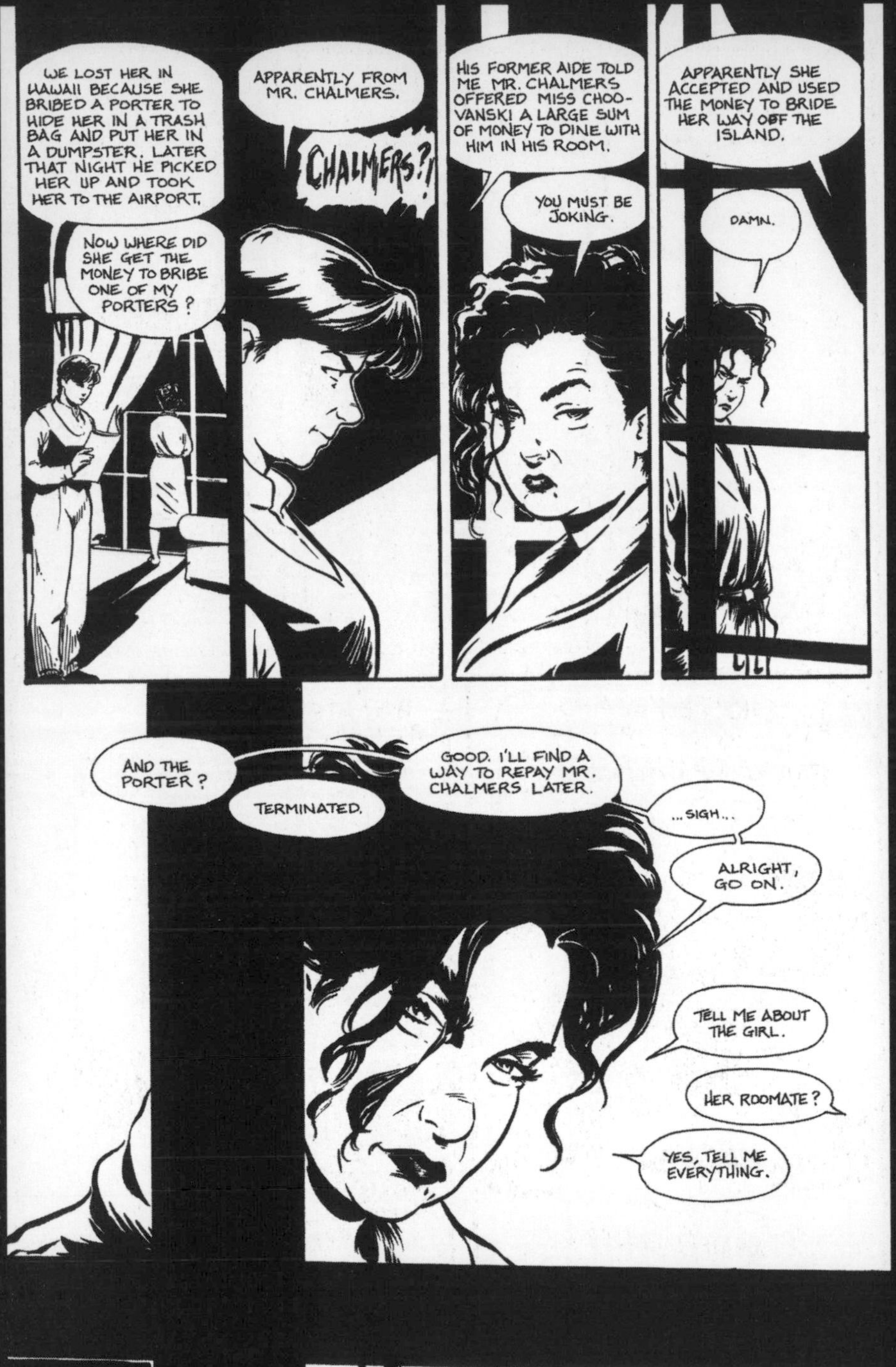
WE LOST HER IN HAWAII BECAUSE SHE BRIBED A PORTER TO HIDE HER IN A TRASH BAG AND PUT HER IN A DUMPSTER. LATER THAT NIGHT HE PICKED HER UP AND TOOK HER TO THE AIRPORT.
NOW WHERE DID SHE GET THE MONEY TO BRIBE ONE OF MY PORTERS?
APPARENTLY FROM MR. CHALMERS.
CHALMERS?!
HIS FORMER AIDE TOLD ME MR. CHALMERS OFFERED MISS CHOOVANSKI A LARGE SUM OF MONEY TO DINE WITH HIM IN HIS ROOM.
YOU MUST BE JOKING.
APPARENTLY SHE ACCEPTED AND USED THE MONEY TO BRIDE HER WAY OFF THE ISLAND.
DAMN.
AND THE PORTER?
TERMINATED.
GOOD. I'LL FIND A WAY TO REPAY MR. CHALMERS LATER.
...SIGH...
ALRIGHT, GO ON.
TELL ME ABOUT THE GIRL.
HER ROOMATE?
YES, TELL ME EVERYTHING.

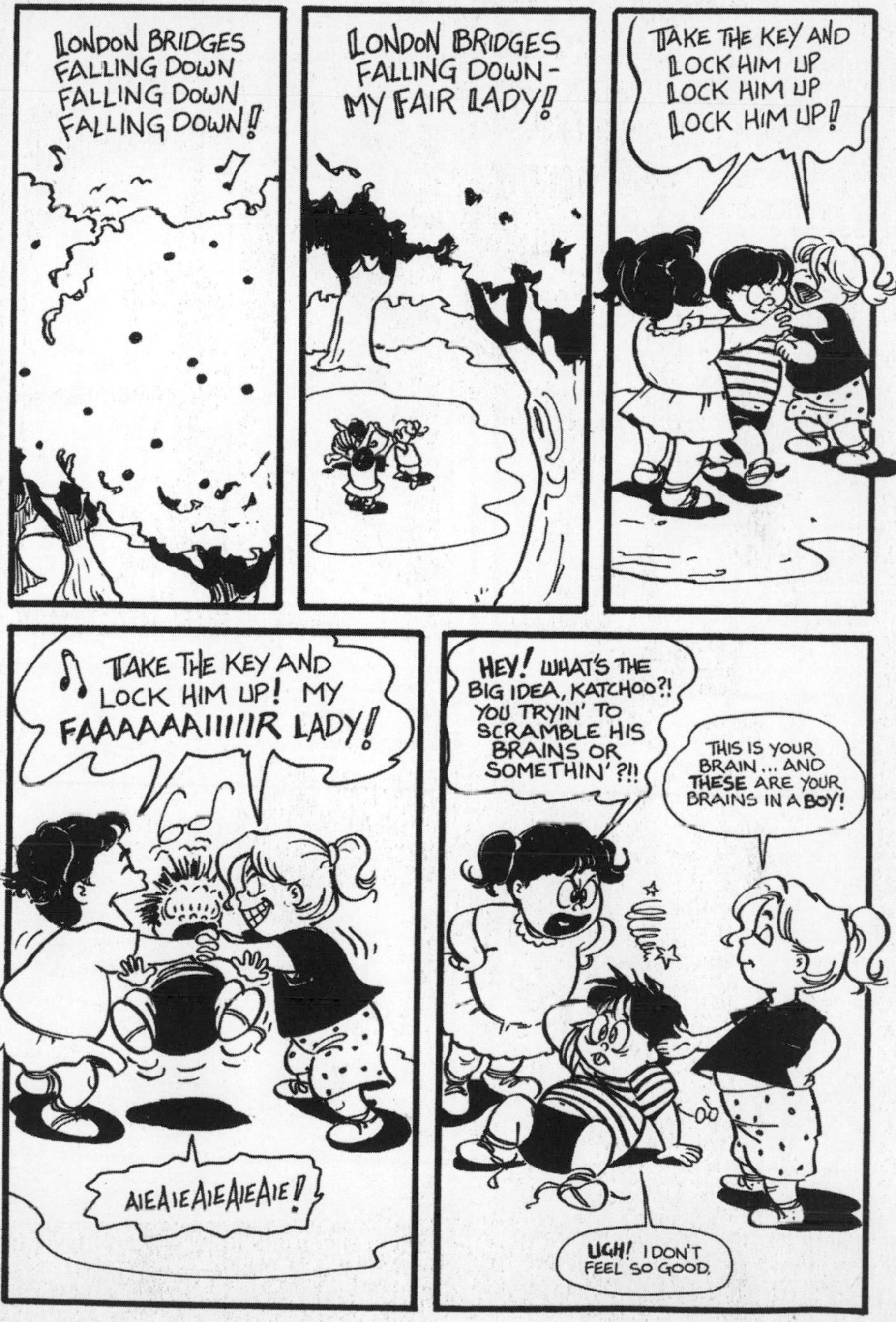
LONDON BRIDGES FALLING DOWN FALLING DOWN FALLING DOWN!
LONDON BRIDGES FALLING DOWN- MY FAIR LADY!
TAKE THE KEY AND LOCK HIM UP LOCK HIM UP LOCK HIM UP!
TAKE THE KEY AND LOCK HIM UP! MY FAAAAAAIIIIIR LADY!
AIEAIEAIEAIEAIE!
HEY! WHAT'S THE BIG IDEA, KATCHOO?! YOU TRYIN' TO SCRAMBLE HIS BRAINS OR SOMETHIN'?!!
THIS IS YOUR BRAIN... AND THESE ARE YOUR BRAINS IN A BOY!
UGH! I DON'T FEEL SO GOOD.

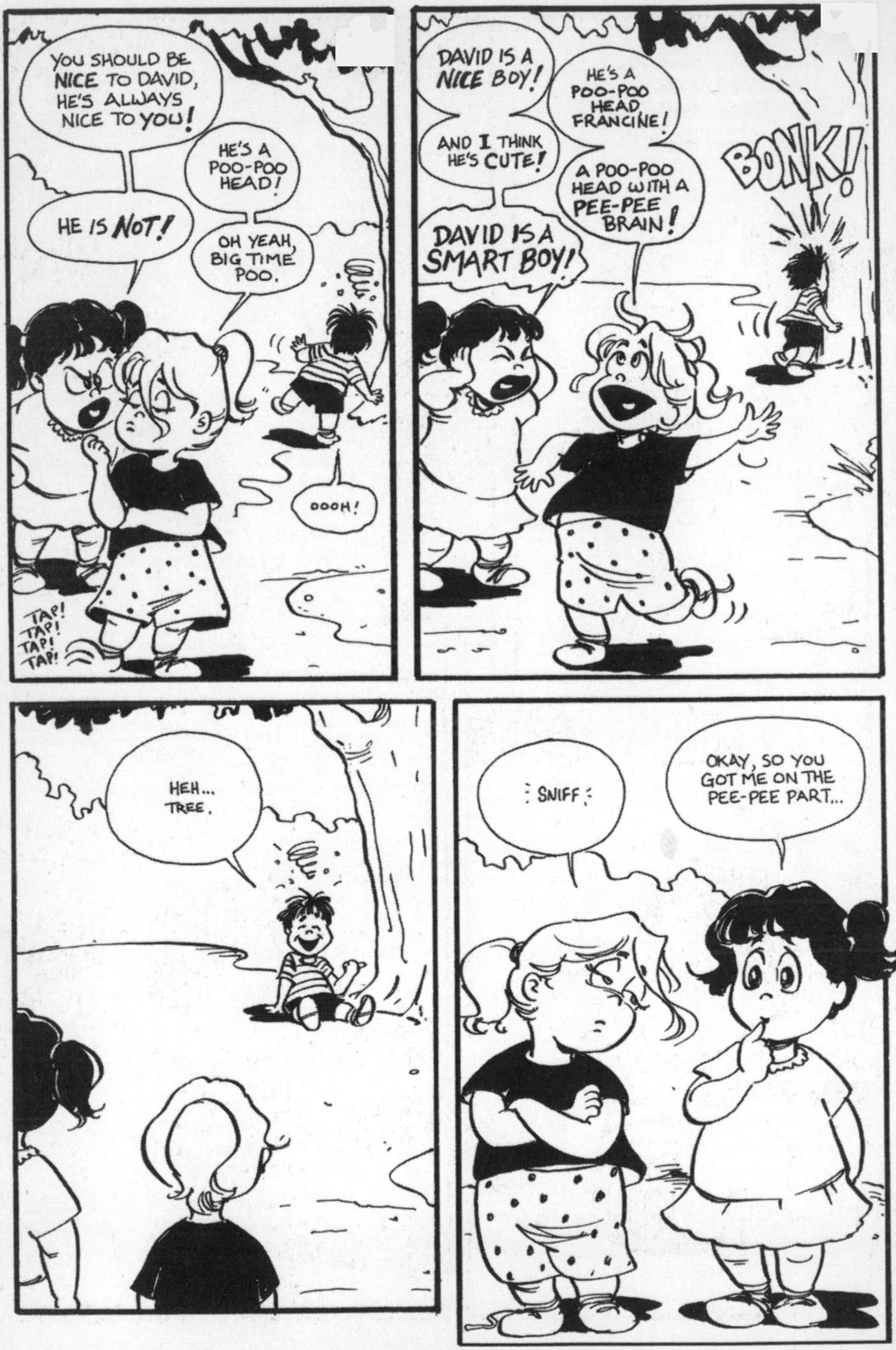
YOU SHOULD BE NICE TO DAVID, HE'S ALWAYS NICE TO YOU!
HE'S A POO-POO HEAD!
HE IS NOT!
OH YEAH, BIG TIME POO.
OOOH!
TAP! TAP! TAP! TAP!
DAVID IS A NICE BOY!
HE'S A POO-POO HEAD FRANCINE!
AND I THINK HE'S CUTE!
A POO-POO HEAD WITH A PEE-PEE BRAIN!
DAVID IS A SMART BOY!
BONK!
HEH... TREE.
SNIFF
OKAY, SO YOU GOT ME ON THE PEE-PEE PART...

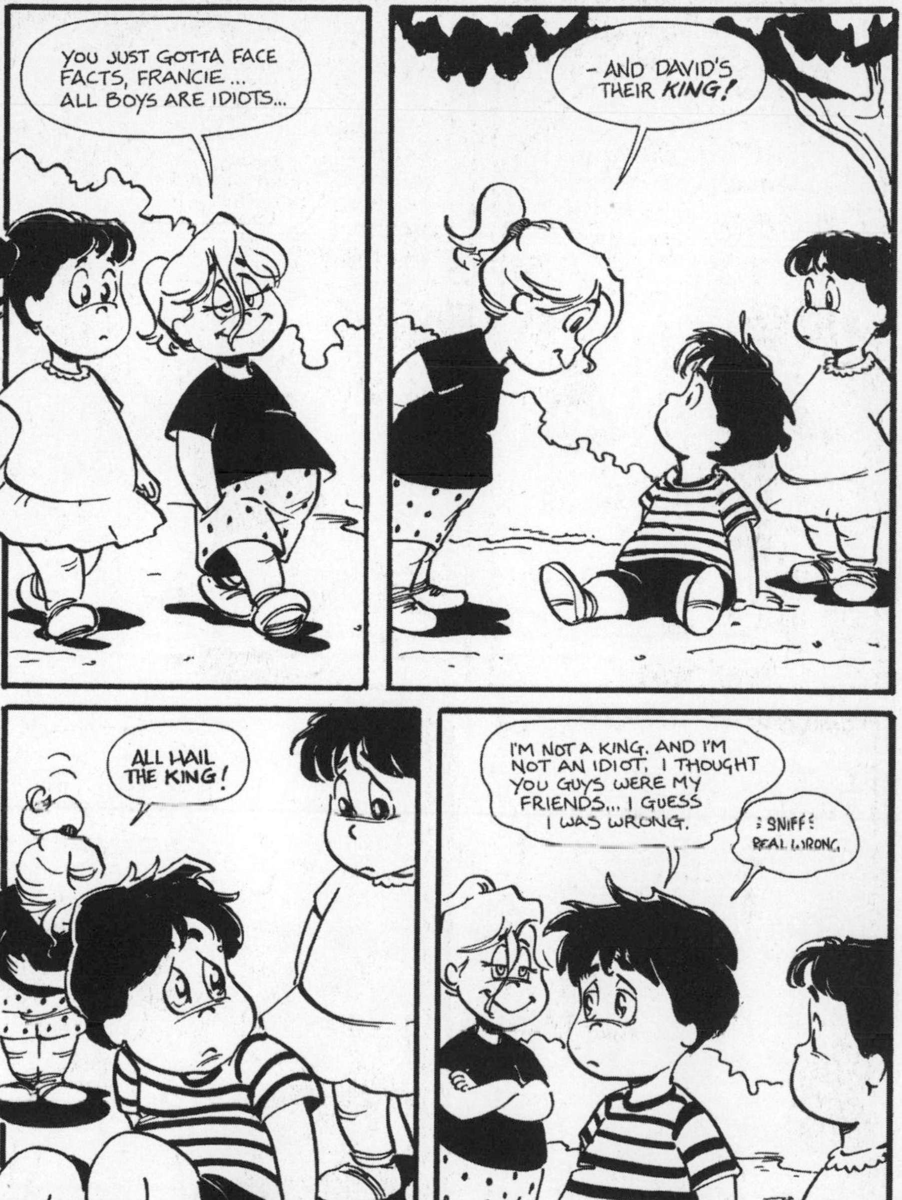
YOU JUST GOTTA FACE FACTS, FRANCIE ... ALL BOYS ARE IDIOTS...
- AND DAVID'S THEIR *KING!*
ALL HAIL THE KING!
I'M NOT A KING. AND I'M NOT AN IDIOT. I THOUGHT YOU GUYS WERE MY FRIENDS... I GUESS I WAS WRONG.
:SNIFF: REAL WRONG.

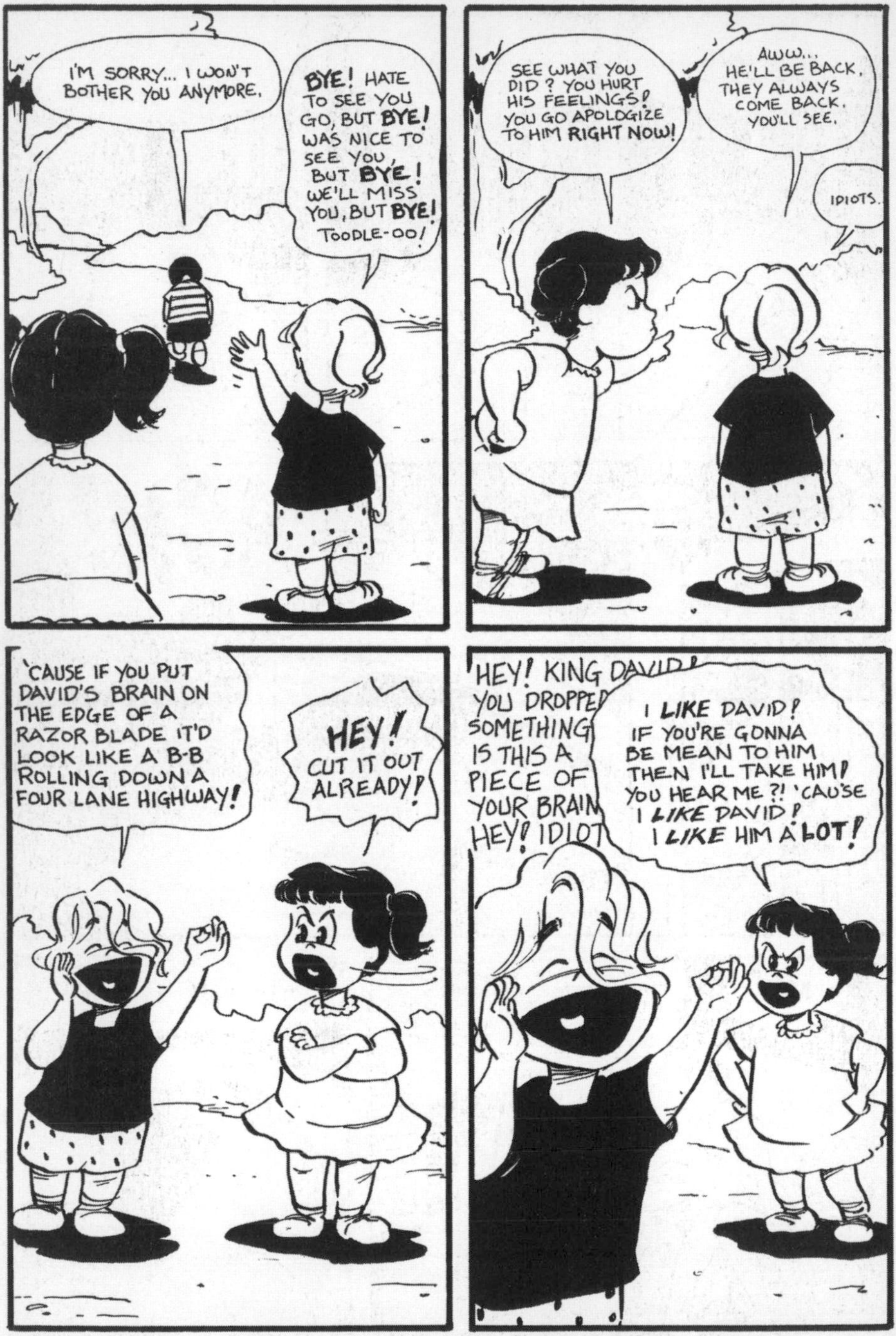
I'M SORRY... I WON'T BOTHER YOU ANYMORE.
BYE! HATE TO SEE YOU GO, BUT BYE! WAS NICE TO SEE YOU, BUT BYE! WE'LL MISS YOU, BUT BYE! TOODLE-OO!
SEE WHAT YOU DID? YOU HURT HIS FEELINGS! YOU GO APOLOGIZE TO HIM RIGHT NOW!
AWW... HE'LL BE BACK. THEY ALWAYS COME BACK. YOU'LL SEE.
IDIOTS.
'CAUSE IF YOU PUT DAVID'S BRAIN ON THE EDGE OF A RAZOR BLADE IT'D LOOK LIKE A B-B ROLLING DOWN A FOUR LANE HIGHWAY!
HEY! CUT IT OUT ALREADY!
I LIKE DAVID! IF YOU'RE GONNA BE MEAN TO HIM THEN I'LL TAKE HIM! YOU HEAR ME?! 'CAUSE I LIKE DAVID! I LIKE HIM A LOT!

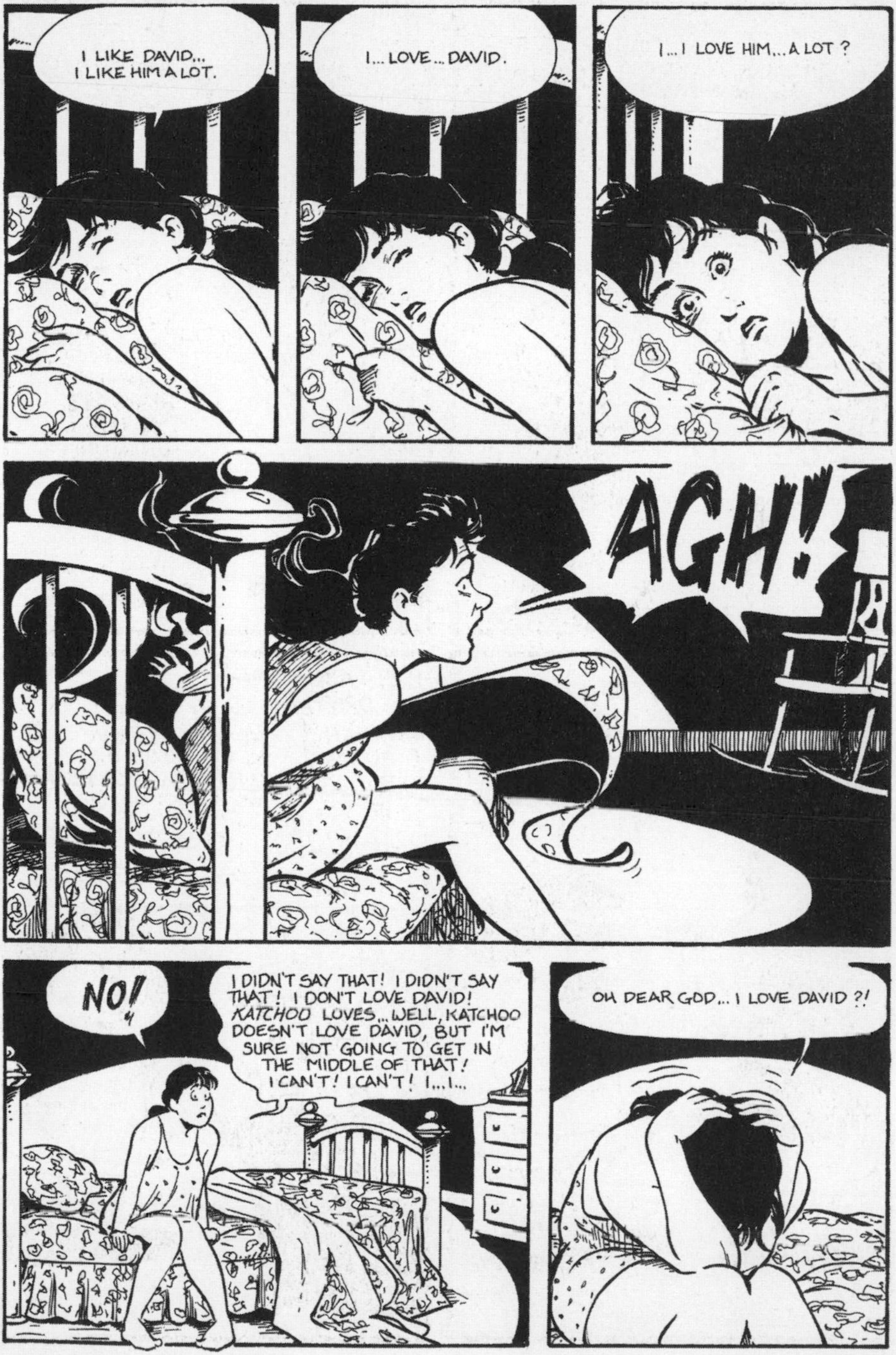
I LIKE DAVID...
I LIKE HIM A LOT.
I... LOVE... DAVID.
I... I LOVE HIM... A LOT ?
AGH!!
NO!
I DIDN'T SAY THAT! I DIDN'T SAY THAT! I DON'T LOVE DAVID! *KATCHOO* LOVES... WELL, KATCHOO DOESN'T LOVE DAVID, BUT I'M SURE NOT GOING TO GET IN THE MIDDLE OF THAT! I CAN'T! I CAN'T! I... I...
OH DEAR GOD... I LOVE DAVID ?!

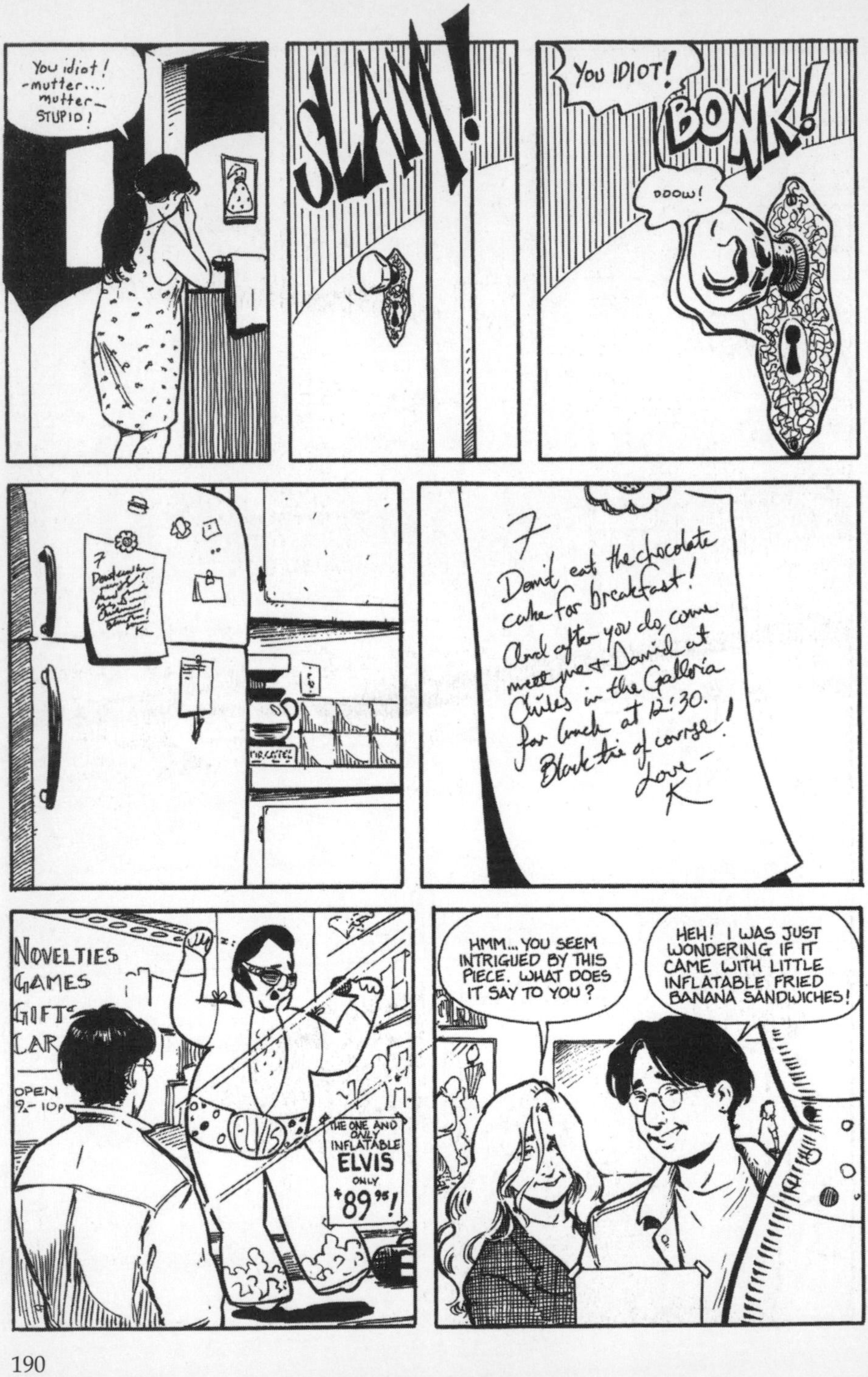
You idiot! -mutter.... mutter— STUPID!
SLAM!
YOU IDIOT!
BONK!
OOOW!
7
Don't eat the chocolate
cake for breakfast!
And after you do, come
meet me + David at
Chiles in the Galleria
for lunch at 12:30.
Black tie of course!
Love—
K
NOVELTIES
GAMES
GIFTS
CAR
OPEN 9A-10P
THE ONE AND ONLY INFLATABLE ELVIS ONLY $89 95!
ELVIS
HMM... YOU SEEM INTRIGUED BY THIS PIECE. WHAT DOES IT SAY TO YOU?
HEH! I WAS JUST WONDERING IF IT CAME WITH LITTLE INFLATABLE FRIED BANANA SANDWICHES!

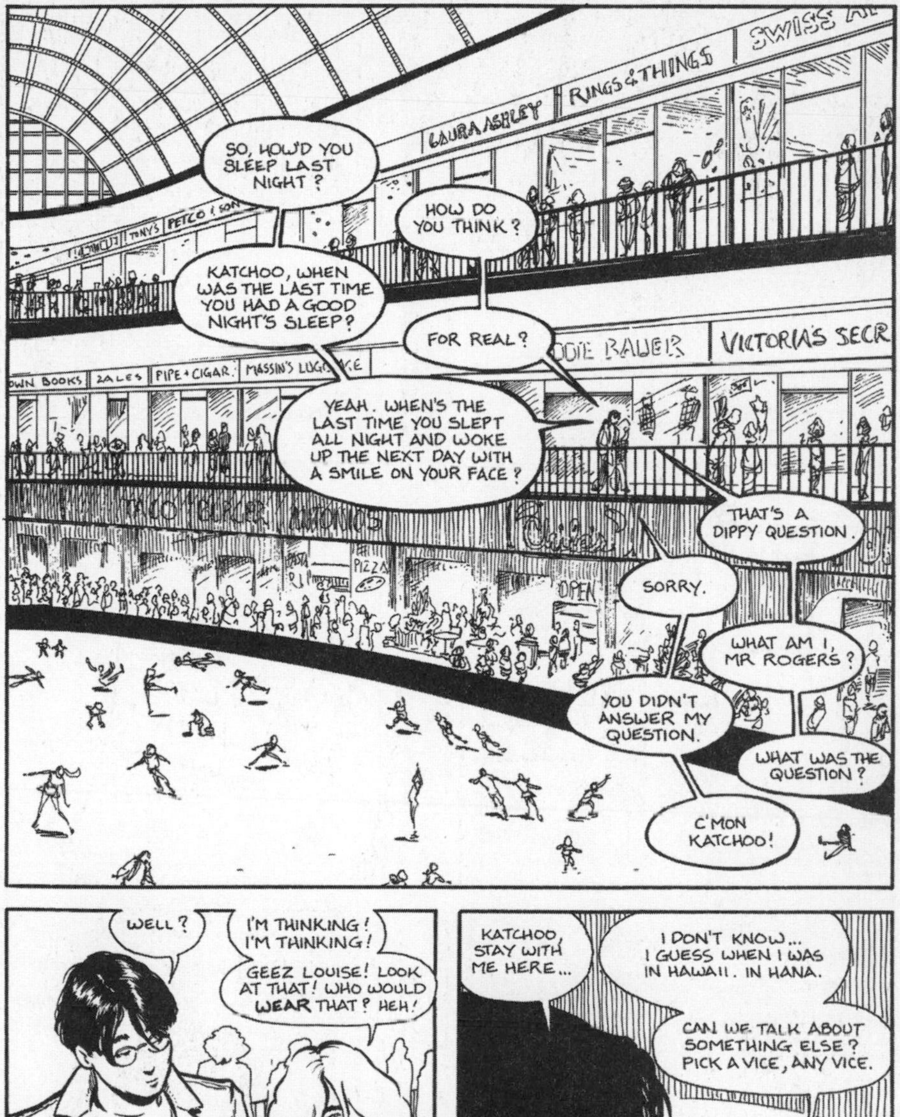
SO, HOW'D YOU SLEEP LAST NIGHT?
HOW DO YOU THINK?
KATCHOO, WHEN WAS THE LAST TIME YOU HAD A GOOD NIGHT'S SLEEP?
FOR REAL?
YEAH. WHEN'S THE LAST TIME YOU SLEPT ALL NIGHT AND WOKE UP THE NEXT DAY WITH A SMILE ON YOUR FACE?
THAT'S A DIPPY QUESTION.
SORRY.
WHAT AM I, MR ROGERS?
YOU DIDN'T ANSWER MY QUESTION.
WHAT WAS THE QUESTION?
C'MON KATCHOO!
WELL?
I'M THINKING! I'M THINKING!
GEEZ LOUISE! LOOK AT THAT! WHO WOULD **WEAR** THAT? HEH!
KATCHOO, STAY WITH ME HERE...
I DON'T KNOW... I GUESS WHEN I WAS IN HAWAII. IN HANA.
CAN WE TALK ABOUT SOMETHING ELSE? PICK A VICE, ANY VICE.

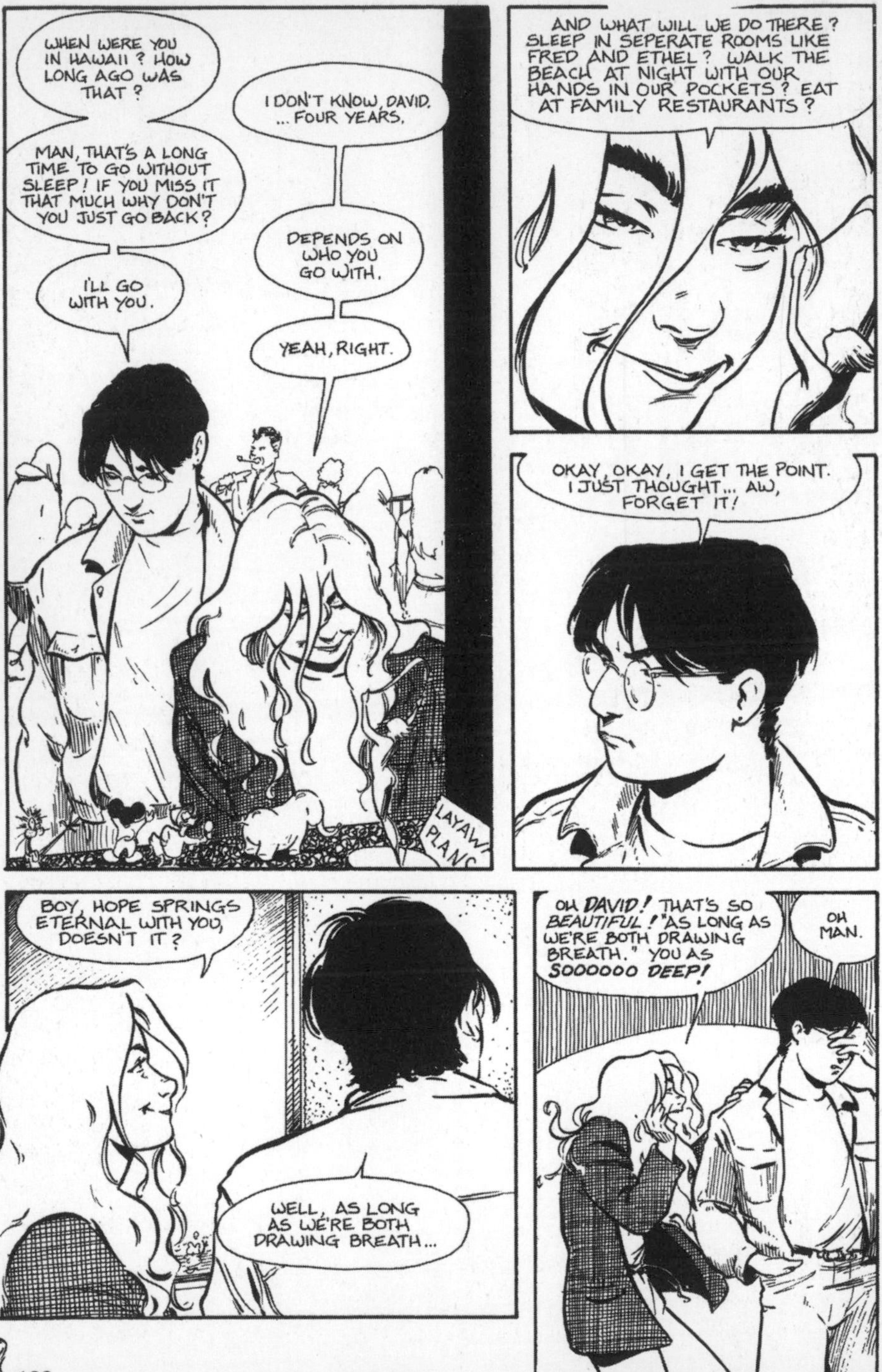
WHEN WERE YOU IN HAWAII? HOW LONG AGO WAS THAT?
I DON'T KNOW, DAVID. ... FOUR YEARS.
MAN, THAT'S A LONG TIME TO GO WITHOUT SLEEP! IF YOU MISS IT THAT MUCH WHY DON'T YOU JUST GO BACK?
DEPENDS ON WHO YOU GO WITH.
I'LL GO WITH YOU.
YEAH, RIGHT.
LAYAW PLANS
AND WHAT WILL WE DO THERE? SLEEP IN SEPERATE ROOMS LIKE FRED AND ETHEL? WALK THE BEACH AT NIGHT WITH OUR HANDS IN OUR POCKETS? EAT AT FAMILY RESTAURANTS?
OKAY, OKAY, I GET THE POINT. I JUST THOUGHT... AW, FORGET IT!
BOY, HOPE SPRINGS ETERNAL WITH YOU, DOESN'T IT?
WELL, AS LONG AS WE'RE BOTH DRAWING BREATH...
OH DAVID! THAT'S SO BEAUTIFUL! "AS LONG AS WE'RE BOTH DRAWING BREATH." YOU AS SOOOOOO DEEP!
OH MAN.

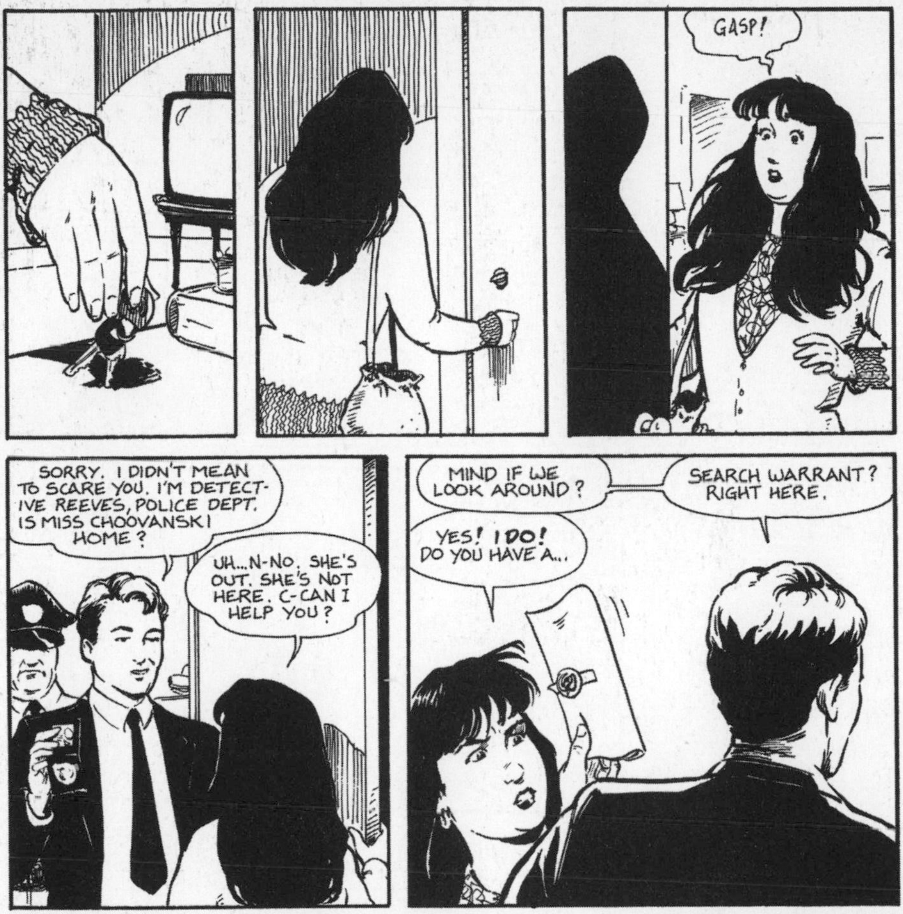
GASP!
SORRY. I DIDN'T MEAN TO SCARE YOU. I'M DETECTIVE REEVES, POLICE DEPT. IS MISS CHOOVANSKI HOME?
UH...N-NO. SHE'S OUT. SHE'S NOT HERE. C-CAN I HELP YOU?
MIND IF WE LOOK AROUND?
YES! I DO! DO YOU HAVE A...
SEARCH WARRANT? RIGHT HERE.
CHECK THE BEDROOMS.
DO YOU MIND TELLING ME WHAT IS GOING ON HERE?!
ARE YOU FRANCINE PETERS?
YES!
WELL, IT'S SIMPLE, MISS PETERS. YOUR ROOMATE IS UNDER SUSPICION OF FELONIOUS ASSAULT OF A POLICE OFFICER.
WHA...? YOU MUST BE JOKING!

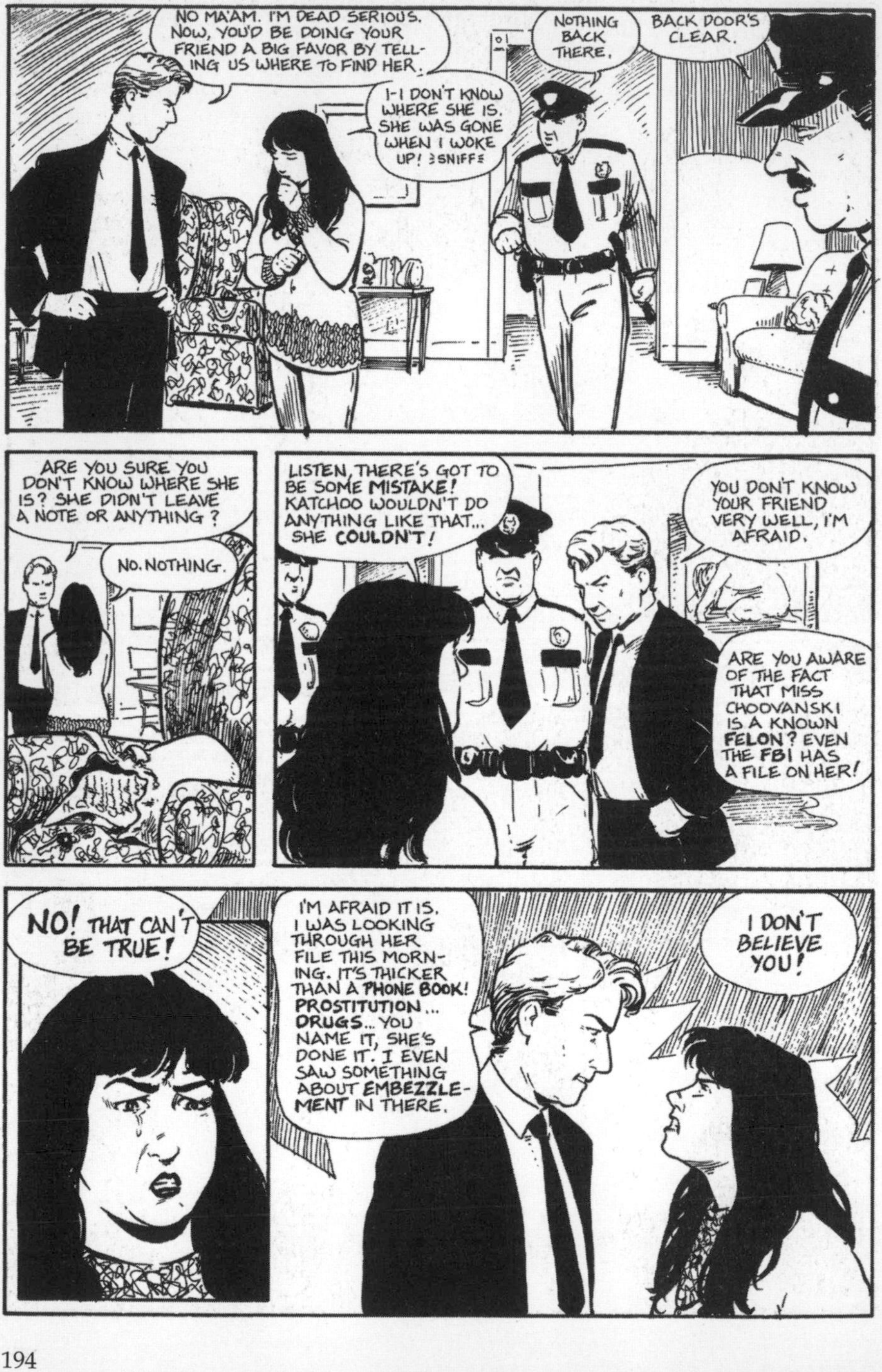
NO MA'AM. I'M DEAD SERIOUS. NOW, YOU'D BE DOING YOUR FRIEND A BIG FAVOR BY TELLING US WHERE TO FIND HER.
I-I DON'T KNOW WHERE SHE IS. SHE WAS GONE WHEN I WOKE UP! ≡SNIFF≡
NOTHING BACK THERE.
BACK DOOR'S CLEAR.
ARE YOU SURE YOU DON'T KNOW WHERE SHE IS? SHE DIDN'T LEAVE A NOTE OR ANYTHING?
NO. NOTHING.
LISTEN, THERE'S GOT TO BE SOME MISTAKE! KATCHOO WOULDN'T DO ANYTHING LIKE THAT... SHE COULDN'T!
YOU DON'T KNOW YOUR FRIEND VERY WELL, I'M AFRAID.
ARE YOU AWARE OF THE FACT THAT MISS CHOOVANSKI IS A KNOWN FELON? EVEN THE FBI HAS A FILE ON HER!
NO! THAT CAN'T BE TRUE!
I'M AFRAID IT IS. I WAS LOOKING THROUGH HER FILE THIS MORNING. IT'S THICKER THAN A PHONE BOOK! PROSTITUTION... DRUGS... YOU NAME IT, SHE'S DONE IT. I EVEN SAW SOMETHING ABOUT EMBEZZLEMENT IN THERE.
I DON'T BELIEVE YOU!

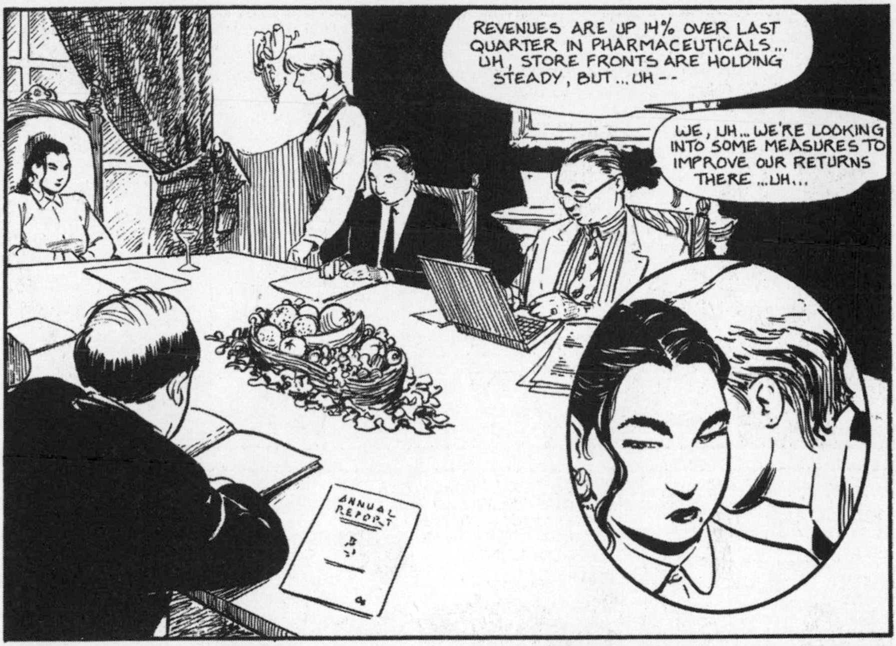
REVENUES ARE UP 14% OVER LAST QUARTER IN PHARMACEUTICALS... UH, STORE FRONTS ARE HOLDING STEADY, BUT... UH --
WE, UH... WE'RE LOOKING INTO SOME MEASURES TO IMPROVE OUR RETURNS THERE ...UH...
ANNUAL REPORT

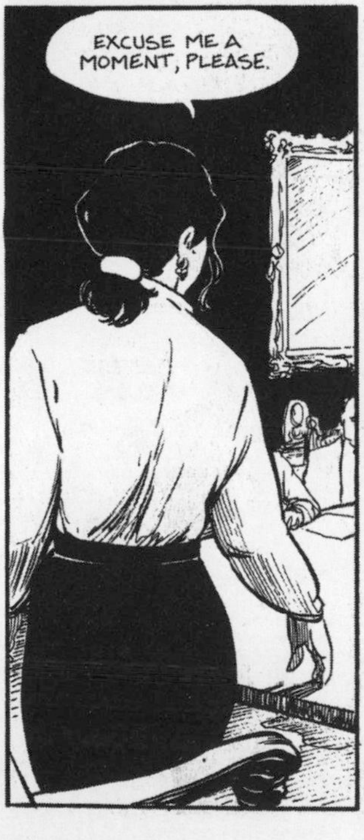
EXCUSE ME A MOMENT, PLEASE.

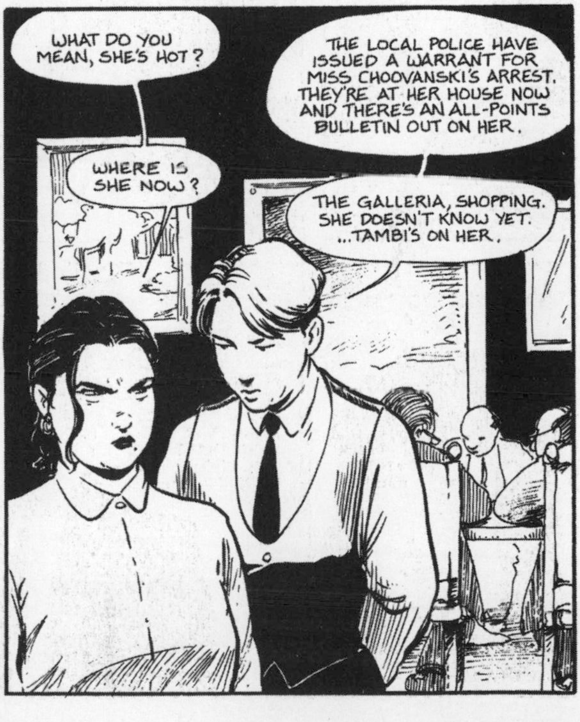
WHAT DO YOU MEAN, SHE'S HOT?
THE LOCAL POLICE HAVE ISSUED A WARRANT FOR MISS CHOOVANSKI'S ARREST. THEY'RE AT HER HOUSE NOW AND THERE'S AN ALL-POINTS BULLETIN OUT ON HER.
WHERE IS SHE NOW?
THE GALLERIA, SHOPPING. SHE DOESN'T KNOW YET. ...TAMBI'S ON HER.

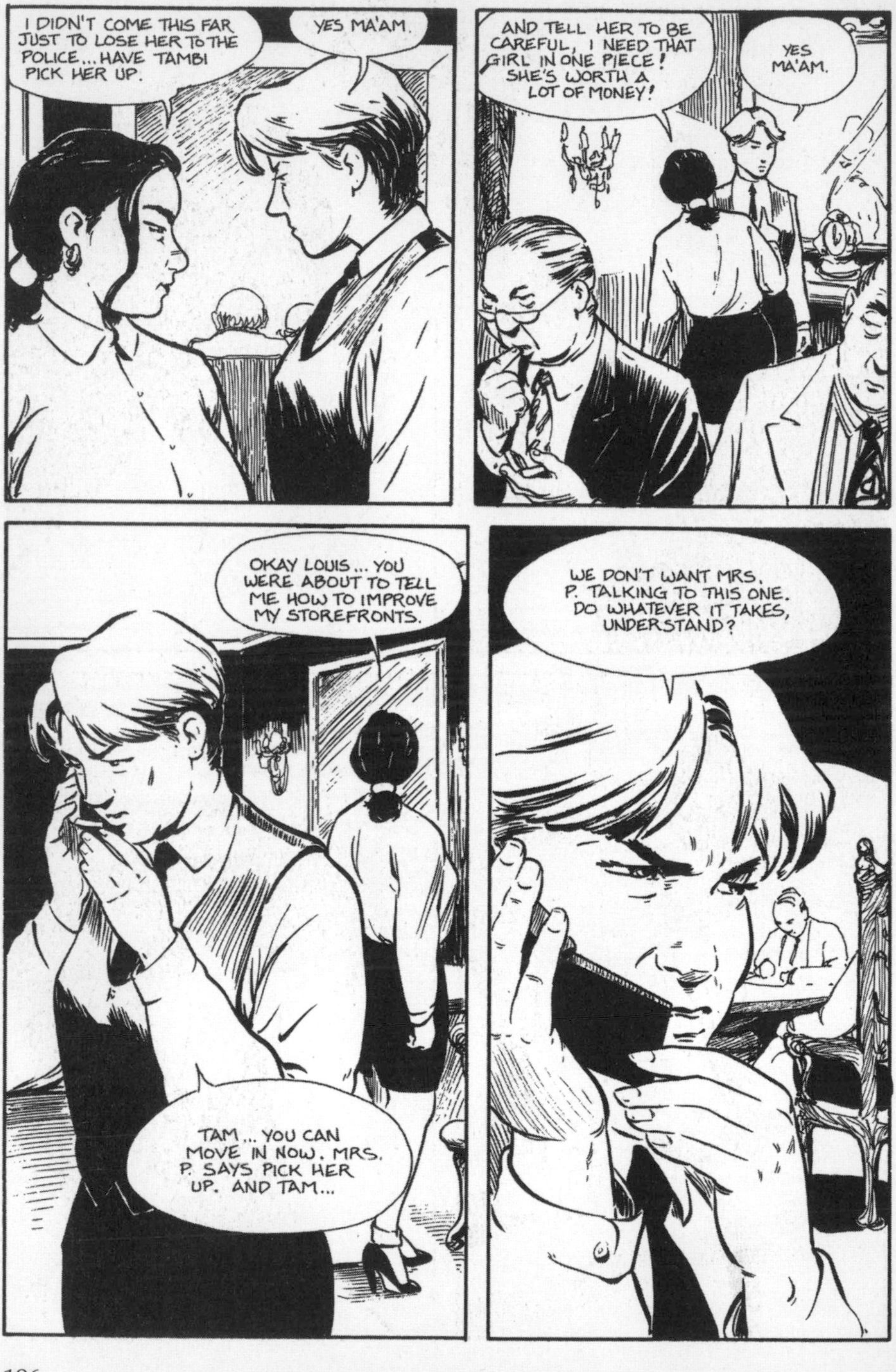
I DIDN'T COME THIS FAR JUST TO LOSE HER TO THE POLICE... HAVE TAMBI PICK HER UP.
YES MA'AM.
AND TELL HER TO BE CAREFUL, I NEED THAT GIRL IN ONE PIECE! SHE'S WORTH A LOT OF MONEY!
YES MA'AM.
OKAY LOUIS... YOU WERE ABOUT TO TELL ME HOW TO IMPROVE MY STOREFRONTS.
TAM... YOU CAN MOVE IN NOW. MRS. P. SAYS PICK HER UP. AND TAM...
WE DON'T WANT MRS. P. TALKING TO THIS ONE. DO WHATEVER IT TAKES, UNDERSTAND?

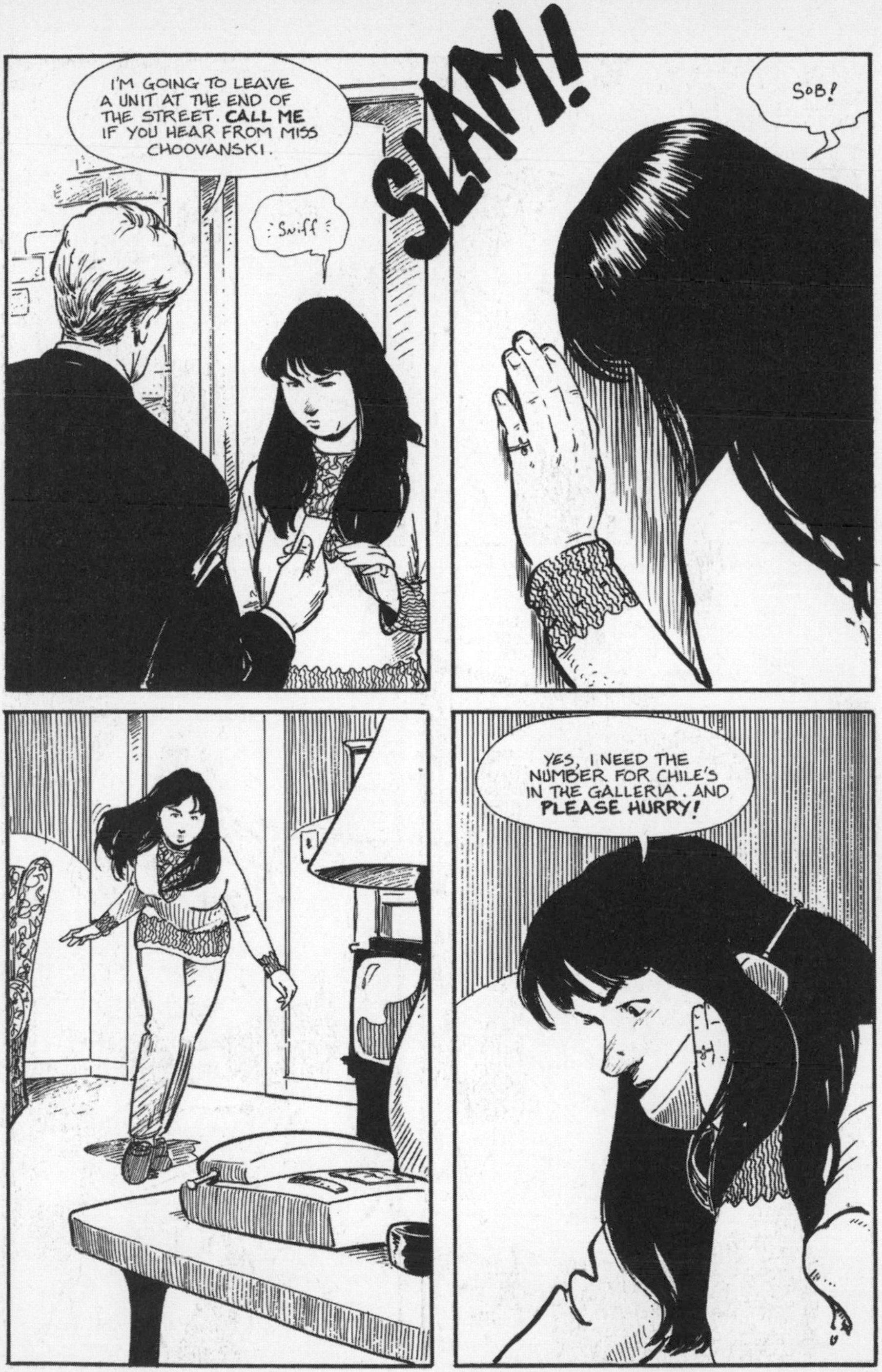
I'M GOING TO LEAVE A UNIT AT THE END OF THE STREET. CALL ME IF YOU HEAR FROM MISS CHOOVANSKI.
Sniff
SLAM!
SOB!
YES, I NEED THE NUMBER FOR CHILE'S IN THE GALLERIA. AND PLEASE HURRY!
SOB...

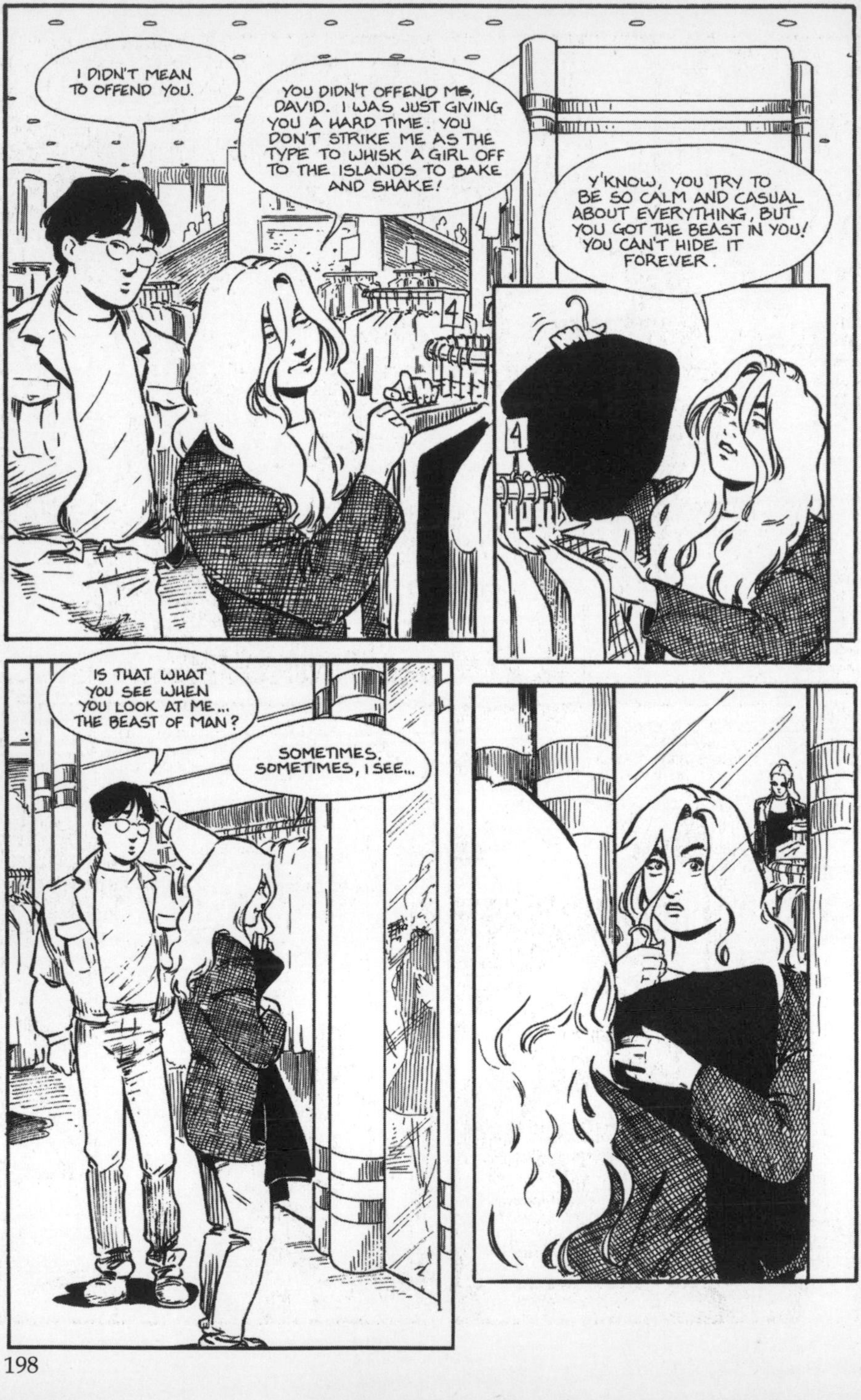
I DIDN'T MEAN TO OFFEND YOU.
YOU DIDN'T OFFEND ME, DAVID. I WAS JUST GIVING YOU A HARD TIME. YOU DON'T STRIKE ME AS THE TYPE TO WHISK A GIRL OFF TO THE ISLANDS TO BAKE AND SHAKE!
Y'KNOW, YOU TRY TO BE SO CALM AND CASUAL ABOUT EVERYTHING, BUT YOU GOT THE BEAST IN YOU! YOU CAN'T HIDE IT FOREVER.
IS THAT WHAT YOU SEE WHEN YOU LOOK AT ME... THE BEAST OF MAN?
SOMETIMES. SOMETIMES, I SEE...

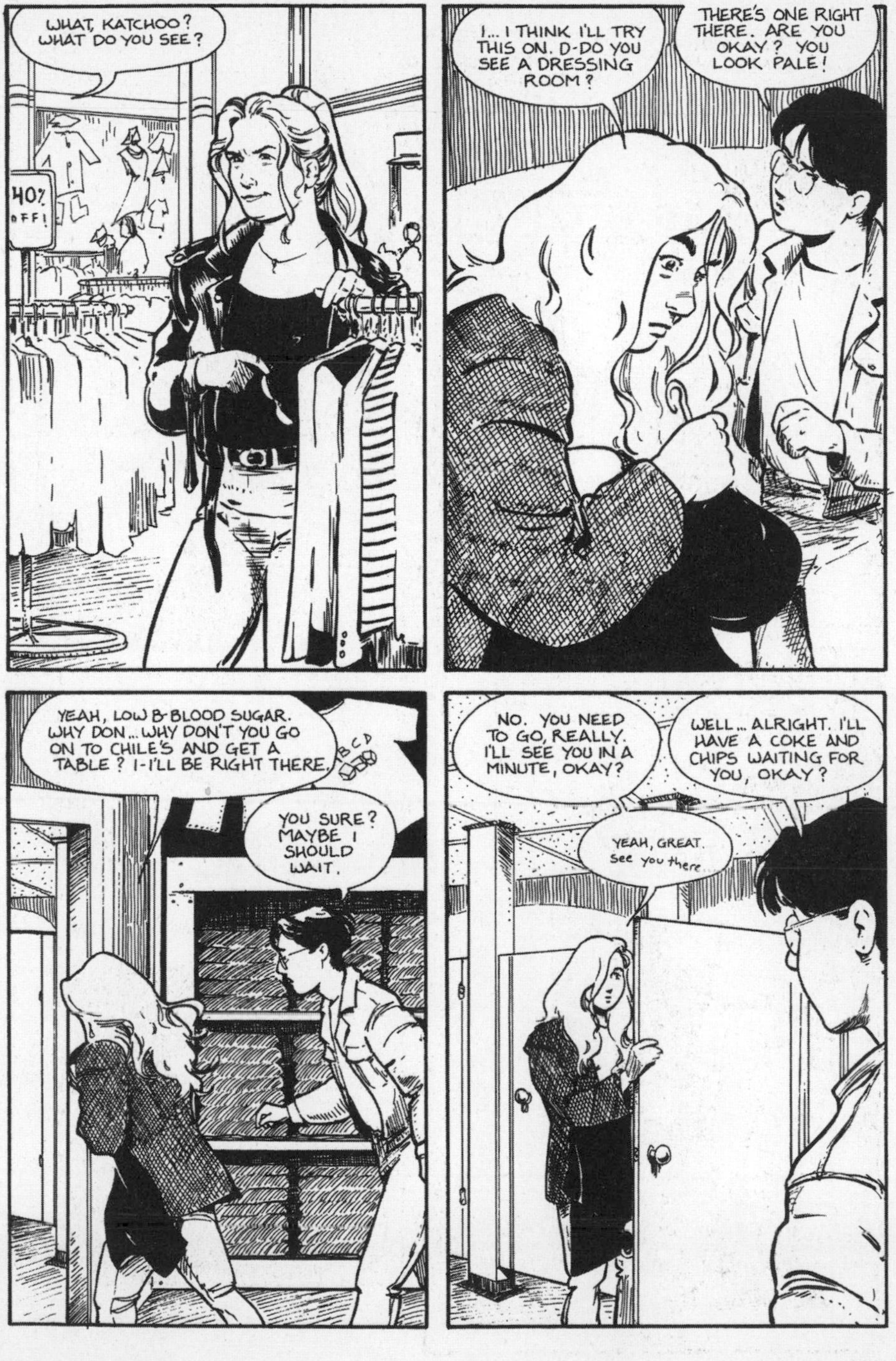
40% OFF!
WHAT, KATCHOO? WHAT DO YOU SEE?
I... I THINK I'LL TRY THIS ON. D-DO YOU SEE A DRESSING ROOM?
THERE'S ONE RIGHT THERE. ARE YOU OKAY? YOU LOOK PALE!
YEAH, LOW B-BLOOD SUGAR. WHY DON... WHY DON'T YOU GO ON TO CHILE'S AND GET A TABLE? I-I'LL BE RIGHT THERE.
YOU SURE? MAYBE I SHOULD WAIT.
NO. YOU NEED TO GO, REALLY. I'LL SEE YOU IN A MINUTE, OKAY?
WELL... ALRIGHT. I'LL HAVE A COKE AND CHIPS WAITING FOR YOU, OKAY?
YEAH, GREAT. See you there...

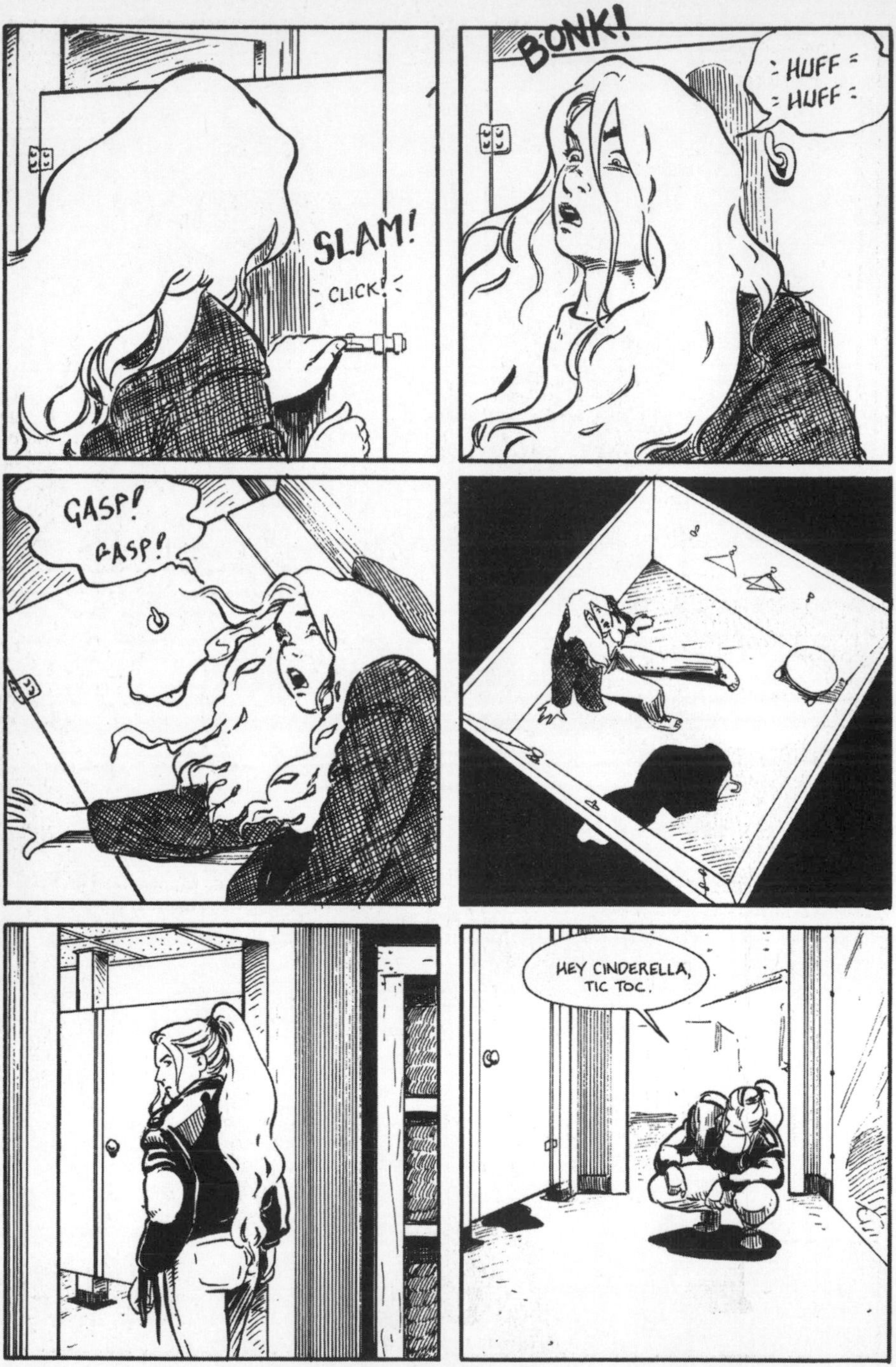
SLAM!
CLICK!
BONK!
HUFF
HUFF
GASP!
GASP!
HEY CINDERELLA, TIC TOC.

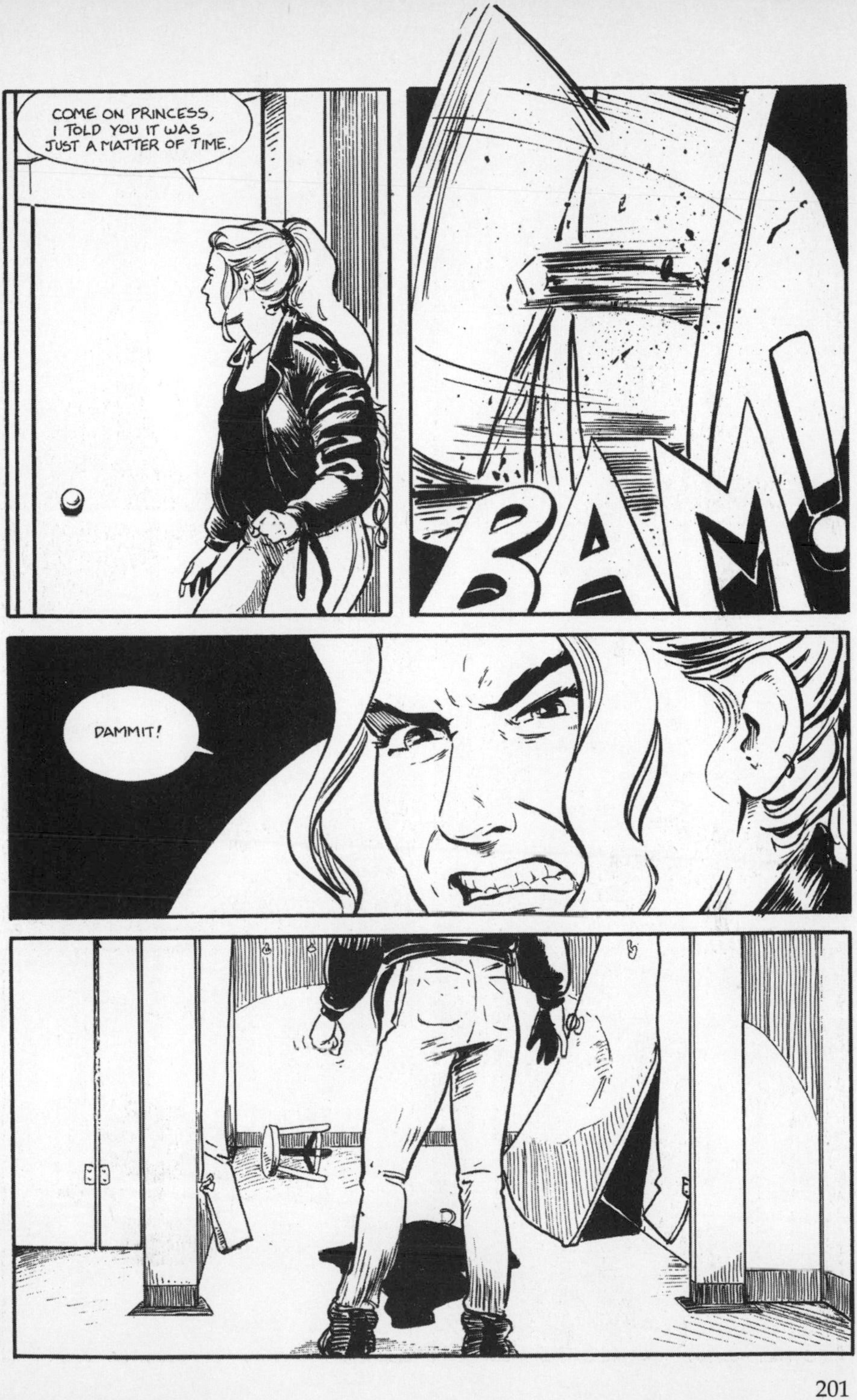

COME ON PRINCESS, I TOLD YOU IT WAS JUST A MATTER OF TIME.
BAM!
DAMMIT!

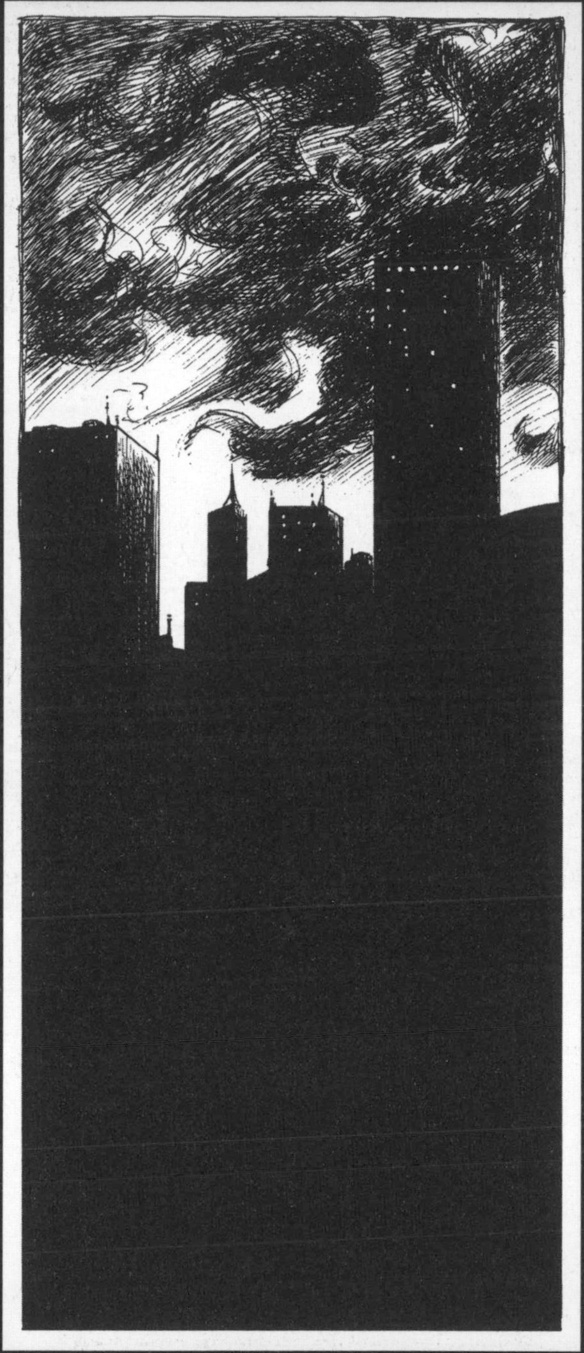

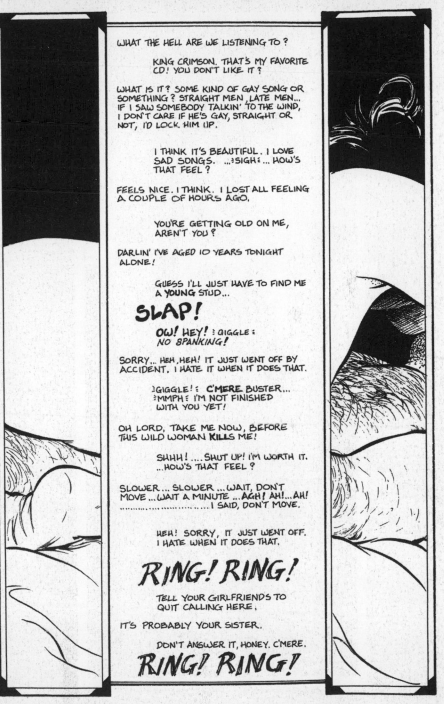

WHAT THE HELL ARE WE LISTENING TO?

KING CRIMSON. THAT'S MY FAVORITE CD! YOU DON'T LIKE IT?

WHAT IS IT? SOME KIND OF GAY SONG OR SOMETHING? STRAIGHT MEN, LATE MEN... IF I SAW SOMEBODY TALKIN' TO THE WIND, I DON'T CARE IF HE'S GAY, STRAIGHT OR NOT, I'D LOCK HIM UP.

I THINK IT'S BEAUTIFUL. I LOVE SAD SONGS. ...≷SIGH≷... HOW'S THAT FEEL?

FEELS NICE. I THINK. I LOST ALL FEELING A COUPLE OF HOURS AGO.

YOU'RE GETTING OLD ON ME, AREN'T YOU?

DARLIN' I'VE AGED 10 YEARS TONIGHT ALONE!

GUESS I'LL JUST HAVE TO FIND ME A YOUNG STUD...

SLAP!

OW! HEY! ≷GIGGLE≷ NO SPANKING!

SORRY... HEH, HEH! IT JUST WENT OFF BY ACCIDENT. I HATE IT WHEN IT DOES THAT.

≷GIGGLE!≷ C'MERE BUSTER... ≷MMPH≷ I'M NOT FINISHED WITH YOU YET!

OH LORD, TAKE ME NOW, BEFORE THIS WILD WOMAN KILLS ME!

SHHH!....SHUT UP! I'M WORTH IT. ...HOW'S THAT FEEL?

SLOWER... SLOWER...WAIT, DON'T MOVE...WAIT A MINUTE ...AGH! AH!...AH! ....I SAID, DON'T MOVE.

HEH! SORRY, IT JUST WENT OFF. I HATE WHEN IT DOES THAT.

RING! RING!

TELL YOUR GIRLFRIENDS TO QUIT CALLING HERE.

IT'S PROBABLY YOUR SISTER.

DON'T ANSWER IT, HONEY. C'MERE.

RING! RING!

203

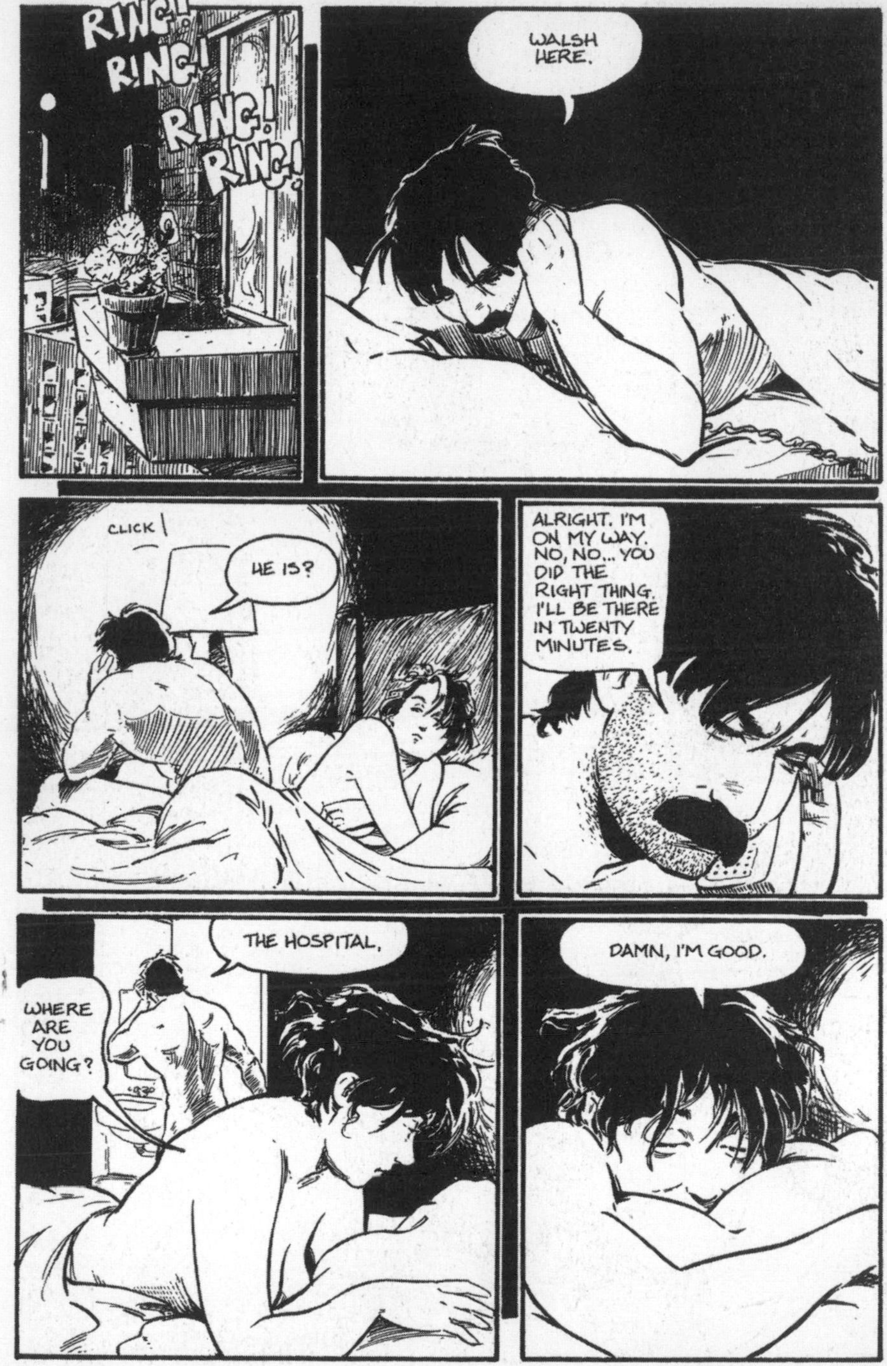
RING!
RING!
RING!
RING!
WALSH HERE.
CLICK!
HE IS?
ALRIGHT. I'M ON MY WAY. NO, NO... YOU DID THE RIGHT THING. I'LL BE THERE IN TWENTY MINUTES.
WHERE ARE YOU GOING?
THE HOSPITAL.
DAMN, I'M GOOD.

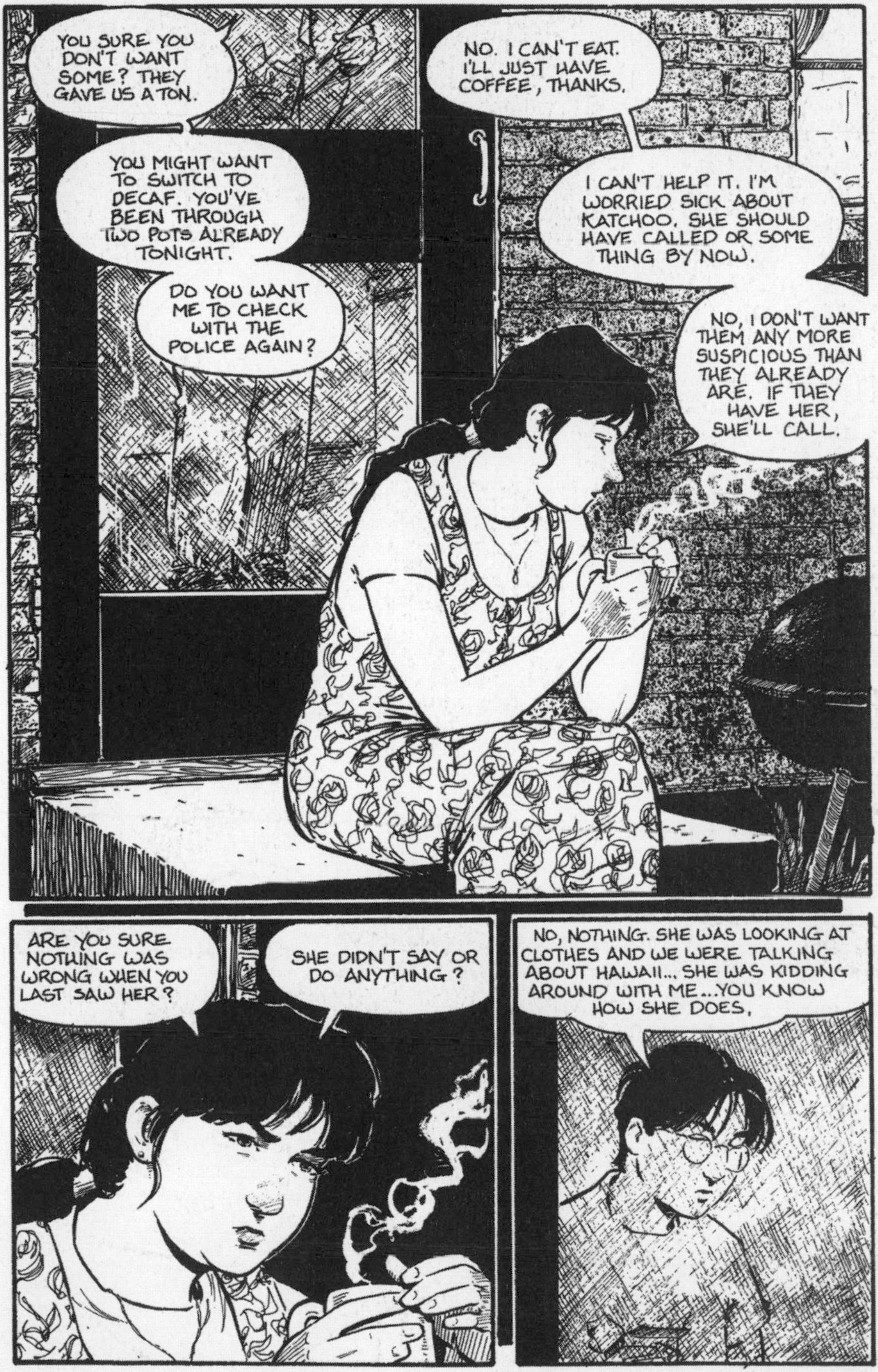
YOU SURE YOU DON'T WANT SOME? THEY GAVE US A TON.
NO. I CAN'T EAT. I'LL JUST HAVE COFFEE, THANKS.
YOU MIGHT WANT TO SWITCH TO DECAF. YOU'VE BEEN THROUGH TWO POTS ALREADY TONIGHT.
I CAN'T HELP IT. I'M WORRIED SICK ABOUT KATCHOO. SHE SHOULD HAVE CALLED OR SOME THING BY NOW.
DO YOU WANT ME TO CHECK WITH THE POLICE AGAIN?
NO, I DON'T WANT THEM ANY MORE SUSPICIOUS THAN THEY ALREADY ARE. IF THEY HAVE HER, SHE'LL CALL.
ARE YOU SURE NOTHING WAS WRONG WHEN YOU LAST SAW HER?
SHE DIDN'T SAY OR DO ANYTHING?
NO, NOTHING. SHE WAS LOOKING AT CLOTHES AND WE WERE TALKING ABOUT HAWAII... SHE WAS KIDDING AROUND WITH ME...YOU KNOW HOW SHE DOES.

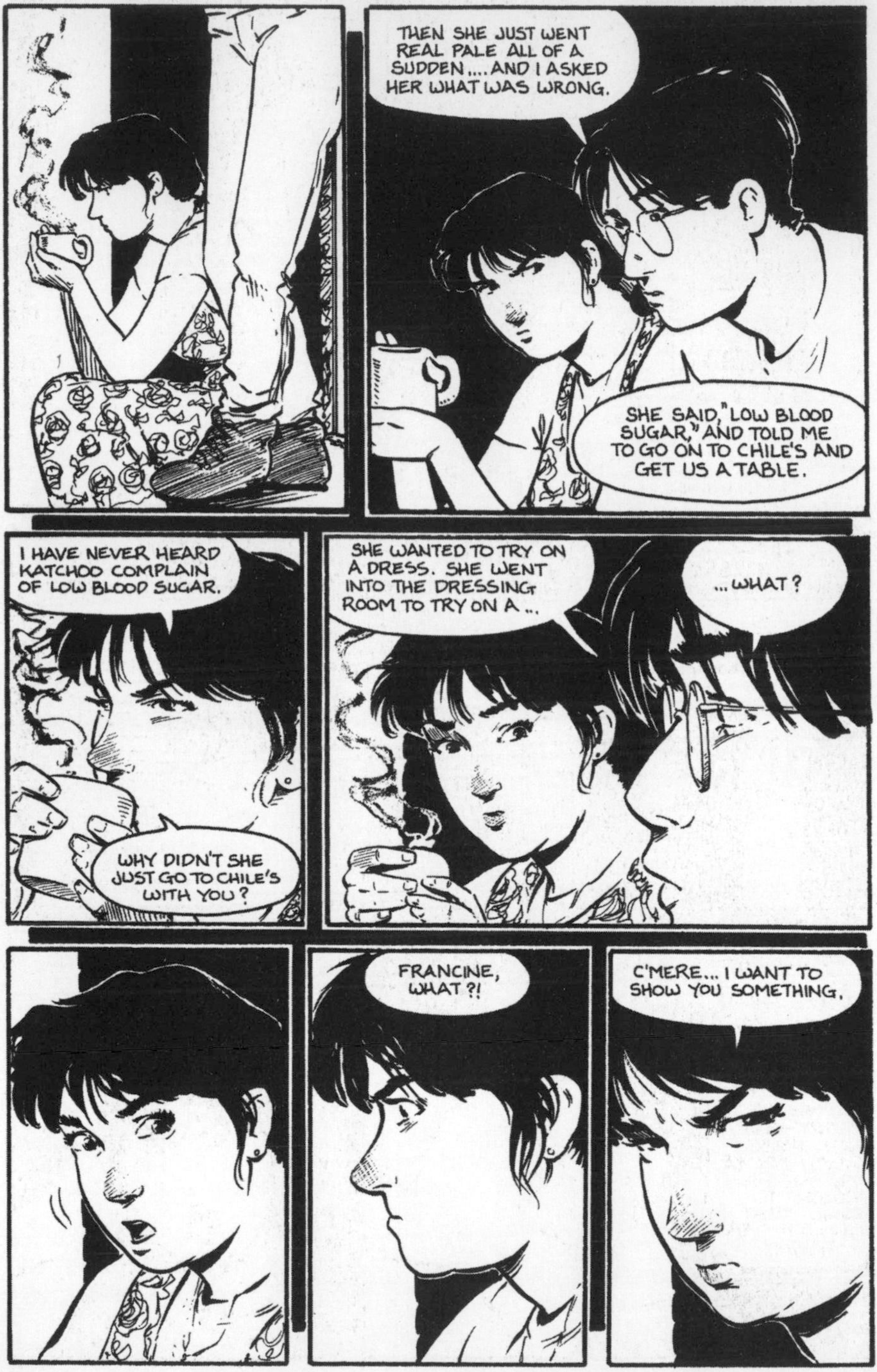
THEN SHE JUST WENT REAL PALE ALL OF A SUDDEN.... AND I ASKED HER WHAT WAS WRONG.
SHE SAID, "LOW BLOOD SUGAR," AND TOLD ME TO GO ON TO CHILE'S AND GET US A TABLE.
I HAVE NEVER HEARD KATCHOO COMPLAIN OF LOW BLOOD SUGAR.
WHY DIDN'T SHE JUST GO TO CHILE'S WITH YOU?
SHE WANTED TO TRY ON A DRESS. SHE WENT INTO THE DRESSING ROOM TO TRY ON A...
...WHAT?
FRANCINE, WHAT?!
C'MERE... I WANT TO SHOW YOU SOMETHING.

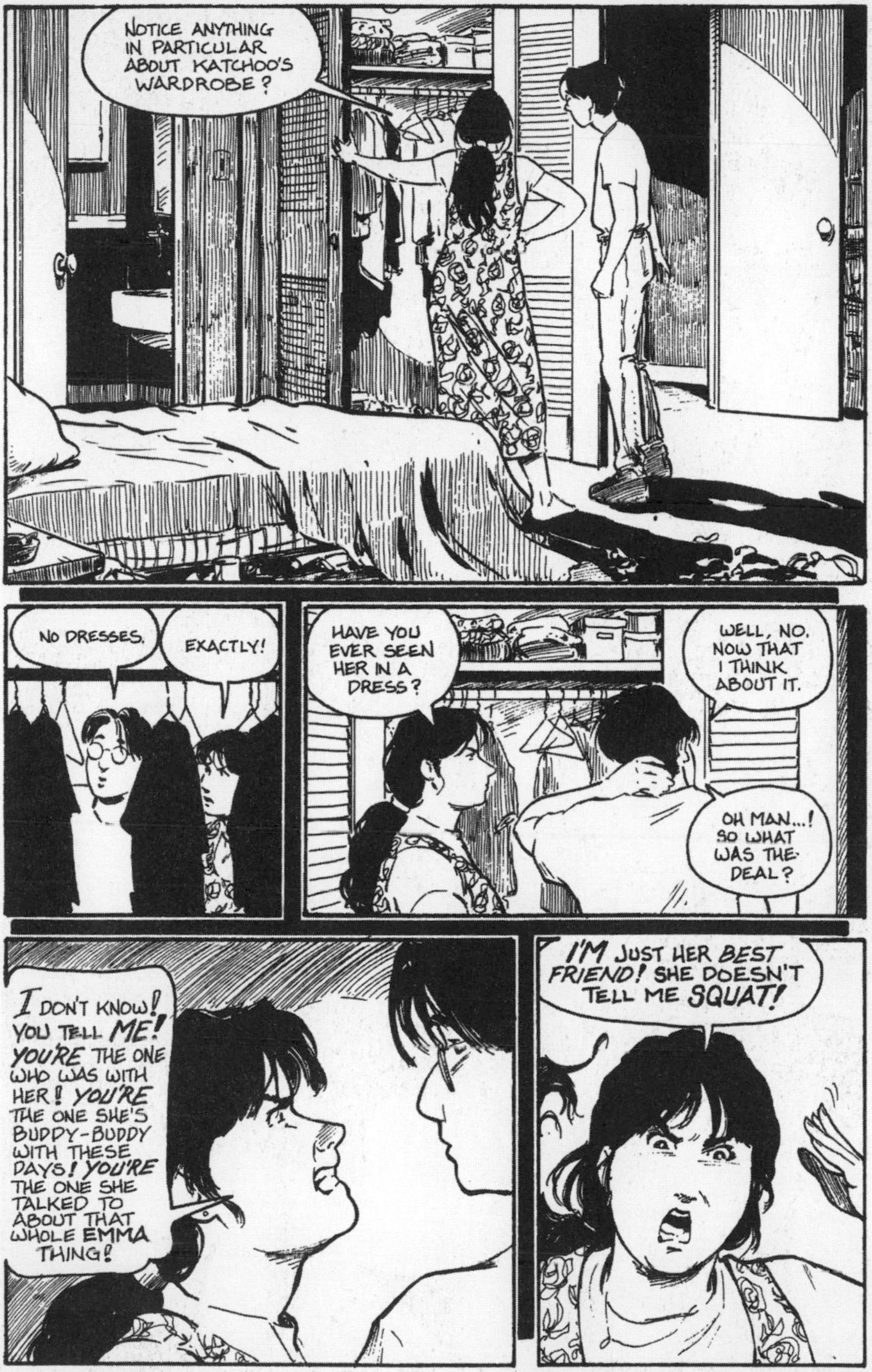
NOTICE ANYTHING IN PARTICULAR ABOUT KATCHOO'S WARDROBE?
NO DRESSES.
EXACTLY!
HAVE YOU EVER SEEN HER IN A DRESS?
WELL, NO. NOW THAT I THINK ABOUT IT.
OH MAN...! SO WHAT WAS THE DEAL?
I DON'T KNOW! YOU TELL ME! YOU'RE THE ONE WHO WAS WITH HER! YOU'RE THE ONE SHE'S BUDDY-BUDDY WITH THESE DAYS! YOU'RE THE ONE SHE TALKED TO ABOUT THAT WHOLE EMMA THING!
I'M JUST HER BEST FRIEND! SHE DOESN'T TELL ME SQUAT!

208

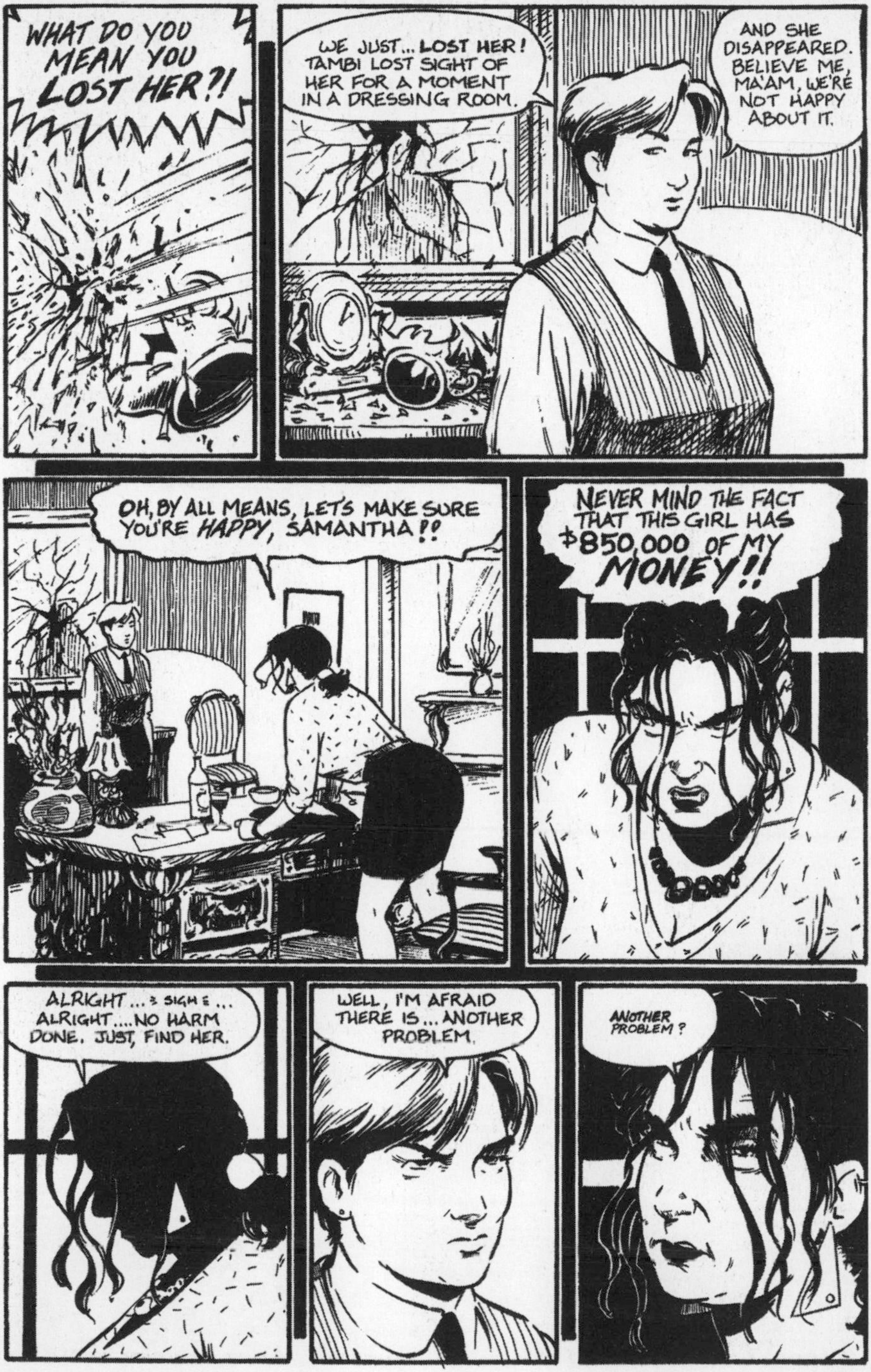
WHAT DO YOU MEAN YOU LOST HER?!
WE JUST... LOST HER! TAMBI LOST SIGHT OF HER FOR A MOMENT IN A DRESSING ROOM.
AND SHE DISAPPEARED. BELIEVE ME, MA'AM, WE'RE NOT HAPPY ABOUT IT.
OH, BY ALL MEANS, LET'S MAKE SURE YOU'RE HAPPY, SAMANTHA!!
NEVER MIND THE FACT THAT THIS GIRL HAS $850,000 OF MY MONEY!!
ALRIGHT... sigh ... ALRIGHT.... NO HARM DONE. JUST, FIND HER.
WELL, I'M AFRAID THERE IS... ANOTHER PROBLEM.
ANOTHER PROBLEM?

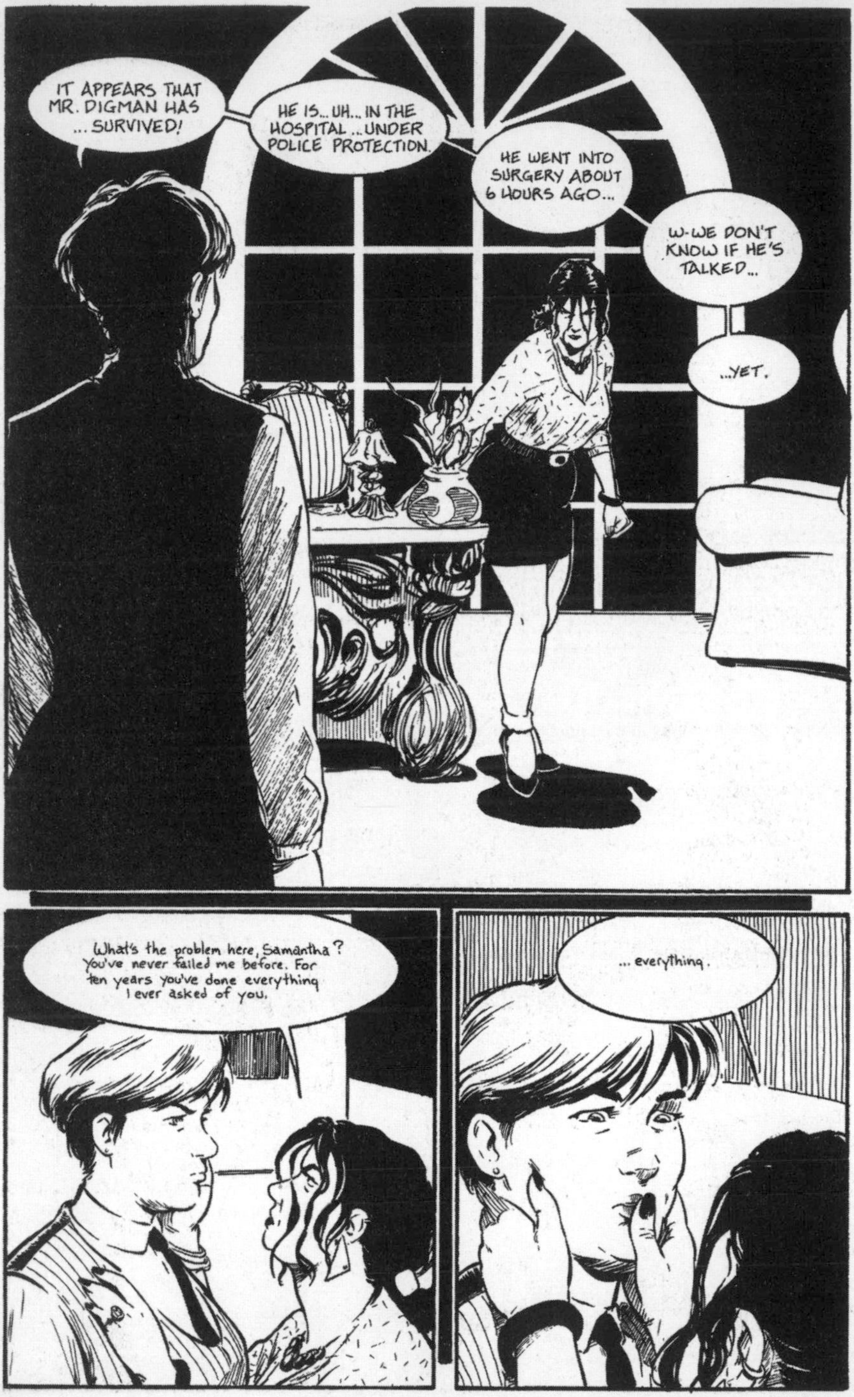
IT APPEARS THAT MR. DIGMAN HAS ... SURVIVED!
HE IS... UH... IN THE HOSPITAL ... UNDER POLICE PROTECTION.
HE WENT INTO SURGERY ABOUT 6 HOURS AGO...
W-WE DON'T KNOW IF HE'S TALKED...
...YET.
What's the problem here, Samantha? You've never failed me before. For ten years you've done everything I ever asked of you.
... everything.

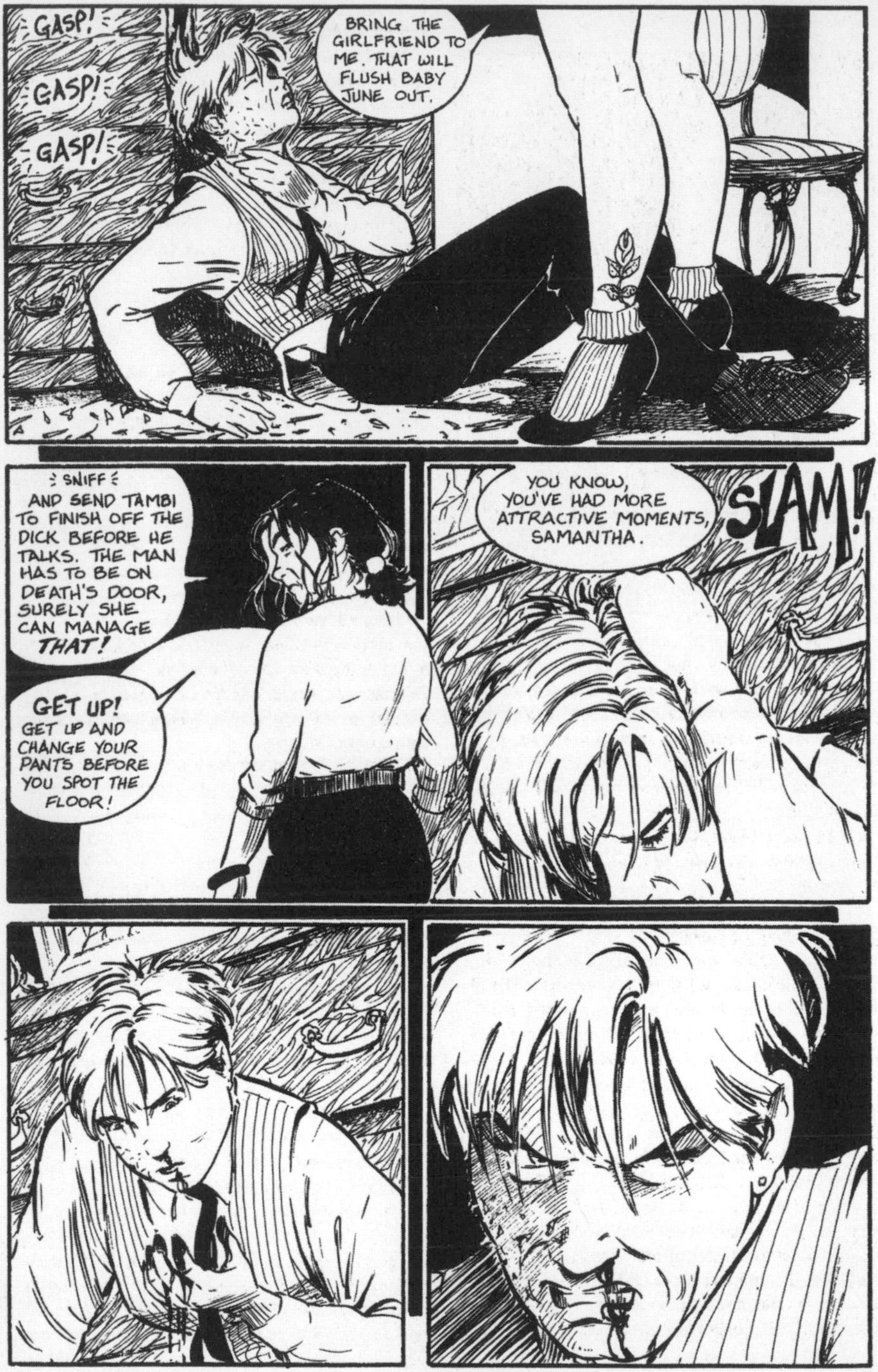

GASP!
GASP!
GASP!
BRING THE GIRLFRIEND TO ME. THAT WILL FLUSH BABY JUNE OUT.
SNIFF
AND SEND TAMBI TO FINISH OFF THE DICK BEFORE HE TALKS. THE MAN HAS TO BE ON DEATH'S DOOR, SURELY SHE CAN MANAGE THAT!
GET UP! GET UP AND CHANGE YOUR PANTS BEFORE YOU SPOT THE FLOOR!
YOU KNOW, YOU'VE HAD MORE ATTRACTIVE MOMENTS, SAMANTHA.
SLAM!

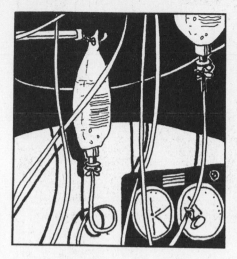

Detective Walsh stepped around the galvanized mop bucket that slid slowly across the floor in a soapy spill of dirty water.

"Excuse me," he said quietly.

The janitor never looked up, but waited, motionless, with his chin in his chest, for the detective to pass. Somewhere around the corner Walsh could hear the muted whirring of someone waxing the floors of the sleeping hospital, removing the tracks of yesterday. Walsh made his way towards the critical care unit.

A handsome black man in police uniform sat in a chair positioned outside the large double doors that led into the CCU.

"Hey, Jesse. Who'd you piss off?" Walsh said as he approached the entrance.

"Man, I'm tellin' you!" the officer replied with a pained expression. "What ever happened to the ol' 9 to 5, you know? I mean, who's supposed to be watchin' my wife in the middle of the night while I'm watching this guy, know what I mean?"

"I hear ya, buddy. I hear ya," Walsh smiled as he opened one of the wide oak doors and stepped through. The door closed silently behind him and the officer resumed the careful cleaning of his fingernails with a pocket knife.

The critical care unit of Ben County Hospital was designed in hub and wheel fashion. A large nurses station filled the center of the circular lobby and served as a command center for monitoring the nine rooms that circled the crowded rotunda. All but one of the rooms were occupied, their guests in various stages of hope.

Walsh stood by the entrance for a moment until he saw a room to the right with an officer and several plain clothesmen huddled by the foot of the bed. He walked slowly towards the room, taking another look around the lobby. Habit.

The small room was dark except for a dim overhead bed light that lit the body beneath it in an eery black-orange glow. Wayne Digman, former police officer and college all-star, lay under a scaffold of tubes and probes. Monitors and rolling carts jammed the area by the bed, pulsing, chirping and beeping in a medical symphony. Digman's face was half obscured by bandages and a respirator extended from his throat. A clean white sheet was folded down to his stomach revealing a massive, hairy torso wrapped tight in bandages and a number of tubes that either fed or drained dark fluids off to the side. Digman's bare arms lay motionless by his side, except for the continuous twitching of the index finger of his right hand. Nerve damage, Walsh decided. Three IV's ran up Digman's left arm that lay wrapped in a splint to keep him from bending his arm back on the needles.

Walsh pursed his lips and took a deep breath. The scene was made more unsettling by the lack of blood. Except for the swelling and the bruises, Digman was spotless with clean white bandages. Like most modern victims, Walsh noted, the real damage was internal.

Detective Reeves left the hushed conversation in the corner to come over and greet him, a grim smile on his face. "Sorry to get you out of bed," he said.

"That's alright," Walsh replied, rubbing the back of his neck. "You probably saved my life."

"I wouldn't know," Reeves smiled tightly. "You're the only couple I know still acts like they're on their honeymoon."

"Well, when you marry the right woman...." Walsh smiled into his hand as he wiped his face. He turned his attention to the detective and sighed heavily, "So, what's goin' on here? Where're we at?"

"He's in and out. Woke up about 45 minutes ago and answered a couple of questions for the nurses. I thought I'd better get you down here."

"How's he doing?" Walsh asked.

"Uh, not so good," Reeves replied, pointing to the bed. "They have him on this kidney dialysis thing, and whatever that wicked looking thing is plugged into his throat. He needs a kidney, but it's complicated. Since he came in under a John Doe and he's not with the force anymore the insurance is a big problem. But, I'll tell you, Mike, whoever did this is some piece of work."

"Yeah, well, everybody's tough with a baseball bat," Walsh replied. " Hell, for all we know he walked into some gang's territory... "

"No." Reeves said flatly, "This was done by hand. The bruises are focused and deep, the internal damage is pinpoint. Accurate. No, this was done by hand, by somebody who knew where to hit, like a surgeon with their fists. And they're strong."

"Any word yet from the lab on the strip of bandage we found in his hand?" Walsh muttered as he flipped through Digman's chart.

"The blood samples don't match his type, or your suspect's, Katina Choovanski."

"What about the strands of hair?"

"Well, they're female, bleached blonde. Our assailant, or one of the assailants anyway, is a brunette with bleached blonde hair. But I tell you, you're going to have a hard time convincing me a woman did this, " Reeves said.

"You'd be amazed at some of the things I've seen a woman do." Walsh said as he stepped carefully towards the head of the bed, pausing a moment to make sure he didn't interfere with one of the many tubes and wires running from the bed. He leaned over and spoke softly to Digman, "Wayne? Wayne, can you hear me?"

Digman eyes opened slightly and closed again.

"Wayne? It's me, Mike Walsh. Can you tell me who did this to you buddy?" Walsh whispered.

Digman's head flinched and his body shivered once before the big man's eyes fluttered briefly and closed again. He looked asleep except for the slight movement his head made every time the respirator pushed air into his lungs. Walsh looked back at Reeves who chewed on a piece of gum nervously, staring intently at the scene. Reeves gave the detective a puzzled look with a shrug of his shoulders. Walsh turned back to Digman. "Wayne? Can you tell me who did this to you?"

Digman turned his head toward Walsh, his movements slow and pained. Silently, he mouthed the word, "Parker."

"Parker?" Walsh frowned, "Parker who?"

Digman tried to lick his lips, but his mouth was dry. He continued slowly, his lips and tongue working without air, "Mrs. Parker... file on desk."

On hearing this, Walsh snapped his fingers behind his back at Reeves, who turned and spoke briefly with the uniformed officer that stood next to him. The officer left immediately for Digman's one room office on the south end of downtown.

Digman's head twitched in a small intense spasm and stopped. One of the monitors by the bed fluttered twice, then resumed its rhythmic sucking, fluttering sound. With great effort, Digman closed, then opened, his eyes and tried to look at the detective. The bandages across his nose and upper lip prevented him from closing his mouth all the way.

"Who's Mrs. Parker?" Walsh asked again.

"Mafia," Digman mouthed, then closed his eyes and seemed to drift away again.

"Excuse me, gentlemen," came a woman's voice from behind, "I need to ask you to leave now. I need to check Mr. Digman's status."

Walsh stood up straight and ran his hands through his hair with a heavy sigh. Reeves reached over and tapped him on the arm, "C'mon Mike, let's go grab a cup of coffee while they do their thing."

Walsh turned to follow Reeves and the other detective, smiling at the nurse who stood patiently by the foot of the bed, waiting for him to step by.

She was tall and statuesque, a little over six feet. Walsh noted her size and broad shoulders as he squeezed between her and the wall. She smiled a tight, polite smile that seemed to only accent her sharp features. She was pretty enough, even with no makeup and her blonde hair pulled tight in a bun behind her white nurse's cap, but there was something oddly cold and unattractive about her as well. Something... military.

Walsh paused at the door and turned to look at Digman, who lay sleeping, as the nurse bent over to check his pulse. Her hands were large and strong, like a man's, her long fingers easily wrapping around Digman's fat wrist. Walsh stared at the muscles in her arms as they filled out the short sleeves of the uniform. This woman has a serious workout, he noted with some admiration. She looked up at Walsh briefly, her gaze cool and unemotional. She lay Digman's hand back on the bed and began to attach a blood pressure strap to his arm in the quick, efficient manner that one acquires through years of routine. Walsh sighed, rubbing the back of his neck. She knows what she's doing, he thought to himself, and turned to leave.

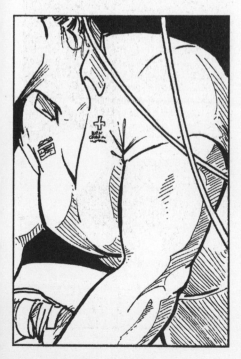

Reeves was waiting for Walsh by the elevators that would take them to the basement cafeteria. "Did you get a look at her?" Reeves chuckled as he pushed the down button, "Damnation! What a body! Can you imagine dating someone stronger than you? Talk about a woman that could kill you!"

Walsh and Reeves stared at each other as the words hung between them.

"Did you see her hands?" Walsh said quietly.

"No, but I saw the back of her neck. Mike, she has dark roots. She's bleached blonde."

"Shit!" Walsh snapped, and immediately began running full speed back down the hall. "Seal off the exits!" he shouted back to Reeves, who was already giving the command over a 2 way radio.

Walsh burst loudly through the CCU doors with Jesse, the guard, close on his heels. "What's goin' on?" Jesse asked. Walsh didn't answer but ran across the small lobby directly to Digman's room and stopped in his tracks inside the doorway. Two nurses and a doctor were bent over Digman's body, the doctor barking instructions as he worked Digman's chest with his hands. One nurse was checking the tubing and IV bags around Digman's bed, giving the status of each one out loud as she moved around the bed.

Reeves ran into the room with two uniformed officers on his heels and pulled up beside Walsh at the foot of the bed. The medical symphony had lost it's rhythm. Only the steady monotone alarm of several monitors sounded as they stood and watched the doctor pump Digman's chest for three minutes before he stood up and wiped his brow.

Three men from cardiology came hurrying into the room with a cart and chest spreader, but the doctor waved them off.

Behind him, Walsh could hear Reeves outside the doorway checking the posts around the building. All the replies came back the same, "Nothing here."

Walsh bit his lip and suppressed a string of profanities as he watched one of the nurses turn off the monitors one by one. The doctor noted the time and cause of death, sudden cardiac arrest, to one of the nurses.

"Nothing," Reeves said quietly to Walsh as he walked out of the room into the lobby where several nurses stood off to one side watching and whispering.

"What do you want to do, Mike?" Reeves asked.

"I want Mrs. Parker's ass!" Walsh growled between his teeth. "This is now priority one, got it? I want the file Digman talked about brought to me, right now. Do a complete, complete records search.

Give me everything you can find on her, state, federal, international, everything! If she's with the syndicate there should be something."

"What about the APB on Katina Choovanski?"

"Drop it. Pull the watch off her house. I want every man you got combing the city for this blonde body builder. If Miss Choovanski turns up I want to talk to her, but I think we know who we're looking for now."

"Right. Listen, Mike, I'm sorry I didn't clue onto the nurse sooner. I knew there was something different about her when I saw her. I just assumed..."

"I know. Me too. Sometimes you just can't tell who the bad guys are."

David put the last of the chinese food in a beat up, pink tupperware bowl and closed the lid. The refrigerator was packed, so he balanced the bowl on top of an opened can of fruit cocktail and rinsed his hands. Folding the dish towel neatly, he hung it back on the oven handle and turned off the lights. He checked the front door locks and peeked out the curtains, the street was empty. The sound of running water in the hall bath finally stopped. David turned and left the room, turning out the lights as he went. Francine came out of the bathroom wiping her nose with a tissue, her eyes red, her face pale and splotchy. She'd been crying for some time. She walked into her bedroom and slumped onto the bed. David followed her in and sat next to her gingerly.

"You okay?" he asked tenderly.

"Yeah," Francine sniffed. She folded her tissue nervously and wiped her eyes, the tears welling up and streaming down her face again.

"It's just... everytime I ever need help, she's there, you know? I mean, last year... she went to jail for me, you know?" Francine's voice broke.

"And now she needs me, I mean really needs me...and I can't do anything to help her. I don't know what's going on, I don't even know where she is!" Francine sobbed and fell into David's arms, crying hard for a long, long time.

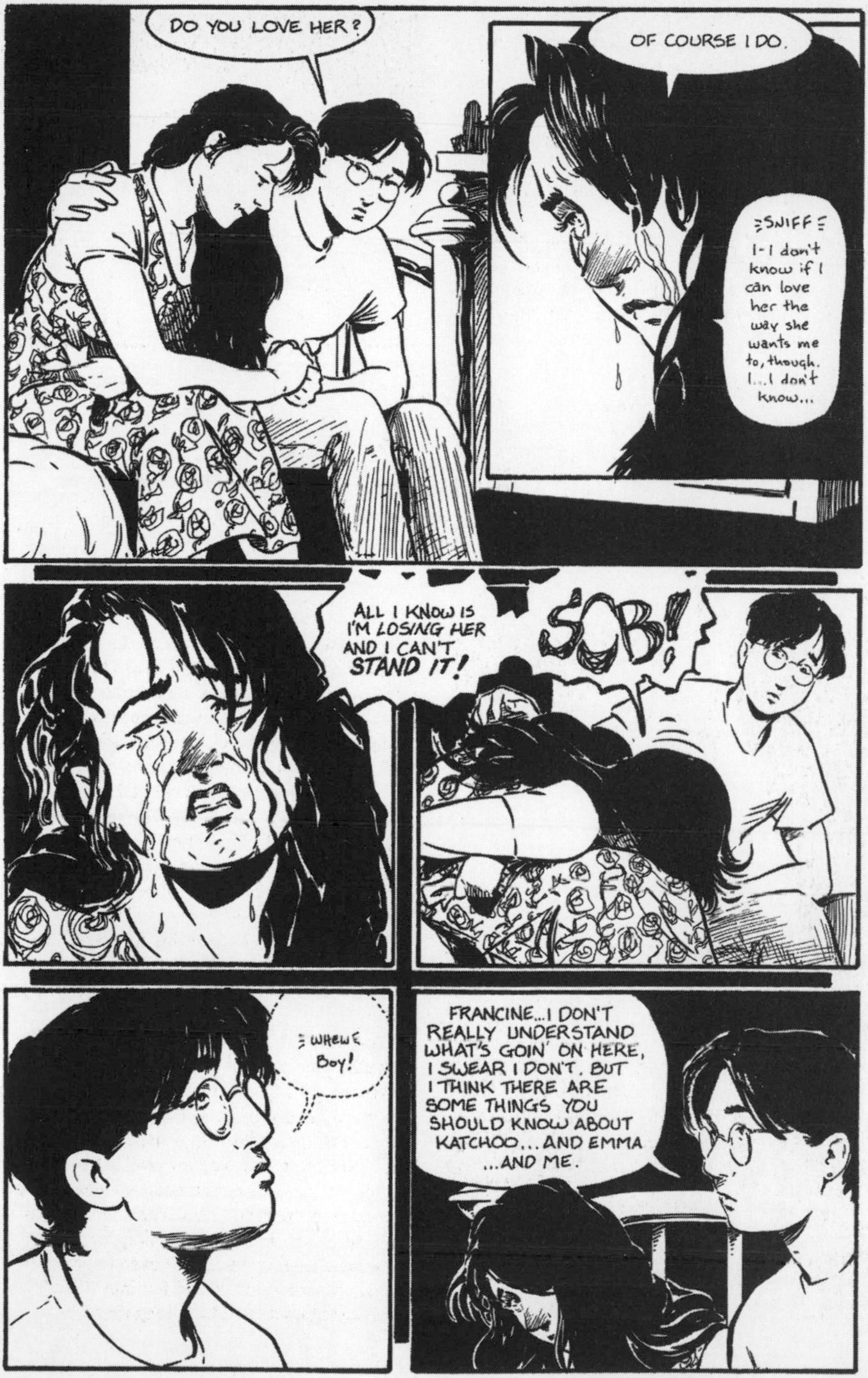
DO YOU LOVE HER?
OF COURSE I DO.
≡SNIFF≡
I-I don't know if I can love her the way she wants me to, though. I...I don't know...
ALL I KNOW IS I'M LOSING HER AND I CAN'T STAND IT!
SOB!
≡WHEW≡ Boy!
FRANCINE...I DON'T REALLY UNDERSTAND WHAT'S GOIN' ON HERE, I SWEAR I DON'T. BUT I THINK THERE ARE SOME THINGS YOU SHOULD KNOW ABOUT KATCHOO... AND EMMA ...AND ME.

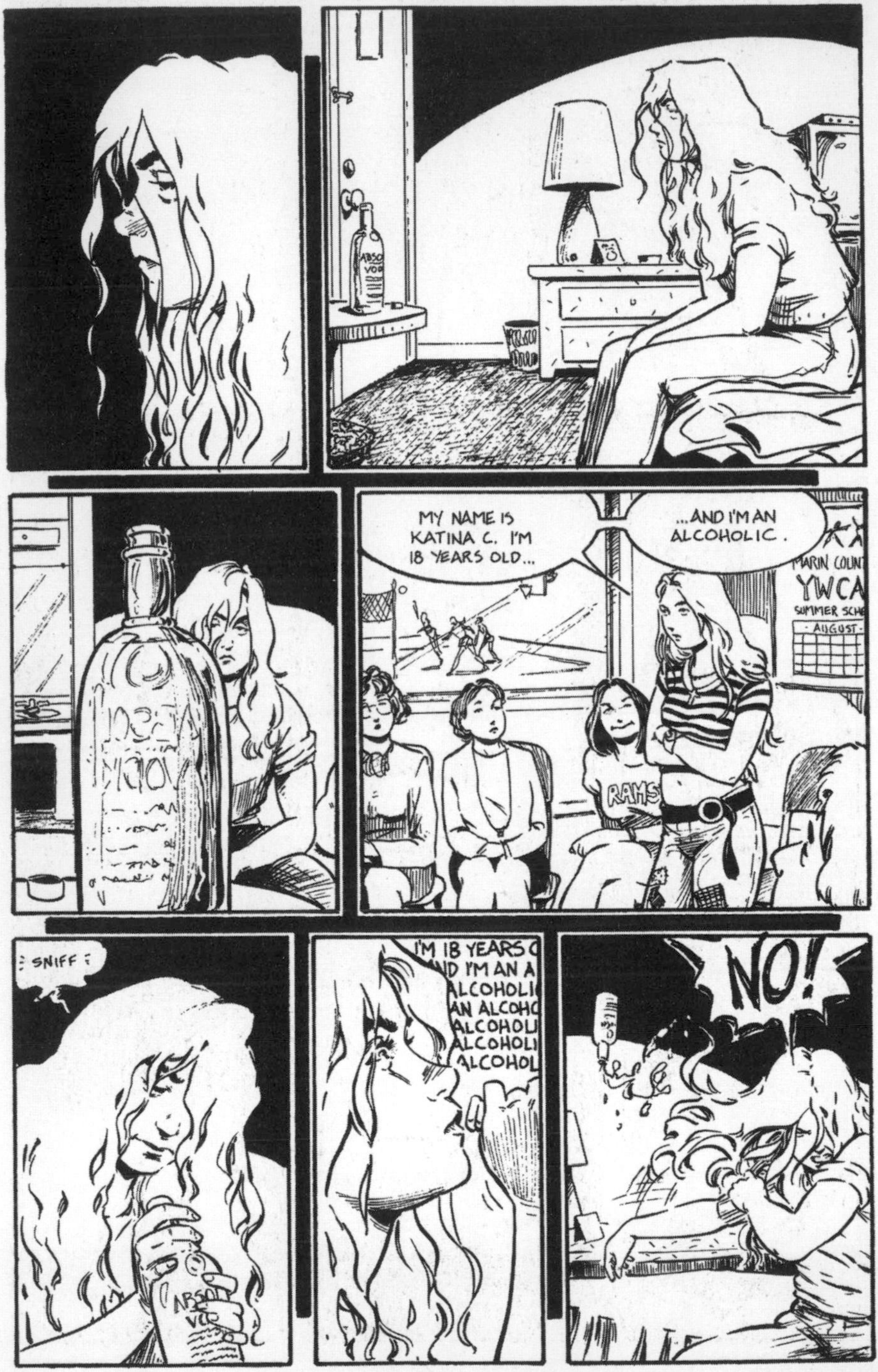
MY NAME IS KATINA C. I'M 18 YEARS OLD...
...AND I'M AN ALCOHOLIC.
YWCA
AUGUST
RAMS
SNIFF
ALCOHOLIC
NO!

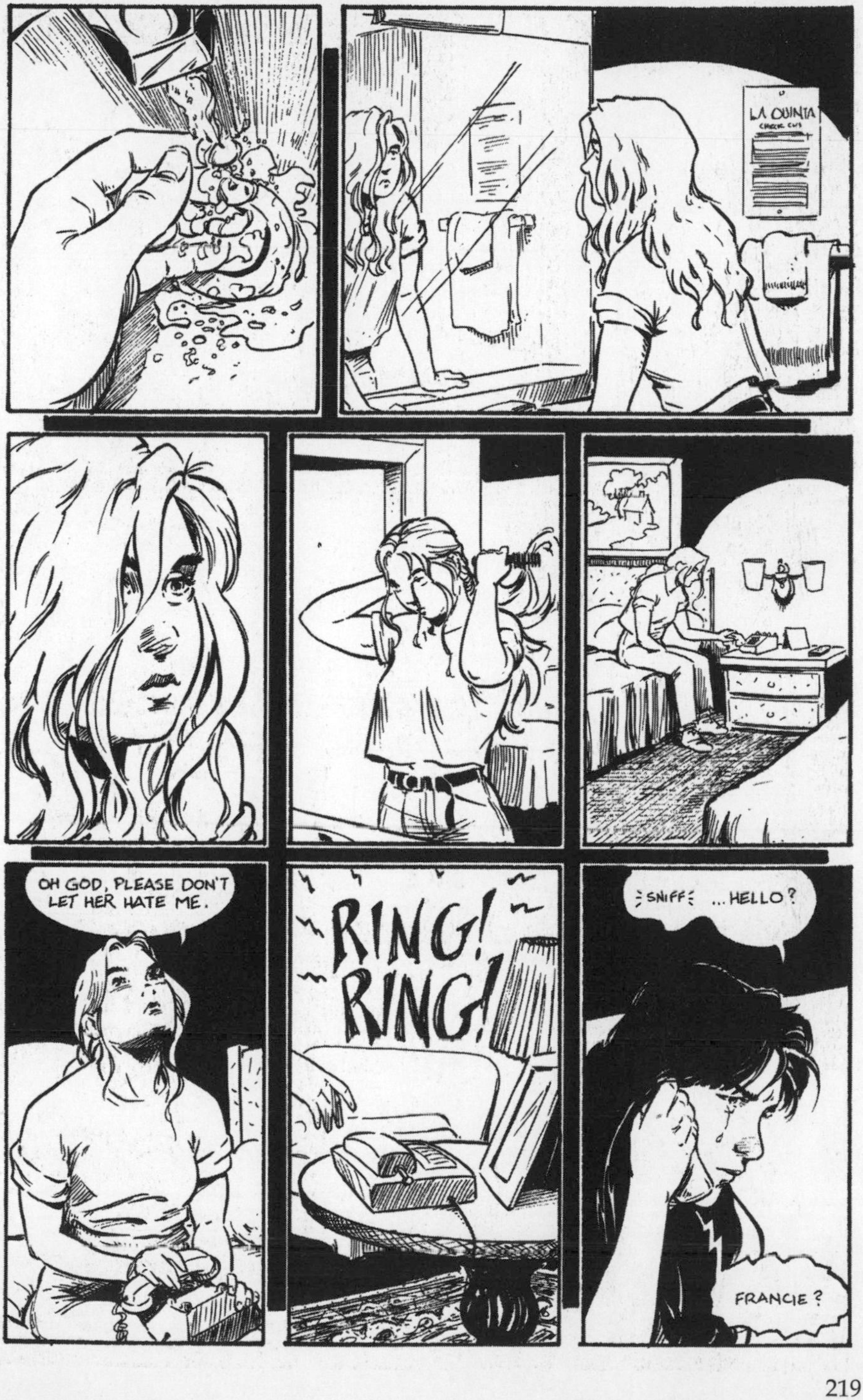
LA QUINTA
OH GOD, PLEASE DON'T LET HER HATE ME.
RING! RING!
SNIFF ...HELLO?
FRANCIE?

KATCHOO! OMIGOD! ARE YOU OK?

I'M FINE. I'M IN A HOTEL OUTSIDE OF TOWN.

THE POLICE CAME LOOKING FOR YOU. THEY SAID YOU ASSAULTED A COP.

WHAT? I DON'T KNOW ANYTHING ABOUT A COP.

THEY SAID A LOT OF OTHER THINGS ABOUT YOU, TOO.

FRANCINE, LISTEN... I - I NEED TO TELL YOU SOMETHING...

I'M IN TROUBLE. I MEAN, **BIG** TROUBLE!

I - I DID SOMETHING FOUR YEARS AGO, WITH EMMA, THAT I SHOULDN'T HAVE...

THIS IS WHEN YOU WERE LIVING IN L.A.?

HOW DID YOU KNOW ABOUT LA?

DAVID TOLD ME.

HE **WHAT**?!

DON'T BE MAD AT HIM, KATCHOO I MADE HIM TELL ME EVERY-THING... ABOUT YOU AND EMMA... AND ALL THAT...

OH FRANCINE... I'M SORRY...

KATCHOO, *DON'T!* LISTEN, IT DOESN'T MATTER, OKAY? **I LOVE YOU!** UNDERSTAND? I LOVE YOU AND NOTHING IS EVER GOING TO CHANGE THAT!

oh Francie...

I DON'T CARE IF YOU GO BY KATCHOO OR BABY JUNE, YOU'LL ALWAYS BE...

WHAT?! W-WAIT! WAIT! HOW DID YOU KNOW I WAS CALLED *BABY JUNE* ?!

DAVID TOLD ME. HE'S BEEN TELLING ME HOW YOU WERE THIS REAL EXCLUSIVE CALL GIRL FOR ALL THE RICH WOMEN IN HOLLYWOOD AND THEY CALLED YOU BABY JUNE.

FRANCINE, I DID NOT TELL HIM THAT! I MEAN, IT'S ALL TRUE... BUT, THAT IS *NOT* WHAT I TOLD HIM! THERE'S *NO WAY* HE COULD POSSIBLY KNOW THAT! .....UNLESS....

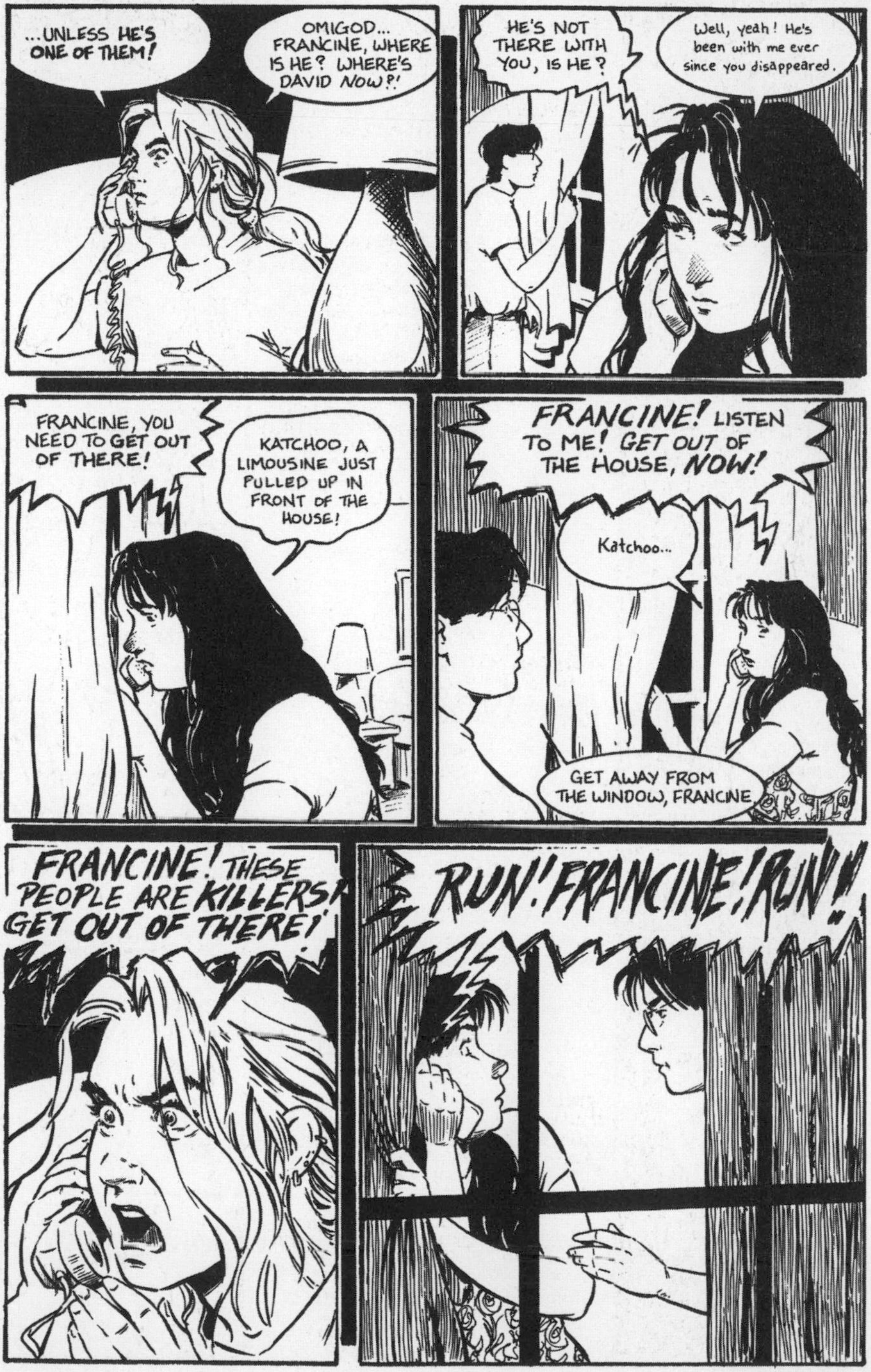
...UNLESS HE'S ONE OF THEM!
OMIGOD... FRANCINE, WHERE IS HE? WHERE'S DAVID NOW?!
HE'S NOT THERE WITH YOU, IS HE?
Well, yeah! He's been with me ever since you disappeared.
FRANCINE, YOU NEED TO GET OUT OF THERE!
KATCHOO, A LIMOUSINE JUST PULLED UP IN FRONT OF THE HOUSE!
FRANCINE! LISTEN TO ME! GET OUT OF THE HOUSE, NOW!
Katchoo...
GET AWAY FROM THE WINDOW, FRANCINE
FRANCINE! THESE PEOPLE ARE KILLERS! GET OUT OF THERE!
RUN! FRANCINE! RUN!!

Do you remember yesterdays?
Do you remember what I was like down?
I feel that madness come my ~~way~~
I must drink ~~to~~ the vicious ~~clowns~~.
I don't know if ~~they~~ ~~found~~ your ears
But I used to have a lot of names
Then one so tender pushed me here
~~And~~ I watched as they fade away.
~~Again~~ I wake up on the tiles
It's like I was never gone.
And just before the pain comes on,
Remember, this is where I started from.

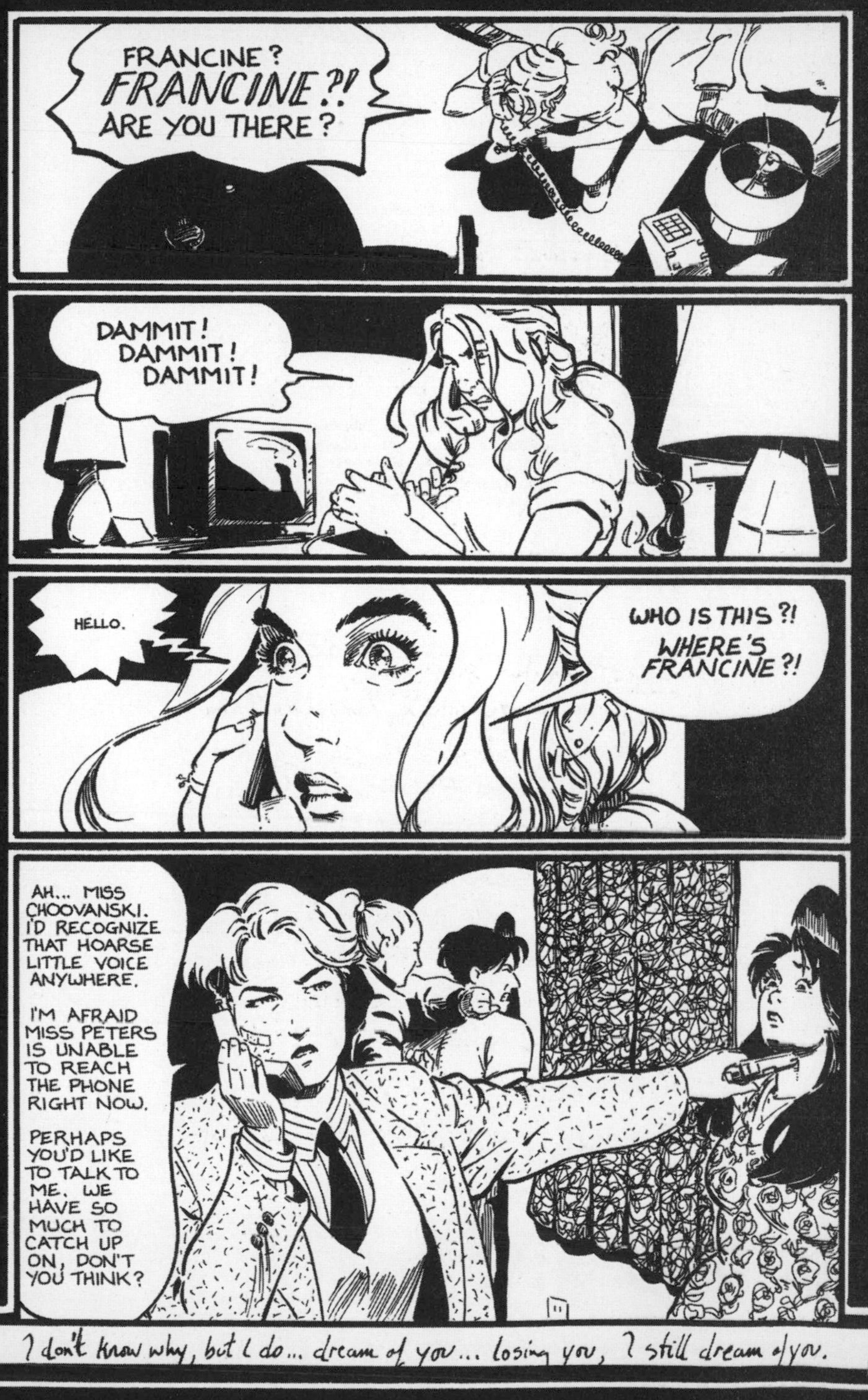
FRANCINE? FRANCINE?! ARE YOU THERE?
DAMMIT! DAMMIT! DAMMIT!
HELLO.
WHO IS THIS?! WHERE'S FRANCINE?!
AH... MISS CHOOVANSKI. I'D RECOGNIZE THAT HOARSE LITTLE VOICE ANYWHERE. I'M AFRAID MISS PETERS IS UNABLE TO REACH THE PHONE RIGHT NOW. PERHAPS YOU'D LIKE TO TALK TO ME. WE HAVE SO MUCH TO CATCH UP ON, DON'T YOU THINK?
I don't know why, but I do... dream of you... losing you, I still dream of you.

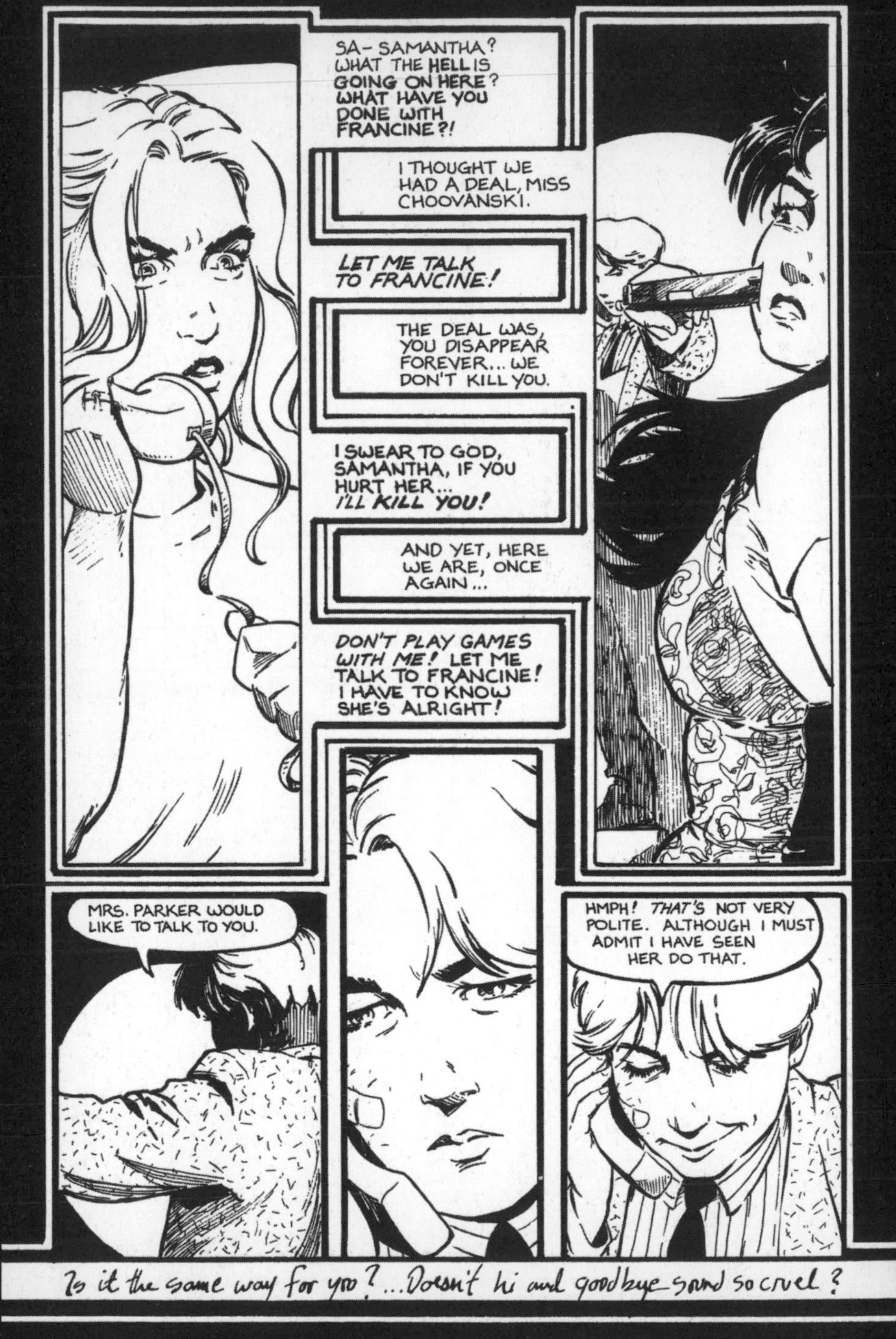
SA-SAMANTHA? WHAT THE HELL IS GOING ON HERE? WHAT HAVE YOU DONE WITH FRANCINE?!
I THOUGHT WE HAD A DEAL, MISS CHOOVANSKI.
LET ME TALK TO FRANCINE!
THE DEAL WAS, YOU DISAPPEAR FOREVER... WE DON'T KILL YOU.
I SWEAR TO GOD, SAMANTHA, IF YOU HURT HER... I'LL KILL YOU!
AND YET, HERE WE ARE, ONCE AGAIN...
DON'T PLAY GAMES WITH ME! LET ME TALK TO FRANCINE! I HAVE TO KNOW SHE'S ALRIGHT!
MRS. PARKER WOULD LIKE TO TALK TO YOU.
HMPH! THAT'S NOT VERY POLITE. ALTHOUGH I MUST ADMIT I HAVE SEEN HER DO THAT.
Is it the same way for you? ...Doesn't hi and goodbye sound so cruel?

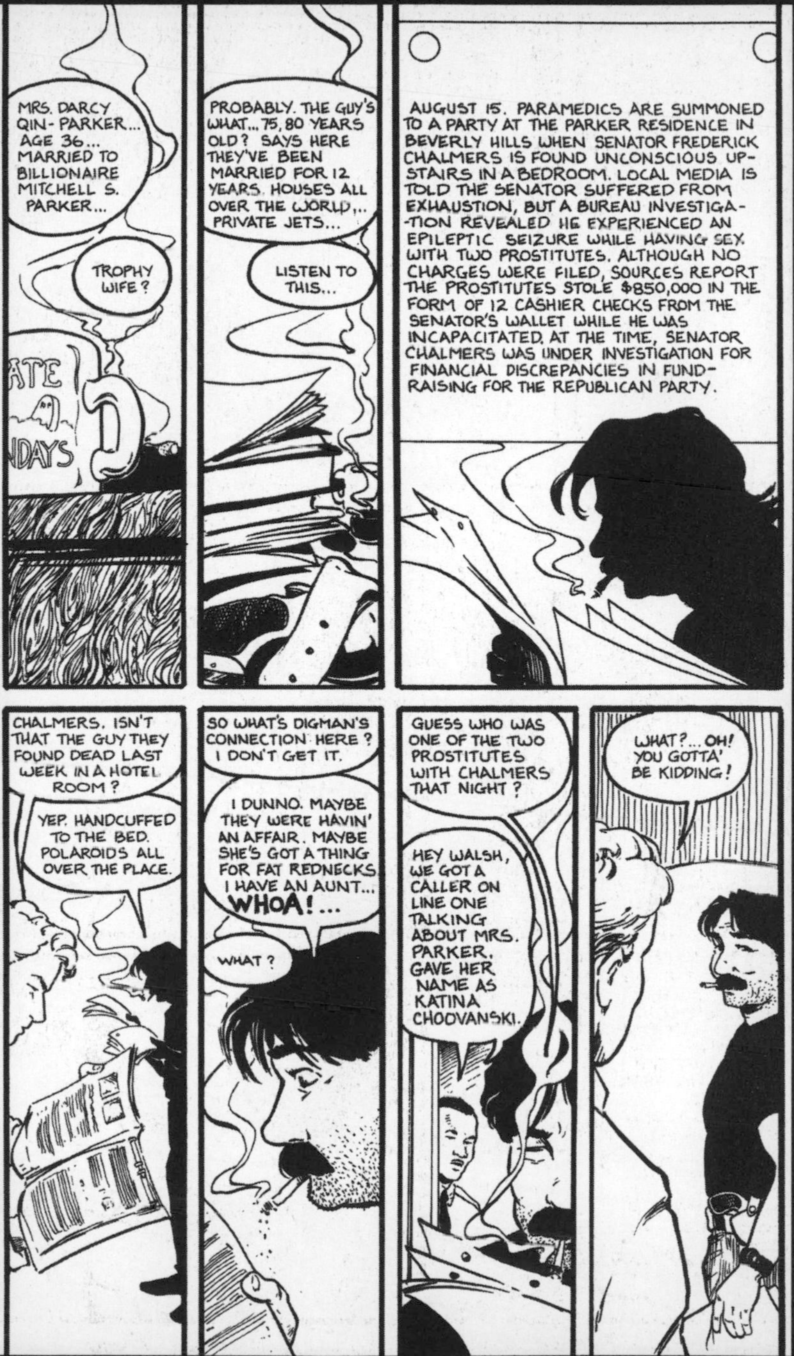
MRS. DARCY QIN-PARKER... AGE 36... MARRIED TO BILLIONAIRE MITCHELL S. PARKER...
TROPHY WIFE?
PROBABLY. THE GUY'S WHAT... 75, 80 YEARS OLD? SAYS HERE THEY'VE BEEN MARRIED FOR 12 YEARS. HOUSES ALL OVER THE WORLD,... PRIVATE JETS...
LISTEN TO THIS...
AUGUST 15. PARAMEDICS ARE SUMMONED TO A PARTY AT THE PARKER RESIDENCE IN BEVERLY HILLS WHEN SENATOR FREDERICK CHALMERS IS FOUND UNCONSCIOUS UPSTAIRS IN A BEDROOM. LOCAL MEDIA IS TOLD THE SENATOR SUFFERED FROM EXHAUSTION, BUT A BUREAU INVESTIGATION REVEALED HE EXPERIENCED AN EPILEPTIC SEIZURE WHILE HAVING SEX WITH TWO PROSTITUTES. ALTHOUGH NO CHARGES WERE FILED, SOURCES REPORT THE PROSTITUTES STOLE $850,000 IN THE FORM OF 12 CASHIER CHECKS FROM THE SENATOR'S WALLET WHILE HE WAS INCAPACITATED. AT THE TIME, SENATOR CHALMERS WAS UNDER INVESTIGATION FOR FINANCIAL DISCREPANCIES IN FUND-RAISING FOR THE REPUBLICAN PARTY.
CHALMERS. ISN'T THAT THE GUY THEY FOUND DEAD LAST WEEK IN A HOTEL ROOM?
YEP. HANDCUFFED TO THE BED. POLAROIDS ALL OVER THE PLACE.
SO WHAT'S DIGMAN'S CONNECTION HERE? I DON'T GET IT.
I DUNNO. MAYBE THEY WERE HAVIN' AN AFFAIR. MAYBE SHE'S GOT A THING FOR FAT REDNECKS. I HAVE AN AUNT... WHOA!...
WHAT?
GUESS WHO WAS ONE OF THE TWO PROSTITUTES WITH CHALMERS THAT NIGHT?
HEY WALSH, WE GOT A CALLER ON LINE ONE TALKING ABOUT MRS. PARKER. GAVE HER NAME AS KATINA CHOOVANSKI.
WHAT?... OH! YOU GOTTA' BE KIDDING!

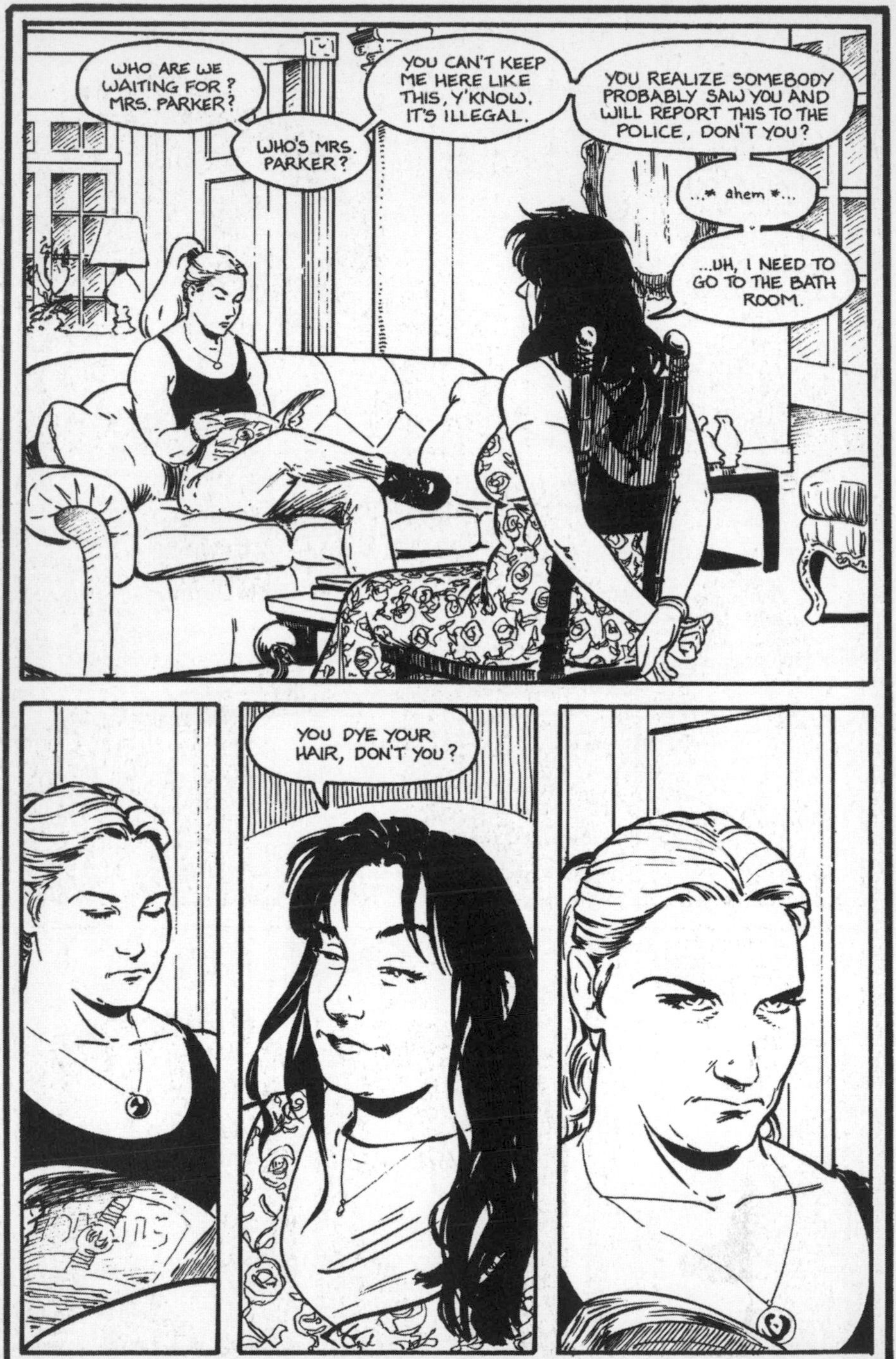
WHO ARE WE WAITING FOR? MRS. PARKER?
WHO'S MRS. PARKER?
YOU CAN'T KEEP ME HERE LIKE THIS, Y'KNOW. IT'S ILLEGAL.
YOU REALIZE SOMEBODY PROBABLY SAW YOU AND WILL REPORT THIS TO THE POLICE, DON'T YOU?
...* ahem *...
...UH, I NEED TO GO TO THE BATH ROOM.
YOU DYE YOUR HAIR, DON'T YOU?

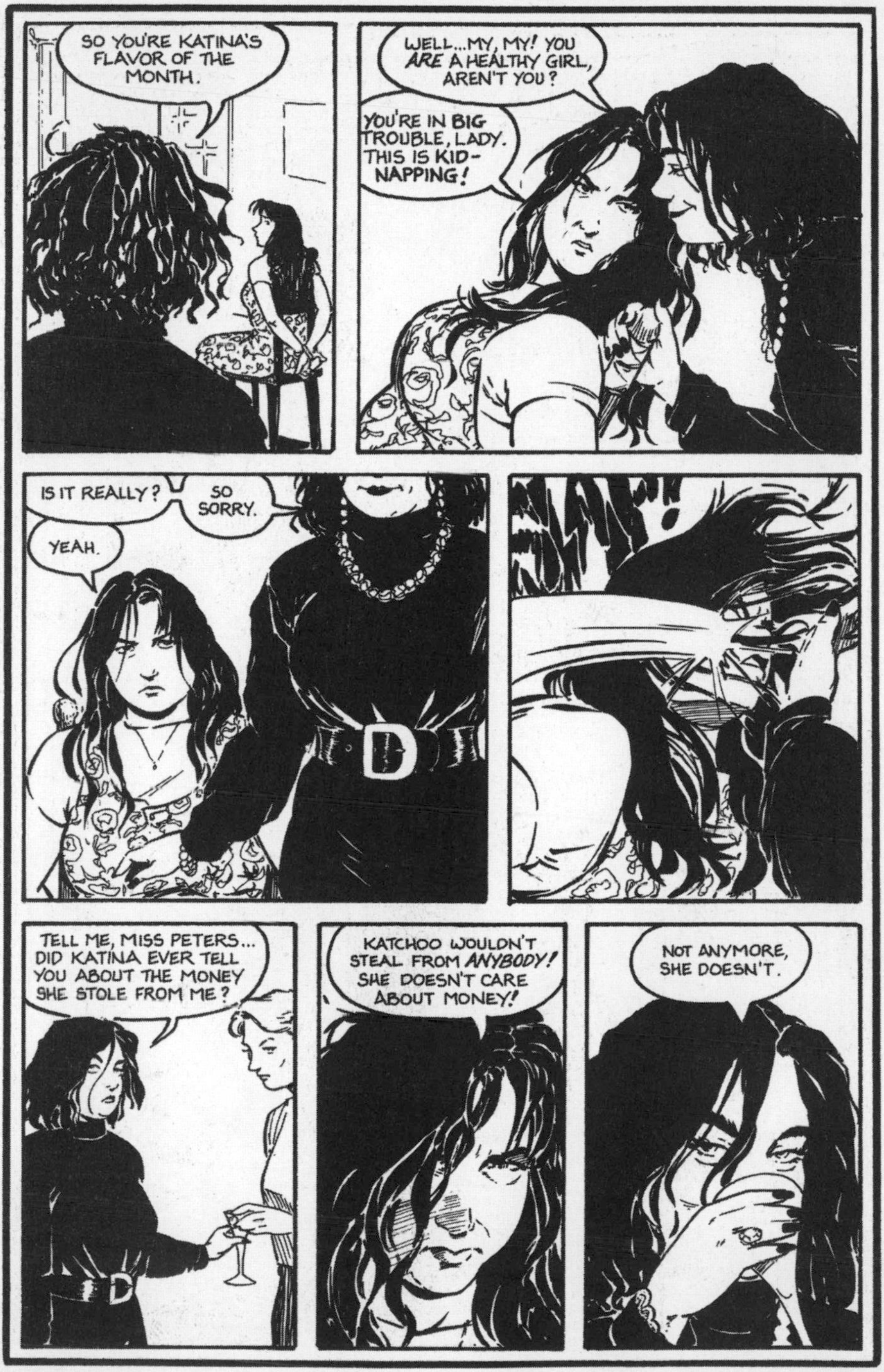
SO YOU'RE KATINA'S FLAVOR OF THE MONTH.
WELL...MY, MY! YOU ARE A HEALTHY GIRL, AREN'T YOU?
YOU'RE IN BIG TROUBLE, LADY. THIS IS KID-NAPPING!
IS IT REALLY?
SO SORRY.
YEAH.
TELL ME, MISS PETERS... DID KATINA EVER TELL YOU ABOUT THE MONEY SHE STOLE FROM ME?
KATCHOO WOULDN'T STEAL FROM ANYBODY! SHE DOESN'T CARE ABOUT MONEY!
NOT ANYMORE, SHE DOESN'T.

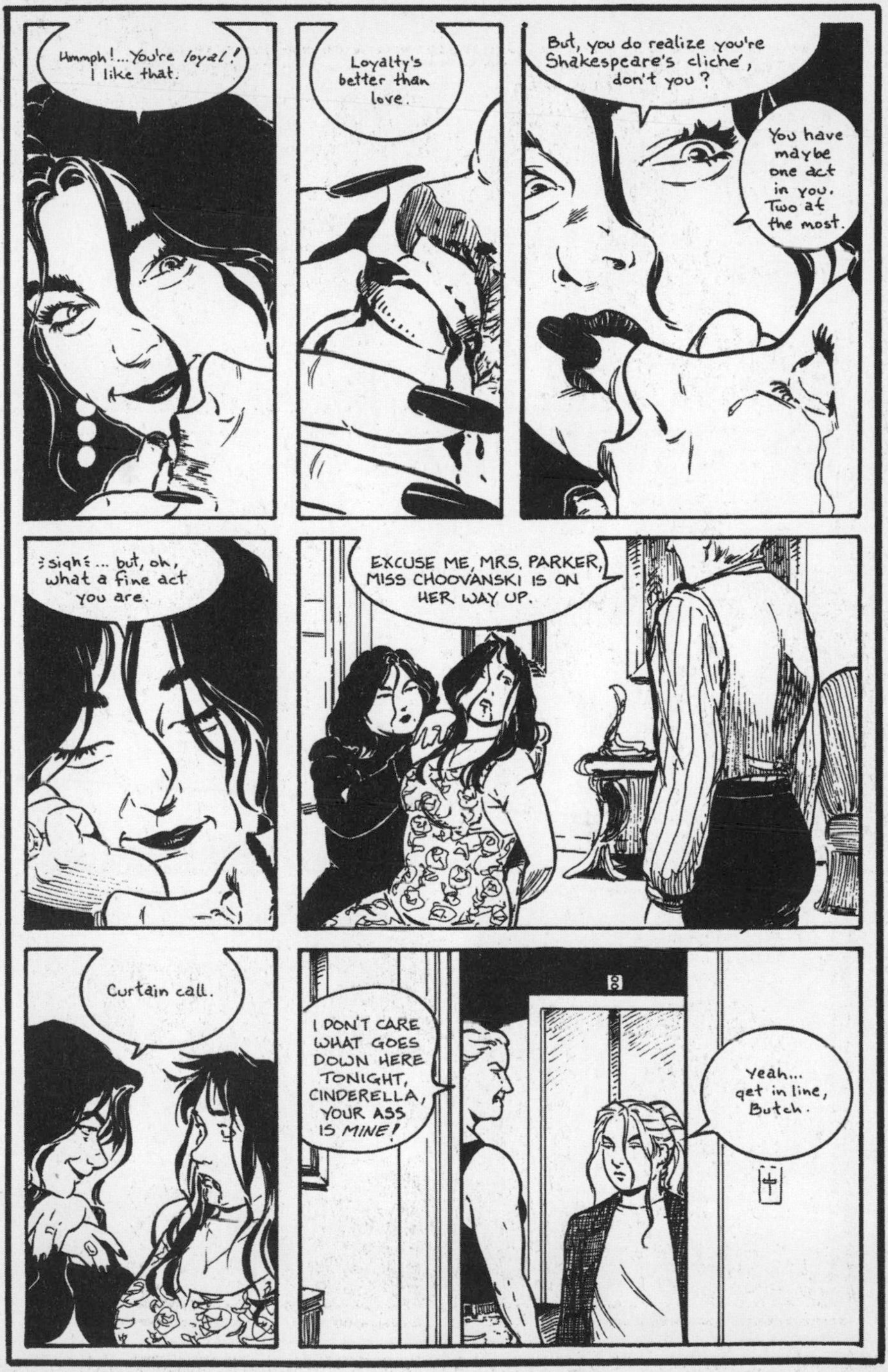
Hmmph!...You're *loyal*! I like that.
Loyalty's better than love.
But, you do realize you're Shakespeare's cliche', don't you?
You have maybe one act in you. Two at the most.
sigh ... but, oh, what a fine act you are.
EXCUSE ME, MRS. PARKER, MISS CHOOVANSKI IS ON HER WAY UP.
Curtain call.
I DON'T CARE WHAT GOES DOWN HERE TONIGHT, CINDERELLA, YOUR ASS IS *MINE*!
Yeah... get in line, Butch.

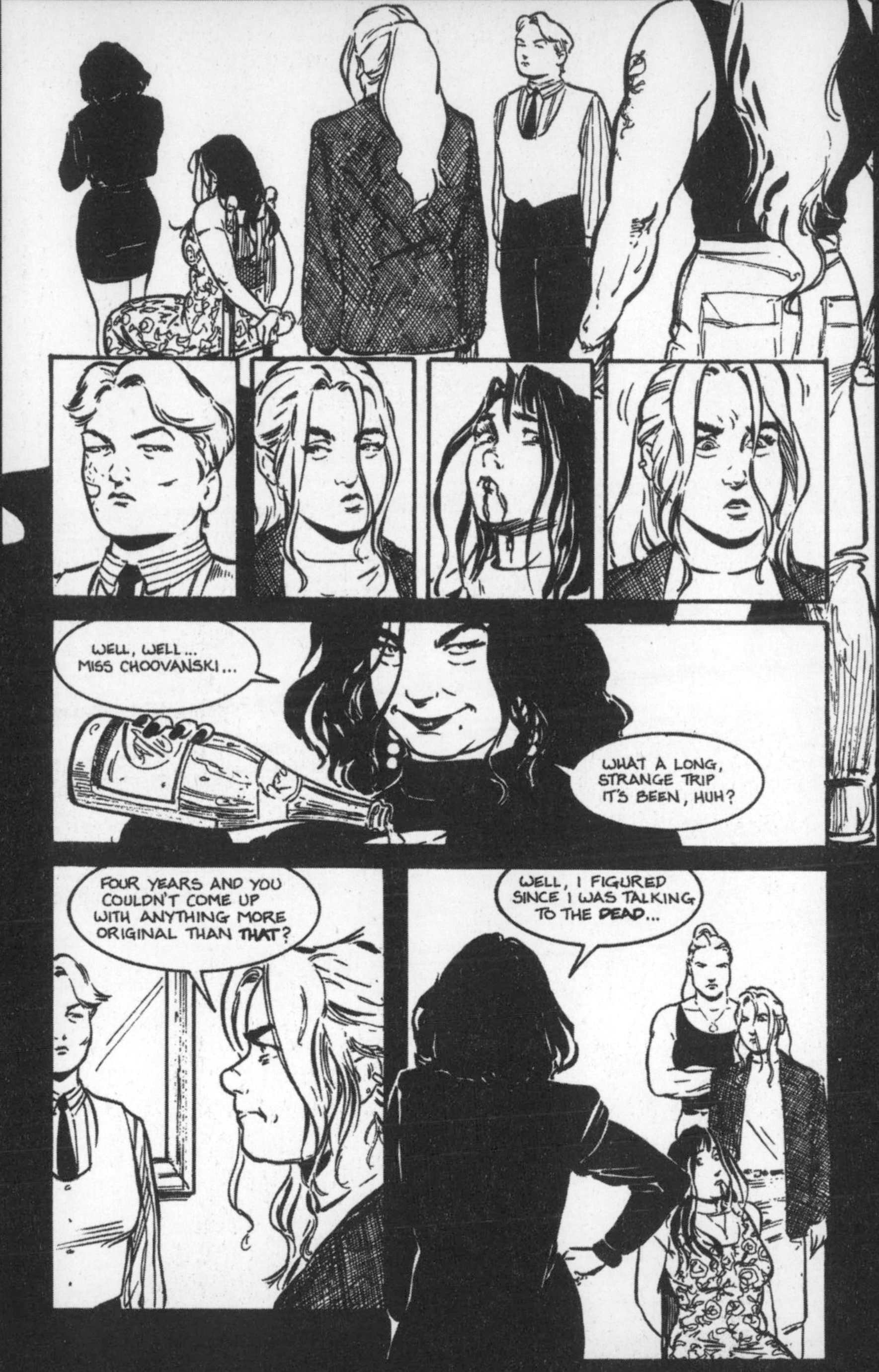

WELL, WELL... MISS CHOOVANSKI...
WHAT A LONG, STRANGE TRIP IT'S BEEN, HUH?
FOUR YEARS AND YOU COULDN'T COME UP WITH ANYTHING MORE ORIGINAL THAN THAT?
WELL, I FIGURED SINCE I WAS TALKING TO THE DEAD...

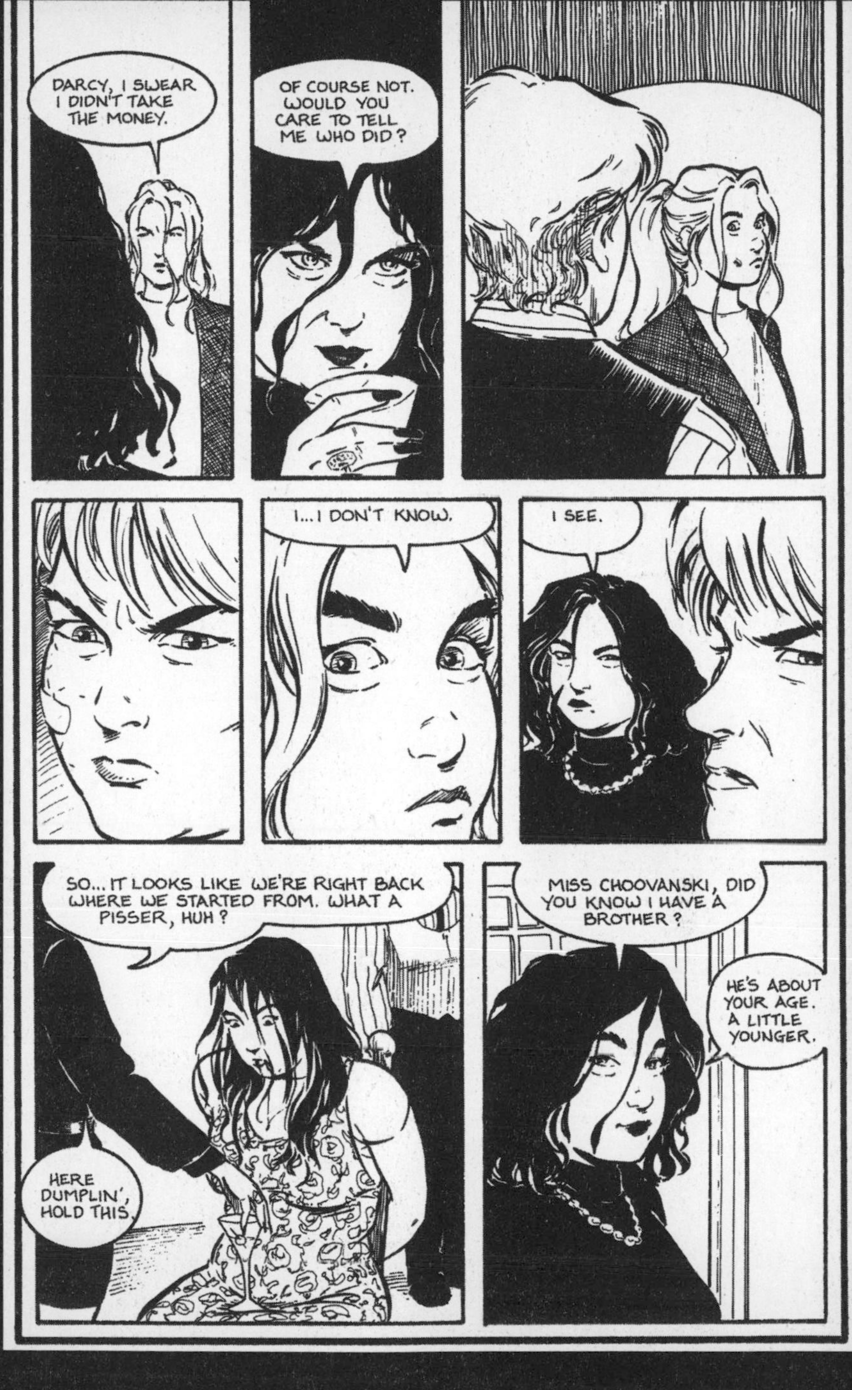
DARCY, I SWEAR I DIDN'T TAKE THE MONEY.
OF COURSE NOT. WOULD YOU CARE TO TELL ME WHO DID?
I... I DON'T KNOW.
I SEE.
SO... IT LOOKS LIKE WE'RE RIGHT BACK WHERE WE STARTED FROM. WHAT A PISSER, HUH?
HERE DUMPLIN', HOLD THIS.
MISS CHOOVANSKI, DID YOU KNOW I HAVE A BROTHER?
HE'S ABOUT YOUR AGE. A LITTLE YOUNGER.

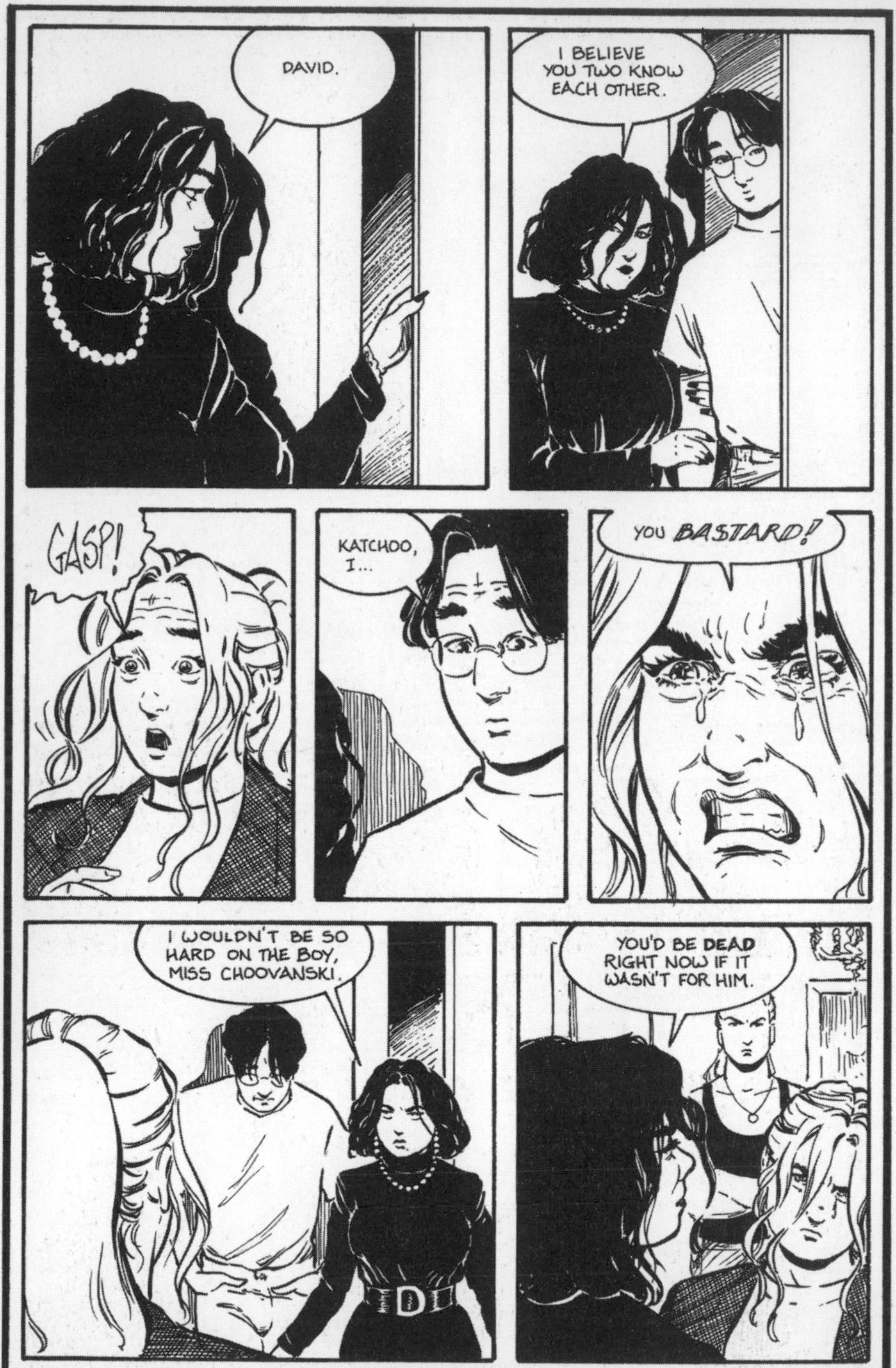
DAVID.
I BELIEVE YOU TWO KNOW EACH OTHER.
GASP!
KATCHOO, I...
YOU BASTARD!
I WOULDN'T BE SO HARD ON THE BOY, MISS CHOOVANSKI.
YOU'D BE DEAD RIGHT NOW IF IT WASN'T FOR HIM.

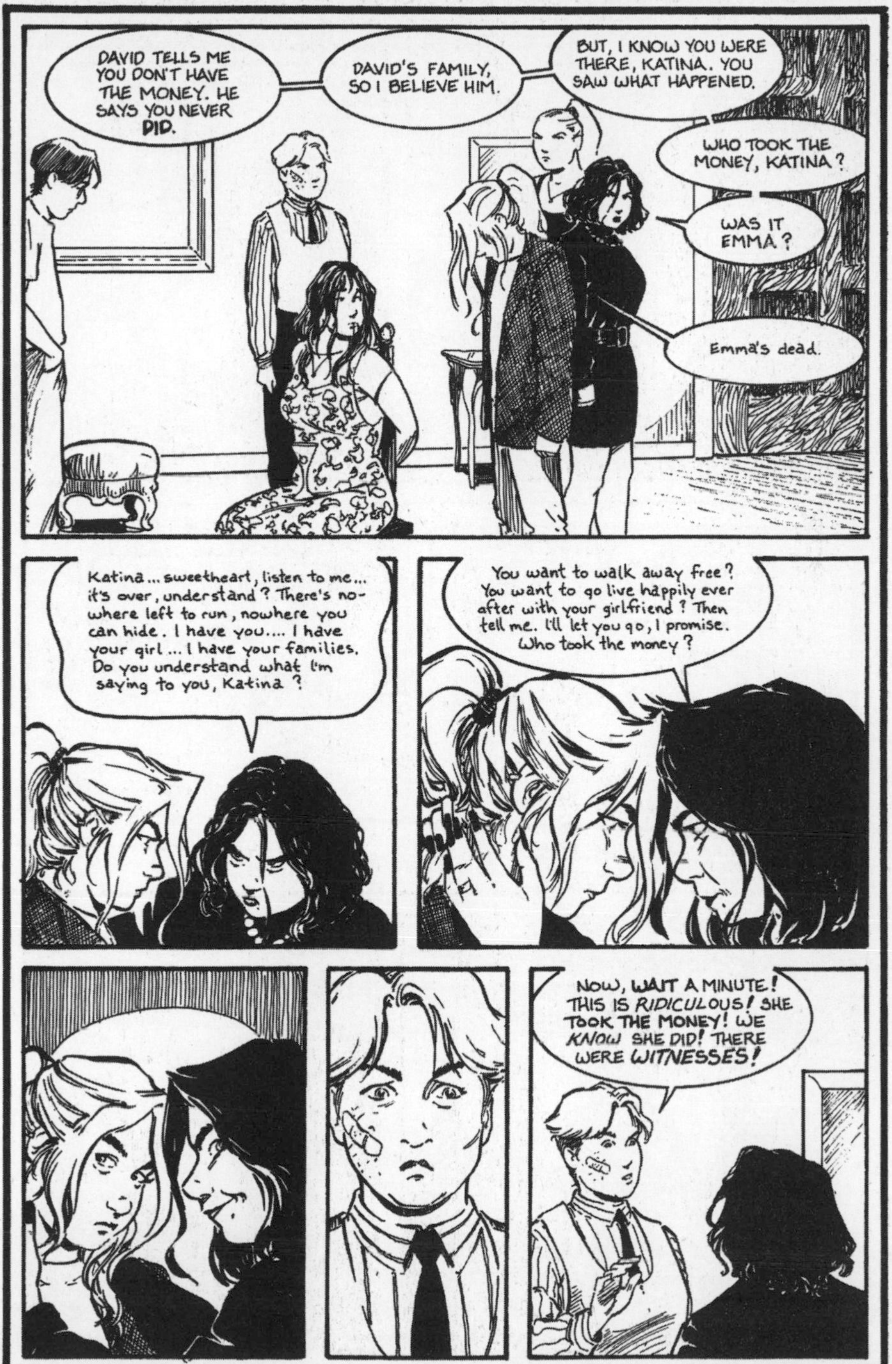
DAVID TELLS ME YOU DON'T HAVE THE MONEY. HE SAYS YOU NEVER DID.
DAVID'S FAMILY, SO I BELIEVE HIM.
BUT, I KNOW YOU WERE THERE, KATINA. YOU SAW WHAT HAPPENED.
WHO TOOK THE MONEY, KATINA?
WAS IT EMMA?
Emma's dead.
Katina... sweetheart, listen to me... it's over, understand? There's nowhere left to run, nowhere you can hide. I have you.... I have your girl... I have your families. Do you understand what I'm saying to you, Katina?
You want to walk away free? You want to go live happily ever after with your girlfriend? Then tell me. I'll let you go, I promise. Who took the money?
NOW, WAIT A MINUTE! THIS IS RIDICULOUS! SHE TOOK THE MONEY! WE KNOW SHE DID! THERE WERE WITNESSES!

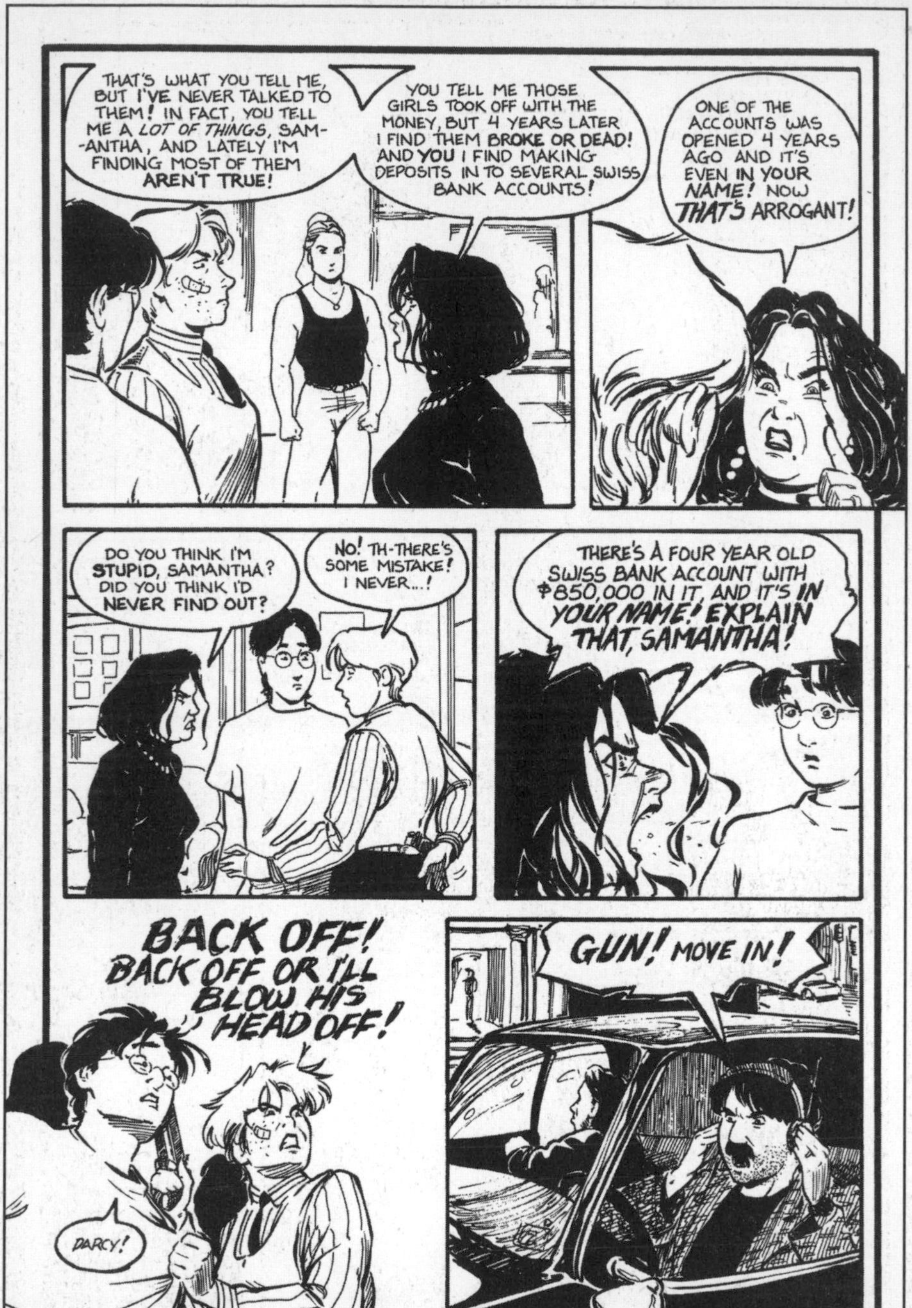

THAT'S WHAT YOU TELL ME, BUT I'VE NEVER TALKED TO THEM! IN FACT, YOU TELL ME A LOT OF THINGS, SAM-ANTHA, AND LATELY I'M FINDING MOST OF THEM AREN'T TRUE!
YOU TELL ME THOSE GIRLS TOOK OFF WITH THE MONEY, BUT 4 YEARS LATER I FIND THEM BROKE OR DEAD! AND YOU I FIND MAKING DEPOSITS IN TO SEVERAL SWISS BANK ACCOUNTS!
ONE OF THE ACCOUNTS WAS OPENED 4 YEARS AGO AND IT'S EVEN IN YOUR NAME! NOW THAT'S ARROGANT!
DO YOU THINK I'M STUPID, SAMANTHA? DID YOU THINK I'D NEVER FIND OUT?
NO! TH-THERE'S SOME MISTAKE! I NEVER...!
THERE'S A FOUR YEAR OLD SWISS BANK ACCOUNT WITH $850,000 IN IT, AND IT'S IN YOUR NAME! EXPLAIN THAT, SAMANTHA!
BACK OFF! BACK OFF OR I'LL BLOW HIS HEAD OFF!
DARCY!
GUN! MOVE IN!

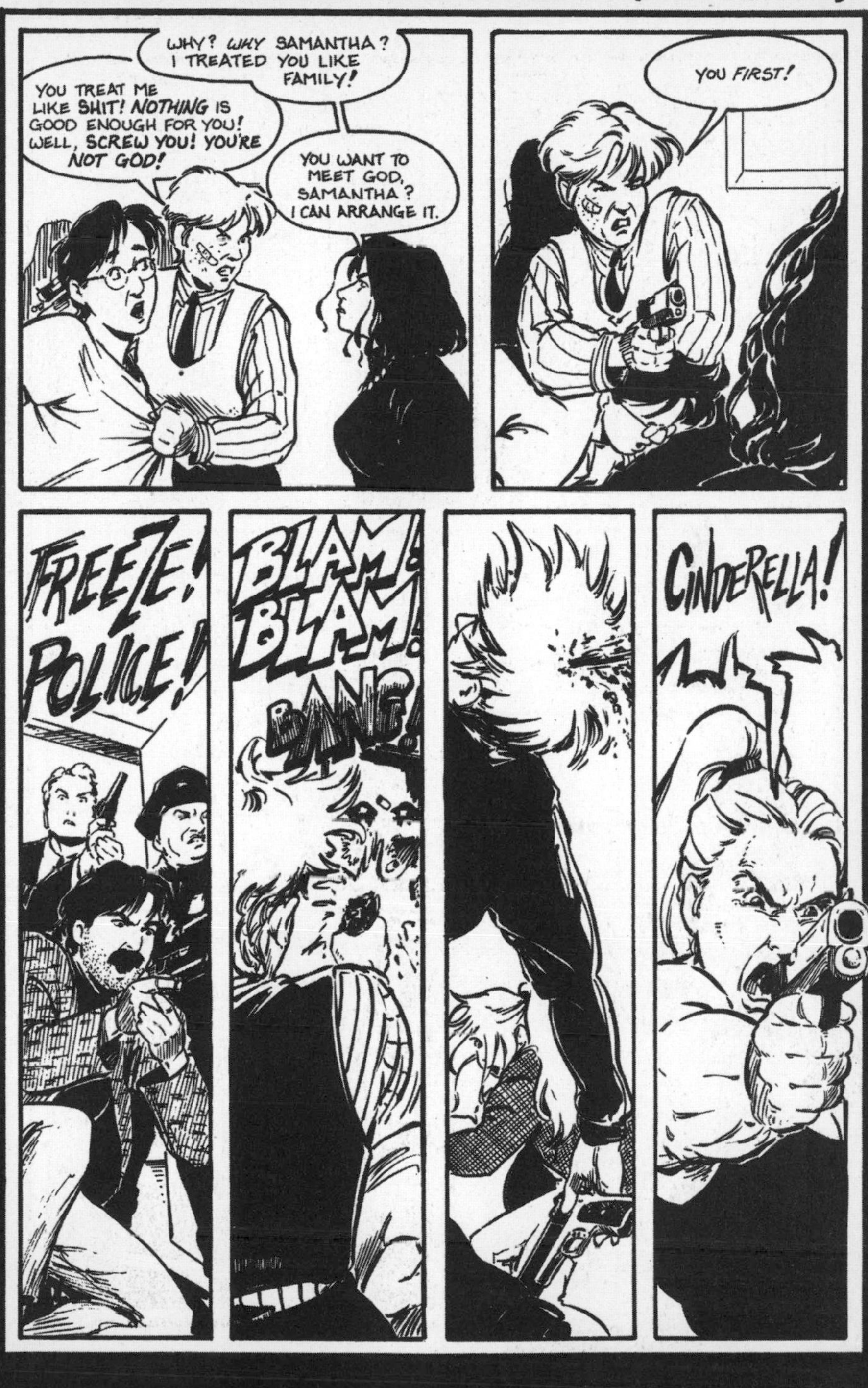
WHY? WHY SAMANTHA? I TREATED YOU LIKE FAMILY!
YOU TREAT ME LIKE SHIT! NOTHING IS GOOD ENOUGH FOR YOU! WELL, SCREW YOU! YOU'RE NOT GOD!
YOU WANT TO MEET GOD, SAMANTHA? I CAN ARRANGE IT.
YOU FIRST!
FREEZE! POLICE!
BLAM! BLAM!
CINDERELLA!

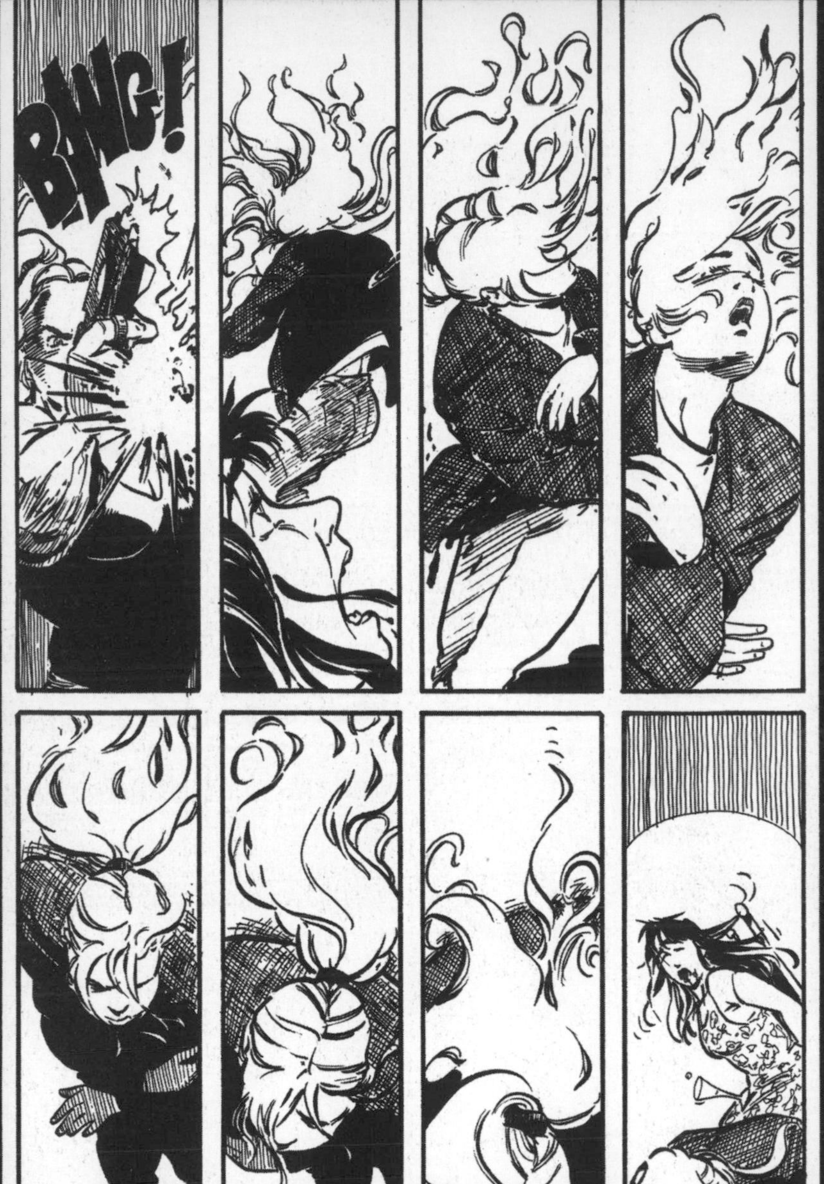
BANG!

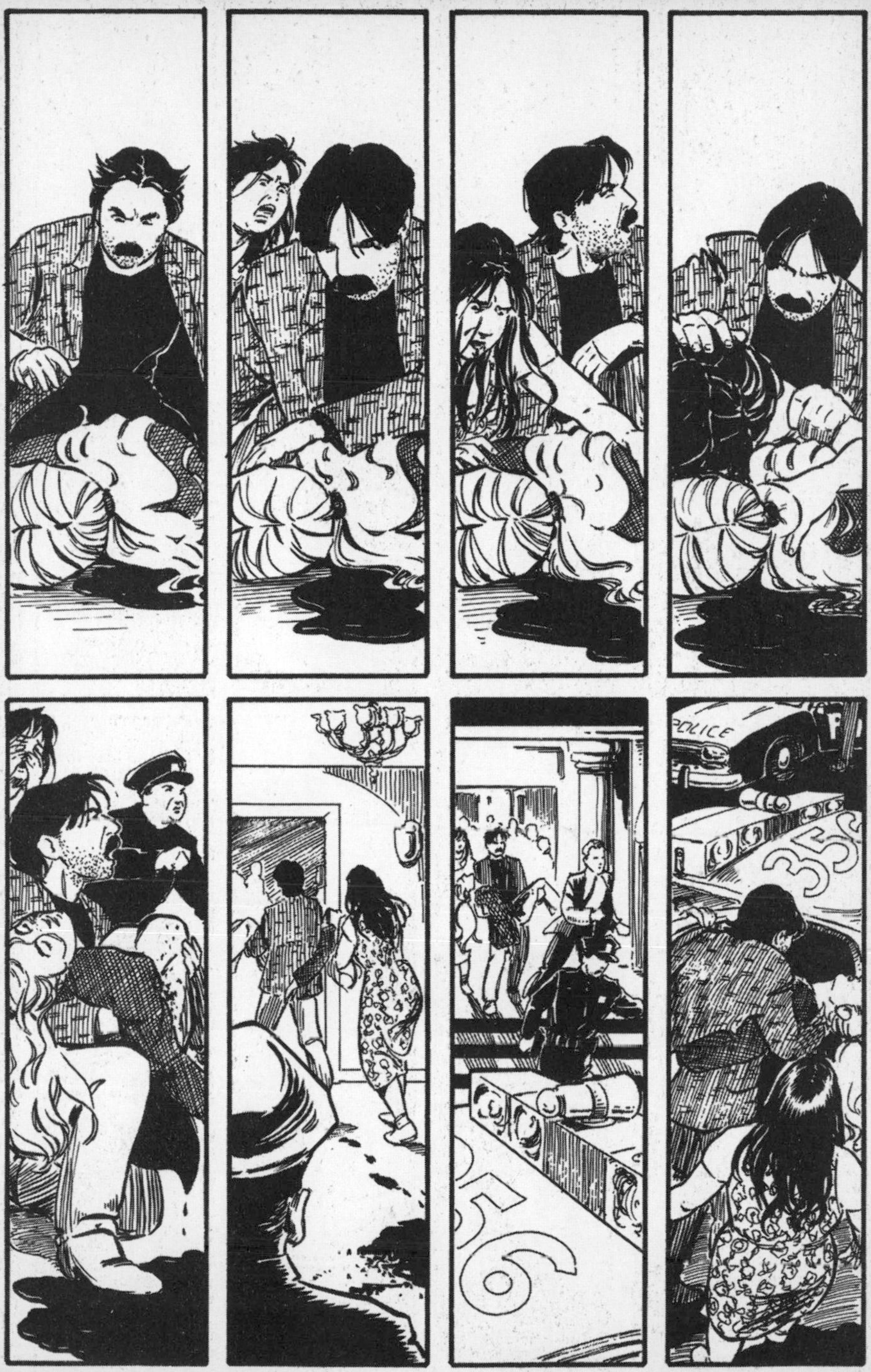
POLICE

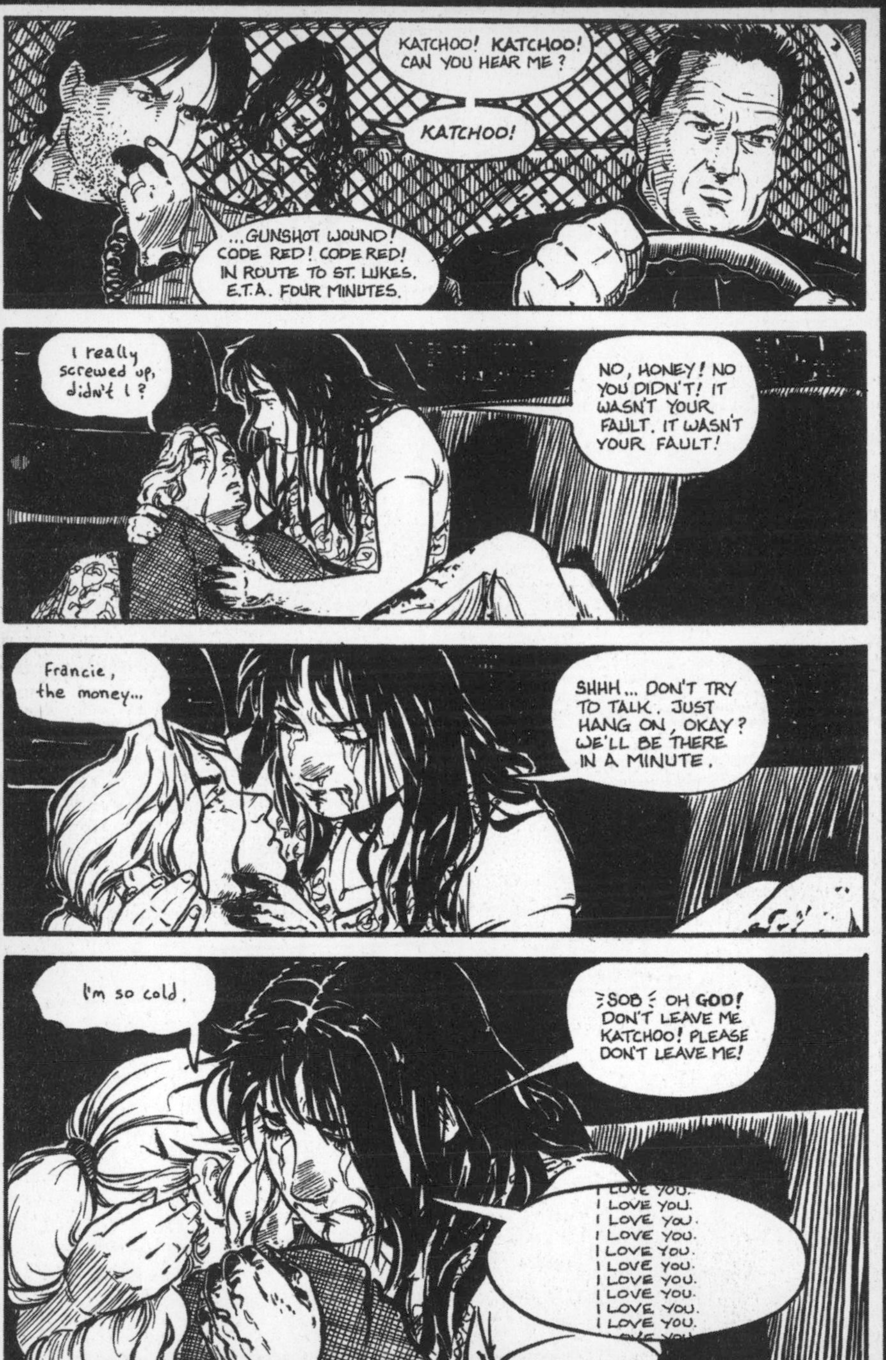
KATCHOO! KATCHOO! CAN YOU HEAR ME?
KATCHOO!
...GUNSHOT WOUND! CODE RED! CODE RED! IN ROUTE TO ST. LUKES. E.T.A. FOUR MINUTES.
I really screwed up, didn't I?
NO, HONEY! NO YOU DIDN'T! IT WASN'T YOUR FAULT. IT WASN'T YOUR FAULT!
Francie, the money...
SHHH... DON'T TRY TO TALK. JUST HANG ON, OKAY? WE'LL BE THERE IN A MINUTE.
I'm so cold.
SOB OH GOD! DON'T LEAVE ME KATCHOO! PLEASE DON'T LEAVE ME!
I LOVE YOU.
I LOVE YOU.
I LOVE YOU.
I LOVE YOU.
I LOVE YOU.
I LOVE YOU.
I LOVE YOU.
I LOVE YOU.
I LOVE YOU.
I LOVE YOU.

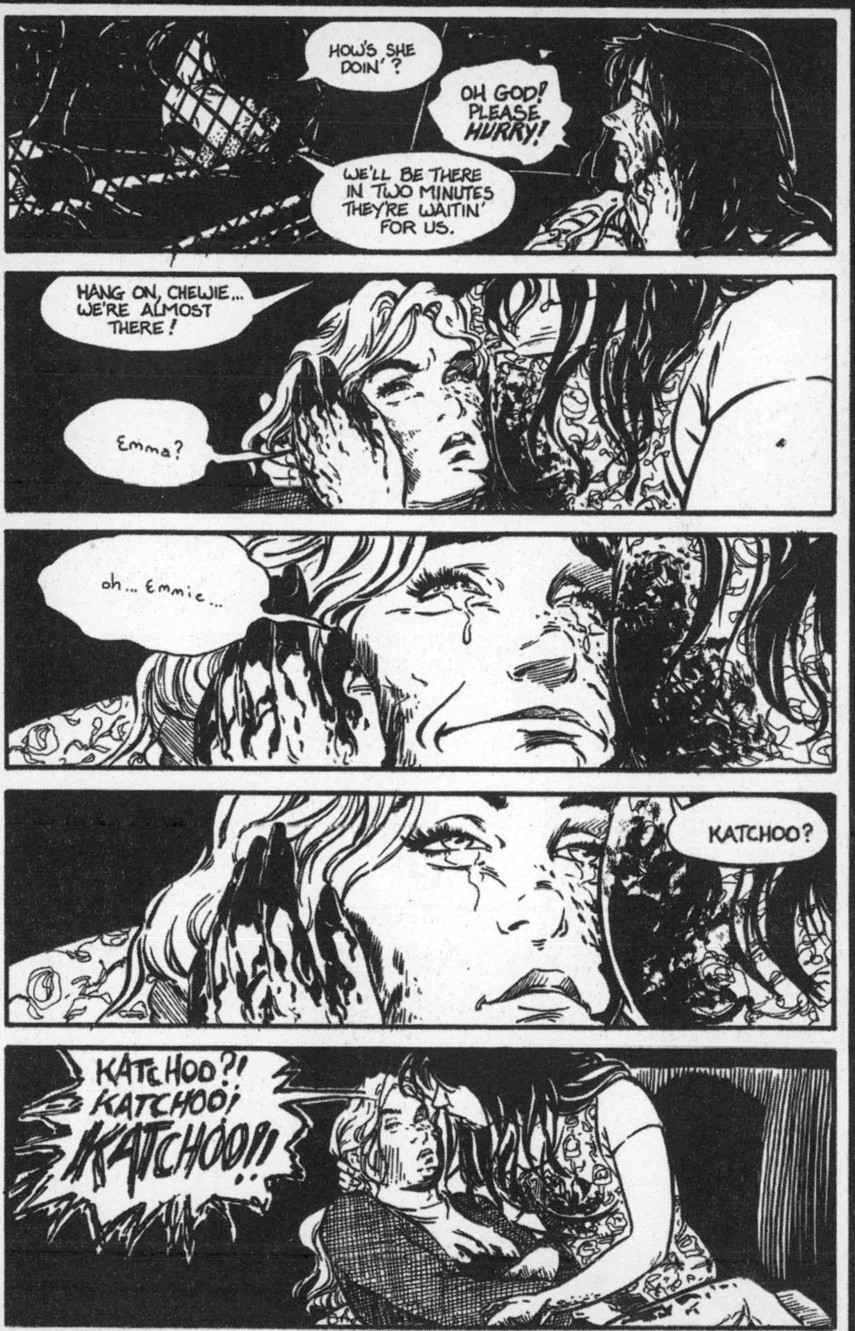
HOW'S SHE DOIN'?
OH GOD! PLEASE HURRY!
WE'LL BE THERE IN TWO MINUTES THEY'RE WAITIN' FOR US.
HANG ON, CHEWIE... WE'RE ALMOST THERE!
Emma?
oh... Emmie...
KATCHOO?
KATCHOO?! KATCHOO! KATCHOO!!

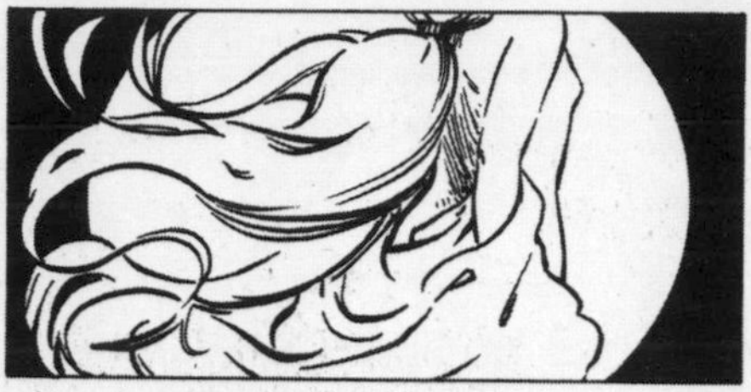

Somewhere far away, the sky cries
out in thunder.
And there's nothing I can do.
So I wait. And I watch. And
I feel his breath against my face.
Cool and brave.
His salt licks my skin, his promise
brushes my hair.
His fury drives the wind to touch
my cheek,
And whisper something I can't hear.
I think he loves me. I think he
comes to see me.
I am young.
I will learn.

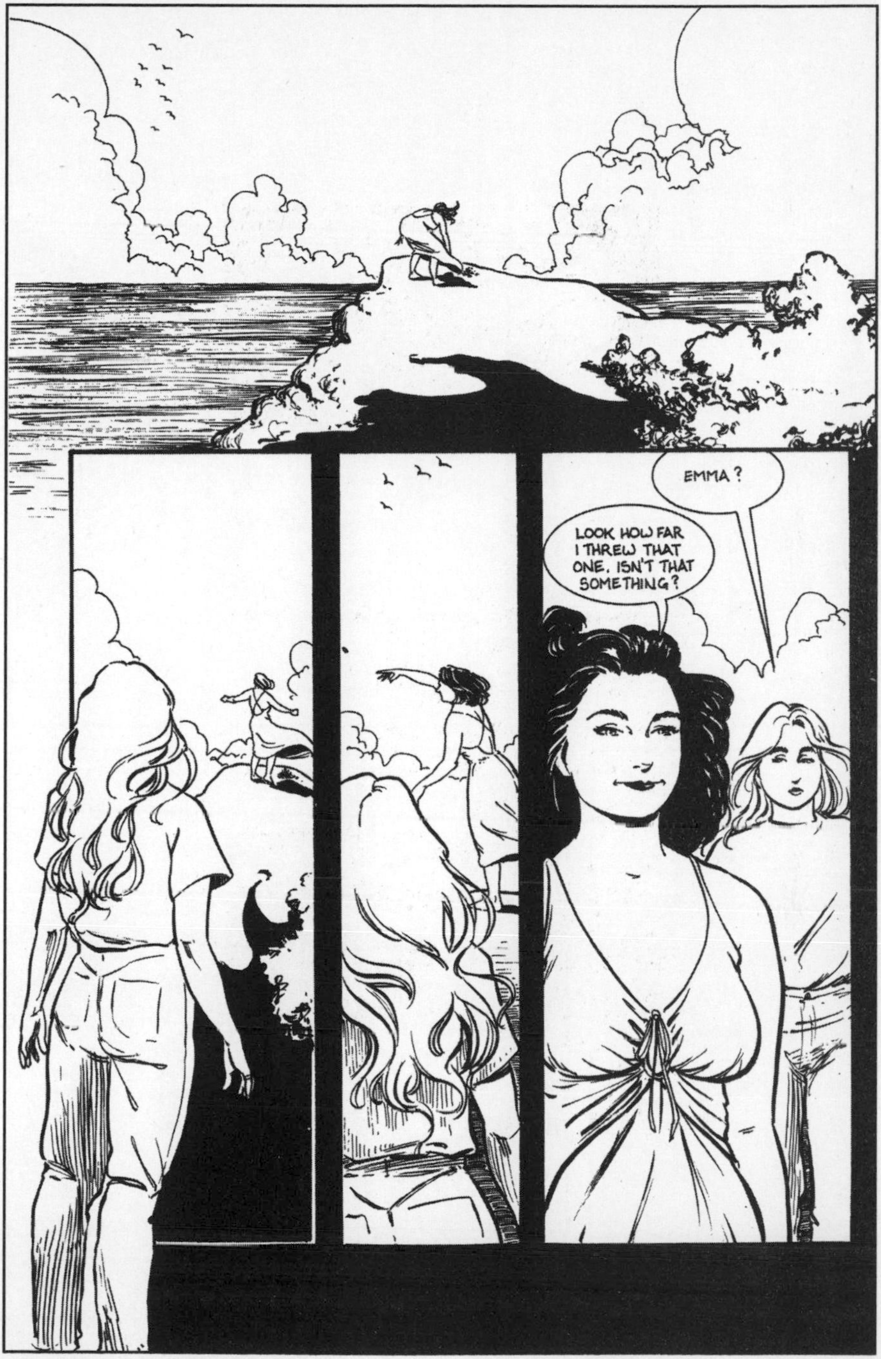
EMMA?
LOOK HOW FAR I THREW THAT ONE. ISN'T THAT SOMETHING?

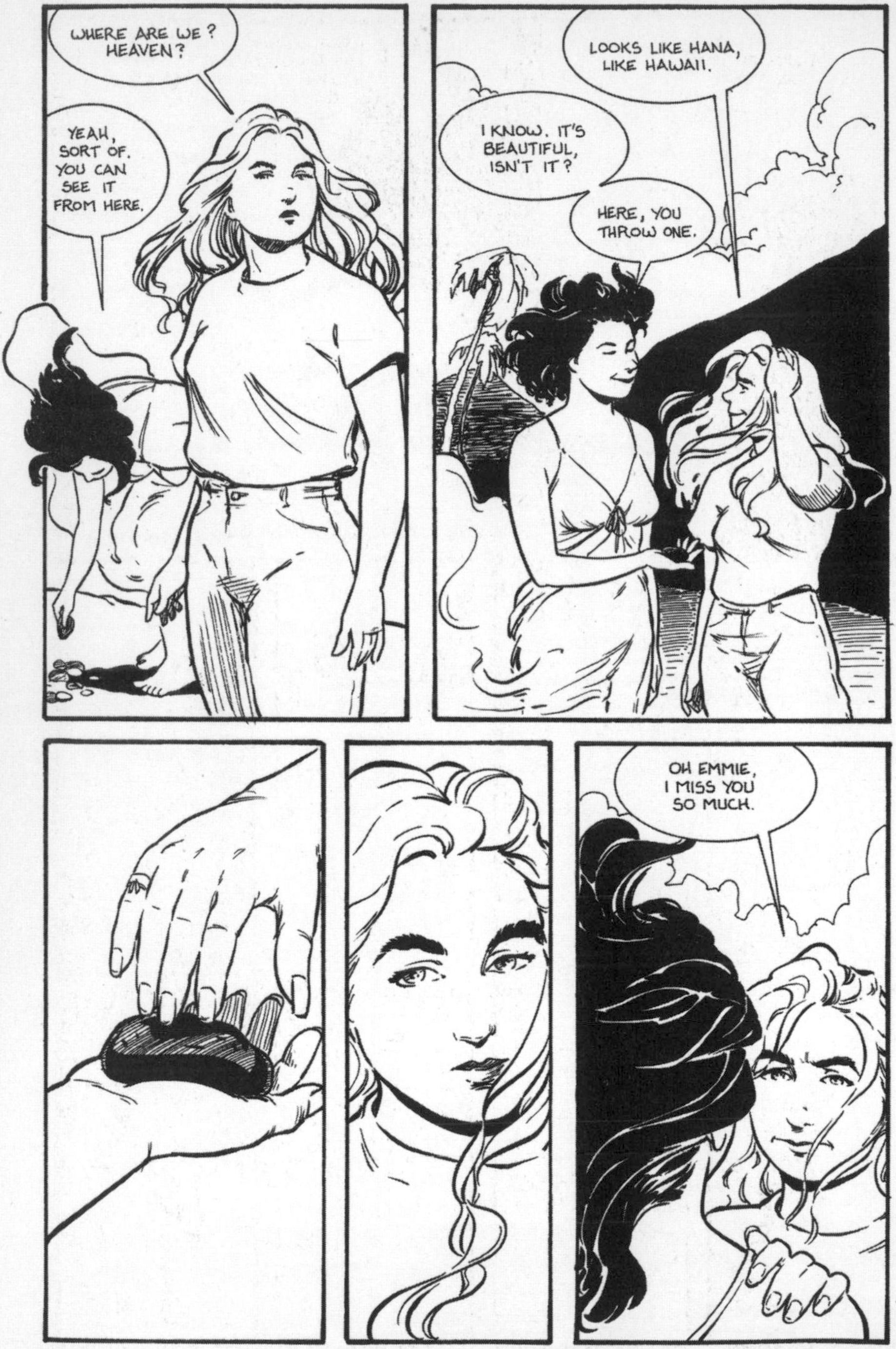
WHERE ARE WE? HEAVEN?
YEAH, SORT OF. YOU CAN SEE IT FROM HERE.
LOOKS LIKE HANA, LIKE HAWAII.
I KNOW. IT'S BEAUTIFUL, ISN'T IT?
HERE, YOU THROW ONE.
OH EMMIE, I MISS YOU SO MUCH.

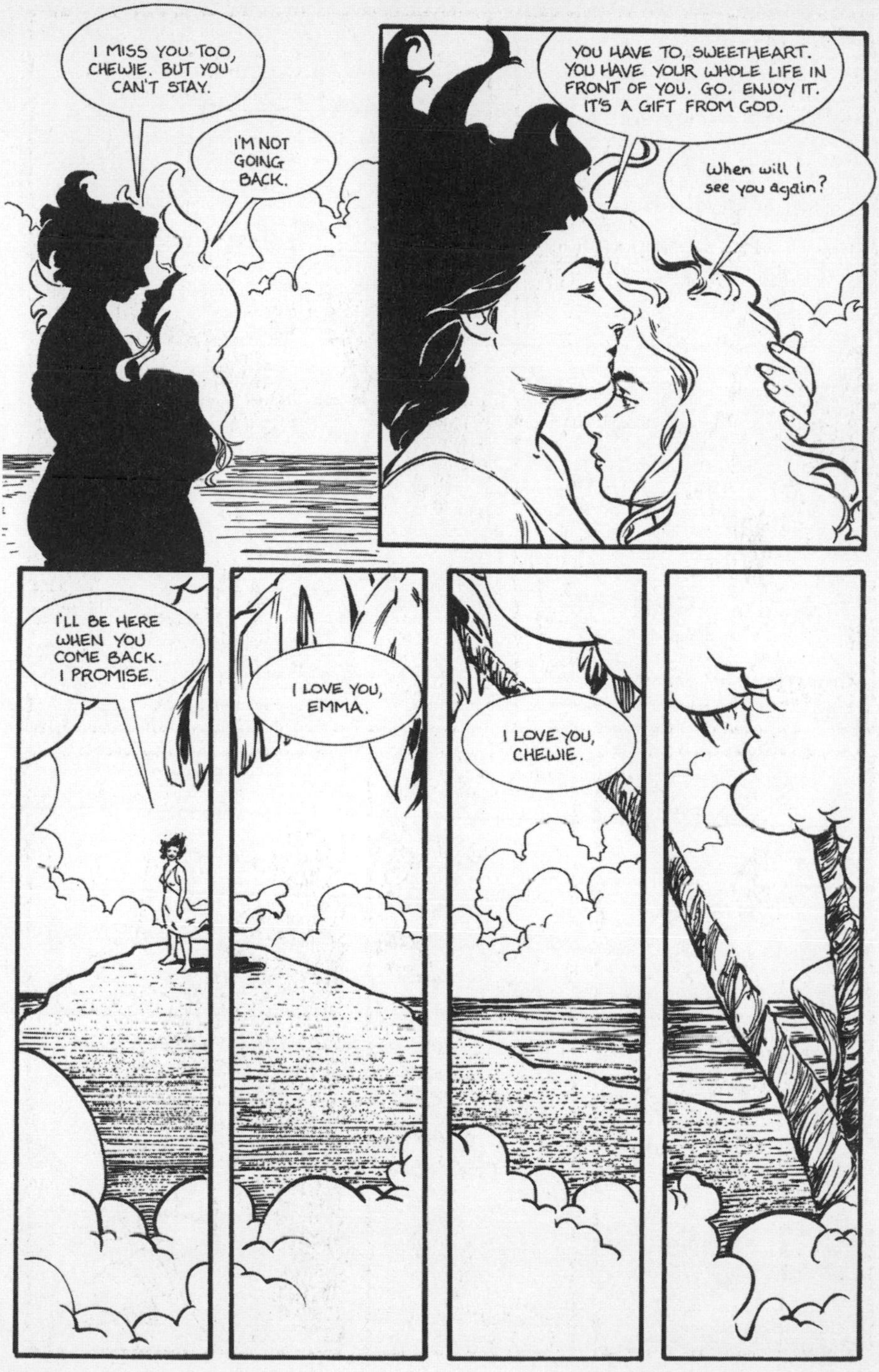
I MISS YOU TOO, CHEWIE. BUT YOU CAN'T STAY.
I'M NOT GOING BACK.
YOU HAVE TO, SWEETHEART. YOU HAVE YOUR WHOLE LIFE IN FRONT OF YOU. GO. ENJOY IT. IT'S A GIFT FROM GOD.
When will I see you again?
I'LL BE HERE WHEN YOU COME BACK. I PROMISE.
I LOVE YOU, EMMA.
I LOVE YOU, CHEWIE.

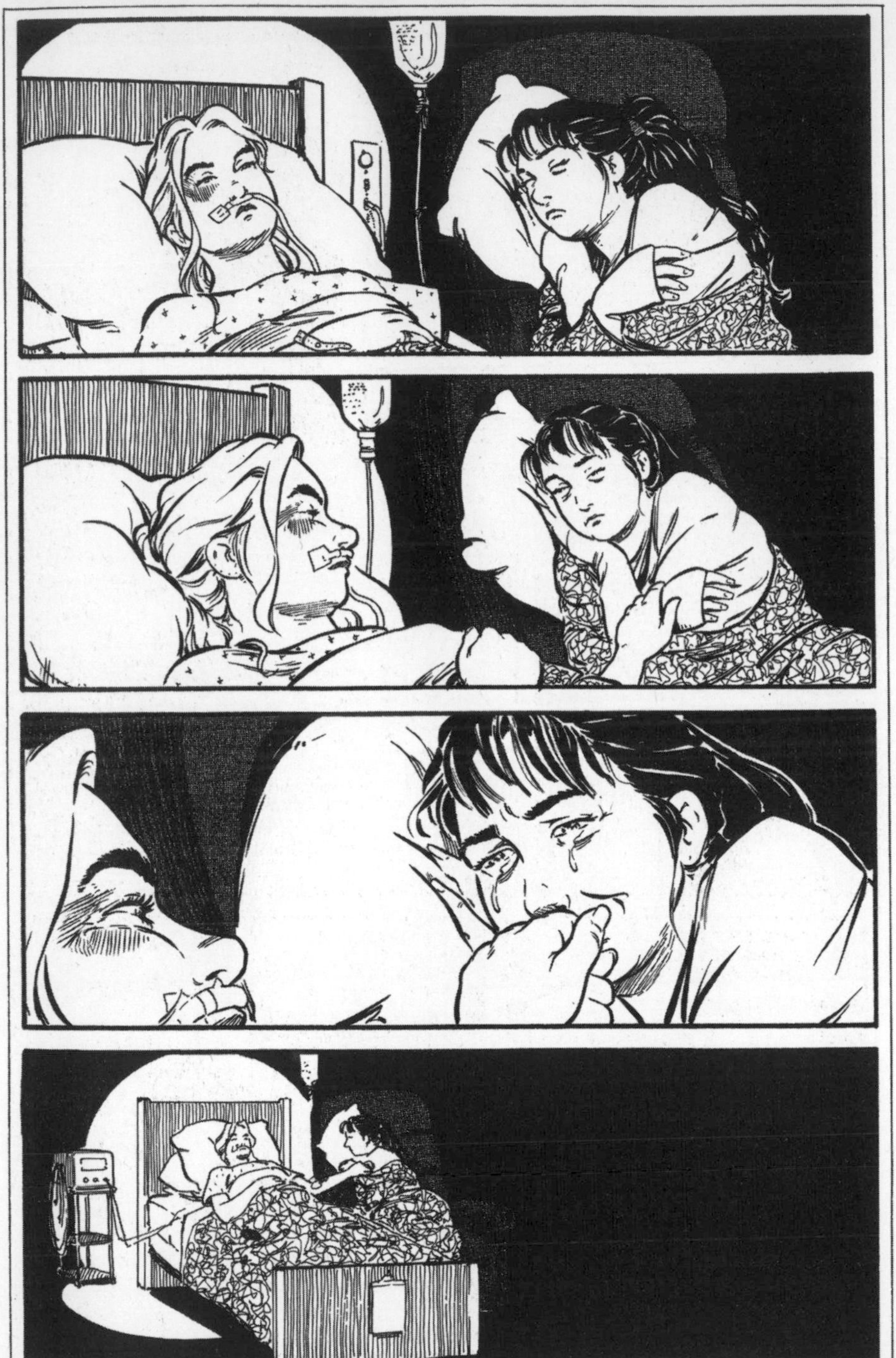

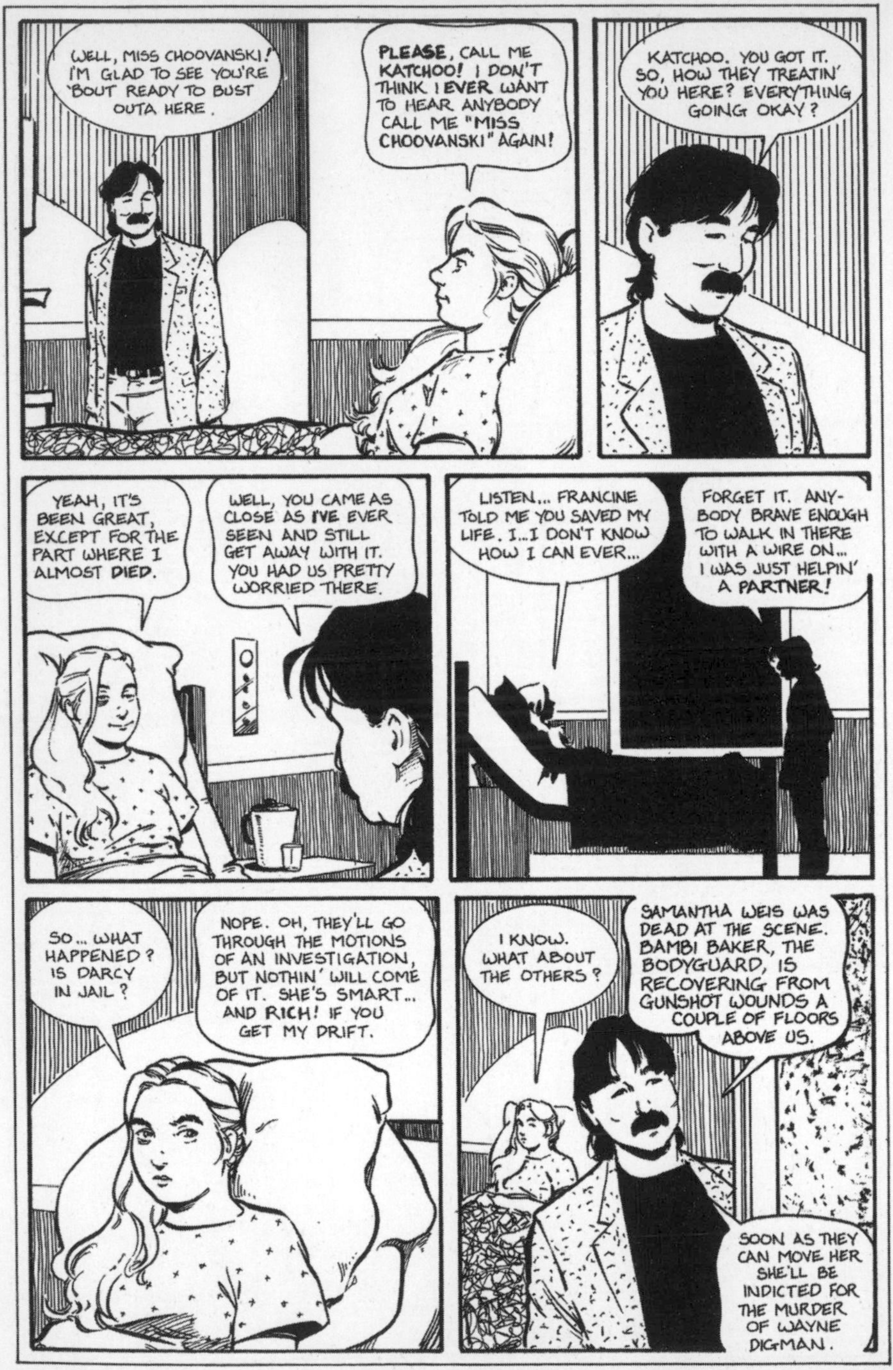
WELL, MISS CHOOVANSKI! I'M GLAD TO SEE YOU'RE 'BOUT READY TO BUST OUTA HERE.
PLEASE, CALL ME KATCHOO! I DON'T THINK I EVER WANT TO HEAR ANYBODY CALL ME "MISS CHOOVANSKI" AGAIN!
KATCHOO. YOU GOT IT. SO, HOW THEY TREATIN' YOU HERE? EVERYTHING GOING OKAY?
YEAH, IT'S BEEN GREAT, EXCEPT FOR THE PART WHERE I ALMOST DIED.
WELL, YOU CAME AS CLOSE AS I'VE EVER SEEN AND STILL GET AWAY WITH IT. YOU HAD US PRETTY WORRIED THERE.
LISTEN... FRANCINE TOLD ME YOU SAVED MY LIFE. I...I DON'T KNOW HOW I CAN EVER...
FORGET IT. ANYBODY BRAVE ENOUGH TO WALK IN THERE WITH A WIRE ON... I WAS JUST HELPIN' A PARTNER!
SO... WHAT HAPPENED? IS DARCY IN JAIL?
NOPE. OH, THEY'LL GO THROUGH THE MOTIONS OF AN INVESTIGATION, BUT NOTHIN' WILL COME OF IT. SHE'S SMART... AND RICH! IF YOU GET MY DRIFT.
I KNOW. WHAT ABOUT THE OTHERS?
SAMANTHA WEIS WAS DEAD AT THE SCENE. BAMBI BAKER, THE BODYGUARD, IS RECOVERING FROM GUNSHOT WOUNDS A COUPLE OF FLOORS ABOVE US.
SOON AS THEY CAN MOVE HER SHE'LL BE INDICTED FOR THE MURDER OF WAYNE DIGMAN.

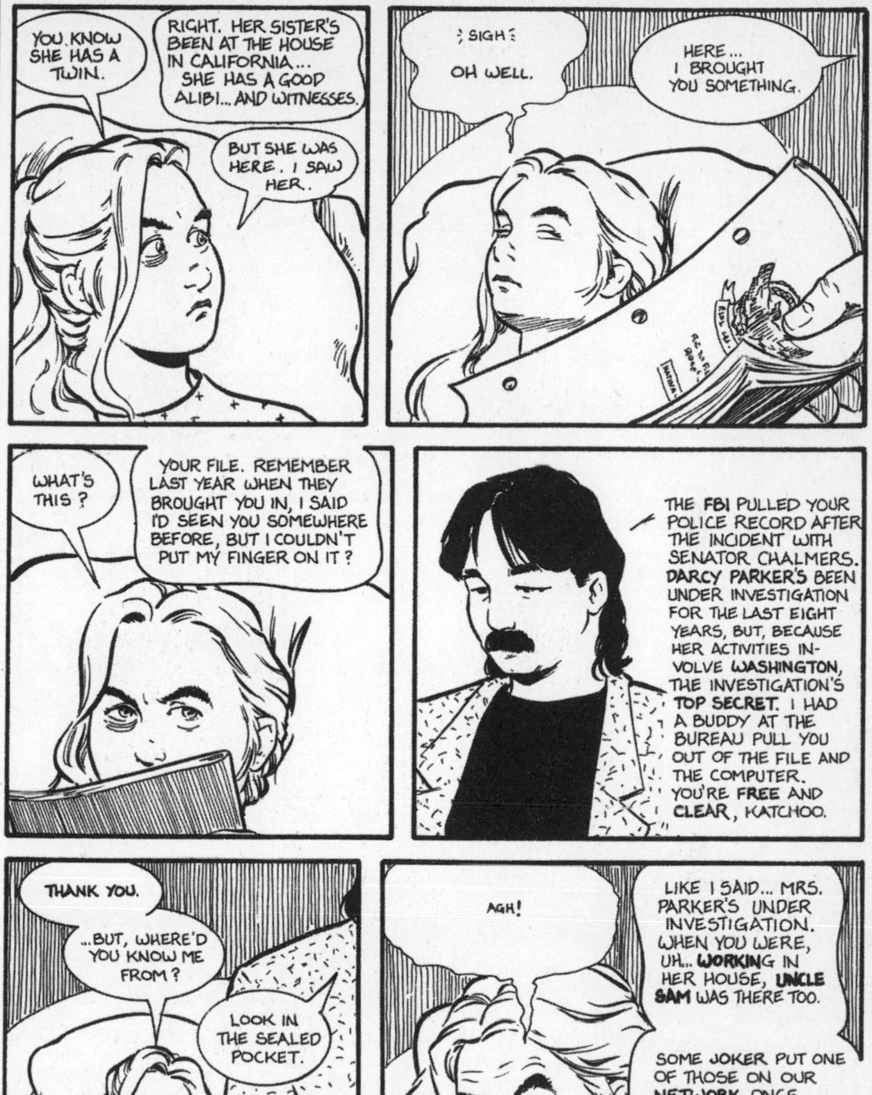
YOU KNOW SHE HAS A TWIN.
RIGHT. HER SISTER'S BEEN AT THE HOUSE IN CALIFORNIA... SHE HAS A GOOD ALIBI... AND WITNESSES.
BUT SHE WAS HERE. I SAW HER.
SIGH
OH WELL.
HERE... I BROUGHT YOU SOMETHING.
WHAT'S THIS?
YOUR FILE. REMEMBER LAST YEAR WHEN THEY BROUGHT YOU IN, I SAID I'D SEEN YOU SOMEWHERE BEFORE, BUT I COULDN'T PUT MY FINGER ON IT?
THE FBI PULLED YOUR POLICE RECORD AFTER THE INCIDENT WITH SENATOR CHALMERS. DARCY PARKER'S BEEN UNDER INVESTIGATION FOR THE LAST EIGHT YEARS, BUT, BECAUSE HER ACTIVITIES INVOLVE WASHINGTON, THE INVESTIGATION'S TOP SECRET. I HAD A BUDDY AT THE BUREAU PULL YOU OUT OF THE FILE AND THE COMPUTER. YOU'RE FREE AND CLEAR, KATCHOO.
THANK YOU.
...BUT, WHERE'D YOU KNOW ME FROM?
LOOK IN THE SEALED POCKET.
AGH!
LIKE I SAID... MRS. PARKER'S UNDER INVESTIGATION. WHEN YOU WERE, UH... WORKING IN HER HOUSE, UNCLE SAM WAS THERE TOO.
SOME JOKER PUT ONE OF THOSE ON OUR NETWORK ONCE WITH SOME STUPID CAPTION UNDER IT. ...YOU KNOW, A JOKE TO GO WITH THE MORNING COFFEE AND ALL THAT. IT'S AN AWFUL THING TO DO, I KNOW. I'M SORRY. ...ANYWAY, I FIGURED YOU'D WANT ALL THIS, BACK IN YOUR HANDS.

Freddie Femurs nursed the imported beer from the bottle he kept propped to his mouth and watched the blonde waitress who never responded to his smile talk warmly with a table nearby.

"So, you're really gonna go through with it, huh?" said Chuck. It was the first thing that crossed his mind. The silence was awkward for him and he felt compelled to say something.

"Go through with what?" Freddie replied. He watched the blonde closely, searching for clues.

"The wedding. You and Casey. You're finally going to tie the knot, huh? You must be getting pretty excited."

Freddie looked at Chuck as if he'd just peed on himself. He was beginning to wonder why he continued to meet Chuck here every Friday afternoon for a beer. When they had worked together at McNeil and Lambart's it had been to Freddie's advantage to strike up a friendship with Chuck, who held the enviable position of personnel advisor to McNeil himself. Now that Freddie had left the firm to strike out on his own, Chuck was just a pain in the butt, but still of some use as an inside man. Freddie reminded himself of this as he forced a tight smile. "Oh....yeah. I suppose," he replied.

"Listen to you," Chuck laughed, "Mr. Cool. You're marrying Casey Jansen, man! You're going to Hawaii to marry the hottest aerobics instructor in town! All I've got to say is you better be in shape. Know what I mean?"

"It's not like you think. Casey's a great girl and all that, but...it's not like you think."

"What do you mean?"

Freddie finished off the rest of his beer and set the bottle by the edge of the table. The callous blonde waitress glided by and picked up the bottle on the run, disappearing into the crowd. The image of her blue jeaned bottom burned in Freddie's brain for several moments after she left.

Freddie turned to Chuck and leaned forward in confidence, "Can you keep a secret?" he whispered, " I mean, you have to swear to me this will go no further."

Chuck wiped his mouth with the back of his hand and leaned forward to tent the table in secrecy. "I'm here for you, buddy," he said.

"We were at her mother's last weekend and she shows me pictures of Casey when she was in high school. I didn't even recognize her! Turns out she's had two nose jobs! She's had her chin done, her lips puffed..."

"Puffed?" Chuck frowned.

"Puffed. I mean it's bad enough she's got these implants I'm not allowed to squeeze or lay on, now I'm wondering what's going to happen to her face if she gets too close to a microwave, you know?"

"Hey, I never thought of that," Chuck nodded solemnly.

Chuck wiped his mouth with the back of his hand and leaned forward to tent the table in secrecy, "I'm here for you, buddy."

"Then Casey gets all upset because her mother shows me these pictures and I have to lie to her and tell her it doesn't matter, but inside I'm thinking, "Geez, who the hell are you, really?"

Freddie glared his point home to Chuck for several moments, awaiting his reaction.

Chuck leaned back and shook his head, "Oh man."

The ice queen brought Freddie another beer, and for once he didn't acknowledge her. The thought crossed his mind she might notice this and it would bother her the rest of the night. That would be a good thing.

Chuck and Freddie slumped over their beers in wrinkled business suits and loosened ties, listening to the music and the din of the growing happy hour crowd. Freddie evaluated every woman in the bar on a desert island basis. Chuck pretended to contemplate his friends dilemma while watching ESPN on the television set reflected in the mirror behind him. When they broke to commercial, Chuck sniffed, sat up straight and ordered another beer. He smiled hopefully at his companion and attempted to turn the mood, "Aw, it'll work out, buddy. Casey's a sweet girl. You two look good together."

Freddie smirked as he stuffed a palm full of nuts into his mouth, "Yeah. We *look* good alright."

Chuck tried harder, "Better than when you were with Francine. She was too tall for you."

Freddie smiled for the first time. "Francine. Yeah." he said, " She was like, 5, 9... 5, 10 something... 6 feet in heels."

"Big girl."

"And getting bigger. Casey and I ran into her at the grocery store about a month ago, and man, she was fat! She's put on thirty pounds. Why do women let themselves go like that?" Freddie shook his head.

"Francine's pretty though."

"When she wants to be. She can be a real slob, too."

"Yeah, but that can be cool too, sometimes, you know?" Chuck interjected, "I mean, she wasn't real uptight about her appearance all the time, like some women."

"You mean like Casey," Freddie frowned.

"Oh no, no! I didn't mean..."

"And how come you know so much about Francine, huh?" Freddie scowled.

Chuck shifted uneasily in his seat, "Well, I wasn't going to say anything, but I guess I can tell you now that you're getting married. I mean, it's all in the past now, right?"

"What's in the past?"

"Francine. And me. We... we were together for awhile. You know, your basic summer romance type thing," Chuck laughed nervously.

Freddie evaluated every woman in the bar on a desert island basis.

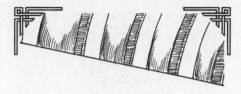

"What? When was this?" Freddie snapped back.

"Before you knew her, I don't know, two... three years ago."

"You never told me this."

"Well, I didn't want to piss you off, you know? Once you guys got together, I figured I'd just keep my mouth shut."

"Mm hmm," Freddie murmured as he pulled a long, slow drink from his bottle. "What do you mean you were... 'together'?"

"I mean we were a couple, man. We practically lived together."

"Serious?"

"Depends on what you mean by serious. If you go by intensity, then yeah, it was serious. It was intense, man. Francine was intense. I thought she was going to kill me sometimes."

"What do you mean?" Freddie perked up, ready to hear another man's troubles with the woman who had eluded him.

"Oh, Francine's a sweet girl and all, you know, real laid back and kind of ditzy. But the sex... the sex was incredible! I mean, it's like she couldn't get enough, you know? After we broke up I realized she had some emotional problems, real insecure. But at the time... man, it was fun! We did it all the time, every night. Even when we went out she would, like... grab me, at the most inappropriate times. It was like a game she played. I'd be dying and she thought it was funny!"

"FRANCINE?!" Freddie exclaimed in disbelief.

"Yeah! One time I took her to Cancun for the weekend and she bought this little string bikini especially for the trip.... I thought I was going to have a stroke! I was a drooling idiot the whole time we were there. I took lots of pictures!" Chuck laughed. "I loved that bikini so much she gave it to me on the plane ride home. I still have it. Man! She was hot."

"Alright, I get the point! Francine was hot." Freddie groaned.

"She wasn't just hot, man, she was *hot to trot!*"

"I said I get the point, okay? Can we drop it?"

Chuck rocked his bottle slowly back and forth upon the table, smiling smugly, "Yep, she was ooooooone hot patootie!"

"Hey! I said SHUT UP!"

Chuck watched the vein on Freddie's forehead pulse and pound. "I'm sorry, you still care for her, don't you?" he said, regretting his confession. "I shouldn't be telling you this. Besides, you were with her too. You don't need to hear my version of what it's like to be with Francine. I'm sure it was the same for you."

Freddie's stomach turned sour. That was just the point, it hadn't been like that at all between him and Francine.

In the entire year they were together, she had never slept with him. She refused to.

"Even when we went out she would, like... grab me, at the most inappropriate times. It was like a game she played."

253

Freddie winced as the memory of Francine overwhelmed him. Whether Freddie wanted to admit it or not, he missed her. He missed her slow, southern drawl and the way she used to look at him when they danced. He missed those big brown eyes, the squeezable breasts and pouting belly. He missed the soft, red lips that had never criticised him.

Nobody else felt like Francine. Nobody else smelled like her. She used to laugh and say it was the baby powder, but Freddie knew it was more than that. He didn't know the word for it, but there was something special about Francine. It radiated from her like body heat. It warmed her breath and flushed her cheeks and hung on every word she said. It swelled her breasts, it tilted her hips, it filled her thighs and moved her around him in slow motion. It sparkled in her eyes when he handed her an ice cream cone and chuckled deeply in the back of her throat when she laughed at his jokes.

God help him, it drove him crazy.

Freddie had wanted Francine more than he wanted anyone or anything in his life. She said she loved him too, but... nothing happened. He invested a year of his life trying to win her confidence, trying to reassure her. Trying to make her. The harder he tried the more she resisted. It became an obsession with him, a challenge to every fiber of his manhood.

Nothing.

Despite her protests and chaste demeanour, Francine drove him to despair seducing him with her desperate struggle to restrain herself, to quiet the sensuous woman within. A woman that screamed to Freddie like a third voice in the arguments and mumbled like a forgotten widow during their conversations. Like a siren on the rocks, the woman within Francine called to Freddie, and her unspoken message was clear, "You've never been with anybody like me."

Freddie knew it was the truth. It drove him insane with desire, and in the end, it drove him away.

She refused to sleep with him. She said every man left her once she gave herself to him. Freddie was different, she said. She loved him, she didn't want to lose him. So she hid her desires from him. He was denied.

This tormented Freddie. Francine was a riddle he could not solve. Any man could have her but the one she loved? Any man but him?

As time went on, Freddie found himself increasingly abusive with Francine, angrily attempting to get what he wanted by losing his special status.

Needless to say, it ended badly.

Her unspoken message was clear, "You've never been with anybody like me."

254

"She met you."

Frustrated with his dilemma, Freddie had begun an affair with Barbara, an administrative assistant in his office. Francine caught them making love in his office one rainy afternoon in November. She burst through the door wearing nothing but a coat and satin underwear.

She'd come to surrender.

The next day they met in the park. Freddie told Francine it was over between them, despite her pleas and promises that she would do anything to keep them together. Later those words haunted him; the lost opportunity intoxicating. If he'd kept his head, he could have taken her at her word and ended up with what he'd wanted all along. But at the time he wanted only to deny her a happy ending, to punish her for his year of frustration. If she'd wanted to break up with him, he would have begged her to stay. Since she wanted him back, he left her.

In retrospect, Freddie cursed himself for not taking advantage of the situation. He'd finally broken Francine's spirit. He could have had everything his way from that moment on. That would have been a good thing, wouldn't it?

A few months later, Freddie met Casey, the kind of girl he understood and was comfortable with. He thought marrying Casey would make him forget Francine. He was wrong. It only made him realize how much he missed her...

"If it makes you feel any better, it got real old," Chuck muttered.

...and this clod across the table wasn't helping matters one bit.

"She was kind of suffocating, you know? She was so insecure, so..." Chuck searched for the proper word, "...dependent. She needed a lot of love, the kind where you're together every minute of your lives. After awhile I saw that's what it was really about and it scared me."

Chuck's face fell and his eyes stayed fixed on a peanut he worried back and forth across his napkin. "But, to tell you the truth, Freddie, I think I did fall in love with her," he mumbled, "I mean, sure, she had problems, but who doesn't, you know? Maybe if I'd had the chance to tell her that..."

Freddie swallowed his anger and took several deep breaths to compose himself. Information was better than warfare.

"So," he smiled grimly, "what happened? If you loved her, why'd you break up? Why'd you dump her?"

Chuck looked up at Freddie with tears in his eyes, "I didn't. She left me."

"Why?"

"She met you."

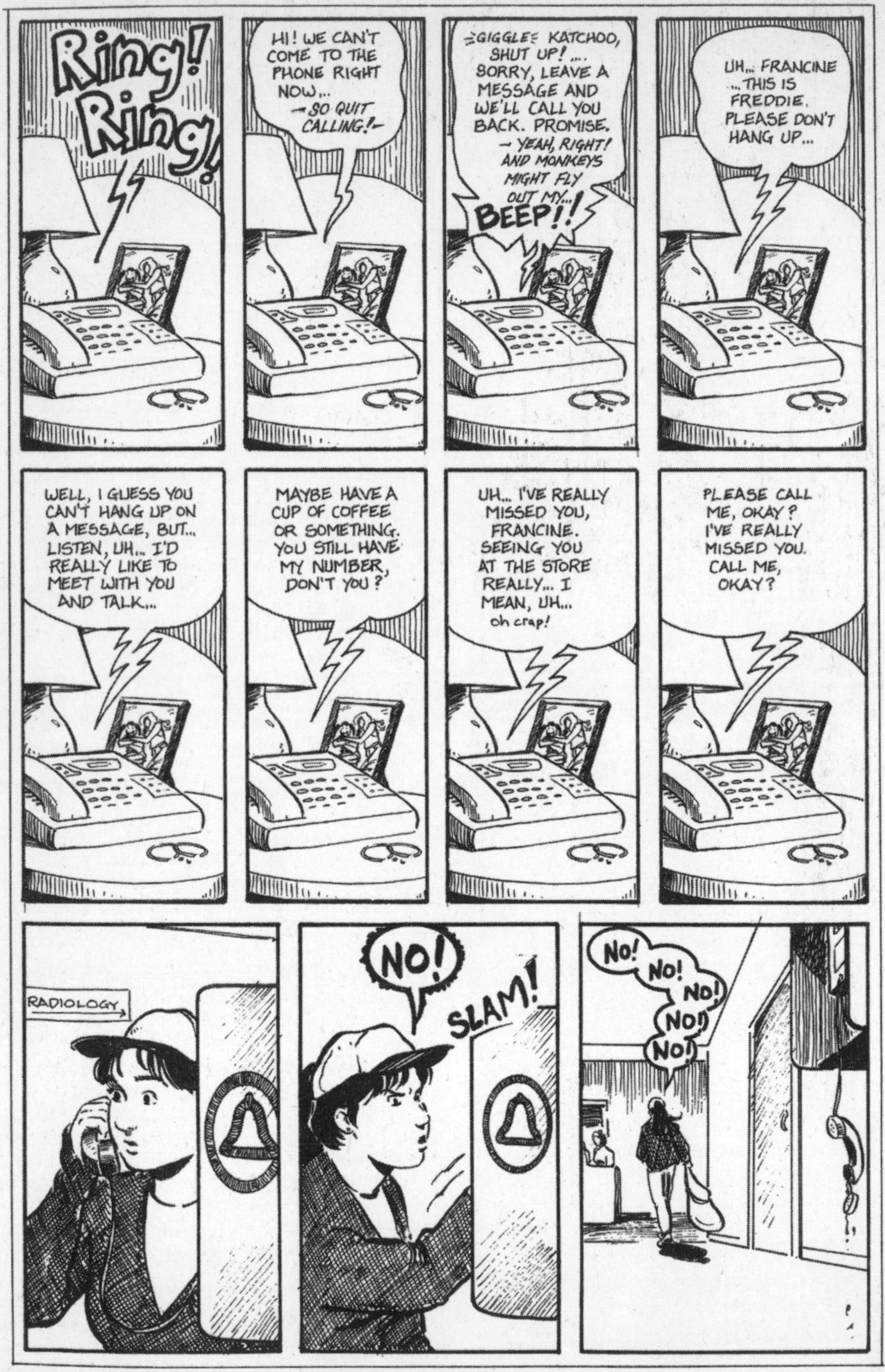
Ring! Ring!
HI! WE CAN'T COME TO THE PHONE RIGHT NOW...
—SO QUIT CALLING!—
=GIGGLE= KATCHOO, SHUT UP! .... SORRY, LEAVE A MESSAGE AND WE'LL CALL YOU BACK. PROMISE.
—YEAH, RIGHT! AND MONKEYS MIGHT FLY OUT MY...
BEEP!!
UH... FRANCINE ...THIS IS FREDDIE. PLEASE DON'T HANG UP...
WELL, I GUESS YOU CAN'T HANG UP ON A MESSAGE, BUT... LISTEN, UH... I'D REALLY LIKE TO MEET WITH YOU AND TALK...
MAYBE HAVE A CUP OF COFFEE OR SOMETHING. YOU STILL HAVE MY NUMBER, DON'T YOU?
UH... I'VE REALLY MISSED YOU, FRANCINE. SEEING YOU AT THE STORE REALLY... I MEAN, UH...
oh crap!
PLEASE CALL ME, OKAY? I'VE REALLY MISSED YOU. CALL ME, OKAY?
RADIOLOGY
NO!
SLAM!
No! No! No! No! No!

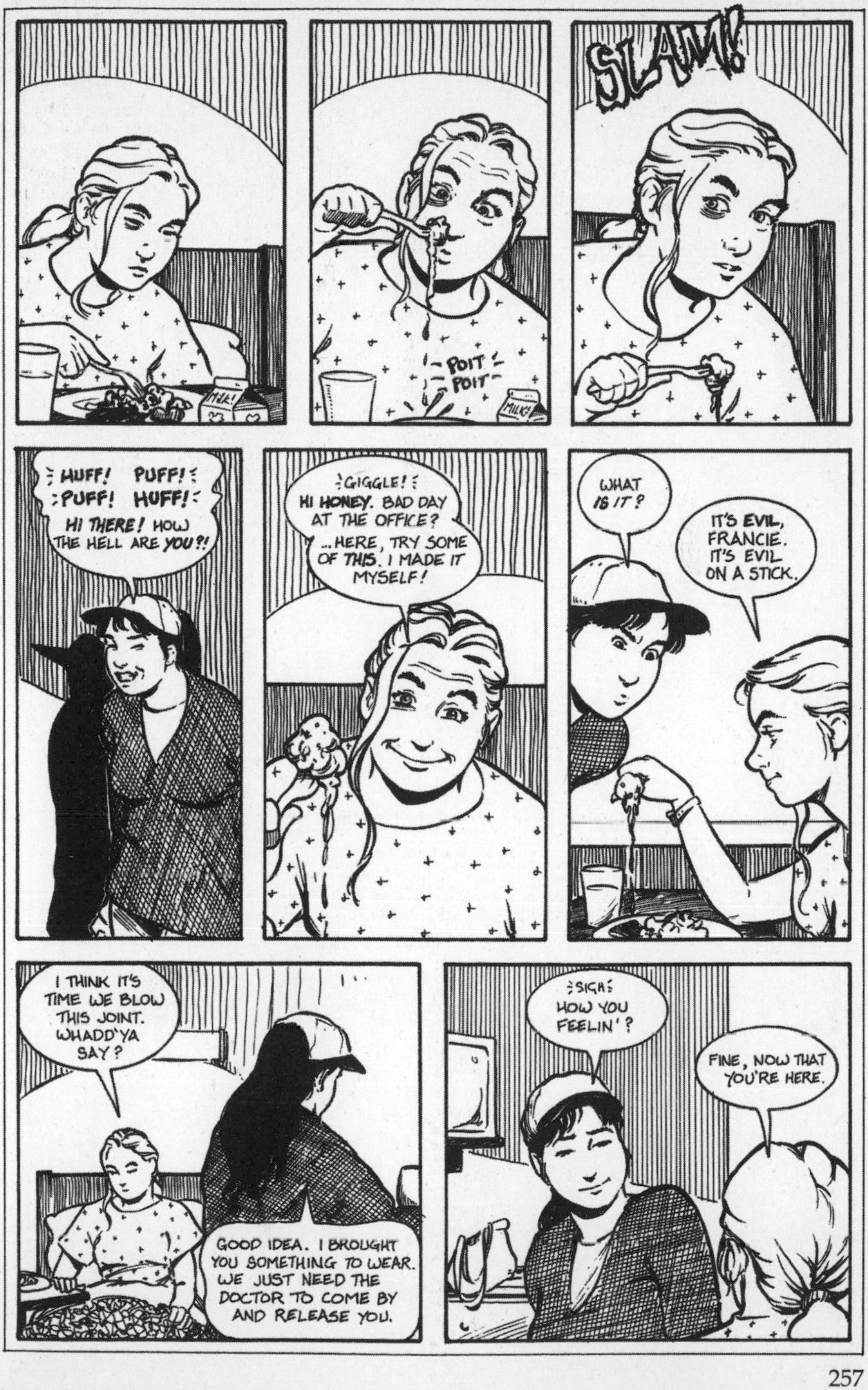
SLAM!
POIT POIT
HUFF! PUFF! PUFF! HUFF!
HI THERE! HOW THE HELL ARE YOU?!
GIGGLE! HI HONEY. BAD DAY AT THE OFFICE? ...HERE, TRY SOME OF THIS. I MADE IT MYSELF!
WHAT IS IT?
IT'S EVIL, FRANCIE. IT'S EVIL ON A STICK.
I THINK IT'S TIME WE BLOW THIS JOINT. WHADD'YA SAY?
GOOD IDEA. I BROUGHT YOU SOMETHING TO WEAR. WE JUST NEED THE DOCTOR TO COME BY AND RELEASE YOU.
SIGH HOW YOU FEELIN'?
FINE, NOW THAT YOU'RE HERE.

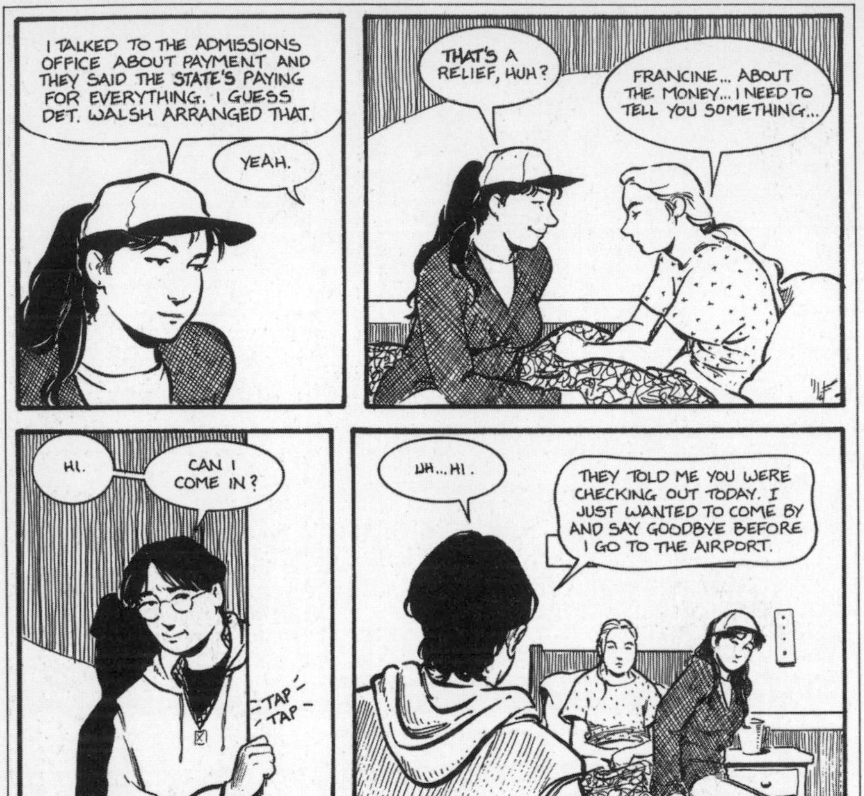

I TALKED TO THE ADMISSIONS OFFICE ABOUT PAYMENT AND THEY SAID THE STATE'S PAYING FOR EVERYTHING. I GUESS DET. WALSH ARRANGED THAT.
YEAH.
THAT'S A RELIEF, HUH?
FRANCINE... ABOUT THE MONEY... I NEED TO TELL YOU SOMETHING...
HI.
CAN I COME IN?
TAP TAP
UH... HI.
THEY TOLD ME YOU WERE CHECKING OUT TODAY. I JUST WANTED TO COME BY AND SAY GOODBYE BEFORE I GO TO THE AIRPORT.
I'M, UH... I'M GOING BACK TO NEW YORK THIS AFTERNOON. I JUST WANTED TO MAKE SURE YOU GUYS WERE GONNA BE, UH...
...okay.

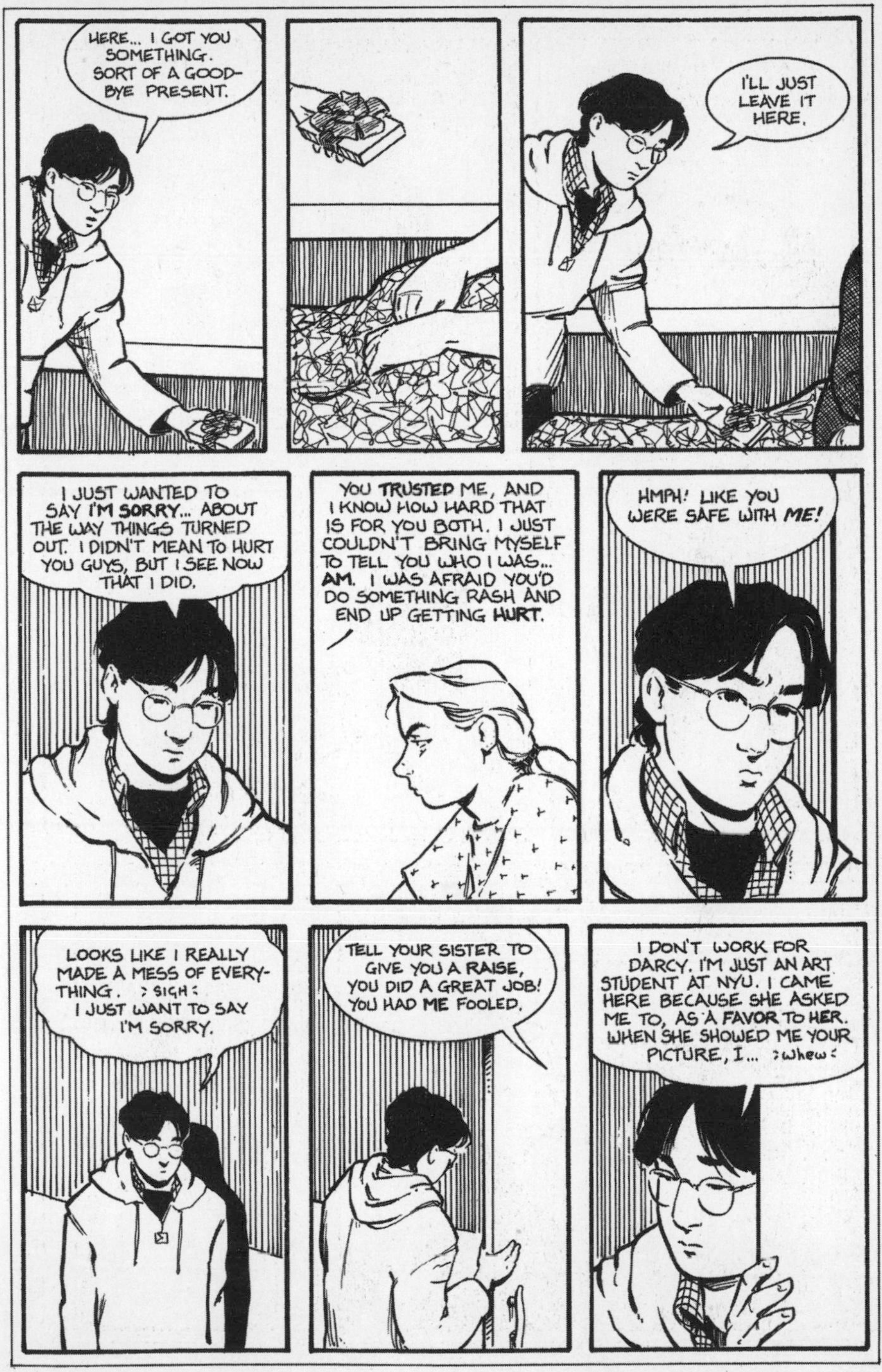
HERE... I GOT YOU SOMETHING. SORT OF A GOOD-BYE PRESENT.
I'LL JUST LEAVE IT HERE.
I JUST WANTED TO SAY I'M SORRY... ABOUT THE WAY THINGS TURNED OUT. I DIDN'T MEAN TO HURT YOU GUYS, BUT I SEE NOW THAT I DID.
YOU TRUSTED ME, AND I KNOW HOW HARD THAT IS FOR YOU BOTH. I JUST COULDN'T BRING MYSELF TO TELL YOU WHO I WAS... AM. I WAS AFRAID YOU'D DO SOMETHING RASH AND END UP GETTING HURT.
HMPH! LIKE YOU WERE SAFE WITH ME!
LOOKS LIKE I REALLY MADE A MESS OF EVERYTHING. >SIGH< I JUST WANT TO SAY I'M SORRY.
TELL YOUR SISTER TO GIVE YOU A RAISE, YOU DID A GREAT JOB! YOU HAD ME FOOLED.
I DON'T WORK FOR DARCY. I'M JUST AN ART STUDENT AT NYU. I CAME HERE BECAUSE SHE ASKED ME TO, AS A FAVOR TO HER. WHEN SHE SHOWED ME YOUR PICTURE, I... >whew<

LOOK, I DON'T UNDER-STAND WHAT'S GOING ON BETWEEN YOU AND DARCY. AND I DON'T CARE WHO TOOK THE MONEY, SHE HAS MORE MONEY THAN SHE CAN SPEND ANYWAY.

ALL I KNOW IS I'VE LOST THE BEST FRIEND I EVER HAD.

...AND NO AMOUNT OF MONEY IS WORTH THAT.

≥ SIGH. ⋜

WHAT IS IT?

≥ SNIFF ⋜

THAT LOOKS LIKE THE BEACH HOUSE IN YOUR PICTURES OF HAWAII.

IT IS. THAT'S THE HOUSE I STAYED AT WITH EMMA.

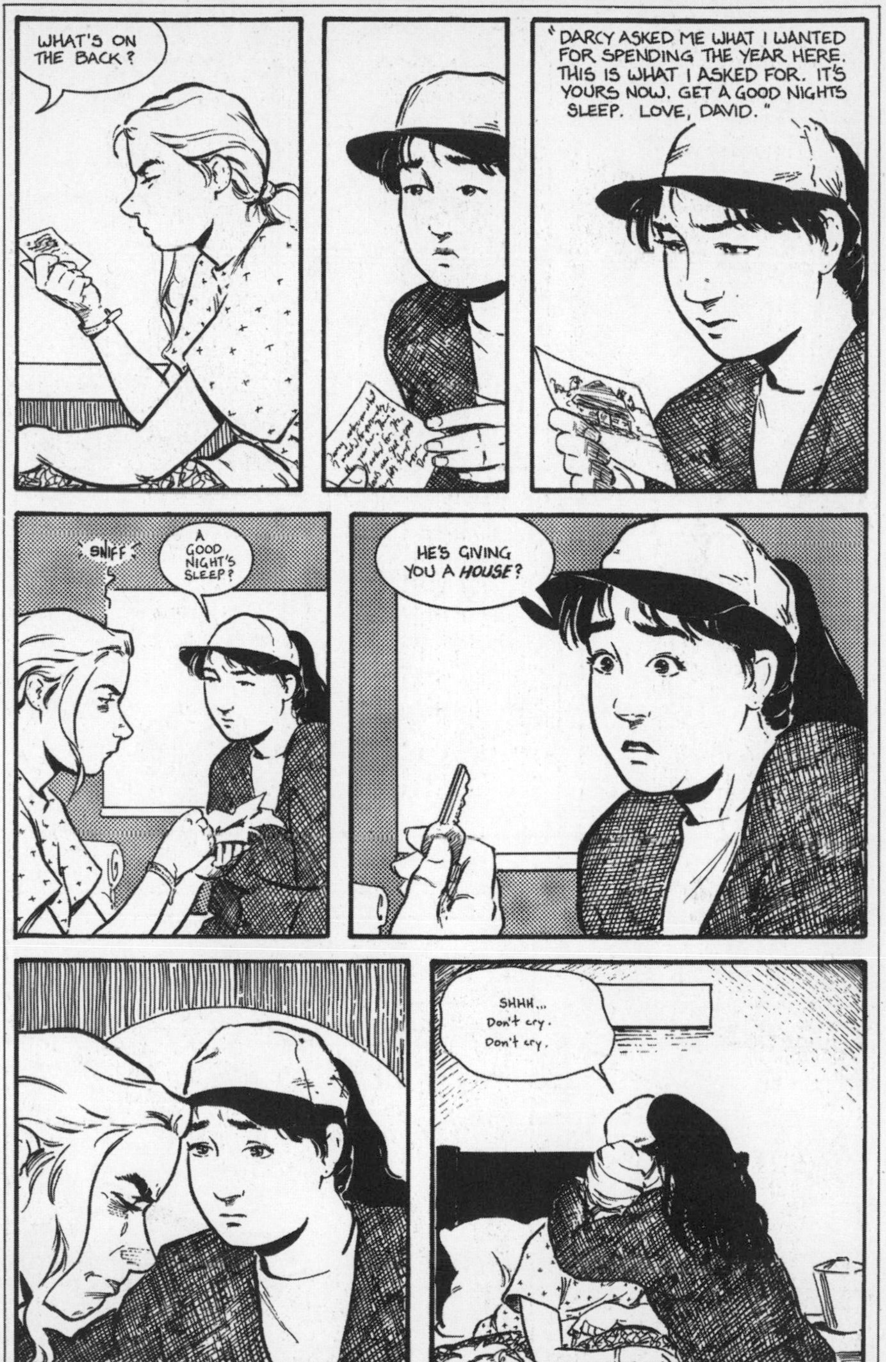
WHAT'S ON THE BACK?
"DARCY ASKED ME WHAT I WANTED FOR SPENDING THE YEAR HERE. THIS IS WHAT I ASKED FOR. IT'S YOURS NOW. GET A GOOD NIGHTS SLEEP. LOVE, DAVID."
SNIFF
A GOOD NIGHT'S SLEEP?
HE'S GIVING YOU A *HOUSE*?
SHHH... Don't cry. Don't cry.

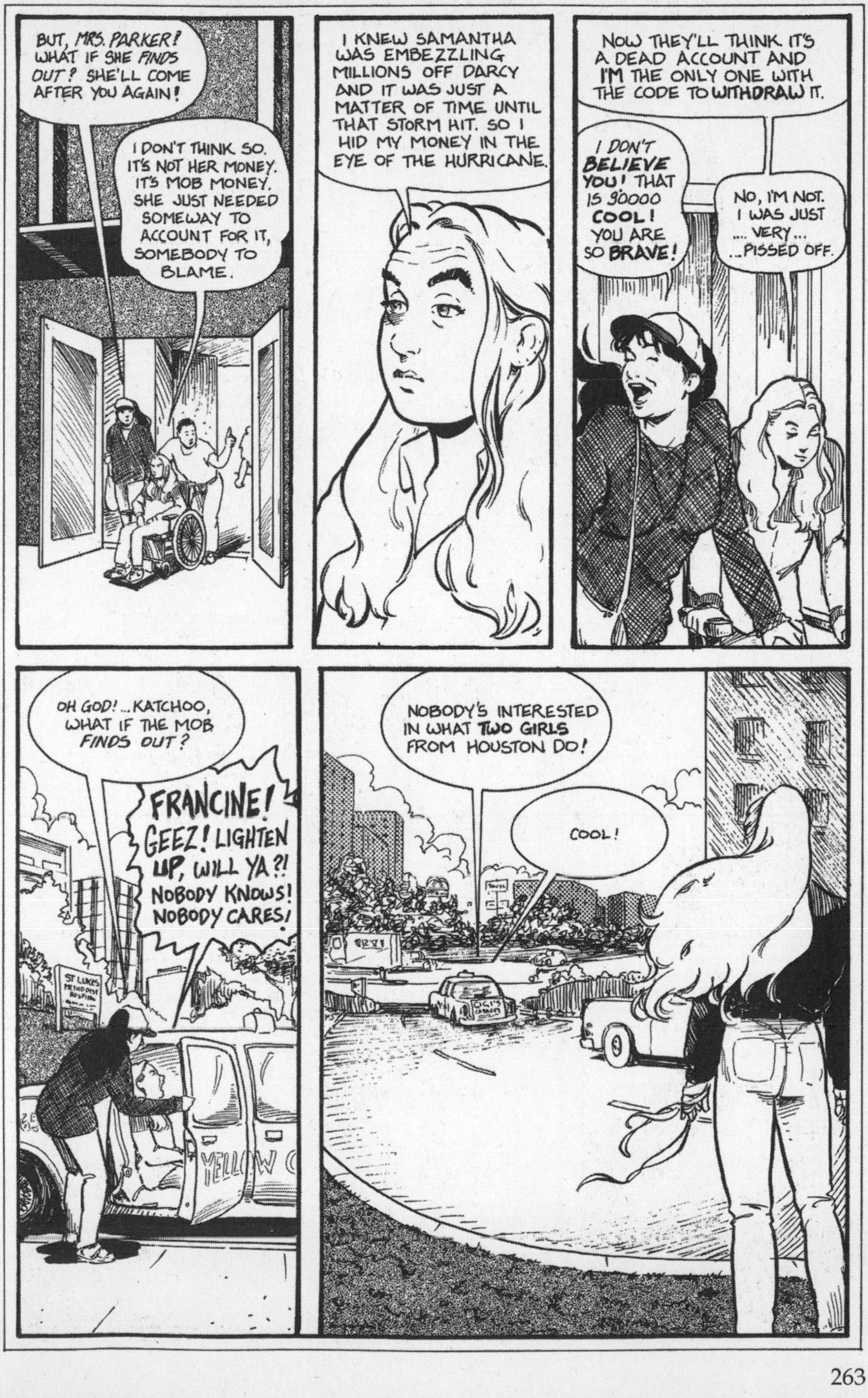
BUT, MRS. PARKER? WHAT IF SHE FINDS OUT? SHE'LL COME AFTER YOU AGAIN!
I DON'T THINK SO. IT'S NOT HER MONEY. IT'S MOB MONEY. SHE JUST NEEDED SOMEWAY TO ACCOUNT FOR IT, SOMEBODY TO BLAME.
I KNEW SAMANTHA WAS EMBEZZLING MILLIONS OFF DARCY AND IT WAS JUST A MATTER OF TIME UNTIL THAT STORM HIT. SO I HID MY MONEY IN THE EYE OF THE HURRICANE.
NOW THEY'LL THINK IT'S A DEAD ACCOUNT AND I'M THE ONLY ONE WITH THE CODE TO WITHDRAW IT.
I DON'T BELIEVE YOU! THAT IS SOOOO COOL! YOU ARE SO BRAVE!
NO, I'M NOT. I WAS JUST ... VERY... ...PISSED OFF.
OH GOD! ...KATCHOO, WHAT IF THE MOB FINDS OUT?
FRANCINE! GEEZ! LIGHTEN UP, WILL YA?! NOBODY KNOWS! NOBODY CARES!
ST LUKES METHODIST HOSPITAL
YELLOW C
NOBODY'S INTERESTED IN WHAT TWO GIRLS FROM HOUSTON DO!
COOL!

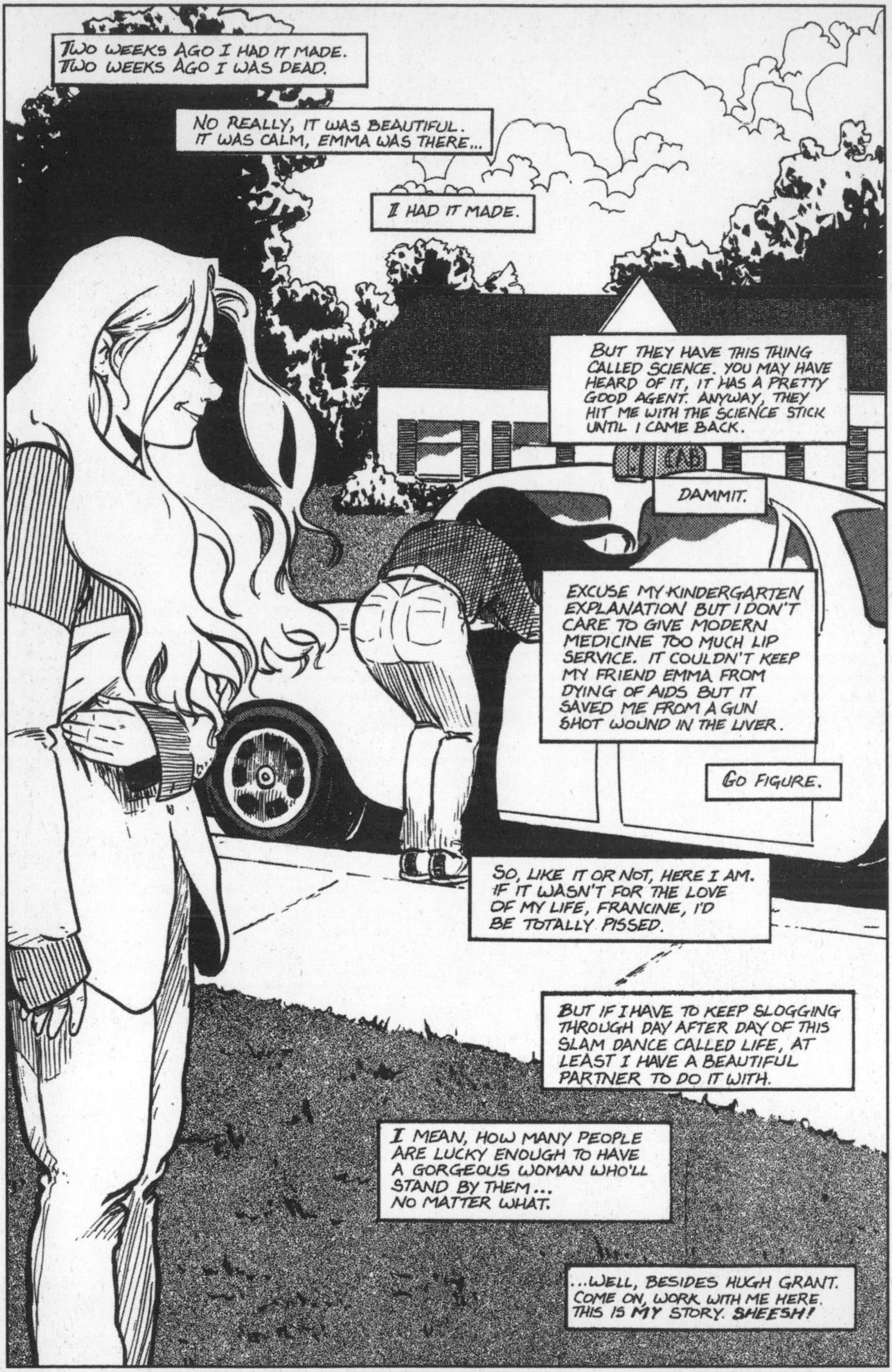
TWO WEEKS AGO I HAD IT MADE.
TWO WEEKS AGO I WAS DEAD.
NO REALLY, IT WAS BEAUTIFUL. IT WAS CALM, EMMA WAS THERE...
I HAD IT MADE.
BUT THEY HAVE THIS THING CALLED SCIENCE. YOU MAY HAVE HEARD OF IT, IT HAS A PRETTY GOOD AGENT. ANYWAY, THEY HIT ME WITH THE SCIENCE STICK UNTIL I CAME BACK.
CAB
DAMMIT.
EXCUSE MY KINDERGARTEN EXPLANATION BUT I DON'T CARE TO GIVE MODERN MEDICINE TOO MUCH LIP SERVICE. IT COULDN'T KEEP MY FRIEND EMMA FROM DYING OF AIDS BUT IT SAVED ME FROM A GUN SHOT WOUND IN THE LIVER.
GO FIGURE.
SO, LIKE IT OR NOT, HERE I AM. IF IT WASN'T FOR THE LOVE OF MY LIFE, FRANCINE, I'D BE TOTALLY PISSED.
BUT IF I HAVE TO KEEP SLOGGING THROUGH DAY AFTER DAY OF THIS SLAM DANCE CALLED LIFE, AT LEAST I HAVE A BEAUTIFUL PARTNER TO DO IT WITH.
I MEAN, HOW MANY PEOPLE ARE LUCKY ENOUGH TO HAVE A GORGEOUS WOMAN WHO'LL STAND BY THEM... NO MATTER WHAT.
...WELL, BESIDES HUGH GRANT. COME ON, WORK WITH ME HERE. THIS IS MY STORY. SHEESH!

265

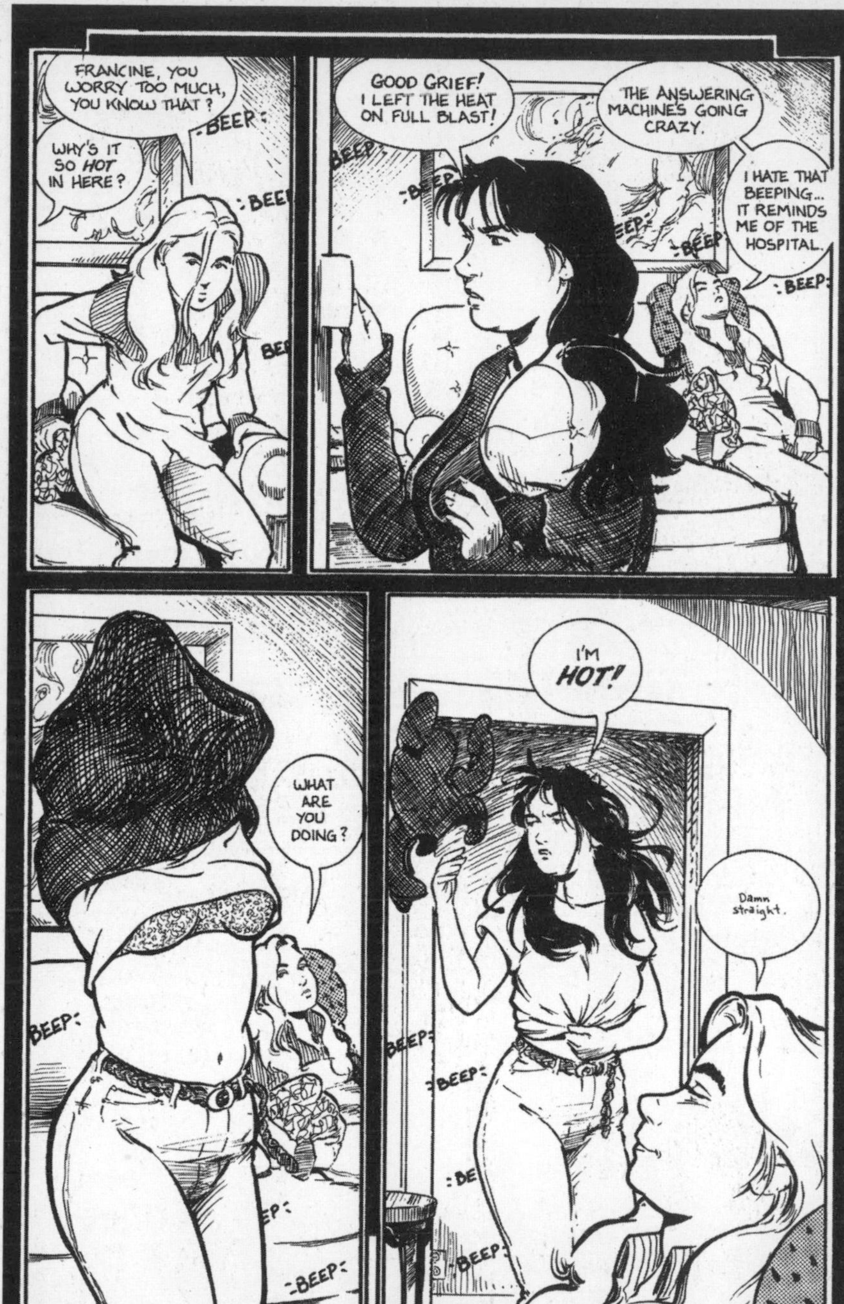
FRANCINE, YOU WORRY TOO MUCH, YOU KNOW THAT?
WHY'S IT SO *HOT* IN HERE?
BEEP
BEEP
GOOD GRIEF! I LEFT THE HEAT ON FULL BLAST!
THE ANSWERING MACHINE'S GOING CRAZY.
I HATE THAT BEEPING... IT REMINDS ME OF THE HOSPITAL.
BEEP
WHAT ARE YOU DOING?
BEEP
BEEP
I'M *HOT!*
Damn straight.
BEEP
BEEP
BEEP

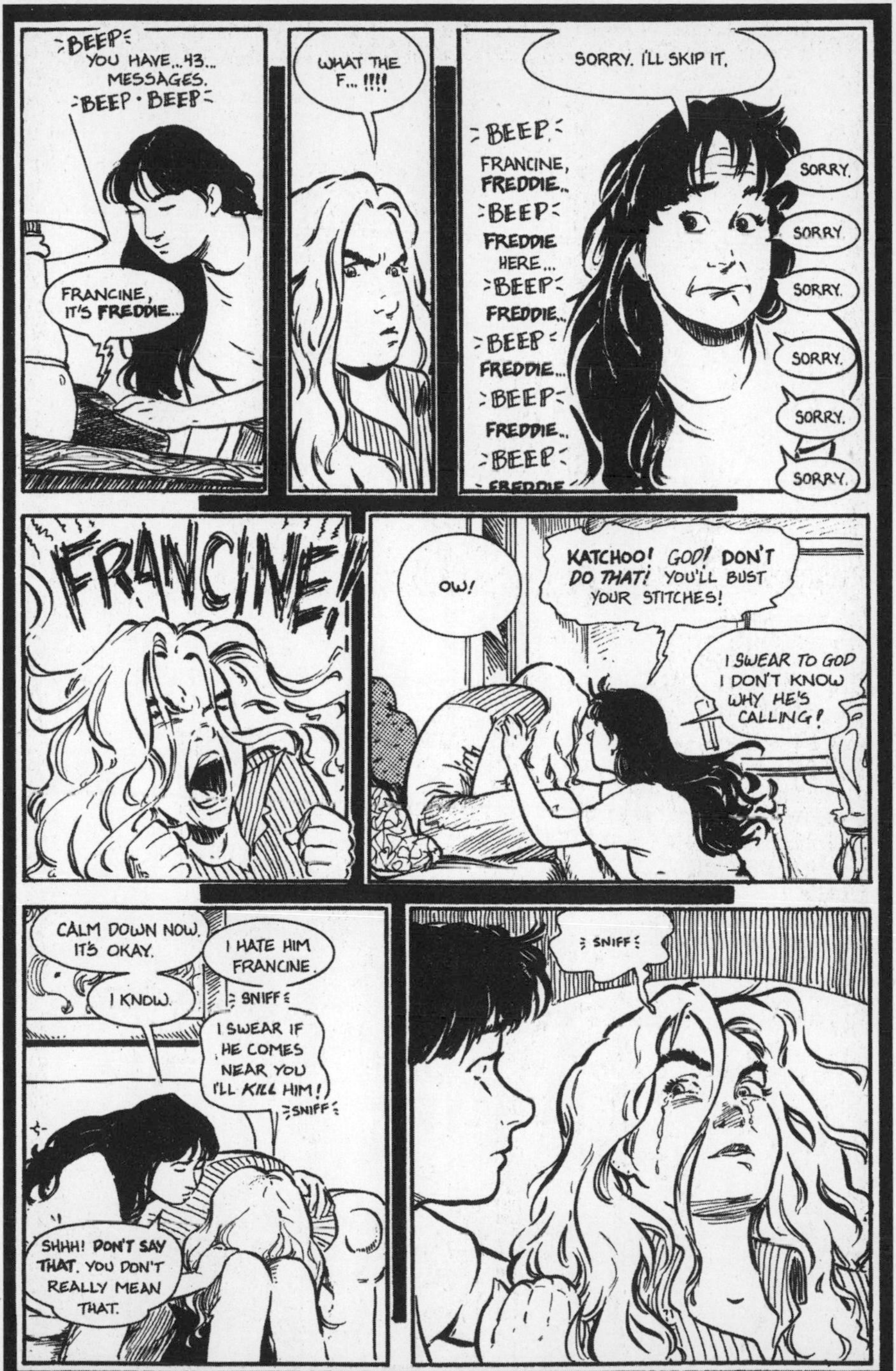
BEEP
YOU HAVE... 43... MESSAGES.
BEEP • BEEP
FRANCINE, IT'S FREDDIE...
WHAT THE F... !!!!
SORRY. I'LL SKIP IT.
BEEP
FRANCINE, FREDDIE..
BEEP
FREDDIE HERE...
BEEP
FREDDIE..
BEEP
FREDDIE...
BEEP
FREDDIE..
BEEP
SORRY.
SORRY.
SORRY.
SORRY.
SORRY.
SORRY.
FRANCINE!
OW!
KATCHOO! GOD! DON'T DO THAT! YOU'LL BUST YOUR STITCHES!
I SWEAR TO GOD I DON'T KNOW WHY HE'S CALLING!
CALM DOWN NOW. IT'S OKAY.
I HATE HIM FRANCINE.
I KNOW.
SNIFF
I SWEAR IF HE COMES NEAR YOU I'LL KILL HIM!
SNIFF
SHHH! DON'T SAY THAT. YOU DON'T REALLY MEAN THAT.
SNIFF

268

269

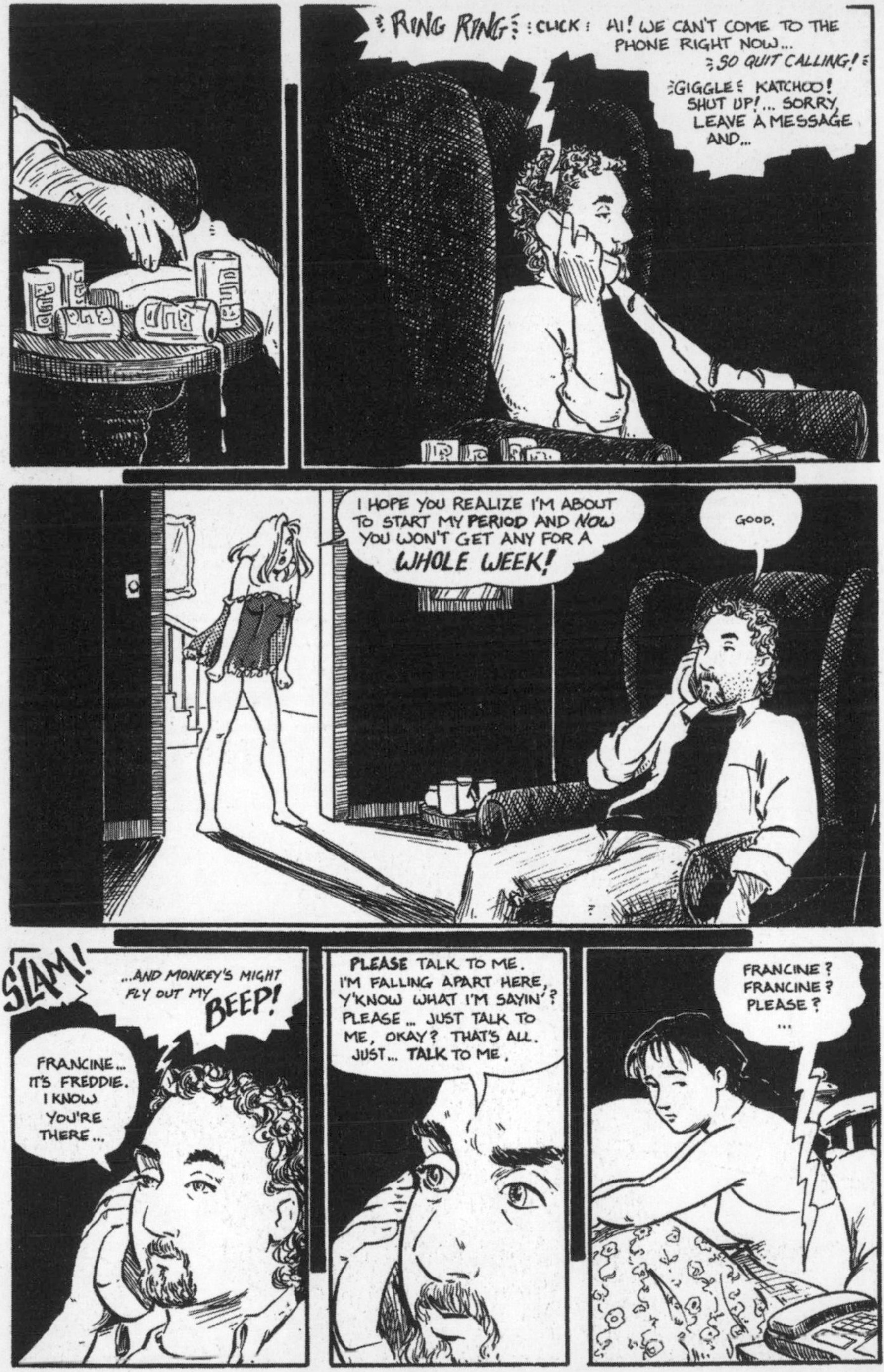
RING RING
CLICK
HI! WE CAN'T COME TO THE PHONE RIGHT NOW...
SO QUIT CALLING!
GIGGLE KATCHOO! SHUT UP!... SORRY, LEAVE A MESSAGE AND...
I HOPE YOU REALIZE I'M ABOUT TO START MY PERIOD AND NOW YOU WON'T GET ANY FOR A WHOLE WEEK!
GOOD.
SLAM!
...AND MONKEY'S MIGHT FLY OUT MY BEEP!
FRANCINE... IT'S FREDDIE. I KNOW YOU'RE THERE...
PLEASE TALK TO ME. I'M FALLING APART HERE, Y'KNOW WHAT I'M SAYIN'? PLEASE... JUST TALK TO ME, OKAY? THAT'S ALL. JUST... TALK TO ME.
FRANCINE? FRANCINE? PLEASE? ...

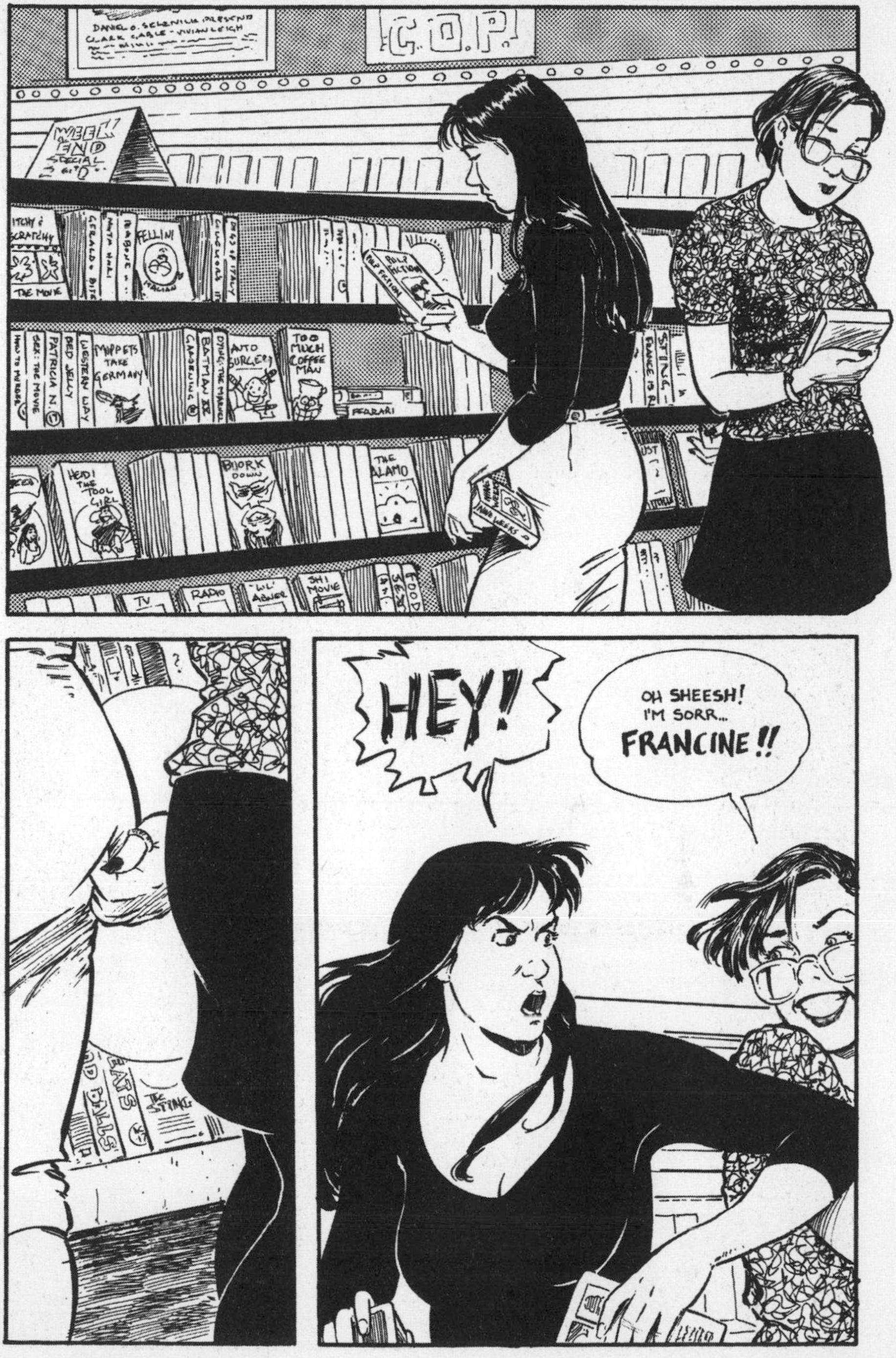
C.O.P.
WEEK END SPECIAL
ITCHY & SCRATCHY THE MOVIE
FELLINI
PULP FICTION
MUPPETS TAKE GERMANY
AUTO SURGERY
TOO MUCH COFFEE MAN
FERRARI
HEIDI THE TOOL GIRL
BJORK DOWN
THE ALAMO
TV
RADIO
LI'L ABNER
HEY!
OH SHEESH! I'M SORR... FRANCINE!!

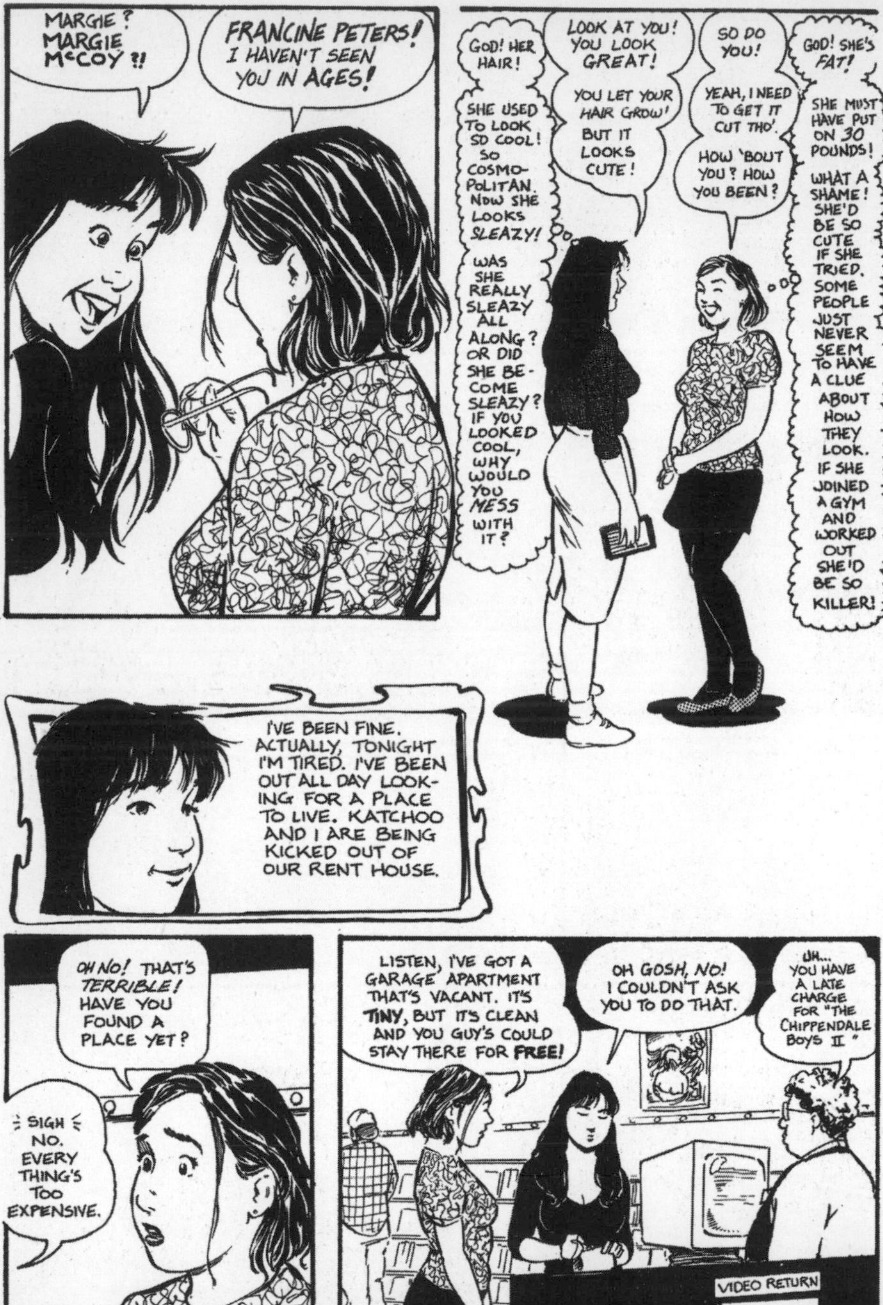
MARGIE? MARGIE McCOY?!
FRANCINE PETERS! I HAVEN'T SEEN YOU IN AGES!
GOD! HER HAIR!
SHE USED TO LOOK SO COOL! SO COSMO-POLITAN. NOW SHE LOOKS SLEAZY!
WAS SHE REALLY SLEAZY ALL ALONG? OR DID SHE BE-COME SLEAZY? IF YOU LOOKED COOL, WHY WOULD YOU MESS WITH IT?
LOOK AT YOU! YOU LOOK GREAT!
YOU LET YOUR HAIR GROW!
BUT IT LOOKS CUTE!
SO DO YOU!
YEAH, I NEED TO GET IT CUT THO'.
HOW 'BOUT YOU? HOW YOU BEEN?
GOD! SHE'S FAT!
SHE MUST HAVE PUT ON 30 POUNDS!
WHAT A SHAME! SHE'D BE SO CUTE IF SHE TRIED. SOME PEOPLE JUST NEVER SEEM TO HAVE A CLUE ABOUT HOW THEY LOOK. IF SHE JOINED A GYM AND WORKED OUT SHE'D BE SO KILLER!
I'VE BEEN FINE. ACTUALLY, TONIGHT I'M TIRED. I'VE BEEN OUT ALL DAY LOOK-ING FOR A PLACE TO LIVE. KATCHOO AND I ARE BEING KICKED OUT OF OUR RENT HOUSE.
OH NO! THAT'S TERRIBLE! HAVE YOU FOUND A PLACE YET?
SIGH NO. EVERY THING'S TOO EXPENSIVE.
LISTEN, I'VE GOT A GARAGE APARTMENT THAT'S VACANT. IT'S TINY, BUT IT'S CLEAN AND YOU GUY'S COULD STAY THERE FOR FREE!
OH GOSH, NO! I COULDN'T ASK YOU TO DO THAT.
UH... YOU HAVE A LATE CHARGE FOR "THE CHIPPENDALE BOYS II"
VIDEO RETURN

273

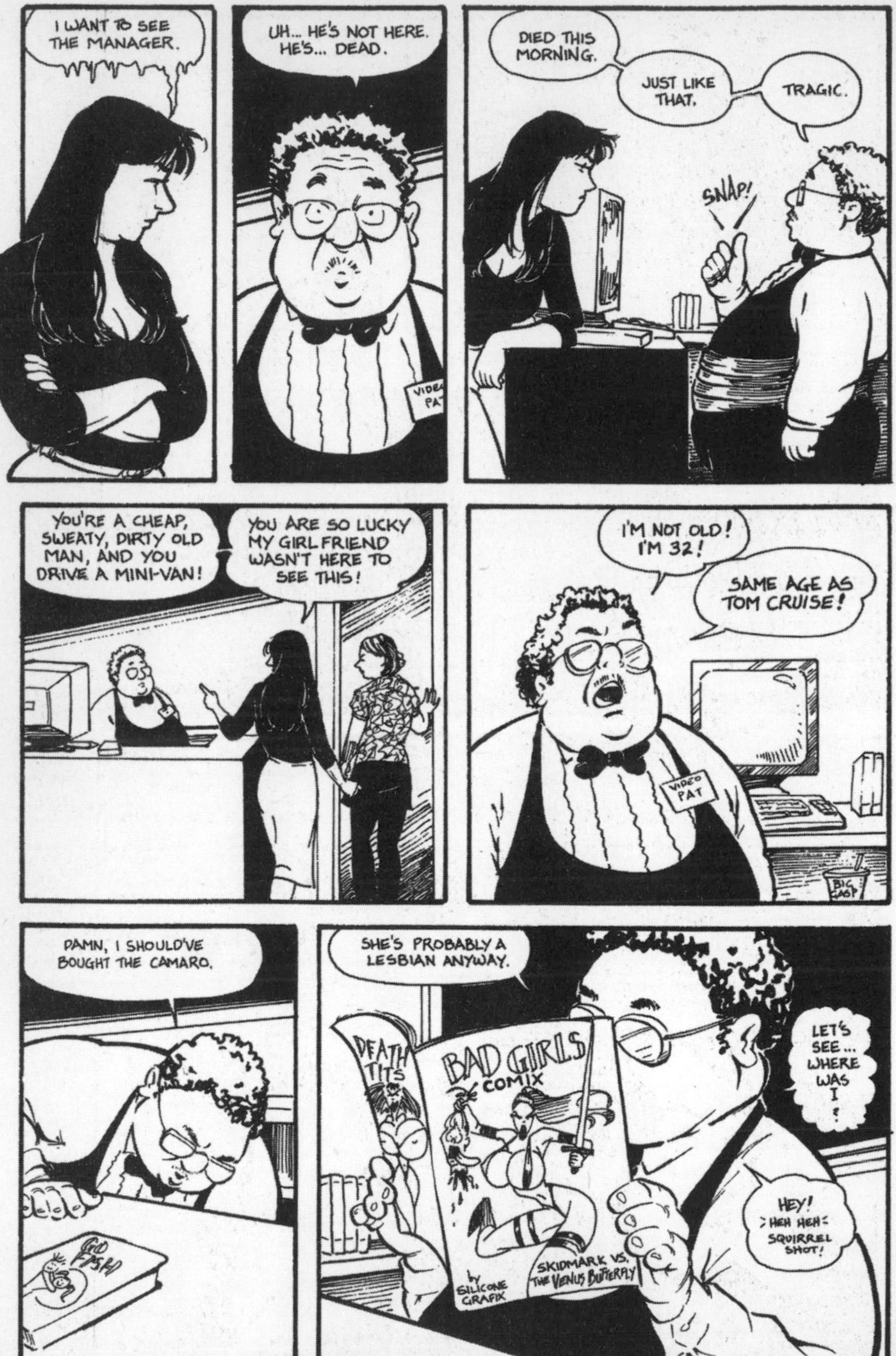
I WANT TO SEE THE MANAGER.
UH... HE'S NOT HERE. HE'S... DEAD.
VIDEO PAT
DIED THIS MORNING.
JUST LIKE THAT.
TRAGIC.
SNAP!
YOU'RE A CHEAP, SWEATY, DIRTY OLD MAN, AND YOU DRIVE A MINI-VAN!
YOU ARE SO LUCKY MY GIRLFRIEND WASN'T HERE TO SEE THIS!
I'M NOT OLD! I'M 32!
SAME AGE AS TOM CRUISE!
VIDEO PAT
BIG GASP
DAMN, I SHOULD'VE BOUGHT THE CAMARO.
SHE'S PROBABLY A LESBIAN ANYWAY.
DEATH TITS
BAD GIRLS COMIX
by SILICONE GRAFIX
SKIDMARK VS. THE VENUS BUTTERFLY
LET'S SEE... WHERE WAS I?
HEY! >HEH HEH< SQUIRREL SHOT!

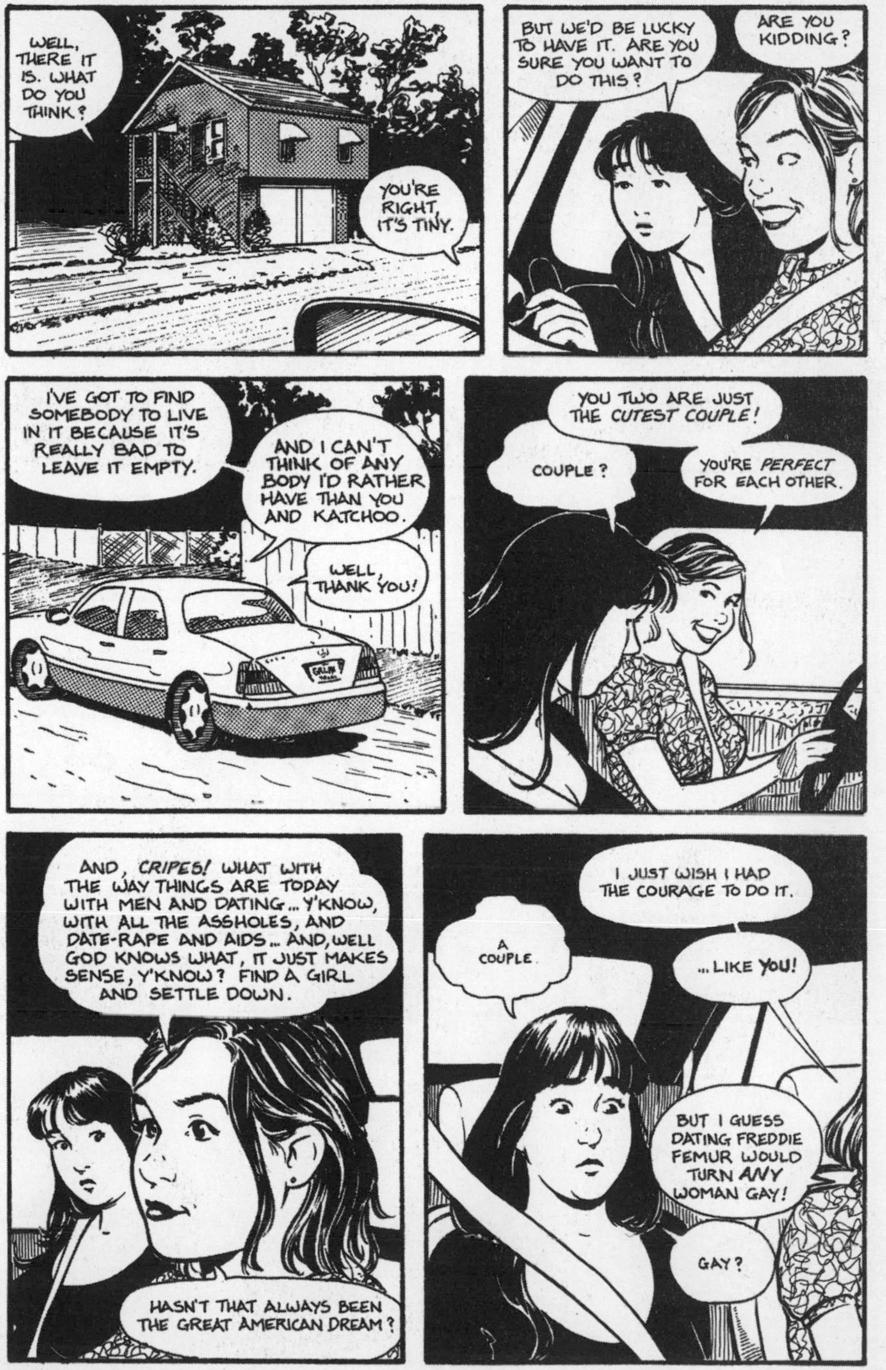
WELL, THERE IT IS. WHAT DO YOU THINK?
YOU'RE RIGHT, IT'S TINY.
BUT WE'D BE LUCKY TO HAVE IT. ARE YOU SURE YOU WANT TO DO THIS?
ARE YOU KIDDING?
I'VE GOT TO FIND SOMEBODY TO LIVE IN IT BECAUSE IT'S REALLY BAD TO LEAVE IT EMPTY.
AND I CAN'T THINK OF ANY BODY I'D RATHER HAVE THAN YOU AND KATCHOO.
WELL, THANK YOU!
YOU TWO ARE JUST THE *CUTEST COUPLE*!
COUPLE?
YOU'RE *PERFECT* FOR EACH OTHER.
AND, *CRIPES!* WHAT WITH THE WAY THINGS ARE TODAY WITH MEN AND DATING... Y'KNOW, WITH ALL THE ASSHOLES, AND DATE-RAPE AND AIDS... AND, WELL GOD KNOWS WHAT, IT JUST MAKES SENSE, Y'KNOW? FIND A GIRL AND SETTLE DOWN.
HASN'T THAT ALWAYS BEEN THE GREAT AMERICAN DREAM?
I JUST WISH I HAD THE COURAGE TO DO IT.
A COUPLE.
...LIKE YOU!
BUT I GUESS DATING FREDDIE FEMUR WOULD TURN *ANY* WOMAN GAY!
GAY?

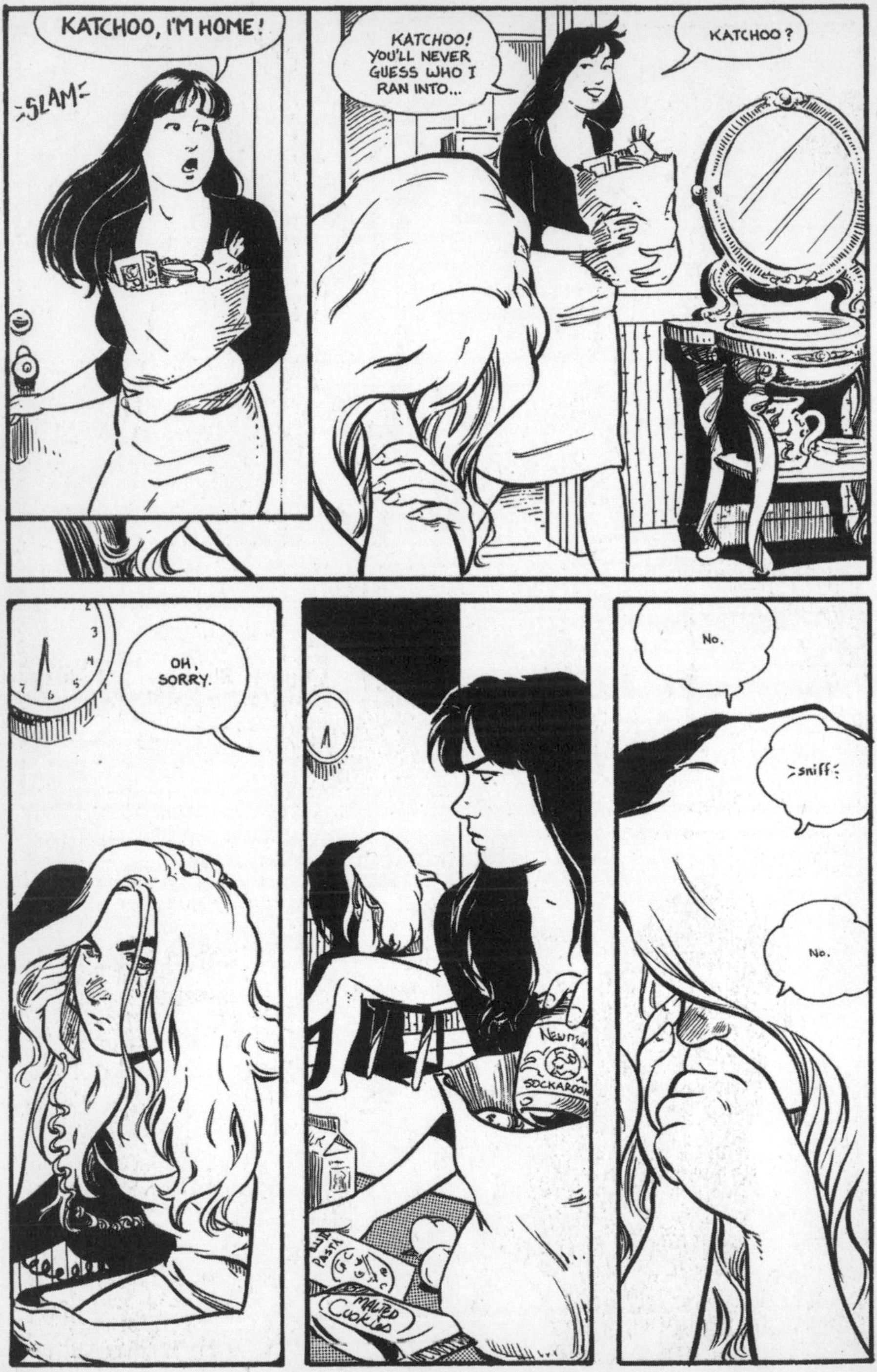
KATCHOO, I'M HOME!
SLAM
KATCHOO! YOU'LL NEVER GUESS WHO I RAN INTO...
KATCHOO?
OH, SORRY.
NEWMAN'S
SOCKAROONS
PASTA
MALTED COOKIES
No.
sniff
No.

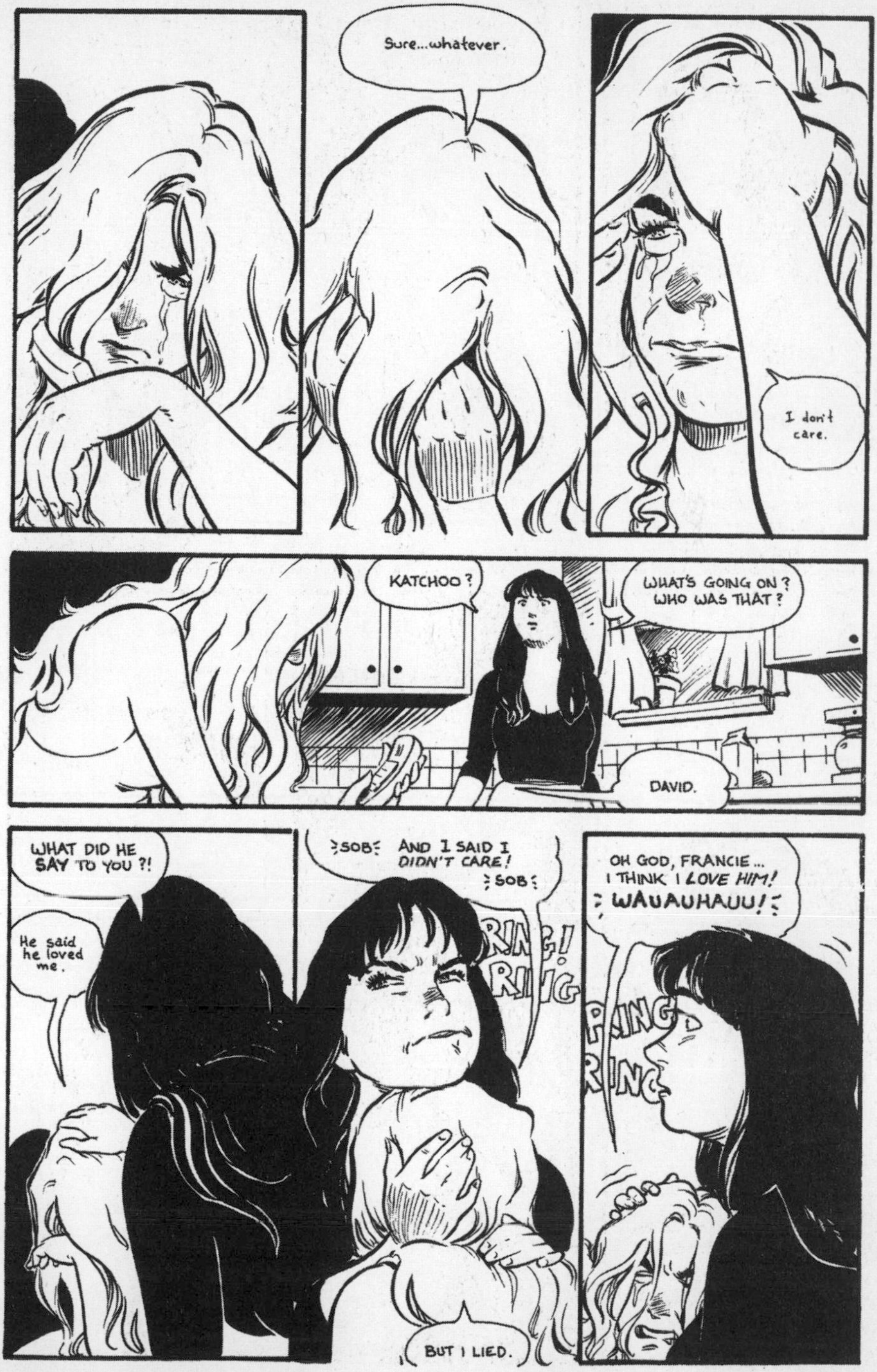

Sure...whatever.
I don't care.
KATCHOO?
WHAT'S GOING ON? WHO WAS THAT?
DAVID.
WHAT DID HE SAY TO YOU?!
He said he loved me.
SOB AND I SAID I DIDN'T CARE! SOB
RING! RING
BUT I LIED.
OH GOD, FRANCIE... I THINK I LOVE HIM! WAUAUHAUU!
RING RING

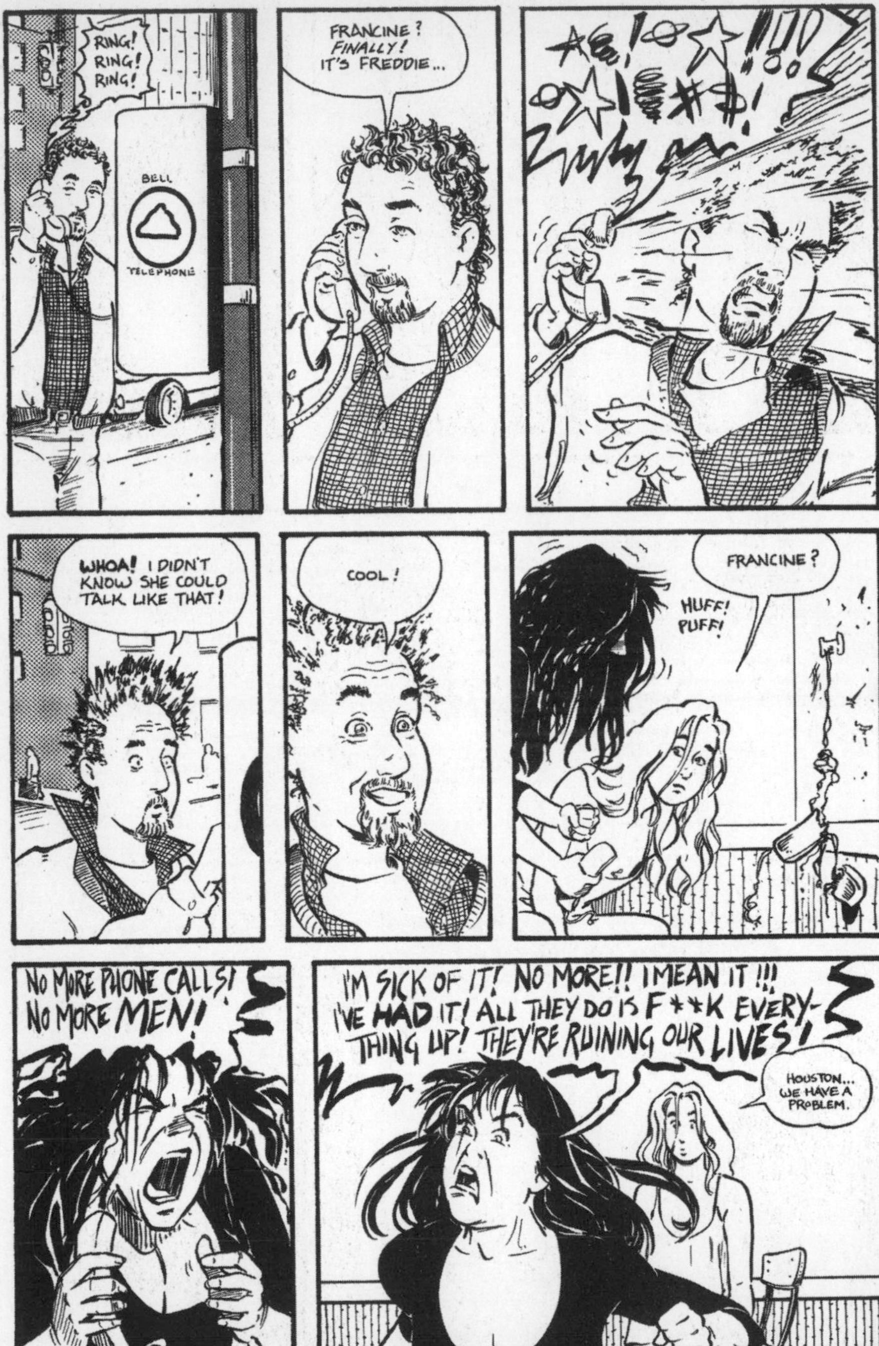

RING! RING! RING!
BELL
TELEPHONE
FRANCINE? FINALLY! IT'S FREDDIE...
WHOA! I DIDN'T KNOW SHE COULD TALK LIKE THAT!
COOL!
FRANCINE?
HUFF! PUFF!
NO MORE PHONE CALLS! NO MORE MEN!
I'M SICK OF IT! NO MORE!! I MEAN IT!!! I'VE HAD IT! ALL THEY DO IS F**K EVERY-THING UP! THEY'RE RUINING OUR LIVES!
HOUSTON... WE HAVE A PROBLEM.

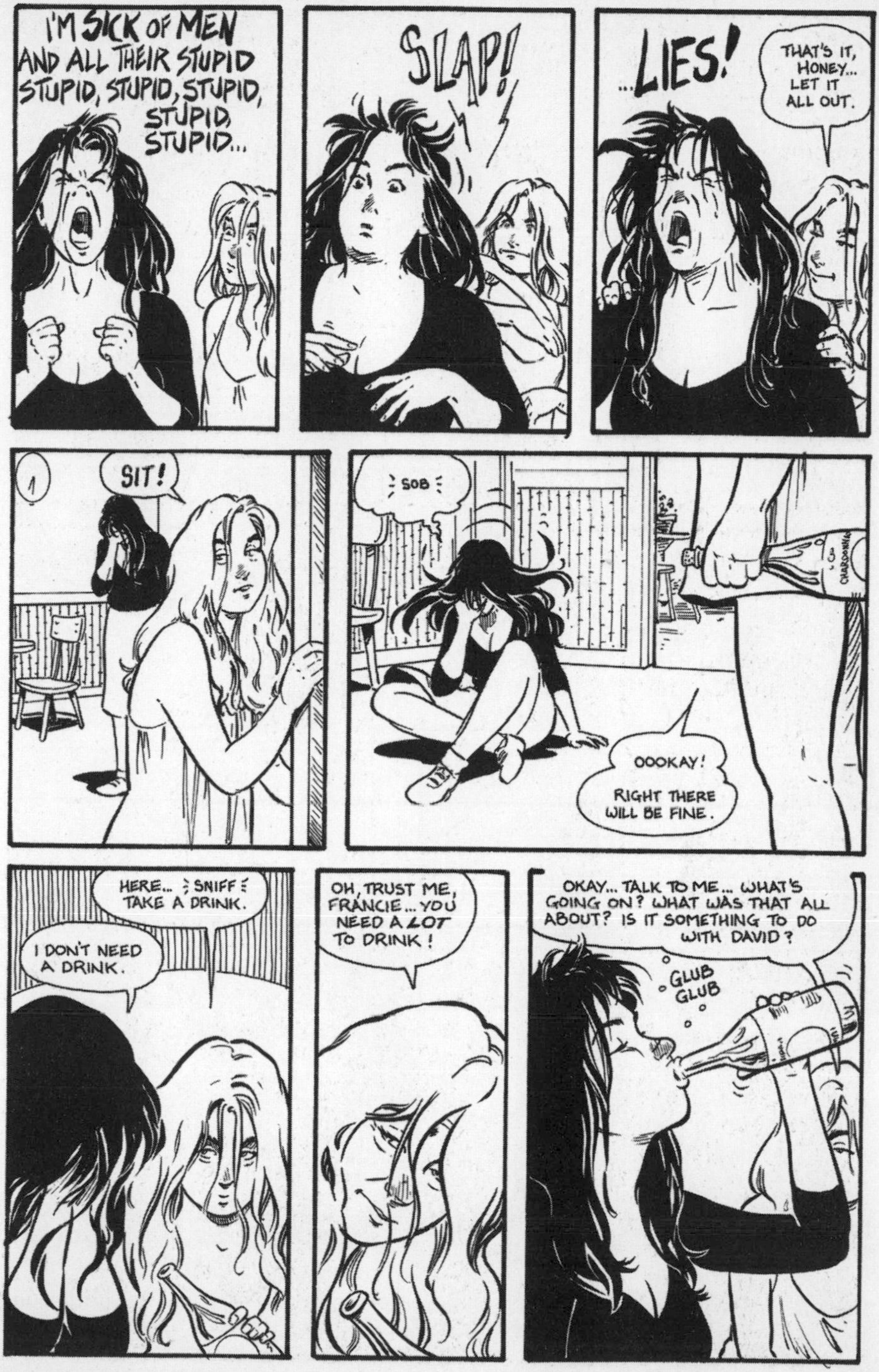

I'M SICK OF MEN AND ALL THEIR STUPID STUPID, STUPID, STUPID, STUPID, STUPID...
SLAP!
...LIES!
THAT'S IT, HONEY... LET IT ALL OUT.
SIT!
SOB
OOOKAY!
RIGHT THERE WILL BE FINE.
HERE... SNIFF TAKE A DRINK.
I DON'T NEED A DRINK.
OH, TRUST ME, FRANCIE... YOU NEED A LOT TO DRINK!
OKAY... TALK TO ME... WHAT'S GOING ON? WHAT WAS THAT ALL ABOUT? IS IT SOMETHING TO DO WITH DAVID?
GLUB GLUB

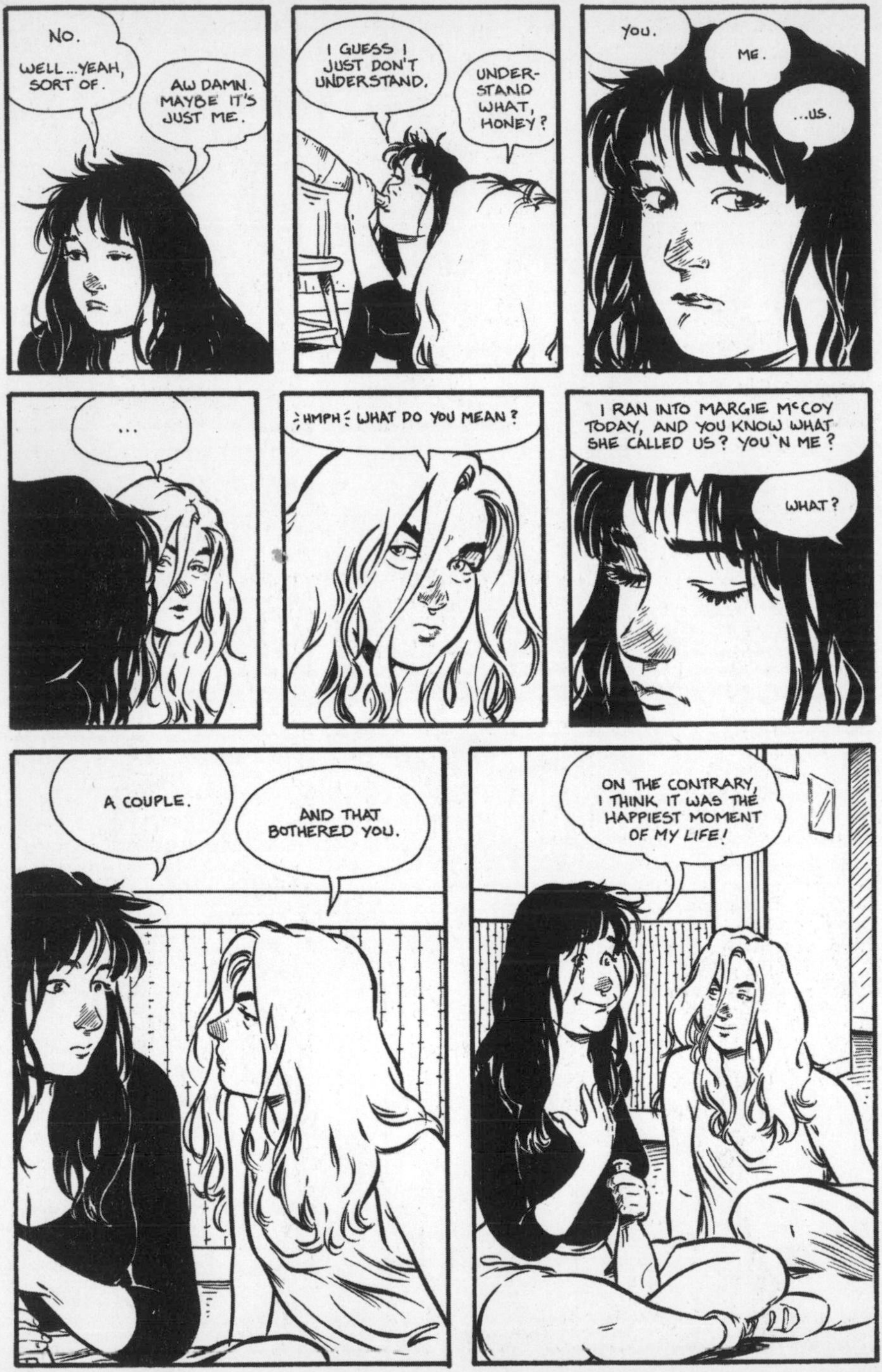

NO.
WELL... YEAH, SORT OF.
AW DAMN. MAYBE IT'S JUST ME.
I GUESS I JUST DON'T UNDERSTAND.
UNDER-STAND WHAT, HONEY?
YOU.
ME.
...US.
...
HMPH WHAT DO YOU MEAN?
I RAN INTO MARGIE McCOY TODAY, AND YOU KNOW WHAT SHE CALLED US? YOU'N ME?
WHAT?
A COUPLE.
AND THAT BOTHERED YOU.
ON THE CONTRARY, I THINK IT WAS THE HAPPIEST MOMENT OF MY LIFE!

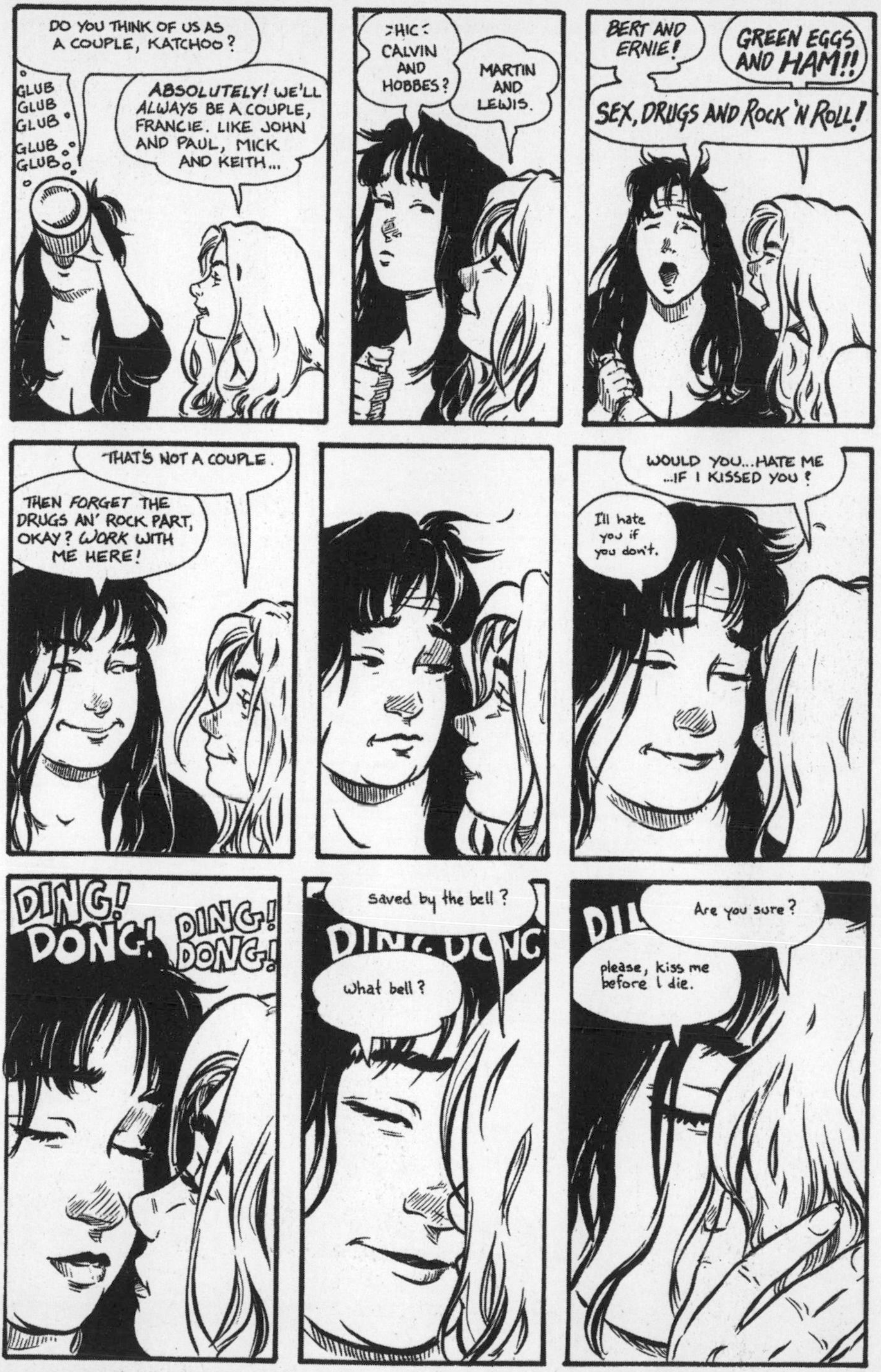
DO YOU THINK OF US AS A COUPLE, KATCHOO?
GLUB GLUB GLUB GLUB GLUB
ABSOLUTELY! WE'LL ALWAYS BE A COUPLE, FRANCIE. LIKE JOHN AND PAUL, MICK AND KEITH...
HIC
CALVIN AND HOBBES?
MARTIN AND LEWIS.
BERT AND ERNIE!
GREEN EGGS AND HAM!!
SEX, DRUGS AND ROCK 'N ROLL!
THAT'S NOT A COUPLE.
THEN FORGET THE DRUGS AN' ROCK PART, OKAY? WORK WITH ME HERE!
WOULD YOU...HATE ME ...IF I KISSED YOU?
I'll hate you if you don't.
DING! DONG! DING! DONG!
saved by the bell?
what bell?
Are you sure?
please, kiss me before I die.

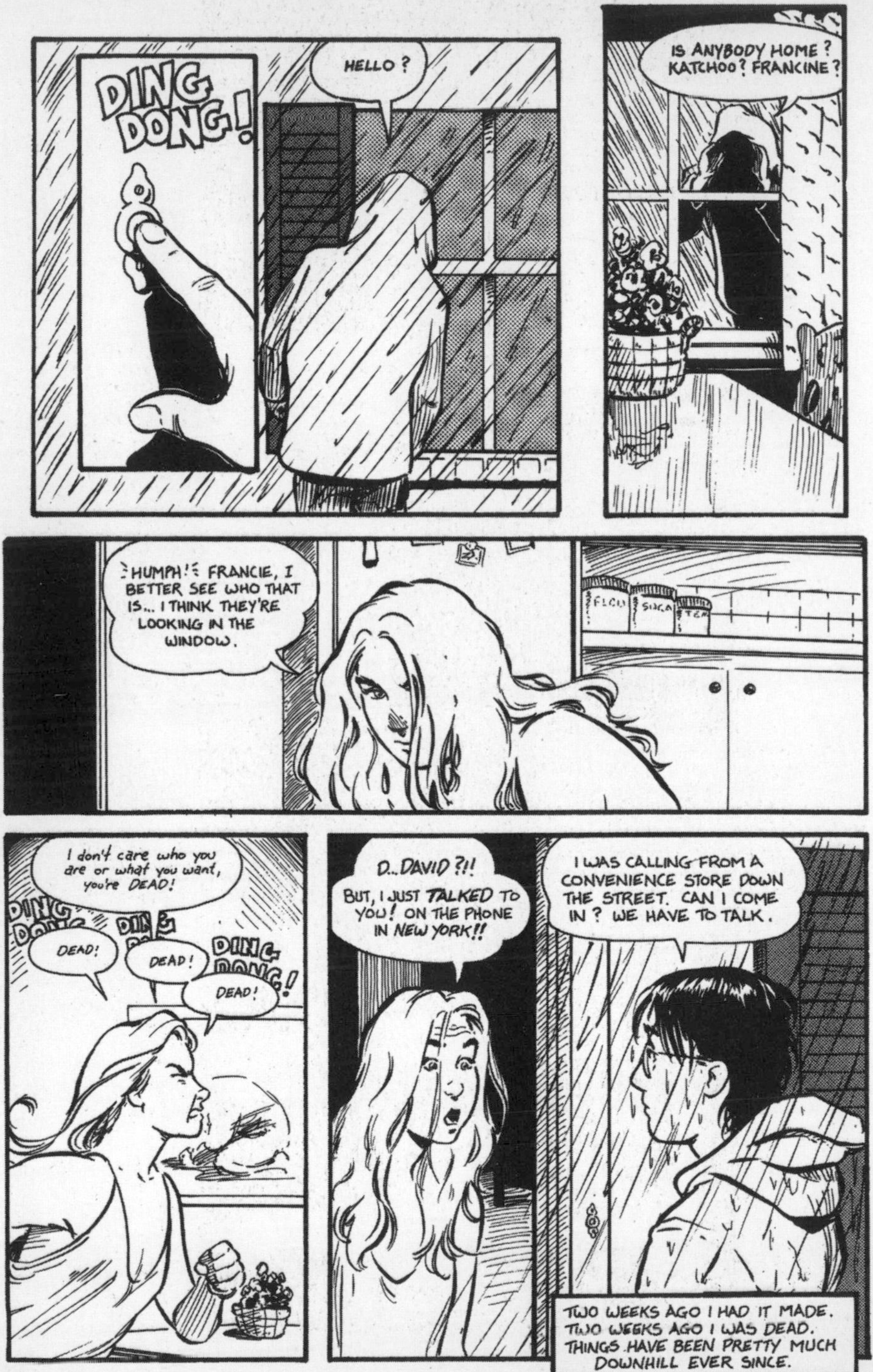
DING DONG!
HELLO?
IS ANYBODY HOME? KATCHOO? FRANCINE?
HUMPH! FRANCIE, I BETTER SEE WHO THAT IS... I THINK THEY'RE LOOKING IN THE WINDOW.
I don't care who you are or what you want, you're DEAD!
DING DONG
DEAD!
DEAD!
DEAD!
DING DONG!
D...DAVID?!!
BUT, I JUST TALKED TO YOU! ON THE PHONE IN NEW YORK!!
I WAS CALLING FROM A CONVENIENCE STORE DOWN THE STREET. CAN I COME IN? WE HAVE TO TALK.
TWO WEEKS AGO I HAD IT MADE. TWO WEEKS AGO I WAS DEAD. THINGS HAVE BEEN PRETTY MUCH DOWNHILL EVER SINCE.

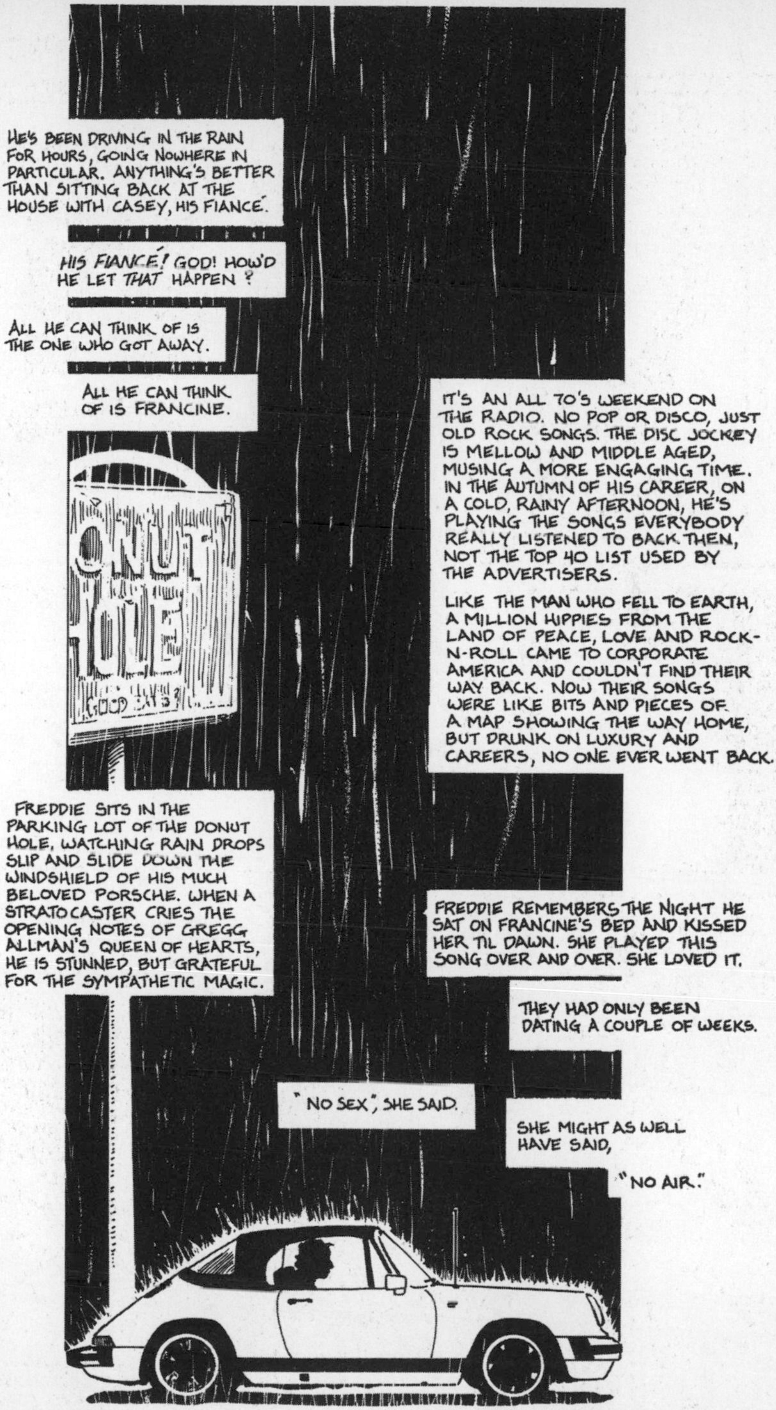
HE'S BEEN DRIVING IN THE RAIN FOR HOURS, GOING NOWHERE IN PARTICULAR. ANYTHING'S BETTER THAN SITTING BACK AT THE HOUSE WITH CASEY, HIS FIANCÉ.
HIS FIANCÉ! GOD! HOW'D HE LET THAT HAPPEN ?
ALL HE CAN THINK OF IS THE ONE WHO GOT AWAY.
ALL HE CAN THINK OF IS FRANCINE.
IT'S AN ALL 70'S WEEKEND ON THE RADIO. NO POP OR DISCO, JUST OLD ROCK SONGS. THE DISC JOCKEY IS MELLOW AND MIDDLE AGED, MUSING A MORE ENGAGING TIME. IN THE AUTUMN OF HIS CAREER, ON A COLD, RAINY AFTERNOON, HE'S PLAYING THE SONGS EVERYBODY REALLY LISTENED TO BACK THEN, NOT THE TOP 40 LIST USED BY THE ADVERTISERS.
LIKE THE MAN WHO FELL TO EARTH, A MILLION HIPPIES FROM THE LAND OF PEACE, LOVE AND ROCK-N-ROLL CAME TO CORPORATE AMERICA AND COULDN'T FIND THEIR WAY BACK. NOW THEIR SONGS WERE LIKE BITS AND PIECES OF A MAP SHOWING THE WAY HOME, BUT DRUNK ON LUXURY AND CAREERS, NO ONE EVER WENT BACK.
FREDDIE SITS IN THE PARKING LOT OF THE DONUT HOLE, WATCHING RAIN DROPS SLIP AND SLIDE DOWN THE WINDSHIELD OF HIS MUCH BELOVED PORSCHE. WHEN A STRATOCASTER CRIES THE OPENING NOTES OF GREGG ALLMAN'S QUEEN OF HEARTS, HE IS STUNNED, BUT GRATEFUL FOR THE SYMPATHETIC MAGIC.
FREDDIE REMEMBERS THE NIGHT HE SAT ON FRANCINE'S BED AND KISSED HER TIL DAWN. SHE PLAYED THIS SONG OVER AND OVER. SHE LOVED IT.
THEY HAD ONLY BEEN DATING A COUPLE OF WEEKS.
"NO SEX", SHE SAID.
SHE MIGHT AS WELL HAVE SAID,
"NO AIR."

"AND AFTER ALL THAT
WE'VE BEEN THROUGH,
I FIND THAT WHEN I
THINK OF YOU,
A WARM SOUTH WIND
RUNS THROUGH
AND THROUGH.
AND IN MY HEART
THERE'S ONLY YOU."

FREDDIE PURSES HIS LIPS
AGAINST THE LUMP THAT
FILLS HIS THROAT. THERE
WOULD NEVER BE ANOTHER
GIRL LIKE FRANCINE.

NEVER.

SHE WAS THE SEXIEST,
MOST BEAUTIFUL, MOST
INTOXICATING, SEXIEST,
MOST... SEXY... SEX...

OH GOD! SHE WAS PERFECT!
EXCEPT FOR THAT LITTLE
TONGUE THINGY SHE DID TO
HER TEETH AFTER SHE ATE,
BUT OTHER THAN THAT...

OH, LORD HELP HIM, WHERE
DID IT ALL GO WRONG?

"AND I WILL ALWAYS KEEP
ON TRYIN'
TO GATHER THIS STRANGE
PEACE OF MIND.
WITHOUT IT THERE'D BE
LONELY ME,
AND, OH DARLING,
LONELY YOU."

HEY! HE WAS LONELY! HE
WAS MORE LONELY THAN
HE'D BEEN HIS ENTIRE
LIFE. ALL ALONE IN A
SEA OF PEOPLE. IN HIS
PORSCHE. IN HIS OWN BED.

EVEN GOD SAID IT WASN'T
GOOD FOR MAN TO BE
ALONE, IN HIS OWN BED.

GOD WANTED HIM TO HAVE
FRANCINE, DAMMIT!

THAT'S IT! HE WAS ON A
MISSION FROM GOD!

HE HAD TO BE WITH
FRANCINE AGAIN. SHE
HAD TO TAKE HIM BACK!

HE SHOULD DO SOMETHING.
HE SHOULD GO OVER
THERE RIGHT NOW AND
TELL HER HOW HE FEELS

"I LOVE YOU, QUEEN OF
HEARTS.
DON'T TELL ME WHEN
TO STOP,
TELL ME WHEN TO START."

THAT'S WHAT HE OUGHT
TO DO. THAT'S WHAT
A REAL MAN WOULD DO.

HE COULD PICTURE
HIMSELF DOING THAT.

WELL, HE COULD!

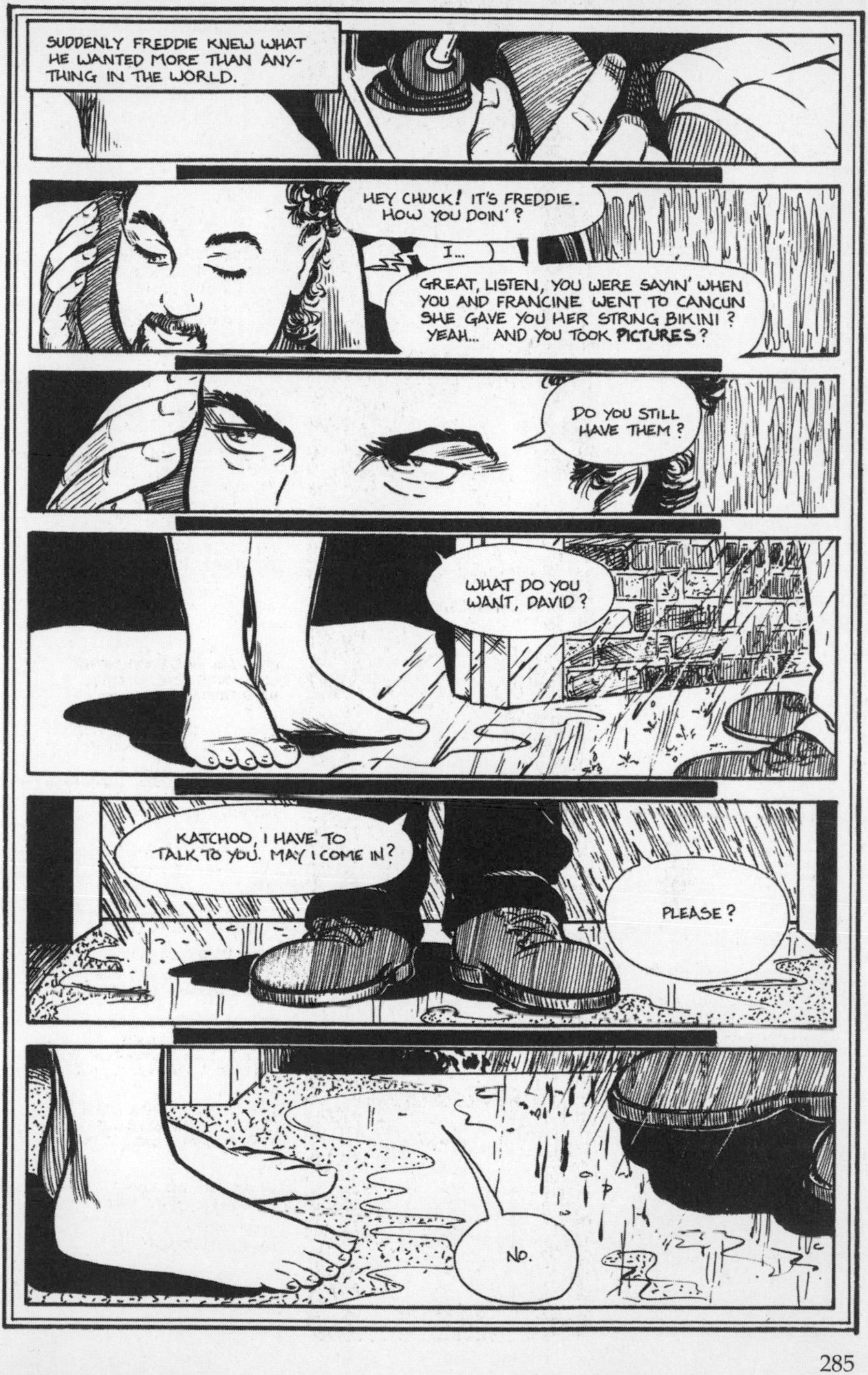
SUDDENLY FREDDIE KNEW WHAT HE WANTED MORE THAN ANY-THING IN THE WORLD.
HEY CHUCK! IT'S FREDDIE. HOW YOU DOIN'?
I...
GREAT, LISTEN, YOU WERE SAYIN' WHEN YOU AND FRANCINE WENT TO CANCUN SHE GAVE YOU HER STRING BIKINI? YEAH... AND YOU TOOK PICTURES?
DO YOU STILL HAVE THEM?
WHAT DO YOU WANT, DAVID?
KATCHOO, I HAVE TO TALK TO YOU. MAY I COME IN?
PLEASE?
NO.

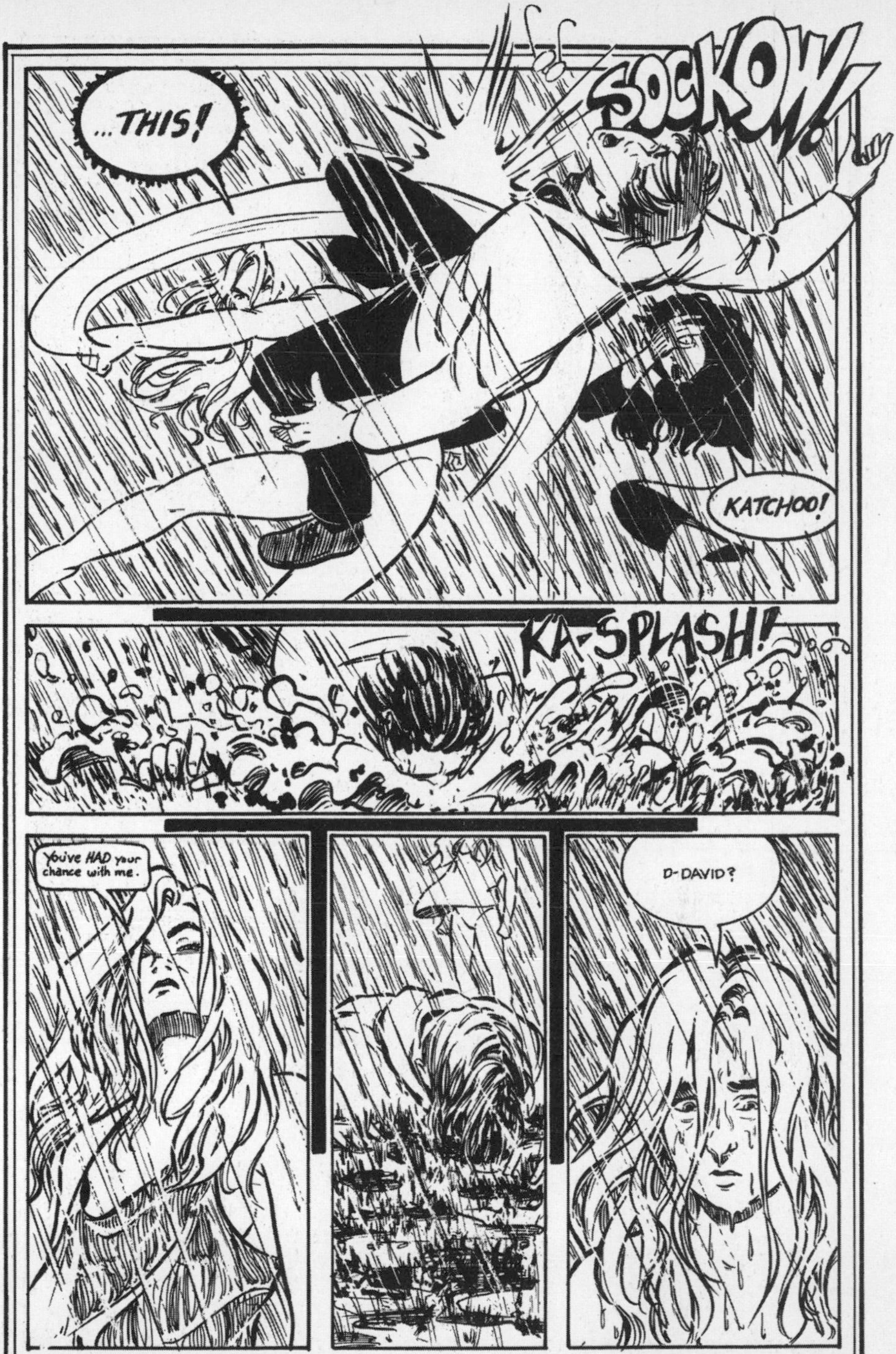
...THIS!
SOCKOW!
KATCHOO!
KA-SPLASH!
You've HAD your chance with me.
D-DAVID?

288

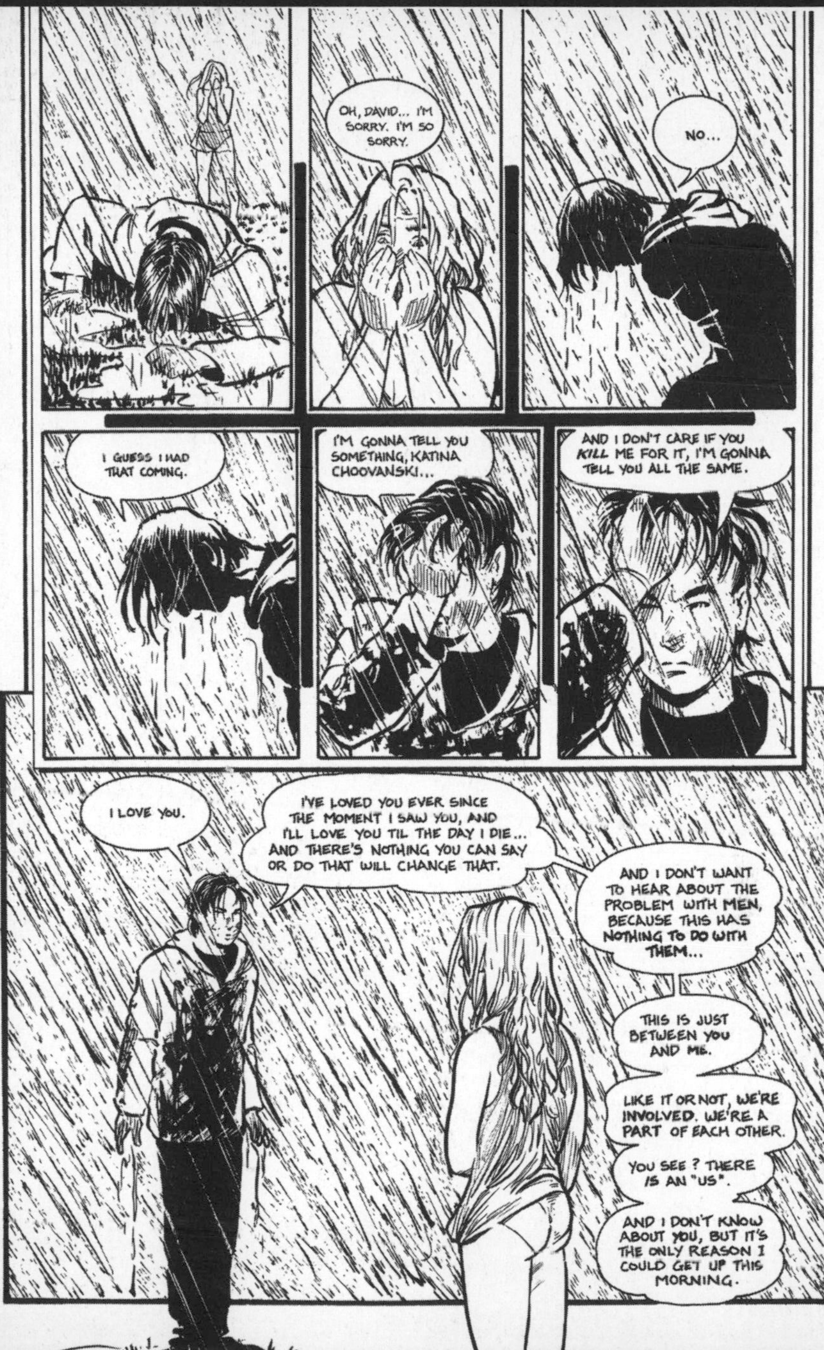
OH, DAVID... I'M SORRY. I'M SO SORRY.
NO...
I GUESS I HAD THAT COMING.
I'M GONNA TELL YOU SOMETHING, KATINA CHOOVANSKI...
AND I DON'T CARE IF YOU *KILL* ME FOR IT, I'M GONNA TELL YOU ALL THE SAME.
I LOVE YOU.
I'VE LOVED YOU EVER SINCE THE MOMENT I SAW YOU, AND I'LL LOVE YOU TIL THE DAY I DIE... AND THERE'S NOTHING YOU CAN SAY OR DO THAT WILL CHANGE THAT.
AND I DON'T WANT TO HEAR ABOUT THE PROBLEM WITH MEN, BECAUSE THIS HAS NOTHING TO DO WITH THEM...
THIS IS JUST BETWEEN YOU AND ME.
LIKE IT OR NOT, WE'RE INVOLVED. WE'RE A PART OF EACH OTHER.
YOU SEE? THERE IS AN "US".
AND I DON'T KNOW ABOUT YOU, BUT IT'S THE ONLY REASON I COULD GET UP THIS MORNING.

290

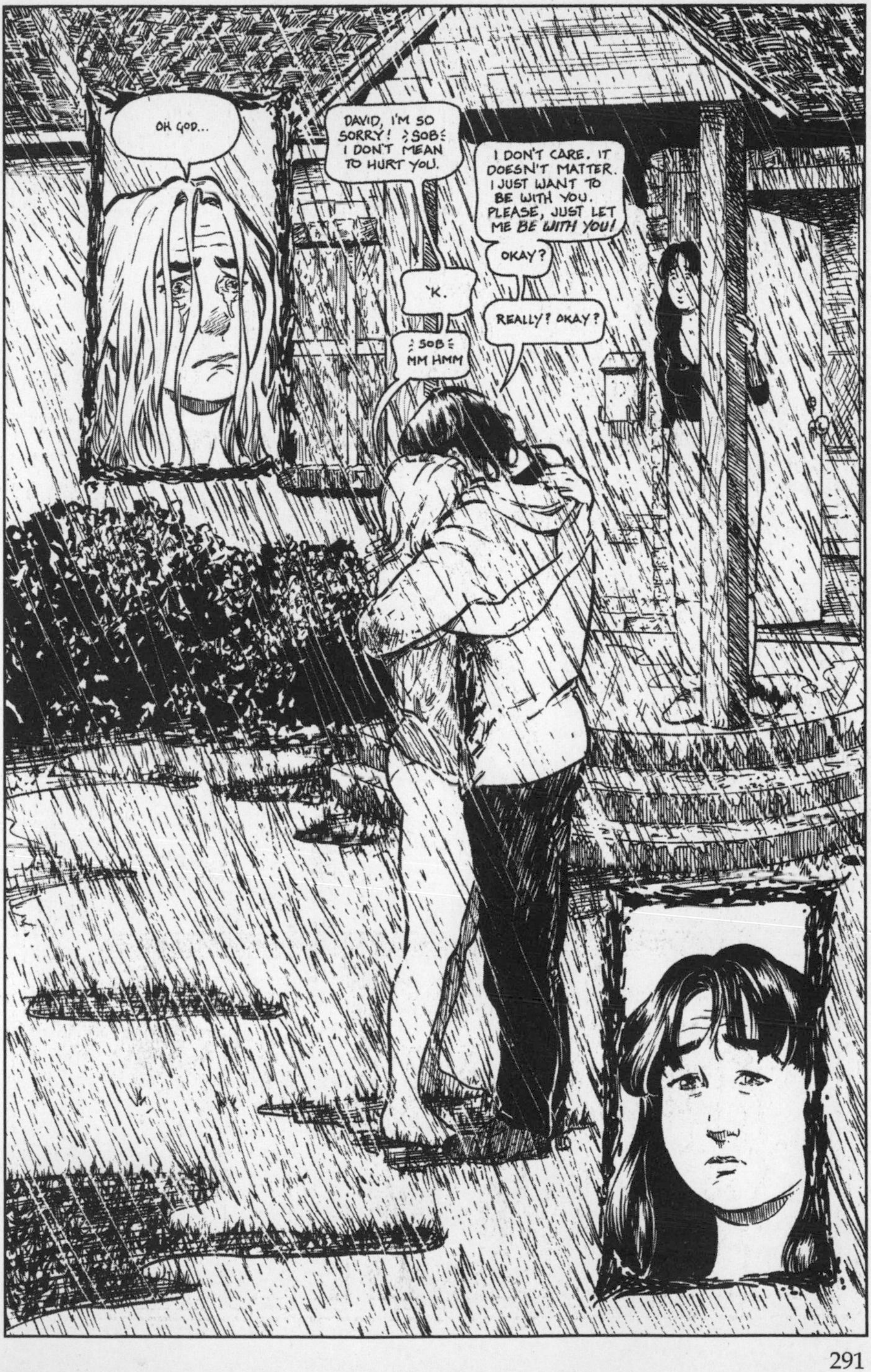
OH GOD...
DAVID, I'M SO SORRY! SOB I DON'T MEAN TO HURT YOU.
I DON'T CARE. IT DOESN'T MATTER. I JUST WANT TO BE WITH YOU. PLEASE, JUST LET ME BE WITH YOU!
OKAY?
'K.
REALLY? OKAY?
SOB MM HMM

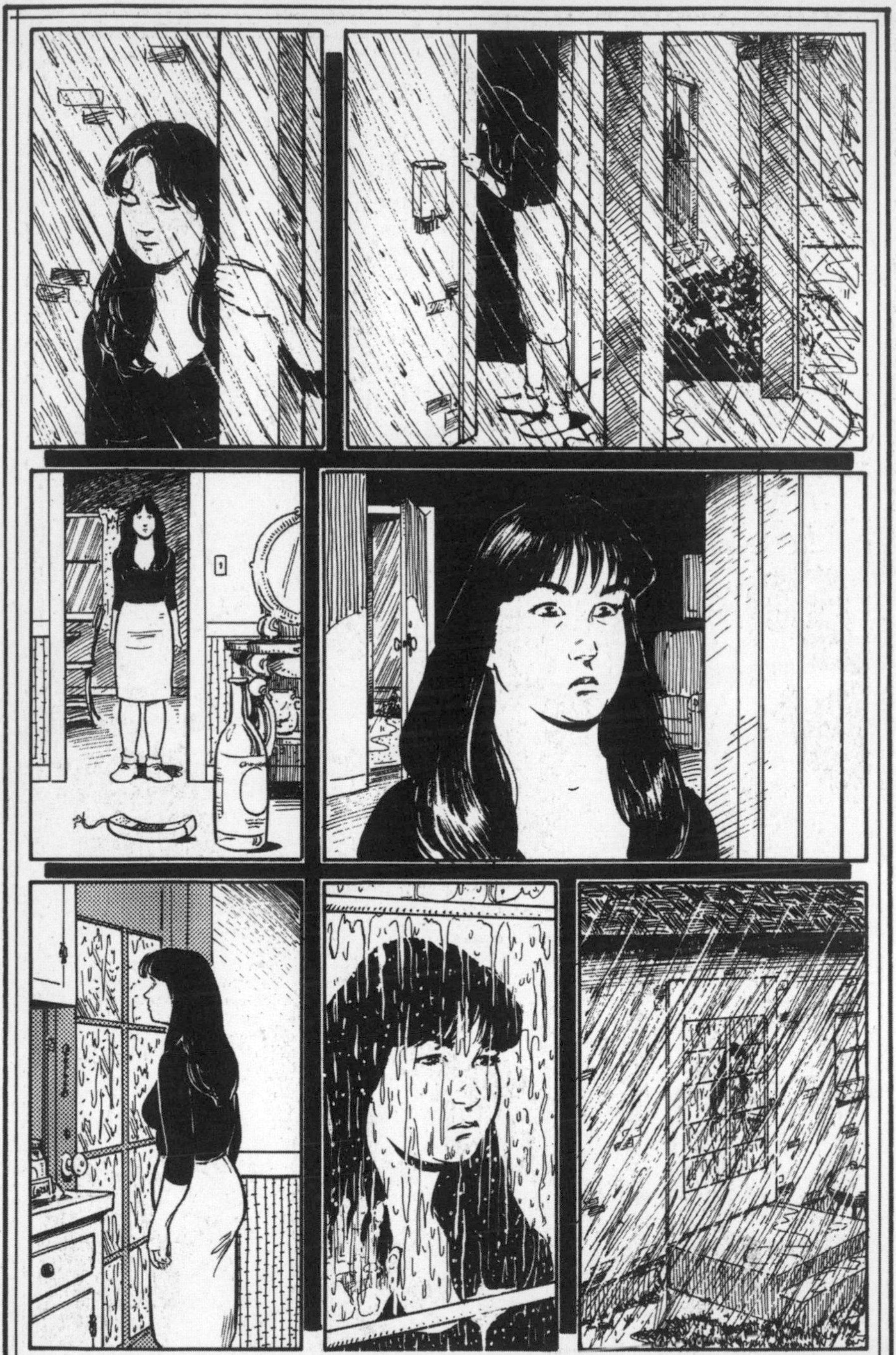

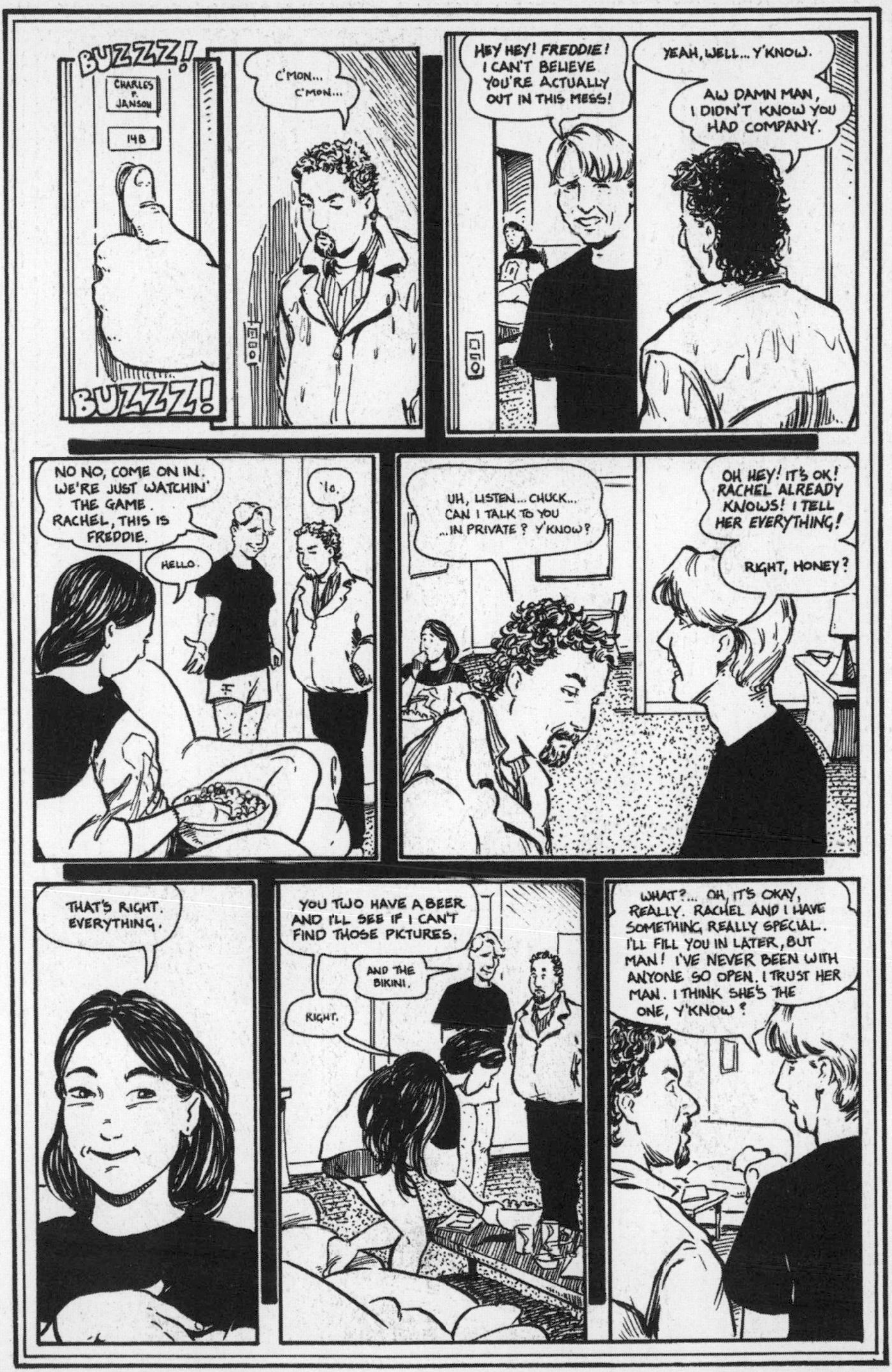
BUZZZ!
CHARLES F. JANSON
148
BUZZZ!
C'MON... C'MON...
HEY HEY! FREDDIE! I CAN'T BELIEVE YOU'RE ACTUALLY OUT IN THIS MESS!
YEAH, WELL... Y'KNOW.
AW DAMN MAN, I DIDN'T KNOW YOU HAD COMPANY.
NO NO, COME ON IN. WE'RE JUST WATCHIN' THE GAME. RACHEL, THIS IS FREDDIE.
'lo.
HELLO.
UH, LISTEN... CHUCK... CAN I TALK TO YOU ...IN PRIVATE? Y'KNOW?
OH HEY! IT'S OK! RACHEL ALREADY KNOWS! I TELL HER EVERYTHING!
RIGHT, HONEY?
THAT'S RIGHT. EVERYTHING.
YOU TWO HAVE A BEER AND I'LL SEE IF I CAN'T FIND THOSE PICTURES.
AND THE BIKINI.
RIGHT.
WHAT?... OH, IT'S OKAY, REALLY. RACHEL AND I HAVE SOMETHING REALLY SPECIAL. I'LL FILL YOU IN LATER, BUT MAN! I'VE NEVER BEEN WITH ANYONE SO OPEN. I TRUST HER MAN. I THINK SHE'S THE ONE, Y'KNOW?

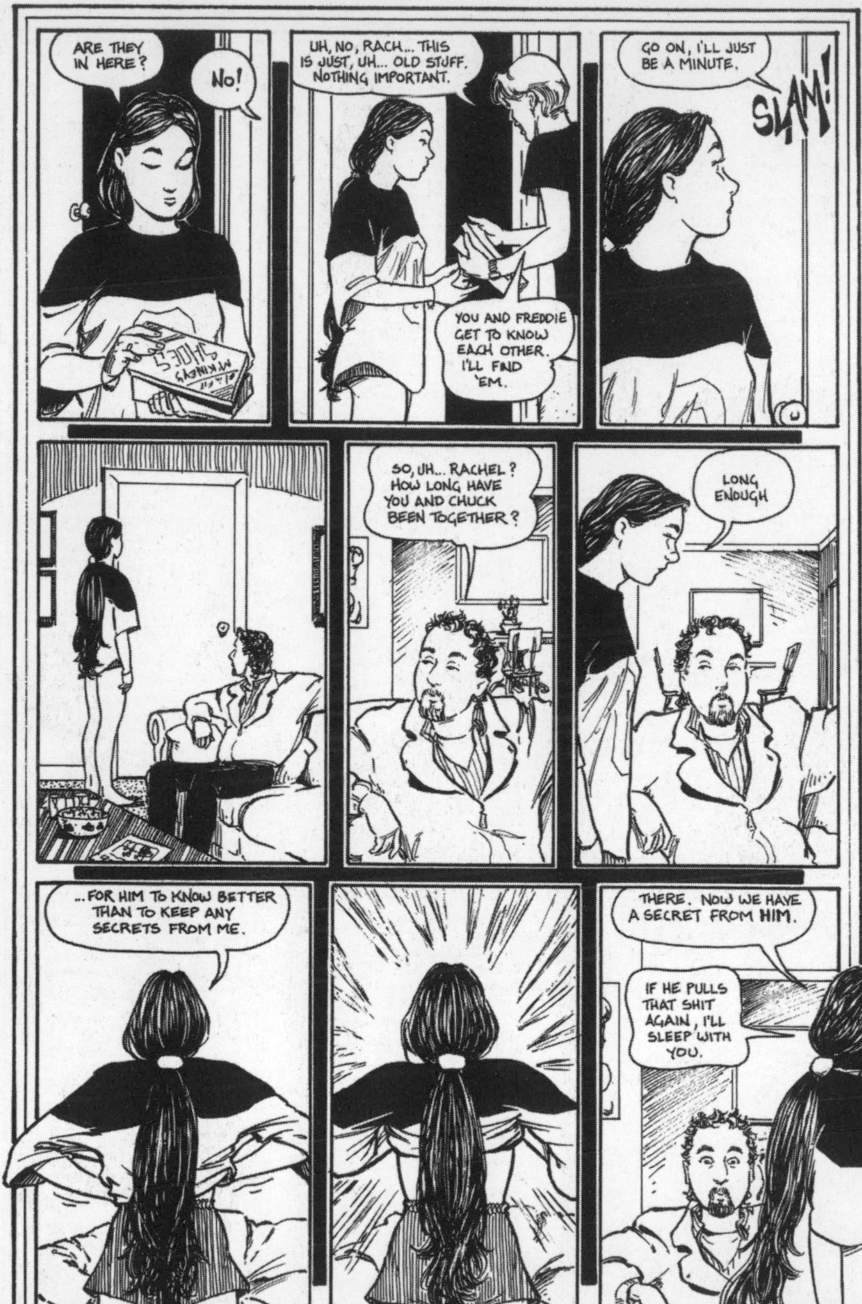
ARE THEY IN HERE?
NO!
UH, NO, RACH... THIS IS JUST, UH... OLD STUFF. NOTHING IMPORTANT.
YOU AND FREDDIE GET TO KNOW EACH OTHER. I'LL FIND 'EM.
GO ON, I'LL JUST BE A MINUTE.
SLAM!
SO, UH... RACHEL? HOW LONG HAVE YOU AND CHUCK BEEN TOGETHER?
LONG ENOUGH
...FOR HIM TO KNOW BETTER THAN TO KEEP ANY SECRETS FROM ME.
THERE. NOW WE HAVE A SECRET FROM HIM.
IF HE PULLS THAT SHIT AGAIN, I'LL SLEEP WITH YOU.

295

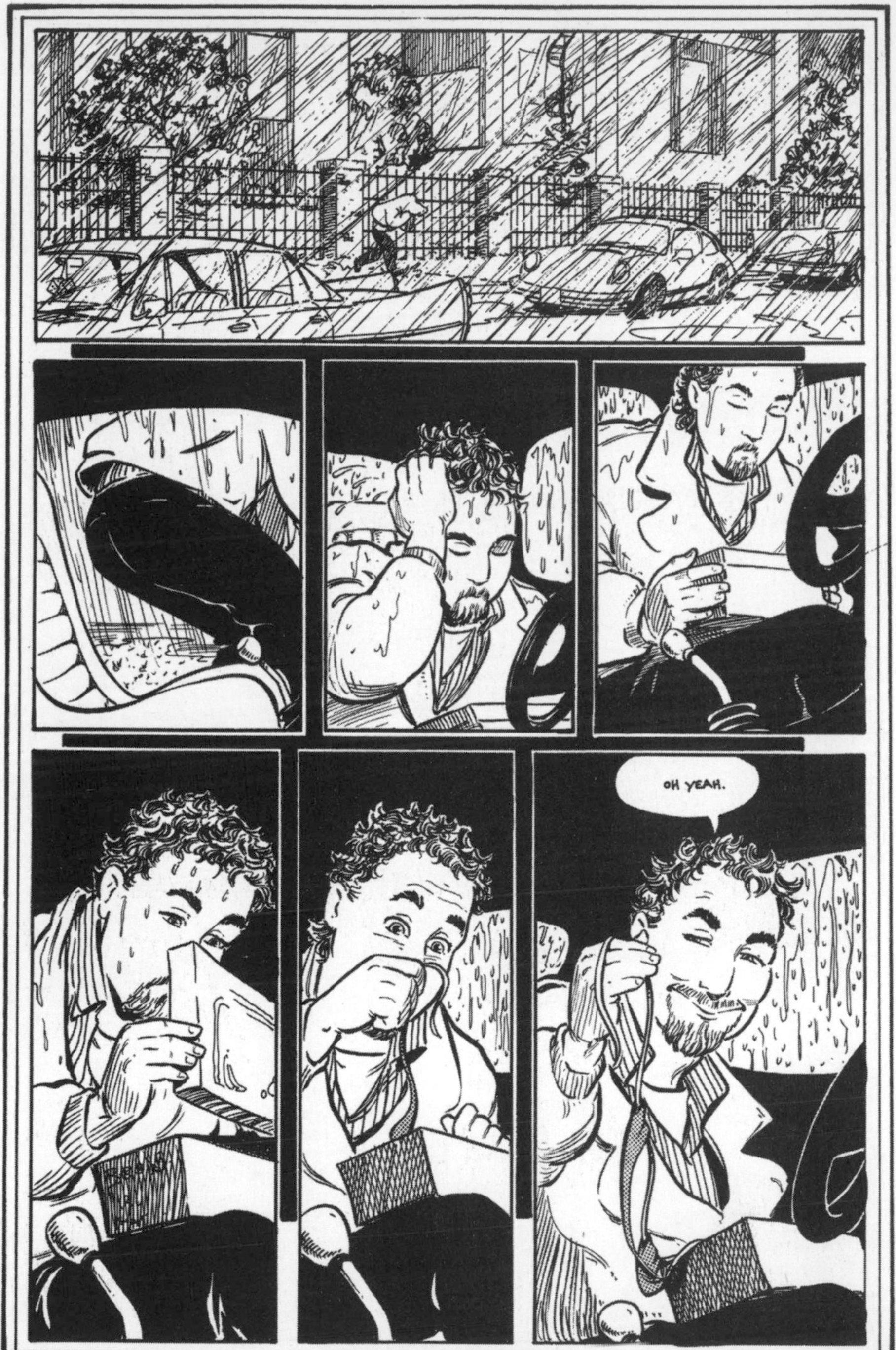
OH YEAH.

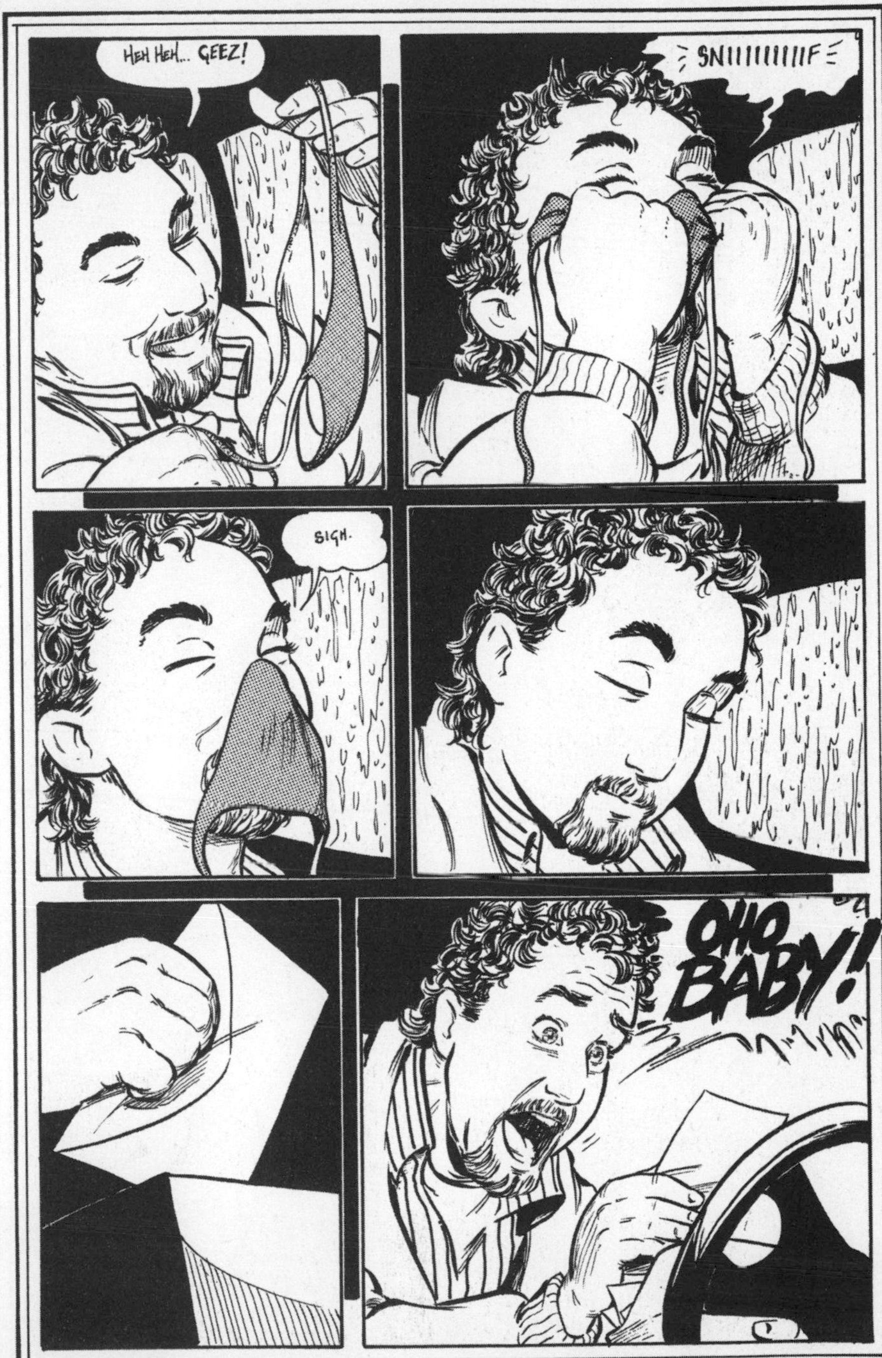
HEH HEH... GEEZ!
SNIIIIIIIIIF
SIGH.
OHO BABY!

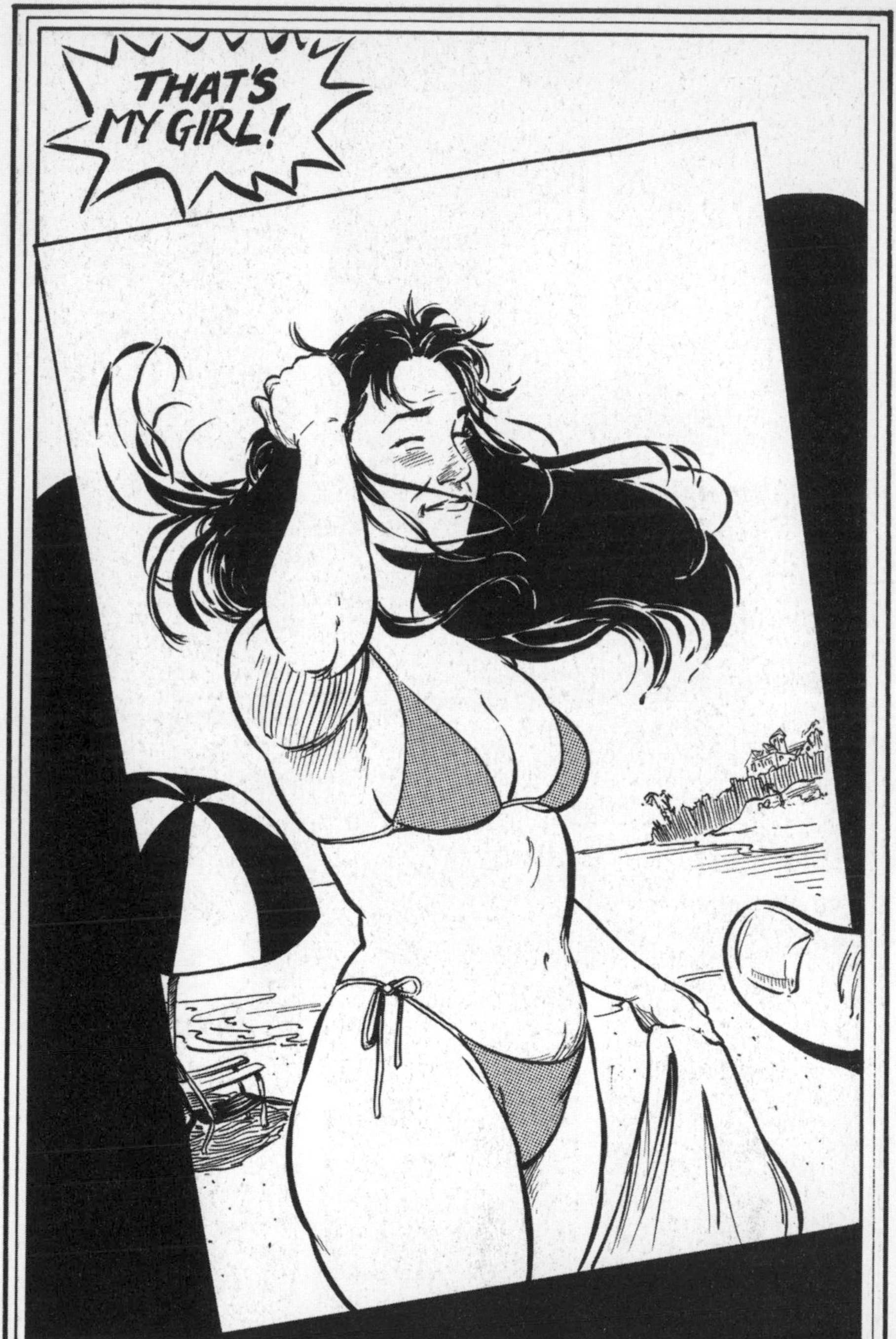
THAT'S MY GIRL!

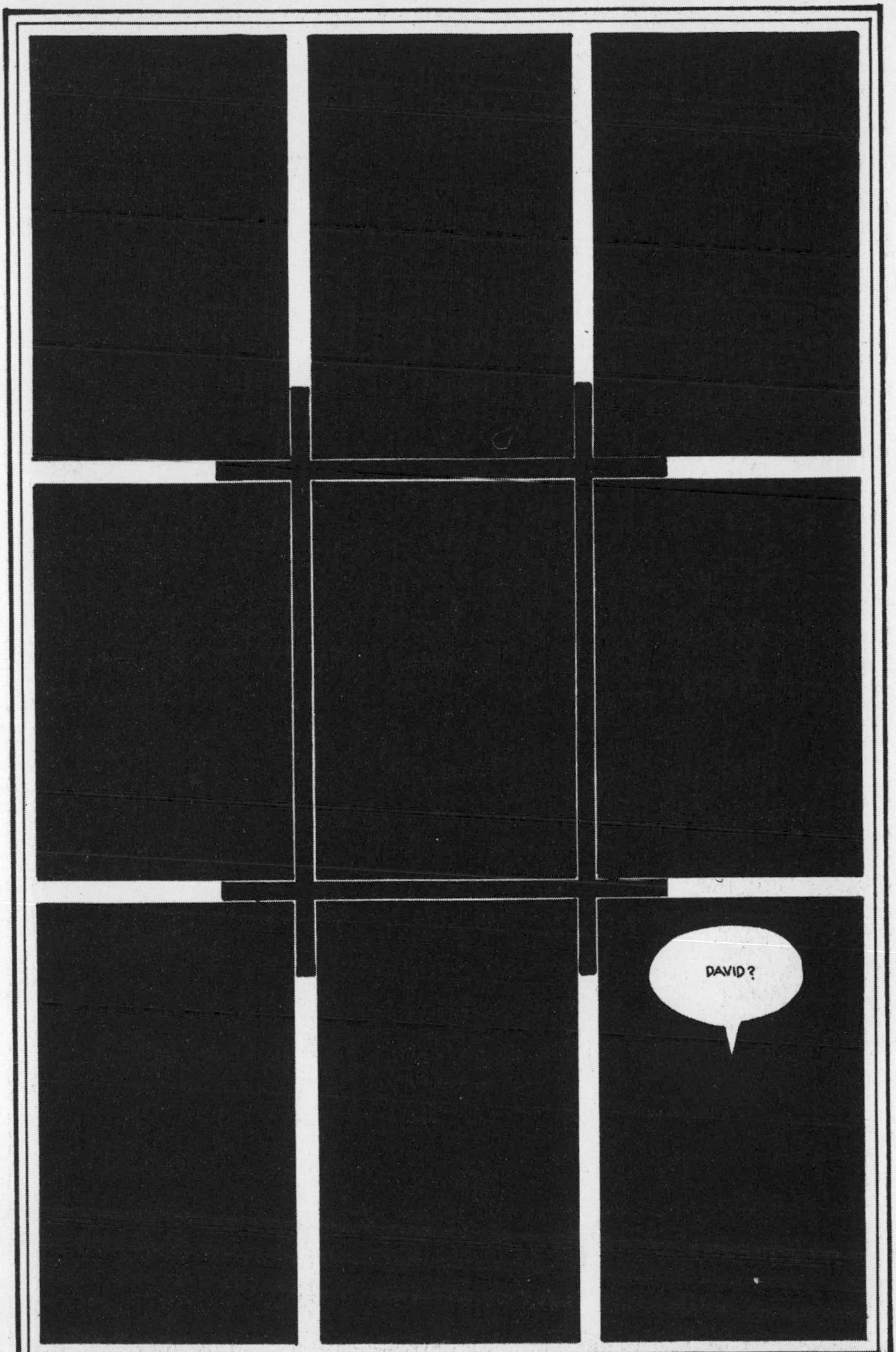
DAVID?

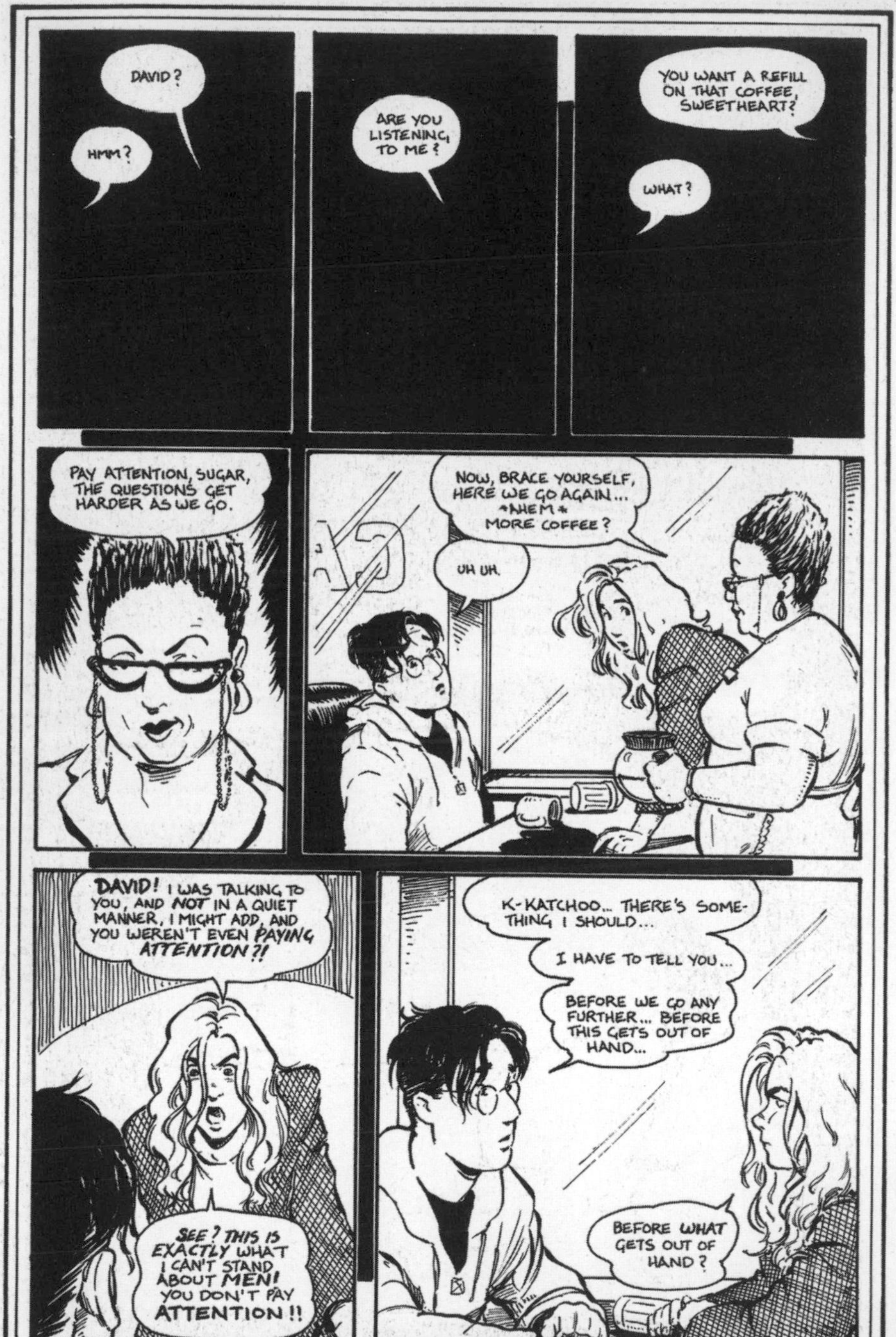
DAVID?
HMM?
ARE YOU LISTENING, TO ME?
YOU WANT A REFILL ON THAT COFFEE, SWEETHEART?
WHAT?
PAY ATTENTION, SUGAR, THE QUESTIONS GET HARDER AS WE GO.
NOW, BRACE YOURSELF, HERE WE GO AGAIN... *AHEM* MORE COFFEE?
UH UH.
DAVID! I WAS TALKING TO YOU, AND NOT IN A QUIET MANNER, I MIGHT ADD, AND YOU WEREN'T EVEN PAYING ATTENTION?!
SEE? THIS IS EXACTLY WHAT I CAN'T STAND ABOUT MEN! YOU DON'T PAY ATTENTION!!
K-KATCHOO... THERE'S SOMETHING I SHOULD...
I HAVE TO TELL YOU...
BEFORE WE GO ANY FURTHER... BEFORE THIS GETS OUT OF HAND...
BEFORE WHAT GETS OUT OF HAND?

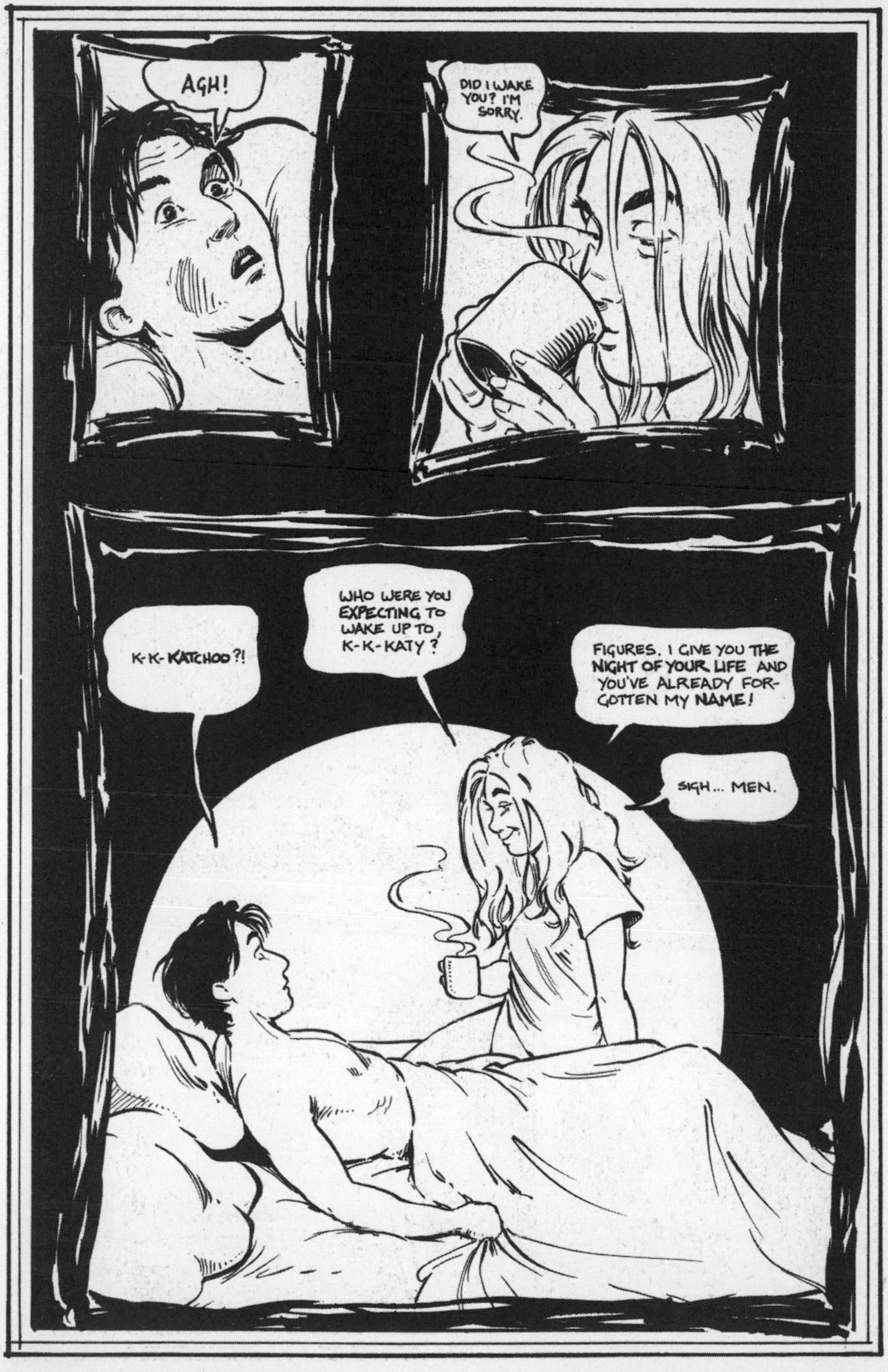
AGH!
DID I WAKE YOU? I'M SORRY.
K-K-KATCHOO?!
WHO WERE YOU EXPECTING TO WAKE UP TO, K-K-KATY?
FIGURES. I GIVE YOU THE NIGHT OF YOUR LIFE AND YOU'VE ALREADY FOR-GOTTEN MY NAME!
SIGH... MEN.

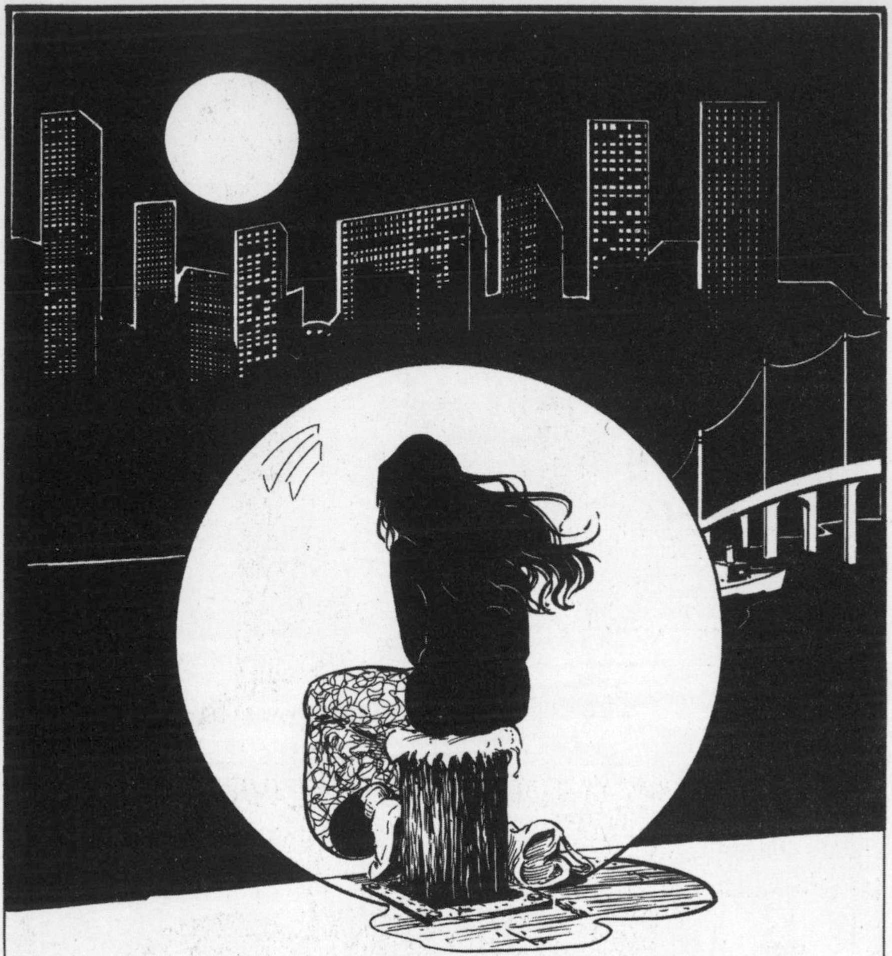

If you're leaving me
please don't tell me
You're still pleasing me
Do I fail you
I will wonder today
if tomorrow you'll stay
I can hear your voice turn cold
when you turn to me I know
I'm the one who won't let go
Are you blaming me
for holding on
when you let me know
it's my last chance
And I know it's gone

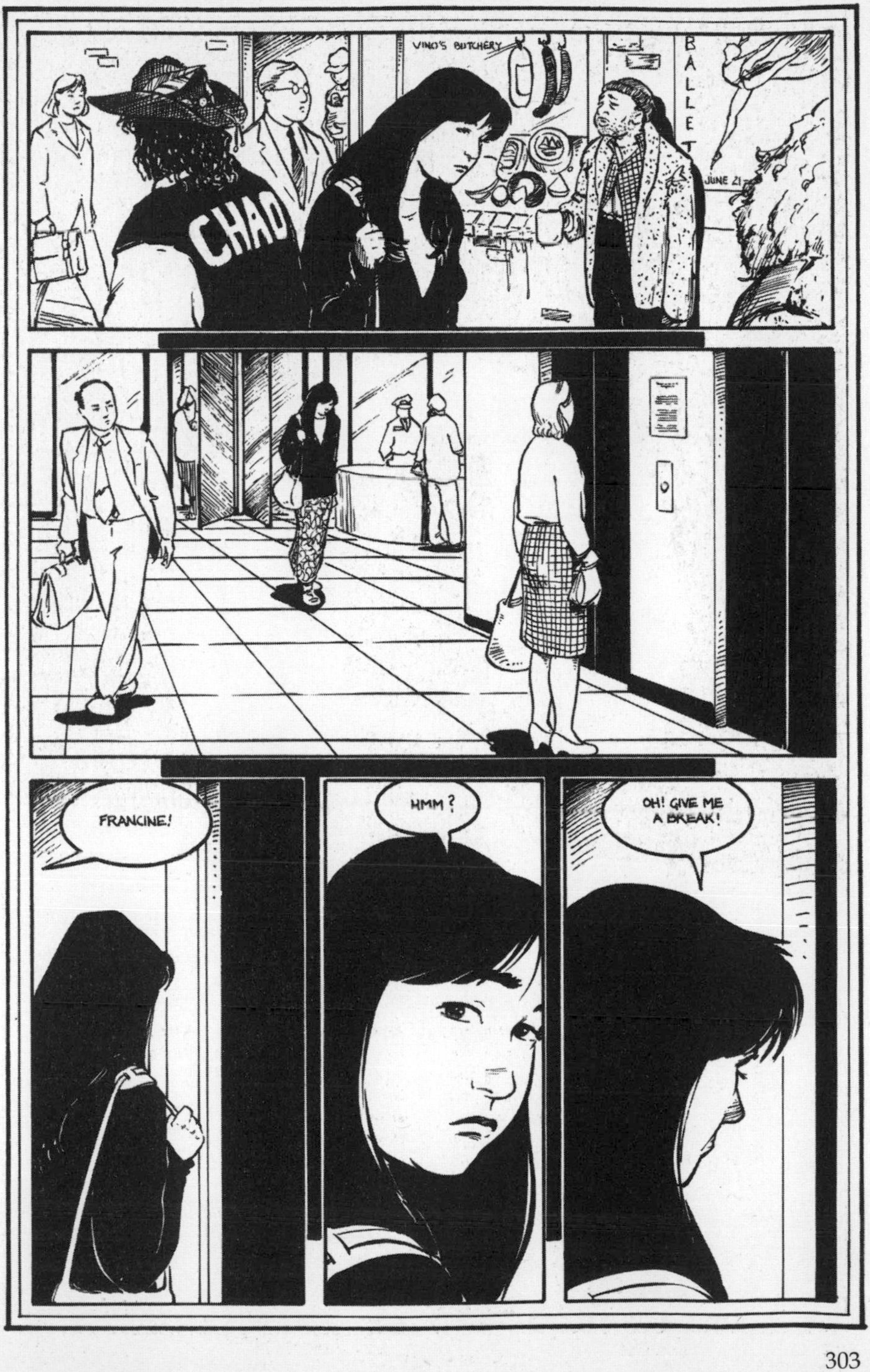
VINO'S BUTCHERY
BALLET
JUNE 21
CHAO
FRANCINE!
HMM?
OH! GIVE ME A BREAK!

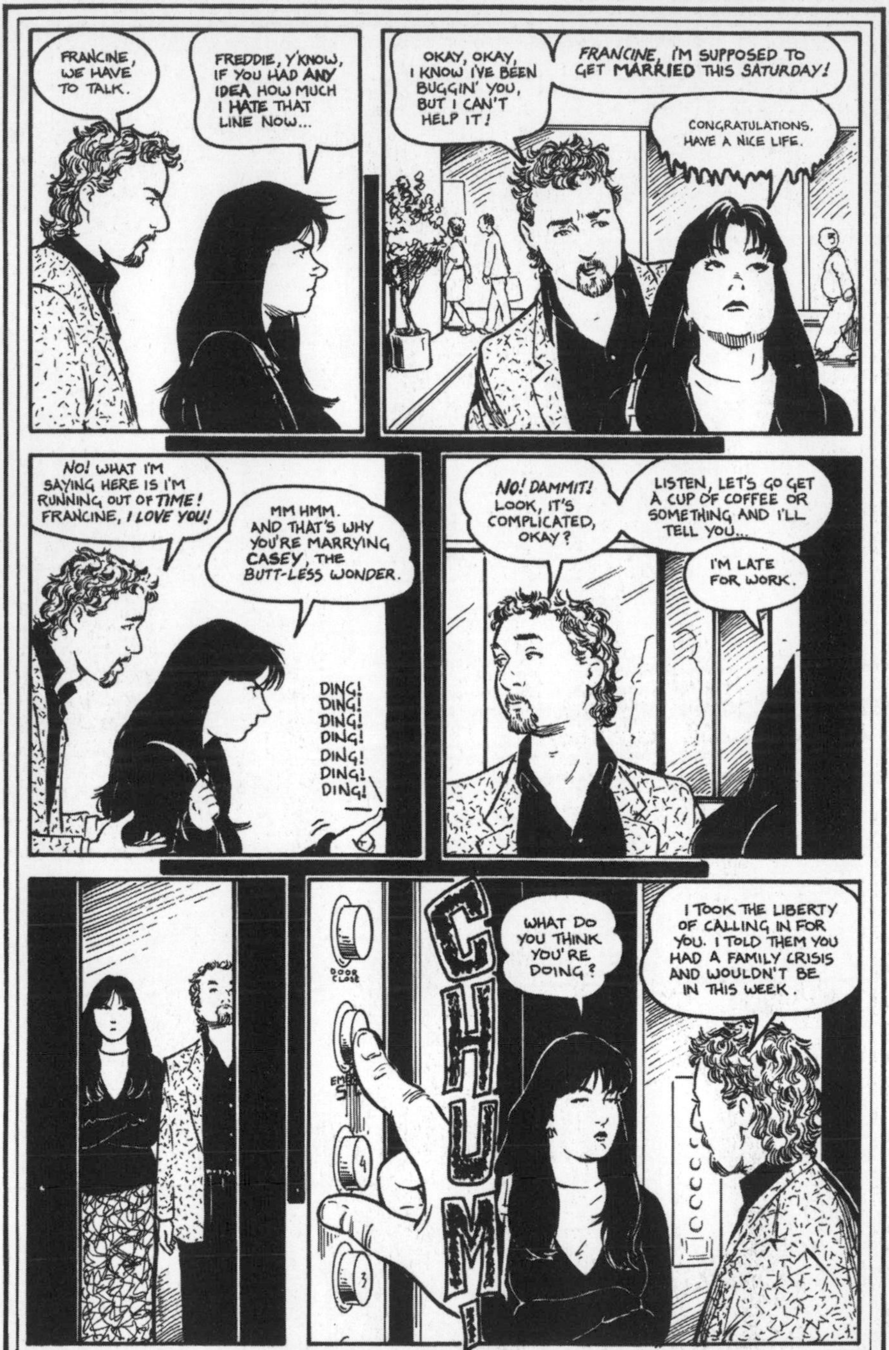
FRANCINE, WE HAVE TO TALK.
FREDDIE, Y'KNOW, IF YOU HAD ANY IDEA HOW MUCH I HATE THAT LINE NOW...
OKAY, OKAY, I KNOW I'VE BEEN BUGGIN' YOU, BUT I CAN'T HELP IT!
FRANCINE, I'M SUPPOSED TO GET MARRIED THIS SATURDAY!
CONGRATULATIONS. HAVE A NICE LIFE.
NO! WHAT I'M SAYING HERE IS I'M RUNNING OUT OF TIME! FRANCINE, I LOVE YOU!
MM HMM. AND THAT'S WHY YOU'RE MARRYING CASEY, THE BUTT-LESS WONDER.
DING! DING! DING! DING! DING! DING! DING!
NO! DAMMIT! LOOK, IT'S COMPLICATED, OKAY?
LISTEN, LET'S GO GET A CUP OF COFFEE OR SOMETHING AND I'LL TELL YOU...
I'M LATE FOR WORK.
DOOR CLOSE
CHUNK!
WHAT DO YOU THINK YOU'RE DOING?
I TOOK THE LIBERTY OF CALLING IN FOR YOU. I TOLD THEM YOU HAD A FAMILY CRISIS AND WOULDN'T BE IN THIS WEEK.

305

307

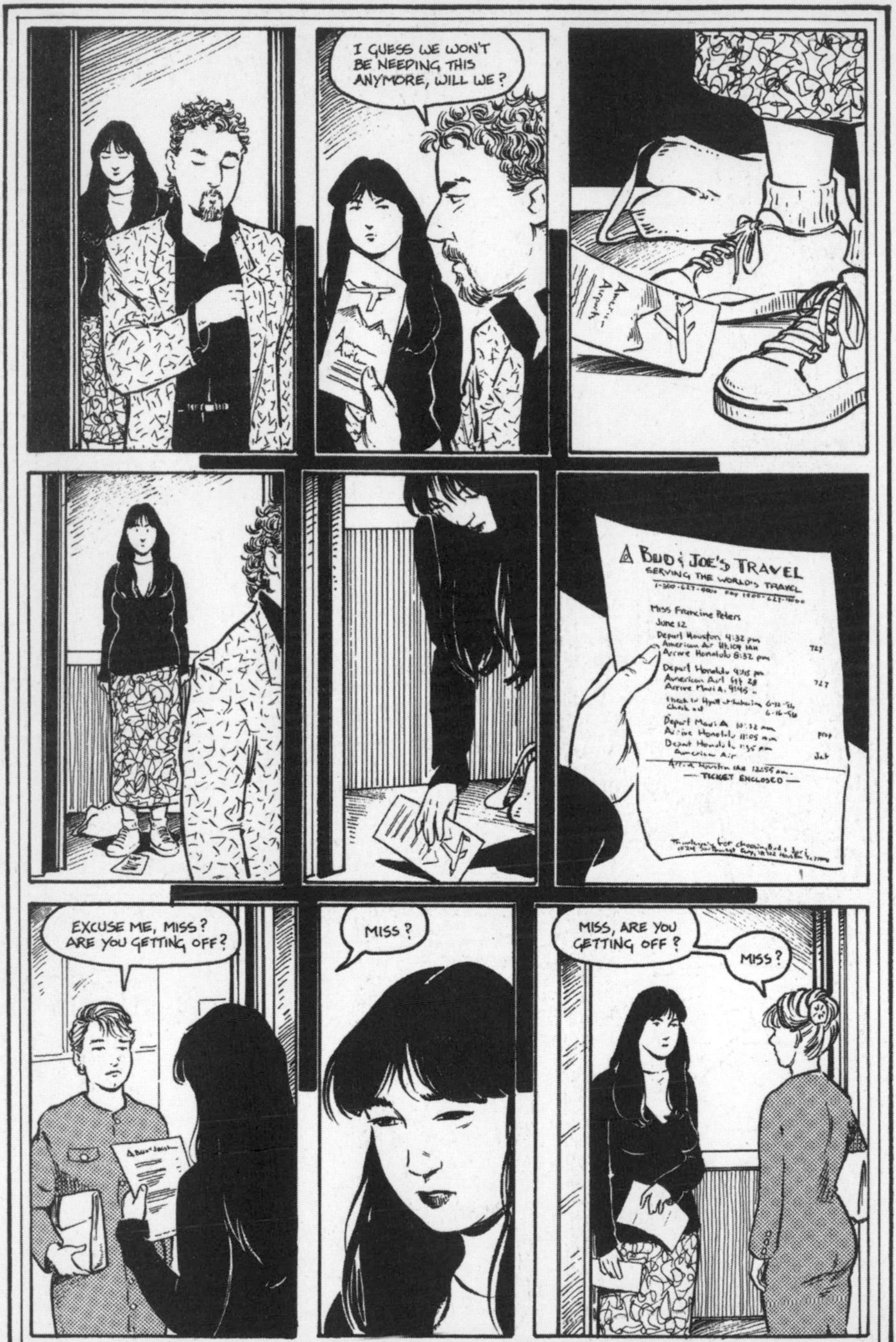
I GUESS WE WON'T BE NEEDING THIS ANYMORE, WILL WE?
BUD & JOE'S TRAVEL
SERVING THE WORLD'S TRAVEL
Miss Francine Peters
June 12
Depart Houston 4:32 pm
Arrive Honolulu 8:32 pm
Depart Honolulu 9:15 pm
Depart Maui A 10:32 am
Depart Honolulu 11:35 pm
American Air
— TICKET ENCLOSED —
EXCUSE ME, MISS? ARE YOU GETTING OFF?
MISS?
MISS, ARE YOU GETTING OFF?
MISS?

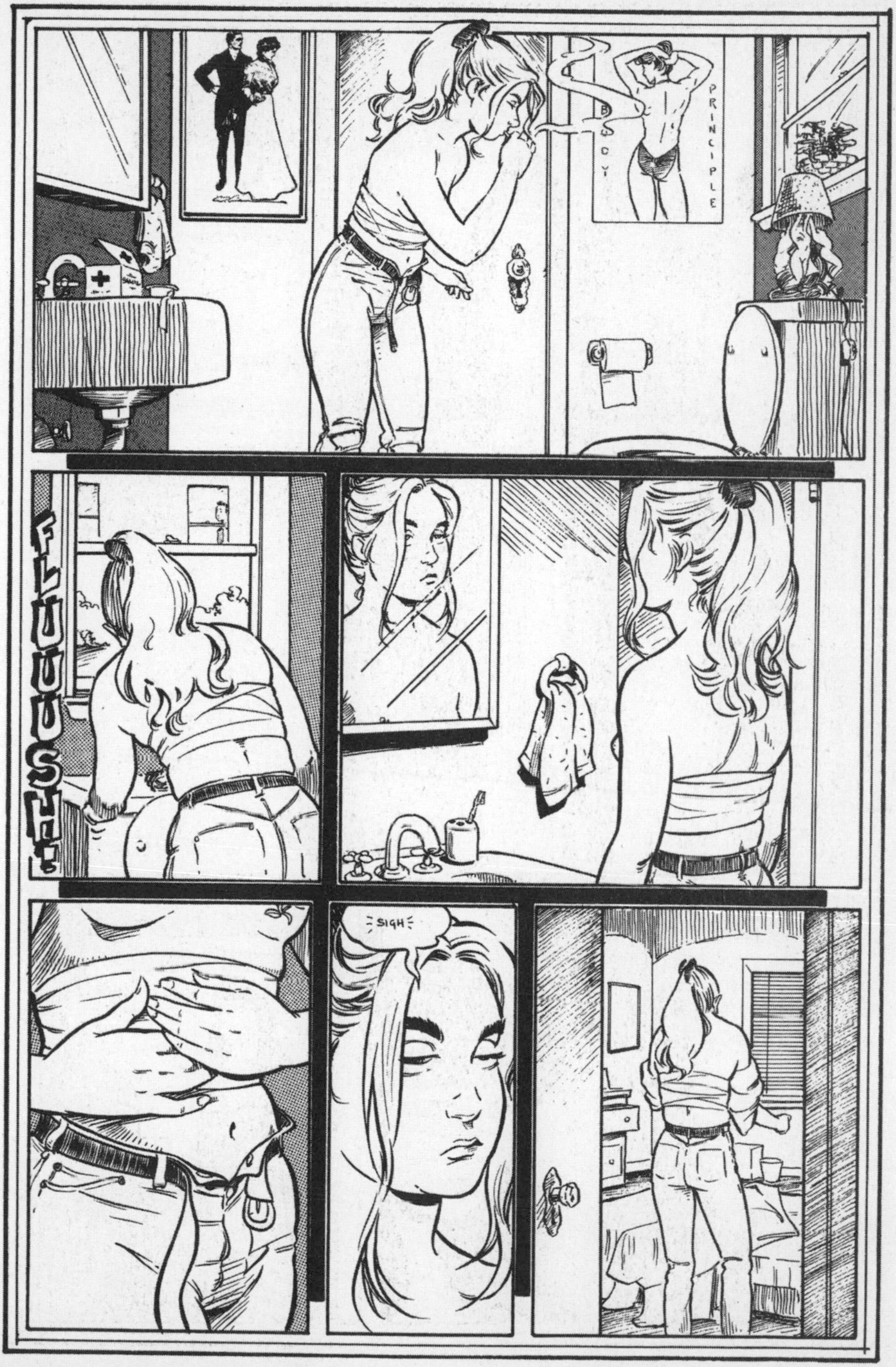
PRINCIPLE
FLUUUUSH!
SIGH

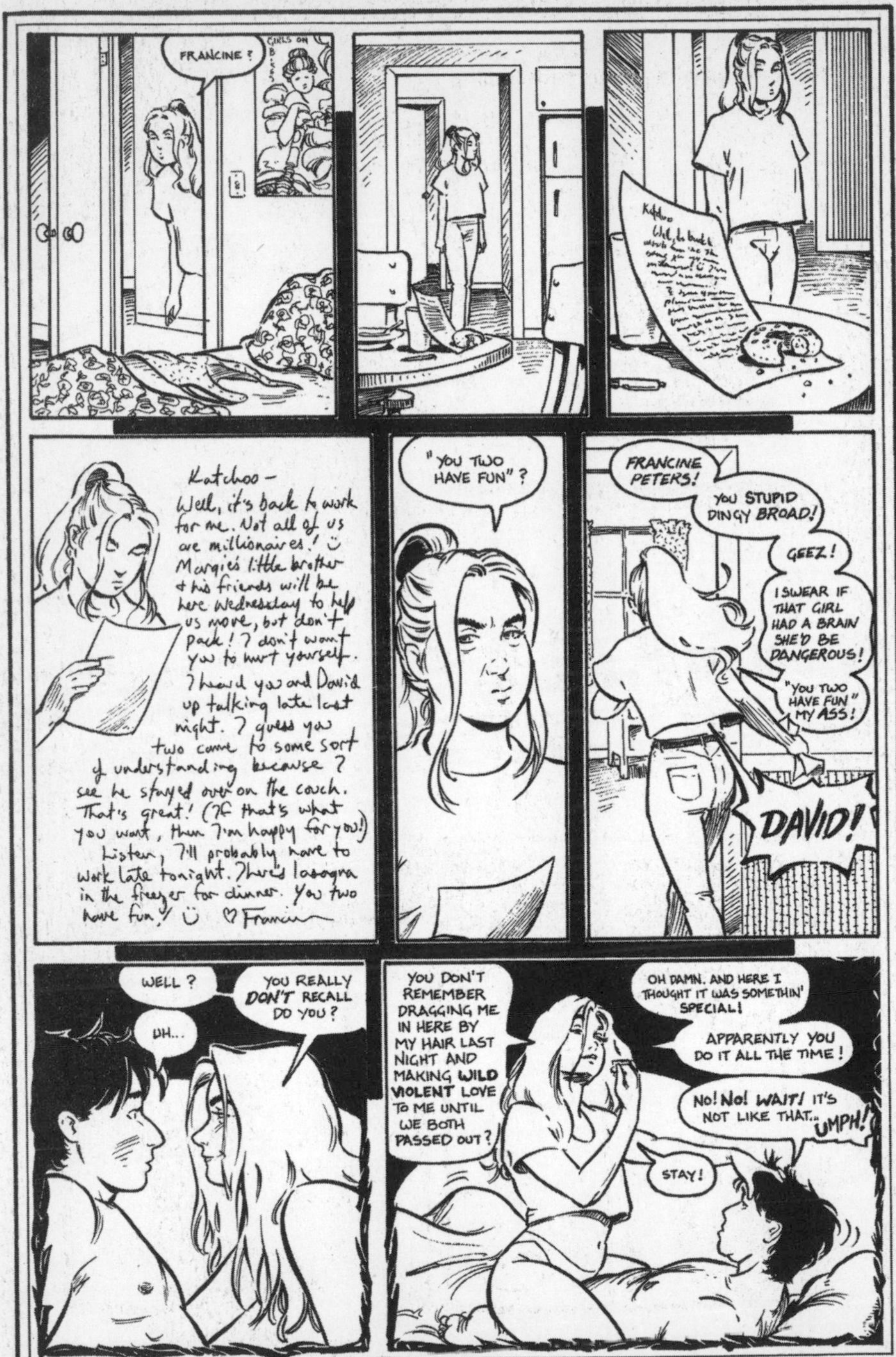
FRANCINE?
GIRLS ON BIKES
Katchoo—
Well, it's back to work for me. Not all of us are millionaires! ☺ Margie's little brother & his friends will be here Wednesday to help us move, but don't pack! I don't want you to hurt yourself.
I heard you and David up talking late last night. I guess you two came to some sort of understanding because I see he stayed over on the couch. That's great! (If that's what you want, then I'm happy for you!)
Listen, I'll probably have to work late tonight. There's lasagna in the freezer for dinner. You two have fun! ☺ ♡ Francine
"YOU TWO HAVE FUN"?
FRANCINE PETERS!
YOU STUPID DINGY BROAD!
GEEZ!
I SWEAR IF THAT GIRL HAD A BRAIN SHE'D BE DANGEROUS!
"YOU TWO HAVE FUN" MY ASS!
DAVID!
WELL?
UH...
YOU REALLY DON'T RECALL DO YOU?
YOU DON'T REMEMBER DRAGGING ME IN HERE BY MY HAIR LAST NIGHT AND MAKING WILD VIOLENT LOVE TO ME UNTIL WE BOTH PASSED OUT?
OH DAMN. AND HERE I THOUGHT IT WAS SOMETHIN' SPECIAL!
APPARENTLY YOU DO IT ALL THE TIME!
NO! NO! WAIT! IT'S NOT LIKE THAT... UMPH!
STAY!

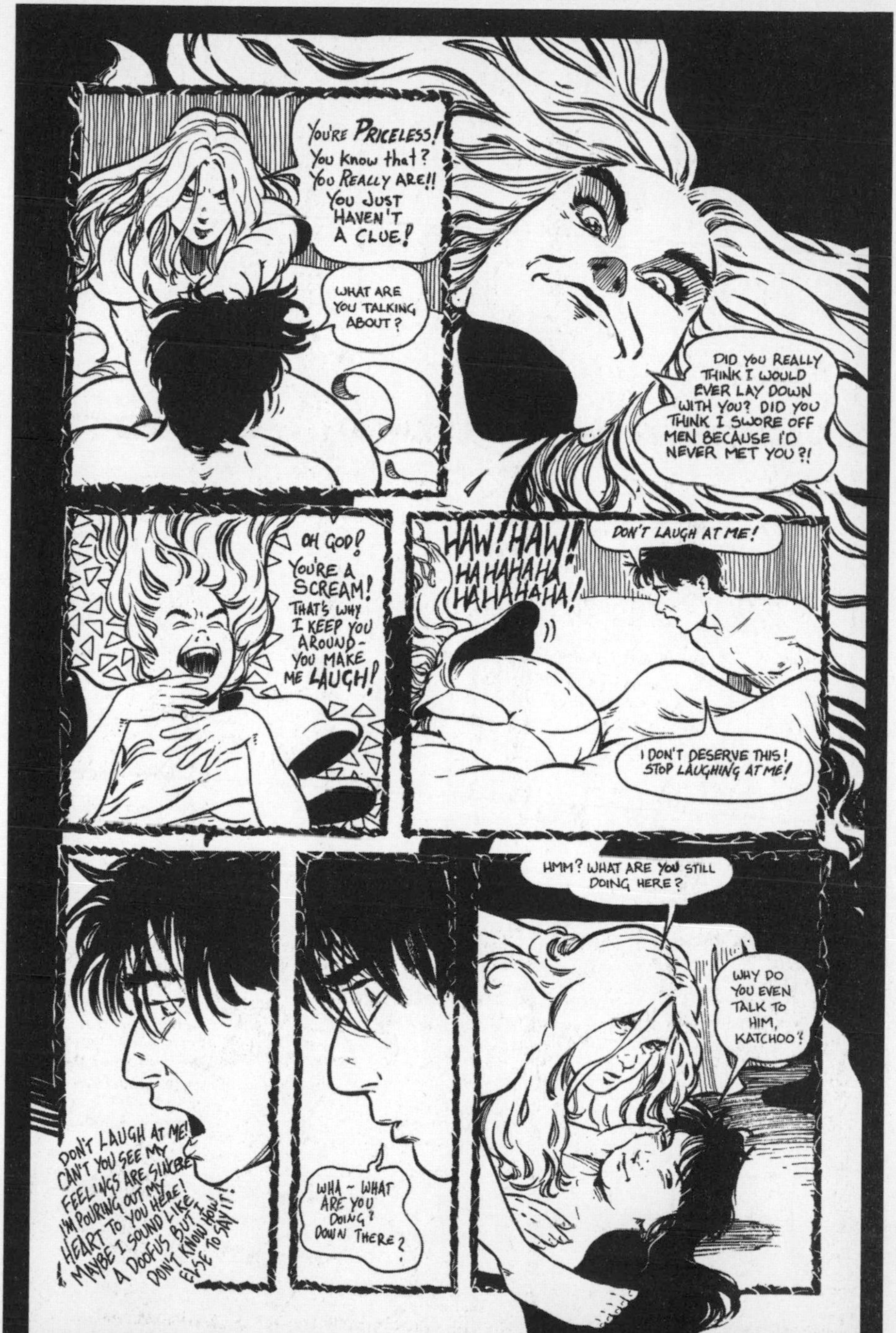
You're PRICELESS! You know that? You REALLY ARE!! You JUST HAVEN'T A CLUE!
WHAT ARE YOU TALKING ABOUT?
DID YOU REALLY THINK I WOULD EVER LAY DOWN WITH YOU? DID YOU THINK I SWORE OFF MEN BECAUSE I'D NEVER MET YOU?!
OH GOD! You're A SCREAM! THAT'S WHY I KEEP YOU AROUND - YOU MAKE ME LAUGH!
HAW! HAW! HAHAHAHA HAHAHAHA!
DON'T LAUGH AT ME!
I DON'T DESERVE THIS! STOP LAUGHING AT ME!
DON'T LAUGH AT ME! CAN'T YOU SEE MY FEELINGS ARE SINCERE! I'M POURING OUT MY HEART TO YOU HERE! MAYBE I SOUND LIKE A DOOFUS BUT I DON'T KNOW HOW ELSE TO SAY IT!
WHA ~ WHAT ARE YOU DOING? DOWN THERE?
HMM? WHAT ARE YOU STILL DOING HERE?
WHY DO YOU EVEN TALK TO HIM, KATCHOO?

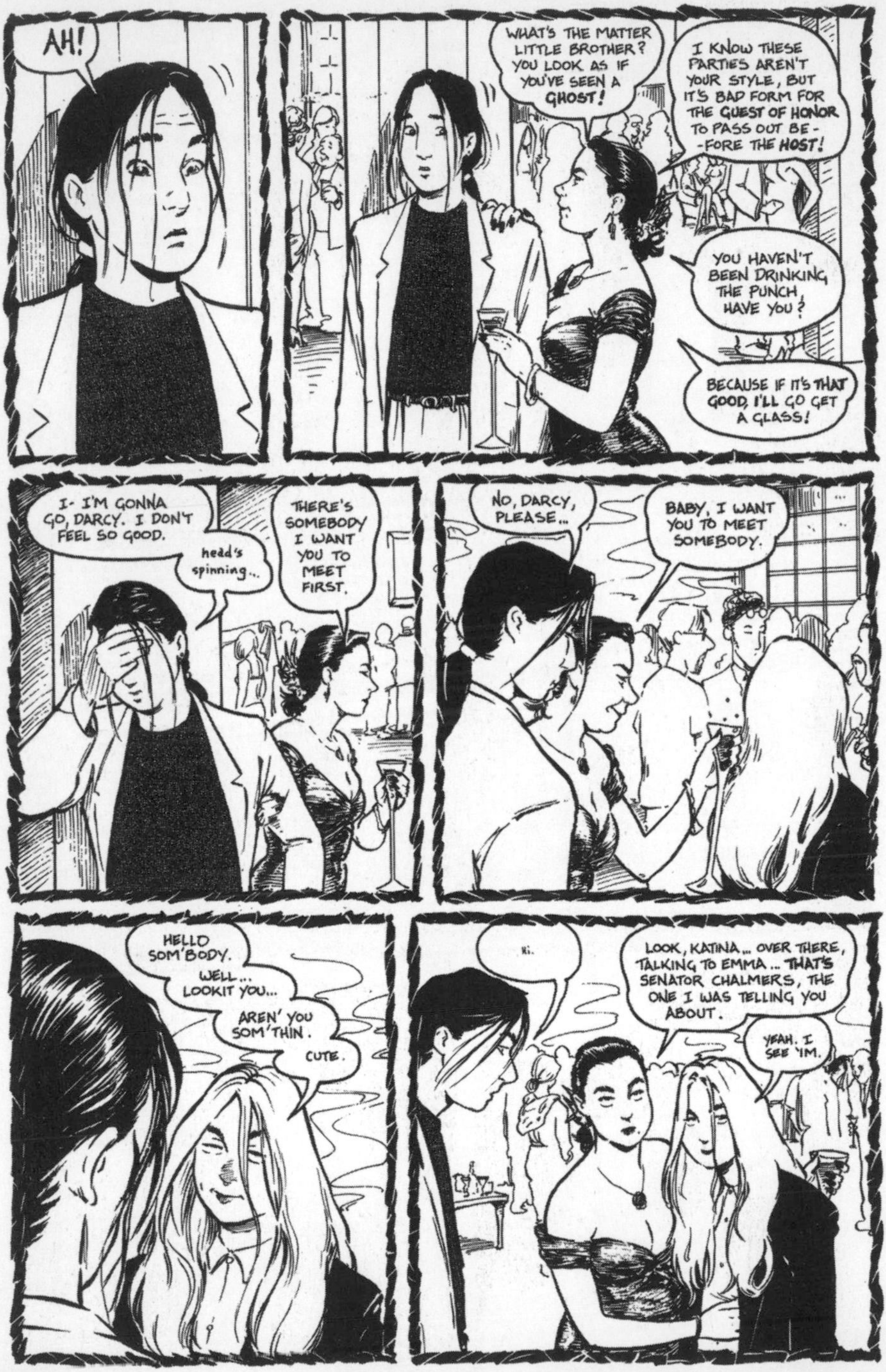
AH!
WHAT'S THE MATTER LITTLE BROTHER? YOU LOOK AS IF YOU'VE SEEN A GHOST!
I KNOW THESE PARTIES AREN'T YOUR STYLE, BUT IT'S BAD FORM FOR THE GUEST OF HONOR TO PASS OUT BE--FORE THE HOST!
YOU HAVEN'T BEEN DRINKING THE PUNCH, HAVE YOU?
BECAUSE IF IT'S THAT GOOD, I'LL GO GET A GLASS!
I- I'M GONNA GO, DARCY. I DON'T FEEL SO GOOD.
head's spinning...
THERE'S SOMEBODY I WANT YOU TO MEET FIRST.
NO, DARCY, PLEASE...
BABY, I WANT YOU TO MEET SOMEBODY.
HELLO SOM'BODY.
WELL... LOOKIT YOU...
AREN' YOU SOM'THIN.
CUTE.
hi.
LOOK, KATINA... OVER THERE, TALKING TO EMMA... THAT'S SENATOR CHALMERS, THE ONE I WAS TELLING YOU ABOUT.
YEAH. I SEE 'IM.

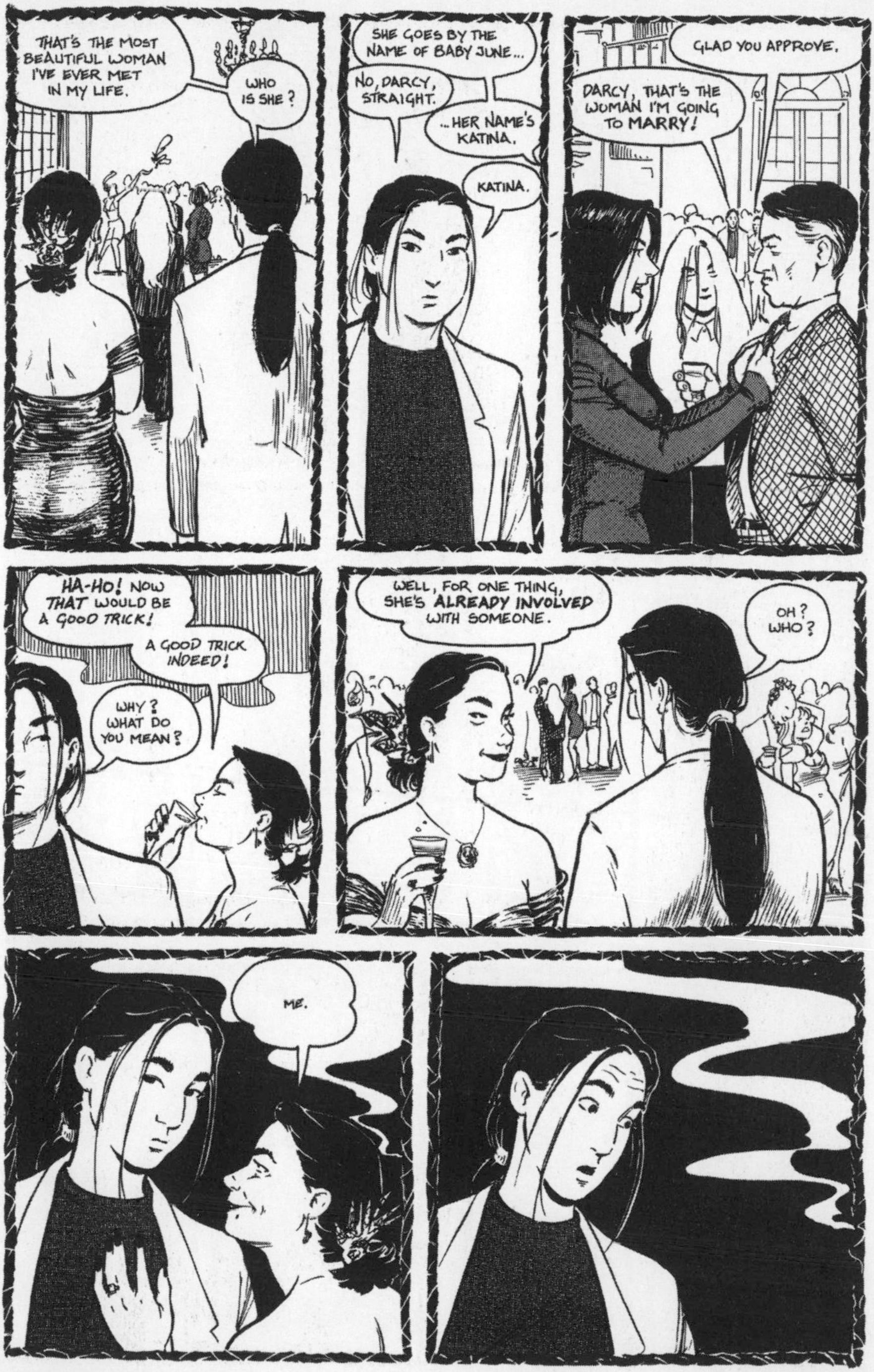
THAT'S THE MOST BEAUTIFUL WOMAN I'VE EVER MET IN MY LIFE.
WHO IS SHE ?
SHE GOES BY THE NAME OF BABY JUNE...
NO, DARCY, STRAIGHT.
...HER NAME'S KATINA.
KATINA.
GLAD YOU APPROVE.
DARCY, THAT'S THE WOMAN I'M GOING TO MARRY!
HA-HO! NOW THAT WOULD BE A GOOD TRICK!
A GOOD TRICK INDEED!
WHY? WHAT DO YOU MEAN?
WELL, FOR ONE THING, SHE'S ALREADY INVOLVED WITH SOMEONE.
OH? WHO?
ME.

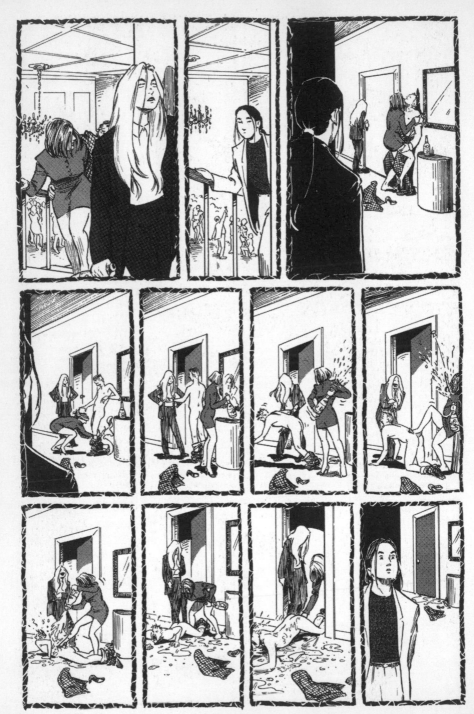

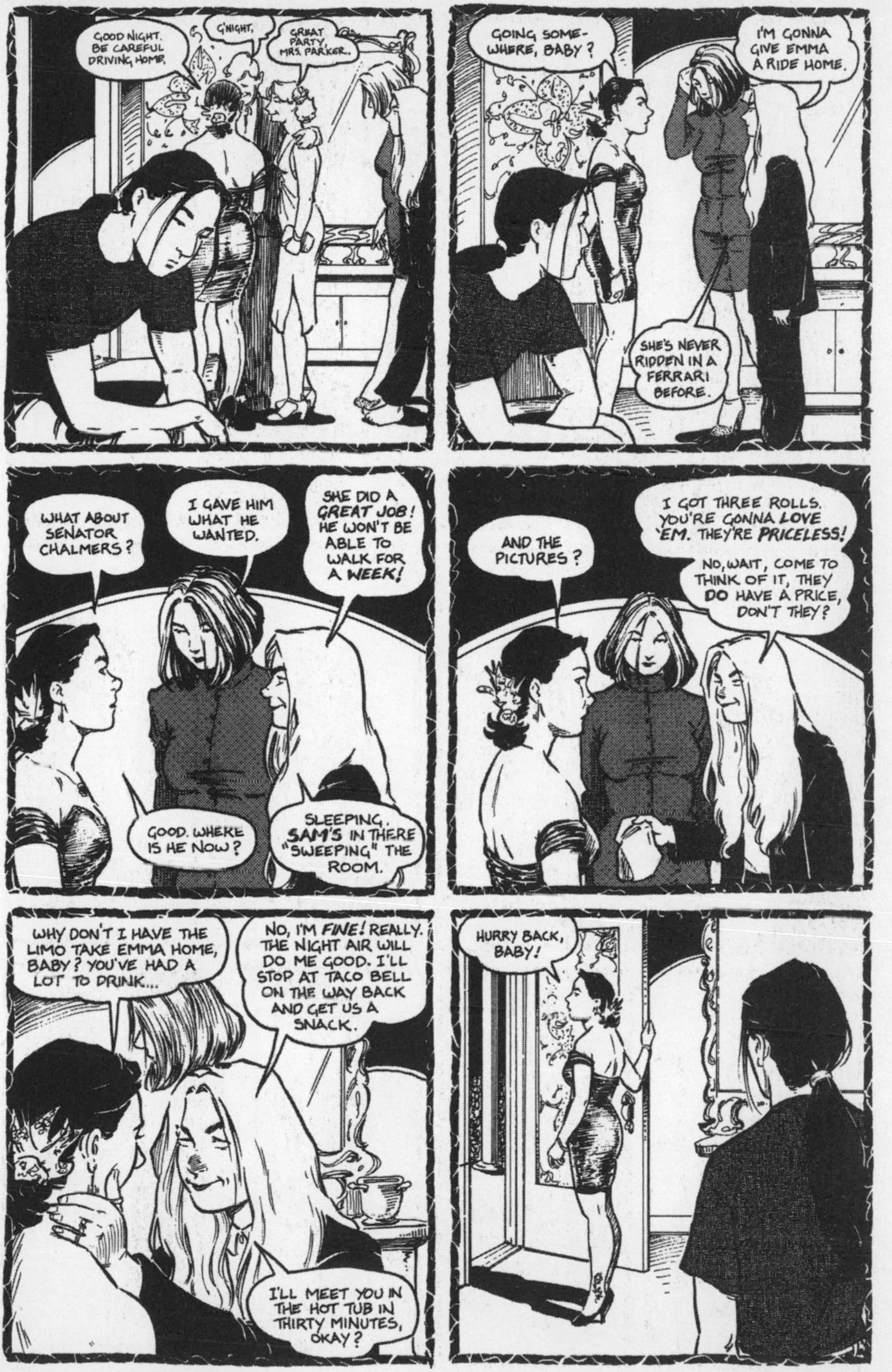
GOOD NIGHT. BE CAREFUL DRIVING HOME.
G'NIGHT.
GREAT PARTY, MRS. PARKER.
GOING SOME-WHERE, BABY?
I'M GONNA GIVE EMMA A RIDE HOME.
SHE'S NEVER RIDDEN IN A FERRARI BEFORE.
WHAT ABOUT SENATOR CHALMERS?
I GAVE HIM WHAT HE WANTED.
SHE DID A GREAT JOB! HE WON'T BE ABLE TO WALK FOR A WEEK!
GOOD. WHERE IS HE NOW?
SLEEPING. SAM'S IN THERE "SWEEPING" THE ROOM.
AND THE PICTURES?
I GOT THREE ROLLS. YOU'RE GONNA LOVE 'EM. THEY'RE PRICELESS!
NO, WAIT, COME TO THINK OF IT, THEY DO HAVE A PRICE, DON'T THEY?
WHY DON'T I HAVE THE LIMO TAKE EMMA HOME, BABY? YOU'VE HAD A LOT TO DRINK...
NO, I'M FINE! REALLY. THE NIGHT AIR WILL DO ME GOOD. I'LL STOP AT TACO BELL ON THE WAY BACK AND GET US A SNACK.
I'LL MEET YOU IN THE HOT TUB IN THIRTY MINUTES, OKAY?
HURRY BACK, BABY!

316

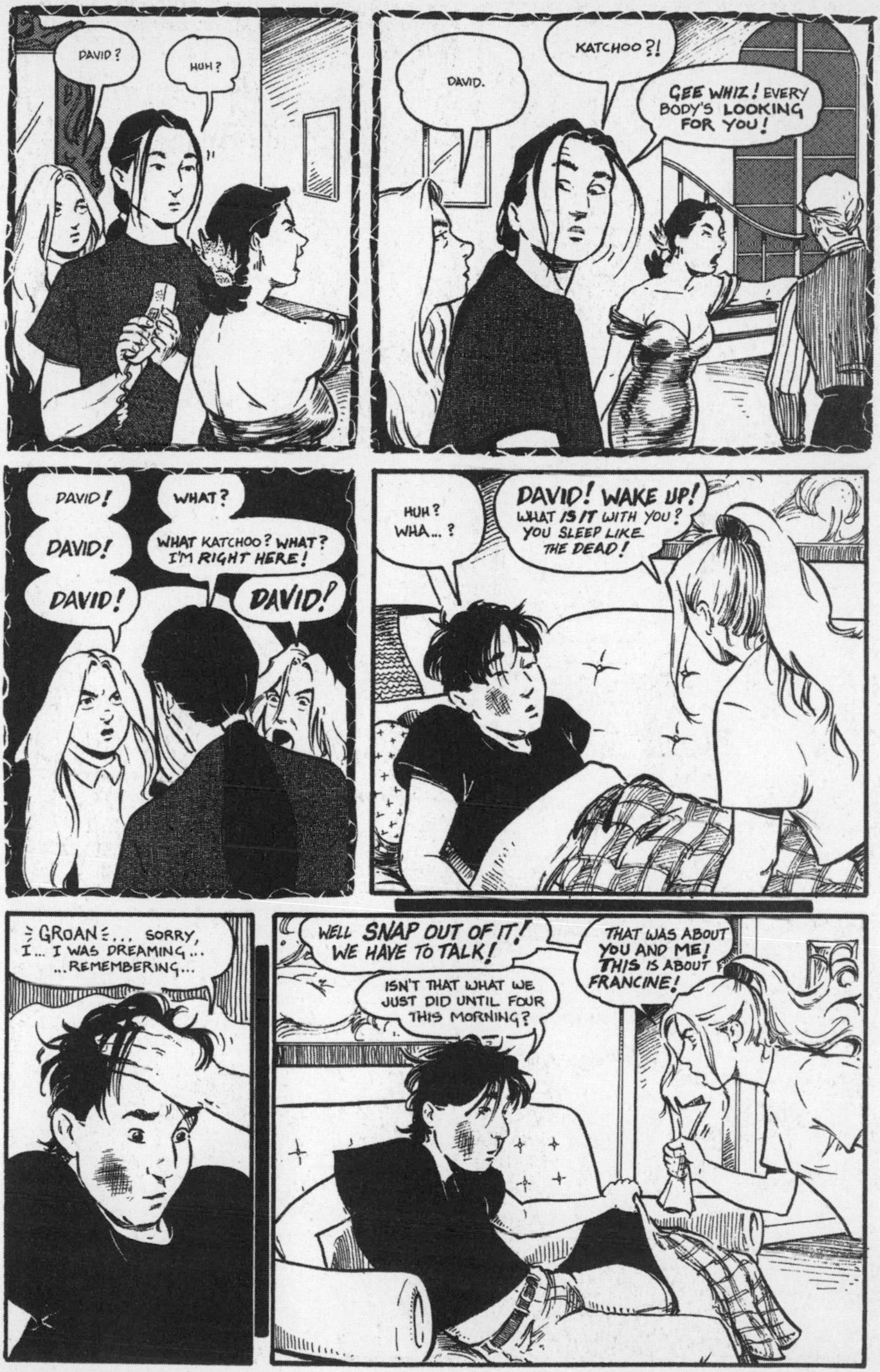
DAVID?
HUH?
DAVID.
KATCHOO?!
GEE WHIZ! EVERY BODY'S LOOKING FOR YOU!
DAVID!
DAVID!
DAVID!
WHAT?
WHAT KATCHOO? WHAT? I'M RIGHT HERE!
DAVID!
HUH? WHA...?
DAVID! WAKE UP! WHAT IS IT WITH YOU? YOU SLEEP LIKE THE DEAD!
≡GROAN≡... SORRY, I... I WAS DREAMING... ...REMEMBERING...
WELL SNAP OUT OF IT! WE HAVE TO TALK!
ISN'T THAT WHAT WE JUST DID UNTIL FOUR THIS MORNING?
THAT WAS ABOUT YOU AND ME! THIS IS ABOUT FRANCINE!

318

319

All of my life
I was waiting for you
How is it we never met?
Here in the latter days
Time on my own
I find too much to regret.
All of the time I spend
Thinking of you
Nothing to say but I call.
Over and Over
It plays on my mind
How come you come and you go?
How is it happening only to me?
Now after all of the time we spent
I was careless and made a slip
Suddenly your love is
Too much to lose
Now I've fallen in love with you.
Were you waiting for
My heart to break?
Though I've fallen
In love with you
I have fallen in love
Too late.

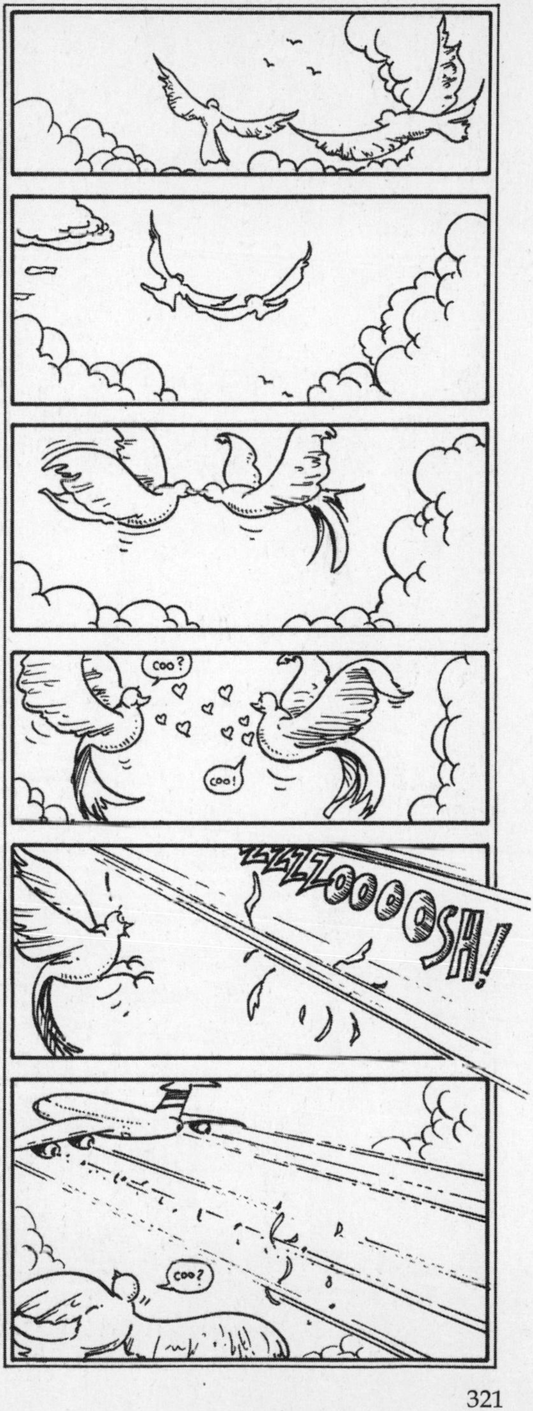
COO?
COO!
!
ZZZZZOOOOSH!
COO?

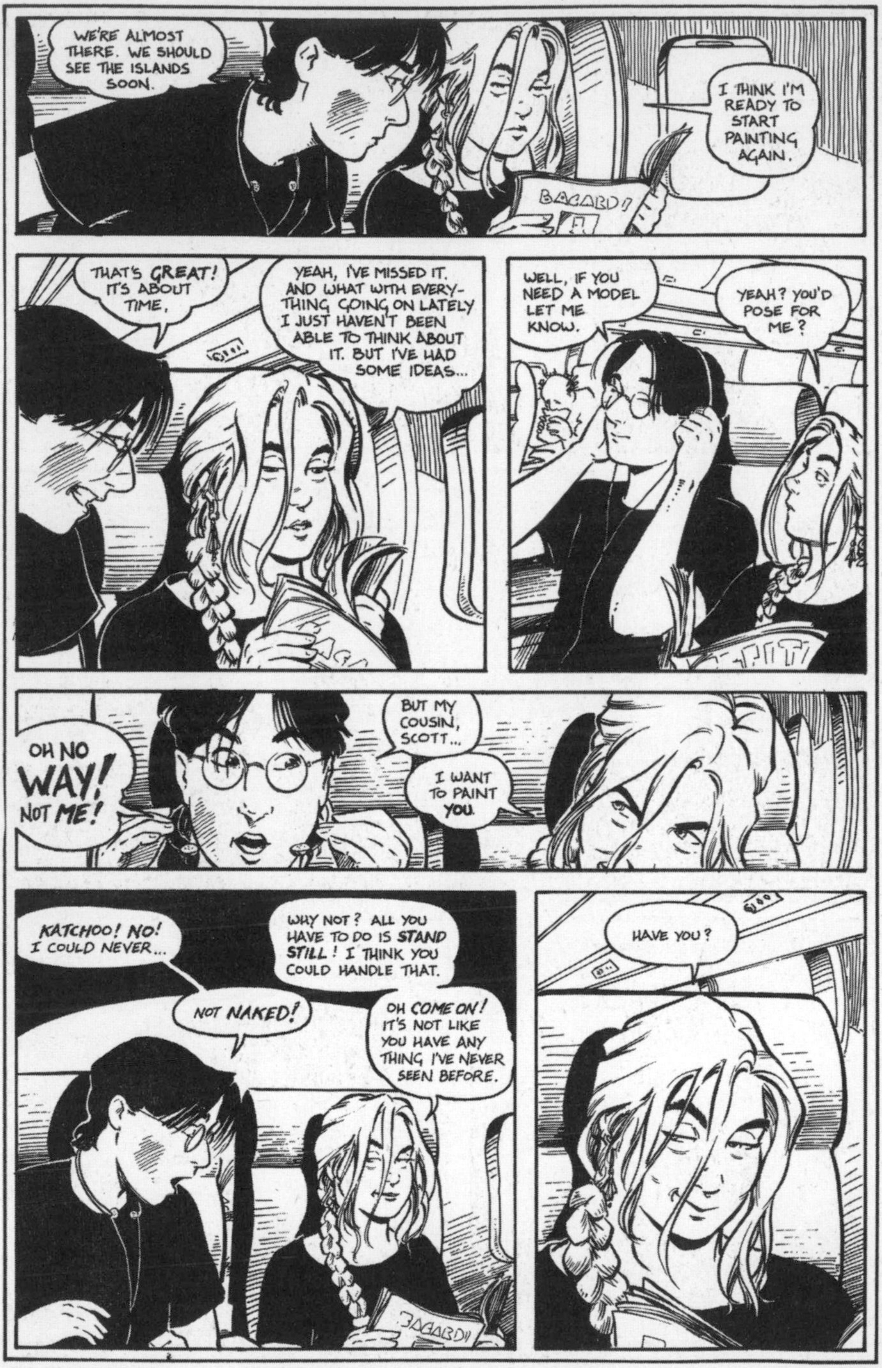
WE'RE ALMOST THERE. WE SHOULD SEE THE ISLANDS SOON.
I THINK I'M READY TO START PAINTING AGAIN.
BACARDI
THAT'S GREAT! IT'S ABOUT TIME.
YEAH, I'VE MISSED IT. AND WHAT WITH EVERYTHING GOING ON LATELY I JUST HAVEN'T BEEN ABLE TO THINK ABOUT IT. BUT I'VE HAD SOME IDEAS...
WELL, IF YOU NEED A MODEL LET ME KNOW.
YEAH? YOU'D POSE FOR ME?
BUT MY COUSIN, SCOTT...
I WANT TO PAINT YOU.
OH NO WAY! NOT ME!
KATCHOO! NO! I COULD NEVER...
WHY NOT? ALL YOU HAVE TO DO IS STAND STILL! I THINK YOU COULD HANDLE THAT.
NOT NAKED!
OH COME ON! IT'S NOT LIKE YOU HAVE ANY THING I'VE NEVER SEEN BEFORE.
HAVE YOU?

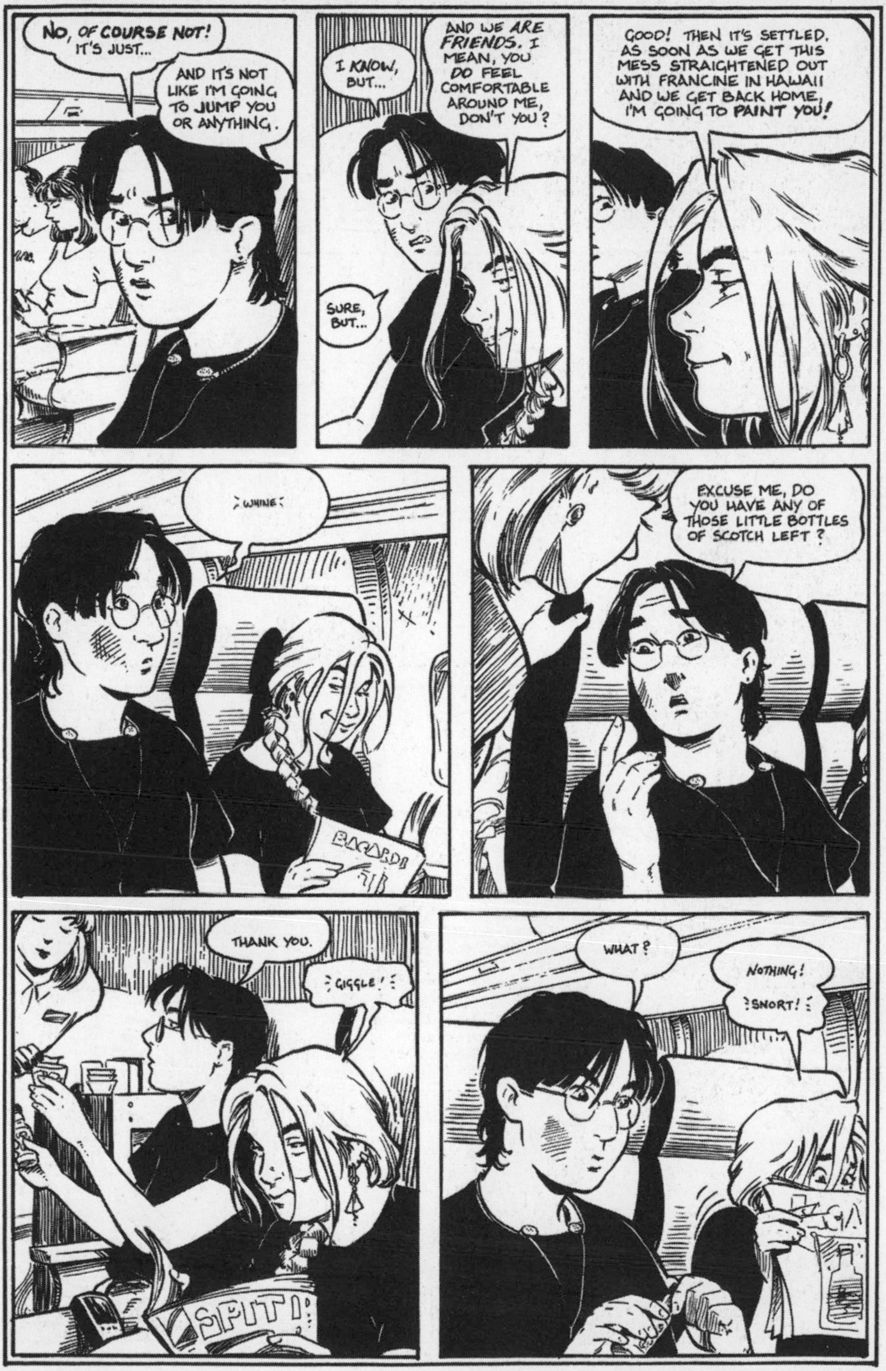
NO, OF COURSE NOT! IT'S JUST...
AND IT'S NOT LIKE I'M GOING TO JUMP YOU OR ANYTHING.
I KNOW, BUT...
AND WE ARE FRIENDS. I MEAN, YOU DO FEEL COMFORTABLE AROUND ME, DON'T YOU?
SURE, BUT...
GOOD! THEN IT'S SETTLED. AS SOON AS WE GET THIS MESS STRAIGHTENED OUT WITH FRANCINE IN HAWAII AND WE GET BACK HOME, I'M GOING TO PAINT YOU!
WHINE
BACARDI
EXCUSE ME, DO YOU HAVE ANY OF THOSE LITTLE BOTTLES OF SCOTCH LEFT?
THANK YOU.
GIGGLE!
SPIT!
WHAT?
NOTHING!
SNORT!

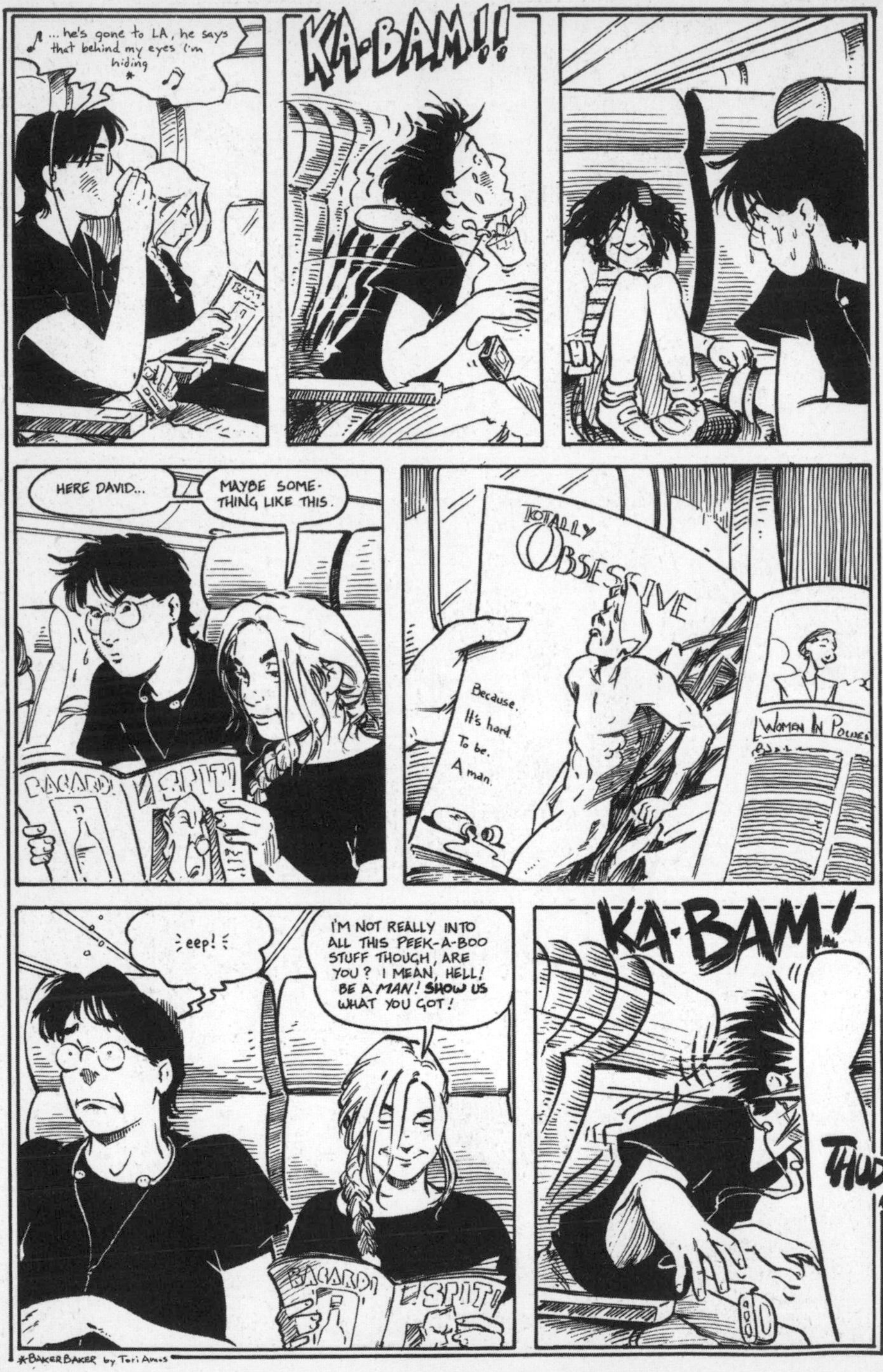
... he's gone to LA, he says that behind my eyes i'm hiding *
KA-BAM!!
HERE DAVID...
MAYBE SOMETHING LIKE THIS.
TOTALLY OBSESSIVE
Because. It's hard. To be. A man.
WOMEN IN POLITICS
BACARDI
SPIT!
eep!
I'M NOT REALLY INTO ALL THIS PEEK-A-BOO STUFF THOUGH, ARE YOU? I MEAN, HELL! BE A MAN! SHOW US WHAT YOU GOT!
BACARDI
SPIT!
KA-BAM!
THUD!
*BAKER BAKER by Tori Amos

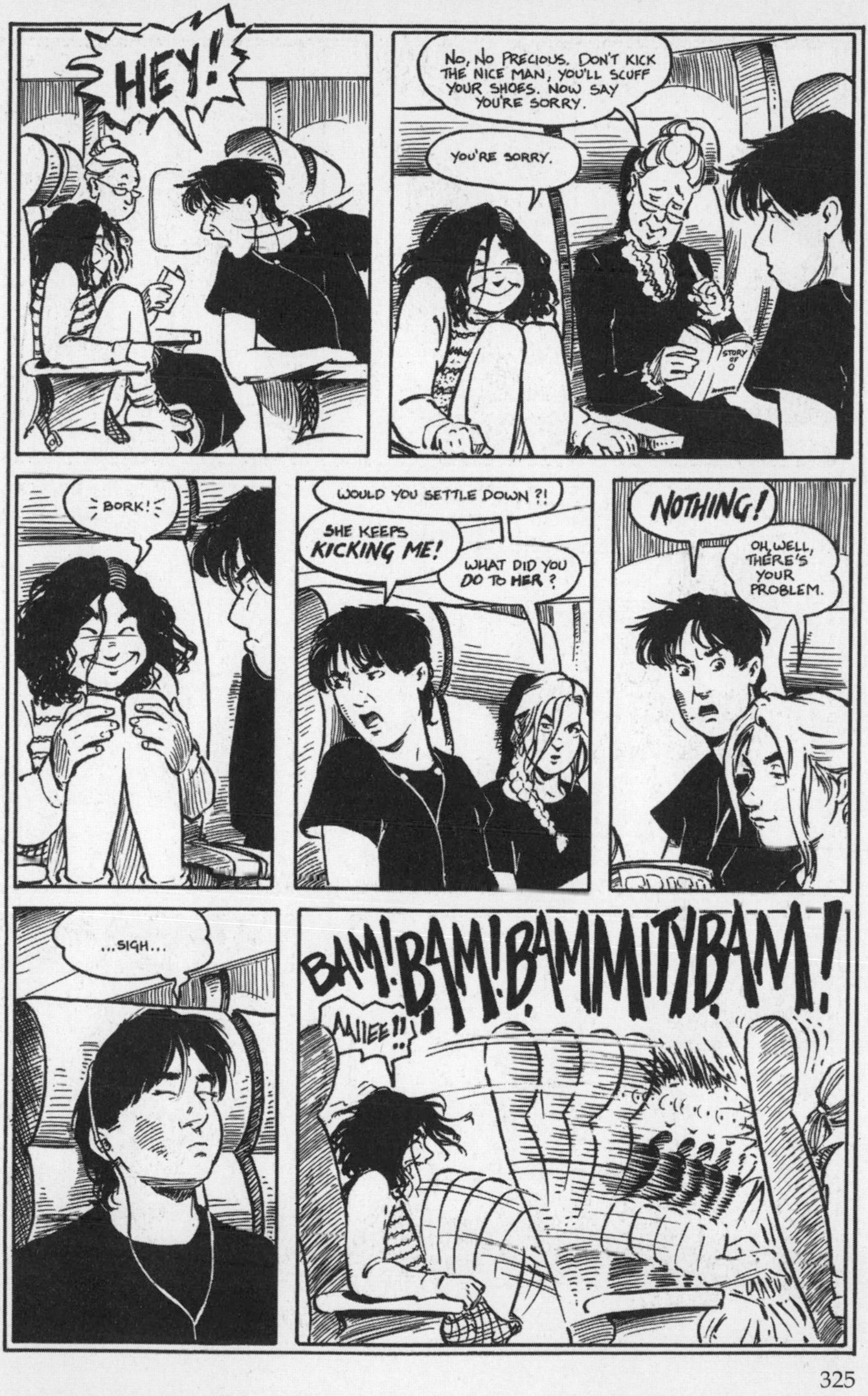
HEY!
No, No Precious. Don't kick the nice man, you'll scuff your shoes. Now say you're sorry.
You're sorry.
BORK!
Would you settle down?!
She keeps KICKING ME!
What did you DO TO HER?
NOTHING!
Oh, well, there's your problem.
...SIGH...
BAM! BAM! BAMMITYBAM!
AAIIEE!!

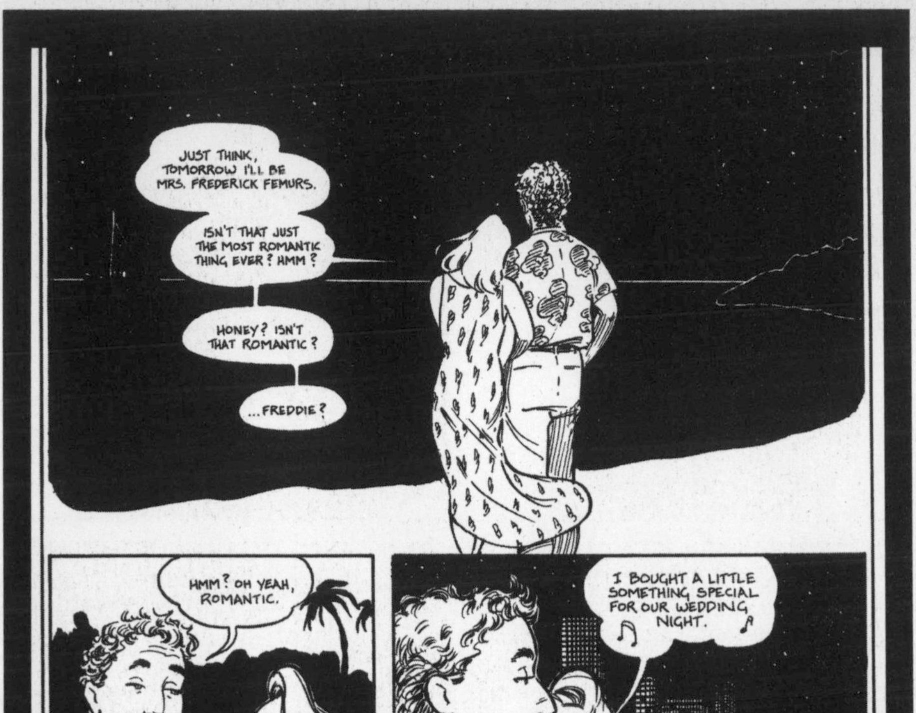

JUST THINK, TOMORROW I'LL BE MRS. FREDERICK FEMURS.
ISN'T THAT JUST THE MOST ROMANTIC THING EVER? HMM?
HONEY? ISN'T THAT ROMANTIC?
...FREDDIE?
HMM? OH YEAH, ROMANTIC.
I BOUGHT A LITTLE SOMETHING SPECIAL FOR OUR WEDDING NIGHT.
...SIGH... YEAH? DOES IT REQUIRE BATTERIES?
OH YOU! YOU'RE AWFUL!
SLAP!
HEY! IF IT'S NOT BANNED IN SEVEN STATES IM NOT INTERESTED.
WELL, WHEN YOU SEE IT ON ME YOU CAN TELL ME IF IT SHOULD BE BANNED OR NOT.
I THINK I LIKE IT ALREADY.

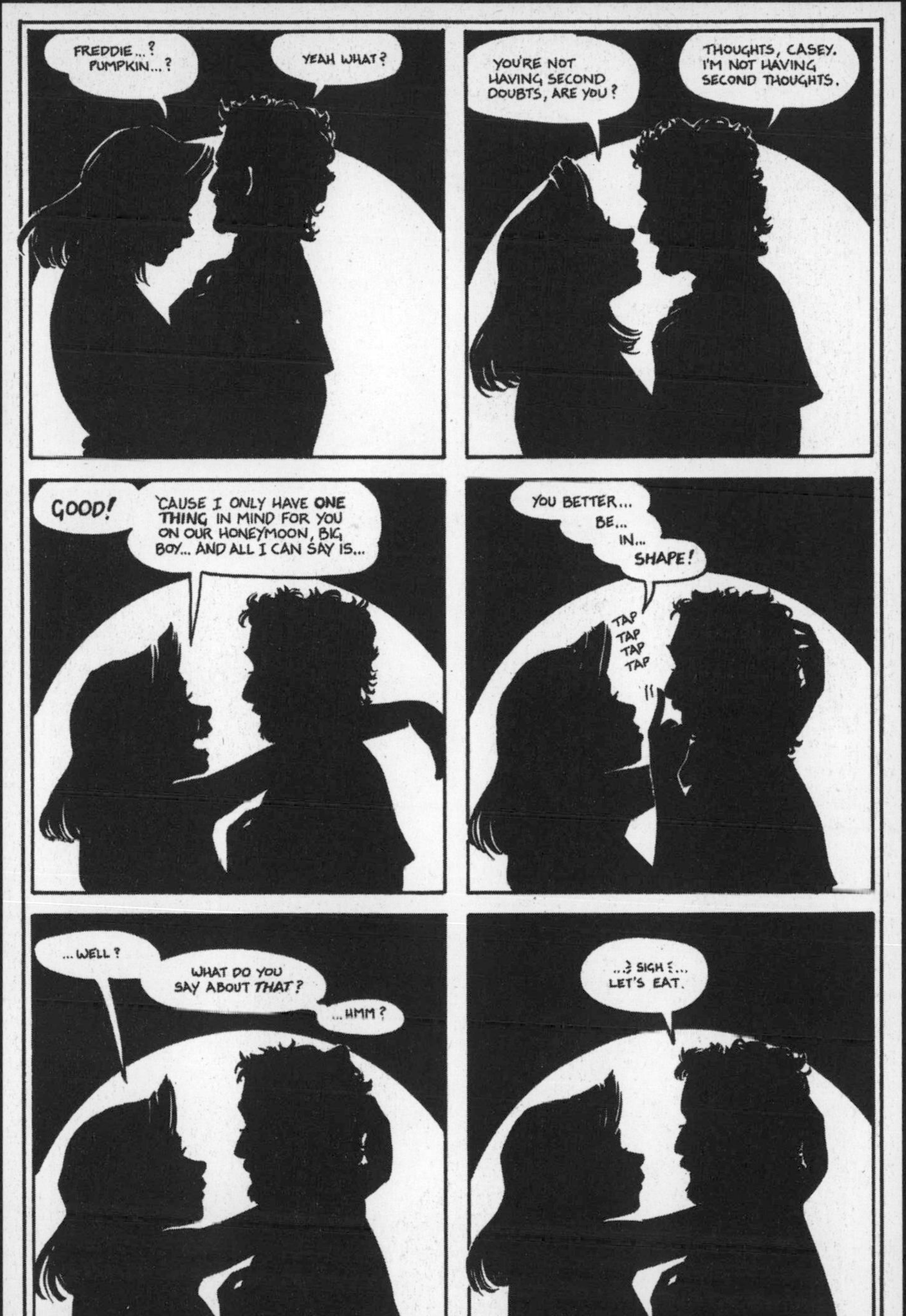
FREDDIE...? PUMPKIN...?
YEAH WHAT?
YOU'RE NOT HAVING SECOND DOUBTS, ARE YOU?
THOUGHTS, CASEY. I'M NOT HAVING SECOND THOUGHTS.
GOOD!
'CAUSE I ONLY HAVE ONE THING IN MIND FOR YOU ON OUR HONEYMOON, BIG BOY... AND ALL I CAN SAY IS...
YOU BETTER... BE... IN... SHAPE!
TAP TAP TAP TAP
...WELL?
WHAT DO YOU SAY ABOUT THAT?
...HMM?
...⟩ SIGH ⟨... LET'S EAT.

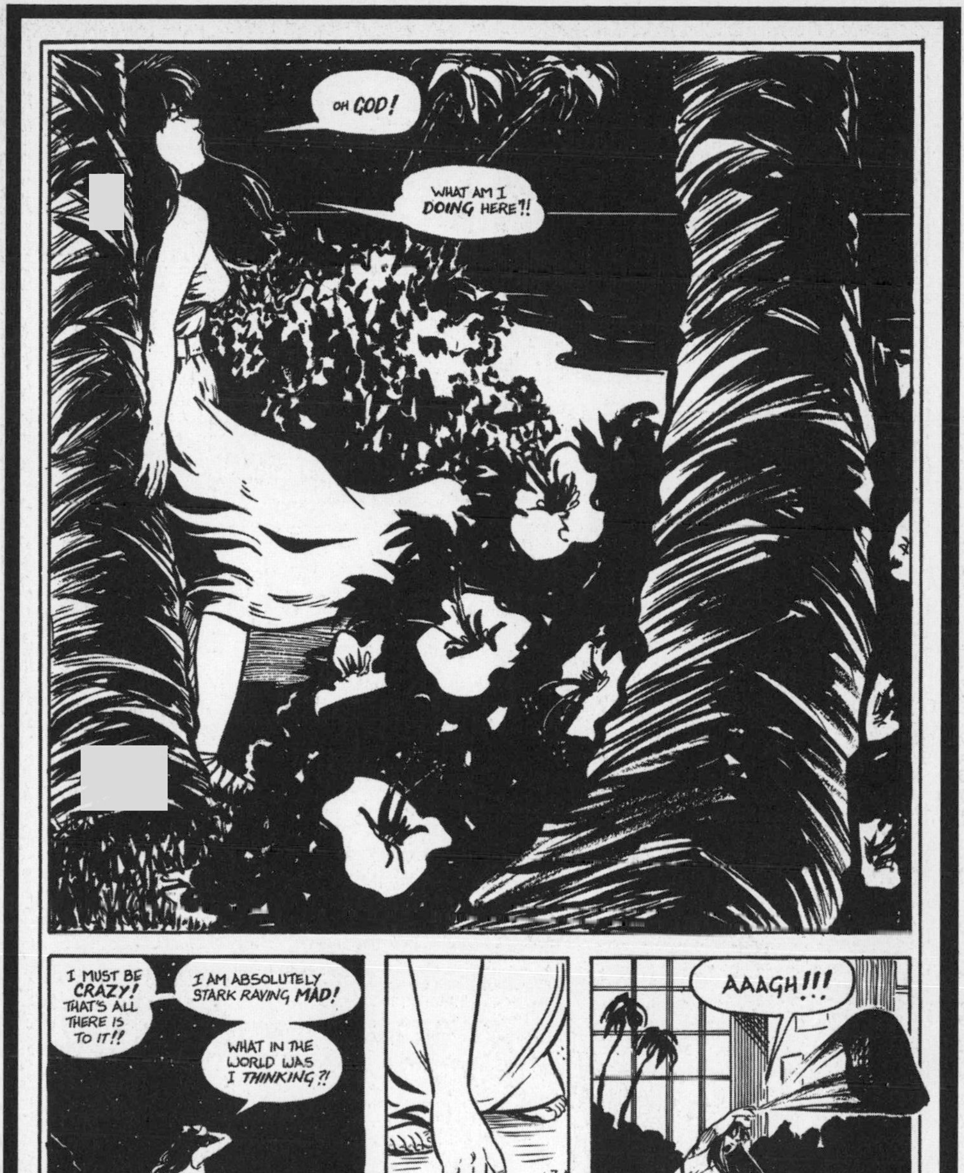
OH GOD!
WHAT AM I DOING HERE?!!
I MUST BE CRAZY! THAT'S ALL THERE IS TO IT!!
I AM ABSOLUTELY STARK RAVING MAD!
WHAT IN THE WORLD WAS I THINKING?!
AAAGH!!!

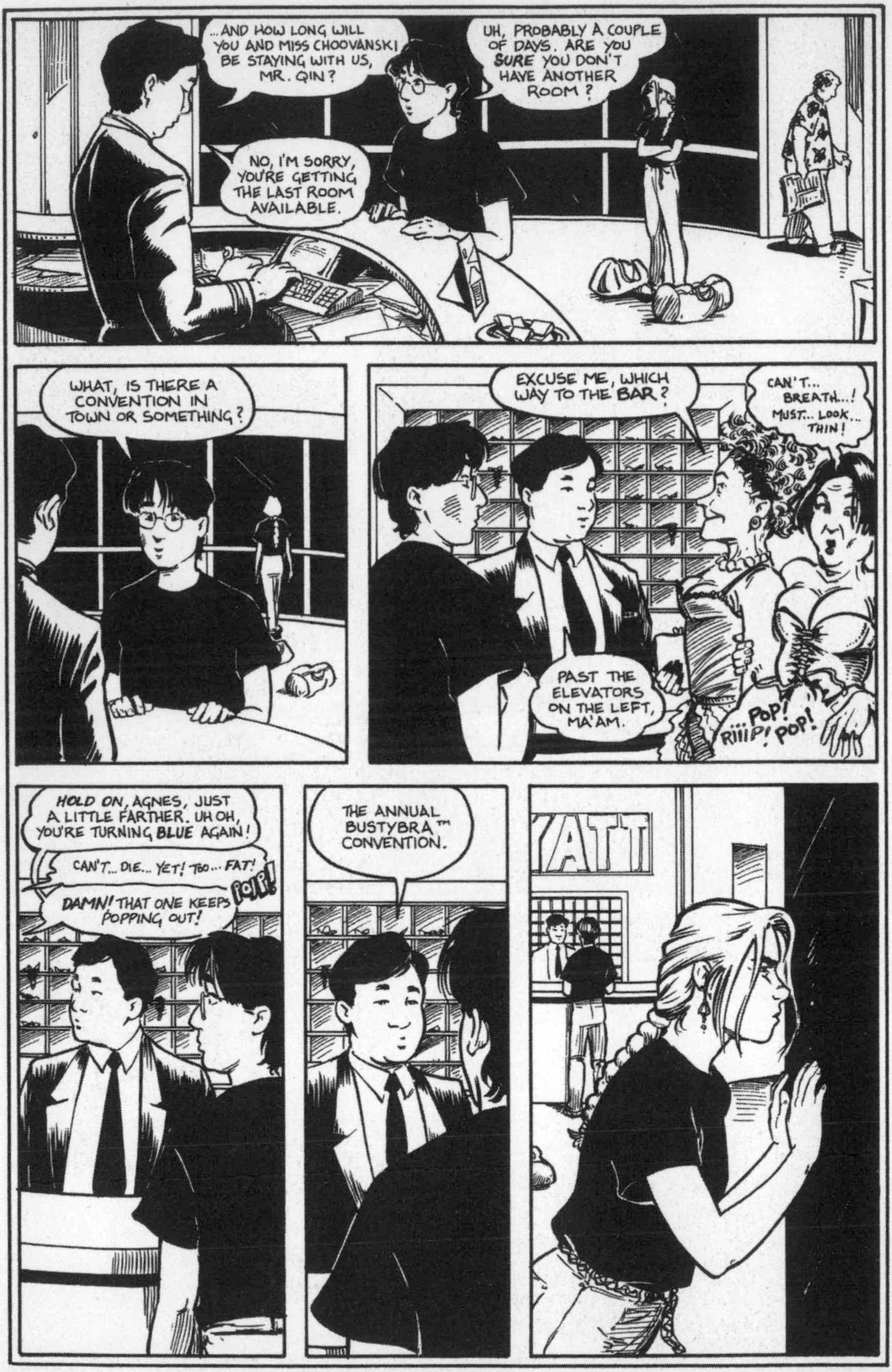
...AND HOW LONG WILL YOU AND MISS CHOOVANSKI BE STAYING WITH US, MR. QIN?
UH, PROBABLY A COUPLE OF DAYS. ARE YOU SURE YOU DON'T HAVE ANOTHER ROOM?
NO, I'M SORRY, YOU'RE GETTING THE LAST ROOM AVAILABLE.
WHAT, IS THERE A CONVENTION IN TOWN OR SOMETHING?
EXCUSE ME, WHICH WAY TO THE BAR?
CAN'T... BREATH...! MUST... LOOK... THIN!
PAST THE ELEVATORS ON THE LEFT, MA'AM.
...POP! RIIIP! POP!
HOLD ON, AGNES, JUST A LITTLE FARTHER. UH OH, YOU'RE TURNING BLUE AGAIN!
CAN'T... DIE... YET! TOO... FAT!
DAMN! THAT ONE KEEPS POPPING OUT!
POP!
THE ANNUAL BUSTYBRA™ CONVENTION.
YATT

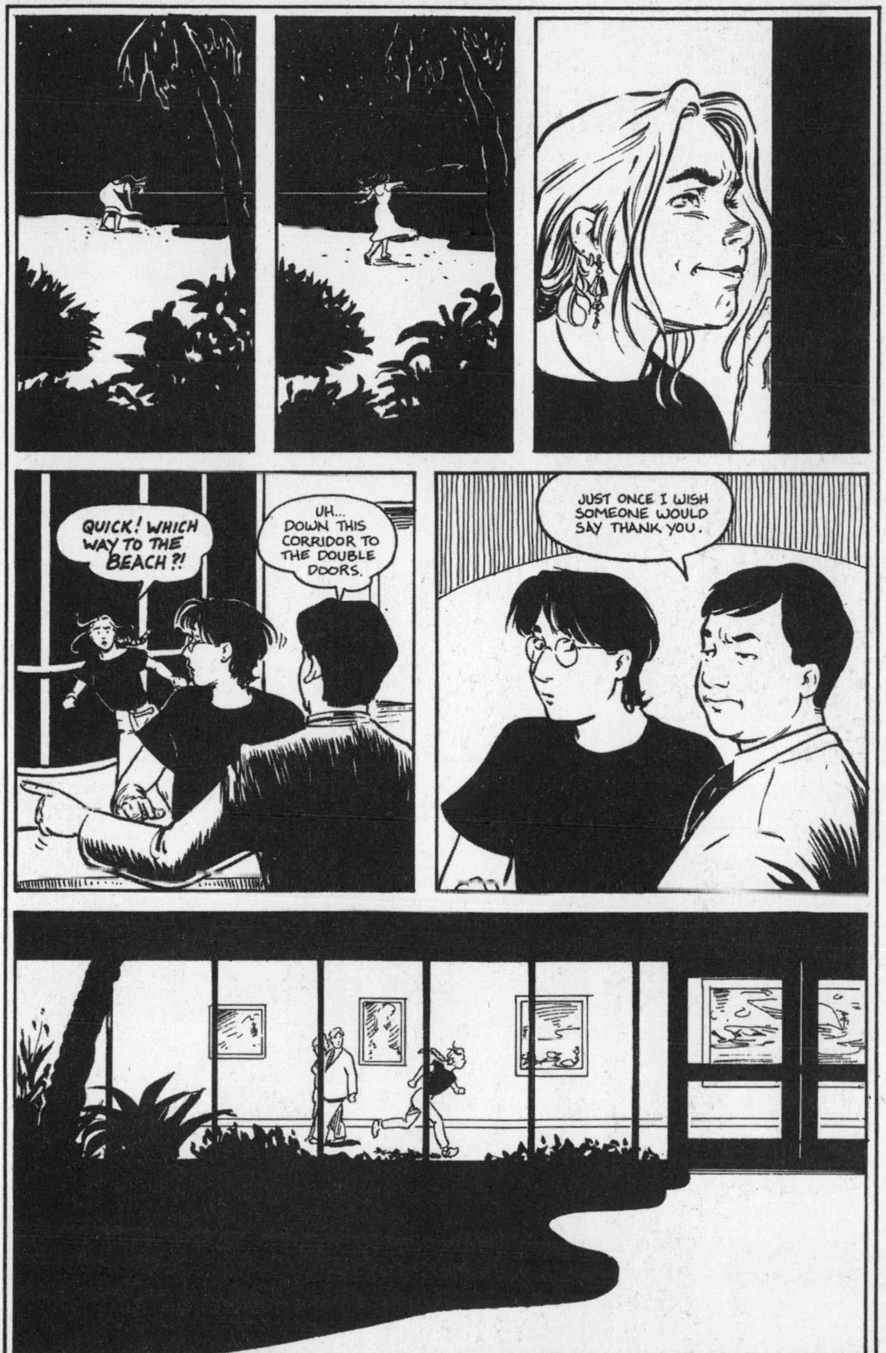
QUICK! WHICH WAY TO THE BEACH?!
UH... DOWN THIS CORRIDOR TO THE DOUBLE DOORS.
JUST ONCE I WISH SOMEONE WOULD SAY THANK YOU.

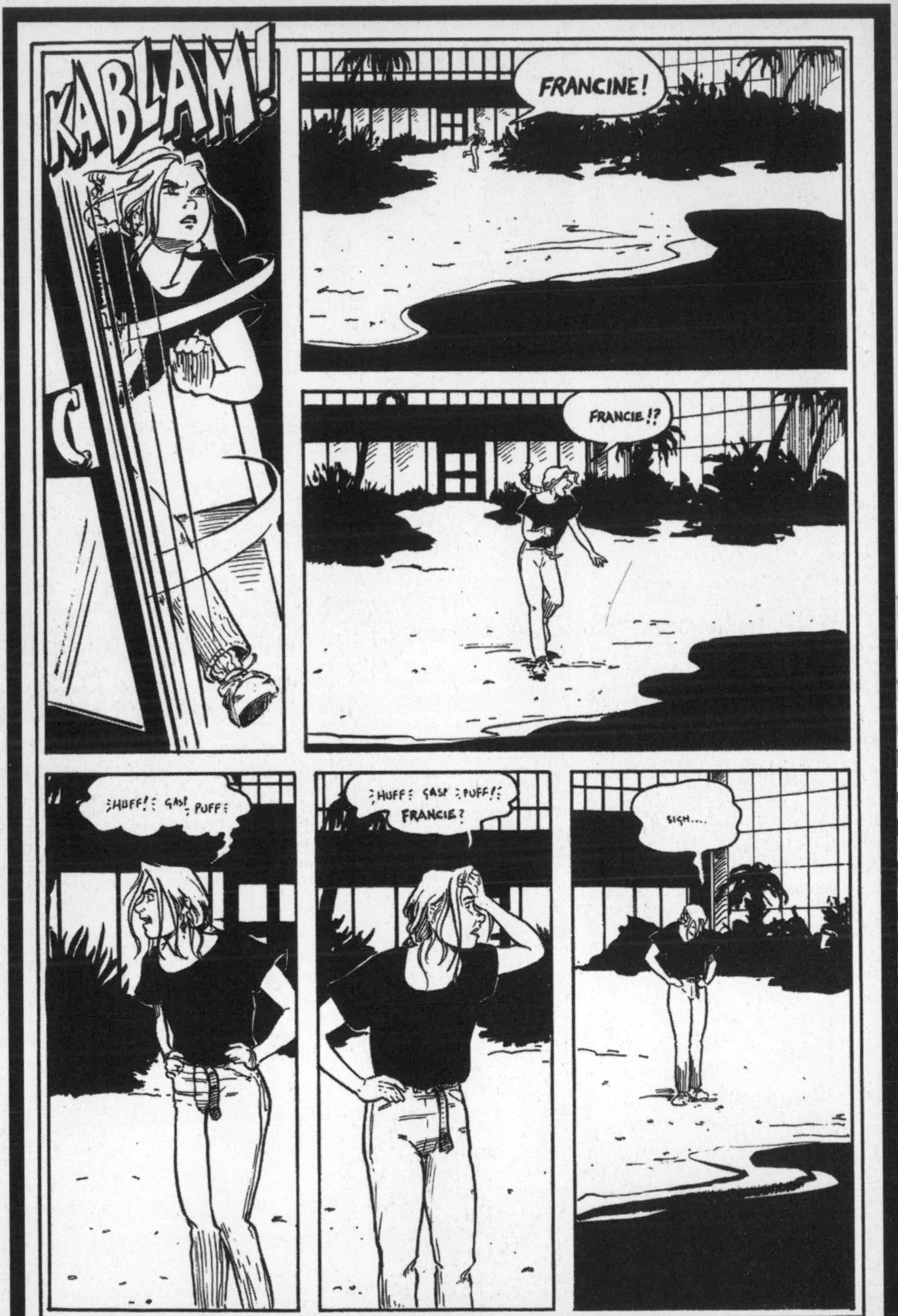
KABLAM!
FRANCINE!
FRANCIE!?
HUFF! GASP! PUFF
HUFF! GASP PUFF!
FRANCIE?
SIGH....

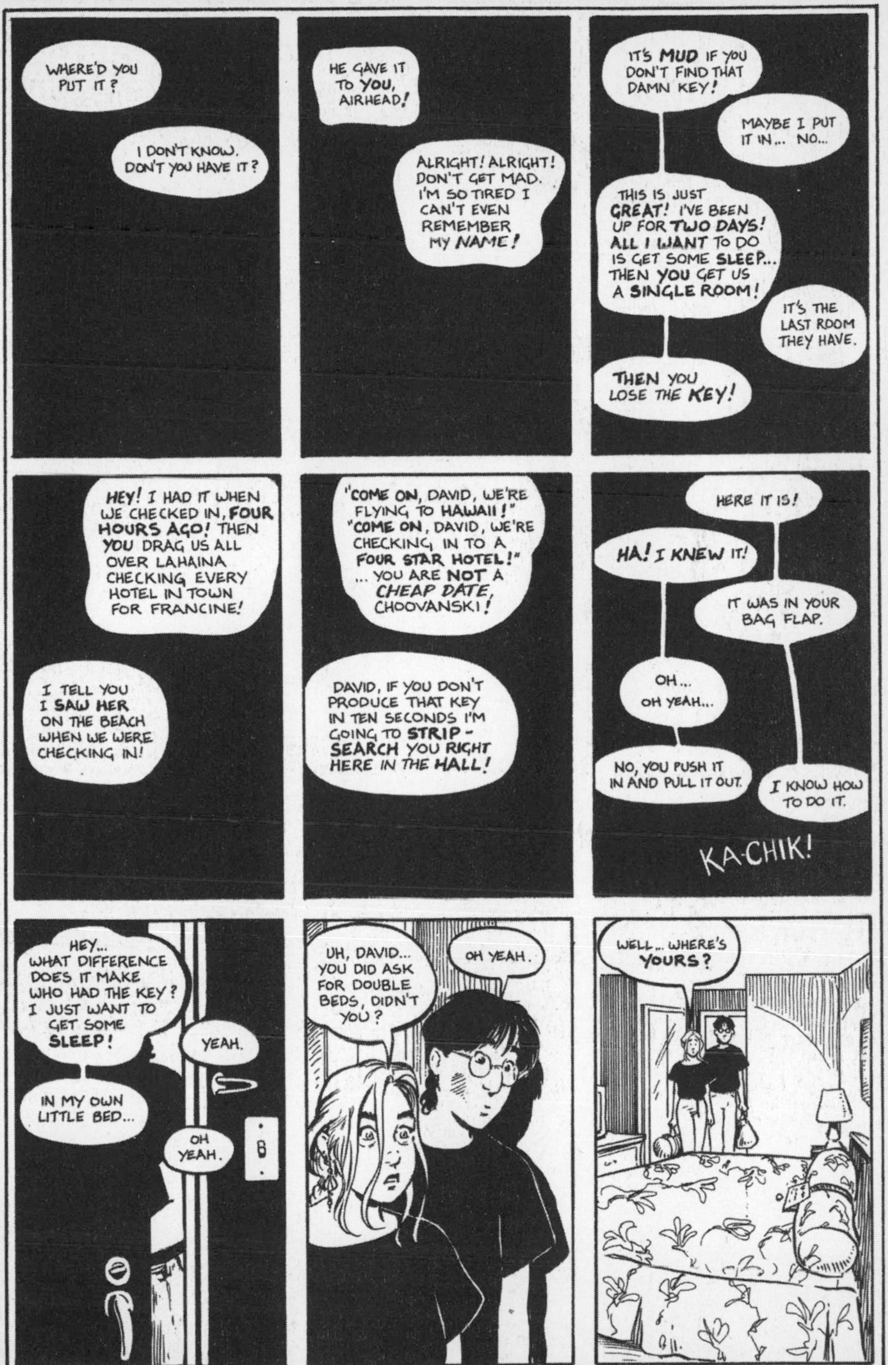
WHERE'D YOU PUT IT?
I DON'T KNOW. DON'T YOU HAVE IT?
HE GAVE IT TO YOU, AIRHEAD!
ALRIGHT! ALRIGHT! DON'T GET MAD. I'M SO TIRED I CAN'T EVEN REMEMBER MY NAME!
IT'S MUD IF YOU DON'T FIND THAT DAMN KEY!
MAYBE I PUT IT IN... NO...
THIS IS JUST GREAT! I'VE BEEN UP FOR TWO DAYS! ALL I WANT TO DO IS GET SOME SLEEP... THEN YOU GET US A SINGLE ROOM!
IT'S THE LAST ROOM THEY HAVE.
THEN YOU LOSE THE KEY!
HEY! I HAD IT WHEN WE CHECKED IN, FOUR HOURS AGO! THEN YOU DRAG US ALL OVER LAHAINA CHECKING EVERY HOTEL IN TOWN FOR FRANCINE!
I TELL YOU I SAW HER ON THE BEACH WHEN WE WERE CHECKING IN!
"COME ON, DAVID, WE'RE FLYING TO HAWAII!" "COME ON, DAVID, WE'RE CHECKING IN TO A FOUR STAR HOTEL!" ... YOU ARE NOT A CHEAP DATE, CHOOVANSKI!
DAVID, IF YOU DON'T PRODUCE THAT KEY IN TEN SECONDS I'M GOING TO STRIP-SEARCH YOU RIGHT HERE IN THE HALL!
HERE IT IS!
HA! I KNEW IT!
IT WAS IN YOUR BAG FLAP.
OH... OH YEAH...
NO, YOU PUSH IT IN AND PULL IT OUT.
I KNOW HOW TO DO IT.
KA-CHIK!
HEY... WHAT DIFFERENCE DOES IT MAKE WHO HAD THE KEY? I JUST WANT TO GET SOME SLEEP!
YEAH.
IN MY OWN LITTLE BED...
OH YEAH.
UH, DAVID... YOU DID ASK FOR DOUBLE BEDS, DIDN'T YOU?
OH YEAH.
WELL... WHERE'S YOURS?

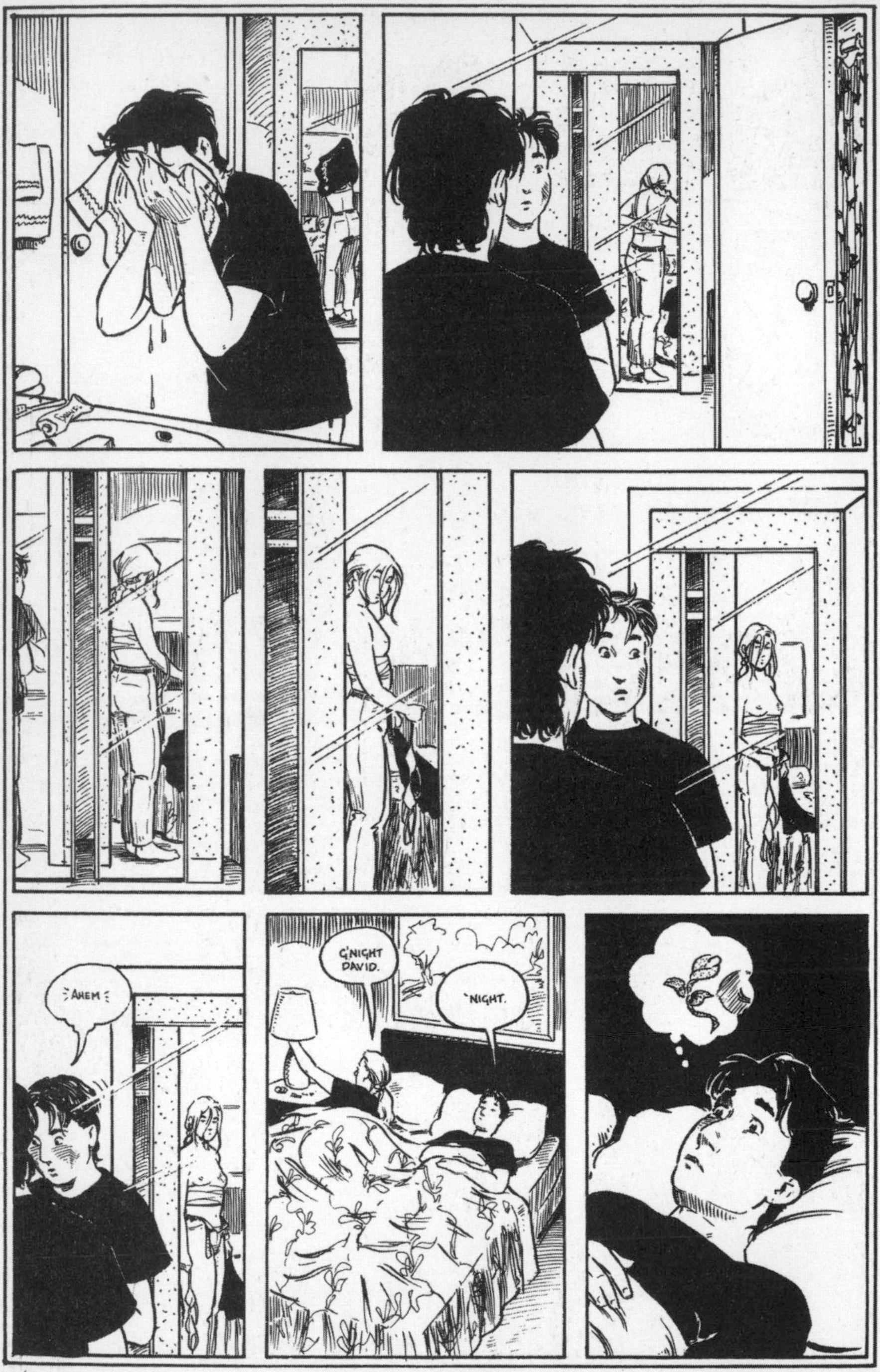
AHEM
G'NIGHT DAVID.
'NIGHT.

337

338

339

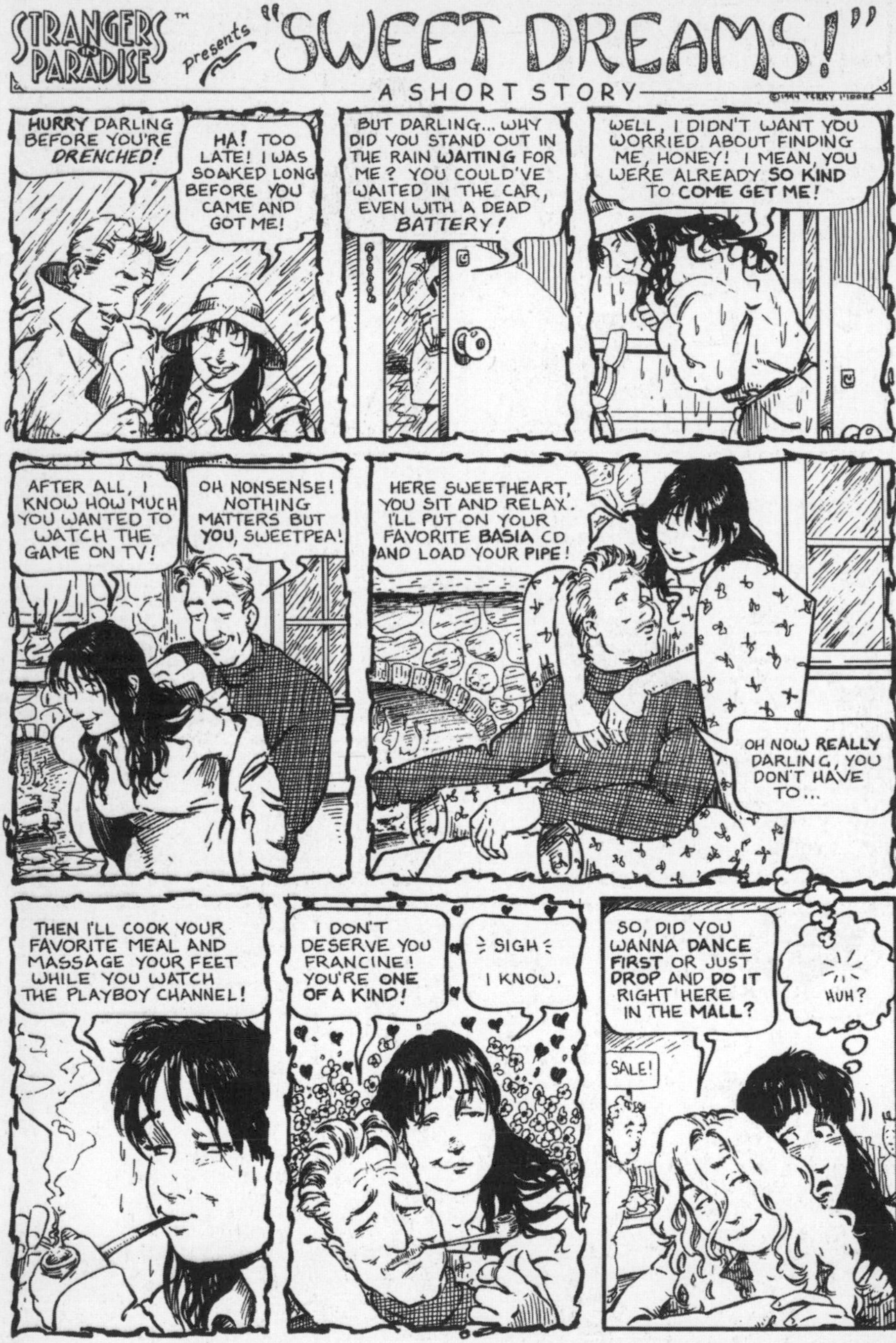
STRANGERS IN PARADISE™ presents "SWEET DREAMS!"
A SHORT STORY
HURRY DARLING BEFORE YOU'RE DRENCHED!
HA! TOO LATE! I WAS SOAKED LONG BEFORE YOU CAME AND GOT ME!
BUT DARLING... WHY DID YOU STAND OUT IN THE RAIN WAITING FOR ME? YOU COULD'VE WAITED IN THE CAR, EVEN WITH A DEAD BATTERY!
WELL, I DIDN'T WANT YOU WORRIED ABOUT FINDING ME, HONEY! I MEAN, YOU WERE ALREADY SO KIND TO COME GET ME!
AFTER ALL, I KNOW HOW MUCH YOU WANTED TO WATCH THE GAME ON TV!
OH NONSENSE! NOTHING MATTERS BUT YOU, SWEETPEA!
HERE SWEETHEART, YOU SIT AND RELAX. I'LL PUT ON YOUR FAVORITE BASIA CD AND LOAD YOUR PIPE!
OH NOW REALLY DARLING, YOU DON'T HAVE TO...
THEN I'LL COOK YOUR FAVORITE MEAL AND MASSAGE YOUR FEET WHILE YOU WATCH THE PLAYBOY CHANNEL!
I DON'T DESERVE YOU FRANCINE! YOU'RE ONE OF A KIND!
SIGH
I KNOW.
SO, DID YOU WANNA DANCE FIRST OR JUST DROP AND DO IT RIGHT HERE IN THE MALL?
HUH?
SALE!

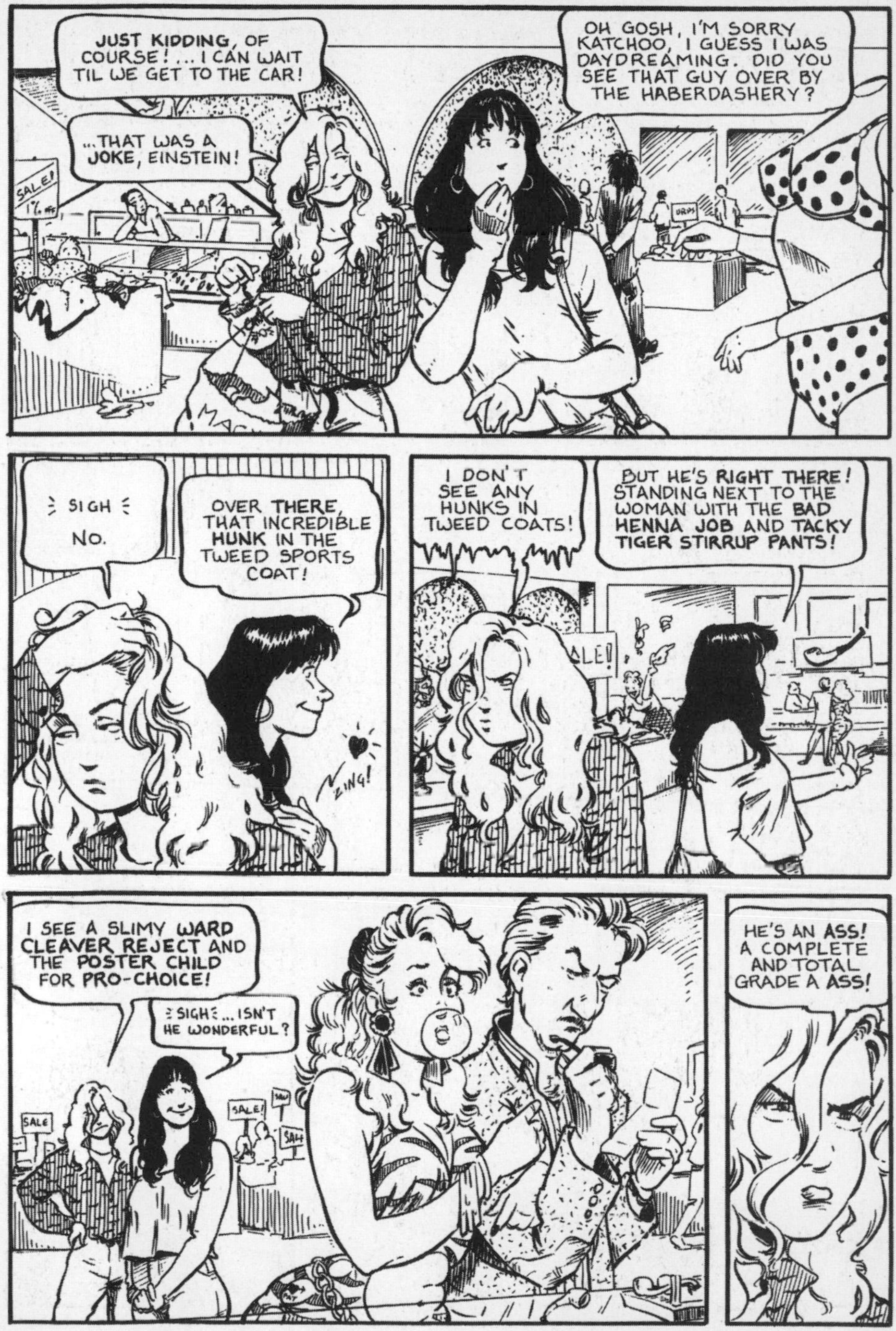
JUST KIDDING, OF COURSE! ... I CAN WAIT TIL WE GET TO THE CAR!
...THAT WAS A JOKE, EINSTEIN!
SALE! 1% OFF
OH GOSH, I'M SORRY KATCHOO, I GUESS I WAS DAYDREAMING. DID YOU SEE THAT GUY OVER BY THE HABERDASHERY?
SIGH
No.
OVER THERE, THAT INCREDIBLE HUNK IN THE TWEED SPORTS COAT!
ZING!
I DON'T SEE ANY HUNKS IN TWEED COATS!
BUT HE'S RIGHT THERE! STANDING NEXT TO THE WOMAN WITH THE BAD HENNA JOB AND TACKY TIGER STIRRUP PANTS!
I SEE A SLIMY WARD CLEAVER REJECT AND THE POSTER CHILD FOR PRO-CHOICE!
SIGH ... ISN'T HE WONDERFUL?
SALE
SALE!
HE'S AN ASS! A COMPLETE AND TOTAL GRADE A ASS!

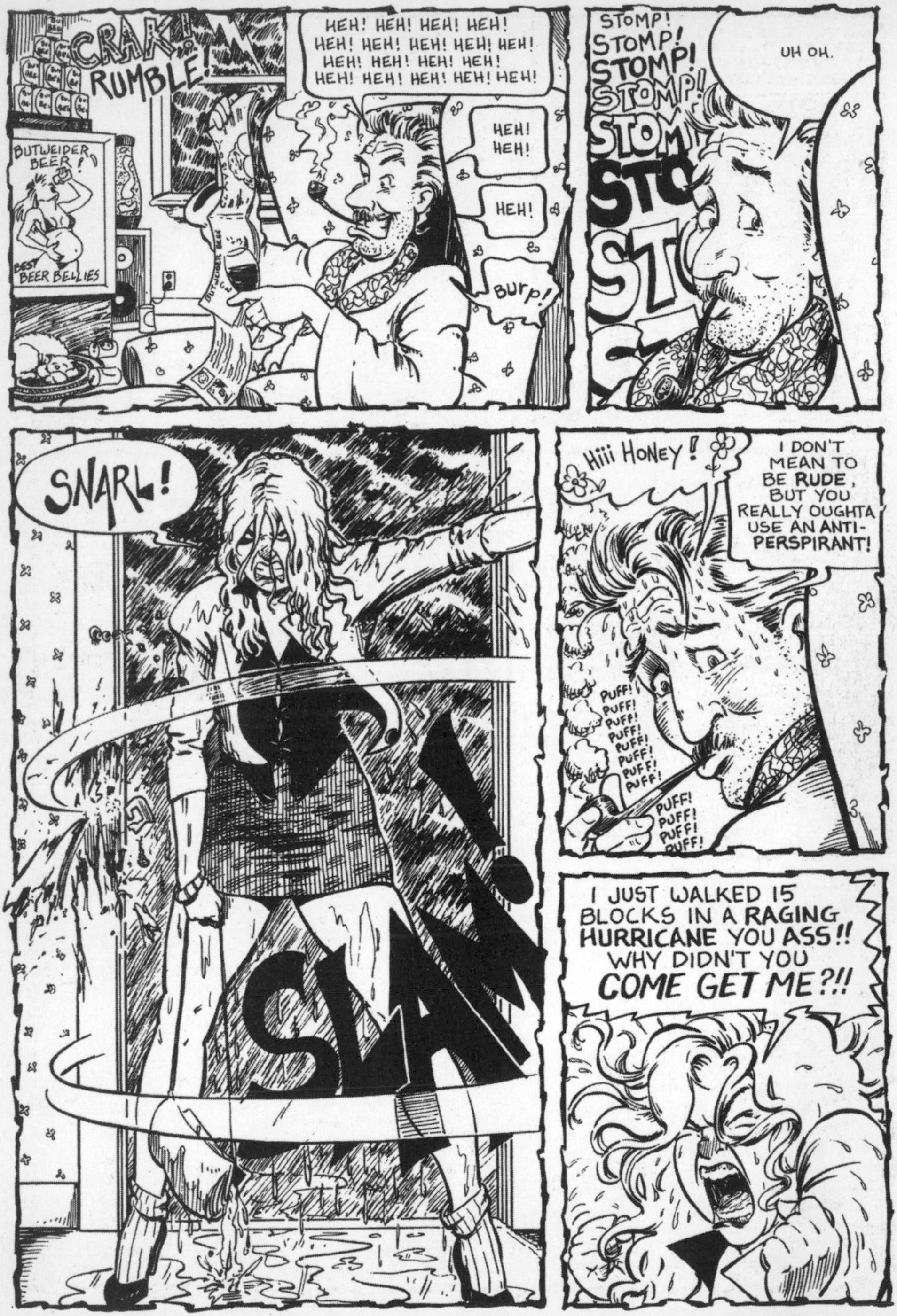
CRAK!
RUMBLE!
BUTWEIDER BEER!
BEST BEER BELLIES
HEH! HEH! HEH! HEH! HEH! HEH! HEH! HEH! HEH! HEH! HEH! HEH! HEH! HEH! HEH! HEH! HEH! HEH!
HEH! HEH!
HEH!
Burp!
STOMP! STOMP! STOMP! STOMP! STOM STO ST
UH OH.
SNARL!
SLAM!
Hiii Honey!
I DON'T MEAN TO BE RUDE, BUT YOU REALLY OUGHTA USE AN ANTI-PERSPIRANT!
PUFF! PUFF! PUFF! PUFF! PUFF! PUFF! PUFF! PUFF!
PUFF! PUFF! PUFF! PUFF!
I JUST WALKED 15 BLOCKS IN A RAGING HURRICANE YOU ASS!! WHY DIDN'T YOU COME GET ME?!!

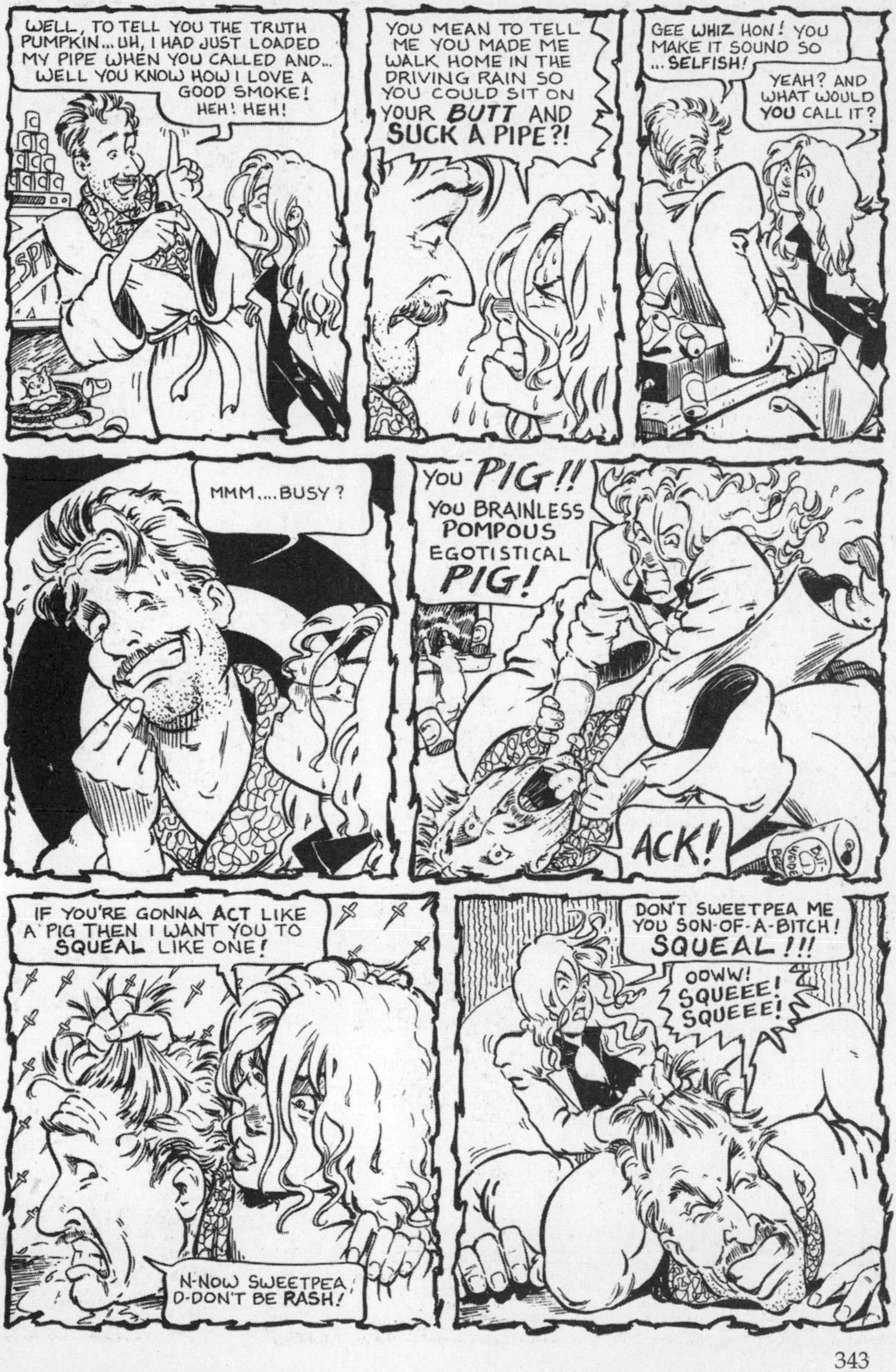
WELL, TO TELL YOU THE TRUTH PUMPKIN... UH, I HAD JUST LOADED MY PIPE WHEN YOU CALLED AND... WELL YOU KNOW HOW I LOVE A GOOD SMOKE! HEH! HEH!
YOU MEAN TO TELL ME YOU MADE ME WALK HOME IN THE DRIVING RAIN SO YOU COULD SIT ON YOUR BUTT AND SUCK A PIPE?!
GEE WHIZ HON! YOU MAKE IT SOUND SO ...SELFISH!
YEAH? AND WHAT WOULD YOU CALL IT?
MMM.... BUSY?
YOU PIG!! YOU BRAINLESS POMPOUS EGOTISTICAL PIG!
ACK!
IF YOU'RE GONNA ACT LIKE A PIG THEN I WANT YOU TO SQUEAL LIKE ONE!
N-NOW SWEETPEA D-DON'T BE RASH!
DON'T SWEETPEA ME YOU SON-OF-A-BITCH! SQUEAL!!!
OOWW! SQUEEE! SQUEEE!

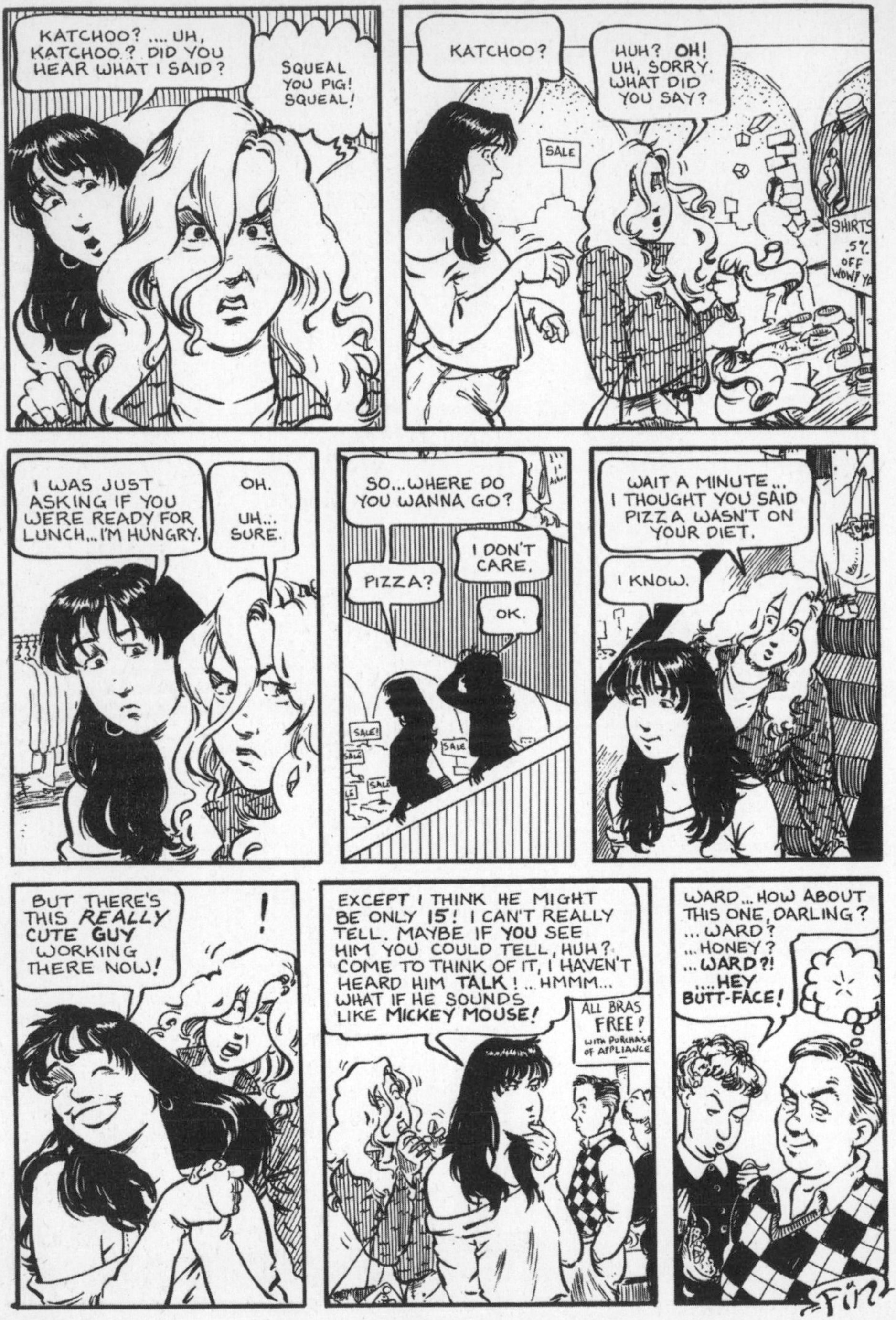
KATCHOO? .... UH, KATCHOO.? DID YOU HEAR WHAT I SAID?
SQUEAL YOU PIG! SQUEAL!
KATCHOO?
HUH? OH! UH, SORRY. WHAT DID YOU SAY?
SALE
SHIRTS .5% OFF WOW! YA
I WAS JUST ASKING IF YOU WERE READY FOR LUNCH... I'M HUNGRY.
OH. UH... SURE.
SO... WHERE DO YOU WANNA GO?
PIZZA?
I DON'T CARE.
OK.
SALE!
SALE
WAIT A MINUTE... I THOUGHT YOU SAID PIZZA WASN'T ON YOUR DIET.
I KNOW.
BUT THERE'S THIS REALLY CUTE GUY WORKING THERE NOW!
!
EXCEPT I THINK HE MIGHT BE ONLY 15! I CAN'T REALLY TELL. MAYBE IF YOU SEE HIM YOU COULD TELL, HUH? COME TO THINK OF IT, I HAVEN'T HEARD HIM TALK! ... HMMM... WHAT IF HE SOUNDS LIKE MICKEY MOUSE!
ALL BRAS FREE! WITH PURCHASE OF APPLIANCE
WARD... HOW ABOUT THIS ONE, DARLING? ... WARD? ... HONEY? ... WARD?! .... HEY BUTT-FACE!
Fin